THE
LEGAL
ENVIRONMENT
OF BUSINESS

THE LEGAL ENVIRONMENT OF BUSINESS.

SECOND EDITION

ROBERT N. CORLEY
ASSOCIATE PROFESSOR OF BUSINESS LAW
UNIVERSITY OF ILLINOIS

ROBERT L. BLACK
ASSOCIATE PROFESSOR OF BUSINESS LAW
UNIVERSITY OF ILLINOIS

McGRAW–HILL BOOK COMPANY
NEW YORK   ST. LOUIS   SAN FRANCISCO
TORONTO   LONDON   SYDNEY

PREFACE

In preparing this second edition, we have sought to accomplish the same basic objectives and have followed the philosophy and approach of the first edition, but with a substantial expansion of subject matter. The first edition was an attempt to provide a course in law which met the criteria of the various studies which had been made relating to education for business. Courses dealing solely with substantive private law had been challenged, and it was believed that the student of these times should be made aware of the environment in which business operates rather than be required to memorize detailed rules of private law. It was recognized that a major part of this environment is legal in nature. Woodrow Wilson's words, "every citizen should know what law is, how it came into existence, what relation its form bears to its substance, and how it gives society its fibre and strength and poise of frame," formed our basic premise.

We believe that all educated persons and especially businessmen need an understanding of the general nature of law and our judicial system. Moreover, modern business practices demand that business school graduates be familiar with those aspects of the law that form the legal environment in which business operates. These consist mainly of taxation and public regulation and control of business activity, especially in the marketing and labor areas. Practically every business decision must be considered and implemented in the light of its legal limitations and ramifications. This edition is, as the first was, an attempt to accomplish these same goals by acquainting the student with the legal environment of business activity.

There were several reasons for our decision to revise the first edition. The first and foremost of these was to expand the text to include materials sufficient for a full semester's course. This was in response to the encouraging demand for an environmental approach to law. As the first edition was an experiment, it was intended to supplement the then existing business law texts; this edition is designed for a full, separate course. The second motivating factor was that we recognized some obvious defects in the first edition. We have sought here to improve upon the former text materials by expanding the coverage of some of the old areas of law they dealt with, by adding some completely new areas (particularly in the field of private law, which originally was largely ignored), and by substituting some new cases for old ones. The final motivation for this revision was the need to update the first book, particularly in the public law areas which have seen many new and dramatic developments in the past few years.

This edition is divided into three parts. The first follows the original format by dealing with "law" generally—its meaning and nature, the sources of law, the factors that shape it, and the process by which law is applied to resolve human conflicts in organized society. The second part follows the original format to a large degree, being concerned with the environment of business as it results from the law. It reveals the attitude of government toward business and shows the basis, historical development, and current trends of public control in such areas as taxation, regulation of commerce, competition, freedom of contract, and labor-management relations. In addition to refining the original materials, other substantial changes have been made in the second part. The treatment of government regulation of competition has been expanded from one to four chapters, which deal with the historical and economic factors that have led to government regulation of competition, the history of antitrust legislation, legal aspects of mergers, and antitrust aspects of marketing policies, respectively. Also, a completely new chapter has been added concerning the private law of business organizations from the standpoint of the major factors to be considered when selecting the form of business enterprise. In addition, the chapter concerned with labor has been reorganized and expanded in its coverage. Part Three, on law and society, is entirely new. It contains chapters on the private law of property (including political, social, and economic effects of a society's concept of property, as well as a section on the contract as a method of creating and transferring property rights); current trends in the law of private wrongs, or torts; the basic freedoms of the Bill of Rights and business (which includes many of the very recent landmark cases dealing with this topic); and, finally, the legal profession (professional ethics, the attorney–client relationship, and the role of lawyers and judges in our society). For those who desire to teach the broad environmental approach exclusively, we feel certain that ample material is presented here for the basis of a complete course at either the graduate or undergraduate level. While our prime objective has been to provide a text for use in the business curriculum, we believe that this book is also very suitable for use in a course designed to contribute to the general education of liberal arts, engineering, or agriculture students. Some may want to build their business law program by starting with an introductory course using this text, followed by one or more separate courses concentrating on the technical aspects of private law, such as contracts or negotiable instruments, for those students who need or have interest in them. Those teachers of business law who still wish to place primary emphasis on the traditional private law approach will find this book useful as an introduction to law and business, enriching and supplementing the subject matter of their present courses.

We take this opportunity to reiterate our position on the role of education in the law for business students. We feel that nonprofessional courses in law should not attempt, and are not attempting, to produce lawyers. A study in depth of some facets of the law is desirable and contributes to an appreciation of the importance of variations in factual situations. It also provides an excellent tool to illustrate and develop analytical reasoning. However, undue concentration on all the minutiae and technicalities of law in a given area results in a law course that merely simulates professional law school courses and is not likely to serve the needs of the educated layman or future businessman. The objective here is to contribute to the general educational and cultural background of the student, to stimulate his interest in philosophy (for law is what translates the moral thought of philosophy into reality by defining enforceable rights and duties), and to make him aware of the nature and type of legal limitations which confront business. In our view, it is unwise to give the student an impression that he "knows" the law or the answers to legal problems. Yet laymen, and especially businessmen, should be equipped to evaluate the law critically, to recognize when they should seek the advice of counsel, and to utilize that advice in the decision-making process.

The materials in this book include text discussions, summaries of important legislation, articles, speeches, and decided cases—both landmark decisions and very recent ones. The student will become familiar with the philosophies and works of many of the great legal scholars, such as Cardozo, Hughes, Brandeis, Pound, Stone, Corbin, Douglas, and Marshall. The judicial decisions which have led to a regulated economy with government policy and control as a primary limitation on business activity are presented, along with some of the cases disapproving governmental action, so that the student will have an idea of the location of the boundary lines of legal forces in the environment of business. To conserve space, portions of the articles and cases presented have been omitted, along with most of their footnotes and citations of authority.

The authors are grateful for the fine work of Joyce Taylor, Betty Hampel, and Grace Meyers, who assisted in the final preparation of the manuscript.

The authors also express their gratitude to Professor Arthur L. Corbin and the *Yale Law Journal* for permission to reprint excerpts from Corbin, *Legal Analysis and Terminology*; the Yale University Press for permission to reprint excerpts from Cardozo, *The Nature of the Judicial Process*; Professor H. E. Willis for permission to reprint excerpts from Willis, *Introduction to Anglo-American Law*; Associate Justice William O. Douglas for permission to reprint excerpts from Douglas, *Stare Decisis*; The University of Chicago Press for permission to reprint excerpts from *Levi, An Introduction to Legal Reasoning*; the New York County Lawyers' Association for permission to reprint excerpts from an address given by Associate Justice Benjamin N. Cardozo; Professor Philip B. Kurland for permission to reprint excerpts from Kurland, *Recent Trends in United States Supreme Court Decisions*; the Yale University Press for permission to reprint excerpts from Pound, *An Introduction to the Philosophy of Law*; the Marshall Jones Company for permission to reprint excerpts from Pound, *The Spirit of the Common Law*; the *Illinois Bar Journal* and Mr. Anthony Lewis for permission to reprint excerpts from Lewis, *The Changing Role of the Supreme Court of the U.S.A.*; the *Illinois Bar Journal* and Mr. Robert W. Bergstrom for permission to reprint excerpts from Bergstrom, *Marxism, Senator Sherman and Our Economic System*; and the American Bar Association and the *American Bar Association Journal* for permission to reprint excerpts from the following articles: Harlan, *The Bill of Rights and the Constitution;* Murphy, *The Constitution: Interpretation and Intent;* Cole, *Administrative Agencies and Judicial Powers;* Cooper, *Turning the Spotlight on State Administrative Procedure;* Rowe, *Mergers and the Law: New Directions for the Sixties;* Bergan, *The Role of Law in Labor Relations;* Marshall, *The Unreality of Accident Litigation: A Plea for a New Approach;* and Hofstadter, *In Memoriam: Louis Dembitz Brandeis.*

ROBERT N. CORLEY

ROBERT L. BLACK

CONTENTS

LIST OF CASES

PART ONE

LAW
Its Nature, Formation, and Application

LAW

1 INTRODUCTION

Perhaps no word of such common usage is so incapable of exact definition or expresses a variety of concepts so well as does the word "law." For example, "law" is used to describe specific statutory enactments and also to denote a general system of rules for governing conduct. Popular uses of the terms "law," "legal," and "illegal" are illimitable. The meaning of these words in any particular situation must be determined from the context in which they are used. This chapter is devoted to a discussion of some of the various definitions of law, as well as legal terminology and classifications of law.

2 SOME DEFINITIONS OF LAW

In his commentaries on the law, Blackstone defined law generally as "that rule of action which is prescribed by some superior and which the inferior is bound to obey." [1] He defined civil law as a "rule of civil conduct prescribed by the supreme power in a state, commanding what is right and prohibiting what is wrong." [2] It can be seen that Blackstone viewed law as flowing from a superior to an inferior person by a command. These definitions and concepts have been generally rejected in the United States, where the constitutional system has established that law stems from the people and flows to the government and that there is no power superior to the people.

Blackstone's definition also fails to describe many areas of our law because such laws as those pertaining to contracts and torts do not "command compliance" in the technical sense but are so constructed that an aggrieved party is given a remedy against one who violates accepted legal principles in these areas. Civil courts, except in unusual situations, do not require compliance but instead impose liability for noncompliance.

However, Blackstone's theory was followed by Justice Stone when he said:

[1] Blackstone, *Commentaries* 38.
[2] Blackstone, *Commentaries* 44.

Law emanates from the sovereign not from its creatures. The sum total of all those rules of human conduct for which there is a state sanction . . . [is law]. Law in its essence is made up of those rules of human conduct which are made mandatory by the state upon all its citizens and without which social order and well-being could not exist.

The American Law Institute has defined law as "the body of principles, standards, and rules which the courts . . . apply in the decision of controversies brought before them." [3] It further pointed out that law is made up of three elements: (1) formulated legislation including constitutions, statutes, treaties, local ordinances, and bylaws, (2) rules of law adopted by the courts, and (3) "the system of legal concepts and the traditional legal technique which forms the basis of its judicial action." [4] Subsequent chapters will discuss laws created by legislation and judicial decision, and the court procedures and techniques established to enforce these laws. The Institute's analysis of the elements composing law actually designates those sources to which courts turn in search of the law.

Justice Oliver Wendell Holmes, in what is perhaps the most succinct definition of law, said "Law is a statement of the circumstances in which the public force will be brought to bear through courts." [5]

Other judges have stated that law is "a rule of reason applied to existing conditions," [6] that "it is an expression of the public will," [7] and that it is "that which must be obeyed and followed by citizens subject to sanctions or legal consequences." [8]

Professor H. E. Willis, in his *Introduction to Anglo-American Law,*[9] stated that law was "a scheme for controlling the conduct of people." He emphasized that law was concerned with social interests and that where social interests recognized a right in one person, courts would create machinery to assist the person with this right in obtaining redress against the person with the duty or obligation, in the event the duty were not performed or the obligation were not fulfilled. By his concept, the law has four characteristics:

1   It is a scheme of social control.
2   It is for the protection of social interests.
3   It accomplishes its purpose by the recognition of a capacity in persons to influence the conduct of others.
4   It affords the machinery of the courts and legal procedures to help the person with the capacity.

[3] *Restatement, Conflict of Laws,* § 3 (1934).
[4] *Ibid.*
[5] *American Banana Co. v. United Fruit Co.,* 213 U.S. 347, 356 (1909).
[6] *City of Milwaukee v. Milwaukee Ry. & Light Co.,* 173 Wis. 400, 180 N.W. 339 (1920).
[7] *Ware v. Hylton,* 3 U.S. (3 Dall.) 199, 212 (1796).
[8] *Koenig v. Flynn,* 258 N.Y. 292, 179 N.E. 705 (1932).
[9] By permission from Willis, *Introduction to Anglo-American Law* 10–11 (Indiana University Studies, Vol. XIII, No. 69, 1926).

In rejecting Blackstone's definition, Willis concluded: "Order through generality, equality, and certainty, and not compulsion, is the fundamental characteristic of the law. . . . Law is a scheme of social control, for the protection of social interests, by means of capacities of influence, backed and sanctioned by the power of the state." [10]

3   LAW AND JUSTICE

"Law" and "justice" are not synonymous, just as legal justice and social justice are not synonymous. Justice has been defined as "that which is founded in equity, honesty, and right." [11] It is the attempt of honorable men to do that which is fair. Justice is the purpose and end of government and civil society. It is apparent that the achievement of justice is dependent upon the concept of right and wrong in the society involved. The purpose of justice in our society, as stated in the Declaration of Independence, is to secure for all men "life, liberty, and the pursuit of happiness."

Social justice recognizes more rights and duties than does legal justice, although the trend of the law is toward equating these concepts. Perfect justice would require that all persons discharge all their obligations and duties so that all other persons might enjoy all their rights and privileges. Our society through law determines which rights and duties will be protected and strives through its judicial system for perfect justice. Of course, the law is incapable of perfect justice because it is in the hands of imperfect men and operates with imperfect procedures. As law tends to achieve perfect justice, legal justice and social justice tend to merge.

Pound attempted to define law in terms of justice when he said that the science of law is "that organized body of knowledge that has to do with the administration of justice by public or regular tribunals in accordance with principles or rules of general character and more or less uniform application." [12]

As the judicial process and those forces which affect it are discussed in subsequent chapters, the student is exhorted to develop his own concept of law and justice and to test critically the judicial decisions studied to determine whether they meet his standard.

4   CLASSIFICATION OF SUBJECT MATTER

It is not possible to classify the many subject matters of the law into categories that will be completely acceptable. There have been numerous

[10] *Id.* at 11.
[11] *Spencer v. Terry's Estate,* 133 Mich. 39, 94 N.W. 372 (1903).
[12] 1 Pound, *Library American Law and Practice* 1.

attempts at such a classification, but each has been vulnerable to the criticism of being either "too inclusive" or "too exclusive." The law has often been described as "a seamless web" in which principles of law are hopelessly and endlessly intertwined with each other. For this reason, any attempted classification or description of the many and varied legal subjects is necessarily inaccurate. The following classifications are, however, generally accepted by most legal scholars.

Law may be generally divided into matters of public law and matters of private law. Public law includes such subject areas as constitutional law, administrative law, and criminal law. In each of these areas, society or "the people" are directly involved and their interests are represented by some governmental agency, officer, or official whose obligation it is to see that justice is accomplished and the ends of society are fulfilled. The public law provides a major portion of the legal environment of business, and for this reason, much of the material in subsequent chapters is concerned with the constitutional and administrative areas of the public law and their application to business.

The criminal law is generally subdivided into felonies, misdemeanors, and treason. This classification is based on the punishment which may be imposed in the event of a conviction. Felonies are punishable by fine or imprisonment in a penitentiary for a period of one year or more, while misdemeanors are punishable by a fine or a jail sentence of less than one year. Treason fits neither definition since it is usually punishable by a mandatory death penalty. The criminal law includes many crimes which may be committed by a corporate enterprise as well as those which may be committed by individuals. Some of these, such as violating the antitrust laws, will be discussed later in this book.

Private law encompasses those legal problems and relationships which exist between individuals, as contrasted with those in which society is involved. Private law is traditionally separated into the law of contracts, the law of torts, and the law of property. The body of law known as contracts is concerned with the legal relationships created between individuals by their own agreement and contains several subbodies of law which are frequently treated as separate classifications. For example, the law of sales, the law of commercial paper, and the law of secured transactions are subjects concerned with special contractual situations. Each has its own body of legal principles and many of these principles conflict with traditional general contract law.

The law of torts is concerned with wrongs committed by one person against another or his property. It is predicated upon the fundamental concept that a member of a civilized society will not injure another member or his property either intentionally or by the lack of exercise of due care and caution in the conduct of his affairs. This body of law, which is designed to give damages to the victim of the tort, is the major source of litigation in this country since it includes suits for personal injuries based on a theory of negligence. Tens of thousands of tort cases are filed each year as a result of automobile accidents, and more tens of thousands of cases are settled without suit being filed. Many torts are labeled intentional as contrasted with negligent. An example of such a tort action is a suit for defamation of character, which is known as libel if the defamation is written and slander if it is oral. Trespass actions comprise still another area of intentional tort litigation. There are three types of trespass: trespass to the person, usually referred to as assault and battery; trespass to goods, frequently called conversion of goods; and trespass to land. It should be noted that frequently conduct which is tortious is also criminal—for example, assault and battery. In such cases, society brings suit for the wrong to society, but the victim must bring his own civil suit if he wishes to be compensated for the wrong done to him. Some activities are actually a hybrid between a tort and a crime. These are sometimes referred to as public torts and include such misconduct as violation of traffic laws. A criminal-type punishment is often imposed.

There is a growing body of tort law that is concerned with business torts. These include suits for damages because an individual or a corporate business has interfered with the employer-employee relationship or with some other contract of someone else. For instance, if A employs B, and C encourages A to discharge B, B may have a tort action against C for the damage caused by his discharge. Business may also have tort liability for violating statutes such as the antitrust laws.

Another growing area of litigation is difficult to classify as either *ex contractu* (arising from a contract) or *ex delicto* (arising from a tort). This area is concerned with the liability of manufacturers and sellers for injuries caused by their products. The theory of such a suit may be negligence, for example, a suit against a soft drink bottler by a person who swallowed a dead mouse with the contents. It also may be on a theory of breach of warranty (contract), as in a case where a purchaser of canned goods which contain ground glass sues the retailer who sold him the goods. In the latter case, there would be no negligence but liability for another reason. In many instances, the actual theory has become obscured and the traditional classification confusing.

Tort liability also includes cases predicated on theories of nuisance and strict liability. Under the latter, liability is imposed if an injury occurs, regardless of fault. It is most commonly invoked against public carriers for injury to property being shipped.

The law of property is concerned with the rights and duties arising out of the ownership and possession of real estate and personal property. Property is considered to be a "bundle of rights." These rights are frequently created by contract and protected by the law of torts. Thus, some legal scholars do not consider property to be a separate classification. The concept of private property is of great importance and is dealt with in detail in Chapter 15.

Another important classification or distinction in the law is the one between substance and procedure. This is discussed in the next section.

5   DISTINCTION BETWEEN PROCEDURE AND SUBSTANCE

Substantive law defines the legal relationships of people with other people or as between them and the state. Thus, the rules of contract law are substantive in nature. Procedural law is concerned with the method and means by which substantive law is made and administered. In other words, substantive rules of law define rights and duties, while procedural rules of law provide the machinery for the enforcement of those rights and duties. Every organ of society has rules by which it conducts its affairs or "proceeds." There are rules of law relating to legislative procedure which govern the steps that must be taken for a statute to be valid. A typical rule of legislative procedure might require that all bills be read to the assembly twice before adoption. Failure to follow this rule of procedure might void the legislature's attempt to create rights or duties in the statute.

Administrative agencies also have rules of procedure which vary from agency to agency. For example, the National Labor Relations Board and the Internal Revenue Service each have procedures which must be followed in matters before these agencies.

Judicial procedures involve the method of conducting law suits, appeals, and the enforcement of judgments. The rules for conducting civil trials are different from those for criminal trials. For example, each party may call the other party to the witness stand for the purpose of cross-examination in a civil trial, but the defendant may not be required to testify in a criminal case. Procedural problems also arise concerning the papers which are filed in the lawsuit, the admission of evidence, and the various other techniques involved in trying the case. They are the rules of the game. It would appear that many rules which are classified as procedural in character might be just as easily classified as substantive because they actually affect rights and duties. Chapter 6 deals with the procedural aspects of law in greater depth.

6   LEGAL TERMINOLOGY

Prior to undertaking a study of law, it would be helpful to understand certain basic terminology. The study of law is essentially concerned with "rules of law." A rule of law, using Holmes's definition, is a statement that if certain facts exist, then the judicial branch of government will take certain action or refuse to take certain action at the request of someone involved. In other words, a rule of law is a prediction as to what a court will or will not do in a given factual situation. It is then obvious that facts create legal issues which are resolved by using rules of law. The student should therefore be aware of the tremendous importance of facts to the law. A majority of our legal procedures are designed to ascertain the facts.

Legal relations exist between two persons and usually are complex in that there is a variety of rights and duties in each party with regard to the specific subject matter in question. For purposes of analyzing basic legal relationships, Professor Arthur L. Corbin, formerly professor of law at Yale University, suggests the following definitions:

From   LEGAL ANALYSIS AND TERMINOLOGY [13]
Arthur L. Corbin, Professor of Law, Yale University

Assuming that we wish to determine the legal relations of A and B, we may ask ourselves the following questions:

1   What may A (or B) do, without societal penalty assessed for the benefit of the other?
2   What must A (or B) do, under threat of societal penalty assessed for the benefit of the other?
3   What can A (or B) do, so as to change the existing legal relations of the other? (This has no reference to mere physical power.)

If we determine that A may conduct himself in a certain way, he has a privilege with respect to B, and B has no-right that A shall not so conduct himself.

If we determine that A must conduct himself in a certain manner, he has a duty to B, and B has a right against A.

If we determine that by his own voluntary act A *can* change B's legal relations with A (or with X), A has a legal *power* and B has a *liability*.

If we determine that A *cannot* by his own voluntary act change the legal relations of B, then A has a *disability* and B has an *immunity*.

Having isolated these definite concepts and chosen these specific terms with which to express them—all being found in the actual decisions and usage of the courts—Professor Wesley N. Hohfeld then arranged them in the following pairs of *opposites* and *correlatives*:

Opposites {	right	privilege	power	immunity
	no-right	duty	disability	liability
Correlatives {	right	privilege	power	immunity
	duty	no-right	liability	disability

[13] By permission from Corbin, Legal Analysis and Terminology, 29 *Yale L.J.* 163 (Dec. 1919).

Each pair of correlatives must always exist together; when some person (A) has one of the pair, another person (B) necessarily has the other. One of the terms expresses the relation of A to B; the other term expresses the relation of B to A.

No pair of opposites can exist together. That is, when a person has a right, he cannot have a no-right with respect to the same subject matter and the same person. When he has a privilege, he cannot have a duty.

The following grouping of terms may be useful:

May	permission	privilege—no-right
Must (may not)	compulsion	right—duty
Can	danger or possibility (of new relations)	power—liability
Cannot	safety (from new relations)	immunity—disability

Observe that when we assert that some fact or group of facts will operate to create a particular legal relation we are stating a *rule of law*. The mere statement that a certain legal relation exists is a statement of *fact*. Thus: (a) A owes B $100—statement of fact. (b) C owns Blackacre—statement of fact. (c) An offer creates a power in the offeree—rule of law. (d) The delivery of a deed conveys title to land—rule of law. (e) The delivery of a release under seal discharges a debtor (creates privilege in place of duty)—rule of law.

We may now proceed to the more formal definition of the eight named legal relations. . . .

1   Right: A legal relation between two persons. . . . It is the legal relation of A to B when society commands action or forbearance by B and will at the instance of A in some manner penalize disobedience.

A, knowing that he has a particular right, can answer the question, "What *must another do* for me?" (The court will aid me by using compulsion if he does not do it.) . . .

2   Duty: . . . It is the legal relation of a person, B, who is commanded by society to act or to forbear for the benefit of another person, A, either immediately or in the future, and who will be penalized by society for disobedience.

B, knowing that he has a particular duty, can answer this question, "What must I do for another?" (A court will use compulsion against me if I do not do it.)

3   Privilege: . . . The legal relation of A to B when A (with respect to B) is *free* or *at liberty* to conduct himself in a certain matter as he pleases; when his conduct is not regulated for the benefit of B by the command of society; and when he is not threatened with

any penalty for disobedience, for the reason that society has made no command.

A, knowing that he has a particular privilege, can answer this question, "What *may* I do?" (A court will not prevent me or penalize me.)

Observe carefully that the concept *privilege* does not itself include a *right* to non-interference by another person, although such a privilege and such a right very commonly are found together. Being the opposite of duty, it is another name for *no duty*. If I am under no duty to A, I am with respect to A privileged. . . .

4   No-Right: . . . The legal relation of a person (A) in whose behalf society commands nothing of another (B). A has no control over B. A, knowing that he has no-right against B, can answer this question, "What *may* another person (B) do?" (A court will not prevent him or penalize him.)

5   Power: . . . The legal relation of A to B when A's own voluntary act will cause new legal relations either between B and A or between B and a third person.

A, knowing that he has a particular power, can answer this question, "What new legal relations can I create between B and myself or others?"

A sharp distinction must be drawn between *legal* power and *physical* power. Thus a person may have a legal power to make a will even though he is too weak physically to sign his name; i.e., he has the legal power but is physically unable to do the volitional act by which it is to be exercised.

6   Liability: . . . The relation of A to B when A may be brought into new legal relations by the voluntary act of B. A is *liable* to have new legal relations created for himself through the exercise by B of B's power. The new relations may be with third persons, or with B, or with both; but the liability-power relation is between A and B only.

A, knowing that he has a certain liability, can answer this question, "What new legal relations can B create between me and himself or others?"

7   Immunity: . . . The relation of A to B when B has no legal power (has disability) to affect some one or more of the existing legal relations of A. As to that particular existing relation A has an immunity with respect to B.

A, knowing that he has a certain immunity, can answer this question, "Which one of my existing relations is safe from alteration by B?"

8   Disability: . . . The relation of A to B when by no voluntary act of his own can A extinguish one (or more) of the existing legal relations of B.

A, knowing that he has a particular disability, can answer this question, "What existing legal relation of another person (B) is it impossible for me to extinguish?" . . .

Res judicata and stare decisis are two additional terms which must be distinguished and understood. Res judicata comes from Latin and literally means that the thing has been decided. As a legal principle it means that a final decision in a lawsuit by a competent court is conclusive and final of the rights and duties of the parties on all points and matters decided. This prevents successive suits involving the same question between the same parties and brings disputes to a final conclusion. A matter once litigated and legally determined is conclusive between the parties in all subsequent proceedings. The case which follows illustrates this concept.

CUMMINGS V. DRESHER
218 N.E.2d 688 (N.Y. 1966)

DESMOND, CHIEF JUDGE: There was a collision between an automobile owned by Martin Cummings and driven by Mary Cummings and an automobile driven by Bernard Dresher. The car driven by Bernard Dresher was owned by Standard Electric Co., Inc., and in it Henry Dresher was a passenger. Driver Bernard Dresher and passenger Henry Dresher as coplaintiffs sued driver Mary Cummings and owner Martin Cummings in the Federal District Court for damages for personal injuries sustained by the two Dresher brothers. The issues up for determination in that *Dresher v. Cummings* suit included, therefore, questions as to the negligence of either or both the Dreshers and either or both of the defendants Cummings. Returning their verdict, the jury told the Federal Judge that it found in favor of the passenger Henry Dresher against defendants Cummings and found also that Mrs. Cummings was "guilty of negligence" and that "plaintiff" (apparently meaning driver Bernard Dresher) "was guilty" of contributory negligence to a very minor degree. The Judge, to "complete" the verdict, instructed the Clerk to ask the jury whether it intended a verdict of no cause of action in Bernard Dresher's suit. The jurors replied that such was their intention. Judgment was thereupon entered in favor of Mr. and Mrs. Cummings dismissing the complaint of Bernard Dresher and the judgment was affirmed by the Federal Court of Appeals 325 F.2d 156 (2d Cir.). At the close of these Federal court proceedings it was completely clear that the jury had found that driver Mary Cummings had been found guilty of negligence and that, therefore, she as driver and her husband as owner had to pay damages to passenger Henry Dresher. Equally clear was the Federal court jury's finding that driver Bernard Dresher had been guilty of contributory negligence and so, notwithstanding the found negligence of driver Mary Cummings, Bernard Dresher could not recover against the defendants Cummings.

Despite this definite and unmistakable Federal court jury finding as to both drivers being at fault, driver Mary Cummings and her husband brought the present suit against driver Dresher and the corporate owner of the Dresher car. The courts below, for inscrutable reasons, held that the Federal court judgment was not determinative here. We do not understand why in a reasonable, prompt and nonrepetitious judicial system the negligence or no of these two drivers must be decided all over again, after having once been settled after a jury trial in which all these same people were parties and all the same issues tried and decided. "One who has had his day in court should not be permitted to litigate the question anew. . . ." Under such circumstances the judgment is held to be conclusive upon those who were parties to the action in which the judgment was rendered. Where a full opportunity has been afforded to a party to the prior action and he has failed to prove his freedom from liability or to establish liability or culpability on the part of another, there is no reason for retrying these issues. . . . [REVERSED]

Stare decisis is the concept by which courts adhere to decided cases as precedent. When a court once determines that a certain rule of law is applicable to a certain set of facts, then it will follow that rule in all future cases involving essentially the same facts and thus the same issue. Under stare decisis the same rules of law are applicable between different sets of parties. This doctrine, which is the basis of our common law, is the subject of the major portion of the subject matter of Chapter 3.

In subsequent chapters, additional terms peculiar to the legal system will be discussed. Caution should be exercised to make sure that the meaning of each term is understood in the context in which it is used.

7   THE JUDICIAL PROCESS—IN GENERAL

The American Law Institute's definition of law, set forth on page 4, indicates that law comes from constitutions, treaties, statutes, ordinances, and decided cases. The latter source provides the basis for the "common law." In the event of litigation, a determination of the law applicable to the facts involved is necessary to a final disposition of the case. In addition, law plays a major role in the determination of the facts by supplying the fact-finding procedures. How do courts or judges make the determination or find the law of the case? Is there a hierarchy or priority as between the many sources? What factors enter into the decision? How do courts resolve or reconcile conflicting laws? When may courts refuse to follow a law or precedent? What formulas do courts use in reaching their decisions? What processes are followed that enable a court to reach one result rather than another? The purpose of the chapters which follow is to attempt an answer to these questions in detail. However, it is noted at this point that the judicial system has established a general priority among the various sources of law. Constitutions prevail over statutes, and statutes prevail over common-law principles established in court decisions. Courts will not turn to case decisions for law if a statute is directly in point, but it should be remembered that statutes usually deal in generalities and require interpretation. Since cases deal with specific problems, interpretation is necessary to fill in the gaps of the legislation and to eliminate the ambiguities caused by the general language of statutes.

Decisions which provide precedent for future cases are those which are appealed to reviewing courts. These courts are generally concerned only with questions of law, and their decisions are printed so that judges and lawyers may study them and use them as a basis for research in finding the law. The decisions set forth later in the text are cases which have been decided by a court of review. All cases which have been decided are available to interested persons, for use in legal research, as are the statutory enactments of legislatures.

Case law as a basis for law and judicial decisions often provides only the point of departure from which the difficult labor of the reviewing court begins. Courts of review must examine and compare cases cited as authority to them, to determine whether the principles or rules of law therein contained should be followed or rejected on some ground, such as changing conditions. In reaching and preparing its decision, the court must consider whether the law as announced will provide justice in the case at bar and will establish sound precedent for future cases involving similar issues.

The chapters immediately following discuss the various sources of law and the nature of the judicial process so that some understanding of law will be developed prior to the examination of some of the more important legal principles that compose the environment in which business operates.

CHAPTER TWO

WRITTEN LAW

1 INTRODUCTION

"Written law" in the narrow sense includes constitutions drafted and adopted by the people, treaties entered into by the executive branch of the Federal government and ratified by the Senate, and statutes and ordinances enacted by legislative bodies such as Congress, state general assemblies, and city councils. In this chapter these various types of written law and their interpretation will be discussed.

2 CONSTITUTIONS

Under a constitutional system such as ours, the constitution of the governmental unit is its basic and supreme law. All other laws, written or unwritten, must be in harmony with it or they are void. By and large, state constitutions are modeled after the Federal Constitution, and as such, provide the same general organization for government, by dividing it into executive, legislative, and judicial branches, giving each branch checks and balances on the others. This concept of separation of powers is testimony to the strong fear the founders of this country felt that too much power might be concentrated in any branch of government. Separation of powers is not an abstract concept. Many day-to-day problems and disputes involve this doctrine and are determined by its application. The case which follows illustrates its use in a dispute between a city council and local judges.

CARLSON V. STATE
220 N.E.2d 532 (Ind. 1966)

A city judge of Hammond, Indiana, prepared his budget for the operation of his court and presented it to the city council for approval. The city council reduced it from $71,042.50 to $53,247.50. The judge sued the city to force it to appropriate the money. The city council contended that it could fix the budget in the exercise of its legislative function. The judge argued that the legislative body may not interfere with the judicial process by exercising its legislative discretion in this manner. The lower court found for the judge, and the council appealed.

ARTERBURN, JUSTICE: . . . It is trite to say, but nevertheless requires repeating here, that our State, as well as our Federal government, is divided into three parts: executive, legislative and judicial—each an independent and integral part of the government. This division is created by the Constitution and is inherent in the functions of each department.

It follows that the judicial function may not be controlled by the executive or the legislative branch, and the same barriers exist with reference to controlling the discretionary actions of the executive department and the legislative department. It is axiomatic that the courts must be independent and must not be subject to the whim of either the executive or legislative departments. The security of human rights and the safety of free institutions require freedom of action on the part of the court. Courts from time immemorial have been the refuge of those who have been aggrieved and oppressed by official and arbitrary actions under the guise of governmental authority. It is the protector of those oppressed by unwarranted official acts under the assumption of authority. Our sense of justice tells us that a court is not free if it is under financial pressure, whether it be from a city council or other legislative body, in the consideration of the rights of some individual who is affected by some alleged autocratic or unauthorized official action of such a body. One who controls the purse strings can control how tightly those purse strings are drawn, and the very existence of a dependent. Justice, as well as the security of human rights and the safety of free institutions requires freedom of action of courts in hearing cases of those aggrieved by official actions, to their injury. . . .

The courts are under a constitutional mandate to administer justice freely and without any restraint coming from any other governmental authority. Unless a court has abused its discretion with respect to exercise of its authority, we will not disturb the decrees by which such authority is exercised.

We find that the respondent court had authority to provide for the payment of expenses necessary for its proper functioning in the absence of any showing of abuse of such discretion.

It is suggested that the right of a court to determine what is reasonably necessary as to the amount of money for its proper functioning, is granting an arbitrary and unlimited power to a court or a judge, which may be unwisely used. In *Knox County Council v. State ex rel. McCormick* . . . Judge Fansler points out that such power is not necessarily unlimited, but those contending that the exercise in a particular case is extravagant, arbitrary or unwarranted, may be heard thereon and the question reviewed by us on appeal. In this case it appears that the appellants had the opportunity to introduce any evidence they saw fit to show that the requests of the appellee city judge were arbitrary, extravagant, and unwarranted, and the trial judge below, in issuing the mandate, had the opportunity to review this issue. However, no evidence of that character convinced the trial judge of any extravagant or arbitrary action on the part of the respondent court. The court or the judge thereof is better informed in that particular area than may be members of a legislative body or council who may desire from time to time to pull the purse strings too tight upon the operations of some court which falls within its disfavor. The courts frequently have to rule upon the act or refusal to act of those controlling the purse strings in rendering justice. Threats of retaliation or fears of strangulation should not hang over such judicial functions.

However, be that as it may, there comes a time when a judge or any other public official must make an accounting to the voters for his actions, if arbitrary, extravagant or not in the public interest, and that is true of a city judge or any judge in the State of Indiana, or if not the judge, then the one who exercises the appointing power. What has just been said about courts may also be said with reference to legislative bodies. There is no absolute protection against the extravagance of such bodies in fixing their own salaries or expenditure of money for their own quarters and operations except the accounting that comes at the polls. [JUDGMENT AFFIRMED]

The doctrine of separation of powers will be further explored in subsequent chapters. It plays a major role in law created by judicial decisions as well as in administrative law. In the latter, an interesting constitutional and ideological problem is presented since administrative agencies perform all three functions of government to some degree. This matter is discussed in Chapter 4.

In addition to providing a government's organization, constitutions define the powers and functions of the various branches. Historically there was a distinction in this respect between the Federal and state constitutions. The Federal Constitution when ratified was a delegation of authority from the states, which were the basic sovereigns, to the Federal government. All powers not contained therein were retained by the states. In other words, the Federal Constitution contains grants of power to the Federal government, which was established by the states. On the other hand, state governments have all powers not denied them by the Federal or their own constitution. State constitutions, therefore, generally contain limitations on the power of state government.

Early court interpretation of the Constitution strictly limited the Federal government to those grants of authority enumerated, and "states' rights" were held to be supreme in all other areas. As the need for a strong central government developed, this distinction was eroded by legislation as well as judicial decision, which placed more and more power in the hands of Congress and the President. The distinction, however, still exists in part, and many legal problems arise in connection with the location of the boundary between Federal and state power.

Article I of the Constitution of the United States illustrates both the organizational and functional aspects of Constitutions. It vests all legislative powers in a Congress consisting of a Senate and a House of Representatives and in Section 8, below, grants specific powers to the Congress.

THE CONSTITUTION OF THE UNITED STATES
Article I, Section 8

The Congress shall have Power To lay and collect Taxes, Duties, Imposts and Excises, to pay the Debts and provide for the common Defence and general Welfare of the United States; but all Duties, Imposts and Excises shall be uniform throughout the United States;

To borrow Money on the credit of the United States;

To regulate Commerce with foreign Nations, and among the several States and with the Indian Tribes;

To establish an uniform Rule of Naturalization, and uniform Laws on the subject of Bankruptcies throughout the United States;

To coin Money, regulate the Value thereof, and of foreign Coin, and fix the Standard of Weights and Measures;

To provide for the Punishment of counterfeiting the Securities and current Coin of the United States;

To establish Post Offices and Post Roads;

To promote the Progress of Science and useful Arts, by securing for limited Times to Authors and Inventors the exclusive Right to their respective Writings and Discoveries;

To constitute Tribunals inferior to the supreme Court;

To define and punish Piracies and Felonies committed on the high Seas, and Offences against the Law of Nations;

To declare War, grant Letters of Marque and Reprisal, and make Rules concerning Captures on Land and Water;

To raise and support Armies, but no Appropriation of Money to that Use shall be for a longer Term than two Years;

To provide and Maintain a Navy;

To make Rules for the Government and Regulation of the land and naval Forces;

To provide for calling forth the Militia to execute the Laws of the Union, suppress Insurrections and repel Invasions;

To provide for organizing, arming, and disciplining, the Militia, and for governing such Part of them as may be employed in the Service of the United States, reserving to the States respectively, the Appointment of the Officers, and the Authority of training the Militia according to the discipline prescribed by Congress;

To exercise exclusive Legislation in all Cases whatsoever, over such District (not exceeding ten Miles square) as may, by Cession of particular States, and the Acceptance of Congress, become the Seat of the Government of the United States, and to exercise like Authority over all Places purchased by the Consent of the Legislature of the State in which the Same shall be, for the Erection of Forts, Magazines, Arsenals, dock-Yards, and other needful Buildings;—And

To make all Laws which shall be necessary and proper for carrying into Execution the foregoing Powers, and all other Powers vested by this Constitution in the Government of the United States, or in any Department or Officer thereof.

In addition to grants of power, the Constitution contains guarantees of individual rights, and limitations on the exercise of power by both the Federal and state governments. Many of these rights are contained in the so-called Bill of Rights which consists of the first ten amendments to the Constitution. These amendments are made applicable to the states by the Fourteenth Amendment. Justice Harlan in the discussion which follows discusses the role of the Bill of Rights in the Constitution and also mentions the doctrines of Federalism, often called "states' rights," and separation of powers.

THE BILL OF RIGHTS AND THE CONSTITUTION [1]
John M. Harlan, Associate Justice of the Supreme Court of the United States

---

We . . . begin by recalling the specific provisions of the Bill of Rights. They speak with such eloquent simplicity and clarity as to defy paraphrasing, and their words should be read in full.

AMENDMENT I

Congress shall make no law respecting an establishment of religion, or prohibiting the free exercise thereof; or abridging the freedom of speech, or of the press; or the right of the people peaceably to assemble, and to petition the Government for a redress of grievances.

[1] 50 *A.B.A.J.* 918 (Oct., 1964). Used by permission from the American Bar Association and the *American Bar Association Journal.*

AMENDMENT II

A well regulated Militia, being necessary to the security of a free State, the right of the people to keep and bear Arms, shall not be infringed.

AMENDMENT III

No Soldier shall, in time of peace be quartered in any house, without the consent of the Owner, nor in time of war, but in a manner to be prescribed by law.

AMENDMENT IV

The right of the people to be secure in their persons, houses, papers, and effects, against unreasonable searches and seizures, shall not be violated, and no Warrants shall issue, but upon probable cause, supported by Oath or affirmation, and particularly describing the place to be searched, and the persons or things to be seized.

AMENDMENT V

No person shall be held to answer for a capital, or otherwise infamous crime, unless on a presentment or indictment of a Grand Jury, except in cases arising in the land or naval forces, or in the Militia, when in actual service in time of War or public danger; nor shall any person be subject for the same offense to be twice put in jeopardy of life or limb; nor shall be compelled in any criminal case to be a witness against himself, nor be deprived of life, liberty, or property, without due process of law; nor shall private property be taken for public use, without just compensation.

AMENDMENT VI

In all criminal prosecutions, the accused shall enjoy the right to a speedy and public trial, by an impartial jury of the State and district wherein the crime shall have been committed, which district shall have been previously ascertained by law, and to be informed of the nature and cause of the accusation; to be confronted with the witnesses against him; to have compulsory process for obtaining witnesses in his favor, and to have the Assistance of Counsel for his defense.

AMENDMENT VII

In Suits at common law, where the value in controversy shall exceed twenty dollars, the right of trial by jury shall be preserved, and no fact tried by a jury, shall be otherwise reexamined in any Court of the United States, than according to the rules of the common law.

AMENDMENT VIII

Excessive bail shall not be required, nor excessive fines imposed, nor cruel and unusual punishments inflicted.

AMENDMENT IX

The enumeration in the Constitution of certain rights, shall not be construed to deny or disparage others retained by the people.

AMENDMENT X

The powers not delegated to the United States by the Constitution, nor prohibited by it to the States, are reserved to the States respectively, or to the people.

While these amendments symbolize the respect for the individual that is the cornerstone of American political concepts, it would be a grave mistake to regard them as the full measure of the bulwarks of our free society. Except for the first three amendments, they are largely procedural protections against particular kinds of arbitrary governmental action and touch the activities of relatively few people; standing alone they do not account for the broad spectrum of freedoms which the people of this country enjoy. They were indeed not a part of the original handiwork of the framers of the Constitution.

The men who wrote the Constitution recognized, with unmatched political wisdom, that true liberty can rise no higher or be made more secure than the spirit of a people to achieve and maintain it. Their prime concern was to devise a form of government for the new nation under which such a spirit might thrive and find the fullest opportunity for expression. The amendments comprising the Bill of Rights followed only after the structure of government had been established by the Constitution proper. They resulted not so much from what the framers considered to be new ideological imperatives as from fears among the states that the national government might seek to tamper with individual rights already largely assured under the laws of the various states. The movement for a Bill of Rights was given added impetus by the passage of the Northwest Ordinance, under which the Federal Government was to administer the western territories, all claims to sovereignty over which had been relinquished by the states. That instrument, passed by the Continental Congress sitting at Federal Hall in New York at the same time as the Constitutional Convention was meeting in Philadelphia, contained what amounted to a formal Bill of Rights of its own.

For the most part the rights assured by these first ten amendments against federal invasion were simply those enjoyed by Englishmen under the institutions of the mother country, having their origins in the provisions of Magna Charta, that famed fountainhead of individual liberty. There were, however, two notable extensions of those rights: freedom of religion and freedom of speech and press, the former stemming from what had been growing colonial practice, and the latter being spurred by the prosecution and acquittal of John Peter Zenger for seditious libel, which had taken place in New York in 1735.

In short, as the debates at the Constitutional Convention and the terms of the Constitution itself both reveal, the framers proceeded on a premise which many years later Judge Learned Hand was to state in the following words: "Liberty lies in the hearts of men and women; when it dies there, no constitution, no law, no court can save it; no constitution, no law, no court even can do much to help it." They staked their faith that liberty would prosper in the new nation not primarily upon declarations of individual rights but upon the kind of government the Union was to have. And they determined that in a government of divided powers lay the best promise for realizing the free society it was their object to achieve.

The matter had a double aspect: *first,* the division of governmental authority between the states and the central government; *second,* the distribution of power within the federal establishment itself. The former, doubtless born not so much of political principle as of the necessity for achieving a more perfect union than had proved possible under the Articles of Confederation, was solved by making the authority of the Federal Government supreme within the sphere of powers expressly or impliedly delegated to it and reserving to the states all other powers—a reservation which subsequently found express protection in the Bill of Rights through the provisions of the Tenth Amendment. The second aspect of the governmental structure was solved, purely as a matter of political theory, by distributing the totality of federal power among the legislative, executive and judicial branches of the government, each having defined functions. Thus eventuated the two great constitutional doctrines of federalism—often inaccurately referred to as the doctrine of states' rights—and separation of powers.

These doctrines lie at the root of our constitutional system. It is manifest that no view of the Bill of Rights or interpretation of any of its provisions which fails to take due account of them can be considered constitutionally sound.

As was previously indicated, state constitutions generally do not enumerate powers granted but provide for the types of activity and legislation which is forbidden, such as ex post facto laws and laws impairing the obligation of contract. The following example contains excerpts which prohibit special legislation favoring or discriminating against any individual, group, or locality in the state in question.

CONSTITUTION OF THE STATE OF ILLINOIS
Article IV, Section 22

The General Assembly shall not pass local or special laws in any of the following enumerated cases, that is to say: For—

Granting divorces;
Changing the names of persons or places; . . .
Regulating county and township affairs;
Regulating the practice in courts of justice; . . .
Providing for the management of common schools;
Regulating the rate of interest on money;
The opening and conducting of any election, or designating the place of voting; . . .
The protection of game or fish; . . .
Remitting fines, penalties or forfeitures; . . .
Changing the law of descent; . . .
Granting to any corporation, association or individual any special or exclusive privilege, immunity or franchise whatever.
In all other cases where a general law can be made applicable, no special law shall be enacted.

State constitutions also authorize the delegation to local governments of certain responsibility and authority, including the authority to enact local laws in the form of ordinances, resolutions, or bylaws.

The case which follows illustrates the application of a state constitutional prohibition against special legislation.

LORTON V. BROWN COUNTY COMMUNITY UNIT SCH. DIST. NO. 1
220 N.E.2d 161 (Ill. 1966)

UNDERWOOD, JUSTICE: Emma Lorton, a private kindergarten teacher, slipped and fell upon the floor of a school building in the basement of which the private kindergarten was operated with the knowledge and consent of the board of education of Brown County Community Unit School District No. 1. . . . She filed a two-count complaint seeking damages for the resulting injuries from the district and its board of education in the amount of $10,000. . . . Plaintiff . . . alleged that defendants' agent had been given by plaintiff the information usually furnished in the required six-months notice (by statute), and in reliance upon statements by such agents plaintiff failed to seek legal counsel or file written notice of her injury.

A motion to dismiss this complaint was allowed. An amended complaint was then filed alleging in greater detail the acts of defendants' agents upon which plaintiff relies in failing to secure counsel or give timely notice, and adding a third count in which it was alleged that The Home Indemnity Company was defendants' insurer, that its agents caused plaintiff to believe payment of her claim was being considered and that in reliance thereon she refrained from securing legal counsel or giving notice. This count sought a declaratory judgment that the insurer be estopped from asserting failure to file timely notice as a defense to the action. Motions by all defendants to dismiss the amended complaint were allowed and judgment was entered against plaintiff which she now seeks to reverse. . . .

Section 3 of the act in question provides that written notice must be filed with the proper authority within six months from the date of the injury, and section 4 provides that the failure to file such notice requires dismissal of any action filed on account of such injury. Plaintiff maintains that these provisions violate section 22 of article IV of the Illinois constitution, which states in part: "The General Assembly shall not pass local or special laws in any of the following enumerated cases, . . . Granting to any corporation, association or individual any special or exclusive privilege, immunity or franchise whatever," since no such notice requirement exists as to other similar municipal corporations.

In *Harvey v. Clyde Park District*, 32 Ill. 2d 60, 65, 203 N.E.2d 573, 576, this court, in determining that a statutory provision purporting to immunize Park Districts from liability for negligence of their agents, employees, etc. violated section 22 of article IV, observed that "Many of the activities that frequently give rise to tort liability are common to all governmental units. . . . From the perspective of the injured party, or from the point of view of ability to insure against liability for negligent operation, there is no reason why one who is injured by a park district truck should be barred from recovery, while one who is injured by a city or village truck is allowed to recover, and one injured by a school district truck is allowed to recover only within a prescribed limit. And to the extent that recovery is permitted or denied on an arbitrary basis, a special privilege is granted in violation of section 22 of article IV."

The court there surveyed the various statutory schemes governing governmental unit tort liability and stated: "If the child involved in the present case had been injured on a slide negligently maintained in a park operated by a city or village there is no legislative impediment to full recovery. If the child had been injured on a slide negligently maintained by a school district, or by the sovereign State, limited recovery is permitted. But if the child had been injured on a slide negligently maintained by a forest preserve district, or, as was actually the case, by a park district, the legislature has barred recovery." . . .

We believe the rationale of *Harvey* is controlling here, for if plaintiff's injury had occurred upon the property of a county, township, or drainage district, her cause of action would not have been barred by failure to file written notice within six months of the injury. If, however, the injury had occurred upon the property of a city or village . . . public or private school . . . as was actually the case, or the Metropolitan Transit Authority . . . the failure to file written notice within 6 months from the date of injury would wholly bar her from recovery. As in *Harvey,* there is in this pattern "no discernible relationship to the realities of life." . . . It is interesting to note that the General Assembly, responding to the suggestion in *Harvey,* enacted in 1965 the Local Governmental and Governmental Employees Tort Immunity Act . . . containing uniform provisions relating to notices of injuries, the effect of failure to secure such notices, and limitations of actions thereon involving "local public entities."

It does not matter that the notice requirement here is procedural in nature, for failure to file completely bars the action. The courts of this State must be open to all those similarly situated upon the same conditions, and where procedures are provided which are applicable to some and not applicable to others under substantially like circumstances and there are no discernible logical reasons apparent for the variations, they must fall as violative of section 22 of article IV of the Illinois constitution. . . .

We therefore hold that the notice provisions of the act questioned herein are null and of no force and effect. . . . [REVERSED]

Thus constitutions provide the organization and powers of government. In so doing, they establish the legal framework for society and the methods for making law. Written laws flow directly from constitutional grants or limitations, and unwritten or case law flows indirectly from the same source.

3 TREATIES

The President is given the power to make treaties, with the advice and consent of the Senate, in Article II, Section 2 of the Constitution. This power has grown in its importance to the economic life and defense of the nation, as the United States has become a leader in world affairs.

The treaties of most countries affect only their external relations with other countries. The United States is unique in that its treaties are part of the "supreme Law of the Land," and thus have the internal force of the

Constitution and laws enacted by Congress. Because of this, many persons have argued for a limitation on the treaty-making power, as well as the power of the President to make "executive agreements" with the heads of other governments. Article VI of the Constitution provides in part: "This Constitution, and the Laws of the United States which shall be made in Pursuance thereof; and all Treaties made, or which shall be made, under the Authority of the United States, shall be the supreme Law of the Land; and the Judges in every State shall be bound thereby, any Thing in the Constitution or Laws of any State to the Contrary notwithstanding."

Note that the language employed makes the laws enacted by Congress binding only if made within the limitations of the Constitution but apparently provides no such restriction on the effect of treaties made "under the Authority of the United States." In the following case, the issue before the Supreme Court was the effect of a treaty on the right of the state of Missouri to control migratory birds within its borders.

STATE OF MISSOURI V. HOLLAND
252 U.S. 416 (1920)

HOLMES, JUSTICE: This is a bill in equity brought by the State of Missouri to prevent a game warden of the United States from attempting to enforce the Migratory Bird Treaty Act of July 3, 1918, . . . and the regulations made by the Secretary of Agriculture in pursuance of the same. The ground of the bill is that the statute is an unconstitutional interference with the rights reserved to the States by the Tenth Amendment, and that the acts of the defendant done and threatened under that authority invade the sovereign right of the State and contravene its will manifested in statutes. The State also alleges a pecuniary interest, as owner of the wild birds within its borders and otherwise admitted by the Government to be sufficient, but it is enough that the bill is a reasonable and proper means to assert the alleged quasi sovereign rights, of a State. . . . A motion to dismiss was sustained by the District Court on the ground that the act of Congress is constitutional. . . . The State appeals.

On December 8, 1916, a treaty between the United States and Great Britain was proclaimed by the President. It recited that many species of birds in their annual migrations traversed certain parts of the United States and of Canada, that they were of great value as a source of food and in destroying insects injurious to vegetation, but were in danger of extermination through lack of adequate protection. It therefore provided for specified closed seasons and protection in other forms, and agreed that the two powers would take or propose to their law-making bodies the necessary measures for carrying the treaty out. . . . The above mentioned Act of July 3, 1918, entitled an act to give effect to the convention, prohibited the killing, capturing or selling any of the migratory birds included in the terms of the treaty except as permitted by regulations compatible with those terms, to be made by the Secretary of Agriculture. Regulations were proclaimed on July 31, and October 25, 1918. . . . It is unnecessary to go into any details, because, as we have said, the question raised is the general one whether the treaty and statute are void as an interference with the rights reserved to the States.

To answer this question it is not enough to refer to the Tenth Amendment, reserving the powers not delegated to the United States, because by Article II, § 2, the power to make treaties is delegated expressly, and by Article VI treaties made under the authority of the United States, along with the Constitution and laws of the United States made in pursuance thereof, are declared the supreme law of the land. If the treaty is valid there can be no dispute about the validity of the Statute under Article I, § 8, as a necessary and proper means to execute the powers of the Government. The language of the Constitution as to the supremacy of treaties being general, the question before us is narrowed to an inquiry into the ground upon which the present supposed exception is placed.

It is said that a treaty cannot be valid if it infringes the Constitution, that there are limits, therefore, to the treaty-making power, and that one such limit is that what an act of Congress could not do unaided, in derogation of the powers reserved to the States, a treaty cannot do. An earlier act of Congress that attempted by itself and not in pursuance of a treaty to regulate the killing of migratory birds within the States had been held bad in the District Court. . . . Those decisions were supported by arguments that migratory birds were owned by the States in their sovereign capacity for the benefit of their people, and that under cases like *Geer v. Connecticut,* 161 U.S. 519, this control was one that Congress had no power to displace. The same argument is supposed to apply now with equal force.

Whether the two cases cited were decided rightly or not they cannot be accepted as a test of the treaty power. Acts of Congress are the supreme law of the land only when made in pursuance of the Constitution, while treaties are declared to be so when made under the authority of the United States. It is open to question whether the authority of the United States means more than the formal acts prescribed to make the convention. We do not mean to imply that there are no qualifications to the treaty-making power; but they must be ascertained in a different way. It is obvious that there may be matters of the sharpest exigency for the national well being that an act of Congress could not deal with but that a treaty followed by such an act could, and it is not lightly to be assumed that, in matters requiring national action, "a power which must belong to and somewhere reside in every civilized government" is not to be found. *Andrews v. Andrews,* 188 U.S. 14, 33. What was said in that case with regard to the powers of the States applies with equal force to the powers of the nation in cases where the States individually are incompetent to act. We are not yet discussing the particular case before us but only are considering the validity of the test proposed. With regard to that we may add that when we are dealing with words that also are a constituent act, like the Constitution of the United States, we must realize that they have called into life a being the development of which could not have been foreseen completely by the most gifted of its begetters. It was enough for them to realize or to hope that they had created an organism; it has taken a century and has cost their successors much sweat and blood to prove that they created a nation. The case before us must be considered in the light of our whole experience and not merely in that of what was said a hundred years ago. The treaty in question does not contravene any prohibitory words to be found in the Constitution. The only question is whether it is forbidden by some invisible radiation from the general terms of the Tenth Amendment. We must consider what this country has become in deciding what the Amendment has reserved.

The State as we have intimated founds its claim of exclusive authority upon an assertion of title to migratory birds, an assertion that is embodied in statute. No doubt it is true that as between a State and its inhabitants the State may regulate the killing and sale of such birds, but it does not follow that its authority is exclusive of permanent powers. To put the claim of the State upon title is to lean upon a slender reed. Wild birds are not in the possession of anyone; and possession is the beginning of ownership. The whole foundation of the State's rights is the presence within their jurisdiction of birds that yesterday had not arrived, tomorrow may be in another State and in a week a thousand miles away. If we are to be accurate we cannot put the case of the State upon higher ground than that the treaty deals with creatures that for the moment are within the state borders, that it must be carried out by officers of the United States within the same territory, and that but for the treaty the State would be free to regulate this subject itself.

As most of the laws of the United States are carried out within the States and as many of them deal with matters which in the silence of such laws the State might regulate, such general grounds are not enough to support Missouri's claim. Valid treaties of course "are as binding within the territorial limits of the States as they are elsewhere throughout the dominion of the United States." *Baldwin v. Franks*, 120 U.S. 678, 683. No doubt the great body of private relations usually fall within the control of the State, but a treaty may override its power. We do not have to invoke the later developments of constitutional law for this propositiion; it was recognized as early as *Hopkirk v. Bell*, 3 Cranch 454, with regard to statutes of limitation, and even earlier, as to confiscation, in *Ware v. Hylton*, 3 Dall. 199. It was assumed by Chief Justice Marshall with regard to the escheat of land to the State in *Chirac v. Chirac*, 2 Wheat. 259, 275. . . . So as to a limited jurisdiction of foreign consuls within a State. *Wildenhus's* case,

120 U.S. 1. . . . . Further illustration seems unnecessary, and it only remains to consider the application of established rules to the present case.

Here a national interest of very nearly the first magnitude is involved. It can be protected only by national action in concert with that of another power. The subject-matter is only transitorily within the State and has no permanent habitat therein. But for the treaty and the statute there soon might be no birds for any powers to deal with. We see nothing in the Constitution that compels the Government to sit by while a food supply is cut off and the protectors of our forests and our crops are destroyed. It is not sufficient to rely upon the States. The reliance is vain, and were it otherwise, the question is whether the United States is forbidden to act. We are of opinion that the treaty and statute must be upheld. *Carey v. South Dakota,* 250 U.S. 118. [DECREE AFFIRMED]

The development of the European Common Market has presented economic challenges which our Federal government may desire to meet by joining its activities, and it has reaffirmed the importance of the treaty-making power to the economic life of the United States.

In *United States v. Curtis-Wright Corp.,*[2] the Supreme Court had occasion to discuss the difference in the powers of the Federal government over foreign affairs and internal affairs. Justice Sutherland, speaking for the court, noted:

. . . It will contribute to the elucidation of the question if we first consider the differences between the powers of the federal government in respect of foreign or external affairs and those in respect of domestic or internal affairs. That there are differences between them, and that these differences are fundamental, may not be doubted.

The two classes of powers are different, both in respect of their origin and their nature. The broad statement that the federal government can exercise no powers except those specifically enumerated in the Constitution and such implied powers as are necessary and proper to carry into effect the enumerated powers, is categorically true only in respect of our internal affairs. In that field, the primary purpose of the Constitution was to carve from the general mass of legislative powers then possessed by the states such portions as it was thought desirable to vest in the federal government, leaving those not included in the enumeration still in the states. Carter v. Carter Coal Co., 298 U.S. 238, 294. That this doctrine applied only to powers which the states had, is self evident. And since the states severally never possessed international powers, such powers could not have been carved from the mass of state powers but obviously were transmitted to the United States from some other source. . . .

[2] 299 U.S. 304 (1936).

Rulers come and go; governments end and forms of government change; but sovereignty survives. A political society cannot endure without a supreme will somewhere. Sovereignty is never held in suspense. When, therefore, the external sovereignty of Great Britain in respect of the colonies ceased, it immediately passed to the Union. . . .

4   LEGISLATION

Legislation, in the technical sense, is a process by which general rules for the course of human conduct are consciously enacted for the general population by government. Legislation differs from law arising from an adjudicated case in that the latter is specific in application, is retroactive in effect, and involves secondary rights while the former is general in application, is prospective in effect, and involves primary rights. The doctrine of separation of powers indicates that the function of making laws, or legislation, is the province of the legislature. This function must be distinguished from the administrative function of the executive branch and the judicial function, but, as we shall see, the borders of these branches of government are not capable of exact location and each branch performs some of the functions of the other. While some persons would deny that courts or the executive legislate, this denial is without merit. This chapter uses the word "legislate" in the technical sense and not in its broader aspect which would include the creation of all laws.

When a problem of society has been recognized to exist, the legislative process involves the answering of the following questions by the governmental body entrusted with the legislative function: (1) Does the problem in question exist because of defects or voids in the system of control of human conduct now in use? (2) Could and would the problem be solved by legislation? (3) Should the problem be solved by this legislative body, or should it be solved by some other social force or legislative body? (4) What law should be adopted, that is, what is the best solution to the problem? (5) How should the selected law or rule of conduct be enforced? Each of these questions has been answered whenever legislation is adopted, the answers being controlled in part by social forces operating within the legislative body, and in part by social forces operating upon it from without. In addition, the answers involve value judgments which are influenced to a great extent by the background, experience, and conscious or subconscious motivations of the legislator.

Issues which are basic to our political system are raised by the foregoing questions. In determining whether legislation should be adopted or not, the argument often is reduced to one of "individualism" versus "paternalism" in government, with one side arguing for less governmental activity and the other for an expanding role of government. Question 3 requires a decision whether the best solution to the problem exists at the local, state, or Federal level. The proposal of Federal aid to education raised many arguments on the foregoing points. Question 5 involves a selection from the variety of sanctions available to a legislative body, such as declaring certain conduct to be criminal for which fine or imprisonment is imposed; allowing civil remedies such as injunctions or causes of action for dollar damages; or simply granting or denying licenses to applicants.

Each state in its constitution and by statute has prescribed the procedural steps to be followed in enacting legislation. These usually require a number of readings of the bill and its formal presentation to the governor after its passage. Occasionally, in a controversy concerning the validity of a statute, a party challenging the statute may do so on the basis of the procedures followed by the legislative body. For example, several state constitutions provide that statutes are effective July 1, *after* passage. Legislative bodies in those states frequently "stop the clock" at midnight on June 30, ignoring the actual date, with the purpose of having their closing actions take effect immediately instead of being delayed for one year. In recent years, courts in some states have tended to allow the effective date of such statutes to be challenged.

Similarly, some state constitutions have procedural rules providing for the maximum time that a regular legislative session is permitted to last, such as West Virginia, where a regular session may not exceed 60 days. In a 1963 case,[3] the Supreme Court of Appeals of West Virginia held that a Sunday "blue" law passed by the legislature of that state was void and of no effect, because it contravened the foregoing provision. The evidence in that case disclosed that the official clock had been stopped at 11:58 P.M. on the sixtieth day to prolong the session in question, but that, in fact, the bill had been enacted early in the morning of the sixty-first day.

The case which follows involves several aspects of legislative procedure. While the exact procedural rules will vary from state to state, this case does illustrate the types of legal problems which might arise concerning such rules. Note that the requirement of approval by the governor is a part of the concept of separation of powers, and provides a check on legislative action. Most constitutions require a two-thirds majority to pass a statute over a veto.

RICHARDS FURNITURE CORP. V. BOARD OF COUNTY COMMISSIONERS
196 A.2d 621 (Md. 1964)

PRESCOTT, JUSTICE: . . .

The appellant challenges the validity of an Act of the General Assembly, set forth below. It has literally "thrown the book" at the Act. It states nine

[3] *State ex rel. Heck's Discount Centers, Inc., v. Winters,* 132 S.E.2d 374 (W. Va. 1963).

separate questions to be answered, with the eighth subdivided into three questions and the ninth into six. . . .

Richards, a Maryland Corporation, rents space and sells furniture in a large building built and owned by the Ritchie Highway Farmers Market, Inc. (Market), known as and called the Ritchie Highway Farmers Market. . . .

The evidence indicates that the Market building, in its entirety, is open for business on Wednesdays and Thursdays from 4:00 to 10:00 P.M.; Fridays and Saturdays from 10:00 A.M. to 10:00 P.M.; and on Sundays from 12:00 noon to 6:00 P.M. The evidence further reveals that approximately 30,000 automobiles visit the Market each week, of which one-third of the total arrive every Sunday. In short, about one-third of the weekly business is transacted on Sundays. Not only does the Market, by its advertisements, hold itself out as the sole and responsible owner of the Market, containing a number of shops and selling a variety of goods, but it exercises a great deal of control over the merchants who occupy space within the Market building. . . . It is also significant that the occupants of the entire building are accommodated by one large parking lot, which is owned and operated by the Market. . . .

The Act complained of reads as follows:

In Anne Arundel County, in addition to the articles of merchandise herein before mentioned, retailers may sell, barter, deal in, and deliver on Sunday the following articles of merchandise . . . [many articles of merchandise, not relevant here]; provided, however, that nothing in this subtitle shall be construed to prevent the operation of any retail establishment on Sunday, the operation of which does not entail the employment of more than one person, not including the owner or proprietor. Every market or department store in which stalls or departments are rented or concessions given to individual merchants or vendors shall be considered as one establishment and each stall or department thereof is not a separate establishment." [*The emphasized portion above was added by the amendment of 1962.*]

I, II, III, IV, V

We shall consider the first five of appellant's contentions under this heading. It asserts that the Maryland Constitution prohibits a special session of the General Assembly from enacting "a non-emergency local bill," citing Article II, Section 16, and Article III, Sections 14, 15, and 27, thereof. It admits finding no Maryland decision to this effect and that the Constitution does not explicitly state any such prohibition, but argues the above sections implicitly do so. We do not find it necessary to set forth the sections in detail. The Maryland Constitution is not a grant of powers to the General Assembly, but a statement of limitations on its otherwise plenary powers. . . .

A careful reading of the Constitution reveals that the only constitutional limitations on extraordinary, or special, sessions are: (1) that the session be convened by a proclamation of the Governor (formerly this was not required); (2) the session shall last no longer than thirty days; and (3) no additional compensation, except mileage and other allowances provided by law, shall be allowed members for such sessions. Section 15 provides that the General Assembly, once properly convened, shall be the sole judge of how long "the public interest may require" (within certain limitations) it to continue in session. There can be little doubt that, at a special session, the public interest requires the Legislature to remain in session, within the thirty-day limit, as long as any necessary and proper legislation is under consideration and before it. . . .

We find no express nor implied provision in the Constitution preventing the passage of a "non-emergency local bill" at a special session. It is generally held that in the absence of constitutional limitation, the legislative power of a Legislature, when convened in extraordinary session, is as broad as its powers in its regular sessions. . . .

We, therefore, hold that the General Assembly was not prohibited from passing the Act because it was a non-emergency local bill.

What we have said above also nearly answers the next four of appellant's contentions. However, we shall add a few further comments concerning them.

The appellant next attacks the Act on the ground that it was not within the Governor's proclamation. The Constitution of Maryland grants no authority to the Governor to limit, by his proclamation, the powers of the Legislature. In the absence of such a restrictive provision, the authorities hold, as stated above, that the powers of the Legislature at a special session are as broad as at its general ones. . . .

Appellant also claims it "was denied its constitutional rights because of a lack of notice of the intended legislation." It does not state the constitutional provisions alleged to have been violated, nor does it cite any case in support of this contention. It cites one or more cases which deal with the title requirements of Article III, Section 29, and seems to argue from certain language in the opinions of cases decided thereunder (which deal with titles) that "notice" of proposed legislation must be given to each citizen and corporation affected by it. Unless the Constitution so provides, due process does not require that notice and hearing be provided in order to validate legislation. There is no provision for such notice in the Maryland Constitution. We may note, however, that "notice" is inherent in the legislative process in this State. Under our democratic form of government, the Senators and Delegates are elected as representatives of the people. Ample safeguards in the Constitution provide that these representatives shall have notice of proposed legislation: each bill must be read on three different days in each House (unless a two-thirds vote authorizes otherwise), Article III, Section 27; no bill shall be read a third time unless actually engrossed or printed, *Ibid.*; and a journal of the proceedings in both Houses must be made and published, Article III, Section 22. We find no merit in this contention.

In arguing that it "was denied its constitutional rights because of the lack of opportunity for a hearing or the right to petition the legislature," appellant again cites cases dealing with titles to bills under Section 29 of Article III. Our constitution, as stated above, does not require that a hearing be held upon suggested legislation; Article 13 of the Declaration of Rights provides: "That every man hath a right to petition the Legislature for the redress of grievances in a peaceable and orderly manner. . . ."

It is clear, we think, that the authors and the people who actually adopted our Declaration of Rights intended no more than to permit any person or peaceable assembly of persons, without fear of reprisal or prosecution, to communicate directly with the legislative body by way of a statement of grievances and a petition requesting a correction of wrongs previously committed. The appellant is seeking herein not a right to petition for the redress of an alleged grievance after the passage of a law which it does not like, but the right of a hearing and a right to petition before the passage of the law. The right guaranteed by Article 13 provides no assistance to the appellant in this regard. . . .

Under its argument that "the action of the Legislature as a whole constitutes unfair and unequal treatment to plaintiff," appellant lists no less than seventeen alleged errors in what it terms "outline form." Many of them are repetitions of claimed errors under other headings. Although all of them have been considered, we think only two deserve brief consideration in this opinion: (1) "K. Non-descriptive title of the bill"; and (2) "L. Reading of the bill by title only." The title complied with Section 29 of Article III, and a reading of a bill by a reading of its title only is a sufficient "reading" thereof to satisfy the constitutional provision relating to three readings.

VI and VII

Under these headings, appellant contends that "the Governor vetoed (the Act) by reason of his failure to sign it within six days after presentation to him," and "a litigant . . . may inquire behind the forms of authentication (of a bill) and the General Assembly actions. . . ." The special session ended on March 9, 1962. On the same day, the Chief Clerk of the House of Delegates delivered the Bill to the Secretary of State, who, on March 12, 1962, handed it, together with other bills, to the Governor. The Governor acknowledged their receipt by letter, and, in accordance with normal procedure, forwarded them to the Attorney General for review as to form and legal sufficiency. The authenticated copy of the Bill states in a memorandum signed by the Chief Clerk of the House that it was sealed and presented to the Governor on March 23, 1962; and it was signed by him on the same day.

Appellant argues that the authentication on the Bill is not conclusive, it has a right to go behind the same, and the Governor's letter and the testimony of the Chief Clerk "imply" that the Bill was "presented" on March 12, 1962. It is true that in a proper case the courts may inquire beyond the forms of authentication on a bill to determine whether it has been constitutionally enacted. However, an act which has been duly authenticated and published as law, as the Bill in the instant case has, bears a strong presumption that all constitutional provisions have been complied with, and it has been validly enacted into law; and this presumption continues to exist until the contrary is clearly made to appear. And a statute which has been duly authenticated is not to be impeached by parol evidence alone.

The appellant's effort to impeach the certification by the Chief Clerk that the Bill was presented to the Governor on March 23, 1962, falls far short of what is necessary to accomplish such an impeachment; and demonstrates, we think, a failure to comprehend the true meaning of the "presentation" of a bill to the Governor as provided for by Article 2, Section 17, of the Constitution and Code (1957), Article 41, Section 45. Such a presentation to the Governor for his signature is a formal act and anticipates that the bill will be sealed with the great seal and actually and formally "presented" to the Governor for his signature by the Secretary of the Senate or Chief Clerk of the House, who in the presence of the Governor, shall make a memorandum thereon in writing of the day and hour of its presentation, and sign the same: The mere informal receipt by the Governor's office of a bill for other purposes is not a requirement of law, and carries with it no legal significance such as to require action by the Governor in any specified time. If this were not true, many practical difficulties would be encountered on such occasions as when several hundred bills passed by the General Assembly are delivered to the Governor before he has had time carefully to consider them and to have the Attorney General pass upon their validity. We hold that the Bill was actually presented to the Governor on March 23, 1962, and that this was a reasonable and legal time after passage of the Bill for its presentation.

The remainder of appellant's argument under these headings is answered by a short quotation. . . .

After it has been presented to the Governor, there are three ways in which such a bill may become a law: (1) By being signed by the Governor. (2) By being passed over his veto. (3) By his failure to return the bill within six days after its receipt by him unless the General Assembly has adjourned and thereby prevented its return. In the case before us, the Legislature (as in the case at bar) had adjourned before the bill was presented to the Governor, and, therefore, under the provisions of the Constitution, Article II, Section 17, it could only become a law by the signature of the Governor.

VIII

. . . We do not find the statute vague or indefinite in a constitutional sense. It is unnecessary to elaborate upon this point in great detail. The Act is couched in plain and simple language, which may be easily understood by persons of ordinary intelligence. This is all that is required of a statute in order to prevent it from being vague and indefinite in a constitutional sense.

. . . The Act was constitutionally enacted and appellant's business operations on Sundays were prohibited by it. . . .

Further discussion of the problem of the validity of Sunday closing or "blue" laws is found in Chapter 17.

5   INTERPRETATION OF LEGISLATION

While there would be no need for interpretation of a statute which was direct, clear, and precise, most legislation is by its very nature general, being stated to cover a multitude of fact situations. Thus, courts constantly are faced with the problem of finding the meaning of general statutes as applied to the specific facts of the cases before them. They must fill in the "gaps" of the legislation or eliminate an ambiguity by construing the legislative intent. The application of a general principle to a particular situation makes honest differences of opinion inevitable. Since language is an imperfect method of communication between human beings, a determination that no ambiguity exists is itself an act of interpretation.

One technique of statutory interpretation is to examine the legislative history of an act to determine the purpose of the legislation, or the evil it was designed to correct. Courts try to find the legislature's answers to the five questions referred to above by examining committee reports, amendments which were rejected, and other matters which transpired prior to the adoption of the statute. While this technique frequently is followed, the truth often is that the individual members of the legislature voted for the statute for many different reasons, and the legislative history does not give a clear meaning to the language used in the statute. History *may* supply the legislative intent, but many of the questions of interpretation which confront courts were never even visualized by the legislature. The real problem often is to determine what the legislature *would have* intended, had it considered the question.

The legislative intent is, therefore, either nonexistent or undiscoverable in many cases; in many others, a resort to legislative history affords an accurate and compelling guide to legislative meaning.

Judges frequently differ on the meaning of legislative history and some judges will choose to ignore it when resort to it will indicate that their opinion on the meaning of the statute was not intended. In the case which follows, the dissent relied on legislative history but the majority chose to ignore it. Notice that a person's liberty was taken by interpreting a statute but that the Justices themselves could not agree on its meaning. How, then, could the defendant, Caminetti, have been expected to know "the law" and govern his conduct accordingly? There are several rules of statutory construction used by both the majority and dissenting judges in the Caminetti case, besides its legislative history, to ascertain the meaning of the language of the statute in issue.

CAMINETTI V. UNITED STATES
242 U.S. 470 (1916)

Petitioner was convicted for violation of the so-called White Slave Traffic Act for transporting in interstate commerce a certain woman with the intention and purpose that she should become his mistress and concubine. He appealed, contending that the statute was intended to reach only "commercialized vice" or the traffic in women for gain, and in support of his position relied on the legislative history of the act.

DAY, JUSTICE: It is elementary that the meaning of a statute must, in the first instance, be sought in the language in which the act is framed, and if that is plain, and if the law is within the constitutional authority of the lawmaking body which passed it, the sole function of the courts is to enforce it according to its terms. . . .

Where the language is plain and admits of no more than one meaning, the duty of interpretation does not arise, and the rules which are to aid doubtful meanings need no discussion. . . . There is no ambiguity in the terms of this act. It is specifically made an offense to knowingly transport or cause to be transported, etc., in interstate commerce, any woman or girl for the purpose of prostitution or debauchery, or for "any other immoral purpose," or with the intent and purpose to induce any such woman or girl to become a prostitute or to give herself up to debauchery, or to engage in any other immoral practice.

Statutory words are uniformly presumed, unless the contrary appears, to be used in their ordinary and usual sense, and with the meaning commonly attributed to them. To cause a woman or girl to be transported for the purposes of debauchery, and for an immoral purpose, to wit, becoming a concubine or mistress, for which Caminetti and Diggs were convicted; or to transport an unmarried woman, under eighteen years of age, with the intent to induce her to engage in prostitution, debauchery, and other immoral practices, for which Hays was convicted, would seem by the very statement of the facts to embrace transportation for purposes denounced by the act, and therefore fairly within its meaning.

While such immoral purpose would be more culpable in morals and attributed to baser motives if accompanied with the expectation of pecuniary gain, such considerations do not prevent the lesser offense against morals of furnishing transportation in order that a woman may be debauched, or become a mistress or a concubine, from being the execution of purposes within the meaning of this law. To say the contrary would shock the common understanding of what constitutes an immoral purpose when those terms are applied, as here, to sexual relations.

In *United States v. Bitty,* 208 U.S. 393, . . . it was held that the act of Congress against the importation of alien women and girls for the purpose of prostitution "and any other immoral purpose" included the importation of an alien woman to live in concubinage with the person importing her. In that case this court said:

All will admit that full effect must be given to the intention of Congress as gathered from the words of the statute. There can be no doubt as to what class was aimed at by the clause forbidding the importation of alien women for purposes of "prostitution." It refers to women who, for hire or without hire offer their bodies to indiscriminate intercourse with men. The lives and example of such persons are in hostility to "the idea of the family, as consisting in and springing from the union for life of one man and one woman in the holy estate of matrimony; the sure foundation of all that is stable and noble in our ciivlization; the best guaranty of that reverent morality which is the source of all beneficent progress in social and political improvement." Murphy v. Ramsey, 114 U.S. 15, 45. . . . Now the addition in the last statute of the words, "or for any other immoral purpose," after the word "prostitution," must have been made for some practical object. Those added words show beyond question that Congress had in view the protection of society against another class of alien women other than those who might be brought here merely for purposes of "prostitution." In forbidding the importation of alien women "for any other immoral purpose," Congress evidently thought that there were purposes in connection with the importations of alien women which, as in the case of importations for prostitution, were to be deemed immoral. It may be admitted that, in accordance with the familiar rule of ejusdem generis, *the immoral purpose referred to by the words "any other immoral purpose" must be one of the same general class or kind as the particular purpose of "prostitution" specified in the same clause of the statute. 2 Lewis's Sutherland, Stat. Constr. § 423, and authorities cited. But that rule cannot avail the accused in this case; for the immoral purpose charged in the indictment is of the same general class or kind as the one that controls in the importation of an alien woman for the purpose strictly of prostitution. The prostitute may, in the popular sense, be more degraded in character than the concubine, but the*

latter none the less must be held to lead an immoral life, if any regard what-
ever be had to the views that are almost universally held in this country as
to the relations which may rightfully, from the standpoint of morality, exist
between man and woman in the matter of sexual intercourse.

This definition of an immoral purpose was given prior to the enactment of the act now under consideration, and must be presumed to have been known to Congress when it enacted the law here involved.

But it is contended that though the words are so plain that they cannot be misapprehended when given their usual and ordinary interpretation, and although the sections in which they appear do not in terms limit the offense defined and punished to acts of "commercialized vice," or the furnishing or procuring of transportation of women for debauchery, prostitution, or immoral practices for hire, such limited purpose is to be attributed to Congress and engrafted upon the act in view of the language of § 8 and the report which accompanied the law upon its introduction into and subsequent passage by the House of Representatives.

In this connection, it may be observed that while the title of an act cannot overcome the meaning of plain and unambiguous words used in its body . . . the title of this act embraces the regulation of interstate commerce "by prohibiting the transportation therein for immoral purposes of women and girls, and for other purposes." It is true that § 8 of the act provides that it shall be known and referred to as the "White Slave Traffic Act," and the report accompanying the introduction of the same into the House of Representatives set forth the fact that a material portion of the legislation suggested was to meet conditions which had arisen in the past few years, and that the legislation was needed to put a stop to a villainous interstate and international traffic in women and girls. Still, the name given to an act by way of designation or description, or the report which accompanies it, cannot change the plain import of its words. If the words are plain, they give meaning to the act, and it is neither the duty nor the privilege of the courts to enter speculative fields in search of a different meaning.

Reports to Congress accompanying the introduction of proposed laws may aid the courts in reaching the true meaning of the legislature in cases of doubtful interpretation. . . . But, as we have already said, and it has been so often affirmed as to become a recognized rule, when words are free from doubt they must be taken as the final expression of the legislative intent, and are not to be added to or subtracted from by considerations drawn from titles or designating names or reports accompanying their introduction, or from any extraneous source. In other words, the language being plain, and not leading to absurd or wholly impracticable consequences, it is the sole evidence of the ultimate legislative intent. . . .

The fact, if it be so, that the act as it is written opens the door to blackmailing operations upon a large scale, is no reason why the courts should refuse to enforce it according to its terms, if within the constitutional authority of Congress. Such considerations are more appropriately addressed to the legislative branch of the government, which alone has authority to enact and may, if it sees fit, amend the law. *Lake County v. Rollins,* 130 U.S. 673. [JUDGMENT AFFIRMED]

[A total of five justices shared the viewpoint expressed by the foregoing opinion. However, three of the justices joined in the reasoning expressed by the following dissenting opinion, taking the stand that Caminetti ought not have been convicted under the language of the statute.]

MC KENNA, JUSTICE, dissenting: Undoubtedly, in the investigation of the meaning of a statute we resort first to its words, and, when clear, they are decisive. The principle has attractive and seemingly disposing simplicity, but that it is not easy of application, or, at least, encounters other principles, many cases demonstrate. The words of a statute may be uncertain in their signification or in their application. If the words be ambiguous, the problem they present is to be resolved by their definition; the subject matter and the lexicons become our guides. But here, even, we are not exempt from putting ourselves in the place of the legislators. If the words be clear in meaning, but the objects to which they are addressed be uncertain, the problem then is to determine the uncertainty. And for this a realization of conditions that provoked the statute must inform our judgment. Let us apply these observations to the present case.

The transportation which is made unlawful is of a woman or girl "to become a prostitute or to give herself up to debauchery, or to engage in any other immoral practice." Our present concern is with the words "any other immoral practice," which, it is asserted, have a special office. The words are clear enough as general descriptions; they fail in particular designation; they are class words, not specifications. Are they controlled by those which precede them? If not, they are broader in generalization and include those that precede them, making them unnecessary and confusing. To what conclusion would this lead us? "Immoral" is a very comprehensive word. It means a dereliction of morals. In such sense it covers every form of vice, every form of conduct that is contrary to good order. It will hardly be contended that in this sweeping sense it is used in the statute. But, if not used in such sense, to what is it limited and by what limited? If it be admitted that it is limited at all, that ends the imperative effect assigned to it in the opinion of the court. But not insisting quite on that, we ask again, By what is it limited? By its context, necessarily, and the purpose of the statute.

For the context I must refer to the statute; of the purpose of the statute Congress itself has given us illumination. It devotes a section to the declaration that the "act shall be known and referred to as the 'White Slave Traffic Act.'" And its prominence gives it prevalence in the construction of the statute. It cannot be pushed aside or subordinated by indefinite words in other sentences, limited even there by the context. It is a peremptory rule of construction that all parts of a statute must be taken into account in ascertaining its meaning, and it cannot be said that § 8 has no object. Even if it gives only a title to the act, it has especial weight. . . . But it gives more than a title; it makes distinctive the purpose of the statute. The designation "white slave traffic" has the sufficiency of an axiom. If apprehended, there is no uncertainty as to the conduct it describes. It is commercialized vice, immoralities having a mercenary purpose, and this is confirmed by other circumstances.

The author of the bill was Mr. Mann, and in reporting it from the House committee on interstate and foreign commerce he declared for the committee that it was not the purpose of the bill to interfere with or usurp in any way the police power of the states, and further, that it was not the intention of the bill to regulate prostitution or the places where prostitution or immorality was practised, which were said to be matters wholly within the power of the states, and over which the Federal government had no jurisdiction. And further explaining the bill, it was said that the sections of the act had been "so drawn that they are limited to the cases in which there is an act of transportation in interstate commerce of women for the purposes of prostitution." And again:

The White Slave Trade.—A material portion of the legislation suggested and proposed is necessary to meet conditions which have arisen within the past few years. The legislation is needed to put a stop to a villainous interstate and international traffic in women and girls. The legislation is not needed or intended as an aid to the states in the exercise of their police powers in the suppression or regulation of immorality in general. It does not attempt to regulate the practice of voluntary prostitution, but aims solely to prevent panderers and procurers from compelling thousands of women and girls against their will and desire to enter and continue in a life of prostitution. Cong. Rec. vol. 50, pp. 3368, 3370.

In other words, it is vice as a business at which the law is directed, using inter-state commerce as a facility to procure or distribute its victims.

In 1912 the sense of the Department of Justice was taken of the act in a case where a woman of twenty-four years went from Illinois, where she lived, to Minnesota, at the solicitation and expense of a man. She was there met by him and engaged with him in immoral practices like those for which petitioners were convicted. The assistant district attorney forwarded her statement to the Attorney General, with the comment that the element of traffic was absent from the transaction and that therefore, in his opinion, it was not "within the spirit and intent of the Mann Act." Replying, the Attorney General expressed his concurrence in the view of his subordinate.

Of course, neither the declarations of the report of the committee on interstate commerce of the House nor the opinion of the Attorney General are conclusive of the meaning of the law, but they are highly persuasive. The opinion was by one skilled in the rules and methods employed in the interpretation or construction of laws, and informed, besides, of the conditions to which the act was addressed. The report was by the committee charged with the duty of investigating the necessity for the act, and to inform the House of the results of that investigation, both of evil and remedy. The report of the committee has, therefore, a higher quality than debates on the floor of the House. The representations of the latter may indeed be ascribed to the exaggerations of advocacy or opposition. The report of a committee is the execution of a duty and has the sanction of duty. There is a presumption, therefore, that the measure it recommends has the purpose it declares and will accomplish it as declared.

This being the purpose, the words of the statute should be construed to execute it, and they may be so construed even if their literal meaning be otherwise. In *Church of the Holy Trinity v. United States,* 143 U.S. 457, 36 L. Ed. 226, 12 Sup. Ct. 511, there came to this court for construction an act of Congress which made it unlawful for anyone in any of the United States "to prepay the transportation, or in any way assist or encourage the importation or migration of any alien or aliens, any foreigner or foreigners, into the United States . . . under contract or agreement . . . to perform labor or *service of any kind* (italics mine) in the United States, its territories or the District of Columbia." The Trinity Church made a contract with one E. W. Warren, a resident of England, to remove to the city of New York and enter its service as rector and pastor. The church was proceeded against under the act and the circuit court held that it applied, and rendered judgment accordingly, 36 Fed. 303.

It will be observed that the language of the statute is very comprehensive,—fully as much so as to the language of the act under review,—having no limitation whatever from the context: and the circuit court, in submission to what the court considered its imperative quality, rendered judgment against the church. This court reversed the judgment, and, in an elaborate opinion by Mr. Justice Brewer, declared that "it is a familiar rule that a thing may be within the letter of the statute and yet not within the statute, because not within its spirit, nor within the intention of its makers." And the learned justice further said: "This has been often asserted, and the reports are full of cases illustrating its application."

It is hardly necessary to say that the application of the rule does not depend upon the objects of the legislation, to be applied or not applied as it may exclude or include good things or bad things. Its principle is the simple one that the words of a statute will be extended or restricted to execute its purpose.

Another pertinent illustration of the rule is *Reiche v. Smythe,* 13 Wall. 162, 20 L. Ed. 566, in which the court declared that if at times it was its duty to regard the words of a statute, at times it was also its duty to disregard them, limit or extend them, in order to execute the purpose of the statute. And applying the principle, it decided that in a tariff act the provision that a duty should be imposed on horses, etc., and other *live animals* imported from foreign countries should not include canary birds, ignoring the classification of nature. And so again in *Silver v. Ladd,* 7 Wall. 219, 19 L. Ed. 138, where the benefit of the Oregon Donation Act was extended by making the words "single man" used in the statute mean an unmarried woman, disregarding a difference of genders clearly expressed in the law.

The rule that these cases illustrate is a valuable one and in varying degrees has daily practice. It not only rescues legislation from absurdity (so far the opinion of the courts admits its application), but it often rescues it from invalidity,—a useful result in our dual form of governments and conflicting jurisdictions. It is the dictate of common sense. Language, even when most masterfully used, may miss sufficiency and give room for dispute. Is it a wonder, therefore, that when used in the haste of legislation, in view of conditions perhaps only partly seen or not seen at all, the consequences, it may be, beyond present foresight, it often becomes necessary to apply the rule? And it is a rule of prudence and highest sense. It rescues from crudities, excesses, and deficiencies, making legislation adequate to its special purpose, rendering unnecessary repeated qualifications and leaving the simple and best exposition of a law the mischief it was intended to redress. Nor is this judicial legislation. It is seeking and enforcing the true sense of a law notwithstanding its imperfection or generality of expression.

There is much in the present case to tempt to a violation of the rule. Any measure that protects the purity of women from assault or enticement to degradation finds an instant advocate in our best emotions; but the judicial function cannot yield to emotion—it must, with poise of mind, consider and decide. It should not shut its eyes to the facts of the world and assume not to know what everybody else knows. And everybody knows that there is a difference between the occasional immoralities of men and women and that systematized and mercenary immorality epitomized in the statute's graphic phrase "white slave traffic." And it was such immorality that was in the legislative mind, and not the other. The other is occasional, not habitual,—inconspicuous,—does not offensively obtrude upon public notice. Interstate commerce is not its instrument as it is of the other, nor is prostitution its object or its end. It may, indeed, in instances, find a convenience in crossing state lines, but this is its accident, not its aid.

There is danger in extending a statute beyond its purpose, even if justified by a strict adherence to its words. The purpose is studied, all effects measured, not left at random,—one evil practice prevented, opportunity given to another. The present case warns against ascribing such improvidence to the statute under review. Blackmailers of both sexes have arisen, using the terrors of the construction now sanctioned by this court as a help—indeed, the means—for their brigandage. The result is grave and should give us pause. It certainly will not be denied that legal authority justifies the rejection of a construction which leads to mischievous consequences, if the statute be susceptible of another construction.

United States v. Bitty, 208 U.S. 393, 52 L. Ed. 543, 28 Sup. Ct. 396, is not in opposition. The statute passed upon was a prohibition against the importation of alien women or girls,—a statute, therefore, of broader purpose than the one under review. Besides, the statute finally passed upon was an amendment to a prior statute, and the words construed were an addition to the prior statute, and necessarily, therefore, had an added effect. The first statute prohibited the importation of any alien woman or girl into the United States *for the purpose of prostitution* (italics mine). The second statute repeated the words and added *"or for any other immoral purpose."* Necessarily there was an enlargement of purpose, and besides, the act was directed against the importation of foreign corruption, and was construed accordingly. The case, therefore, does not contradict the rule; it is an example of it.

For these reasons I dissent from the opinion and judgment of the court, expressing no opinion of the other propositions in the cases.

I am authorized to say that the Chief Justice and Mr. Justice Clarke concur in this dissent.

In the foregoing case, there were three rules of statutory interpretation mentioned in the majority opinion and two others in the dissent in addition to its resort to legislative history. They were:

Majority

1. *Unless contrary intent appears, statutory words are uniformly presumed to be used in their ordinary and usual sense, and with the meaning commonly attributed to them.*
2. *Statutes which are consistent with one another, and which relate to the same subject matter, are* in pari materia *and should be construed together, and effect be given to them all, although they may contain no reference to one another and were passed at different times.*
3. *Where a general word in a statute follows particular and specific words of the same nature as itself, it takes its meaning from them, and is presumed to be restricted to the same genus as those words* (e.g., *a statute naming "ox, cow, heifer, steer, or other cattle" does not include a bull). This rule is called* ejusdem generis.

Dissent

1. *The meaning of a doubtful word may be ascertained by reference to the meaning of words with which it is associated. (This rule is sometimes referred to as* noscitur a sociis; *it is similar to the rule of* in pari materia *but is applied to sentences and sections of a single statute.)*

2. *A thing may be within the letter of the statute and yet not within the statute, because not within its spirit nor within the intention of the makers.*

The dissent might have used still another rule of statutory construction:

Criminal statutes (and taxing laws) should be strictly constructed.

It becomes apparent that, because there are many rules of statutory construction and because they themselves are so general, a rule could be found to support almost any view as to the meaning of the language of a given statute. The difficulty of statutory construction is further illustrated by examining two frequently quoted rules.

1. *Statutes in derogation of the common law are to be strictly construed.*
2. *Remedial statutes are to be liberally construed.*

The problem of the above two rules is simply stated: Every statute in derogation of the common law is remedial in some sense; and, every remedial statute is in derogation of the common law. How are statutes to be construed—strictly or liberally? Volumes have been written on the problems of statutory interpretation, but as Judge Learned Hand said, "They haven't advanced us very far."

The case which follows involves a statute in derogation of the common law. It was not strictly construed. The decision of the court hinged mainly on the interpretation of the word "negligence," as it was used in a statute. Recall that, strictly speaking, the tort of negligence involves the injury of another person or his property proximately caused by *carelessness*, thus distinguishing it from a tort resulting from an *intentional* wrongful act, such as trespass to the person.

JAMISON V. ENCARNACION
281 U.S. 635 (1929)

Plaintiff, a longshoreman, sued defendant, his employer, for personal injuries incurred when he was struck by another employee while loading a barge. The jury awarded plaintiff $2,500 and the defendant appealed, contending that the applicable statutes only created liability for negligence and since the tort was intentional there was no liability. The Court of Appeals of New York held that the word "seamen" in the Federal Employers' Liability Act included "stevedores" and that "negligence" included "misconduct."

BUTLER, JUSTICE: The question is whether "negligence" as there used includes the assault in question. The measure was adopted for the relief of a large class of persons employed in hazardous work in the service described.

It abrogates the common-law rule that makes every employee bear the risk of injury or death through the fault or negligence of fellow servants, and applies the principle of respondeat superior (section 1), eliminates the defense of contributory negligence and substitutes a rule of comparative negligence (section 3 [45 U.S.C.A. § 53]), abolishes the defense of assumption of risk, where the violation of a statute enacted for the safety of employees is a contributing cause (section 4 [45 U.S.C.A. § 54]), and denounces all contracts, rules, and regulations calculated to exempt the employer from liability created by the act (section 5 [45 U.S.C.A. § 55]).

The reports of the House and Senate committees having the bill in charge condemn the fellow-servant rule as operating unjustly when applied to modern conditions in actions against carriers to recover damages for injury or death of their employees, and show that a complete abrogation of that rule was intended. The act, like an earlier similar one that was held invalid because it included subjects beyond the reach of Congress, is intended to stimulate carriers to greater diligence for the safety of their employees and of the persons and property of their patrons. . . .

The rule that statutes in derogation of the common law are to be strictly construed does not require such an adherence to the letter as would defeat an obvious legislative purpose or lessen the scope plainly intended to be given to the measure. . . . The act is not to be narrowed by refined reasoning or for the sake of giving "negligence" a technically restricted meaning. It is to be construed liberally to fulfill the purposes for which it was enacted, and to that end the word may be read to include all the meanings given to it by courts, and within the word as ordinarily used. *Miller v. Robertson*, 266 U.S. 243. . . .

As the Federal Employers' Liability Act (45 U.S.C.A. §§ 51–59) does not create liability without fault, . . . it may reasonably be construed in contrast with proposals and enactments to make employers liable in the absence of any tortious act, for the payment of compensation for personal injuries or death of employees arising in the course of their employment.

"Negligence" is a word of broad significance and may not readily be defined with accuracy. Courts usually refrain from attempts comprehensively to state its meaning. While liability arises when one suffers injury as the result of any breach of duty owed him by another chargeable with knowledge of the probable result of his conduct, actionable negligence is often deemed —and we need not pause to consider whether rightly—to include other elements. Some courts call willful misconduct evincing intention or willingness to cause injury to another gross negligence. . . . And it has been held that the use of excessive force causing injury to an employee by the superintendent of a factory in order to induce her to remain at work was not a trespass as distinguished from a careless or negligent act. . . . While the assault of which plaintiff complains was in excess of the authority conferred by the employer upon the foreman, it was committed in the course of the discharge of his duties and in furtherance of the work of the employer's business. As unquestionably the employer would be liable if plaintiff's injuries had been caused by mere inadvertence or carelessness on the part of the offending foreman, it would be unreasonable and in conflict with the purpose of Congress to hold that the assault, a much graver breach of duty, was not negligence within the meaning of the act. . . . [JUDGMENT AFFIRMED]

One common complaint of lawyers in statutory construction cases is that judges, under the guise of liberally construing a statute, frequently construe the facts of the case. Another similar problem arises when the trial judge admits that he does not know the meaning of the statute but makes a decision stating words to the effect that "The appellate court can reverse me if I'm wrong." The appellate court often then affirms the trial judge, stating that great deference is owed to his decision, and the burden is on the appellant to show that it was clearly wrong.

The cases which follow further illustrate some of the problems of statutory construction and the resulting difficulty that even a lawyer has in knowing what the law is. Each case is preceded by the major rule of construction used by the court. Notice also that such other matters as the objectives of the legislation as stated in preambles and debates, statements by executives in requesting the particular legislation, prior judicial decisions involving the same subject matter, and the title of the act are used as extrinsic aids to judicial interpretations.

A   STATUTES WILL BE CONSTRUED TO OPERATE RETROACTIVELY ONLY WHERE THAT IS THE CLEAR LEGISLATIVE INTENT

SCHEFFLER V. RINGHOFER
214 N.E.2d 575 (Ill. 1966)

BRYANT, PRESIDING JUSTICE: This is an appeal from an order granting summary judgment and dismissing the appellant's complaint for failure to state a cause of action.

This action has been brought by Anne Marie Scheffler as administratrix of the estate of her deceased son, Ralph. The complaint alleged that on July 26, 1957 Ralph, then being three and one-half years old, fell through the screen in a window of a third floor apartment in a building owned by the appellees. It was also alleged that the screens were negligently allowed to fall into disrepair by the appellees. The appellees then filed an answer in which they denied that the fall was occasioned by any negligent act of theirs.

The appellees made a motion for summary judgment. They alleged that there was no agreement between them and the tenant of the apartment from which the deceased fell as to the furnishing of any protective devices on the windows. It was also alleged that the screens were in the windows for the purpose of keeping out insects and were not placed there for the purpose of keeping children from falling out. They also cited *Crawford v. Orner & Shayne Inc.*, 331 Ill. App. 568, 73 N.E.2d 615 (1947) for the proposition that "a landlord has no duty to furnish screens for the purpose of keeping persons from falling out of a window."

The appellant then added a Count II to her complaint alleging that the appellees had violated Chap. 75 of the Municipal Code of Chicago, which chapter required that there be guard rails on windows having a sill less than two feet from the floor. It was also alleged that the window from which the deceased fell was less than two feet from the floor. The appellees then filed a motion to strike Count II of the complaint alleging that Chap. 75 was passed after the erection of the building where the accident occurred and that this chapter was prospective in operation and had no retroactive operation. On February 26, 1964 the motion was granted and Count II of the complaint was ordered stricken. On November 30, 1964 a motion for summary judgment was granted. . . .

The appellant's theory of the case before this court has been that the appellees violated their statutory duty in not providing guard rails at the window from which the deceased fell in accordance with Chap. 75 of the Municipal Code of Chicago . . . the appellant's appeal must fail. Chap. 75 of the Municipal Code of Chicago operates prospectively only and has no application to buildings already in existence when the law was passed. This is the general rule in construing any statute and it has long been settled that a statute will operate retroactively only where that is the clear legislative intent. . . . [ORDER AFFIRMED]

B   CRIMINAL STATUTES MUST BE WORDED CLEARLY ENOUGH TO INFORM A REASONABLE MAN OF THE NATURE OF THE OFFENSE PROHIBITED

PEOPLE V. BYRON
215 N.E.2d 345 (N.Y. 1966)

The defendant was convicted of violating a statute relating to mufflers. An intermediate or reviewing court reversed the conviction holding the statute unconstitutional for vagueness. The state appealed.

KEATING, JUSTICE: . . . On May 28, 1964, defendant was stopped by a State trooper and issued a uniform traffic ticket charging him with violating the Vehicle and Traffic Law which provides: "Mufflers. Prevention of noise. Every motor vehicle, operated or driven upon the highways of the state, shall at all times be equipped with an adequate muffler in constant operation and properly maintained to prevent any excessive or unusual noise and no such muffler or exhaust system shall be equipped with a cut-out, bypass, or similar device. . . ."

At the hearing, the trooper supplied a bill of particulars alleging that defendant operated his 1958 Studebaker without an adequate muffler, that the vehicle made a loud noise much in excess of the noise made by other vehicles which passed, that the muffler was in a bad state of repair and that defendant admitted it was in a bad state of repair and had been for some time. . . .

The prosecution in this case was for a "traffic infraction," not a crime, but such a prosecution is penal in nature and the rules of criminal law are generally applicable. As the County Judge stated, a criminal statute must be sufficiently definite, clear and positive to give unequivocal warning to citizens of the rule which is to be obeyed. It is also true, of course, that all presumptions and intendments favor the validity of a statute and mere doubt does not afford sufficient reason for a judicial declaration of invalidity.

It is our opinion that the statute in question states with sufficient clarity the rule which is to be obeyed. The test is whether a reasonable man subject to the statute would be informed of the nature of the offense prohibited and what is required of him. Such warning must be unequivocal but this requirement does not preclude the use of ordinary terms to express ideas which find adequate interpretation in common usage and understanding.

The evil sought to be prevented is "excessive or unusual noise." What is usual noise in the operation of a car has become common knowledge and anything in excess of that is excessive or unusual and any ordinary motorist should have no difficulty in ascertaining whether or not excessive or unusual noise accompanied the operation of his vehicle. The purpose of the statute, as made clear on its face, is not to *prohibit* noise but to *minimize* noise. We think the statute sufficiently describes the evil to be prevented and informs the motorist of his duty, not to eliminate all noise, but to have a properly maintained muffler to prevent unusual noise. When his muffler is in such a state of disrepair that the noise exceeds the usual level, the motorist has violated the statute.

The words of the Supreme Court upholding an ordinance prohibiting the use of instruments emitting "loud and raucous noises" are applicable here: "While these are abstract words, they have through daily use acquired a content that conveys to any interested person a sufficiently accurate concept of what is forbidden. . . ." [ORDER REVERSED AND MATTER REMITTED TO THE COUNTY COURT FOR FURTHER PROCEEDINGS NOT INCONSISTENT WITH THE OPINION HEREIN]

C THE MEANING OF A STATUTE MAY BE ESTABLISHED INDIRECTLY BY THE FAILURE OF THE LEGISLATIVE BODY TO ACT IN AN AREA IN WHICH THE LAW HAS BEEN BASED ON JUDICIAL DECISION OR ON INTERPRETATION BY THE EXECUTIVE BRANCH OF GOVERNMENT CHARGED WITH ITS ADMINISTRATION

STRAT-O-SEAL MANUFACTURING CO. V. SCOTT
218 N.E.2d 227 (Ill. 1966)

A taxpayer brought suit to enjoin the use of public funds for payment of public assistance to workers on strike and their families. The trial court found for the defendant, and the taxpayer appealed, contending that by such payments the State was not neutral in labor disputes and that the workers were not in need due to unavoidable causes. Taxpayer also pointed out that workers on strike could not receive unemployment compensation and thus the State had inconsistent positions.

SMITH, JUSTICE: . . . Plaintiffs argue that it is indeed anomalous to hold that a striker is voluntarily unemployed and ineligible for unemployment compensation benefits and, at the same time, hold that he is out of work due to "unavoidable cause" and thus eligible for general assistance benefits. Such patently inconsistent intent should not be charged to our legislators, it is said. If an anomaly does exist, it would appear that it is now about sixteen years old. In practice it has resulted in a denial of unemployment compensation to strikers and the allowance of aid to striking employees and their families under the Public Assistance Code. It seems hardly conceivable that this was not known to our legislators. They did nothing. Late in the 73rd General Assembly, Senate Bill 358 passed the Senate and was sent to the House incorporating into the Public Assistance Code the basically same provisions as to strikers which are in the Unemployment Compensation Act. Either for lack of time or insufficient votes or pure indifference—and for our purposes at this point it makes no difference—the bill did not pass. If the Public Assistance Code as it now exists denies payments to strikers and their families, no amendments are necessary. If the legislature felt that such payments should be specifically denied—and it knew or should have known that administratively they weren't being denied—it either failed or refused to say so. Devoid of legislative capacity, we see no reason for us to do a remodeling job when it would seem that the legislature likes the structure as it is and as it is being administered now. The Unemployment Compensation Act suggests that the legislature knows what language to use to specifically express its intention.

The present policy was generated by an unpublished opinion of the Attorney General to the State's Attorney of Will County dated May 5, 1950, in which he said:

> . . . It is my opinion that subject to the approval of the Illinois Public Aid Commission, if otherwise eligible, a person "in need" due to "unavoidable causes," is entitled to receive Public Assistance, even though he may be out of employment because of a strike.

A second opinion dated January 19, 1962, *Ops. Att'y Gen.* 189 (1962), reads in part as follows:

> . . . The Illinois Public Aid Commission also has this authority under Paragraph 607 of the Illinois Public Assistance Code, and nothing in the statutory sections discussed herein precludes the payment of Aid to Dependent Childen to the childen of persons engaged in a labor strike, where the other tests of eligibility are met.

Both sides concede that the issue before this Court is a matter of first impression in the courts of this State. This being true, these opinions of the Attorney General as Chief Law Officer of the State of Illinois "will be accorded considerable weight." . . . These opinions as well as administrative policy pursued as a result of them and the fact that the legislature has seen fit to remain quiescent through several successive sessions suggests and indicates "legislative acquiescence in the contemporary and continuous interpretation" which they announced. It would seem that we too ought to fold our tents and steal away.

To avoid our departure, plaintiffs suggest that final construction of statutes is for the courts and not for an executive or administrative branch of government and that an erroneous construction by such branches, even though somewhat aged, is not binding on the courts. This is true. Even though not binding, we have already indicated that it is and should be persuasive. In addition, we do not regard the interpretation given the Public Assistance Code over the years as patently erroneous. We cannot accept plaintiff's thesis that one who voluntarily participates or acquiesces in a strike cannot be considered unemployed for "unavoidable causes," or that one who voluntarily withholds his services from his employer by electing to go on a strike has "refused" employment which is available to him or that he has not "for good cause" refused a bona fide offer of suitable employment by refusing to remain on the job in the face of a bona fide strike. . . .

[AFFIRMED]

D   THE SPIRIT OF A LAW PREVAILS OVER A LITERAL
INTERPRETATION

ECK V. UNITED ARAB AIRLINES, INC.
203 N.E.2d 640 (N.Y. 1964)

The plaintiff, a resident of California, brought this action in the New York courts against the defendant, United Arab Airlines, an Egyptian corporation, for damages for injuries she sustained in a crash in Sudan. The trial court denied the defendant airline's motion to dismiss the complaint under Article 28 of the Warsaw Convention, which provides: "An action for damages *must* be brought, at the option of the plaintiff, *in the territory of one of the High Contracting Parties,* either *before the court of the domicile of the carrier or of his principal place of business, or where he has a place of business through which the contract has been made,* or *before the court at the place of destination."* [EMPHASIS ADDED] On review, the Appellate Division reversed, holding that New York was not one of the jurisdictions where suit may be brought under the Warsaw Convention, and dismissed the suit for lack of jurisdiction. The plaintiff then perfected this appeal to the Court of Appeals of New York.

BURKE, JUSTICE: . . . Plaintiff, a California resident, was a member of the Far West Ski Association, which contracted with Scandanavian Airlines System (SAS) on her behalf for passage in the early part of 1962 by air from Los Angeles to several countries in Europe, finally returning to Los Angeles. Plaintiff also arranged with the Oakland, California, office of SAS for the purchase of tickets for a side air trip while she was abroad between several cities in Europe and the Middle East. One of the flights listed in the ticket SAS obtained for the plaintiff was to be on defendant United Arab Airlines Flight No. 796 from Jerusalem to Cairo. Subsequently plaintiff was injured when Flight No. 796 crashed on March 16, 1962 in Wadi Halfa, Sudan, a place not scheduled as a stop on the flight, but where the pilot was diverted in an attempt to avoid bad weather at Cairo.

The defendant carrier maintains a place of business, a ticket office, in New York City. This office would have sold the plaintiff passage on the same United Arab Airlines flight that SAS ticketed her on. When the defendant opened its United States office in New York it anticipated that it would be amenable to suits there for claims arising out of any carriage sold by that office. If the plaintiff had purchased her ticket in that office the defendant would have to concede jurisdiction to our courts. But by happenstance the plaintiff made her purchase of a seat on Flight No. 796 in the SAS office which for our purposes could have been right next door. . . .

It is argued that article 28 expressly provides that a place of business, other than a principal place of business, outside the domicile of the carrier, will support jurisdiction only if the contract of carriage was made through that office. Defendant quotes that part of the article that, it asserts, places jurisdiction in the court "in the territory of one of the High Contracting Parties . . . *where he* [the carrier] *has a place of busines through which the contract has been made."* This is the basis for the result reached by the Appellate Division.

The crux of the problem is that the Appellate Division reached its conclusion by applying mechanically the *literal* translation of a phrase without an analysis of the treaty. The court overlooked the canon that, when a treaty is invoked, *what is to be applied are its principles if its purposes are to be observed presently as in the past.* . . . The reasoning which supports a strictly literal reading of the phrase might not have done violence to the overall scheme and design of the Convention under the conditions existing when the treaty was drafted. At that time it would have been in harmony with the methods under which the carriers were operating and with the objectives of the Convention. . . . Now, however, almost a half century later, when the carriers have radically changed their methods of booking passage, the whole scheme of the treaty in relation to international air travel makes it imperative to analyze this self-executing treaty in assigning meaning to any part of it. In doing this it must be recognized that the literal wording of one particularly applicable section of the entire treaty should not set the limits of our interpretive examination. . . . The proper procedure now is to examine the treaty as a whole, along with its history, and, in particular, to look into the problems which it was intended to solve.

This process displays the purpose underlying the treaty's adoption. The overall principle of the Convention was one of allowing only a regulated burden to be the responsibility of the then struggling carriers. The purposes were to *provide uniform rules of limitation concerning the liability* of international air carriers to their passengers and to *provide a uniform remedy for these passengers* to the extent that this remedy would not burden the carrier more than the Convention provisions allowed. These principles were expected to be operative with respect to conditions developing after the enactment of the Convention. In this light, the particular wording of article 28, with which we are here concerned, appears to have been intended to limit the bringing of suits to only those forums where the terms of the Convention were in force and would be applied. Moreover, the intent was to avoid suits in countries where the carrier had no office for the making of transportation contracts and where no passage on the carriers' aircraft had been purchased.

Allowing this suit does not run contrary to the Convention's provisions. Rather it gives a meaningful effect to the underlying principles by applying them to the realities of international air travel in these times. In 1926 these principles were put into a specific written formula which was meant to deal not only with the circumstances of an infant industry in that era but also accommodate itself consistently to changing conditions as the industry grew. The formula did not speak to the right to sue belonging to a traveler who purchased passage on one carrier from another carrier in a country where the first carrier itself maintained an office, because such a procedure was unknown. Travel agents and connecting carriers then cleared the bookings through the local officers. At the time of the enactment of the Convention, if a carrier had a ticket office in any particular country it would be a very exceptional case if the carriage was not booked through the airline's office there. Hence the phrase relied on by respondent then meant the office through which, *in the ordinary course of business,* the contract would be made. Today the volume of business done by the carriers requires a vast network of international communications and other ticket routing procedures—procedures not possible when this article was drafted in Paris in 1926, and ratified by this country in 1934.

. . . If the drafters of the treaty intended to discriminate against a passenger who purchased a ticket in a territory where the carrier had an office, but which the ultimate carrier decided should be cleared through an office outside that territory, such an intention should have been expressed. It cannot be implied, as such a change would take from the passengers, without notice, the very relief which the treaty gave them and intended that they continue to have. . . . A literal interpretation of the single clause in the convention, therefore, is at odds with the tenor of the document. . . . The interpretation given to the Convention by the Appellate Division would allow a passenger who purchased transportation through United Arab Airlines office in New York City to sue here, but compel a copassenger in the same accident who purchased transportation through another carrier in New York City in the same block to go abroad to bring suit. This construction rejects the fundamental rule set forth in the Convention.

Throughout subdivision (1) of article 28 the emphasis is on the distinction between absence or presence of the carrier in a territory, i.e., "domicile," "place of business," "destination." By the use of the words "where he has a place of business through which the contract has been made," the treaty barred a suit in a place where only a ticket was sold and where the carrier did not have an office. The clause also forbids a suit in a territory where the carrier had an office if the ticket was not purchased in that territory. . . . But because the place of business and the place of contracting were at that time in a single office, the phrase dealing with only known circumstances should not be read as exclusive. . . .

The preference of this court for being faithful to purpose rather than coldly literal is well established. In the case of *River Brand Rice Mills v. Latobe Brewing Co.,* 305 N.Y. 36, 110 N.E.2d 545 (1953) we said: " '[A] thing which is within the letter of the statute is not within the statute unless it be within the intention of the lawmakers, but a case within the intention of a statute is within the statute, though an exact literal construction would exclude it. . . .' " In the case of *New York Post Corp. v. Leibowitz,* 2

N.Y.2d 677, 163 N.Y.S.2d 409, 143 N.E.2d 256 (1957) Judge FULD wrote: "In construing statutory provisions, the spirit and purpose of the statute and the objectives sought to be accomplished by the legislature must be borne in mind." (2 N.Y.2d, 685, 163 N.Y.S.2d, 415, 143 N.E.2d, 260.) . . .

The provisions can be read in an excessively literal manner, but it is unreasonable to think that the signatories intended such an unwarranted construction. We will not deny the plaintiff the right to sue here since the purposes of the Convention in respect to consistency of remedy must be heeded, and analogous cases should be dealt with in a similar fashion.

Accordingly, the order of the Appellate Division should be reversed and the motion to dismiss the complaint should be denied, and the action remanded to the Supreme Court for further proceedings.

[Two of the Judges of the Court of Appeals of New York disagreed with the interpretation of the majority, favoring an interpretation based on the plain meaning of the words of the Warsaw Convention, and joined in the dissent which follows.]

BERGAN, JUSTICE, dissenting: The ratification of the Warsaw Convention by any of its high contracting parties necessarily took into account the domestic court system of each signatory when it came to providing for jurisdiction over actions arising in pursuance of the Convention. In respect of its judicial structure the United States differs from countries possessing a nationwide court of common jurisdiction over private lawsuits; and ratification of the Convention by the United States was with the territorial distribution of jurisdiction among the several State courts in mind.

Article 28 prescribes that an action may be brought "in the territory of one of the High Contracting Parties." But that clause does not authorize actions in any court within that territory. Jurisdiction is expressly limited to a specified court. An action must be brought in "the court . . . where he [the carrier] has a place of business through which the contract has been made."

In the United States this means the court in a State in which the specified conditions of jurisdiction can be met. Such an action cannot be brought in New York merely because a ticket was sold in California and because California is within the territory of the United States. The article defines "the court" as that court which exercises a territorial jurisdiction where the carrier has made the transportation contract in its place of business.

In some countries this might well mean any court in the Nation where the same national court has local jurisdiction everywhere. But the jurisdictional condition prescribed by article 28 is not met in New York unless the contract is made by the carrier through its office in this State.

General domestic policies of long standing suggest an absence of jurisdiction. New York has had no contact with the litigation. Neither party is a resident of New York; the contract was made in California; the accident which gives rise to the action occurred in Wadi Halfa, several thousand miles from our territory; the defendant is an Egyptian corporation; and its office in New York had nothing to do with plaintiff's contract.

What would have been the consequence had plaintiff made the contract in New York is irrelevant. The contract was not made here, but in California. Nor is the growth of air travel a new or decisive factor in deciding the jurisdictional question. The careful language of the Convention in respect of jurisdiction means the same thing now that it meant in 1926 when it was drafted and in 1934 when adopted by the United States.

The text states plainly that jurisdiction is conferred on a court in the place where (a) the carrier sued has a regular place of business; and (b) the contract is made through that place of business. These words are controlling on the question of our jurisdiction and they can be read in no other sense.

The order of the Appellate Division should be affirmed.

E   THE PLAIN MEANING OF THE WORDS OF A STATUTE SHOULD BE FOLLOWED

RINNERT V. INDIANAPOLIS MORRIS PLAN CORP.
220 N.E.2d 256 (III. 1966)

A statute was repealed by express provision of the Uniform Commercial Code effective on July 1, 1962. The repealed statute provided that an owner may sue and recover one-third of the value of property sold by a mortgagee or assignee of a mortgage if the mortgagee or assignee failed to deliver a statement with respect to the sale. Plaintiff's property was mortgaged in February, 1962, and was sold in May, 1964. The Uniform Commercial Code provided that transactions validly entered into before July, 1962, may be terminated, completed, consummated, or enforced as required or permitted by statutes repealed by the Uniform Commercial Code.

Plaintiff brought suit under the repealed statute for one-third of the value of the property sold because defendants did not deliver the required statement. The lower court dismissed the suit.

MORAN, JUSTICE: . . .

The Uniform Commercial Code . . . provides that:

Transactions validly entered into before the effective date specified in Section 10-101 (July 1, 1962) and the rights, duties, and interests flowing from them remain valid thereafter and may be terminated, completed, consummated or enforced as required or permitted by any statute or other law amended or repealed by this Act as though such repeal or amendment had not occurred.

This savings provision makes former law applicable to transactions entered into prior to the effective date. The defendant, however, argues that Sec. 10-102(2) provides only that rights, duties, and interests flowing from *transactions* remain valid thereafter, not rights, duties and interests flowing from *repealed statutes.*

Our Supreme Court has recently stated that "[t]he plain meaning of the language used is always the safest guide to follow in construing any act and the courts have no right to read into a statute words not found therein either by express inclusion or by fair implication." . . . The plain meaning of the savings provision is that rights, duties, and interests flowing from a transaction, whether statutory or not, may be terminated, completed, or consummated under the provisions of the old statutes when the transaction was entered into prior to July 1, 1962. This is the same interpretation which other jurisdictions have given to the identical provision. . . .

The penalty provision of Ch. 95, Sec. 27, was applicable to the sale of the mortgaged property and therefore the complaint should not have been dismissed.

The judgment of the trial court is reversed and this case is remanded for further proceedings not inconsistent with this opinion. [REVERSED AND REMANDED]

F   PENAL STATUTES ARE TO BE STRICTLY CONSTRUED

MC GILL v. 830 s. MICHIGAN HOTEL
216 N.E.2d 273 (Ill. 1966)

MURPHY, JUSTICE: Plaintiff, Winifred McGill, proceeding *pro se,* seeks to recover statutory damages for violation of her civil rights. She appeals from an order which struck her fourth amended complaint and dismissed her action.

Plaintiff, a hotel guest, bases her action on a series of weekly rent increases which commenced November 7, 1960, and have remained effective to the present time. Plaintiff alleges these rent increases were and continue to be violations of sections 125 and 126 of Chapter 38, Ill. Rev. Stat. 1961, and Article 13 of Chapter 38, Ill. Rev. Stat., effective as of January 1, 1962. . . .

In her fourth amended complaint, plaintiff alleges, in summary that she is a white person, and on September 12, 1960, became a tenant of the defendant, 830 S. Michigan Hotel, and occupied Room 410 at a weekly rental of $21.50; that because she received Negro visitors in her room, the weekly rental for plaintiff's room was increased to $26 on November 7, 1960, to $28 on December 10, 1960, and to $30 on January 16, 1961, for a total increase of 40% over a 10-week period; and defendants have continued to charge her the highest figure only because of her Negro visitors. Plaintiff further alleges there has been no equal increase in the weekly rentals asked of other guests at 830 S. Michigan Hotel from September 12, 1960, up to the present time; that "the defendants have not redecorated and repaired plaintiff's room, #410 when and as they have the rooms surrounding room #410"; and that "the defendants have wilfully, maliciously, illegally and unconscionably exploited plaintiff's desire and necessity to live in the area of the 830 S. Michigan Hotel, and the difficulties which she faces in securing suitable accommodations, because she is a white woman who associates with Negroes, by continuing each week to charge her an excessive and discriminatory rate for her room. . . ."

The complaint also alleges:

20. *Shortly after September 12, 1960, and at various times thereafter, plaintiff, who is white, received Negro visitors at the 830 S. Michigan Hotel.*

21. *On various occasions while plaintiff was receiving a Negro visitor at the 830 S. Michigan Hotel, the defendants . . . committed the following acts:*

   a. *K. Golden untruthfully told plaintiff that guests of the 830 S. Michigan Hotel are not permitted to receive visitors.*

   b. *K. Golden refused to provide plaintiff with a written notice stating that guests of the 830 S. Michigan Hotel are not permitted to receive visitors.*

   c. *K. Golden and various agents and/or employees of the 830 S. Michigan Hotel and/or Modern Management Company told plaintiff and her Negro visitor that if she did not "dismiss her guest," they would call the police and have them arrested for "loitering."*

The Illinois Criminal Code in effect on September 12, 1960, contained a "Civil Rights" act entitled "An Act to protect all citizens in their civil and legal rights and fixing a penalty for violation of the same," and sections 125 and 126 are pertinent here.

125. *All persons entitled to equal enjoyment of accommodations—Discrimination in price on account of race or color prohibited.) § 1. All persons within the jurisdiction of said State of Illinois shall be entitled to the full and equal enjoyment of the accommodation, advantages, facilities and privileges of inns, restaurants, eating houses, hotels, . . . subject only to the conditions and limitations established by laws and applicable alike to all citizens; . . .*

126. *Penalty.) § 2. That any person who shall violate any of the provisions of the foregoing section by denying to any citizen, except for reasons applicable alike to all citizens of every race and color, and regardless of color or race, the full enjoyment of any of the accommodations, advantages, facili-*

ties or privileges in said section enumerated, or by aiding or inciting such denial, shall for every such offense, forfeit and pay a sum not less than twenty-five ($25) dollars nor more than five hundred ($500) dollars to the person aggrieved thereby, to be recovered in any court of competent jurisdiction, in the county where said offense was committed; and shall also, for every such offense be deemed guilty of a misdemeanor, and upon conviction thereof, shall be fined not to exceed five hundred dollars ($500), or shall be imprisoned not more than one year, or both.

The foregoing sections were repealed as of January 1, 1962.

The provisions of Article 13, Chapter 38, Illinois Criminal Code, entitled "Violation of Civil Rights," became effective January 1, 1962, and have continued in effect up to this time.

13-1. Definitions.) (a) . . . A public place of accommodation or amusement includes inns, . . . hotels, . . . and all other places of public accommodation and amusement.

(b) . . . An operator of a public place of accommodation or amusement is any owner, lessee, proprietor, manager, superintendent, agent, or occupant of the public place of accommodation or amusement, or an employee of any such person or persons.

13-2. Elements of the Offense.) A person commits a violation of civil rights when:

(a) He denies to another the full and equal enjoyment of the facilities and services of any public place of accommodation or amusement because of race, religion, color or national ancestry; . . .

13-3. Sanctions.) . . .

(b) Suit for Damages. Any operator of a public place of accommodation or amusement who commits a violation of civil rights shall be liable to the person aggrieved thereby for not less than $100 nor more than $1000, to be recovered in an action at law in any court of competent jurisdiction.

Plaintiff prays for damages of $500 "for each discriminatory, unlawful written statement of rent due on room #410 which they submitted to plaintiff from November 7, 1960 to December 31, 1961, and of $1,000 for each unlawful, discriminatory written statement of rent due on room #410 which they have submitted to plaintiff since January 1, 1962, with the costs being assessed against defendants."

Although a motion to dismiss admits all facts well pleaded in the complaint, the indispensable requirement of the complaint is that the allegations state a cause of action. The . . . complaint is to be construed most strongly against plaintiff, but she is entitled to the reasonable intendments of the language used. . . .

Therefore, the issue on appeal is whether plaintiff's fourth amended complaint alleges ultimate facts sufficient to state a cause of action for the violation of plaintiff's civil rights and sufficient to bring the instant situation within the provisions of sections 125 and 126 and Article 13 of the Illinois Criminal Code.

Defendants contend that "plaintiff has no remedy under the Illinois Civil Rights Statute for any alleged discriminations against her for reasons other than her own race and color. She cannot prevail in her cause of action under the statute because of defendants' purported practice of discriminations against Negroes. No relief is provided for discrimination against third parties. The discrimination must be direct and personal and must be because of her own race and color. . . . [Plaintiff's] fourth amended complaint affirmatively shows that she, a white person, was not discriminated against because of her race or color."

Defendants also contended that Article 13 of Chapter 38 is not applicable to the facts presented by the fourth amended complaint, because the last purported discriminatory rate increase occurred one year prior to the effective date of said statute.

The Illinois authorities on this facet of civil rights are limited. The authorities cited from other states are not sufficiently in point to warrant extended discussion.

As to sections 125 and 126, in *Pickett v. Kuchan,* 323, Ill. 138, 140, 153 N.E. 667, 668, 49 A.L.R. 499 (1926), where our Supreme Court affirmed a verdict and judgment for damages for refusal to sell plaintiff a ticket of admission to a show given in appellant's theater, the court said:

> *The right of the state to regulate theaters and all places of public amusement is universally recognized. . . . The Legislature undoubtedly had the power to pass the act in question. Whether it acted wisely is a matter for it to determine. The judiciary have nothing to do with the wisdom or policy of legislation.*

The foregoing case is a good illustration of the fact that the rules of construction are used as an aid to find the intent of the legislature, the primary goal of courts in statutory interpretation. If the court feels for some reason that the application of a particular rule will not achieve that end, it will ignore the rule.

And at page 141, 153 N.E. at page 668:

> *Its purpose is to regulate, for the promotion of the public good, certain businesses in which the public have an interest, and it is therefore remedial. The remedy for the breach of a remedial statute is an action in case to recover damages for the injuries sustained.*

Defendants assert that "under the law of Illinois, the Civil Rights Act, being penal in its nature and being in derogation of the common law, must be strictly construed in determining its scope and effect even though it is intended as a remedial act." Cited is *Cedar Park Cemetery Ass'n. v. Cooper,* 408 Ill. 79, 83, . . . where the court said:

> *When a statute is penal in its nature, it cannot be extended by intendment or implication to embrace matters beyond its terms. . . . Where a statute has remedial features and is at the same time in derogation of the common law, it will be strictly construed when determining what persons come within ⋅ the statute.*

However correct this statement may be, it is equally true that penal laws are not to be construed so strictly as to defeat the obvious intention of the legislature. . . . Hence, we believe that the general rules of statutory construction should be applied here. "A statute or ordinance must be construed according to its intent and meaning and a situation that is within the object, spirit and meaning of the statute is regarded as within the statute, although not within the letter; and a situation that is within the letter is not regarded as within the statute unless also within its object, spirit and meaning." . . .

Both the new and the old "Civil Rights" acts provide that a person commits a violation of civil rights when he denies to another the full and equal enjoyment of the accommodations, facilities and services of a hotel because of race or color (§ 125), or race, religion, color or national ancestry (Article 13-2(a)). We believe that the alleged unexplained rent increases following the alleged acts of hotel employees informing "plaintiff and her Negro visitor that if she did not 'dismiss her guest,' they would call the police and have them arrested for 'loitering,' " and "untruthfully" telling plaintiff that "guests of the 830 S. Michigan Hotel are not permitted to receive visitors," would be considered by reasonable men to be acts of discrimination against plaintiff that fall "within the object, spirit and meaning of the statute . . . although not within the letter." . . . In our opinion, the race of the plaintiff is not the test of the violation. The determinative question is, were the rent increases and the attempted deprivation of plaintiff of the full and equal enjoyment of her hotel accommodations "because of race," either plaintiff's or her Negro visitors? If the acts complained of were, as alleged, "because of race," they come within the scope of the philosophy of the Illinois "Civil Rights" acts. Otherwise, the general purpose of the acts would be severely limited.

We hold that the fourth amended complaint alleges a prima facie cause of action for statutory damages under both acts and, therefore, the complaint should be answered.

For the reasons given, the order striking the fourth amended complaint and dismissing the action is reversed and the cause remanded for further proceedings consistent with the views expressed herein. [REVERSED AND REMANDED WITH DIRECTIONS]

The foregoing case is a good illustration of the fact that the rules of construction are used as an aid to find the intent of the legislature, the primary goal of courts in statutory interpretation. If the court feels for some reason that the application of a particular rule will not achieve that end, it will ignore the rule.

6   TRENDS IN WRITTEN LAW

The American Law Institute in the last several years has published *Restatements of the Law* in many fields such as contracts, torts, trusts, and conflicts of laws. These treatises have been drafted from the generally accepted principles of the common law found in numerous court decisions and have been prepared in reference form similar to a statute to assist in promoting certainty and clarity in the law. The statements of the law found in these compilations are prima facie correct. In the broadest sense, "written law" includes those references, which, although they do not have the force of legislation, are relied upon heavily by the courts and cited frequently with favor. The *Restatements of the Law* are under continual review and are revised as required.

The need for certainty and uniformity in the laws as between the states provided the impetus for several uniform statutes in areas previously controlled by court decisions, such as the Uniform Negotiable Instruments Law, the Uniform Sales Act, and the Uniform Partnership Act. The National Conference of Commissioners on Uniform State Laws, appointed by the governors of the various states, drafted these laws and has attempted to secure their passage in as many states as possible. Recently a desire for modernization, uniformity throughout the country, and consistency in *all* aspects of commercial law resulted in a draft by the Commissioners on Uniform Laws and the American Law Institute of a proposed statute known as the Uniform Commercial Code, which replaces and repeals many of the old uniform acts. In one internally consistent body of laws, the Code deals with all the aspects of a commercial transaction, or sale of personal property, from the contract of sale itself, to the security device which may be used to ensure the seller payment, the negotiable instrument given the seller by the buyer (such as a check or note), and the document of title to goods being sold. The Code also concerns itself with other commercial matters such as bulk sales, investment securities, and the bank collection process. The Code had few adoptions until 1961, but as of this writing, forty-nine states have enacted it.

The field of commercial law is not the only area of new codification. Many states are adopting revised criminal codes which contain modern procedures and concepts. In addition, the past few years have seen dynamic changes in both state and Federal statutes setting forth civil procedures and revising court systems. The future will undoubtedly bring many further developments to improve the administration of justice. The trend, despite some objection, is to cover more areas of the law with statutes and to rely less on precedent in judicial decisions, or common law, as a source of law.

CHAPTER THREE

LAW BY JUDICIAL DECISION

1 STARE DECISIS

In addition to the written law of constitutions, treaties, and statutes, there is a body of law sometimes referred to as "unwritten law," or judge-made law, which is created by judicial decisions. The common law is based on the doctrine of "stare decisis," the principle that prior decisions provide precedents which should be followed in subsequent cases involving the same question of law. In other words, where a rule of law has been announced and followed by courts so that the rule has become settled by judicial decisions, a precedent is established for future cases. Judicial decisions create precedent where there is no legislation as well as by interpreting legislation. The common law originated in England and was used by the colonies as the basis of their judicial systems. Most of the other states also followed English precedent when establishing their laws. Many state constitutions specifically adopt the common law except where changed by statute.

Not all common-law rules require several decisions for acceptance as precedent, but a decision standing alone will not necessarily invoke the doctrine of stare decisis where the decision has not been cited by the courts for many years, or is lacking in reason. The doctrine is generally only applicable to rules of law announced by courts of review, and it is these decisions that are available for legal research.

Stare decisis arose from the desire of courts as well as society for certainty and predictability in the law. In addition, following precedent was expedient. The common law, through precedent, settled many legal issues and brought stability into many areas of the law, such as contracts, enabling individuals to act in reliance upon prior decisions, with reasonable certainty as to the results of their conduct.

Notwithstanding the fact that the common law arose out of a desire for certainty, and is designed to create it, the fact of the matter is that the common law creates a great deal of uncertainty in the minds of laymen about the law. The sheer volume of judicial decisions, each possibly creating precedent, makes "the law" beyond the comprehension of lawyers let alone laymen. Large law firms employ lawyers whose sole task is to search the case reports for "the law" to be used in lawsuits and in advising their clients. Each lawyer must have access to literally hundreds of volumes so that he can find "the law." Since the total body of ruling case law is beyond the grasp of lawyers, it is obvious that laymen who are supposed to know the law and govern their conduct accordingly do not know the law and are somewhat bewildered by it. One legal scholar in discussing this anomaly, observed:

> *It is the judges that make the common law. Do you know how they make it? Just as a man makes laws for his dog. When your dog does anything you want to break him of, you wait till he does it, and then beat him for it. This is the way you make laws for your dog: and this is the way the judges make laws for you and me. They won't tell a man beforehand what it is he should not do—they won't so much as allow of his being told: they lie by till he has done something which they say he should not have done, and then they hang him for it. What way, then, has any man of coming at this dog-law? Only by watching their proceedings: by observing in what cases they have hanged a man, in what cases they have sent him to jail, in what cases they have seized his goods, and so forth.*[1]

There are other problems inherent in a legal system based in part on precedent. These are compounded in a country which consists of fifty sovereign states because each of these creates its own body of common law and the rules are frequently in conflict. Moreover, the Federal legal system is superimposed on the state systems, thus creating additional bodies of judge-made laws. The methods of determining the applicable precedent where conflicts exist between the laws of different jurisdictions are discussed later in this chapter.

One significant problem involving case law arises because conflicting precedents previously announced by the state where the action was brought are frequently presented by the parties to an action. One of the major tasks of the courts in such cases is to determine which precedent is applicable to the case at bar, and which is correct, if the cited authorities are in actual conflict. In addition, even today, many questions of law arise on which there has been no prior decision, or in areas where the only authority is by implication. In such situations, the judicial process is "legislative" in character and involves the creation of law, not merely its discovery. It should also be noted that there is a distinction between precedent and mere dicta. A judicial decision, as authority for future cases, is coextensive only with the facts upon which it is founded and the rules of law upon which the decision actually is predicated. Frequently courts make comments on matters not necessary to the decision reached. Such expressions, called "dicta," lack the force of an adjudication and, strictly speaking, are not precedent which the court will be required to follow within the rule of stare decisis. However, dicta or implication in prior cases may be followed if sound and just, and

---

[1] 5 Bentham, *Works* 235, quoted in 1 Steffen & Levi, *Cases and Materials on the Elements of the Law* 207 (3d ed. 1946).

dicta which has been repeated frequently is often given the force of precedent.

2 REJECTION OF STARE DECISIS

Courts in general hesitate to renounce precedent and usually assume that a principle or rule of law announced in a former judicial decision, if unfair or contrary to public policy, will be changed by legislation. Precedent has more force on trial courts than on courts of review, which have the power to make precedent in the first instance. However, stare decisis does not mean that former decisions *always* will be followed, even by trial courts. A former ruling may have been erroneous or the conditions upon which it was based may have changed or may no longer exist. The doctrine does not require courts to multiply their errors by using former mistakes as authority and support for new errors. Thus, just as legislatures change the law by new legislation, so also do courts change the law, from time to time, by reversing former precedents. Judges are subject to social forces and changing circumstances just as are legislatures. (The forces affecting decisions are discussed in Chapter 5.) The personnel of courts change, and each new generation of judges deems it a responsibility to reexamine precedents and to adapt them to the world of the times.

The changing of precedent is a strange phenomenon indeed. A party to a case who would lose under an established rule, argues against stagnation and in favor of ignoring the rule of stare decisis. If he successfully convinces the court to change its view, he is armed with a new precedent, and he becomes the advocate of the *status quo* for the new rule. Those who attacked stare decisis become champions of its cause. Justice William O. Douglas of the United States Supreme Court, in a speech before the New York City Bar, quoted Thomas Jefferson on the subject of stare decisis: "The problem of constitutional adjudication . . . is to keep our age unfettered by the fears or limited vision of another." Additional portions of this speech, which follow, illustrate some of the bases for rejecting precedent, and discuss those situations in which the doctrine of stare decisis will be or should be rejected.

STARE DECISIS [2]
William O. Douglas, Associate Justice of the Supreme Court of the United States

---

Most lawyers, by training and practice, are all too apt to turn their interests and their talents toward the finding not the creating of precedents. This

[2] The Eighth Annual Benjamin N. Cardozo Lecture delivered before the Association of the Bar of the City of New York on April 12, 1949. By permission from Justice William O. Douglas.

lawyerly search is for moorings where clients can be safely anchored. But the search has, as well, a deeper, more personal impetus. For the lawyer himself shares the yearning for security that is common to all people everywhere. And this yearning grows as the world seems to grow more *insecure*.

We live in an age of doubt and confusion. Rules that once seemed fixed and certain today seem beclouded. Principles of law have been challenged and judges asked to refashion them. Many raised their voices in protest. Some were special pleaders with a stake in existing law. Others had a sincere belief that the foremost function of law in these days of stress and strain is to remain steady and stable so as to promote security. Thus judges have been admonished to hold steadfast to ancient precedents lest the courts themselves add fresh doubt, confusion, and concern over the strength of our institutions.

This search for a static security—in the law or elsewhere—is misguided. The fact is that security can only be achieved through constant change, through the wise discarding of old ideas that have outlived their usefulness, and through the adapting of others to current facts. There is only an illusion of safety in a Maginot Line. Social forces like armies can sweep around a fixed position and make it untenable. A position that can be shifted to meet such forces and at least partly absorb them alone gives hope of security.

I speak here of long-term swings in the law. I do not suggest that *stare decisis* is so fragile a thing as to bow before every wind. The law is not properly susceptible to whim or caprice. It must have the sturdy qualities required of every framework that is designed for substantial structures. Moreover, it must have uniformity when applied to the daily affairs of men.

Uniformity and continuity in law are necessary to many activities. If they are not present, the integrity of contracts, wills, conveyances, and securities is impaired. (See *United States v. Title Ins. Co.*, 265 U.S. 472, 486–487.) And there will be no equal justice under law if a negligence rule is applied in the morning but not in the afternoon. *Stare decisis* serves to take the capricious element out of law and to give stability to a society. It is a strong tie which the future has to the past.

It is easy, however, to overemphasize *stare decisis* as a principle in the lives of men. Even for the experts law is only a prediction of what judges will do under a given set of facts—a prediction that makes rules of law and decisions not logical deductions but functions of human behavior. There are usually plenty of precedents to go around; and with the accumulation of decisions, it is no great problem for the lawyer to find legal authority for most propositions. The difficulty is to estimate what effect a slightly different shade of facts will have and to predict the speed of the current in a changing stream of the law. The predictions and prophecies that lawyers make are indeed appraisals of a host of imponderables. The decisions of yesterday or of the last century are only the starting points.

As for laymen, their conception of the rules of law that govern their conduct is so nebulous that in one sense, as Gray said, the law in its application to their normal affairs is to a very considerable extent *ex post facto.*

The place of *stare decisis* in constitutional law is even more tenuous. A judge looking at a constitutional decision may have compulsions to revere past history and accept what was once written. But he remembers above all else that it is the Constitution which he swore to support and defend, not the gloss which his predecessors may have put on it. So he comes to formulate his own views, rejecting some earlier ones as false and embracing others. He cannot do otherwise unless he lets men long dead and unaware of the problems of the age in which he lives do his thinking for him.

This reexamination of precedent in constitutional law is a personal matter for each judge who comes along. When only one new judge is appointed during a short period, the unsettling effect in constitutional law may not be great. But when a majority of a Court is suddenly reconstituted, there is likely to be substantial unsettlement. There will be unsettlement until the new judges have taken their positions on constitutional doctrine. During that time—which may extend a decade or more—constitutional law will be in flux. That is the necessary consequence of our system and to my mind a healthy one. The alternative is to let the Constitution freeze in the pattern which one generation gave it. But the Constitution was designed for the vicissitudes of time. It must never become a code which carries the overtones of one period that may be hostile to another.

So far as constitutional law is concerned *stare decisis* must give way before the dynamic component of history. Once it does, the cycle starts again. Today's new and startling decision quickly becomes a coveted anchorage for new vested interests. The former proponents of change acquire an acute conservatism in their new *status quo.* It will then take an oncoming group from a new generation to catch the broader vision which may require an undoing of the work of our present and their past. . . .

Much of what courts do is little understood by laymen. Very few portions of the press undertake to show the social, economic, or political significance of the work of the judiciary or to educate the public on long-term trends. Lawyers often do not see the broader view which is exposed by the narrow and intensely personal efforts of a client to vindicate a position or gain an advantage. Yet the work of a court may send a whole economy in one direction or help shape the manifest destiny of an era. Two illustrations from different periods of our history will indicate what I mean.

For at least a decade or more it was commonly assumed that the Fourteenth Amendment was adopted to protect Negroes in their newly won rights. Other interests had sought to creep under its wing. Thus corporations claimed they were persons within the meaning of the equal protection clause. Woods (then circuit judge) thought the language of the Amendment and its history too clear to admit of doubt on the point. In 1870 he rejected the contention in *Insurance Co. v. New Orleans,* 1 Woods 85. Sixteen years passed. Woods was now a member of the Court on which Waite was Chief Justice. A railroad company pressed its claim that California's tax assessment against it violated the Equal Protection Clause of the Fourteenth Amendment. Before the point was even argued, Waite announced from the bench that the Court did not care to hear argument on the question whether the clause applied to corporations. "We are all of opinion that it does," he said. (*Santa Clara Co. v. Southern Pac. R.R.,* 118 U.S. 394, 396.) Thus without argument or opinion on the point the *Santa Clara* case became one of the most momentous of all our decisions. It was not long before the same constitutional doctrine was extended to the Due Process Clause. Again the decision was cryptic and oracular, without exposition or explanation.

These decisions, whether right or wrong, sound or unsound, may have changed the course of our industrial history. Corporations were now armed with constitutional prerogatives. And so armed, they proceeded to the development and exploitation of a continent in a manner never equaled before or since. Some think these decisions helped give corporations what Parrington has called "the freedom of buccaneers." They doubtless did release some of the dynamic quality of the drive that built industrial America in a brilliant (albeit ruthless) way.

These unexplained (and certainly not obvious) decisions are now so implicit in the financial and industrial undertaking of the nation that a recent challenge of them had a resounding effect. Such is the hold of *stare decisis* on the profession.

A half century passed and the Court made another decision whose impact on industrial America was almost as profound.

In 1918 the Court in the *Dagenhart* case (*Hammer v. Dagenhart,* 247 U.S. 251) had decided that Congress had no power to regulate the production of goods for commerce where the goods themselves were harmless. It thus struck down a child labor law. A process of erosion soon set in. Distinctions and qualifications were made in a long line of decisions. Finally in 1941 in a case involving the constitutionality of the Fair Labor Standards Act (*United States v. Darby,* 312 U.S. 100) a unanimous Court overruled the earlier five-to-four decision. Stone's exposition of the Commerce Clause in the *Darby* case was undoubtedly more faithful to Marshall's conception of it than that espoused by a bare majority of the Court in the *Dagenhart* case. However that may be, the *Darby* case gave sanction to a new centralized force in American industrial and social life.

Some have thought that but for the philosophy which it represents and the power of the Federal Government which it sanctions, the nation would not have been able to marshall all the strength and to develop all the ingenuity and resourcefulness necessary to deal with the increasingly national problems of the age.

The decision of the Court in the *Santa Clara* case protected the forces of free enterprise that were building America. We can never know how much the spectre of socialism and the fear of assaults on capitalism contributed to the decision. But the end result is plain: the Court itself became part of the dynamic component of history. It did not live aloof from the turbulence of the times. It was part of the life of the community, absorbed from it the dominant attitudes and feelings of the day, and moved with the impetus of the era.

The Court in the *Darby* case was likewise extremely sensitive to the critical problems of another day. The whole of the democratic world had long been reexamining the conditions that had produced the misery of depressions. It is a soul-searching decision when one is asked to deny the existence of the power of government to correct a social evil. The unanimity of the Court in the *Darby* case indicated how high experience had piled since *Dagenhart* was decided.

Neither the Court in the *Santa Clara* case nor the Court in the *Darby* case was insensitive to the implications of the decisions. Precedents are made or unmade not on logic and history alone. The choices left by the generality of a constitution relate to policy. That is why laymen and lawyers alike must look widely and diversely for understanding. The problem of the judge is to keep personal predilections from dictating the choice and to be as faithful as possible to the architectural scheme. We can get from those who preceded a sense of the continuity of a society. We can draw from their learning a feel for the durability of a doctrine and a sense of the rights of principles. But we have experience that they never knew. Our vision may be shorter or longer. But it is ours. It is better that we make our own history than be governed by the dead. We too must be dynamic components of history if our institutions are to be vital, directive forces in the life of our age.

One can respect the policy decision both in the *Santa Clara* case and in the *Darby* case. But whatever the view on the merits all will agree, I think, that the recent Court was more faithful to the democratic tradition. It wrote in words that all could understand why it did what it did. That is vital to the integrity of the judicial process. . . .

The study of changes in judicial precedents gives, of course, a distorted view. It is like the study of pathological cases in social or medical sciences. The norm is robust and enduring. The case that gets into the books often has an unsettling effect. Yet we are apt to forget that "the fact that a case is in the reports at all is in itself uncertain." The great body of law is unperturbed by events that may rock a nation.

When the changing stream of public law is studied there are three considerations to keep in mind.

First. We have had only one major dispute that struck at the vitals of our federalism. That was the Civil War. Our controversies and quarrels even at the level of constitutional law have been of a lesser kind. They have been disputes calling for adjustment within the framework of our Charter not for repudiation of it. As one of my Brethren recently stated, they have not involved reconsideration of our basic constitutional tenets which have been accepted since the days of Marshall. They have entailed arguments over the application of established doctrine. The problem has been to free the system for growth unhampered by the crippling restraints which men of cramped and narrow vision placed on it. In considering the charges leveled against those of any period who are responsible for giving new or broader interpretations to the Constitution or discarding precedents it is well to remember these words of Thayer.

And so it happens, as one looks back over our history and the field of political discussions in the past, that he seems to see the whole region strewn with the wrecks of the Constitution,—of what people have been imagining and putting forward as the Constitution. That it was unconstitutional to buy Louisiana and Florida; that it was unconstitutional to add new states to the Union from territory not belonging originally to it; that it was unconstitutional to govern the territories at all; that it was unconstitutional to charter a bank, to issue paper money, to make it a legal tender, to enact a protective tariff,—that these and a hundred other things were a violation of the Constitution has been solemnly and passionately asserted by statesmen and lawyers. Nothing that is now going forward can exceed the vehemence of denunciation, and the pathetic and conscientious resistance of those who lifted up their voices against many of these supposed violations of the Constitution. The trouble has been, then as now, that men imputed to our fundamental law their own too narrow construction of it, their own theory of its purposes and its spirit, and sought thus, when the question was one of mere power, to restrict its great liberty.

Second. It is sometimes thought to be astute political management of a shift in position to proclaim that no change is under way. That is designed as a sedative to instill confidence and allay doubts. It has been a tool of judges as well as other officials. Precedents, though distinguished and qualified out of existence, apparently have been kept alive. The theory is that the outward appearance of stability is what is important.

The idea that any body of law, particularly public law, should appear to stay put and not be in flux is an interesting phenomenon that Frank has explored in *Law and the Modern Mind*. He points out how it is—in law and in other fields too—that men continue to chant of the immutability of a rule in order to "cover up the transformation, to deny the reality of change, to conceal the truth of adaption behind a verbal disguise of fixity and universality." But the more blunt, open, and direct course is truer to democratic traditions. It reflects the candor of Cardozo. The principle of full disclosure has as much place in government as it does in the market place. A judiciary that discloses what it is doing and why it does it will breed understanding. And confidence based on understanding is more enduring than confidence based on awe.

Third. From age to age the problem of constitutional adjudication is the same. It is to keep the power of government unrestrained by the social or economic theories that one set of judges may entertain. It is to keep one age unfettered by the fears or limited vision of another. There is in that connection one tenet of faith which has crystallized more and more as a result of our long experience as a nation. It is this: If the social and economic problems of state and nation can be kept under political management of the people, there is likely to be long-run stability. It is when a judiciary with life tenure seeks to write its social and economic creed into the Charter that instability is created. For then the nation lacks the adaptability to master the sudden storms of an era. It must be remembered that the process of constitutional amendment is a long and slow one.

That philosophy is reflected in what Thomas Jefferson wrote about the Constitution,

Some men look at constitutions with sanctimonious reverence, and deem them like the ark of the covenant, too sacred to be touched. They ascribe to the men of the preceding age a wisdom more than human, and suppose what they did to be beyond amendment. I knew that age well; I belonged to it, and labored with it. It deserved well of its country. It was very like the present, but without the experience of the present; and forty years of experience in government is worth a century of book-reading; and this they would say themselves, were they to rise from the dead.

Jefferson's words are *a fortiori* germane to the fashioning of constitutional law and to the lesser lawmaking in which the judiciary necessarily indulges.

Justice Douglas's position is that a stagnant Constitution with rigid application will not meet the needs of our changing times. He urges that the words of justices of the Supreme Court of days gone by—justices who could not foresee the social and economic problems of our country today—should not hamstring today's court, which has the responsibility of deciding today's cases in light of changing conditions. Agreeing with the stand that the court should alter Constitutional construction to meet new conditions, Walter F. Murphy, assistant professor of politics at Princeton University, wrote: "The sociological approach is old and it is necessary." [3] Rejecting the notion that the court should be bound by the "intent" of the original framers as to the meaning of the Constitution, Professor Murphy states:

[3] Murphy, The Constitution: Interpretation and Intent, 45 *A.B.A.J.* 592, 594 (June, 1959). Used by permission from the American Bar Association and the *American Bar Association Journal.*

Not only is there grave danger of an unacceptable (and unworkable) system coming from an "intent" search, but such an investigation is really incomplete unless it takes into account the intent of the ratifiers as well as of the drafters. Just how such a research project would be undertaken would stagger the collective imagination of the historical profession. And it is highly improbable that, even if such a compilation could be made, it would reflect a clear, consistent purpose in many instances. It is difficult to "imagine how any known method of psychoanalysis, or plain crystal-ball gazing applied to such records or to the people who left them could give thoroughly reliable and irrefutable answers concerning the intention of these later framers." [4]

Professor Murphy further states: "The sociological method is at least as old as the Court itself. . . ." He continues:

No scholar today would seriously argue that John Marshall's opinions were not heavily colored by his social views—his concept of the order and scaling of society and also his concept of proper social arrangements. His whole line of decisions reflects a deep concern for protection of vested interests and a supporting desire for strong national government. Pure logic and the wording of constitutional clauses were Marshall's instruments, not his masters. What the Framers had intended was seldom as important to him as what they should—as good Federalists—have intended. [5]

It is the foregoing approach to constitutional interpretation which has led to more power in government generally and in particular is permitting government to interfere more and more in economic life and business activity. Mr. David Lawrence, editor of the *U.S. News & World Report,* is extremely critical of the "sociological" method of constitutional interpretation. His viewpoint is presented in the excerpts from an editorial which follow.

DOWNGRADING THE CONSTITUTION [6]
David Lawrence

There has arisen in America a cult which believes that the "spirit" of the Constitution is more important than the letter of the document.

The argument is that when the Founding Fathers gave us a written Constitution—subject to amendment—they nevertheless vested autocratic powers of interpretation in the Supreme Court.

The late President Franklin D. Roosevelt was among the first to downgrade the Constitution as having provided "too cumbersome" a process of

---

[4] *Id.* at 594 [quoting from Anderson, The Intention of the Framers: A Note on Constitutional Interpretation, 49 *Am. Pol. Sci. Rev.* 340, 350 (1955)].
[5] *Id.* at 592.
[6] Reprinted from *U.S. News & World Report* 104 (Dec. 17, 1962), published at Washington.

amendment. He proposed in 1937 to circumvent it instead by a simple law of Congress which would allow the President to "pack" the Supreme Court with six additional Justices who would conform to the views of his Administration.

While this scheme was defeated in Congress, "courtpacking" by appointment has persisted.

President Kennedy, on August 28 [1962], speaking to a group of students at the White House, said:

"Well, the American Constitution is an extraordinary document and it is certainly the most extraordinary written Constitution in the history of the world, but it has required men to make it work, and it still does today. After all, the Constitution was written for an entirely different period in our nation's history. It was written under entirely different conditions. It was written during a period of isolation. It was written at a time when there were 13 different units which had to be joined together and which, of course, were extremely desirous of limiting the central power of the government."

This is a disparagement of the original Constitution and confuses political doctrine with the external principles of human rights, for principles of law do not change with the times. The basis of American constitutional law is the English common law. In defining the rights of man, our concepts of justice go back through the centuries.

Principles of justice are immutable just as are the Ten Commandments. The constitutional provisions guaranteeing freedom of speech, freedom of the press and freedom of worship were not "written for an entirely different period in our nation's history." They were written for all times.

The exact application of principles may vary according to changing conditions or to the circumstances of each case, but the fundamental law written into the Constitution cannot be altered except by a two-thirds vote of both houses of Congress and ratification by three fourths of the States. If this method is "cumbersome," the people alone can change it by amendment.

Yet today we observe, for example, a President of the United States issuing executive orders in which he proclaims new laws, including some which Congress has specifically refused to pass. We see Presidents employing federal troops whenever it is believed that violence may ensue in any state, even though States and cities alone are specifically given the right and obligation to exercise police power, except in cases of "insurrection."

But since when may every "internal disorder" be called an "insurrection"? A President could become a military dictator overnight and disregard all local governmental authority by calling every case of disorder an "insurrection."

When the original Constitution was being drafted, fears of usurpation were openly expressed. Alexander Hamilton, writing in "The Federalist" in 1788, summed up the views of those who felt the ultimate decision should be vested in whole or in part in the legislative body, instead of in a court. He was opposed to this procedure, but the contention of his critics now has proved to be singularly prophetic. He wrote:

The arguments, or rather suggestions, upon which this charge is founded, are to this effect: "The authority of the proposed Supreme Court of the United States, which is to be a separate and independent body, will be superior to that of the Legislature. The power of construing the laws, according to the spirit of the Constitution, will enable the Court to mould them into whatever shape it may think proper; especially as its decisions will not be in any manner subject to the revision or correction of the legislative body. This is as unprecedented as it is dangerous." . . .

In the first place, there is not a syllable in the plan under consideration which directly empowers the national courts to construe the laws according to the spirit of the Constitution.

But the Constitution today is being downgraded on the very ground that the "spirit," rather than the letter, of the document should be followed. . . . [Copyright 1963 U.S. News & World Report, Inc.]

The fact that precedent is to be given great weight in the areas of the private law does not mean that courts will continue to follow a rule of law where the reasoning behind the rule no longer exists. The case which follows illustrates the rejection of such a rule of law.

MYERS V. DROZDA
141 N.W.2d 852 (Nebr. 1966)

SMITH, JUSTICE: An infant girl and her father urge us to repudiate the court-made rule which has exempted nonprofit charitable hospitals from liability for negligent injuries to patients. In the district court the rule of exemption produced a summary judgment for the hospital on the personal injury claim of the girl and the derivative claim of her father. These appeals followed.

For purposes of review we assume the truth of the following statements. Defendant Lutheran Medical Center is a charitable corporation operating a nonprofit hospital. While the baby girl was a patient in the surgical quarters of the hospital, an employee of defendant hospital negligently anesthetized her. As a result she suffered a cardiac arrest. Defendant hospital carried hospital professional liability insurance with limits of $10,000 per claim and $30,000 aggregate.

In 1912 we adopted a policy of partial immunity which protected parties like defendant hospital. In 1955 we affirmed that policy. Today we reexamine it.

The rationale of exemption has these four labels: "Trust fund," "respondeat superior," "implied waiver," and "public policy." Under the trust fund theory the diversion of assets to satisfy tort judgments would breach the trust. Respondeat superior is said to govern a business for profit but not a charity. An implied waiver by a patient of his tort claim is defended as a fair conclusion from the patient-hospital relationship. The public policy contains the assumption that liability would dissipate the assets of charities.

Although the law of trusts and agency has exempted the hospital from tort liability to its patients, the law has not been applied to the claim of the invitee; a physician may recover, a patient may not.

Implied waiver is a fiction. Of many illustrations we choose one—plaintiff's allegations. At the same time of the "waiver" the age of the girl was 1 year. ". . . Waiver . . . amounts merely to imposing immunity as a rule of law in the guise of assumed contract or renunciation of right, when all other reasons are found insufficient to support the distinction."

The foreboding that tort liability would dissipate assets was dispelled years ago by the following language in *President & Directors of Georgetown College v. Hughes:* . . .

No statistical evidence has been presented to show that the mortality or crippling of charities has been greater in states which impose full or partial liability than where complete or substantially full immunity is given. Nor is there evidence that deference of donation has been greater in the former. Charities seem to survive and increase in both, with little apparent heed to whether they are liable for torts or difference in survival capacity. . . .

What is at stake, so far as the charity is concerned, is the cost of reasonable protection, the amount of the insurance premium as an added burden on its finances, not the awarding over in damages of its entire assets. . . .

Whether immunity is founded on the "trust fund" theory, the rule of respondeat superior, so-called "public policy," or the more indefensible doctrine of "implied waiver," is not for us a controlling consideration. . . . They are merely different names for the same idea, cast according to the predilection of the user. . . . The differences in foundation do not affect even the extent of the departure.

If this exemption formerly met a need, it has had its day. In 1942 four states apparently imposed unqualified liability. In 1955 we named 22 states, exclusive of Nebraska, which had granted some degree of immunity, and we said that 10 of them had recently reaffirmed their position. Afterward courts in 8 of the 22 states abrogated the immunity, and 5 of the 10 "recent" decisions were overruled. Two legislatures intervened on one side or the other. It is doubtful that any court has overruled a decision declaring a charity to be nonexempt. Liability probably represents the majority view. The judicial trend is unmistakable.

Defendant hospital relies upon our prior announcement that any change ought to be made by the Legislature. If we endorsed legislation by silence, we erred. Stare decisis "was intended, not to effect a 'petrifying rigidity,' but to assure the justice that flows from certainty and stability. . . . We would be abdicating 'our own function, in a field peculiarly nonstatutory,' were we to insist on legislation and 'refuse to reconsider an old and unsatisfactory court-made rule.' "

. . . *[J]udges of an earlier generation declared the immunity simply because they believed it to be a sound instrument of judicial policy which would further the moral, social and economic welfare of the people of the State. When judges of a later generation firmly reach a contrary conclusion they must be ready to discharge their own judicial responsibilities in conformance with modern concepts and needs. . . .*

The old rule being clearly wrong, we hold that nonprofit charitable hospitals are not exempt from tort liability to their patients. Contrary decisions are overruled to the extent of their inconsistency.

The point of departure from precedent remains to be determined. Loss of exemption may be retrospective, partially retrospective, or prospective. The choice is influenced by these broad considerations: The reasons for overruling the prior decisions; the public interest in institutional stability; justifiable reliance upon the exemption; and uniformity of application to parties similarly situated.

Other courts have considered some of those policy factors. Several decisions removed the exemption prospectively except for the cases being decided. Three reasons were given. First, the charitable corporation may have relied on the old rule whether or not insurance coverage existed. Second, announcement of prospective operation would be dictum. Third, if the effort and expense of challenge were to go unrewarded, appellant would have no incentive to contest the old rule.

We too think that the new rule should be partially retrospective; however, insurance is insignificant. A differentiating factor between a charity and its insurer is reliance. An insured charity does not rely justifiably on the exemption within the limits of the insurer's liability. The impact of liability upon an insurer should be relatively light because of its ability to spread the loss. ". . . [O]rdinarily it is impossible to trace the impact of particular legal doctrine upon liability insurance rates." Factors concerning dictum and reward carry some weight but not much.

In conclusion the new rule applies to all causes of action arising after April 22, 1966, the filing date of this opinion. In respect to other causes of action the new rule applies if, but only if, the nonprofit charitable hospital was insured against liability on the claim of the patient, and then only to the extent of the maximum applicable amount of its insurance coverage.

The judgment is reversed, and the causes are remanded for proceedings consistent with this opinion. [REVERSED AND REMANDED]

3   SCOPE OF PRECEDENT

Each state has its own statutory laws and its own body of judge-made precedent. These laws cover both matters of substance and matters of procedure. Generally, the decisions of one state are considered to be applicable precedent only in that state. The decisions of other states, however, may be considered by way of analogy when there are no previous decisions on the point in question in the state where a case is being heard. For example, precedent of other states is frequently referred to in cases involving the construction of statutes such as the Uniform Acts where each state has adopted the same statute. Where there is no precedent a case is one of "first impression," and in such cases, each state is free to decide for itself questions concerning its common law and interpretation of its own constitution and statutes.

In addition to this system of fifty distinct bodies of state precedent there is the Federal legal system. The Federal courts have their own body of procedural law and their own body of substantive law on questions arising under the Federal Constitution, codes, statutes, or treaties. Decisions of the United States Supreme Court on Federal questions involving the United States Constitution, treaties, Federal statutes, and matters of interstate commerce are binding on state courts, while decisions of lower Federal courts are generally held not to be binding. Federal courts also have jurisdiction of cases involving citizens of different states under the Constitution, even though no Federal question is in issue. In the case which follows, it is established that there is no body of Federal common law, and that in suits based on diversity of citizenship, the Federal courts use the substantive law of the states in which they are sitting to determine the rights and duties of the parties. In such cases, the Federal courts do use their own rules of procedure, however. Thus, just as state courts are bound by Federal precedent in certain situations, so also are Federal courts bound by state precedent in others.

ERIE RAILROAD V. TOMPKINS
304 U.S. 64 (1938)

BRANDEIS, JUSTICE: The question for decision is whether the oft-challenged doctrine of *Swift v. Tyson* shall now be disapproved.

Tompkins, a citizen of Pennsylvania, was injured on a dark night by a passing freight train of the Erie Railroad Company while walking along its right of way at Hughestown in that state. He claimed that the accident occurred through negligence in the operation, or maintenance, of the train; that he was rightfully on the premises as licensee because on a commonly used beaten footpath which ran for a short distance alongside the tracks;

and that he was struck by something which looked like a door projecting from one of the moving cars. To enforce that claim he brought an action in the federal court for Southern New York, which has jurisdiction because the company is a corporation of that state. It denied liability; and the case was tried by a jury.

The Erie insisted that its duty to Tompkins was no greater than that owed to a trespasser. It contended, among other things, that its duty to Tompkins, and hence its liability, should be determined in accordance with the Pennsylvania law; that under the law of Pennsylvania, as declared by its highest court, persons who use pathways along the railroad right of way —that is, a longitudinal pathway as distinguished from a crossing—are to be deemed trespassers; and that the railroad is not liable for injuries to undiscovered trespassers resulting from its negligence, unless it be wanton or willful. Tompkins denied that any such rule had been established by the decisions of the Pennsylvania courts; and contended that, since there was no statute of the state on the subject, the railroad's duty and liability is to be determined in federal courts as a matter of general law.

The trial judge refused to rule that the applicable law precluded recovery. The jury brought in a verdict of $30,000; and the judgment entered thereon was affirmed by the Circuit Court of Appeals, which held (2 Cir., 90 F.2d 603, 604) that it was unnecessary to consider whether the law of Pennsylvania was as contended, because the question was one not of local but of general law, and that

> . . . *upon questions of general law the federal courts are free, in absence of a local statute, to exercise their independent judgment as to what the law is; and it is well settled that the question of the responsibility of a railroad for injuries caused by its servants is one of general law. . . . Where the public has made open and notorious use of a railroad right of way for a long period of time and without objection, the company owes to persons on such permissive pathway a duty of care in the operation of its trains. . . . It is likewise generally recognized law that a jury may find that negligence exists toward a pedestrian using a permissive path on the railroad right of way if he is hit by some object projecting from the side of the train.*

The Erie had contended that application of the Pennsylvania rule was required, among other things, by section 34 of the Federal Judiciary Act of September 24, 1789, c. 20, 28 U.S.C. § 725, 28 U.S.C.A. § 725, which provides: "The laws of the several States, except where the Constitution, treaties, or statutes of the United States otherwise require or provide, shall be regarded as rules of decision in trials at common law, in the courts of the United States, in cases where they apply."

Because of the importance of the question whether the federal court was free to disregard the alleged rule of the Pennsylvania common law, we granted certiorari. . . .

First. *Swift v. Tyson,* 16 Pet. 1, 18, 10 L. Ed. 865, held that federal courts exercising jurisdiction on the ground of diversity of citizenship need not, in matters of general jurisprudence, apply the unwritten law of the state as declared by its highest court; that they are free to exercise an independent judgment as to what the common law of the state is—or should be; and that, as there stated by Mr. Justice Story,

The true interpretation of the 34th section limited its application to state laws, strictly local, that is to say, to the positive statutes of the state, and the construction thereof adopted by the local tribunals, and to rights and titles to things having a permanent locality, such as the rights and titles to real estate, and other matters immovable and intra-territorial in their nature and character. It never has been supposed by us, that the section did apply, or was designed to apply, to questions of a fixed and permanent operation, as, for example, to the construction of ordinary contracts or other written instruments, and especially to questions of general commercial law, where the state tribunals are called upon to perform the like functions as ourselves, that is, to ascertain, upon general reasoning and legal analogies, what is the true exposition of the contract or instrument, or what is the just rule furnished by the principles of commercial law to govern the case.

The Court in applying the rule of section 34 to equity cases, in *Mason v. United States,* 260 U.S. 545, 559, . . . said: "The statute, however, is merely declarative of the rule which would exist in the absence of the statute." The federal courts assumed, in the broad field of "general law," the power to declare rules of decision which Congress was confessedly without power to enact as statutes. Doubt was repeatedly expressed as to the correctness of the construction given section 34, and as to the soundness of the rule which it introduced. But it was the more recent research of a competent scholar, who examined the original document, which established that the construction given to it by the Court was erroneous; and that the purpose of the section was merely to make certain that, in all matters except those in which some federal law is controlling, the federal courts exercising jurisdiction in diversity of citizenship cases would apply as their rules of decision the law of the state, unwritten as well as written.

Criticism of the doctrine became widespread after the decision of *Black & White Taxicab & Transfer Co. v. Brown & Yellow Taxicab & Transfer Co.,* 276 U.S. 518. . . . There, Brown & Yellow, a Kentucky corporation owned by Kentuckians, and the Louisville & Nashville Railroad, also a Kentucky corporation, wished that the former should have the exclusive privilege of soliciting passenger and baggage transportation at the Bowling Green, Ky., railroad station; and that the Black & White, a competing Kentucky corporation, should be prevented from interfering with that privilege. Knowing that such a contract would be void under the common law of Kentucky, it was arranged that the Brown & Yellow reincorporate under the law of

Tennessee, and that the contract with the railroad should be executed there. The suit was then brought by the Tennessee corporation in the federal court for Western Kentucky to enjoin competition by the Black & White; an injunction issued by the District Court was sustained by the Court of Appeals; and this Court, citing many decisions in which the doctrine of *Swift v. Tyson* had been applied, affirmed the decree.

Second. Experience in applying the doctrine of *Swift v. Tyson* had revealed its defects, political and social; and the benefits expected to flow from the rule did not accrue. Persistence of state courts in their own opinions on questions of common law prevented uniformity, and the impossibility of discovering a satisfactory line of demarcation between the province of general law and that of local law developed a new well of uncertainties.

On the other hand, the mischievous results of the doctrine had become apparent. Diversity of citizenship jurisdiction was conferred in order to prevent apprehended discrimination in state courts against those not citizens of the state. *Swift v. Tyson* introduced grave discrimination by noncitizens against citizens. It made rights enjoyed under the unwritten "general law" vary according to whether enforcement was sought in the state or in the federal court; and the privilege of selecting the court in which the right should be determined was conferred upon the noncitizen. Thus, the doctrine rendered impossible equal protection of the law. In attempting to promote uniformity of law throughout the United States, the doctrine had prevented uniformity in the administration of the law of the state.

The discrimination resulting became in practice far-reaching. This resulted in part from the broad province accorded to the so-called "general law" as to which federal courts exercised an independent judgment. In addition to questions of purely commercial law, "general law" was held to include the obligations under contracts entered into and to be performed within the state, the extent to which a carrier operating within a state may stipulate for exemption from liability for his own negligence or that of his employee; the liability for torts committed within the state upon persons resident or property located there, even where the question of liability depended upon the scope of a property right conferred by the state, and the right to exemplary or punitive damages. Furthermore, state decisions construing local deeds, mineral conveyances, and even devices of real estate, were disregarded.

In part the discrimination resulted from the wide range of persons held entitled to avail themselves of the federal rule by resort to the diversity of citizenship jurisdiction. Through this jurisdiction individual citizens willing to remove from their own state and become citizens of another might avail themselves of the federal rule. And, without even change of residence, a corporate citizen of the state could avail itself of the federal rule by reincorporating under the provisions of the laws of another state, as was done in the *Taxicab* case.

The injustice and confusion incident to the doctrine of *Swift v. Tyson* have been repeatedly urged as reasons for abolishing or limiting diversity of citizenship jurisdiction. Other legislative relief has been proposed. If only a question of statutory construction were involved, we should not be prepared to abandon a doctrine so widely applied throughout nearly a century. But the unconstitutionality of the course pursued has now been made clear, and compels us to do so.

Third. Except in matters governed by the Federal Constitution or by acts of Congress, the law to be applied in any case is the law of the state. And whether the law of the state shall be declared by its Legislature in a statute or by its highest court in a decision is not a matter of federal concern. There is no federal general common law. Congress has no power to declare substantive rules of common law applicable in a state whether they be local in their nature or "general," whether they be commercial law or a part of the law of torts. And there is no clause in the Constitution that purports to confer such a power upon the federal courts. As stated by Mr. Justice Field when protesting in *Baltimore & Ohio R.R. v. Baugh*, 149 U.S. 368, 401, . . . against ignoring the Ohio common law of fellow-servant liability:

> I am aware that what has been termed the general law of the country— which is often little less than what the judge advancing the doctrine thinks at the time should be the general law on a particular subject—has been often advanced in judicial opinions of this court to control a conflicting law of a state. I admit that learned judges have fallen into the habit of repeating this doctrine as a convenient mode of brushing aside the law of a state in conflict with their views. And I confess that, moved and governed by the authority of the great names of those judges, I have, myself, in many instances, unhesitatingly and confidently, but I think now erroneously, repeated the same doctrine. But, notwithstanding the great names which may be cited in favor of the doctrine, and notwithstanding the frequency with which the doctrine has been reiterated, there stands, as a perpetual protest against its repetition, the constitution of the United States, which recognizes and preserves the autonomy and independence of the states,—independence in their legislative and independence in their judicial departments. Supervision over either the legislative or the judicial action of the states is in no case permissible except as to matters by the constitution specifically authorized or delegated to the United States. Any interference with either, except as thus permitted, is an invasion of the authority of the state, and, to that extent, a denial of its independence.

The fallacy underlying the rule declared in *Swift v. Tyson* is made clear by Mr. Justice Holmes. The doctrine rests upon the assumption that there is "a transcendental body of law outside of any particular State but obligatory within it unless and until changed by statute," that federal courts have the power to use their judgment as to what the rules of common law are; and that in the federal courts "the parties are entitled to an independent judgment on matters of general law":

. . . *But law in the sense in which courts speak of it today does not exist without some definite authority behind it. The common law so far as it is enforced in a State, whether called common law or not, is not the common law generally but the law of that State existing by the authority of that State without regard to what it may have been in England or anywhere else. . . .*

The authority and only authority is the State, and if that be so, the voice adopted by the State as its own (whether it be of its Legislature or of its Supreme Court) should utter the last word.

Thus the doctrine of *Swift v. Tyson* is, as Mr. Justice Holmes said, "an unconstitutional assumption of powers by the Courts of the United States which no lapse of time or respectable array of opinion should make us hesitate to correct." In disapproving that doctrine we do not hold unconstitutional section 34 of the Federal Judiciary Act of 1789 or any other act of Congress. We merely declare that in applying the doctrine this Court and the lower courts have invaded rights which in our opinion are reserved by the Constitution to the several states.

Fourth. The defendant contended that by common law of Pennsylvania as declared by its highest court in *Falchetti v. Pennsylvania R.R.*, 307 Pa. 203, 160 Atl. 859, the only duty owed to the plaintiff was to refrain from willful or wanton injury. The plaintiff denied that such is the Pennsylvania law. In support of their respective contentions the parties discussed and cited many decisions of the Supreme Court of the state. The Circuit Court of Appeals ruled that the question of liability is one of general law; and on that ground declined to decide the issue of state law. As we hold this was error, the judgment is reversed and the case remanded to it for further proceedings in conformity with our opinion. [REVERSED]

Subsequent to the *Erie* case, in diversity of citizenship cases, many Federal decisions have been concerned with whether a given issue is one of substantive law, in which case the applicable state law will be followed, or one of procedure, in which case the Federal practice will be followed. If the state rule of law, whether created by statute or case decision, will affect the *result* of the controversy, the rule is treated as substantive and will be followed by the Federal court.

One further aspect of the scope of precedent must be noted. Article IV, Section 1, of the United States Constitution provides: "Full Faith and

Credit shall be given in each State to the public Acts, Records, and judicial proceedings of every other State. . . ." This does not mean that the precedent in one state is binding in other states, but only that the final decisions or judgments rendered in any given state shall be enforced as between the original parties in other states. Full faith and credit is applicable to the result of a specific decision as it affects the rights of the parties, and not to the reasons or principles upon which it was based.

4   CONFLICTS OF LAW

In litigation involving a transaction or occurrence in only one state, the court may have the problem of selecting the applicable precedent from the conflicting citations of authority from previous decisions of that state made by the attorneys on each side of the case. Obviously, the problem is magnified many times when the transaction or occurrence is interstate in character. For example, suppose that a resident of Illinois boards an airline in St. Louis, Missouri, for a flight to California, and the plane crashes in Nebraska. Assuming that the ticket was purchased in Illinois, the liability of the airline could be based on the statutes and decisions of any one of these four different states. Illinois law might provide a $30,000 maximum liability for wrongful death, Missouri $25,000, Nebraska unlimited, and California still a different amount. The law of torts, though a part of the private law, does vary from state to state in such important matters as the burden of proof and the measure of damages. In such cases, what is the applicable precedent?

Likewise, the law of contracts is not uniform throughout the country, and the following situation would create a similar problem requiring a determination of the applicable precedent to be followed. A manufacturing concern in Illinois orders some new materials from a corporation doing business in Michigan with production facilities in several states, including Arizona. The order for the goods is received in Michigan and transmitted to Arizona for delivery. The Michigan office does not notify the buyer, but the Arizona plant fills the order. The goods are destroyed in Iowa while en route. In determining who must bear the loss, the result may vary depending upon which state's substantive law is used.

The problem of selecting the applicable law frequently arises in other areas of the law, such as marriage and divorce, and the passing of property on death. In the latter situation, for example, the retired person who is planning his estate and has a winter home in Florida, a summer home in Maine, and who was formerly a resident of New York may face a complex state inheritance tax question. It is possible that each of the states mentioned may claim him as a resident and attempt to tax the estate.

As a direct result of the multistate transaction or occurrence, there has developed a body of law, primarily through judicial decisions, which is generally referred to as "conflicts of law." The decisions which comprise this body of law simply determine which state's law is applicable to any given question when more than one state is involved. This usually arises where all or some of the facts occur in one state and the trial is held in another. For example, the conflicts-of-law rule for tort actions is, in most states, that the law of the place of injury is applicable. Thus, if a car accident occurred in Missouri but suit was brought in an Illinois state court, the judge would apply the law of Missouri in determining the rights of the parties. There are several different views held by courts about which law to select in resolving issues involving contracts. Some favor the law of the state where the contract was made, others the law of the place of performance, and still others have adopted the "grouping of contacts" theory which uses the law of the state with the most substantial contact with the contract.

In a multistate situation, the first problem confronting the court is, therefore, the selection of the appropriate state to turn to for legal precedent. Once a determination has been made of which state is appropriate, the court's business then is to review the citations of authority advanced by the opposing attorneys to determine which of that state's case decisions to apply in following the doctrine of stare decisis.

One further complicating factor should be noted in the process of a *Federal* court in selecting the law of the state's precedent it has decided to follow. The Federal court will look at the total body of law of the state in which it is sitting, *including the state's conflicts of law principles.* Thus, in using the law of state X it may in turn look to the law of some other state for the actual precedent. For example, assume that a citizen of the state of Illinois sues a citizen of the state of Indiana in the Federal district court in Indiana for personal injuries received in an automobile accident which occurred in the state of Kentucky. The Federal district court sitting in Indiana will use Federal procedure and the substantive law of the state of *Indiana.* The substantive law of the state of Indiana includes the conflicts-of-law principle that the applicable tort law is the law of the place of injury. The Federal court in Indiana will use the Kentucky tort law since that is the law which would be used by an Indiana state court.

Therefore, it must be recognized that there is a body of law used to decide the inherent conflicts between the precedent of the various states, which is especially significant in our modern society with its ease of communication and transportation. The trend toward uniform statutes and codes has tended to decrease these conflicts, but many of them still exist. So long as we have a Federal system and fifty separate state bodies of substantive law, the area of conflicts of law will continue to be of substantial importance in the application of the doctrine of stare decisis.

5   SEPARATION OF POWERS AND JUDICIAL REVIEW

There are two doctrines which play a major role in our legal system as a result of the use of precedent as a source of law. First of all, there is the doctrine of separation of powers which simply affords to each branch of government its respective duties with the implication that they should not be performed by the others. The doctrine is also the basis of our so-called checks and balances system by which each branch serves in some way as a restricting power in the activities of the other. Separation of powers on the surface would seem to be violated when judges make law. This doctrine, if narrowly followed, would limit the law-making function to the legislature. However, as a practical matter, each branch has certain law-making functions—the Congress by legislation, the courts by judicial decision, and the executive by administrative action, decision, or regulation. (Administrative law making is discussed in Chapter 4.) Since each branch of government in its activities creates laws, it is not surprising that occasionally the action of one is inconsistent with the position of another. We have already seen that legislatures may change judicial decisions by enacting specific statutes. Of course, a court may "change a law" by giving a statute an interpretation which may or may not have been intended. The court may allow a statute to stand as interpreted and thus in one sense is exercising control over the legislative body. The second doctrine is that of judicial review, which empowers courts to review laws passed by the legislative body and to declare them to be unconstitutional and thus void. It also allows the courts to review actions taken by the executive branch and to declare them to be unconstitutional. While the Constitution does not expressly provide that the judiciary shall be the overseer of the government, the net effect of this doctrine is to make it so. Chief Justice Marshall in *Marbury v. Madison* announced the doctrine of judicial review and recognized the concept of separation of powers, using the following language and reasoning:

MARBURY V. MADISON
5 U.S. (1 Cranch) 137 (1803)

MARSHALL, CHIEF JUSTICE: . . . The question, whether an act, repugnant to the constitution, can become the law of the land, is a question deeply interesting to the United States; but, happily, not of an intricacy proportioned to its interest. It seems only necessary to recognise certain principles, supposed to have been long and well established, to decide it. That the people have an original right to establish, for their future government, such principles as, in their opinion, shall most conduce to their own happiness, is the basis on which the whole American fabric has been erected. The exercise of this original right is a very great exertion; nor can it, nor ought it, to be frequently repeated. The principles, therefore, so established, are deemed fundamental; and as the authority from which they proceed is supreme, and can seldom act, they are designed to be permanent.

This original and supreme will organizes the government, and assigns to different departments their respective powers. It may either stop here, or establish certain limits not to be transcended by those departments. The government of the United States is of the latter description. The powers of the legislature are defined and limited; and that those limits may not be mistaken or forgotten, the constitution is written. To what purpose are powers limited, and to what purpose is that limitation committed to writing, if these limits may, at any time, be passed by those intended to be restrained? The distinction between a government with limited and unlimited powers is abolished, if those limits do not confine the persons on whom they are imposed, and if acts prohibited and acts allowed, are of equal obligation. It is a proposition too plain to be contested, that the constitution controls any legislative act repugnant to it; or that the legislature may alter the constitution by an ordinary act.

Between these alternatives, there is no middle ground. The constitution is either a superior paramount law, unchangeable by ordinary means, or it is on a level with ordinary legislative acts, and, like other acts, is alterable when the legislature shall please to alter it. If the former part of the alternative be true, then a legislative act, contrary to the constitution, is not law: if the latter part be true, then written constitutions are absurd attempts on the part of the people, to limit a power, in its own nature, illimitable.

Certainly, all those who have framed written constitutions contemplate them as forming the fundamental and paramount law of the nation, and consequently, the theory of every such government must be, that an act of the legislature, repugnant to the constitution, is void. This theory is essentially attached to a written constitution, and is, consequently, to be considered, by this court, as one of the fundamental principles of our society. It is not, therefore, to be lost sight of, in the further consideration of this subject.

If an act of the legislature, repugnant to the constitution, is void, does it, notwithstanding its invalidity, bind the courts, and oblige them to give it effect? Or, in other words, though it be not law, does it constitute a rule as operative as if it was a law? This would be to overthrow, in fact, what was established in theory; and would seem, at first view, an absurdity too gross to be insisted on. It shall, however, receive a more attentive consideration.

It is, emphatically, the province and duty of the judicial department, to say what the law is. Those who apply the rule to particular cases, must of necessity expound and interpret that rule. If two laws conflict with each other, the courts must decide on the operation of each. So, if a law be in opposition to the constitution; if both the law and the constitution apply to a particular case, so that the court must either decide that case, conformable to the law, disregarding the constitution; or conformable to the constitution, disregarding the law; the court must determine which of these conflicting rules governs the case: this is of the very essence of judicial duty. If then, the courts are to regard the constitution, and the constitution is superior to any ordinary act of the legislature, the constitution, and not such ordinary act, must govern the case to which they both apply.

Those, then, who controvert the principle, that the constitution is to be considered, in court, as a paramount law, are reduced to the necessity of maintaining that courts must close their eyes on the constitution, and see only the law. This doctrine would subvert the very foundation of all written constitutions. It would declare that an act which, according to the principles and theory of our government, is entirely void, is yet, in practice, completely obligatory. It would declare that if the legislature shall do what is expressly forbidden, such act, notwithstanding the express prohibition, is in reality effectual. It would be giving to the legislature a practical and real omnipotence, with the same breath which professes to restrict their powers within narrow limits. It is prescribing limits, and declaring that those limits may be passed at pleasure. That it thus reduces to nothing, what we have deemed the greatest improvement on political institutions, a written constitution, would, of itself, be sufficient, in America, where written constitutions have been viewed with so much reverence, for rejecting the construction. But the peculiar expressions of the constitution of the United States furnish additional arguments in favor of its rejection. The judicial power of the United States is extended to all cases arising under the constitution. Could it be the intention of those who gave this power, to say, that in using it, the constitution should not be looked into? That a case arising under the constitution should be decided, without examining the instrument under which it arises? This is too extravagant to be maintained. In some cases, then, the constitution must be looked into by the judges. And if they can open it at all, what part of it are they forbidden to read or to obey?

There are many other parts of the constitution which serve to illustrate this subject. It is declared, that "no tax or duty shall be laid on articles exported from any state." Suppose, a duty on the export of cotton, of tobacco or of flour; and a suit instituted to recover it. Ought judgment to be rendered in such a case? Ought the judges to close their eyes on the constitution, and only see the law?

The constitution declares "that no bill of attainder or *ex post facto* law shall be passed." If, however, such a bill should be prosecuted under it; must the court condemn to death those victims whom the constitution endeavors to preserve?

"No person," says the constitution, "shall be convicted of treason, unless on the testimony of two witnesses to the same *overt* act, or on confession in open court." Here, the language of the constitution is addressed especially to the courts. It prescribes, directly for them, a rule of evidence not to be departed from. If the legislature should change that rule, and declare one witness, or a confession out of court, sufficient for conviction, must the constitutional principle yield to the legislative act?

From these, and many other selections which might be made, it is apparent, that the framers of the constitution contemplated that instrument as a rule for the government of courts, as well as of the legislature. Why otherwise does it direct the judges to take an oath to support it? This oath certainly applies in an especial manner, to their conduct in their official character. How immoral to impose it on them, if they were to be used as the instruments, and the knowing instruments, for violating what they swear to support!

The oath of office, too, imposed by the legislature, is completely demonstrative of the legislative opinion on this subject. It is these words: "I do solemnly swear, that I will administer justice, without respect to persons, and do equal right to the poor and to the rich; and that I will faithfully and impartially discharge all the duties incumbent on me as _____, according to the best of my abilities and understanding, agreeably to the constitution and laws of the United States." Why does a judge swear to discharge his duties agreeably to the constitution of the United States, if that constitution forms no rule for his government? If it is closed upon him, and cannot be inspected by him? If such be the real state of things, this is worse than solemn mockery. To prescribe, or to take this oath, becomes equally a crime.

It is also not entirely unworthy of observation, that in declaring what shall be the supreme law of the land, the constitution itself is first mentioned; and not the laws of the United States, generally, but those only which shall be made in pursuance of the constitution, have that rank.

Thus, the particular phraseology of the constitution of the United States confirms and strengthens the principle, supposed to be essential to all written constitutions, that a law repugnant to the constitution is void; and that courts, as well as other departments, are bound by that instrument. . . .

The power of courts to declare void actions of the executive or legislature has played an important role in our history and in the law as it is related to business. The following case is a more recent example of the application of the doctrine of judicial review and contains significant discussions of the separation of powers concept, of which judicial review is a part.

YOUNGSTOWN SHEET & TUBE CO. V. SAWYER
343 U.S. 579 (1952)

During the Korean War, a dispute arose between certain steel companies and their employees over the terms and conditions which should be included in new collective-bargaining agreements. The dispute was not settled despite governmental attempts at a settlement, and a nationwide strike was called. Steel was used in the weapons of war and was in short supply. Just prior to the strike, the President, without specific congressional authority, issued an order directing the Secretary of Commerce to take possession of and operate most of the nation's steel mills. This action challenged the validity of that order.

BLACK, JUSTICE: The President's power, if any, to issue the order must stem either from an act of Congress or from the Constitution itself. There is no statute that expressly authorizes the President to take possession of property as he did here. Nor is there any act of Congress to which our attention has been directed from which such a power can fairly be implied. Indeed, we do not understand the Government to rely on statutory authorization for this seizure. . . .

Moreover, the use of the seizure technique to solve labor disputes in order to prevent work stoppages was not only unauthorized by any congressional enactment; prior to this controversy, Congress had refused to adopt that method of settling labor disputes. . . .

It is clear that if the President had authority to issue the order he did, it must be found in some provision of the Constitution. And it is not claimed that express constitutional language grants this power to the President. The contention is that presidential power should be implied from the aggregate of his powers under the Constitution. Particular reliance is placed on provisions in Article II which say that "The executive Power shall be vested in a President . . ."; and that he "shall be Commander in Chief of the Army and Navy of the United States."

The order cannot properly be sustained as an exercise of the President's military power as Commander in Chief of the Armed Forces. The Government attempts to do so by citing a number of cases upholding broad powers in military commanders engaged in day-to-day fighting in a theater of war. Such cases need not concern us here. Even though "theater of war" be an expanding concept, we cannot with faithfulness to our constitutional system hold that the Commander in Chief of the Armed Forces has the ultimate power as such to take possession of private property in order to keep labor disputes from stopping production. This is a job for the Nation's lawmakers, not for its military authorities.

Nor can the seizure order be sustained because of the several constitutional provisions that grant executive power to the President. In the framework of our Constitution, the President's power to see that the laws are faithfully executed refutes the idea that he is to be a lawmaker. The Constitution limits his functions in the lawmaking process to the recommending of laws he thinks wise and the vetoing of laws he thinks bad. And the Constitution is neither silent nor equivocal about who shall make laws which the President is to execute. The first section of the first article says that "All legislative Powers herein granted shall be vested in a Congress of the United States. . . ." After granting many powers to the Congress, Article I goes on to provide that Congress may "make all Laws which shall be necessary and proper for carrying into Execution the foregoing Powers, and all other Powers vested by this Constitution in the Government of the United States, or in any Department or Officer thereof."

The President's order does not direct that a congressional policy be executed in a manner prescribed by Congress—it directs that a presidential policy be executed in a manner prescribed by the President. The preamble of the order itself, like that of many statutes, sets out reasons why the President believes certain policies should be adopted, proclaims these policies as rules of conduct to be followed, and again, like a statute, authorizes a government official to promulgate additional rules and regulations consistent with the policy proclaimed and needed to carry that policy into execution. The power of Congress to adopt such public policies as those proclaimed by the order is beyond question. It can authorize the taking of private property for public use. It can make laws regulating the relationships between employers and employees, prescribing rules designed to settle labor disputes, and fixing wages and working conditions in certain fields of our economy. The Constitution does not subject this lawmaking power of Congress to presidential or military supervision or control.

It is said that other Presidents without congressional authority have taken possession of private business enterprises in order to settle labor disputes. But even if this be true, Congress has not thereby lost its exclusive constitutional authority to make laws necessary and proper to carry out the powers vested by the Constitution "in the Government of the United States, or any Department or Officer thereof."

The Founders of this Nation entrusted the lawmaking power to the Congress alone in both good and bad times. It would do no good to recall the historical events, the fears of power and the hopes for freedom that lay behind their choice. Such a review would but confirm our holding that this seizure cannot stand. . . .

[The *Youngstown Sheet & Tube* case contained concurring opinions, and a dissent in which three of the nine justices joined. While six members of the Court agreed on the result, there were five separate methods of stating the result. Many of the principles and much of the philosophy underlying the doctrine of judicial review were set forth in Mr. Justice Frankfurter's concurring opinion, which follows in part.]

FRANKFURTER, JUSTICE, concurring: . . . A constitutional democracy like ours is perhaps the most difficult of man's social arrangements to manage successfully. Our scheme of society is more dependent than any other form of government on knowledge and wisdom and self-discipline for the achievement of its aims. For our democracy implies the reign of reason on the most extensive scale. The Founders of this Nation were not imbued with the modern cynicism that the only thing that history teaches is that it teaches nothing. They acted on the conviction that the experience of man sheds a good deal of light on his nature. It sheds a good deal of light not merely on the need for effective power, if a society is to be at once cohesive and civilized, but also on the need for limitations on the power of governors over the governed.

To that end they rested the structure of our central government on the system of checks and balances. For them the doctrine of separation of powers was not mere theory; it was a felt necessity. Not so long ago it was fashionable to find our system of checks and balances obstructive to effective government. It was easy to ridicule that system as outmoded—too easy. The experience through which the world has passed in our own day has made vivid the realization that the Framers of our Constitution were not inexperienced doctrinaires. These long-headed statesmen had no illusion that our people enjoyed biological or psychological or sociological immunities from the hazards of concentrated power. It is absurd to see a dictator in a representative product of the sturdy democratic traditions of the Mississippi Valley. The accretion of dangerous power does not come in a day. It does come, however slowly, from the generative force of unchecked disregard of the restrictions that fence in even the most disinterested assertion of authority.

The Framers, however, did not make the judiciary the overseer of our government. They were familiar with the revisory functions entrusted to judges in a few of the states and refused to lodge such powers in this Court. Judicial power can be exercised only as to matters that were the traditional concern of the courts at Westminster, and only if they arise in ways that to the expert feel of lawyers constitute "Cases" or "Controversies." Even as to questions that were the staple of judicial business, it is not for the courts to pass upon them unless they are indispensably involved in a conventional litigation—and then, only to the extent that they are so involved. Rigorous adherence to the narrow scope of the judicial function is especially demanded in controversies that arouse appeals to the Constitution. The attitude with which this Court must approach its duty when confronted with such issues is precisely the opposite of that normally manifested by the general public. So-called constitutional questions seem to exercise a mesmeric influence over the popular mind. This eagerness to settle—preferably forever—a specific problem on the basis of the broadest possible constitutional pronouncements may not unfairly be called one of our minor national traits. . . .

The pole-star for constitutional adjudications is John Marshall's greatest judicial utterance that "it is a *constitution* we are expounding." *McCullouch v. Maryland*, 4 Wheat. 316, 407. That requires both a spacious view in applying an instrument of government "made for an undefined and expanding future," *Hurtado v. California*, 110 U.S. 516, 530, and as narrow a delimitation of the constitutional issues as the circumstances permit. Not the least characteristic of great statesmanship which the Framers manifested was the extent to which they did not attempt to bind the future. It is no less incumbent upon this Court to avoid putting fetters upon the future by needless pronouncements today.

Marshall's admonition that "it is a *constitution* we are expounding" is especially relevant when the Court is required to give legal sanctions to an underlying principle of the Constitution—that of separation of powers. "The great ordinances of the Constitution do not establish and divide fields of black and white." Holmes, J., dissenting in *Springer v. Philippine Islands,* 277 U.S. 189, 209.

The issue before us can be met, and therefore should be, without attempting to define the President's powers comprehensively. I shall not attempt to delineate what belongs to him by virtue of his office beyond the power even of Congress to contract; what authority belongs to him until Congress acts; what kind of problems may be dealt with either by the Congress or by the President or by both, cf. *La Abra Silver Mng. Co. v. United States,* 175 U.S. 423; what power must be exercised by the Congress and cannot be delegated to the President. It is unprofitable to lump together in an undiscriminating hotch-potch past presidential actions claimed to be derived from occupancy of the office, as it is to conjure up hypothetical future cases. The judiciary may, as this case proves, have to intervene in determining where authority lies as between the democratic forces in our scheme of government. But in doing so we should be wary and humble. Such is the teaching of this Court's role in the history of the country. . . .

A scheme of government like ours no doubt at times feels the lack of power to act with complete, all-embracing, swiftly moving authority. No doubt a government with distributed authority subject to be challenged in the courts of law, at least long enough to consider and adjudicate the challenge, labors under restrictions from which other governments are free. It has not been our tradition to envy such governments. In any event our government was designed to have such restrictions. The price was deemed not too high in view of the safeguards which these restrictions afford. I know no more impressive words on this subject than those of Mr. Justice Brandeis:

The doctrine of the separation of powers was adopted by the Convention of 1787, not to promote efficiency but to preclude the exercise of arbitrary power. The purpose was, not to avoid friction, but, by means of the inevitable friction incident to the distribution of the governmental powers among three departments, to save the people from autocracy. Myers v. United States, 272 U.S. 52, 240, 293.

It is not a pleasant judicial duty to find that the President has exceeded his powers and still less so when his purposes were dictated by concern for the Nation's well-being, in the assured conviction that he acted to avert danger. But it would stultify one's faith in our people to entertain even a momentary fear that the patriotism and the wisdom of the President and the Congress, as well as the long view of the immediate parties in interest, will not find ready accommodation for differences on matters which, however close to their concern and however intrinsically important, are overshadowed by the awesome issues which confront the world. . . .

CHAPTER FOUR

LAW BY ADMINISTRATIVE AGENCIES

1 THE ADMINISTRATIVE PROCESS

As our industrial society has grown and become more and more complex, the social and economic problems which confront government have multiplied fantastically. Not only have these problems increased in number, but interrelationships and conflicting social goals have complicated their solution. Also, advances in technology have required special training and experience to make an intelligent attempt at the solution of problems in many areas. Having decided that regulation of one sort or another is desirable, governments of necessity have employed the device of the administrative agency to lighten the burdens imposed on the executive branch, legislative bodies, and courts by this growth and development. The multitude of administrative agencies performing governmental functions today has resulted from limitations due to the lack of time to devote to making, enforcing, and interpreting laws and the lack of expert familiarity with all aspects of all these problems to make informed and effectual decisions concerning them. The President, every governor, every legislator, and every judge cannot at once be equipped with an expert knowledge of all the problems in the fields of transportation, atomic energy, labor relations, television, and radio communications, to name a few. The fact that our society and economy are constantly changing requires that continuous attention be given to all areas which the government is involved in and that regulatory rules be flexible and some degree of discretion be given for their making and enforcement.

The direct day-to-day legal impact on business of the many local, state, and Federal administrative agencies is far greater than the impact of the courts and legislative bodies. Administrative agencies create and enforce the greater bulk of the laws which make up the legal environment of business. A brief examination of the functions of just a handful of the Federal agencies such as the NLRB, the FTC, the ICC, the FCC, and the FPC, will illustrate this impact.

The National Labor Relations Board (NLRB) is involved in all aspects of labor-management relations. This agency annually conducts thousands of hearings involving labor disputes and engages in many other activities as well. The Federal Trade Commission (FTC) is concerned with the whole field of business competition and unfair trade practices including such fundamental aspects of business as advertising, pricing of products, and corporate growth by merger or acquisition.

The Interstate Commerce Commission (ICC) has the responsibility for licensing common carriers in interstate commerce and for approving their rates. There are similar agencies at the state level which set rates and grant licenses for intrastate transportation and communication. The rates for services or products furnished by public utilities such as the telephone, water, gas, and electrical power companies, are set by these agencies in addition to shipping charges.

The Federal Communications Commission (FCC) is responsible for supervising all aspects of television and radio broadcasting and the Federal Power Commission (FPC) is concerned with the production and distribution of natural gas and similar commodities. There are many other Federal agencies such as the Internal Revenue Service (IRS) which regulate and supervise activities which directly affect all our daily lives. Others like the Atomic Energy Commission (AEC) have a limited effect.

It is clear that, collectively, administrative agencies are directly or indirectly involved in practically every aspect of business as well as our private lives.

The functions of administrative bodies generally are described as (1) rule making, (2) adjudicating, (3) prosecuting, (4) advising, (5) supervising, and (6) investigating. These functions are not the concern of all administrative agencies to the same degree. Some agencies are primarily adjudicating bodies, such as the industrial commissions which rule on workmen's compensation claims. Others are primarily supervisory, such as the Securities and Exchange Commission (SEC) which supervises the issue and sale of investment securities. To be sure, most agencies perform all the foregoing functions to some degree in carrying out their responsibilities.

In addition to traditional executive functions, note that the administrative process involves performance of both legislative and judicial functions and therefore is by its very nature in conflict with the doctrine of separation of powers. But, as we have seen, the utilization of administrative agencies is a product of necessity, and practicality demands that this doctrine, however good in theory, give way at least to some extent. In the preceding chapter, the invasion of the legislative field by the judiciary was discussed. In this chapter, the bases for invasion of both the traditional legislative and judicial fields by administrative agencies will be discussed, along with the functions of courts in reviewing the activities of these agencies. Subsequent chapters also contain cases involving the exercise of power by administrative bodies.

2   LEGISLATION BY ADMINISTRATIVE BODIES

The rule-making function in the administrative process is essentially legislative in character. Administrative agencies are usually created by enactments of the legislature in which the legislative branch is generally said to *delegate* certain responsibility to the agency. Aside from the doctrinal question of whether one governmental body can constitutionally perform all three functions of government, there is also the issue of whether a legislature can delegate its law-making function at all to some other person or group. A delegation of legislative authority usually is valid only if limitations are imposed on the exercise of the power and if standards are prescribed by which a court can determine whether these limitations have been exceeded. The standards set must meet certain minimum requirements before the agency in question is validly empowered to act in a certain area, and the rules promulgated by the agency must follow these standards and limitations imposed by the law establishing it, if they are to be upheld. Thus, the standards imposed are at the heart of litigation challenging administrative actions.

Some courts have taken the view that the legislature cannot delegate its law-making function at all, but have concluded that authorizing an administrative agency to "fill in the details" of legislation is valid as not being an exercise of the legislative power. Other courts have stated that the legislature *can* delegate part of its function to an agency as long as sufficient general standards to be used by the agency are included in the grant of authority. The difference in the two foregoing approaches to delegation is largely a matter of semantics. In still other cases, courts have recognized that standards are not possible and that, of necessity, administrative agencies must determine questions of law as well as questions of fact. The following cases illustrate these viewpoints. The first case is an example of a court's approving broad standards; the second is an example of an approved delegation without any standards at all.

HILL V. RELYEA
216 N.E.2d 795 (Ill. 1966)

HOUSE, JUSTICE: The appellant . . . was found to be in need of mental treatment and was ordered detained in the Manteno State Hospital by the circuit court of Will County on April 29, 1965. The superintendent of the hospital granted her an absolute discharge on May 17, 1965, pursuant to authority vested in him by section 10-6 of the Mental Health Code. The appellant filed a motion in the circuit court of Will County asking the court to enter its order discharging her and restoring her person to legal competence in accordance with section 10-7 of the Code. The court denied her motion and held both sections 10-6 and 10-7 of the Code unconstitutional.

Section 10-6 of the Mental Health Code provided: "When a mentally retarded person, or a person in need of mental treatment has been hospitalized on court order, the superintendent of the hospital in which such person is detained ("detained" changed to "hospitalized" by 1965 amendment) shall have the power and authority to grant an absolute discharge or a conditional discharge, as the welfare of such person and of the community may require, under such rules and regulations as may be adopted by the Department."

Section 10-7 of the Code provided that when the superintendent granted an absolute discharge, he should immediately notify in writing the court entering the original order of hospitalization. Upon receipt of such notice the court should "as a matter of record," enter its order discharging such person, and if the person was previously adjudged legally incompetent under any prior statute the court should enter a further order restoring the person to legal competence unless the notice alleged that the patient's condition required continuance of his status as legally incompetent. . . .

The first question is whether the provisions of section 10-6 constitute an unconstitutional delegation of powers by the General Assembly. Appellees argue that the statute fails to provide adequate standards to guide the superintendent's action. Appellants, on the other hand, contend that administrative discretion is controlled by the standard set forth in the statute, whereby the superintendent may discharge patients only "as the welfare of such person and of the community may require, under such rules and regulations as may be adopted by the Department."

There is a distinction between the delegation of true legislative power and the delegation to a subordinate of authority to execute the law. The former involves a discretion as to what the law shall be; the latter is merely an authority or discretion as to its execution, to be exercised under and in pursuance of the law. It is an established rule that the General Assembly cannot delegate its general legislative power to determine what the law shall be. However, it may delegate to others the authority to do those things which the legislature might properly do, but cannot do as understandingly or advantageously. Absolute criteria whereby every detail necessary in the enforcement of a law is anticipated need not be established by the General Assembly. The constitution merely requires that intelligible standards be set to guide the agency charged with enforcement, and the precision of the permissible standard must necessarily vary according to the nature of the ultimate objective and the problems involved.

In this case the legislature gave the superintendent of the hospital the power and authority to discharge patients "as the welfare of such person and of the community may require." The legislature has determined who shall discharge patients and the criteria for discharge but it has granted authority to the Department of Mental Health and to the hospital superintendent to use discretion in executing the law and in granting the discharge. This discretion must be exercised within the standard set forth by the General Assembly. The difficulty in attempting to establish more precise legislative standards is readily apparent. The superintendent of the hospital and his staff examine, work with and treat the hospitalized person. They can determine more understandingly and advantageously when the welfare of the person and of the community may require a discharge or continued hospitalization of such person. Therefore it is desirable to grant to the superintendent and the Department the authority to discharge hospitalized persons and the discretion as to when the welfare of such person requires it. The nature of the objectives to be achieved and the problems to be solved negate the usefulness of setting more precise legislative standards.

The legislature has conferred authority and discretion as to the execution of a law. The authority and discretion is to be exercised under and in pursuance of the standard, "as the welfare of such person and of the community may require," which is found in section 10-6. This is a proper delegation of administrative authority. . . . [REVERSED AND REMANDED, WITH DIRECTIONS]

GECKLER V. REVIEW BD. OF INDIANA EMPLOYMENT SECURITY DIVISION
187 N.E.2d 751 (Ind. 1963)

The Review Board of the Indiana Employment Security Division granted unemployment compensation benefits to Cox. Cox had quit her work voluntarily and the question of whether or not she did so for "good cause" is raised on this appeal by her former employer from the ruling of the board.

RYAN, JUSTICE: . . . The Review Board . . . [said]

Statement of Facts:

This claimant (aged 32) was employed in general office work at this employer's medical laboratory for one year and three months. The claimant's proximate reason for quitting her job on January 14, 1961, after two weeks' notice, was the employer's criticism of the manner in which she operated and maintained the copyflex machine; which criticism upset the claimant because she considered it to be unwarranted and unfair under the circumstances. When the employer informed her that he could get a ten-year-old who could operate the copyflex better than the claimant, she replied that if that's what he wanted, that was what he should have; and that she would just give him notice right then. Also, she testified that although her hours were from 8 a.m. to 5 p.m., she would always get the employer's work handed to her about five or ten minutes to 5:00 and she was to stay there and run those things until they were completed.

These and other differences between the employer and the claimant made her so nervous that she "just couldn't take it any longer." She testified to the referee, that she went home crying every night because she was a nervous wreck. She became convinced that it was impossible for her to perform her work to the satisfaction of her employer.

Findings and Conclusions:

The cogent facts are obscure, but from close analysis of the record it is clearly enough discernible that this employer, dedicated, disciplined, precise, scientific and objective, and this claimant, nervous, temperamental, hypersensitive and subjective, were hopelessly at odds; and that the employment relationship between these two was ultimately bound to become mutually intolerable because of their diametrically opposed personalities. In the case of National Furn. Mfg. Co. v. Review Board, *131 Ind. App. 260, 170 N.E.2d 381, the Court held that the determination of whether or not the claimant had good cause to voluntarily leave his work, is in most cases a fact question to be decided upon the basis of the circumstances attendant to the particular case. In the instant case, it is apparent that the claimant honestly believed that it was impossible for her to continue in the employment.*

The referee heard and observed the witnesses under oath, and weighed the evidence. The majority of the Review Board likewise finds and holds that, under all the circumstances of this case, the claimant did not leave her work voluntarily without good cause on January 14, 1961, but that she honestly believed she was compelled to leave this work; which conviction of the claimant was due to circumstances that she was incapable of controlling.

The question as to what is or is not good cause is one which does not lend itself to any exact rules or definitions of reasonable precision. The problem was adequately pointed out in *State ex el. Standard Oil Co. v. Review Bd.,* 230 Ind. 1 (1951) at page 9, 101 N.E.2d 60 at page 64, where the court stated:

"Good cause" is not defined in the Act. The Board is not authorized to implement the Act by making rules which would lay down conditions and tests of general application to all cases within the legislative framework from which it could be determined to what classes of cases the broad legislative policy above mentioned should not apply. There is no rule or standard, legislative or otherwise, for the ascertainment of what is or is not "good cause" for waiving or modifying the denial of benefits. It seems to us the choice is left wholly to the unbridled discretion of the Board. The Board may find the facts, but, having found them is without any legal yardstick by which to measure the rights of the parties. The Act does not state, even in a general way, in what circumstances or under what conditions the Board shall, or even may, waive or modify the denial of benefits. It establishes no criterion to govern the Board's course. It arms the Board with a high-powered vehicle but no

road map. The attempted delegation of authority involves more than methods or details. It permits the Board such a wide discretion as to vest in them the power not only to find the facts, but to make the law which shall be applied to those facts. The range of the Board's discretion as to what constitutes "good cause" might vary from claim to claim and from day to day, and in the final analysis depend largely, if not entirely, on the changing complexion of the Board itself, for "good cause" might mean one thing to one mind and something entirely different to another. We think the legislature would have no difficulty in drafting a statute which would not leave to the Review Board the legislative power of choice.

The judicial guideposts to be applied to appeals from administrative agencies were laid down in *Warren v. Indiana Telephone Co.*, 217 Ind. 93 (1939) at page 118, where the court stated:

. . . If, however, it should be made to appear that the evidence upon which the agency acted was devoid of probative value; that the quantum of legitimate evidence was so proportionately meager as to lead to the conviction that the finding does not rest upon a rational basis; or that the result of the hearing must have been substantially influenced by improper considerations, the order will be set aside, not because incompetent evidence was admitted, but rather because the proof, taken as a whole, does not support the conclusion reached.

Applying these tenets to this particular case, we are unable to say as a matter of law the determination reached by the Review Board was not correct. [AFFIRMED]

Questions of delegation to administrative agencies have played an important role in the legal history of business. For example, during the early days of the New Deal, delegations were held invalid in two important cases, *Schechter Poultry Corp. v. United States* [1] and *Panama Refining Co. v. Ryan.* [2] These decisions contributed in part to the attempted "court-packing" by President Roosevelt. Many scholars of administrative law believe that the decisions should no longer be considered as precedent and that any delegation is valid. Justice Cardozo in a special concurring opinion in *Schechter Poultry* very vividly applied the rule requiring standards to be included in the delegation when he said:

The delegated power of legislation which has found expression in this code is not canalized within banks that keep it from overflowing. It is unconfined and vagrant. . . . Here in the case before us, is an attempted delegation not confined to any single act nor to any class or group of acts identified

---

[1] 295 U.S. 495 (1935).
[2] 293 U.S. 388 (1935).

or described by reference to a standard. Here in effect is a roving commission to inquire into evils and upon discovery correct them.

The following majority opinion in *Schechter Poultry* discusses the concept of delegating the legislative function:

SCHECHTER POULTRY CORP. V. UNITED STATES
295 U.S. 495 (1935)

The National Industrial Recovery Act of Congress authorized the President to approve "codes of fair competition" for a trade or industry upon application by one or more trade or industrial associations or groups. If no code were applied for by segments of the trade, the President could prescribe one himself, either on his own motion or upon receiving a complaint. Violation of the codes approved was made a criminal offense. Pursuant to the act, the President promulgated a Live Poultry Code to govern the poultry industry in and around New York City. This code contained, among others, provisions prescribing certain trade practices to be followed, minimum wage and maximum hours for employees of members of the industry, and the minimum number of employees to be hired by a member depending on the volume of his business. The defendants were wholesalers in the poultry industry in New York City, who purchased, slaughtered, and resold chickens to retailers. None of their sales were in interstate commerce. The defendants were found guilty in Federal District Court of committing misdemeanors for violating the Live Poultry Code and their convictions were sustained on appeal by the Circuit Court of Appeals. This appeal to the Supreme Court resulted, challenging the act as an unconstitutional delegation of power. The convictions were based, in part, on violations of the requirement of "straight killing" found in the "trade practice" provisions of the code. Actually these provisions required straight *selling,* by prescribing that wholesalers sell their poultry to retailers in the same lots as purchased by the wholesalers, that is, in the same coops as received at the slaughterhouse. Defendants had violated this provision by permitting retail dealers and butchers to select the individual chickens they wanted to buy.

HUGHES, CHIEF JUSTICE: *The Question of the Delegation of Legislative Power.* . . . The Constitution provides that "All legislative powers herein granted shall be vested in a Congress of the United States, which shall consist of a Senate and House of Representatives," Article 1, § 1. And the Congress is authorized "To make all Laws which shall be necessary and proper for carrying into Execution" its general powers. Article 1, § 8, par. 18. The Congress is not permitted to abdicate or to transfer to others the essential legislative functions with which it is thus vested. We have repeatedly recognized the necessity of adapting legislation to complex conditions involving a host of details with which the national Legislature cannot deal directly. We pointed out in the *Panama Refining Co.* case that the Constitution has never been regarded as denying to Congress the necessary resources of flexibility and practicality, which will enable it to perform its function in laying down policies and establishing standards, while leaving to selected instrumentalities the making of subordinate rules within prescribed limits and the determination of facts to which the policy as declared by the Legislature is to apply. But we said that the constant recognition of the necessity and validity of such provisions, and the wide range of administrative authority which has been developed by means of them, cannot be allowed to obscure the limitations of the authority to delegate, if our constitutional system is to be maintained. *Id.,* 293, page 421. . . .

Accordingly, we look to the statute to see whether Congress has overstepped these limitations—whether Congress in authorizing "codes of fair competition" has itself established the standards of legal obligation, thus performing its essential legislative function, or, by the failure to enact such standards, has attempted to transfer that function to others. . . . The question . . . is whether there is any adequate definition of the subject to which the codes are to be addressed. . . .

For a statement of the authorized objectives and content of the "codes of fair competition," we are referred repeatedly to the "Declaration of Policy" in section 1 of title 1 of the Recovery Act (15 U.S.C.A. § 701). Thus the approval of a code by the President is conditioned on his finding that it "will tend to effectuate the policy of this title." Section 3 (a) of the act, 15 U.S.C.A. § 703 (a). The President is authorized to impose such conditions "for the protection of consumers, competitors, employees, and others, and in furtherance of the public interest and may provide such exceptions to and exemptions from the provisions of such code, as the President in his discretion deems necessary to effectuate the policy herein declared." *Id.* The "policy herein declared" is manifestly that set forth in section 1. That declaration embraces a broad range of objectives. Among them we find the elimination of "unfair competitive practices." But, even if this clause were to be taken to relate to practices which fall under the ban of existing law, either common law or statute, it is still only one of the authorized aims described in section 1. It is there declared to be

. . . the policy of Congress . . . to remove obstructions to the free flow of interstate and foreign commerce which tend to diminish the amount thereof; and to provide for the general welfare by promoting the organization of industry for the purpose of cooperative action among trade groups, to induce and maintain united action of labor and management under adequate governmental sanctions and supervision, to eliminate unfair competitive practices, to promote the fullest possible utilization of the present productive

capacity of industries, to avoid undue restriction of production (except as may be temporarily required), to increase the consumption of industrial and agricultural products by increasing purchasing power, to reduce and relieve unemployment, to improve standards of labor, and otherwise to rehabilitate industry and to conserve natural resources.

Under section 3, whatever "may tend to effectuate" these general purposes may be included in the "codes of fair competition." . . .

The government urges that the codes will "consist of rules of competition deemed fair for each industry by representative members of that industry—by the persons most vitally concerned and most familiar with its problems." Instances are cited in which Congress has availed itself of such assistance; as, e.g., in the exercise of its authority over the public domain, with respect to the recognition of local customs or rules of miners as to mining claims, or, in matters of a more or less technical nature, as in designating the standard height of draw-bars. But would it be seriously contended that Congress could delegate its legislative authority to trade or industrial associations or groups so as to empower them to enact the laws they deem to be wise and beneficent for the rehabilitation and expansion of their trade or industries? Could trade or industrial associations or groups be constituted legislative bodies for that purpose because such associations or groups are familiar with the problems of their enterprises? And could an effort of that sort be made valid by such a preface of generalities as to permissible aims as we find in section 1 of title 1? The answer is obvious. Such a delegation of legislative power is unknown to our law, and is utterly inconsistent with the constitutional prerogatives and duties of Congress.

. . . Congress cannot delegate legislative power to the President to exercise an unfettered discretion to make whatever laws he thinks may be needed or advisable for the rehabilitation and expansion of trade or industry.

To summarize and conclude upon this point: Section 3 of the Recovery Act (15 U.S.C.A. § 703) is without precedent. It supplies no standards for any trade, industry, or activity. It does not undertake to prescribe rules of conduct to be applied to particular states of fact determined by appropriate administrative procedure. Instead of prescribing rules of conduct, it authorizes the making of codes to prescribe them. For that legislative undertaking, section 3 sets up no standards, aside from the statement of the general aims of rehabilitation, correction, and expansion described in section 1. In view of the scope of that broad declaration and of the nature of the few restrictions that are imposed, the discretion of the President in approving or prescribing codes, and thus enacting laws for the government of trade and industry throughout the country, is virtually unfettered. We think that the code-making authority thus conferred is an unconstitutional delegation of legislative power. [CONVICTIONS REVERSED]

Justice Cardozo, in the special concurring opinion previously noted, used rather strong language when he said: "This is delegation running riot." While Roosevelt's attempt to pack the court failed, many people believe that he lost the battle but won the war. Since *Schechter Poultry,* the court has approved very broad delegations of legislative authority, as is illustrated by the following case:

YAKUS V. UNITED STATES
321 U.S. 414 (1944)

The Emergency Price Control Act, as amended by the Inflation Control Act, provided for the establishment of the Office of Price Administration and set up a scheme for the promulgation of regulations and orders fixing maximum prices of commodities and rents. These acts were adopted as wartime measures in the interest of national defense and security, with the avowed purposes of stabilizing prices and rents, eliminating speculation and hoarding, and protecting persons with fixed incomes and government from paying excessive prices because of shortages.

The standards which were to guide the Administrator's exercise of his authority to fix prices contained the following language: "The Administrator is authorized after consultation with representative members of the industry, to promulgate regulations fixing prices of commodities which in his judgment will be generally fair and equitable and will effectuate the purposes of this Act." Due consideration was to be given prevailing prices between October 1 and October 15, 1941. In addition, changes in costs of production, transportation, and distribution as well as increases or decreases in profits since 1941 were to be considered in making the regulations.

The petitioners were tried, convicted, sentenced to jail for six months, and fined $1,000 each on charges of violation of the act by the willful sale of wholesale cuts of beef at prices above the maximum prescribed by Revised Maximum Price Regulation No. 169, which had been promulgated by the Administrator. This was an appeal from their conviction.

STONE, CHIEF JUSTICE: Congress enacted the Emergency Price Control Act in pursuance of a defined policy and required that the prices fixed by the Administrator should further that policy and conform to standards prescribed by the Act. The boundaries of the field of the Administrator's permissible action are marked by the statute. It directs that the prices fixed shall effectuate the declared policy of the Act to stabilize commodity prices so as to prevent war-time inflation and its enumerated disruptive causes and effects. In addition the prices established must be fair and equitable, and in fixing them the Administrator is directed to give due consideration, so far as practicable, to prevailing prices during the designated base period, with prescribed administrative adjustments to compensate for enumerated disturbing factors affecting prices. In short the purposes of the Act specified in § 1 denote the objective to be sought by the Administrator in fixing prices—the prevention of inflation and its enumerated consequences. The standards set out in § 2 define the boundaries within which prices having that purpose must be fixed. It is enough to satisfy the statutory requirements that the Administrator finds that the prices fixed will tend to achieve that objective and will conform to those standards, and that the courts in an appropriate proceeding can see that substantial basis for those findings is not wanting.

The Act is thus an exercise by Congress of its legislative power. In it Congress has stated the legislative objective, has prescribed the method of achieving that objective—maximum price fixing—and has laid down standards to guide the administrative determination of both the occasions for the exercise of the price-fixing power, and the particular prices to be established. . . .

The Act is unlike the National Industrial Recovery Act of June 16, 1933, 48 Stat. 195, considered in *Schechter Poultry Corp. v. United States,* 295 U.S. 495, . . . which proclaimed in the broadest terms its purpose "to rehabilitate industry and to conserve natural resources." It prescribed no method of attaining that end save by the establishment of codes of fair competition, the nature of whose permissible provisions was left undefined. It provided no standards to which those codes were to conform. The function of formulating the codes was delegated, not to a public official responsible to Congress or the Executive, but to private individuals engaged in the industries to be regulated. . . .

The Constitution as a continuously operative charter of government does not demand the impossible or the impracticable. It does not require that Congress find for itself every fact upon which it desires to base legislative action or that it make for itself detailed determinations which it has declared to be prerequisite to the application of the legislative policy to particular facts and circumstances impossible for Congress itself properly to investigate. The essentials of the legislative function are the determination of the legislative policy and its formulation and promulgation as a defined and binding rule of conduct—here the rule, with penal sanctions, that prices shall not be greater than those fixed by maximum price regulations which conform to standards and will tend to further the policy which Congress has established. These essentials are preserved when Congress has specified the basic conditions of fact upon whose existence or occurrence, ascertained from relevant data by a designated administrative agency, it directs that its statutory command shall be effective. It is no objection that the determination of facts and the inferences to be drawn from them in the light of the statutory standards and declaration of policy call for the formulation of subsidiary administrative policy within the prescribed statutory framework. . . .

Nor does the doctrine of separation of powers deny to Congress power to direct that an administrative officer properly designated for that purpose have ample latitude within which he is to ascertain the conditions which Congress has made prerequisite to the operation of its legislative command. Acting within its constitutional power to fix prices it is for Congress to say whether the data on the basis of which prices are to be fixed are to be confined within a narrow or a broad range. In either case the only concern of courts is to ascertain whether the will of Congress has been obeyed. This depends not upon the breadth of the definition of the facts or conditions which the administrative officer is to find but upon the determination whether the definition sufficiently marks the field within which the Administrator is to act so that it may be known whether he has kept within it in compliance with the legislative will.

As we have said: "The Constitution has never been regarded as denying to the Congress the necessary resources of flexibility and practicality . . . to perform its function." *Currin v. Wallace, supra,* 306 U.S. at page 15. . . . Hence it is irrelevant that Congress might itself have prescribed the maximum prices or have provided a more rigid standard by which they are to be fixed; for example, that all prices should be frozen at the levels obtaining during a certain period or on a certain date. . . . Congress is not confined to that method of executing its policy which involves the least possible delegation of discretion to administrative officers. . . . It is free to avoid the rigidity of such a system, which might well result in serious hardship, and to choose instead the flexibility attainable by the use of less restrictive standards.

Only if we could say that there is an absence of standards for the guidance of the Administrator's action, so that it would be impossible in a proper proceeding to ascertain whether the will of Congress has been obeyed, would we be justified in over-riding its choice of means for effecting its declared purpose of preventing inflation.

The standards prescribed by the present Act, with the aid of the "statement of the considerations" required to be made by the Administrator, are sufficiently definite and precise to enable Congress, the courts and the public to ascertain whether the Administrator, in fixing the designated prices, has conformed to those standards. . . . Hence we are unable to find in them an unauthorized delegation of legislative power. The authority to fix prices only when prices have risen or threaten to rise to an extent or in a manner inconsistent with the purpose of the Act to prevent inflation is no broader than the authority to fix maximum prices when deemed necessary to protect consumers against unreasonably high prices, sustained in *Sunshine Anthracite Coal Co. v. Adkins, supra,* or the authority to take possession of and operate telegraph lines whenever deemed necessary for the national security or defense, upheld in *Dakota Cent. Tel. Co. v. State of South Dakota,* 250 U.S. 163, . . . or the authority to suspend tariff provisions upon findings that the duties imposed by a foreign state are "reciprocally unequal and unreasonable," held valid in *Field v. Clark, supra.* . . .

The directions that the prices fixed shall be fair and equitable, that in addition they shall tend to promote the purposes of the Act, and that in promulgating them consideration shall be given to prices prevailing in a stated base period, confer no greater reach for administrative determination than the power to fix just and reasonable rates, . . . or the power to regulate radio stations engaged in chain broadcasting "as public interest, convenience or necessity requires," upheld in *National Broadcasting Co. v. United States, supra,* 319 U.S. at page 225, . . . or the power to prohibit "unfair methods of competition" not defined or forbidden by the common law, *Federal Trade Commission v. R. F. Keppel & Bro.,* 291 U.S. 304, . . . or the direction that in allotting marketing quotas among states and producers due consideration be given to a variety of economic factors, sustained in *Mulford v. Smith, supra,* 307 U.S. at pages 48, 49, 59, . . . or the similar direction that in adjusting tariffs to meet differences in costs of production the President "take into consideration . . . in so far as he finds it practicable" a variety of economic matters, sustained in *Hampton Jr. & Co. v. United States, supra,* 276 U.S. 394, or the similar authority, in making classifications within an industry, to consider various named and unnamed "relevant factors" and determine the respective weights attributable to each, held valid in *Opp Cotton Mills v. Administrator, supra.* [AF-FIRMED]

The *Schechter* case illustrates the fact that sometimes even the President can be considered an "administrative agency," if he has been given authority to make rules or adjudicate. The category is very broad and includes such titles as board, office, bureau, department, commissioner, and administrator. According to Professor Kenneth Culp Davis, while the court in the *Schechter* case dwells mostly on the vagueness of standards, the main distinguishing feature of the case from others where the delegation has been approved, such as *Yakus,* is the very broad amount of authority delegated.[3] Professor Davis further indicates that it is improbable that Congress will go as far again, and points to the fact that such sweeping action was avoided through all of World War II.[4]

Some courts have tried to distinguish valid delegations from invalid ones on the following basis: "The true distinction is between the delegation of *power to make* the law, which necessarily involves a discretion as to what it shall be [and would be invalid], and conferring authority or discretion as

---

[3] Davis, *Administrative Law Text (Hornbook Series),* § 2.06 (1959).
[4] *Id.* § 2.01.

to its *execution* to be exercised under and in pursuance of the law [which would be valid]." [5]

There are innumerable examples of delegations which have been approved. Statutes delegating authority to administrative agencies are usually liberally construed in order to accomplish the legislative goal. The trend of modern cases is to hold the delegations valid even though legislative power is given and standards are absent or are vague, as long as there are procedural safeguards or checks on the power which prevent an abuse of its exercise. As a practical matter, legislatures can deal only in generalities. Many of the problems which have arisen in connection with an area of regulation were not even considered by the legislature when it enacted the statute calling for regulation. It would not be possible to deal with all the present and future unforeseeable problems by specific statutes. The necessary flexibility is provided by delegation of the rule-making function to administrative agencies.

3   JUDICIAL POWERS OF ADMINISTRATIVE AGENCIES

The doctrine of separation of powers, as was noted earlier, seemingly conflicts with administrative action in the exercise of judicial functions as well as legislative functions. The American Bar has long been concerned with the extent to which administrative agencies exercise judicial powers. The essay which follows indicates the attitude of many lawyers toward the adjudicating function of administrative bodies, and describes the various activities of some of the many administrative agencies at the Federal level.

ADMINISTRATIVE AGENCIES AND JUDICIAL POWERS [6]
Roy L. Cole [7]

An administrative agency is customarily defined as any governmental authority, other than a court or legislature, which determines or directly affects the rights and obligations of private parties through rule-making or adjudication. The First Congress in 1789 enacted three statutes granting administrative powers, two pertaining to customs and the third initiating the series of pension laws now administered by the Veterans' Administration. Of the fifty-one authorities classified as administrative agencies in 1941 by the Attorney General's Committee on Administrative Procedure, eleven trace their beginnings to legislation enacted prior to the end of the Civil War, but

---

[5] *Cincinnati W. & Z. Ry. v. Clinton,* 1 Ohio St. 77, 88 (1852).
[6] 44 *A.B.A.J.* 953 (Oct., 1958). Used by permission from the American Bar Association and the *American Bar Association Journal.*
[7] Mr. Cole is a member of the Texas Bar (Dallas).

the tremendously powerful "independent" agencies, exercising broad control over nationwide activities, are largely a development of the twentieth century. The modern history of the administrative agency dates from the creation of the Interstate Commerce Commission in 1887. The Federal Reserve System was established in 1913, the Federal Trade Commission in 1914, the Federal Power Commission in 1920, and the Board of Tax Appeals in 1924. With the advent of the New Deal came such important agencies as the Federal Deposit Insurance Corporation, the Securities and Exchange Commission, the Social Security Board, and the National Labor Relations Board. World War II produced such powerful though temporary agencies as the Office of Price Administration, Office of Defense Transportation, the War Production Board and others. Still later came the tremendously important Atomic Energy Commission, and Congress seems sure to establish a space commission to control our relations with the rest of the universe.

A characteristic of these administrative authorities is their exercise of what are historically termed "judicial powers"—the adjudication of controversies directly affecting private individuals. The grant of these powers has often been attributed to a failure of the common law courts to meet the great social problems arising from late nineteenth and early twentieth century industrialization—the individual's inability as a practical matter to obtain legal redress for wrongs committed against him by the new gigantic industrial combines, and the transition from a *laissez-faire* government to one assuming many affirmative responsibilities for the social and economic well-being of the populace as a whole. Another and fairer analysis is that, while judicial failure was sometimes involved, administrative agencies have been created from time to time simply because in each particular situation such an authority seemed to practical men to be the most practical solution to the problem at hand. Certainly the expressed and accepted specific reasons for administrative exercise of traditionally judicial powers are practical and varied ones, among them being:

(a) The need, in adjudication incidental to regulation of modern industrial complexes, for an expertise which can be developed only through the constant attention to a particular field which the courts are unable to give and with the assistance of large staffs whose combined skills cover all the various non-legal areas pertinent to the industries to be regulated.

(b) The necessity for intelligent coordination between policy-making and enforcement.

(c) The necessity of deciding controversies in fields affected by the public interest as "rightly" as possible, taking into account all relevant facts, not merely (as in the courts) those specially selected facts placed in the record by the adversary parties.

(d) The tendency of the judiciary, drawn primarily from conservative, propertied classes, to resist legislative programs antipathetic to those classes even though clearly favored by the majority of the populace as a whole.

(e) The tremendous volume of cases before some agencies which would so overwhelm the courts that they would find themselves unable to perform their normal and important tasks.

The American Bar . . . [has] constantly maintained [its] attack on all administrative exercise of judicial powers, on the ground that such exercise violates the fundamental doctrine of separation of powers and thus imperils the even more fundamental "rule of law."

These broadly based objections have had an almost astonishing lack of success in even retarding continual new and expanded grants of administrative judicial powers. . . .

There is room for doubt as to the correctness of classifying all adjudication as an exercise of judicial power. Although most of us fundamentally believe in a kind of natural law, we realize that the adjudicatory process in the courts is not merely a matter of "discovering" pre-existing law, as Blackstone and his contemporaries maintained, but in the judge's choice of available alternatives amounts actually to making law, and always has. In the words of Theodore Roosevelt, approved by Cardozo: "The chief lawmakers in our country may be, and often are, the judges, because they are the final seat of authority. Every time they interpret contract, property, vested rights, due process of law, liberty, they necessarily enact into law parts of a system of social philosophy; and as such interpretation is fundamental they give direction to all lawmaking."

Since making law is by definition an exercise of legislative power, it is logical to assert that what we call judicial powers are in many instances only adjudicatory techniques, which may as well be proper tools in the exercise of legislative powers as in the exercise of judicial ones. Furthermore, since the courts through judicial action actually make perhaps more law than legislatures, without complaint from the Bar, it appears to many persons that we are in poor position to clamor so strongly for complete abolition of the use of adjudicatory techniques by administrative agencies in the course of their congressional delegated legislative duties. . . .

There is widespread feeling that the judicial process has had its chance and muffed it, that the courts have failed, and would again fail, to meet the challenge posed by Theodore Roosevelt in the words immediately following those quoted above: "The decisions of the courts on economic and social questions depend upon their economic and social philosophy; and for the peaceful progress of our people during the twentieth century we shall owe most to those judges who hold to a twentieth century economic and social philosophy and not to a long outgrown philosophy which was itself the product of primitive economic conditions."

Even among those who do not view the judicial process as having failed, there is a feeling that the passive, impartial character of that process is unsuited to the accomplishment of the affirmative policies entrusted to many regulatory agencies in our complex modern existence. . . .

It is absolutely clear that the principle of complete divestiture of *all* adjudicatory powers of *all* administrative agencies is discredited beyond reasonable hope of revival. This discredit is merited, not only because the dogma is historically and logically unsound, but also because, from a coldly practical standpoint, "a government consisting of three (completely) separate powers would get no farther than a span of three horses without a driver. Our strength comes from the interplay of the powers and the checks and balances among them—our unity from the ultimate responsibility of all branches of government to the electorate and to the court-sustained fundamentals of Christian morality. . . .

If the demand for total abolition of all administrative adjudication is, as I believe, untenable, the opposite extreme is likewise indefensible. To allow Congress to provide for administrative use of adjudicatory techniques as incidental aids in implementing certain definite economic regulatory programs is one thing—to permit administrative adjudication of matters affecting life, liberty and basic individual rights, even with judicial review, is quite another. It is also a threat to our system of checks and balances to allow establishment or continuation of administrative adjudication in areas where there is no affirmative legislative policy to be implemented wholly or partly by the use of adjudicatory techniques; and a similar threat exists in the indefinite continuation of administrative adjudication in agencies of any type which use these techniques to the substantial exclusion of others, and which therefore actually constitute extra-judicial courts. Our solution to the basic problem of administrative exercise of judicial powers lies somewhere in the middle ground, and can be best approached through separate analysis of each class of agency.

Administrative agencies may be classified in various ways, *e.g.*, according to form, function, operational organization or degree of independence. For our purposes the functional analysis seems most fruitful. We have the following types:

1. Claims or "benefit" agencies such as the Veterans' Administration, the Social Security Board and the Bureau of Old Age and Survivors' Insurance, which do not set policy, but merely handle great numbers of small claims on the basis of approving those covered by comprehensive statutes and disapproving those not covered.
2. The Tax Court, formerly the Board of Tax Appeals, which adjudicates controversies under the tax laws between taxpayers and the Commissioner of Internal Revenue.
3. Authorities such as the Attorney General's Immigration and Natu-

ralization Service and the Third Assistant Postmaster General, regulating matters involving life, liberty and freedom of speech and communication.

4 Agencies such as the ICC, SEC, FPC and FCC, which regulate and control nationwide industries in the public interest, and which bear a clear burden of responsibility for their actions and for the success or failure of their efforts. These agencies act primarily through rules and use adjudicatory techniques as supplements to the rule-making power. In this class also fall such departmental divisions as the Commodity Stabilization Service in the Department of Agriculture, with broad regulatory power over certain aspects of nationwide industries, operating similarly to the independent agencies but having less easily identifiable responsibility.

5 Agencies such as the FTC and NLRB, which are regulatory in intent but prosecutory in form, which cut across all industries and fields of endeavor, have no clear burden of responsibility for the results of their efforts, and use adjudicatory techniques as a primary means of establishing and enforcing policy.

A. The clearest case for retention of adjudicatory powers by administrative agencies is in the first category—the claims or benefit agencies. Paradoxically, these are the authorities which make greatest use of adjudication in performing their functions. But the "controversies" which they determine are not really adversary in nature. Certain benefits are granted by Congress to those meeting carefully prescribed statutory conditions. In the vast majority of cases the determination of whether an individual meets those conditions calls merely for mechanical application of the rules to the undisputed facts. There is no real opposition to a claimant—agency personnel are charged with assisting him to obtain benefits to the full extent he is lawfully entitled. There is no necessity for the trial and evidentiary rules of a court. And as a practical matter the judicial system would quite surely be literally overwhelmed by the application of judicial procedures to the millions of claims involved.

B. The clearest case for removal of judicial powers from an administrative agency involves the Tax Court. As the name implies, it is a court, it operates as such, and should be transferred to the judicial branch. Its sole business is the adjudication of highly technical tax controversies between the government and individuals. In this process it deals with the ascertainment of facts of the type which judicial procedures are best fitted to ascertain, and with the interpretation of detailed statutory codes on a subject as to which lawyers are the experts. It has no regulatory, investigatory or policy-making authority, is charged only with the fair and impartial adjudication of cases, and clearly belongs in the judicial system.

C. An equally clear and more urgent case for transfer of adjudicatory functions from administrators to courts is in our third category—authorities exercising control over matters involving life, liberty and freedom of speech and communication. The most important agency in this field is the Immigration and Naturalization Service of the Department of Justice. A special inquiry officer first determines the question of exclusion or deportation. An appeal then lies to the nonstatutory quasi-judicial Board of Immigration Appeals. There is a further right of appeal to the courts in deportation cases and possible review through habeas corpus in exclusion proceedings. But in no case is full judicial review available, although we are here dealing with administrative power which can result, in Justice Brandeis' words, "in loss of both property and life; or of all that makes life worth living." As pointed out by the Hoover Commission's Task Force on Legal Services and Procedure, the arbitrary exclusion of an alien not entitled to constitutional protection not only is inconsistent with humanitarian principles but also many times deeply affects citizens of the United States to whom the alien may be related. The problem in this field is infinitely complicated by what the Hoover Commission Task Force has correctly termed the absolute essentiality to the national security that unauthorized persons be stopped or ejected.

The delicate necessity of preserving both national security and individual liberty is too great to be left largely in the hands of administrators. This is a field in which the experts are the courts, trained in the traditions of the Constitution and the common law which has served so well whenever fundamentals are involved. The functions of the Board of Immigration Appeals must be transferred to the courts generally or to a special Immigration Court.

The allied rights of freedom of speech and expression are subject to several serious and largely unfettered administrative controls. Under a doubtful construction of the Foreign Agent's Registration Act of 1938, as amended in 1942, the Customs Bureau and the Post Office Department destroy, without notice to sender or addressee, any printed matter from other countries which they decide constitutes "foreign propaganda," a term subject to almost any definition. Both the above agencies have broad additional powers to prevent the transmission of material deemed seditious or obscene, and the Postmaster General also has the power to revoke the second-class mail privileges of periodical publications, revocation being the practical equivalent of suppression. Here again we are in a vital field where the judiciary has the expertise and where the dangers of arbitrary action are so vital that only the courts should have the right to act.

D. Our fourth category contains the powerful industry-wide independent regulatory agencies about which (together with the FTC and NLRB) most controversy arises. The highlights of their historical development have been outlined earlier in this article, as have the reasons for the grants to them of the right to exercise judicial powers or adjudicatory techniques. To recapitulate, each of these agencies was formed to cure certain evils which had not been alleviated by the existing branches of government, and to exercise an affirmative, continuing guidance over the future activities of the industry concerned. The Supreme Court aptly expressed the differing functions of administrative and judicial adjudication in this field as follows:

The Communications Act is not designed primarily as a new code for the adjustment of conflicting private rights through adjudication. Rather it expresses a desire on the part of Congress to maintain, through appropriate administrative control, a grip on the dynamic aspect of radio transmission. . . . To a large degree they (administrative agencies) have been a response to the felt need of governmental supervision over economic enterprise—a supervision which could effectively be exercised neither through self-executing legislation nor by the judicial process.

Effective regulation of a complex twentieth-century industry requires a cohesive, integrated instrumentality of control, having adequate staffs with as varied skills as the industry to be regulated, able to focus constant attention on that industry and to initiate action, and with the power to use all techniques, including the adjudicative, necessary to make its control meaningful and effective.

Apart from the complaint of violation of the separation of powers doctrine, already discussed, four main objections have been made to administrative control as represented by the industry-wide agencies:

1 The presence of an inherent "leftist" orientation;
2 A tendency toward totalitarianism, undermining "the rule of law";
3 Bias; and
4 Susceptibility to improper influence.

Certainly an antipathy toward a substantive program is not in itself a valid reason for criticizing the agency administering that program. However, in the early days of the independent regulatory agencies the administrative process was believed, with hope by some and with fear by others, to have an inherent political or social orientation. But "both the thrill and the chill failed to take into account basic factors limiting the managing and planning potentialities of the administrative process." Natural economic forces have in this country proved infinitely more potent than all the regulatory agencies combined in determining social and political orientation. Having observed the changes in aims and policies in the various agencies from time to time to meet the needs and demands of the people resulting from the development of new goods and services by industry, we must now realize that there is no such thing as a permanently built-in administrative viewpoint. The administrative process is instead a maneuverable device, shifting orientation as economic and social developments and varying legislative expressions may direct.

The complaint of totalitarianism is primarily directed at governmental regulation as such. Insofar as it constitutes an accusation that administrative use of adjudicatory techniques violates the principle of "rule of law," it is subject to the gibe that we are really advocating the rule of lawyers. The rule of law certainly must be preserved, but if for the term we accept perhaps the best modern definition—"a state of affairs in which there are legal barriers to governmental arbitrariness and legal safeguards for the protection of the individual"—we can through combined legislative and judicial control of administrative procedures and through judicial review achieve those ends without sacrificing the efficiency of the administrative process.

The accusations of bias seem largely unfair. The twentieth-century agency is created and from time to time revitalized to accomplish positive results—a bias in favor of the basic program is required by the legislative history and the terms of the governing statutes. Cardozo has reminded us that every person, every judge, necessarily views any given situation from a point where he is placed by his own heredity and environment—no one of us can look at the world out of another's eyes. Yet bias must not impair fair-mindedness, especially in adjudication. Careful scholarship seems to have shown that administrative agencies have been subject to isolated lapses in this respect, to no greater extent than have the courts. And charges of bias have been far less frequently heard since the agencies "went conservative" in the late 1940's, lending weight to the belief that many criticisms leveled at administrative authorities are in actuality motivated by antagonism to the substantive programs entrusted to their care.

The very real problem of agency exposure and susceptibility to improper influence is at this time of writing highlighted by congressional investigation of the Federal Communications Commission. This problem is best solved by (a) the formulation and enforcement of a code of ethics for administrators; (b) the enforcement of legislation imposing criminal penalties on persons exerting improper influence; and most importantly, (c) the development among legislators, members of the executive branch of government, politicians and the people generally of the realization that it is as immoral and destructive to attempt to influence administrative decisions as judicial ones. All branches of the government must co-operate to this end, since it is a joint problem of all. As yet, the drastic step of complete removal of administrative adjudicatory powers does not seem justified—if it later does, we can have confidence in the abilities of the judiciary to fill the gap.

On balance, the reasons for continuation of exercise of judicial powers in the industry-regulatory agencies outweigh the objections.

E. By far the greatest difficulty in determining whether judicial powers should be exercised by administrative agencies involves the Federal Trade Commission and the National Labor Relations Board. Most or all of the reasons advanced for the exercise of adjudicatory powers by industry-regulating agencies apply here, but there are far more powerful arguments against FTC and NLRB retention of such functions than apply to the others. The FTC and NLRB, while in a sense regulatory, differ from other independent agencies in the following important particulars.

First, they lack that most important essential of democratic government—precise accountability. It is comparatively easy to tell whether the SEC or the CAB is doing a good job in the public interest in the limited fields in which they function. It is far more difficult to determine the same question when the FTC and NLRB are involved, since their actions are but one of the many factors involved in the health of the general economy which they affect.

Second, instead of a defined and limited area where technical non-legal expertness is essential, their inquiries involve a broad consideration of more intangible social and ethical factors—they deal with fields in which we may assert that courts are, or should be, the more expert.

Third, these agencies are not regulatory in the sense that they lay down rules of general application, but instead are solely investigatory and prosecutory. Here the use, or threat of use, of adjudicatory powers is not in aid of other, more clearly legislative processes, but is the sole technique. While it is noted above that the use of the adjudicatory technique may actually be an exercise of a legislative power, it is nevertheless true that all organisms, in the words of the Supreme Court, "represent an interplay of form and function." In the case of these two agencies, the forms are those of a court, the fundamental policies of their substantive programs have been established, and their adjudicatory functions should now be court-administered.

Finally, there is a widespread public distrust of the essential fairness of these agencies. This is probably explainable in the case of the NLRB as the "inevitable outcome of a statute which gives employers no affirmative rights, imposes no duties upon employees and places upon the Board a duty of acting as prosecutor as well as judge." This distrust has carried over in spite of the 1947 legislation imposing obligations on labor unions and providing complete internal separation of prosecuting and judging functions. The feeling with regard to the FTC, though less intense, arises from similar considerations. And, as Professor Davis has pointed out: "So long as detached and informed opinions differ as to what is justice, one objective in a democratic society is to appear to do justice. That ideal remains unrealized so long as significant groups, whether or not misled, firmly believe that justice is denied."

For the Bar to advocate the transfer to the courts of the adjudicatory functions of the NLRB and the FTC is a bold and self-challenging course. These are the two agencies which, so nearly identical in form to traditional courts, were established almost solely because of a belief that the judiciary's economic and social opinions were so far opposed to the prevailing ideals of the time that the courts would subvert the legislative purpose. This belief was largely justified and was widely held. If the judicial functions of these agencies are transferred to the courts, the Bar and judiciary must thereafter so act as to convince a still slightly suspicious people that their former causes for distrust are abated. In requesting such transfer we represent to the nation that the work of Holmes, Cardozo, Brandeis, Pound, and many others has had its effect—that American common law, attuning itself more closely to the convictions of the past, recognizes the necessity in its work for consideration of contemporary social, industrial and political conditions as well as historical factors, and is therefore entitled to exercise its traditional functions under the conditions of modern society. This is a strong representation and a magnificently challenging one, worthy of the best traditions of the Bench and Bar.

In summary, then, administrative exercise of judicial powers should be permitted in three instances:

1 In claims or "benefit" agencies, where the "adjudications" are not really controversial, do not need formal judicial techniques, and are of such volume as to be impossible of practicable administration by the courts.

2 In industry-regulatory agencies, where continuing supervision of complex industrial organizations requires the constant attention of specialists in the nonlegal fields and where the use of adjudicatory techniques is in addition and supplementary to rule making and other more usual forms of regulations.

3 In agencies (such as FTC and NLRB) administering new and untried economic and social policies cutting across many segments of the nation's life, and which therefore of necessity must use a cautious case-by-case adjudicatory method in determining the proper implementation of such policies. In these instances, administrative adjudication should be permitted only for such period of time as is necessary to develop a generally accepted body of precedent. As soon as this has been done their adjudicatory powers should be transferred to the courts.

Administrative exercise of judicial powers should be denied, or if in existence should be removed, in all other cases, particularly where fundamentals of life, liberty and freedom of expression are involved. Even where administrative adjudication is permissible, judicial review should be preserved and strengthened, and the Bar should continue its efforts to assure that administrative procedures are conducted in accordance with the highest standards of fairness.

In immediate application these recommendations involve transfer to the present court system, or preferably to specialized courts, of the judicial functions of the Immigration and Naturalization Service, the National Labor

Relations Board, the Federal Trade Commission, and certain authorities within the Post Office Department and the Customs Bureau. These changes should be specifically advocated—we only hurt our cause by continuing to demand the elimination of all administrative adjudication on the basis of an irretrievably discredited over-rigid application of the separation of powers doctrine.

Notwithstanding the objections of the organized bar indicated in the preceding essay, the exercise of judicial functions by administrative agencies continues to expand. The criticism is often made that in its judicial capacity an agency acts as prosecutor, finder of facts, and judge. However, similar to the current attitude on delegation of legislative power, the trend is to uphold the granting of judicial power to an administrative agency if the power is restricted by procedural safeguards preventing its abuse. Note that the right to a jury trial does not exist in either formal or informal hearings conducted by administrative bodies. However, the judicial power to hear and decide *criminal* cases cannot be granted to agencies other than courts, because of a stricter standard of procedural "due process of the law" in this area. In the exercise of the judicial function, the agency involved may issue an order requiring certain action or prohibiting certain conduct. The latter order is often referred to as a cease-and-desist order, which is the administrative-law version of a court injunction or decree. Such orders are usually complied with in the event that the affected party does not seek judicial review of the order. Failure to comply with the cease-and-desist order may result in fines, imprisonment, or other sanctions such as loss of a license or permit. Other orders are known as consent orders because they are entered by mutual agreement of the agency and the party involved. Cease-and-desist orders are entered only after the agency hears evidence and makes a finding of fact, but consent orders may be entered at any time.

4   CHECKS ON ADMINISTRATIVE ACTION

It is unlikely today that a court would find that the exercise of executive, judicial, and legislative functions at once by an administrative agency is invalid because of the doctrine of separation of powers. The doctrine itself, however, is still very much alive. The original purpose for separating the functions of government was to create checks and balances on the exercise of governmental power and thereby prevent tyranny. Society views administrative agencies as desirable because they provide needed continuity and consistency in the formulation, application, and enforcing of rules and regulations. And, as we have seen, agencies can accomplish what the other branches cannot, because of limitations imposed on those branches by time, the volume of governmental activity, and the necessity of expert acquaintance with many problems and the factors to be considered in solving them. While in *form* administrative agencies appear to violate the doctrine of separation of powers, in *substance* they are compatible with its underlying purpose, as long as checks and safeguards prevent the abuse of administrative power.

The executive usually has a check on administrative actions, in that he normally is the one who appoints the top officials of an agency.

The legislature can review and control administrative activity by abolishing the agency, providing specific legislation contrary to rules adopted by the agency, more explicitly defining the limitations on the activities of an agency and its rule making, providing additional procedural requirements for the agency's adjudications, or limiting appropriations of funds to the agency.

The courts also provide a check on administrative bodies by judicial review of their actions. Just as the laws enacted by the legislature must be within its power as established by the Constitution or they are void, the rules and regulations promulgated by an administrative body must be within the confines of its grant of power from the legislature, or a court will find them void. However, once having determined that an act of the legislature is constitutional or a rule of an agency is authorized, the courts will not inquire into its wisdom or effectiveness. An unwise or ineffectual law may and should be corrected by political action at the polls; an unwise rule or regulation adopted by an agency may be corrected by the legislature which gave the agency power to make the rule in the first place.

In reviewing administrative quasi-judicial decisions (which may involve both findings of fact and interpretation of rules), courts are reluctant to decide in advance of a hearing that it will not be conducted fairly by the agency in question. In general (although there are exceptions), courts refuse to review administrative actions until a complaining party has exhausted all the administrative remedies and procedures available to him for redress. For example, a person complaining of the enforcement of a zoning ordinance must first seek relief from the zoning board and fail to obtain it from that body before he can seek review by a court.

When it reviews the findings of *fact* made by an administrative body, a court considers these to be prima facie correct. A court of review examines the evidence by analyzing the record of the agency's proceedings and upholds the agency's findings and conclusions on questions of fact if they are supported by substantial evidence in the record as a whole. In other words, the record must contain material evidence from which a reasonable person might reach the same conclusion as did the agency. If substantial evidence in support of the decision is present, the court will not disturb the agency's findings, even though the court itself might have reached a different conclusion on the basis of other conflicting evidence also in the record.

Contrary to popular belief, courts reviewing administrative interpretations of *law* do not always decide questions of law for themselves. According to Professor Kenneth Culp Davis, frequently a court holds an administrative interpretation as final "if it has warrant in the record and rational basis in law." [8] Administrative agencies are frequently called upon to interpret the statute governing the agency and the agency's construction is persuasive to courts. However, courts frequently do replace administrative holdings with their own interpretations of law. Professor Davis lists three major matters which influence courts in deciding whether they should review an agency's interpretation or not. He indicates that a court will be less apt to overrule an agency (1) if the court feels the agency is better equipped to decide the matter (because of the agency's expert knowledge of the problem, for example); (2) if it appears that the legislative intent was to prefer determination of the matter by the agency; (3) if the interpretation of the agency does not have far-reaching, significant effects.[9]

Courts also review the procedural rules established by administrative agencies for the conduct of their hearings. In reviewing such rules, courts are not empowered to substitute their judgment on their own procedures for those of the agency. Judicial responsibility is limited to ensuring consistency with statutes and compliance with the demands of the Constitution for a fair hearing.

The principle that Federal administrative agencies should be free to fashion their own rules of procedure and to pursue methods of inquiry capable of permitting them to discharge their multitudinous duties is an outgrowth of the view that administrative agencies and administrators will be familiar with the industries which they regulate and thus will be in a better position than courts or legislative bodies to design procedural rules adapted to the peculiarities of the industry and the tasks of the agency involved.

The cases which follow illustrate various rules of law concerned with the judicial review of administrative decisions. Each is preceded by a short statement or description of the rule illustrated.

A   THE DOCTRINE OF EXHAUSTION OF REMEDIES

HORAN V. FOLEY
188 N.E.2d 877 (III. 1963)

MURPHY, JUSTICE: This is an action for a declaratory judgment. Plaintiff, John F. Horan, an employee of the Metropolitan Sanitary District of Greater Chicago, seeks a judgment declaring that the defendants, members of the

[8] Davis, *op. cit.*, § 30.14.
[9] *Ibid.*

Civil Service Board of the District, have lost jurisdiction to hear or to determine charges filed against him. Defendants appeal from a judgment on the pleadings in favor of plaintiff, entered after a denial of their motion to dismiss.

The principal question is whether plaintiff was entitled to judicial relief before he had exhausted the administrative remedies available to him. Plaintiff's theory is that he was entitled to challenge the jurisdiction of the Board judicially "without waiting to go through the useless and expensive process of a full hearing before the Board." The complaint alleges all of the factual recitations made in this opinion.

On August 8, 1961, plaintiff was notified by the acting general superintendent of the district that he was suspended from his civil service position for a period of 30 days commencing August 12, 1961. On August 25, 1961, plaintiff was personally served with "Notice and Charges," "Statement of Charges," and "Specifications," by which he was informed that charges had been filed against him and that the Civil Service Board had set the matter for hearing on September 12, 1961. Plaintiff was informed of his right to be heard, with counsel, in his own defense.

On September 8, 1961, plaintiff's attorneys mailed to the Board a "motion to quash and dismiss charges," based upon the contention that the statutory 30 days from date of suspension, within which the Board was empowered to conduct the hearing, would expire prior to September 12, 1961. Plaintiff was absent from Chicago from September 8 until about 1:00 p.m., September 11, 1961. Upon returning home, he was handed, by his wife, two sealed envelopes bearing his name and address. He brought the envelopes to the office of his attorneys, where they were opened in his presence. The envelopes contained "Notice of Resetting" in the matter of charges filed against the plaintiff as aforesaid, advising that the hearing thereon would be held on Monday, September 11, 1961, at 10 o'clock a.m. at the place indicated in the original notice of August 25, 1961. Plaintiff was served neither personally, nor by registered mail, with the "Notice of Resetting."

On September 12, 1961, plaintiff, with his attorneys, appeared at the time and place indicated in the notice served upon him on August 25, 1961. He was there informed that the defendant members of the Board had convened on Monday, September 11, 1961, with respect to the charges filed against him, and that the matter had been "continued" to September 12, 1961. Neither plaintiff nor his attorneys were present on September 11, 1961, and he did not request or consent "to the 'continuance' of any hearing from September 11, 1961, to September 12, 1961."

On September 12, 1961, the Board denied plaintiff's motion to quash and dismiss the charges; it allowed his motion for a bill of particulars, and continued the hearing to October 3, 1961. On that date, plaintiff again moved to quash and dismiss the charges on the ground of the Board's asserted lack of jurisdiction; after consideration, the Board on October 4, 1961, advised plaintiff "that it had determined it had jurisdiction to proceed in the matter of the charges" and continued further hearing to October 16, 1961. Plaintiff then brought this action on October 11, 1961.

Defendants' motion to dismiss, denied by the trial court, was on the ground that the trial court was without jurisdiction of the subject matter, since plaintiff had not exhausted the administrative remedies available to him. As the defendants elected to stand on their motion to dismiss the complaint, the court sustained plaintiff's motion for judgment on the pleadings and declared and found that "defendants herein have no jurisdiction to proceed to a hearing or to determine the charges filed against plaintiff John F. Horan, under date of August 25, 1961, because of the failure of said Board to properly convene for, or to conduct a hearing on said charges within the thirty-day period from plaintiff's suspension under said charges, as required by the statute and rules. . . ."

Defendants' objection to judicial review at this state of the proceedings is based on the doctrine of exhaustion of administrative remedies— "the long settled rule of judicial administration that no one is entitled to judicial relief for a supposed or threatened injury until the prescribed administrative remedy has been exhausted." The doctrine of exhaustion of remedies is followed in the state of Illinois: "The courts of this state have refused to interfere with administrative hearings and have forced complainants to exhaust their administrative remedies before appealing to the judiciary."

Our Supreme Court has indicated that the exhaustion doctrine is subject to limitation. In *Bright v. City of Evanston,* 10 Ill.2d 178, (1956), the court said (pp. 184, 185):

> [W]here it is claimed the effect of an ordinance as a whole is to unconstitutionally impair the value of the property and destroy its marketability, direct judicial relief may be afforded without prior resort to remedies under the ordinance. . . . Under this rule one who seeks relief from an ordinance on the ground that it is void in its entirety is not obliged to pursue the machinery of the ordinance itself for his remedy.
>
> On the other hand, where the claim is merely that the enforcement or application of a particular classification to plaintiff's property is unlawful and void, and no attack is made against the ordinance as a whole, judicial relief is appropriate only after available administrative remedies have been exhausted.

Similarly, when the power of the Chicago Civil Service Commission to demote police officers in large numbers was attacked, our Supreme Court did not require that the police officers therein exhaust their various administrative remedies before seeking judicial relief. There, the attack on the Commission's power was based on its asserted lack of jurisdiction to proceed with the intended demotions. We conclude, here, that the trial court had jurisdiction to consider the merits or sufficiency of plaintiff's complaint.

This being so, we now consider the merits of plaintiff's contention. . . .

We believe that since plaintiff was served personally on August 25, 1961, with a copy of the charges filed against him, the Board properly acquired jurisdiction of plaintiff and the subject matter. The inclusion of a notice of the time and place of the hearing on such charges beyond the required 30 days did not prevent the Board from acquiring jurisdiction nor cause it to lose jurisdiction.

Generally, regulations designed to secure order, system and dispatch in proceedings, cannot be disregarded where the rights of the parties interested may be injuriously affected. However, plaintiff suffered no injury by reason of the original scheduling of the hearing for September 12, nor by the rescheduling it for September 11, which was done within the 30-day period, even though his complaint alleges that the notice of the resetting did not personally reach him before the latter time. Also, plaintiff suffered no injury because the hearing was postponed from the 11th to the 12th without his consent. We conclude that this rescheduling of the hearing date by the Board did not cause it to lose jurisdiction.

We conclude, from the allegations of the complaint, that the defendants had jurisdiction to proceed to a hearing and to determine the charges served personally on plaintiff under date of August 25, 1961. Therefore, the trial court should have sustained defendant's motion to dismiss, because plaintiff had failed to exhaust his administrative remedies.

The judgment of the trial court is reversed and plaintiff's action is ordered dismissed here. [REVERSED AND ORDERED DISMISSED HERE]

B   THE REQUIREMENT THAT AN AGENCY EXERCISE ITS DISCRETION AND USE ITS SPECIAL COMPETENCE

FEDERAL COMMUNICATIONS COMMISSION
V. RCA COMMUNICATIONS, INC.
346 U.S. 87 (1953)

FRANKFURTER, JUSTICE: The Mackay Radio and Telegraph Co. (Mackay) provides radiotelegraph service between the United States and a number of foreign countries. Over the opposition of RCA Communications, Inc. (RCAC), which provides similar service by means of a total of 65 circuits including ones to Portugal and The Netherlands, the Federal Communications Commission authorized Mackay, at that time authorized to communicate with 39 overseas points, to open two new circuits, to Portugal and The Netherlands. RCAC claims that duplicate circuits, already authorized for RCAC and Mackay to 11 other points, are not here "in the public interest," in that Mackay has been unable to show any tangible benefit to the public. . . .

Finding that "over-all competition for telegraph traffic generally" would be increased, and more effective radiotelegraph competition introduced, the Commission concluded that duplicate facilities should be authorized because of the "national policy in favor of competition." From this policy, the Commission said, it follows that "competition" is in the public interest where competition is "reasonably feasible." The Commission, . . . authorized Mackay's proposed service to Portugal and The Netherlands. . . . RCAC sought review and was successful in the Court of Appeals on its claim that an applicant must demonstrate, as the Commission found that Mackay had failed to do here, that tangible benefit to the public would be derived from the authorization. . . .

Congress did not purport to transfer its legislative power to the unbounded discretion of the regulatory body. In choosing among applicants, the Commission was to be guided by the "public interest, convenience, or necessity," a criterion we held not to be too indefinite for fair enforcement. . . . The statutory standard no doubt leaves wide discretion and calls for imaginative interpretation. Not a standard that lends itself to application with exactitude, it expresses a policy, born of years of unhappy trial and error, that is "as concrete as the complicated factors for judgment in such a field of delegated authority permit. . . ."

Congress might have made administrative decision to license not reviewable. Although it is not suggested—or implied by the grant of power to review—that Congress could not have reserved to itself or to the Commission final designation of those who would be permitted to utilize the air waves, precious as they have become with technological advance, it has not done so. On the other hand, the scope of this Court's duty to review administrative determinations under the Federal Communications Act of 1934, has been carefully defined. Ours is not the duty of reviewing determinations of "fact," in the narrow, colloquial scope of that concept. Congress has charged the courts with the responsibility of saying whether the Commission has fairly exercised its discretion within the vagueish, penumbral bounds expressed by the standard of "public interest." It is our responsibility to say whether the Commission has been guided by proper considerations in bringing the deposit of its experience, the disciplined feel of the expert, to bear on applications for licenses in the public interest.

In this case, the Court of Appeals has ruled that the Commission was guided by a misinterpretation of national policy, in that it thought that the maintenance of competition is in itself a sufficient goal of federal communications policy so as to make it in the public interest to authorize a license merely because competition, i.e., duplication of existing facilities, was "reasonably feasible." RCAC relies on the holding of the Court of Appeals that the Commission must decide, in the circumstances of the application, that competition is not merely feasible but beneficial.

The Commission has not in this case clearly indicated even that its own experience, entirely apart from the tangible demonstration of benefit for which RCAC contends, leads it to conclude that competition is here desirable. It seems to have relied almost entirely on its interpretation of national policy. Since the Commission professed to dispose of the case merely upon its view of a principle which it derived from the statute and did not base its conclusion on matters within its own special competence, it is for us to determine what the governing principle is. . . .

In reaching a conclusion that duplicating authorizations are in the public interest wherever competition is reasonably feasible, the Commission is not required to make specific findings of tangible benefit. It is not required to grant authorizations only if there is a demonstration of facts indicating immediate benefit to the public. To restrict the Commission's action to cases in which tangible evidence appropriate for judicial determination is available would disregard a major reason for the creation of administrative agencies, better equipped as they are for weighing intangibles "by specialization, by insight gained through experience, and by more flexible procedure." . . . In the nature of things, the possible benefits of competition do not lend themselves to detailed forecast, . . . but the Commission must at least warrant, as it were, that competition would serve some beneficial purpose such as maintaining good service and improving it. Although we think RCAC's contention that an applicant must demonstrate tangible benefits is asking too much, it is not too much to ask that there be ground for reasonable expectation that competition may have some beneficial effect. Merely to assume that competition is bound to be of advantage, in an industry so regulated and so largely closed as is this one, is not enough. [JUDGMENT VACATED AND CASE REMANDED TO FCC FOR DISPOSITION]

On remand of the foregoing case, the Federal Communications Commission held that competition with RCAC would have a considerable beneficial effect and granted the license to Mackay Radio and Telegraph. RCA Communications again appealed, but the Commission's action was upheld by the United States Circuit Court of Appeals (D.C.).[10]

C THE PROHIBITION ON A COURT'S SUBSTITUTING ITS JUDGMENT FOR THAT OF THE AGENCY

FEDERAL SECURITY ADMINISTRATOR V. QUAKER OATS CO.
318 U.S. 218 (1943)

STONE, CHIEF JUSTICE: The Federal Security Administrator, acting under §§ 401 and 701(e), of the Federal Food, Drug and Cosmetic Act, promulgated regulations establishing "standards of identity" for various milled wheat

[10] 38 F.2d 24 (1956).

products, excluding vitamin D from the defined standard of "farina" and permitting it only in "enriched farina," which was required to contain vitamin B_1, riboflavin, nicotinic acid and iron. The question is whether the regulations are valid as applied to respondent. The answer turns upon (a) whether there is substantial evidence in support of the Administrator's finding that indiscriminate enrichment of farina with vitamin and mineral contents would tend to confuse and mislead consumers; (b) if so, whether, upon such a finding, the Administrator has statutory authority to adopt a standard of identity, which excludes a disclosed non-deleterious ingredient, in order to promote honesty and fair dealing in the interest of consumers; and (c) whether the Administrator's treatment, by the challenged regulations, of the use of vitamin D as an ingredient of a product sold as "farina" is within his statutory authority to prescribe "a reasonable definition and standard of identity." . . .

Respondent, The Quaker Oats Company, has for the past ten years manufactured and marketed a wheat product commonly used as a cereal food, consisting of farina as defined by the Administrator's regulation, but with vitamin D added. Respondent distributes this product in packages labeled "Quaker Farina Wheat Cereal Enriched with Vitamin D," or "Quaker Farina Enriched by the Sunshine Vitamin." The packages also bear the label "Contents 400 U.S.P. units of Vitamin D per ounce, supplied by approximately the addition of 1/5 of 1 percent irradiated dry yeast."

Respondent asserts, and the Government agrees, that the Act as supplemented by the Administrator's standards will prevent the marketing of its product as "farina" since, by reason of the presence of vitamin D as an ingredient, it does not conform to the standard of identity prescribed for "farina," and that respondent cannot market its product as "enriched farina" unless it adds the prescribed minimum quantities of vitamin B_1, riboflavin, nicotinic acid and iron. Respondent challenges the validity of the regulations. . . .

The court below . . . held that because there was no evidence that respondent's product had in fact confused or misled anyone, the Administrator's finding as to consumer confusion was without substantial support in the evidence. It thought that, if anything, consumer confusion was more likely to be created, and the interest of consumers harmed, by the sale of farinas conforming to the standard for "enriched farina," whose labels were not required to disclose their ingredients, than by the sale of respondent's product under an accurate and informative label such as that respondent was using.

The Act does not contemplate that courts should thus substitute their own judgment for that of the Administrator. As passed by the House it appears to have provided for a judicial review in which the court could take additional evidence, weigh the evidence, and direct the Administrator "to take such further action as justice may require." . . . But before enactment, the Conference Committee substituted for these provisions those which became § 701 (f) of the Act. While under that section the Administrator's regulations must be supported by findings based upon "substantial evidence" adduced at the hearing, the Administrator's findings as to the facts if based on substantial evidence are conclusive. In explaining these changes the chairman of the House conferees stated on the floor of the House that "there is no purpose that the court shall exercise the functions that belong to the executive or the legislative branches." . . .

The review provisions were patterned after those by which Congress has provided for the review of "quasi-judicial" orders of the Federal Trade Commission and other agencies, which we have many times had occasion to construe. Under such provisions we have repeatedly emphasized the scope that must be allowed to the discretion and informed judgment of an expert administrative body. . . . These considerations are especially appropriate where the review is of regulations of general application adopted by an administrative agency under its rule-making power in carrying out the policy of a statute with whose enforcement it is charged. . . . Section 401 calls for the exercise of the "judgment of the Administrator." That judgment, if based on substantial evidence of record, and if within statutory and constitutional limitations, is controlling even though the reviewing court might on the same record have arrived at a different conclusion. . . . Taking into account the evidence of public demand for vitamin-enriched foods, their increasing sale, their variable vitamin composition and dietary value, and the general lack of consumer knowledge of such values, there was sufficient evidence of "rational probative force" . . . to support the Administrator's judgment that, in the absence of appropriate standards of identity, consumer confusion would ensue. . . . Respondent's final and most vigorous attack on the regulations is that they fail to establish reasonable definitions and standards of identity, as § 401 requires, in that they prohibit the marketing, under the name "farina," of a wholesome and honestly labeled product consisting of farina with vitamin D added, and that they prevent the addition of vitamin D to products marketed as "enriched farina" unless accompanied by the other prescribed vitamin ingredients which do not coact with or have any dietary relationship to vitamin D. Stated in another form, the argument is that it is unreasonable to prohibit the addition to farina of vitamin D as an optional ingredient while permitting its addition as an optional ingredient to enriched farina, to the detriment of respondent's business.

Since the definition of identity of a vitamin-treated food, marketed under its common or usual name, involves the inclusion of some vitamin ingredients and the exclusion of others, the Administrator necessarily has a large range of choice in determining what may be included and what excluded. It is not necessarily a valid objection to his choice that another could reasonably have been made. The judicial judgment is not to be substituted for the legislative judgment. It is enough that the Administrator has acted within the statutory bounds of his authority, and that his choice among possible alternative standards adapted to the statutory end is one which a rational person could have made. . . .

We conclude that the Administrator did not depart from statutory requirements in choosing these standards of identity for the purpose of promoting fair dealing in the interest of consumers, that the standards which he selected are adapted to that end, and that they are adequately supported by findings and evidence.

D   THE SUBSTANTIAL EVIDENCE RULE

UNIVERSAL CAMERA CORP. V. NATIONAL LABOR RELATIONS BOARD
340 U.S. 474 (1951)

The NLRB ordered Universal Camera Corp. to reinstate, with back pay, an employee whom the Board found was discharged because he gave testimony in another proceeding under the National Labor Relations Act. This order was issued despite the fact that the evidence concerning the reason the company dismissed the employee was conflicting, and the Board's examiner had found as a fact that the employee was discharged for some other reason and had recommended that the proceeding of the employee for reinstatement be dismissed. The Court of Appeals on reviewing the case held the Board's findings were "supported by substantial evidence" but the Court of Appeals did not consider the findings of the Hearing Examiner. This appeal to the Supreme Court resulted.

FRANKFURTER, JUSTICE: The essential issue raised by this case . . . is the effect of the Administrative Procedure Act and the legislation colloquially known as the Taft-Hartley Act, . . . on the duty of the Courts of Appeals when called upon to review orders of the National Labor Relations Board. . . .

I

Want of certainty in judicial review of Labor Board decisions partly reflects the intractability of any formula to furnish definiteness of content for all the impalpable factors involved in judicial review. But in part doubts as to the nature of the reviewing power and uncertainties in its application derive from history, and to that extent an elucidation of this history may clear them away.

The Wagner Act provided: "The findings of the Board as to the facts, if supported by evidence, shall be conclusive." . . . This Court read "evidence" to mean "substantial evidence," . . . and we said that "[s]ubstantial evidence is more than a mere scintilla. It means such relevant evidence as a reasonable mind might accept as adequate to support a conclusion." . . . Accordingly, it "must do more than create a suspicion of the existence of the fact to be established . . . it must be enough to justify, if the trial were to a jury, a refusal to direct a verdict when the conclusion sought to be drawn from it is one of fact for the jury." . . .

The very smoothness of the "substantial evidence" formula as the standard for reviewing the evidentiary validity of the Board's findings established its currency. But the inevitably variant applications of the standard to conflicting evidence soon brought contrariety of views and in due course bred criticism. Even though the whole record may have been canvassed in order to determine whether the evidentiary foundation of a determination by the Board was "substantial," the phrasing of this Court's process of review readily lent itself to the notion that it was enough that the evidence supporting the Board's result was "substantial" when considered by itself. It is fair to say that by imperceptible steps regard for the fact-finding function of the Board led to the assumption that the requirements of the Wagner Act were met when the reviewing court could find in the record evidence which, when viewed in isolation, substantiated the Board's findings. . . .

Criticism of so contracted a reviewing power reinforced dissatisfaction felt in various quarters with the Board's administration of the Wagner Act in the years preceding the war. . . .

Protests against "shocking injustices" and intimations of judicial "abdication" with which some courts granted enforcement of the Board's orders stimulated pressures for legislative relief from alleged administrative excesses. . . .

So far as the history of [the] movement for enlarged review reveals, the phrase "upon the whole record" makes its first appearance into the statute books when Congress with unquestioning—we might even say uncritical—unanimity enacted the Administrative Procedure Act.

One is tempted to say "uncritical" because the legislative history of that Act hardly speaks with that clarity of purpose which Congress supposedly furnishes courts in order to enable them to enforce its true will. On the one hand, the sponsors of the legislation indicated that they were reaffirming the prevailing "substantial evidence" test. But with equal clarity they expressed disapproval of the manner in which the courts were applying their own standard. The committee reports of both houses refer to the practice of agencies to rely upon "suspicion, surmise, implications, or plainly incredible evidence" and indicate that courts are to exact higher standards "in the exercise of their independent judgment" and on consideration of "the whole record."

Similar dissatisfaction with too restricted application of the "substantial evidence" test is reflected in the legislative history of the Taft-Hartley Act. . . . In order to clarify any ambiguity in that statute, however, the conference committee inserted the words "questions of fact, if supported by substantial evidence *on the record considered as a whole.* . . ."

This phraseology . . . became the law.

From the legislative story . . . two concrete conclusions do emerge. One is the identity of aim of the Administrative Procedure Act and the Taft-Hartley Act regarding the proof with which the Labor Board must support a decision. The other is that now Congress has left no room for doubt as to the kind of scrutiny which a court of appeals must give the record before the Board to satisfy itself that the Board's order rests on adequate proof. . . .

The standard of proof specifically required of the Labor Board by the Taft-Hartley Act is the same as that to be exacted by courts reviewing every administrative action subject to the Administrative Procedure Act.

Whether or not it was ever permissible for courts to determine the substantiality of evidence supporting a Labor Board decision merely on the basis of evidence which in and of itself justified it, without taking into account contradictory evidence or evidence from which conflicting inferences could be drawn, the new legislation definitively precludes such a theory of review and bars its practice. The substantiality of evidence must take into account whatever in the record fairly detracts from its weight. This is clearly the significance of the requirement in both statutes that courts consider the whole record. . . .

To be sure, the requirement for canvassing "the whole record" in order to ascertain substantiality does not furnish a calculus of value by which a reviewing court can assess the evidence. Nor was it intended to negative the function of the Labor Board as one of those agencies presumably equipped or informed by experience to deal with a specialized field of knowledge, whose findings within that field carry the authority of an expertness which courts do not possess and therefore must respect. Nor does it mean that even as to matters not requiring expertise a court may displace the Board's choice between two fairly conflicting views, even though the court would justifiably have made a different choice had the matter been before it *de novo*. Congress has merely made it clear that a reviewing court is not barred from setting aside a Board decision when it cannot conscientiously find that the evidence supporting that decision is substantial, when viewed in the light that the record in its entirety furnishes, including the body of evidence opposed to the Board's view. . . .

But a standard leaving an unavoidable margin for individual judgment does not leave the judicial judgment at large even though the phrasing of the standard does not wholly fence it in. The legislative history of these

Acts demonstrates a purpose to impose on courts a responsibility which has not always been recognized. Of course it is a statute and not a committee report which we are interpreting. But the fair interpretation of a statute is often "the art of proliferating a purpose" . . . revealed more by the demonstrable forces that produced it than by its precise phrasing. The adoption in these statutes of the judicially-constructed "substantial evidence" test was a response to pressures for stricter and more uniform practice, not a reflection of approval of all existing practices. To find the change so elusive that it cannot be precisely defined does not mean it may be ignored. We should fail in our duty to effectuate the will of Congress if we denied recognition to expressed Congressional disapproval of the finality accorded to Labor Board findings by some decisions of this and lower courts, or even of the atmosphere which may have favored those decisions.

We conclude, therefore, that the Administrative Procedure Act and the Taft-Hartley Act direct that courts must now assume more responsibility for the reasonableness and fairness of Labor Board decisions than some courts have shown in the past. Reviewing courts must be influenced by a feeling that they are not to abdicate the conventional judicial function. Congress has imposed on them responsibility for assuring that the Board keeps within reasonable grounds. That responsibility is not less real because it is limited to enforcing the requirement that evidence appear substantial when viewed, on the record as a whole, by courts invested with the authority and enjoying the prestige of the Courts of Appeals. The Board's findings are entitled to respect; but they must nonetheless be set aside when the record before a Court of Appeals clearly precludes the Board's decision from being justified by a fair estimate of the worth of the testimony of witnesses or its informed judgment on matters within its special competence or both. . . .

III

The Taft-Hartley Act provides that "The findings of the Board with respect to questions of fact if supported by substantial evidence on the record considered as a whole shall be conclusive." Surely an examiner's report is as much a part of the record as the complaint or the testimony. . . .

It is therefore difficult to escape the conclusion that the plain language of the statutes directs a reviewing court to determine the substantiality of evidence on the record including the examiner's report. The conclusion is confirmed by the indications in the legislative history that enhancement of the statutes and function of the trial examiner was one of the important purposes of the movement for administrative reform. . . .

We do not require that the examiner's findings be given more weight than in reason and in the light of judicial experience they deserve. The "substantial evidence" standard is not modified in any way when the Board and its examiner disagree. We intend only to recognize that evidence supporting a conclusion may be less substantial when an impartial, experienced examiner who has observed the witnesses and lived with the case has drawn conclusions different from the Board's than when he has reached the same conclusion. The findings of the examiner are to be considered along with the consistency and inherent probability of testimony. The significance of his report, of course, depends largely on the importance of credibility in the particular case. To give it this significance does not seem to us materially more difficult than to heed the other factors which in sum determine whether evidence is "substantial."

The direction in which the law moves is often a guide for decision of particular cases, and here it serves to confirm our conclusion. However halting its progress, the trend in litigation is toward a rational inquiry into truth, in which the tribunal considers everything "logically probative of some matter requiring to be proved." [CASE REMANDED TO COURT OF APPEALS]

On remand of the foregoing case, the Circuit Court of Appeals reexamined the record as a whole. Taking into account the recommendations and findings of the Board's examiner, the court found that the NLRB should have dismissed the complaint of the employee, because the record did *not* show substantially that he was discharged because he gave testimony, and accordingly denied enforcement of the Board's order.[11]

E   THE MANIFEST WEIGHT OF THE EVIDENCE RULE

ART V. DEPARTMENT OF REVENUE
215 N.E.2d 243 (III. 1966)

The Department of Revenue found Plaintiff liable for the sales tax on ice cream sold by boys from carts, motor scooters, and bike units. Plaintiff sought to avoid the tax liability.

HOUSE, JUSTICE: . . . Plaintiff operates an ice cream business. He purchases the manufactured product and stores it at two locations in Chicago. Ice cream is packed in small conveyances (carts, motor scooters and bike units) each morning and is then peddled and sold from the vehicles by boys 14 years old and upward. The vehicles are furnished by plaintiff. He supplies the gas to operate the motor scooters and pays the license fees required

[11] 190 F.2d 429 (1951).

of vendors. Some of the boys pay cash and others are charged with the amount taken out. Settlement is made each day, and the unsold packages are returned in the evening for refund or credit. The evidence is conflicting relative to assignment of territories, but a fair reading of the record indicates that some degree of control over territories is retained and exercised by plaintiff.

Each boy, or his parents on his behalf, signed identical instruments furnished by plaintiff designated "Consignment Agreement," paragraph 4 of which reads: "It is further understood that no compensation of any kind shall be due from either party to the other and that no employer-employee relationship exists between vendor and distributor. Said vendor further agrees not to hold himself out to the public as an employee of said distributor and understands that said distributor is not liable for injuries or damages to said vendor or to third persons."

From the foregoing evidence, plaintiff contends that section 1 and 2 of the act (Ill. Rev. Stat. 1963, chap. 120, pars. 440 and 441), are inapplicable because the ice cream products involved in the transaction (except sales from a truck which are admittedly taxable) were not for use or consumption but were transferred to the boys for resale by them. He recognizes the conflict in the testimony but relies heavily on the quoted paragraph of the agreement to sustain his position that no employer-employee relationship exists. . . .

The finding of the Department that plaintiff exercises almost complete control over the boys is justified. Its holding that the relationship of the parties is either employer-employee or principal-agent rather than categorizing the status of the boys as independent contractors is not contrary to the manifest weight of the evidence. No citation of authority is required for the familiar rule that the finding of an administrative agency will not be disturbed unless it is contrary to the manifest weight of the evidence. [JUDGMENT AFFIRMED]

Manifest weight means the obvious preponderance of evidence. In other words the rule involved does not permit a court to set aside an agency's finding unless the evidence obviously points to one result and the finding and decision of the agency are for the opposite result.

Rules D and E above are clearly quite similar. The courts of some jurisdictions may use the former in deciding a case while others will use the latter. Legal scholars may find a difference in degree between the two; they usually believe that the substantial-evidence test requires less proof and less persuasion than does the manifest-weight-of-the-evidence rule. In any event, the application of either of these rules gives prima facie support to the findings of the agency.

F   THE RULE THAT AN AGENCY'S REGULATION IS VALID UNLESS IT IS UNREASONABLE, ARBITRARY, OR CAPRICIOUS

GROSSMAN V. BAUMGARTNER
218 N.E.2d 259 (N.Y. 1966)

The New York City Charter authorized the Board of Health "to add to and to alter, amend or repeal any part of the health code." The Board of Health adopted a regulation prohibiting tattooing. Plaintiff brought suit contending that the regulation was unconstitutional.

FULD, JUSTICE: . . . A statute—or an administrative regulation which is legislative in nature—will be upheld as valid if it has a rational basis, that is, if it is not unreasonable, arbitrary or capricious. In the case before us, there is no warrant for the charge that the Board of Health acted arbitrarily or capriciously or that the regulation under attack was unreasonable. A review of the evidence given by the defendants' witnesses thoroughly demonstrates the compelling medical necessity for section 181.15 of the Health Code. Not only was a connection shown between tattooing and hepatitis but the proof convincingly established that rigorous regulation would be ineffective. The police power is exceedingly broad, and the courts will not substitute their judgment of a public health problem for that of eminently qualified physicians in the field of public health. As the Supreme Court has expressed it, "The judicial function is exhausted with the discovery that the relation between means and end is not wholly vain and fanciful, an illusory pretense." In its wisdom, the board in the case before us decided that the prohibition of lay tattooing was essential for the protection of the public health, and, as stated above, it may not be said that that determination was unreasonable or without justification. It follows, therefore, that the legislation is valid, and this is so notwithstanding that it will occasion the discontinuance of an existing business. [AFFIRMED]

5   STATE ADMINISTRATIVE AGENCIES

It is frequently assumed that the only significant administrative agencies exist at the Federal level in government. While the importance of the Federal administrative agencies to the legal environment of business may stagger the imagination, the role of state and local agencies cannot be considered as anything less than very substantial.

At the local level every business will be regulated and controlled by such agencies as zoning boards, which determine the permissible locations of business enterprises, and various taxing boards, which play a major role in determining the "cost of doing business" in the community. State agencies exist to regulate wages, hours, and working conditions of employees as well as to administer unemployment and workmen's compensation laws. Many states have Fair Employment Practice Commissions to prevent discrimination in hire, pay, or tenure of employment based on race, creed, sex, or national origin. As previously noted, other state agencies regulate rates charged by business in the fields of transportation, gas, water and power supply, and communications.

Clearly, there are not enough legally trained people in this country to staff all of these agencies. Agencies performing quasi-judicial functions are subject to constant criticism from lawyers because of "procedural errors" and related shortcomings as noted in the Cole article, set forth in section 3 of this chapter. The members of the bar have been attempting to bring reform to state administrative procedures to correct their weaknesses. The National Conference of Commissioners on Uniform State Laws prepared a Revised Model State Administrative Procedure Act in 1961. The act recognizes differences between Federal and state agencies. A major one is that state agencies operate in a much smaller area and on a more intimate basis. This means that state officials may have more preconceived ideas. In addition, states have more difficulty in hiring legally trained personnel. The following discussion outlines the nine basic principles of this model statute, which was designed to overcome some of the traditional objections to state administrative agency procedures.

TURNING THE SPOTLIGHT ON STATE ADMINISTRATIVE PROCEDURE [12]
Frank E. Cooper [13]

. . . First, the Revised Model State Act requires a substantial degree of uniformity in procedure by defining "agency" in all-inclusive terms as meaning each state board, commission, department or officer (other than the legislature or the courts) authorized to make rules or determine contested cases. Many officers of state agencies are opposed to the principle of giving the act broad applicability. They prefer that their own agencies be exempted, because they believe they can work out a better code of procedure for their own agencies than can anyone else; and they are eager to improve on it from case to case, devising as they go along. A desire to obtain powers of self-direction, not to say self-determination, is the main reason agencies are generally opposed to administrative procedure acts; the desire that state agencies be denied such powers is the chief reason the Bar approves such legislation.

[12] 49 *A.B.A.J.* 29 (Jan., 1963. Used by permission from the American Bar Association and the *American Bar Association Journal.*
[13] Professor Cooper is chairman of the American Bar Association Section on Administrative Law and professor of law at the University of Michigan.

Second, the Revised Model State Act requires that each agency adopt well-defined courses of procedure, setting forth in formal rules a description of its organization, the method of its operations, the nature and requirements of all formal and informal procedures available and a description of all forms and instructions used by the agency. These requirements should result not only in easing the task of respondents' counsel but also in improving the efficiency of the operations of the agencies.

Third, the Revised Model State Act implements the principle that agency actions should not be in the nature of secret, star-chamber proceedings but should be publicly known. All statements of policy or interpretations utilized by the agency are required to be made available for public inspection. No rule, order or decision may be invoked by the agency for any purpose until it has been made public in the manner prescribed.

Fourth, it is required that all interested parties have a voice in the adoption of agency rules. Except in the case of emergency rules (which may be effective only for a limited time) an agency proposing to adopt a rule must give at least twenty days' notice of its intended action, stating the terms or substance of the proposed rule. Further, the agencies must afford all interested persons reasonable opportunity to participate in the rule-making proceedings by submitting views and information. In stated cases, opportunity for oral hearing must be afforded (thus obviating the possibility that briefs may not be carefully considered). Provision is also made to assure the careful consideration of petitions for the adoption of rules.

Fifth, provisions are made for filing and prompt publication of all administrative rules. The provisions in this respect are skeletal in nature, experience having indicated that many states find it desirable to make detailed provisions, appropriate to their particular conditions, to assure that complete and current statements of all administrative rules are conveniently available. In Wisconsin, for example, a loose-leaf publication is issued monthly.

Sixth, the Revised Model State Act makes broad and explicit provision for obtaining declaratory relief, so that anyone who doubts either the validity or the applicability of an agency rule may obtain a speedy determination of such questions. To achieve these ends, agencies are required to provide by rule for the prompt disposition of petitions for declaratory rulings as to the applicability of any statutory provision or of any rule or order of the agency. Further, provision is made for the determination of the validity or applicability of a rule in a judicial proceeding for a declaratory judgment.

Seventh, ample provision is made to assure that all contested cases shall be decided fairly, on a complete and accurate record affording a basis for a fully informed decision by officers who have duly mastered the record. It is required that the notice initiating the proceeding include a short and plain statement of the matters asserted. Rules of evidence applied in civil cases in the state's courts are to be followed, except that when it is necessary to ascertain facts not reasonably susceptible of proof under such rules, agencies may relax the judicial standards of admissibility and hear evidence of a type commonly relied upon by reasonably prudent men in the conduct of their affairs. When an agency proposes to take official notice of facts within its asserted specialized knowledge, parties shall be notified of the facts which the agency proposes so to notice, and parties shall be given an opportunity to demonstrate that the actual facts are not what the agency had assumed.

Recognizing the dangers inherent in the institutional decision process, but recognizing also the necessity of utilizing it under some circumstances, the Revised Model State Act provides that when a majority of the agency officials who are to render the final decision have not heard the case or read the record, no decision adverse to a party other than the agency shall be made until a proposal for decision is served upon the parties, and an opportunity is afforded each party adversely affected to file exceptions and present briefs and oral argument before the officials who are to render the decision. In this way, parties respondent are guaranteed an opportunity of presenting their views as to the facts and law to the very individuals charged with ultimate responsibility for decision making.

As a further guarantee that decisions shall be carefully considered and fully informed, agencies are required to make specific rulings upon each proposed finding of fact submitted by any party in accordance with agency rules; and it is required that each final decision shall be accompanied by a concise and explicit statement of the underlying facts that support findings of ultimate fact set forth in the language of the applicable statute.

A final guarantee of fairness in the disposition of contested cases is contained in Section 13 of the Revised Model State Act, which places limitations upon resort to *ex parte* consultations as to either facts or law.

Eighth, express recognition is given to the principle that licensees have special rights and privileges of which they should not be summarily deprived. Appropriate provisions are made for the continuance of existing licenses pending application and final disposition of application for renewal. Limits are imposed on revocation or suspension of licenses.

Ninth, the Revised Model State Act provides for prompt, simple and effective judicial review. Appeals are heard in a trial court of general jurisdiction, thus avoiding the burdensome difficulties placed both upon the appellate courts and upon the parties when review is limited to the state supreme court. The reviewing courts are not limited to deciding questions of law, but are authorized to set aside agency findings and decisions which are clearly erroneous in view of the reliable, probative and substantial evidence on the whole record, or which are determined by the court to involve a clearly unwarranted exercise of discretion.

The Revised Model State Act provides a vehicle through which, with proper adaptation to local conditions, the state legislatures can achieve realistic and practical legal reform that will redound to the benefit of millions of American citizens.

6 ADDITIONAL PROBLEMS

The vastness of the administrative process creates many problems other than those relating to the exercise of legislative or judicial powers by these agencies. For example, every rule-making agency publishes its rules, and so many are being published that no one person, company, or law firm can have them all available to *examine,* let alone *know* what they contain. The Federal Register prints these regulations so that persons and businesses will be charged with knowledge of them and will have at least an opportunity to discover what they are.

Not only are there so many rules and regulations that it is impossible to know them or sometimes to find them, the rules and regulations of different agencies are frequently in conflict with each other. One agency often does not know what others are doing, and there is today a tremendous overlapping of responsibilities. For example, at least forty-two Federal departments, agencies, and bureaus are involved with some aspect of education. Transportation problems are under the jurisdiction of the Department of Commerce, the Federal Aviation Agency (FAA), the Coast Guard, the Army Engineers, the Interstate Commerce Commission (ICC), the Civil Aeronautics Board (CAB), the Maritime Commission, and the Department of Housing and Urban Development. Senator Abraham Ribicoff, in a speech on October 20, 1965, on the floor of the Senate, illustrated the problems which result from such overlapping of administrative authority when he noted:

"In the pesticide field, the Department of Agriculture, the Food and Drug Administration, the Public Health Service and the Interior Department all vie with one another, not only in their day-to-day operations but in the policy area too. Interior forbids its constitutent agencies to use in National Forests the same poisons that the Agriculture Department urges the public to spray on lawns, trees and rose bushes. The Public Health Service spends public funds to study the possible connection between the cancer toll and the increased use of pesticides, while the Food and Drug Administration says the housewife's market-basket is 'safe' from pesticide residue." [14]

From the foregoing, it is clear that reorganization and elimination of duplication in the various agencies, as proposed by Senator Ribicoff, is urgently needed. The proliferation of agencies creates a difficult, if not incomprehensible, environment for business and constitutes a waste of the

[14] III *Cong. Rec.* 27499 (1965).

taxpayer's money as well. Even if the number of agencies and their functions were reduced to a minimum, it would still be difficult to keep abreast of the requirements imposed on business. Government, because of the vastness of administrative agencies, often appears "confused, diffused, and disorganized" in the words of Senator Ribicoff. Many people who are daily involved with the administrative process believe that government is in fact "confused, diffused, and disorganized."

Additional problems concerning the administrative process and administrative law will be further illustrated in subsequent chapters concerned with labor law, antitrust law, and other areas of regulation of business. It should be emphasized that this source of law comprises a substantial and probably the major portion of the legal environment of business.

CHAPTER FIVE

FORMULATION OF JUDICIAL DECISIONS

1 INTRODUCTION

Previous chapters have been concerned with written law and the unwritten law announced in judicial decisions. We have seen that courts on occasion strike down legislation by finding it to be unconstitutional, and former precedent by a simple process of overruling it. In addition, courts fill the gaps in legislation by interpretation and create legal principles where legislation is nonexistent. But what formula is used by courts in reaching these decisions? What process is followed that enables a court to reach one result rather than another? What forces tend to bear the heaviest influence in decisions concerned with the public interest?

There is, obviously, no simple answer to these questions. Many persons assume that logic affords the basic tool of the judicial decision. But Justice Holmes stated "the life of the law has not been logic; it has been experience." [1] Other persons argue that courts merely reflect the predominant attitude of the times and that they simply follow the more popular course in decisions where the public is involved.

Justice Benjamin Cardozo, in his lectures on the judicial process,[2] discussed the sources of information to which judges resort in deciding cases. He stated that if the answer were not clearly established by statute or by unquestioned precedent, the problem was twofold: "He [the judge] must first extract from the precedents the underlying principle, the *ratio decidendi;* he must then determine the path or direction along which the principle is to work and develop, if it is not to wither and die." [3] The first part of the problem is to separate legal principles from dicta so that the actual precedent is clear. Commenting on the second aspect of the problem, Cardozo said: "The directive force of a principle may be exerted along the line of logical progression; this I will call the rule of analogy or the method of philosophy; along the line of historical development; this I will call the method of evolution; along the lines of the customs of the community; this I will call the method of tradition; along the lines of justice, morals and

[1] Holmes, *The Common Law,* 1 (1938).
[2] Cardozo, *The Nature of the Judicial Process* (1921). Excerpts are used by permission from the Yale University Press.
[3] *Id.* at 28.

social welfare, the *mores* of the day; and this I will call the method of sociology." [4]

In Cardozo's judgment, the rule of analogy was entitled to certain presumptions and should be followed if possible. He believed that the judge who molds the law by the method of philosophy is satisfying the deep-seated desire of mankind for certainty. History, in indicating the direction of precedent, often makes the path of logic clear and plays an important part in decisions in areas such as real property. Custom or trade practice has supplied much of the direction of the law in the area of business. All judicial decisions are at least in part directed by the judge's viewpoint on the welfare of society. The end served by law must dictate the administration of justice, and ethical considerations, if ignored, will ultimately overturn a principle of law.

Noting the psychological aspects of judges' decisions, Cardozo observed that it is the subconscious forces which keep judges consistent with one another. In so recognizing that all persons, including judges, have a philosophy which gives coherence and direction to their thought and actions whether they admit it or not, he stated:

All their lives, forces which they do not recognize and cannot name, have been tugging at them—inherited instincts, traditional beliefs, acquired conviction; and the resultant is an outlook on life, a conception of social needs, . . . which when reasons are nicely balanced, must determine where choice shall fall. In this mental background every problem finds its setting. We may try to see things as objectively as we please. None the less, we can never see them with any eyes except our own. To that test they are all brought—a form of pleading or an act of parliament, the wrongs of paupers or the rights of princes, a village ordinance or a nation's charter. [5]

In the following comments, Cardozo summarized his view of the judicial process.

From   THE NATURE OF THE JUDICIAL PROCESS [6]
Benjamin N. Cardozo

. . . My analysis of the judicial process comes then to this, and little more: logic, and history, and custom, and utility, and the accepted standards of right conduct, are the forces which singly or in combination shape the progress of the law. Which of these forces shall dominate in any case, must depend largely upon the comparative importance or value of the social interests that will be thereby promoted or impaired. One of the most fundamental

[4] *Id.* at 30–31.
[5] *Id* at 12–13.
[6] *Id.* at 112–115.

social interests is that law shall be uniform and impartial. There must be nothing in its action that savors of prejudice or favor or even arbitrary whim or fitfulness. Therefore in the main there shall be adherence to precedent. There shall be symmetrical development, consistently with history or custom when history or custom has been the motive force, or the chief one, in giving shape to existing rules, and with logic or philosophy when the motive power has been theirs. But symmetrical development may be bought at too high a price. Uniformity ceases to be a good when it becomes uniformity of oppression. The social interest served by symmetry or certainty must then be balanced against the social interest served by equity and fairness or other elements of social welfare. These may enjoin upon the judge the duty of drawing the line at another angle, or staking the path along new courses, of marking a new point of departure from which others who come after him will set out upon their journey.

If you ask how he is to know when one interest outweighs another, I can only answer that he must get his knowledge just as the legislator gets it, from experience and study and reflection; in brief, from life itself. Here, indeed, is the point of contact between the legislator's work and his. The choice of methods, the appraisement of values, must in the end be guided by like considerations for the one as for the other. Each indeed is legislating within the limits of his competence. No doubt the limits for the judge are narrower. He legislates only between gaps. He fills the open spaces in the law. How far he can go without traveling beyond the walls of the interstices cannot be staked out for him upon a chart. He must learn it for himself as he gains the sense of fitness and proportion that comes with years of habitude in the practice of an art. Even within the gaps, restrictions not easy to define, but felt, however impalpable they may be, by every judge and lawyer, hedge and circumscribe his action. They are established by the traditions of the centuries, by the example of other judges, his predecessors and his colleagues, by the collective judgment of the profession, and by the duty of adherence to the pervading spirit of the law. . . . None the less, within the confines of these open spaces and those of precedent and tradition, choice moves with a freedom which stamps its action as creative. The law which is the resulting product is not found, but made. The process, being legislative, demands the legislator's wisdom. . . .

This chapter will attempt to point out some of the more important of the infinite number of factors which play a part in the formulation of judicial decisions. The weight to be given any of these in a particular case cannot be predicted with any degree of certainty. The number of factors involved in any one case is likewise indeterminable. The product of these unknowns applied to a set of facts results in a judicial decision.

While these forces which shape the course of the law are discussed here in terms of their effect on court decisions specifically, it should be recognized that many or all of these same forces also have a profound effect on the type of legislation requested by the executive and his enforcement of existing law; the rule making, enforcement policies, and quasi-judicial decisions of administrative bodies; and the enactment of law by legislatures.

2 LOGIC

The first directive force in the formulation of judicial decisions that Cardozo listed was logic, which he also called the rule of analogy and the method of philosophy. Cardozo considered judicial logic, or the following of prior decisions which are analogous to the case at bar as precedents, to be of prime importance to the judicial process because of the need for certainty in the law. Logic may involve deductive reasoning or inductive reasoning. Deductive reasoning takes the form of a syllogism in which a conclusion concerning a particular circumstance (minor premise) is drawn from a general principle (major premise). Inductive reasoning involves the process of using specific cases to reach a general conclusion. It is often said that application of the doctrine of stare decisis by basing a decision on precedents announced in prior cases is inductive in nature, while applying a statute to a given set of facts is an example of deductive reasoning, but these examples are open to some criticism.

Reasoning is a basic requisite to stability in the law. However, legal reasoning, as the discussion which follows indicates, has certain perculiarities all its own.

From   AN INTRODUCTION TO LEGAL REASONING [7]
Edward H. Levi

This is an attempt to describe generally the process of legal reasoning in the field of case law and in the interpretation of statutes and of the Constitution. It is important that the mechanism of legal reasoning should not be concealed by its pretense. The pretense is that the law is a system of known rules applied by a judge; the pretense has long been under attack. In an important sense legal rules are never clear, and if a rule had to be clear before it could be imposed, society would be impossible. The mechanism accepts the differences of view and ambiguities of words. It provides for the participation of the community in resolving the ambiguity by providing a forum for the discussion of policy in the gap of ambiguity. On serious

---

[7] Reprinted from *An Introduction to Legal Reasoning*, by Edward H. Levi, pp. 1–3, by permission of the University of Chicago Press. Copyright 1948 by the University of Chicago.

controversial questions, it makes it possible to take the first step in the direction of what otherwise would be forbidden ends. The mechanism is indispensable to peace in a community.

The basic pattern of legal reasoning is reasoning by example.* It is reasoning from case to case. It is a three-step process described by the doctrine of precedent in which a proposition descriptive of the first case is made into a rule of law and then applied to a next similar situation. The steps are these: similarity is seen between cases; next the rule of law inherent in the first case is announced; then the rule of law is made applicable to the second case. This is a method of reasoning necessary for the law, but it has characteristics which under other circumstances might be considered imperfections.

These characteristics become evident if the legal process is approached as though it were a method of applying general rules of law to diverse facts—in short, as though the doctrine of precedent meant that general rules, once properly determined, remained unchanged, and then were applied, albeit imperfectly, in later cases. If this were the doctrine, it would be disturbing to find that the rules change from case to case and are remade with each case. Yet this change in the rules is the indispensable dynamic quality of law. It occurs because the scope of a rule of law, and therefore its meaning, depends upon a determination of what facts will be considered similar to those present when the rule was first announced. The finding of similarity or difference is the key step in the legal process.

The determination of similarity or difference is the function of each judge. Where case law is considered, and there is no statute, he is not bound by the statement of the rule of law made by the prior judge even in the controlling case. The statement is mere dictum, and this means that the judge in the present case may find irrelevant the existence or absence of facts which prior judges thought important. It is not what the prior judge intended that is of any importance; rather it is what the present judge, attempting to see the law as a fairly consistent whole, thinks should be the determining classification. In arriving at his result he will ignore what the past thought important; he will emphasize facts which prior judges would have thought made no difference. It is not alone that he could not see the law through the eyes of another, for he could at least try to do so. It is rather that the doctrine of dictum forces him to make his own decision.

Thus it cannot be said that the legal process is the application of known rules to diverse facts. Yet it is a system of rules; the rules are dis-

---

* [footnote by Levi] "Clearly then to argue by example is neither like reasoning from part to whole, nor like reasoning from whole to part, but rather reasoning fom part to part, when both particulars are subordinate to the same term and one of them is known. It differs from induction, because induction starting from all the particular cases proves . . . that the major term belongs to the middle and does not apply the syllogistic conclusion to the minor term, whereas argument by example does make this application and does not draw its proof from all the particular cases." Aristotle, *Analytica Priora* 69a (McKeon ed., 1941).

covered in the process of determining similarity or difference. But if attention is directed toward the finding of similarity or difference, other peculiarities appear. The problem for the law is: When will it be just to treat
different cases as though they were the same? A working legal system must
therefore be willing to pick out key similarities and to reason from them to
the justice of applying a common classification. The existence of some facts
in common brings into play the general rule. If this is really reasoning, then
by common standards, thought of in terms of closed systems, it is imperfect
unless some overall rule has announced that this common and ascertainable
similarity is to be decisive. But no such fixed prior rule exists. It could be
suggested that reasoning is not involved at all; that is, that no new insight
is arrived at through a comparison of cases. But reasoning appears to be
involved; the conclusion is arrived at through a process and was not immediately apparent. It seems better to say there is reasoning, but it is imperfect.*

Therefore it appears that the kind of reasoning involved in the legal
process is one in which the classification changes as the classification is
made. The rules change as the rules are applied. More important, the rules
arise out of a process which, while comparing fact situations, creates the
rules and then applies them. But this kind of reasoning is open to the
charge that it is classifying things as equals when they are somewhat different, justifying the classification by rules made up as the reasoning or classification proceeds. In a sense all reasoning is of this type, but there is an
additional requirement which compels the legal process to be this way. Not
only do new situations arise, but in addition peoples want change. The categories used in the legal process must be left ambiguous in order to permit
the infusion of new ideas. And this is true even where legislation or a constitution is involved. The words used by the legislature or the constitutional
convention must come to have new meanings. Furthermore, agreement on
any other basis would be impossible. In this manner the laws come to express the ideas of the community and even when written in general terms, in
statute or constitution, are molded for the specific case.

But attention must be paid to the process. A controversy as to whether
the law is certain, unchanging, and expressed in rules, or uncertain, changing, and only a technique for deciding specific cases misses the point. It is
both. Nor is it helpful to dispose of the process as a wonderful mystery possibly reflecting a higher law, by which the law can remain the same and
yet change. The law forum is the most explicit demonstration of the mechanism required for a moving classification system. The folklore of law may
choose to ignore the imperfections in legal reasoning,† but the law forum
itself has taken care of them. . . .

---

* [footnote by Levi] The logical fallacy is the fallacy of the undistributed middle or the fallacy of
assuming the antecedent is true because the consequent has been affirmed.
† [footnote by Levi] "That the law can be obeyed even when it grows is often more than the legal
profession itself can grasp." Cohen & Nagel, *An Introduction to Logic and Scientific Method* 371
(1934); see Stone, *The Province and Function of Law* 140-206 (1946).

3   HISTORY

Cardozo stated that the second directive force which influences judicial decisions is exerted along the lines of historical development. He also called this force of history the method of evolution. Its importance is clear. There is an interaction between law and history; each shapes the other. Historical events have shaped the law and provided direction for society. Changes in social conduct and attitudes have given direction to the law. For example, the Constitutional amendment calling for prohibition greatly affected the history of our country; and the historical events which followed prohibition led to its repeal.

We have seen the importance of the legislative history of an act as a factor in the interpretation of statutes in Chapter 2. Other historical events also are used by courts in determining the meaning and even the constitutionality of statutes, as the case which follows illustrates.

UNITED STATES V. BROWN
381 U.S. 437 (1965)

WARREN, CHIEF JUSTICE: In this case we review for the first time a conviction under § 504 of the Labor-Management Reporting and Disclosure Act of 1959, which makes it a crime for a member of the Communist Party to serve as an officer or (except in clerical or custodial positions) as an employee of a labor union. . . .

Respondent has been a working longshoreman on the San Francisco docks, and an open and avowed Communist, for more than a quarter of a century. He was elected to the Executive Board of Local 10 of the International Longshoremen's and Warehousemen's Union for consecutive one-year terms in 1959, 1960, and 1961. On May 24, 1961, respondent was charged in a one-count indictment returned in the Northern District of California with "knowingly and wilfully serv(ing) as a member of an executive board of a labor organization . . . while a member of the Communist Party, in wilful violation of Title 29, United States Code, Section 504." It was neither charged nor proven that respondent at any time advocated or suggested illegal activity by the union, or proposed a political strike. The jury found respondent guilty, and he was sentenced to six months' imprisonment. The Court of Appeals for the Ninth Circuit, sitting *en banc*, reversed and remanded with instructions to set aside the conviction and dismiss the indictment, holding that § 504 violates the First and Fifth Amendments to the Constitution. We granted certiorari.

Respondent urges—in addition to the grounds relied on by the court below—that the statute under which he was convicted is a bill of attainder, and therefore violates Art. I, § 9, of the Constitution. We agree that § 504 is void as a bill of attainder and affirm the decision of the Court of Appeals on that basis. We therefore find it unnecessary to consider the First and Fifth Amendment arguments.

I

The provisions outlawing bills of attainder were adopted by the Constitutional Convention unanimously, and without debate.

No Bill of Attainder or ex post facto Law shall be passed [by the Congress]. Art. I, § 9, cl. 3.

No State shall . . . pass any Bill of Attainder, ex post facto Law, or Law impairing the Obligation of Contracts. . . . Art. I, § 10.

A logical starting place for an inquiry into the meaning of the prohibition is its historical background. The bill of attainder, a parliamentary act sentencing to death one or more specific persons was a device often resorted to in sixteenth, seventeenth and eighteenth century England for dealing with persons who had attempted, or threatened to attempt, to overthrow the government. In addition to the death sentence, attainder generally carried with it a "corruption of blood," which meant that the attainted party's heirs could not inherit his property. The "bill of pains and penalties" was identical to the bill of attainder, except that it prescribed a penalty short of death, e.g., banishment, deprivation of the right to vote, or exclusion of the designated party's sons from Parliament. Most bills of attainder and bills of pains and penalties named the parties to whom they were to apply; a few, however, simply described them. While some left the designated parties a way of escaping the penalty, others did not. The use of bills of attainder and bills of pains and penalties was not limited to England. During the American Revolution, the legislatures of all thirteen States passed statutes directed against the Tories; among these statutes were a large number of bills of attainder and bills of pains and penalties.

While history thus provides some guidelines, the wide variation in form, purpose and effect of ante-constitutional bills of attainder indicates that the proper scope of the Bill of Attainder Clause, and its relevance to contemporary problems, must ultimately be sought by attempting to discern the reasons for its inclusion in the Constitution, and the evils it was designed to eliminate. The best available evidence, the writings of the architects of our constitutional system, indicates that the Bill of Attainder Clause was intended not as a narrow, technical (and therefore soon to be outmoded) prohibition, but rather as an implementation of the separation of powers, a general safeguard against legislative exercise of the judicial function, or more simply trial by legislature. . . .

Thus the Bill of Attainder Clause not only was intended as one implementation of the general principle of fractionalized power, but also reflected the Framers' belief that the Legislative Branch is not so well suited as politically independent judges and juries to the task of ruling upon the blameworthiness of, and levying appropriate punishment upon, specific persons.

Every one must concede that a legislative body, from its numbers and organization, and from the very intimate dependence of its members upon the people, which renders them liable to be peculiarly susceptible to popular clamor, is not properly constituted to try with coolness, caution, and impartiality a criminal charge, especially in those cases in which the popular feeling is strongly excited,—the very class of cases most likely to be prosecuted by this mode.

By banning bills of attainder, the Framers of the Constitution sought to guard against such dangers by limiting legislatures to the task of rule-making. "It is the peculiar province of the legislature, to prescribe general rules for the government of society; the application of those rules to individuals in society would seem to be the duty of other departments." . . . [The Court then discussed several previous bill of attainder cases.]

III

Under the line of cases just outlined § 504 plainly constitutes a bill of attainder. . . . The statute does not set forth a generally applicable rule decreeing that any person who commits certain acts or possesses certain characteristics (acts and characteristics which, in Congress' view make them likely to initiate political strikes) shall not hold union office, and leave to courts and juries the job of deciding what persons have committed the specified acts or possess the specified characteristics. Instead, it designates in no uncertain terms the persons who possess the feared characteristics and therefore cannot hold union office without incurring criminal liability—members of the Communist Party. . . .

The Solicitor General argues that § 504 is not a bill of attainder because the prohibition it imposes does not constitute "punishment." In support of this conclusion, he urges that the statute was enacted for preventive rather than retributive reasons—that its aim is not to punish Communists for what they have done in the past, but rather to keep them from positions where they will in the future be able to bring about undesirable events. . . .

Historical considerations by no means compel restriction of the bill of attainder ban to instances of retribution. A number of English bills of attainder were enacted for preventive purposes—that is, the legislature made a judgment undoubtedly based largely on past acts and associations (as § 504 is) that a given person or group was likely to cause trouble (usually, overthrow the government) and therefore inflicted deprivations upon that person or group in order to keep them from bringing about the feared event. It is also clear that many of the early American bills attainting the Tories were passed in order to impede their effectively resisting the Revolution.

In the progress of the conflict, and particularly in its earliest periods, attainder and confiscation had been resorted to generally, throughout the continent, as a means of war. But it is a fact important to the history of the revolting colonies, that the acts prescribing penalties, usually offered to the persons against whom they were directed the option of avoiding them, by acknowledging their allegiance to the existing governments.

It was a preventative, not a vindictive policy. In the same humane spirit, as the contest approached its close, and the necessity of these severities diminished, many of the states passed laws offering pardons to those who had been disenfranchised, and restoring them to the enjoyment of their property. . . .

Thus Justice Iredell was on solid historical ground when he observed, in *Calder v. Bull,* 3 Dall. 386, 399–400, 1 L.Ed. 648, that "attainders, *on the principle of retaliation and proscription,* have marked all the vicissitudes of party triumph." [EMPHASIS SUPPLIED]

We do not hold today that Congress cannot weed dangerous persons out of the labor movement. . . . Rather, we make again the point . . . that Congress must accomplish such results by rules of general applicability. It cannot specify the people upon whom the sanction it prescribes is to be levied. Under our Constitution, Congress possesses full legislative authority, but the task of adjudication must be left to other tribunals.

This Court is always reluctant to declare that an Act of Congress violates the Constitution, but in this case we have no alternative. As Alexander Hamilton observed:

By a limited constitution, I understand one which contains certain specified exceptions to the legislative authority; such, for instance, as that it shall pass no bills of attainder, no ex post facto laws, and the like. Limitations of this kind can be preserved in practice no other way than through the medium of the courts of justice; whose duty it must be to declare all acts contrary to the manifest tenor of the Constitution void. Without this, all the reservations of particular rights or privileges would amount to nothing.

The judgment of the Court of Appeals is affirmed.

Further aspects of the influence of history on judicial decisions should be noted. First of all, cases decided by the judiciary are historical events;

thus, the following of precedent is an application of history to current controversies. Second, to evaluate the force of history properly, we cannot view
past events in the abstract alone but must look beyond these occurrences
themselves for the traditions which have grown up around them. The tradition resulting from an event compounds its effect on the law. Justice Cardozo noted that the tradition or myth surrounding an historical event
frequently becomes the major force when he stated: [8]

> *Take Magna Charta for example. Today it is not what is written in the
> Charter—if the words are read in the sense in which they were understood
> by those who wrote them—that has any commanding interest, any throbbing
> and vital meaning, for those who walk the earth. What lives in the Charter
> today is the myth that has gathered around it—the things that it has come
> to stand for in the thought of successive generations—not the pristine core
> within, but the incrustations that have formed without.*
>
> *The thought is tellingly expressed by Plucknett in his short history of
> the common law. "The Charter gradually grew bigger than the mere feudal
> details which it contained and came to be a symbol of successful opposition to
> the Crown which resulted in a negotiated peace representing a reasonable
> compromise. As time goes on, therefore, the Charter becomes more and more
> a myth, but nevertheless a very powerful one, and in the Seventeenth Cen-
> tury all the forces of liberalism rallied around it. . . . To explode the 'myth'
> of the great Charter is indeed to get back to its original historical meaning,
> but for all that, the myth has been much more important than the reality, and
> there is still something to be said for the statement that 'the whole of English
> constitutional history is a commentary upon the great Charter.'"*
>
> *Now, what is true of Magna Charta is true, I think of our own constitu-
> tion in many of its provisions; true, for example, of the bill of rights, which
> is much more important for the spirit it enshrines than for this or the other
> privilege or immunity which it professes to secure. Some of them have a vital
> meaning even to this day, others are reminiscent of battles long ago. The
> myth that has enveloped them has become greater than the reality, or rather
> in a sense the genuine reality.*

4   CUSTOM

Cardozo's third directive force which shapes judicial decisions was along
the lines of customs of the community, which he also called the method of
tradition. The influence of custom and usage is of special importance in the
field of business law. For example, a term not stated may be added to a
contract, because of well-established custom and usage in the trade or

---

[8] From *An Address to the New York County Lawyers' Association*, given at its annual dinner Dec.
17, 1931, and published in the *New York County Lawyers' Yearbook* 369 (1932). Used by permission from the New York County Lawyers' Association.

business. The amount of a broker's commission, although not expressly agreed upon, has been determined by reference to usage.[9] Likewise, the questions of whether the buyer or seller of goods is bound to pay the freight for their transportation,[10] or who must bear the expenses of the sales tax,[11] when these matters were not settled by the contract of sale, have been determined by proof of custom.

Although the language employed in contracts by the parties is usually interpreted to have its normal, ordinary meaning, a custom and usage can be shown which changes meaning and therefore the performance required by the contract. Accepted scientific tables of weights and measures define a British barrel as 36 gallons and a United States barrel as 31.5 gallons. However, in the oil industry, a barrel is understood to amount to 42 gallons. In *Harvard Brewing Co. v. Killian*,[12] the court held that in the beer industry, by custom and usage, a barrel could be shown to mean only 31 gallons.

Most commercial law has its roots in the customs and trade practices of merchants. Early common-law courts provided no legal sanctions for the enforcement of commercial transactions. However, merchants, in activities such as buying and selling goods and in employing negotiable instruments as substitutes for money, developed customs and traditions which defined the rights and duties of the parties to these agreements. Usually a "judge" was appointed at fairs by the merchants to hear and render a summary decision on the basis of generally accepted usage, in any disputes which arose. His "judgments" were enforced by the ostracism of any merchant who refused to abide by them. Eventually the common law opened its doors to merchants, recognizing their agreements as creating legal rights and duties. Common-law court decisions in commercial matters gave the force of law to the custom and usage of merchants by following their practice. In modern times, these decisions in many areas have been codified into the uniform acts, such as the Uniform Sales Act, the Uniform Negotiable Instruments Law and more recently, the Uniform Commercial Code. Of course, as the customs involving commercial matters have varied, the law has varied, but it finds its basis in early usage and traditions, or the "law merchant."

5   THE MORES OF THE DAY OR THE METHOD OF SOCIOLOGY

Cardozo indicated that the fourth major force which gives direction to the formulation of judicial decisions is along the lines of justice, morals, and

---

[9] *Vanemburg v. Duffey*, 177 Ark. 663, 7 S.W.2d 336 (1928).
[10] *Carlsten-William Co. v. Marshall Oil Co.*, 187 Iowa 80, 173 N.W. 903 (1919).
[11] *Trueba Bros. v. Early-Foster Co.*, 256 S.W. 909 (Tex. Com. App. 1923).
[12] 222 Mass. 13, 109 N.E. 649 (1915).

social welfare, or the mores of the day, which he also called the method of sociology. This method, he indicated, places the highest value on arriving at judicial decisions which have the greatest social utility or usefulness under current conditions and which are in accord with the presently accepted standards of right conduct. The method of sociology has steadily grown in importance in recent years and in the opinion of many observers is now the dominant force which shapes the judicial opinions of our Supreme Court. It is used by all the justices to a varying degree and most often by those who are "activists."

It is clearly possible to have a system of law which fails to achieve justice. Rigid or strict application of "rules of law" may reach an unjust result. The converse is also possible—a system may achieve a just result without using "rules of law." Historically, our courts have felt that the need for certainty and predictability requires a system using "rules of law," and injustice has sometimes resulted. On occasion, however, they have refused to follow precedent and instead have striven toward a "right" solution, or one which would have greater social utility, in their view, than a mechanical application of previous decisions could provide. The method of sociology has played a significant role in all cases where precedent has been reversed. (See the discussion of rejection of stare decisis in Chapter 3.)

A judge who is influenced by the force of the method of sociology might say to an attorney arguing a case words to this effect: "I'm not concerned with your precedent and authorities; tell me why your client is right and the other party is wrong as a matter both of justice and of social policy." Such a judge is result-conscious and does not want to apply a rigid rule of law which may achieve an unjust result.

The method of sociology is perhaps the most complex of all the forces which shape the law. It includes such elements as the judge's desire to achieve the "correct" result, the judge's own philosophy, political considerations, society's attitudes, and even the effect of emergencies. Each of these influences and the part it can play in shaping a judicial decision is discussed in more detail in the subsections which follow.

A   RESULT DESIRED

It is perhaps shocking to the layman to realize that, in many cases, the result which a court desires to reach controls the statements of legal principles upon which its decision is based. Many people blindly assume that the law always controls the result, but the plain fact of the matter is that often the desired result controls the law applicable to a case at hand. A court frequently decides the outcome of a case and then searches precedent for some basis for its opinion. Similar cases with a different result are

distinguished, statutes are construed or even declared to be unconstitutional, exceptions are made, or precedent is overruled simply to reach what
the court believes to be the correct decision.

It is often said that "hard cases make bad law." Probably one of the
most perplexing aspects of the law to laymen and law students comes from
a study of those judicial decisions which are a product of ambivalence—a
desire by the court to follow precedent, yet a feeling that to do so strictly
will be unjust in the case at hand. Under these circumstances, the court
may attempt to serve both the ends of logic and fairness by *stating* and
laboriously reasoning that a case falls within a rule (when by ordinary logic
it does not), as a pretext for arriving at a just result. If it follows this path,
the court reaches an equitable conclusion without expressly overruling precedent, thereby keeping up the appearance of stability.

As an example of the foregoing, compare the following decisions. *International Paper Co. v. Rockefeller* [13] involved an action for damages for
breach of a contract to cut and deliver 56,000 cords of wood from spruce
growing on a designated tract of land, for $5.50 a cord. The defendant
argued that he should be excused from the agreement, since a forest fire
had destroyed all the tract but about 550 cords remaining on top of a high
mountain, which would cost him $20 a cord to cut and deliver. The court
excused the defendant as to the wood which had been destroyed, but said:
"The defendant is not excused from delivering the live spruce . . . which
survived the fire by the mere fact that its location upon the tract is such
that it would be very expensive for him to deliver it. . . ." [14] This holding
represents the strict, logical, and long-established view that a person who
has made a contractual promise will not be excused simply because he
suffers additional hardship and a financial loss. Only in cases where the act
has become *absolutely impossible* may he ignore his contract. However, in
Mineral Park Land Co. v. Howard,[15] the defendants had contracted to buy
at an agreed price and remove from the plaintiff's land all the gravel needed
to build a certain bridge. After the defendants had removed about one-half
of the gravel needed, they began purchasing elsewhere, since the rest of
plaintiff's gravel was under water and it would cost about 10 to 12 times as
much as dry gravel to remove and ready for use. In its opinion, the court
referred to cases where performance of similar contracts had been excused
after the supply at an agreed source was *totally depleted,* then said:

*The defendants were not binding themselves to take what was not there. And
in determining whether the earth and gravel were "available" we must view
the conditions in a practical and reasonable way. Although there was gravel
on the land, it was so situated that the defendants could not take it by ordi-*

[13] 161 App. Div. 180, 146 N.Y.S. 371 (1914).
[14] *Id.*
[15] 172 Cal. 289, 156 Pac. 458 (1916).

nary means, nor except at a prohibitive cost. To all fair intents then, it was impossible in legal contemplation for defendants to take it. . . . We do not mean to intimate that the defendants could excuse themselves by showing the existence of conditions which would make the performance of their obligations more expensive than they had anticipated, or which would entail a great loss upon them. But where the difference in cost is so great as here, and has the effect, as found, of making performance impracticable, the situation is not different from that of a total absence of earth and gravel. . . .[16] [The court disallowed recovery of damages for breach of contract.]

The Uniform Commercial Code—Sales, 2–615, permits a court to reach what it considers to be a fair result in certain cases without encountering the logical difficulty in defining "impossibility," by providing that a seller of tangible personal property is excused from his contract, if a change in assumed conditions makes performance "impracticable." The Code reflects a trend in court decisions away from predictability and toward liberality and "fairness" in defining what makes a contract "impossible" to perform.

Many of the factors affecting judicial decisions discussed in this chapter simply influence the court in determining the result it will reach rather than in finding "correct" principles of law. The importance of the doctrine of stare decisis varies in inverse proportion to the intensity of the desire of the judge for a certain result of a controversy, in controlling the principles of law to be announced.

B   BACKGROUND AND PHILOSOPHY OF JUDGES

Justice William O. Douglas in his lecture on stare decisis (Chapter 3) discussed the importance of each judge's philosophy on his decisions, particularly in the area of constitutional law. Judges are human beings subject to the same forces, pressures, and prejudices as are other human beings. The sum total of their experiences in life will necessarily affect their judicial decisions. However, this fact need not be viewed as an evil of our system of law. As Charles P. Curtis noted in *A Commonplace Book*, "There are only two ways to be quite unprejudiced and impartial. One is to be completely ignorant. The other is to be completely indifferent." It is not possible in the limited space available to examine the lives of even a few of the judges who have made a great contribution to our system of jurisprudence. However, articles and case opinions written by many of them, which are contained elsewhere in the text, give significant clues to their values and ideas. The following excerpt from a memorial for Justice Brandeis is offered as a single illustration of the influence of the background and philosophy of a great jurist on our legal system.

[16] *Id.*

IN MEMORIAM: LOUIS DEMBITZ BRANDEIS [17]
Samuel H. Hofstadter, Justice of the Supreme Court of the State of New York

October fifth (1961), marks the twentieth anniversary of the death of Louis Dembitz Brandeis—a judge who was a prophet not without honor in his own country even in his own time. . . .

If the United States has succeeded in disciplining its socio-economic system—shifting from the *laissez faire* economy of 1900 to the well-regulated industrial society we are today—without rejecting its basic philosophy nor impinging upon individual opportunity, the accomplishment is due to those who served as "goads and guides" in that process.

That distinguished company must include Brandeis, who contributed so greatly to the success of the American experiment based on the concept that government belongs to the people and not the people to the government. . . .

Unprepossessed with vested status—social or economic—he was forever concerned with the "little fellow," the disinherited and the oppressed. He spoke for the inarticulate masses. As lawyer and as judge, he strove to redress violation of human rights. Ardent for justice, with a regard for realities of the present but rooted soberly in the past, he disdained the arrant professionalism which spawns glittering abstractions that are not meaningful in application.

Many have contributed to the heterogeneous fabric of the American idea. The chief strand which Brandeis contributed was what John Dewey has called "instrumentalism": whereby the usefulness of an idea is to be determined by the consequences of acting on it, rather than by its *a priori* plausibility. Such a device employs knowledge as power. Brandeis rejected, therefore, George Eliot's engaging dictum that there is a saving grace in ignorance; he embraced the saving power of knowledge of the facts "as the generative source of the law." He was not carried away by the one-sidedness of a fanatic nor by the rashness of a radical; he judged with the cool deliberateness of a candid critic. Empiricism was blended with pragmatism—the juridical version of "nature obeys necessity."

At one stage of his career as a lawyer, when he was retained to defend before the Supreme Court the constitutionality of an Oregon statute limiting the working hours of women, he was inspired to write a brief containing very little legal argument but setting forth pages and pages of evidence pertaining to the health, social, moral and safety welfare of the women involved and the economic advantages to the country in general. His success in that case belongs to history. Chief Justice Fuller called him the ablest man to have appeared before the Supreme Court.

The writer dissents from a view recently expressed that "of the three

[17] 47 *A.B.A.J.* 978 (Oct., 1961). Used by permission from the American Bar Association and the *American Bar Association Journal*.

branches of our Government the Presidency alone has nourished individualism. The Congress and the courts must express themselves collectively." The personality of the individual judge may express itself to a degree that his thought has a lasting impact on our society. The greatest leaders are always great teachers; and the greatest judges have utilized their gifts of mind to expound and to suggest.

Thus, some twelve years after his death and fourteen years after his retirement from the Bench, a unanimous Supreme Court, subscribing to the Brandeis philosophy of jurisprudence and utilizing his method, revised its earlier holding and decided in the public school desegregation cases that "separate cannot be equal." The Brandeis legacy was there evident in three respects: that cases must be argued and decided by the application to legal principles of specific facts, rather than subjective dogma; that, so long as the basic import of those principles is not violated, they are sufficiently broad to adapt to changing social needs and conditions; that in applying those principles, adherence to precedent is not an iron rule of rigidity but a golden rule of trial and error—of growth and development, not a lead weight anchored to the initial application.

The technique which Brandeis first introduced in the Oregon case he repeated successfully before various state tribunals as well as the Supreme Court. But it received its greatest impetus from its utilization by him as a member of the Court. In opinion after opinion he piled fact upon fact amassed from legislative reports, findings of administrative agencies and studies of social scientists from this country and Europe. And if the briefs did not supply the facts, he (and his law clerk) sought them out. The crescendo reached its climax in the application of the voluminous data to familiar legal precedents.

Brandeis' insistence on getting at the facts was the technique by which he sought to infuse the experience of life into the law. Factual data were to be used to keep the fingers of the judiciary on the pulse of the nation; to make it aware of and to understand the current problems of society; to appreciate the legislative efforts to cope with the problems; to decide cases in the context of such awareness and understanding. He urged that the courts should not be rigidly bound by earlier decisions influenced by social or economic views and needs no longer prevalent. "A code of law that makes no provision for its amendment provides for its ultimate rejection," he declared. He did not disdain authority; what he objected to was weak authority which merely reproduces the ancient voice of others, without initiative or animation of its own.

Another basic thread running throughout Brandeis' philosophy was the belief that ours is essentially a system of checks and balances. A function of the judiciary was to preserve the balance among our divers entities and diverse institutions. He said that "in a democracy it is the better part of statesmanship to prevent the development of power which overawes the ordinary forces of man. Wherever such power exists it must be broken. The privilege which it begets must be destroyed."

Hence, the economic imbalance among businesses troubled Brandeis. For some years before he came to the Court he was a severe critic of the tendency toward industrial "bigness" and resultant monopoly—"so trapped in its own contradictions that it is no longer a viable method of economic organization." He believed strongly in free, fair competition so that rewards will be proportionate to success; that regulation is essential to the preservation of competition and to its best development; that regulation is more desirable than monopolistic development, later inevitably to be controlled by governmental price fixing.

Brandeis was concerned, too, over the imbalance between capital and labor. He dissented from the decisions that enjoined unions from organizing, striking, picketing or boycotting. But he did not consider that organized labor should have *carte blanche*. When unions acted irresponsibly or unlawfully he was quick to join his associates in holding them accountable for their actions. Indeed, as early as 1902 he advocated that unions be required to incorporate to make them responsible for their actions. He opposed the closed shop demands of labor as strenuously as he opposed the non-union shop demands of industry.

In labor relations, as in all other areas of American life, his central thought was of the public weal. Its influence continues to this day. In a recent labor dispute in which Secretary of Labor Goldberg participated, he succeeded in getting the parties to siphon off certain basic problems from the pending area of bargaining for future arbitrament by a long-term group to consider the public interest involved in those issues. This device was anticipated fifty years ago in the "protocols of peace" that ended the New York Cloak-Maker's strike of 1910, drawn up by Brandeis. They provided for a conciliation and arbitration board which was to confine its attention to new fundamental conflicts that might arise. In effect, the plan provided for a permanent industrial government. It served at the time as a bridge to the more orthodox kind of trade agreement. But it may very well have been the harbinger of the next development in collective bargaining beyond the collective agreement.

It is apparent that Brandeis was far from being a radical as some of his critics regarded him. For instance he recognized that long standing precedents acquiesced in and creating property rights should not lightly be disregarded; and even went so far as to say that in such cases it is more important "that a rule of law be settled, than that it be settled right," particularly where the error could be rectified by legislation. He held a "mystic reverence for the Court," Judge Learned Hand says. His respect for the independence of the judiciary was made manifest in the important role he played in resisting Roosevelt's court-packing plan. He was as interested as his critics in preserving free, democratic, competitive society. But, as an exponent of realist jurisprudence with its insistence on functional realities, he would not fossilize a legal system so that it could not determine justice nor promote the social welfare. He knew that social problems can have only proximate, not ultimate, solution. He agreed with Cardozo that "law must be stable and yet it cannot stand still."

He disapproved, therefore, of raising outmoded concepts to the level of dogmas. Precedent furnishes a floor beneath which legal practice may not sink, but above which it is free to rise. In overruling prior doctrine, a court concededly legislates just as it did when it enunciated the original principle. In the words of Brandeis: "The Court bows down to experience." Precedents are followed until their irrelevance and inutility to current life are demonstrated. There can be little doubt that *Brown v. Board of Education* was the grand climax of many decisions in which Brandeis, while he was on the Bench, had participated that slowly eroded the language in the *Plessy* case —illustrating the "search by courts of last resort for the true rule" by modification which "implies growth [in] the life of the law." Thus, the Brandeis legacy had been put to a high use, indeed!

He shared the conviction of other judicial statesmen that "dissents are a vitalizing influence, that they promote wholesome elements to legal growth, and that each individual member must be true to his own conscience." Thus the principles he propounded in his dissents frequently become the basis for the decisions of the court limiting executive power, equalizing the balance between labor and industry in socio-economic legislation and in civil liberties. So long as even the memory of ordered freedom endures, men will recall the ringing words of Mr. Justice Brandeis' dissent in the *Olmstead* case:

> *The makers of our Constitution undertook to secure conditions favorable to the pursuit of happiness. . . . They knew that only a part of the pain, pleasure and satisfactions of life are to be found in material things. They sought to protect Americans in their beliefs, their thoughts, their emotions and their sensations. They conferred, as against the government, the right to be let alone—the most comprehensive of rights and the right most valued by civilized men. To protect that right, every unjustifiable intrusion by the government upon the privacy of the individual, whatever the means employed, must be deemed a violation of the Fourth Amendment.*

C   POLITICAL INFLUENCES

In many states judges are elected. In other states and in the Federal system, judges are appointed. Political considerations play some part in all such appointments and are controlling in others. An analysis of the party affiliation of the judges appointed by each President would make it appear that the party not in power is almost devoid of members with judicial qualifications. It should be noted however, that many persons upon ascending the bench for life suddenly reject many of their former political philosophies and ideologies, so that attempts to control future judicial action by careful appointment have not and will not necessarily be successful.

The judges who must run for reelection must of necessity recognize and be influenced to some degree by the policies of the political party under whose banner and upon whose platform they must run. At the local level, judges often have substantial amounts of patronage and are sources of power within their party. Only the very naïve believe that political considerations can be divorced from judicial decisions entirely.

In recent years a series of judicial decisions involving the reapportionment of legislative districts at all levels of government have changed the political climate of the entire country. The Supreme Court has transferred the balance of political power from rural America to urban America. In so doing, they have been accused of violating the concept of separation of powers. These cases inspired an unsuccessful attempt to amend the Constitution. The reapportionment issue illustrates the effect of political beliefs on the law and of the law on our political system. A brief look at the development of this area of the law is helpful in understanding the interrelationship of politics and the law.

Prior to 1962, the Supreme Court had held that questions of legislative district apportionment were political questions over which the courts had no jurisdiction. The precedent for this approach was a 1947 decision, *Colegrove v. Green*,[18] in which Justice Frankfurter, speaking for the majority of the court, stated:

> *We are of the opinion that the appellants ask of this Court what it is beyond its competence to grant. This is one of those demands on judicial power which cannot be met by fencing about "jurisdiction." It must be resolved by considerations on the basis of which this Court, from time to time, has refused to intervene in controversies. It has refused to do so because due regard for the effective working of our government revealed this issue to be of a peculiarly political nature and therefore not meant for judicial determination. . . . Nothing is clearer than that this controversy concerns matters that bring courts into immediate and active relations with party contests. From the determination of such issues this Court has traditionally held aloof. It is hostile to a democratic system to involve the judiciary in the politics of the people. . . . If Congress failed in exercising its powers, whereby standards of fairness are offended, the remedy ultimately lies with the people. . . .* To sustain this action would cut very deep into the very being of Congress. Courts ought not to enter the political thicket. *The remedy for unfairness in districting is to secure state legislatures that will apportion properly or to invoke the ample powers of Congress.*

[18] 328 U.S. 549 (1947).

Justice Black, in dissenting in *Colegrove v. Green,* set the pattern for the future when he said:

> The power granted to the state legislatures on this subject is primarily derived from the Federal and not the State Constitution. . . . The constitutionally guaranteed right to vote and the right to have one's vote counted clearly imply policy that state election systems, no matter what their form, should be designed to give approximately equal weight to each vote cast. . . . Here we have before us a state law which abridges the constitutional rights of citizens to cast votes in such a way as to obtain the kind of congressional representation the Constitution guarantees to them. . . . It has always been the rule that where a federally protected right has been invaded the federal courts will provide the remedy to rectify the wrong done.

In 1962, the reasoning of the dissent persuaded the court to reverse *Colegove v. Green,* and in *Baker v. Carr,*[19] the Supreme Court held that legislative apportionment was a justiciable controversy. Justice Brennan, speaking for the majority of the court, said:

> An unbroken line of our precedents sustains the federal court's jurisdiction on the subject matter of federal constitutional claims of this nature. . . . The mere fact that the suit seeks protection of a political right does not mean it presents a political question. . . . Review reveals that in political question cases, it is the relationship between the judiciary and the coordinate branches of the Federal Government, and not the federal judiciary's relationship to the states, which gives rise to the "political question." . . . "Deciding whether a matter has in any measure been committed by the Constitution to another branch of government, or whether the action of that branch exceeds whatever authority has been committed, is itself a delicate exercise in constitutional interpretation, and is a responsibility of this Court as ultimate interpreter of the Constitution. . . ." When a state exercises power wholly within the domain of state interest, it is insulated from federal judicial review. But such insulation is not carried over when a state power is used as an instrument for circumventing a federally protected right. . . . We conclude that the complaint's allegations of a denial of equal protection present a justiciable constitutional cause of action upon which appellants are entitled to a trial and a decision. The right asserted is within reach of judicial protection under the Fourteenth Amendment.

Baker v. Carr, as might be expected, was not a unanimous opinion. Justice Frankfurter, in seeking to maintain the doctrine of *Colegrove v. Green,* argued:

> The Court today reverses a uniform course of decision established by a dozen cases, including one by which the very claim now sustained was unan-

19 369 U.S. 186 (1962).

imously rejected only five years ago. The impressive body of rulings thus cast aside reflected the equally uniform course of our political history regarding the relationship between population and legislative representation—a wholly different matter from denial of the franchise to individuals because of race, color, religion or sex. Such a massive repudiation of the experience of our whole past in asserting a destructively novel judicial power demands a detailed analysis of this Court in our Constitutional scheme. Disregard of inherent limits in the effective exercise of the Court's judicial power not only presages the futility of judicial intervention in the essentially political conflict of forces by which the relation between population and representation has time out of mind been and now is determined. It may well impair the Court's position as the ultimate organ of the Supreme Law of the Land in that vast range of legal problems, often strongly entangled in popular feelings, on which this Court must pronounce. . . .

The notion that representation proportioned to the geographic spread of population is so universally accepted as a necessary element of equality between man and man that it must be taken to be the standard of political equality preserved by the Fourteenth Amendment—that it is, in appellant's words "the basic principle of representative government"—is, to put it bluntly, not true. However desirable and however desired by some among the great political thinkers and framers of our government, it has never been generally practiced, today or in the past. It was not the English system, it was not the colonial system, it was not the system chosen for the national government by the Constitution, it was not the system exclusively or even predominately practiced by the states at the time of the adoption of the Fourteenth Amendment, it is not predominately practiced by the states today. Unless judges, the judges of this Court, are to make their private views of political wisdom the measure of the Constitution—views which in all honesty cannot but give the appearance, if not reflect the reality, of involvement with the business of partisan politics so inescapably a part of apportionment controversies . . . [then] the case is of that class of political controversy which, by nature of its subject, is unfit for federal judicial action.

Once the court declared that the judiciary had jurisdiction over issues of legislative apportionment, a veritable flood of cases followed, challenging legislative bodies at all levels. These decisions have not been met with unanimous accord and, as noted previously, have even resulted in an attempt to amend the Constitution. The proposed amendment, usually referred to as the Dirksen Amendment, would have allowed states by popular vote to have a bicameral legislature with one body being apportioned in part on a geographic basis. While a majority of the United States Senators voted for the amendment, it failed to obtain the required two-thirds support.

Many critics of the reapportionment cases argue that state government is being diluted and weakened. The views of those opposed to reapportionment by judicial decision have been perhaps best stated by a member of the court. Justice Harlan, dissenting in *Wesberry v. Sanders*,[20] said:

> I had not expected to witness the day when the Supreme Court of the United States would render a decision which casts grave doubt on the constitutionality of the composition of the House of Representatives. It is not an exaggeration to say that such is the effect of today's decision. The court's holding that the Constitution requires States to select Representatives either by elections at large or by elections in districts composed "as nearly as is practicable" of equal population places in jeopardy the seats of almost all the members of the present House of Representatives.
>
> In the last congressional election, in 1962, Representatives from 42 States were elected from congressional districts. In all but five of those States, the difference between the populations of the largest and smallest districts exceeded 100,000 persons. A difference of this magnitude in the size of districts the average population of which in each State is less than 500,000 is presumably not equality among districts "as nearly as is practicable," although the Court does not reveal its definition of that phrase. Thus, today's decision impugns the validity of the election of 398 Representatives from 37 States, leaving a "constitutional" House of 37 members now sitting.
>
> Only a demonstration which could not be avoided would justify this Court in rendering a decision the effect of which, inescapably as I see it, is to declare constitutionally defective the very composition of a coordinate branch of the Federal Government. The Court's opinion not only fails to make such a demonstration. It is unsound logically on its face and demonstrably unsound historically. . . .
>
> The Court holds that the provision in Art. I, § 2, for election of Representatives "by the People" means that congressional districts are to be "as nearly as is practicable" equal in population. Stripped of rhetoric and a "historical context," which bears little resemblance to the evidence found in the pages of history, the Court's opinion supports its holding only with the bland assertion that "the principle of a House of Representatives elected 'by the People'" would be "cast aside" if "a vote is worth more in one district than in another," i.e., if congressional districts within a State, each electing a single Representative, are not equal in population. The fact is, however, that Georgia's 10 Representatives are elected "by the People" of Georgia, just as Representatives from other States are elected "by the People of the several States." This is all that the Constitution requires.
>
> Although the Court finds necessity for its artificial construction of Article I in the undoubted importance of the right to vote, that right is not involved in this case. All of the appellants do vote. The Court's talk about "debasement" and "dilution" of the vote is a model of circular reasoning, in which the premises of the argument feed on the conclusion. Moreover, by focusing

exclusively on numbers in disregard of the area and shape of a congressional district as well as party affiliations within the district, the Court deals in abstractions which will be recognized even by the politically unsophisticated to have little relevance to the realities of political life. . . .

There is a further basis for demonstrating the hollowness of the Court's assertion that Article I requires "one man's vote in a congressional election . . . to be worth as much as another's." Nothing that the Court does today will disturb the fact that although in 1960 the population of an average congressional district was 410,481, the States of Alaska, Nevada, and Wyoming each have a Representative in Congress, although their respective populations are 226,167, 285,278, and 330,066. In entire disregard of population, Art. I, § 2, guarantees each of these States and every other State "at Least one Representative." It is whimsical to assert in the face of this guarantee that an absolute principle of "equal representation in the House of equal numbers of people" is "solemnly embodied" in Article I. All that there is is a provision which bases representation in the House, generally but not entirely, on the population of the States. The provision for representation of each State in the House of Representatives is not a mere exception to the principle framed by the majority; it shows that no such principle is to be found.

The upshot of all this is that the language of Art. I, §§ 2 and 4, the surrounding text, and the relevant history are all in strong and consistent direct contradiction of the Court's holding. The constitutional scheme vests in the States plenary power to regulate the conduct of elections for Representatives, and, in order to protect the Federal Government, provides for congressional supervision of the States' exercise of their power. Within this scheme, the appellants do not have the right which they assert, in the absence of provision for equal districts by the Georgia Legislature or the Congress. The constitutional right which the Court creates is manufactured out of whole cloth. . . .

Today's decision has portents for our society and the Court itself which should be recognized. This is not a case in which the Court vindicates the kind of individual rights that are assured by the Due Process Clause of the Fourteenth Amendment whose "vague contours," Rochin v. People of California, 342 U.S. 165, 170, 72 S.Ct. 205, 208, 96 L.Ed. 183, *of course leave much room for constitutional developments necessitated by changing conditions in a dynamic society. Nor is this a case in which an emergent set of facts requires the Court to frame new principles to protect recognized constitutional rights. The claim for judicial relief in this case strikes at one of the fundamental doctrines of our system of government, the separation of powers. In upholding that claim, the Court attempts to effect reforms in a field which the Constitution, as plainly as can be, has committed exclusively to the political process.*

This Court, no less than all other branches of the Government, is bound by the Constitution. The Constitution does not confer on the Court blanket authority to step into every situation where the political branch may be thought to have fallen short. The stability of this institution ultimately depends not only upon its being alert to keep the other branches of government within constitutional bounds but equally upon recognition of the limitations on the Court's own functions in the constitutional system.

What is done today saps the political process. The promise of judicial intervention in matters of this sort cannot but encourage popular inertia in efforts for political reform through the political process, with the inevitable result that the process is itself weakened. By yielding to the demand for a judicial remedy in this instance, the Court in my view does a disservice both to itself and to the broader values of our system of government.

The prevailing view in the cases following *Baker v. Carr* can be seen in *Reynolds v. Sims*,[21] in which Chief Justice Earl Warren said:

Legislators represent people, not trees or acres. Legislators are elected by voters, not farms or cities or economic interests. As long as ours is a representative form of government, and our legislatures are those instruments of government elected directly by and directly representative of the people, the right to elect legislators in a free and unimpaired fashion is a bedrock of our political system. . . . State legislatures are, historically, the fountainhead of representative government in this country. Full and effective participation by all citizens in a state government requires, therefore, that each citizen have an equally effective voice in the election of his state legislature. To sanction minority control of state legislative bodies would appear to deny majority rights in a way that far surpasses any possible denial of minority rights that otherwise might be thought to result. . . . Our constitutional system amply provides for the protection of minorities by means other than giving them majority control of state legislatures. We are told that the matter of apportioning representation in state legislatures is a complex and many-faceted one. We are advised that the states can rationally consider factors other than population in apportioning legislative representation. We are admonished not to restrict the power of the states to impose differing views as to political philosophy on their citizens. We are cautioned about the dangers of entering into political thickets and mathematical quagmires. Our answer is this: a denial of constitutionally protected rights demands judicial protection; our path and our office require no less of us. . . . We hold that, as a basic constitutional standard, the Equal Protection Clause requires that the seats in both houses of a bicameral state legislature must be apportioned on a population basis.

The so-called federal analogy is inapplicable as a sustaining precedent for state legislative apportionment. . . .

So long as divergencies from a strict population standard are based on legitimate considerations incident to the effectuation of a rational state policy,

21 377 U.S. 533 (1964).

some deviations from the equal population principle are constitutionally permissible with respect to the appointment of seats in either or both of the two houses of a bicameral state legislature. . . .

Note that in the *Reynolds* case, the court recognized the impossibility of rigidly applying the one-man, one-vote rule. How much deviation is permissible, and what does the future hold for reapportionment cases? The decision which follows in *Swann v. Adams* suggests an answer to the foregoing questions.

SWANN V. ADAMS
87 S.Ct. 569 (1967)

WHITE, JUSTICE: This case presents still another development in the efforts of the State of Florida to apportion its legislature in accordance with the requirements of the Federal Constitution. There have been previous chapters in this story. The litigation began in 1962. On June 22, 1964, . . . we reversed the judgment of the three-judge District Court upholding the then current legislative apportionment in Florida and remanded the case for further proceedings, consistent with the Court's opinion in *Reynolds v. Sims*, 377 U.S. 533, 84 S.Ct. 1362, 12 L.Ed.2d 506. . . . The District Court then deferred further action until the conclusion of the legislative session which convened on April 6, 1965. The legislature proceeded to reapportion the State on June 29, 1965. The District Court forthwith held the new plan failed to meet the requirements of the Fourteenth Amendment but approved the plan on an interim basis, limiting it to the period ending 60 days after the adjournment of the 1967 session of the Florida Legislature. This Court, finding no warrant for perpetuating what all conceded was an unconstitutional apportionment for another three years, reversed the judgment and remanded the case to the District Court so that a valid reapportionment plan would be made effective for the 1966 elections. . . . The Florida Legislature again acted on the matter in March 1966 by adopting still another reapportionment plan which the appellants promptly attacked in the District Court.

The new plan provides for 48 senators and 117 representatives, and includes what in effect are multimember districts for each house. The senate districts range from 87,595 to 114,053 in population per senator, or from 15.09% over-represented to 10.56% under-represented. The ratio between the largest and the smallest district is thus 1.30:1. The deviation from the average population per senator is greater than 15% in one senatorial district, is greater than 14% in five more districts and is more than 10% in still six other districts. Approximately 25% of the State's population living in one quarter of the total number of senatorial districts is under- or over-represented by at least 10%. The minimum percentage of persons that could elect a majority of 25 senators is 48.38%.

In the house the population per representative ranges from 34,584 to 48,785 or from 18.28% over-represented to 15.27% under-represented. The ratio between the largest and the smallest representative district is 1.41 to 1. Two districts vary from the norm by more than 18% and another by more than 15%, these three districts having seven of the 117 representatives. Ten other districts with 22 representatives vary from the norm by more than 10%. There is thus a deviation of more than 10% in districts which elect 29 of the 117 representatives. 24.35% of the State's population live in these districts. The minimum percentage of persons that could elect 58 representatives is 47.79% and a majority of 59 representatives could be elected by 50.43% of the population.

The District Court recognized that "apportionment must be substantially on a population basis" but that "mathematical exactness or precision is not required." It went on to hold "[s]uch departures as there are from the ideal are not sufficient in number or great enough in percentages to require an upsetting of the legislative plan . . . what deviation there is does not discriminate to any great extent against any section of the state or against either rural or urban interests." Accordingly, the plan was held constitutional. . . .

We reverse for the failure of the State to present or the District Court to articulate acceptable reasons for the variations among the populations of the various legislative districts with respect to both the senate and house of representatives. *Reynolds v. Sims, supra,* recognized that mathematical exactness is not required in state apportionment plans. De minimus deviations are unavoidable, but variations of 30% among senate districts and 40% among house districts can hardly be deemed de minimus and none of our cases suggests that differences of this magnitude will be approved without a satisfactory explanation grounded on acceptable state policy. . . .

Variations from a pure population standard might be justified by such state policy considerations as the integrity of political subdivisions, the maintenance of compactness and contiguity in legislative districts or the recognition of natural or historical boundary lines. Likewise, in *Roman v. Sincock,* 377 U.S. 695, 710, 84 S.Ct. 1449, 1458, 12 L.Ed.2d 620, the Court stated that the Constitution permits "such minor deviations only as may occur in recognizing certain factors that are free from any taint of arbitrariness or discrimination." . . .

The State suggests that the plans approved in three prior cases involved variations of equal or greater magnitude than those revealed by the Florida apportionment, and for that reason the judgment here should be affirmed. But in none of these cases was the issue of the validity of the differences in population between various legislative districts either raised or ruled upon in this Court. There was no occasion to explore whether or not there was ample justification for the challenged variations. . . . In any event, the fact that a 10% or 15% variation from the norm is approved in one State has little bearing on the validity of a similar variation in another State. "What is marginally permissible in one State may be unsatisfactory in another, depending on the particular circumstances of the case." *Reynolds v. Sims*, 533 U.S. 553, 578, 84 S.Ct. 1362, 1390. . . .

All the State suggested in either the lower court or here is that its plan comes as close as "practical" to complete population equality and that the State was attempting to follow congressional district lines. There was, however, no attempt to justify any particular deviations, even the larger ones, with respect to either of these considerations. Moreover, the State's brief states only that the legislature followed "in most instances" the congressional boundaries and with respect to "practicality" it seems quite obvious that the State could have come much closer to providing districts of equal population than it did. . . .

We think the better view is that taken by the three-judge court in Maryland which disapproved a legislative plan involving an over-representation of 14.90% and an under-representation of 14.38% because, as Judge Sobeloff said, there was "no showing in this case that the difference of one-third is unavoidable or justified upon any legally acceptable ground." *Maryland Citizens Committee for Fair Congressional Redistricting, Inc. v. Tawes, D.C.,* 253 F.Supp. 731, 733. . . . [REVERSED]

HARLAN, JUSTICE, dissenting (joined by JUSTICE STEWART):

Reynolds v. Sims, 377 U.S. 533, 84 S.Ct. 1362, laid down a "one man-one vote" mandate for the structuring of all state legislatures, but the Court there recognized, as it does again today, that "mathematical exactness is not required," ante, p. 571, and that variations are acceptable if they "are based on legitimate considerations incident to the effectuation of a rational state policy. . . ." The Court refuses, however, to accept Florida's present legislative apportionment plan, at least on the record before us, because neither the State nor the District Court justified the relatively minor variations in population among some of the districts.

This holding seems to me to stand on its head the usual rule governing this Court's approach to the validity of legislative enactments, state as well as federal, which is of course that they come to us with a strong presumption of regularity and constitutionality. . . . Accordingly, I do not believe the burden is on the State to justify every aspect of a complex plan completely restructuring its legislature, on pain of its being declared constitutionally invalid by the judiciary. I can think of no other area of law in which there is an analogous presumption of invalidity attaching to a legislative enactment of a State in an area of its admitted competence and superior experience. The burden of showing unconstitutionality should be left here, as in other cases, on the attacking party.

I would affirm the judgment of the District Court on the grounds (1) that the plan enacted by the Florida Legislature is in substantial compliance with the rule of *Reynolds v. Sims, supra,* and (2) that the appellants have not shown any invidious purpose for, or effect flowing from, the mathematical variations among certain districts.

D   SOCIETY'S ATTITUDE

The law is greatly influenced by the mood of the people or the attitude of society toward any particular problem. On many questions society's attitude will be divided, which makes it difficult to ascertain whether the court in a given case is reflecting the dominant attitude of the times or is providing leadership in bringing about social change by adopting the philosophy of an enlightened minority. The court usually does not have the benefit of a public opinion poll or an actual vote by the electorate on the great social questions before it. Most reviewing courts are not "politically responsible" in the sense that the voters can replace the judges if they hand down unpopular decisions. Nevertheless, a court of review generally has its ear to the feelings and attitudes of society, and its actions are frequently based on its own best judgment of what those attitudes and beliefs are, concerning the problem at hand. For example, the decisions on questions of obscenity in recent years have tended to hold that very few books or movies are obscene. This has been a period of time during which society's attitude toward sex and morality has been changing. While it can not definitely be determined whether the courts have reflected society's ideas or society has been influenced by the judicial decisions, it is clear that the attitudes of both court and society have moved away from the so-called "Victorian attitude" and toward a much more "liberal" view of the effects of pornography on society. Although there have been strong dissents from the trend of the cases, the rules of law involved clearly have become more permissive, as the following case illustrates. Chapter 17 contains further discussion of the legal problems of balancing the police power to protect public morality with the constitutional guarantees of freedom of speech and of the press in cases of alleged obscenity.

PEOPLE V. KIMMEL
220 N.E.2d 203 (Ill. 1966)

KLINGBIEL, CHIEF JUSTICE: At a jury trial in the circuit court of Cook County Charles Kimmel was found guilty of selling an obscene book, in violation of Section 11-20 of the Criminal Code (Ill. Rev. State. 1965, chap. 38, par. 11-20). He was fined the sum of $2000 and placed on probation for a period of three years. He appeals directly to this court contending that the material is within the range of constitutionally protected expression.

The book is entitled "The Sex Addicts" and tells of a vacation cruise to tropical islands during which the hero and his cabin-mate engage in a series of sexual exploits with various girls they met aboard the ship. The hero has sexual intercourse with several female acquaintances in succession. He finally finds himself falling in love with one of two sisters, with whom he and his roommate had had a "four-way affair" in the girls' cabin, including an exchange of partners. The roommate is portrayed as a man obsessed with the urge to make new conquests who cannot be satisfied with the same girl more than once. The hero was left with the two sisters, and before ending up with the girl of his choice he has relations with both. The book contains the suggestion that the roommate, with his compulsive urge to move from one conquest to another, is mentally ill and ought to see an analyst.

The controlling rules in this kind of case were recently set forth and discussed in *City of Chicago v. University Publishing and Distributing Corp.,* 34 Ill.2d 250, 215 N.E.2d 251, and need not be repeated in detail here. To lose the constitutional protection of free press the material must appeal only to a prurient interest—i.e., a morbid interest in sex—and must go substantially beyond customary limits of candor in the description or representation of it. Before a book can be classed as obscene so as to fall outside constitutional protections it must be patently offensive and without any redeeming social importance. The application of such necessarily vague standards can become extremely difficult in marginal cases, but we think the material in the case at bar, under the constitution as construed by the United States Supreme Court, can hardly be denied protection. True, the cover of this paperback book is rather blatant in suggesting illicit sexual conduct, as are the title and descriptive remarks. And the contents consist principally of a more or less continuous account of sexual engagements and the preliminaries. But there is little violence and none of the descriptions of perverted behavior of the sort portrayed, e.g., in the books held obscene in *People v. Sikora,* 32 Ill. 2d 260, 204 N.E.2d 768. The acts of intercourse are not described in detail, so as to exceed the limits of contemporary candor in such matters, nor do we find repulsive and disgusting language of the kind given protection in *Grove Press, Inc. v. Gerstein,* 378 U.S. 577, 84 S.Ct. 1909.

Publication of the book questioned in the case at bar would obviously be unjustified on any conceivable basis of literary merit although it might be said to deal, to a very slight and superficial extent, with a common social problem. But as it was pointed out in *City of Chicago v. Universal Publishing and Distributing Corp.,* 34 Ill. 2d 250, 215 N.E.2d 251, sex is not synonymous with obscenity, and its portrayal is not of itself sufficient reason to deny the constitutional protection of freedom of speech and press.

In view of our conclusion that the book is not obscene it is unnecessary to consider defendant's other contentions. The judgment is reversed.
[JUDGMENT REVERSED]

The doctrine of "constitutional relativity" stands for the proposition that the meaning of the language found in the Constitution is relative to the time in which it is being interpreted. The doctrine has been recently used rather frequently by the Supreme Court to give effect to society's attitudes. Under this concept great weight is attached to social forces and needs, as the court sees them, in formulating judicial decisions. As the attitudes and problems of society change, the law and the Constitution are changed also. The evolution in interpretation of law is accomplished by the courts' reflection of social evolution. Perhaps no single legal problem better illustrates the power of social pressure than that of school integration. As social forces demanded equality for the Negro, the law, reflecting these demands, has gradually changed. Precedent was overturned and the dominant viewpoint of one portion of the country was dramatically rejected, at least by the Supreme Court in its unanimous holding. Judicial decree, brought about by social change, is accomplishing what was impracticable by legislation. The following is the land-mark case on school integration.

BROWN V. BOARD OF EDUCATION
347 U.S. 497 (1954)

WARREN, CHIEF JUSTICE: These cases come to us from the States of Kansas, South Carolina, Virginia, and Delaware. They are premised on different facts and different local conditions, but a common legal question justifies their consideration together in this consolidated opinion.

In each of the cases, minors of the Negro race, through their legal representatives, seek the aid of the courts in obtaining admission to the public schools of their community on a nonsegregated basis. In each instance, they had been denied admission to schools attended by white children under laws requiring or permitting segregation according to race. This segregation was alleged to deprive the plaintiffs of the equal protection of the laws under the Fourteenth Amendment. In each of the cases other than the Delaware case, a three-judge federal district court denied relief to the plaintiffs on the so-called "separate but equal" doctrine announced by this Court in *Plessy v. Ferguson,* 163 U.S. 537. Under that doctrine, equality of treatment is accorded when the races are provided substantially equal facilities, even though these facilities be separate. In the Delaware case, the Supreme Court of Delaware adhered to that doctrine, but ordered that the plaintiffs be admitted to the white schools because of their superiority to the Negro schools.

The plaintiffs contend that segregated public schools are not "equal" and cannot be made "equal," and that hence they are deprived of the equal protection of the laws. Because of the obvious importance of the question presented, the Court took jurisdiction. Argument was heard in the 1952 Term, and reargument was heard this Term on certain questions propounded by the Court.

Reargument was largely devoted to the circumstances surrounding the adoption of the Fourteenth Amendment in 1868. It covered exhaustively consideration of the Amendment in Congress, ratification by the states, then existing practices in racial segregation, and the views of proponents and opponents of the Amendment. This discussion and our own investigation convince us that, although these sources cast some light, it is not enough to resolve the problem with which we are faced. At best, they are inconclusive. The most avid proponents of the post-War Amendments undoubtedly intended them to remove all legal distinctions among "all persons born or naturalized in the United States." Their opponents, just as certainly, were antagonistic to both the letter and the spirit of the Amendments and wished them to have the most limited effect. What others in Congress and the state legislatures had in mind cannot be determined with any degree of certainty.

An additional reason for the inconclusive nature of the Amendment's history, with respect to segregated schools, is the status of public education at that time. In the South, the movement toward free common schools, supported by general taxation, had not yet taken hold. Education of white children was largely in the hands of private groups. Education of Negroes was almost nonexistent, and practically all of the race were illiterate. In fact, any education of Negroes was forbidden by law in some states. Today, in contrast, many Negroes have achieved outstanding success in the arts and sciences as well as in the business and professional world. It is true that public school education at the time of the Amendment had advanced further in the North, but the effect of the Amendment on Northern States was generally ignored in the congressional debates. Even in the North, the conditions of public education did not approximate those existing today. The curriculum was usually rudimentary; ungraded schools were common in rural areas; the school term was but three months a year in many states; and compulsory school attendance was virtually unknown. As a consequence, it is not surprising that there should be so little in the history of the Fourteenth Amendment relating to its intended effect on public education.

In the first cases in this Court construing the Fourteenth Amendment, decided shortly after its adoption, the Court interpreted it as proscribing all state-imposed discriminations against the Negro race. The doctrine of "separate but equal" did not make its appearance in this Court until 1896 in the case of *Plessy v. Ferguson, supra,* involving not education but transportation. American courts have since labored with the doctrine for over half a century. In this Court, there have been six cases involving the "separate but equal" doctrine in the field of public education. In *Cumming v. County Board of Education,* 175 U.S. 528, and *Gong Lum v. Rice,* 275 U.S. 78, the validity of the doctrine itself was not challenged. In more recent cases, all on the graduate school level, inequality was found in that specific benefits enjoyed by white students were denied to Negro students of the same educational qualifications. *Missouri ex rel. Gaines v. Canada,* 305 U.S. 337; *Sipuel v. Oklahoma,* 332 U.S. 631; *Sweatt v. Painter,* 339 U.S. 629; *McLaurin v. Oklahoma State Regents,* 339 U.S. 637. In none of these cases was it necessary to re-examine the doctrine to grant relief to the Negro plaintiff. And in *Sweatt v. Painter, supra,* the Court expressly reserved decision on the question whether *Plessy v. Ferguson* should be held inapplicable to public education.

In the instant cases, that question is directly presented. Here, unlike *Sweatt v. Painter,* there are findings below that the Negro and white schools involved have been equalized, or are being equalized, with respect to buildings, curricula, qualifications and salaries of teachers, and other "tangible" factors. Our decision, therefore, cannot turn on merely a comparison of these tangible factors in the Negro and white schools involved in each of the cases. We must look instead to the effect of segregation itself on public education.

In approaching this problem, we cannot turn the clock back to 1868 when the Amendment was adopted, or even to 1896 when *Plessy v. Ferguson* was written. We must consider public education in the light of its full development and its present place in American life throughout the Nation. Only in this way can it be determined if segregation in public schools deprives these plaintiffs of the equal protection of the laws.

Today, education is perhaps the most important function of state and local governments. Compulsory school attendance laws and the great expenditures for education both demonstrate our recognition of the importance of education to our democratic society. It is required in the performance of our most basic public responsibilities, even service in the armed forces. It is the very foundation of good citizenship. Today it is a principal instrument in awakening the child to cultural values, in preparing him for later professional training, and in helping him to adjust normally to his environment. In these days, it is doubtful that any child may reasonably be expected to succeed in life if he is denied the opportunity of an education. Such an opportunity, where the state has undertaken to provide it, is a right which must be made available to all on equal terms.

We come then to the question presented: Does segregation of children in public schools solely on the basis of race, even though the physical facilities and other "tangible" factors may be equal, deprive the children of the minority group of equal educational opportunities? We believe that it does.

In *Sweatt v. Painter, supra,* in finding that a segregated law school for Negroes could not provide them equal educational opportunities, this Court relied in large part on "those qualities which are incapable of objective measurement but which make for greatness in a law school." In *McLaurin v. Oklahoma State Regents, supra,* the Court, in requiring that a Negro admitted to a white graduate school be treated like all other students, again resorted to intangible considerations: ". . . his ability to study, to engage in discussions and exchange views with other students, and, in general, to learn his profession." Such considerations apply with added force to children in grade and high schools. To separate them from others of similar age and qualifications solely because of their race generates a feeling of inferiority as to their status in the community that may affect their hearts and minds in a way unlikely ever to be undone. The effect of this separation on their educational opportunities was well stated by a finding in the Kansas case by a court which nevertheless felt compelled to rule against the Negro plaintiffs:

> *Segregation of white and colored children in public schools has a detrimental effect upon the colored children. The impact is greater when it has the sanction of the law; for the policy of separating the races is usually interpreted as denoting the inferiority of the negro group. A sense of inferiority affects the motivation of a child to learn. Segregation with the sanction of law, therefore, has a tendency to [retard] the educational and mental development of negro children and to deprive them of some of the benefits they would receive in a racial[ly] integrated school system.*

Whatever may have been the extent of psychological knowledge at the time of *Plessy v. Ferguson,* this finding is amply supported by modern authority. Any language in *Plessy v. Ferguson* contrary to this finding is rejected.

We conclude that in the field of public education the doctrine of "separate but equal" has no place. Separate educational facilities are inherently unequal. Therefore, we hold that the plaintiffs and others similarly situated for whom the actions have been brought are, by reason of the segregation complained of, deprived of the equal protection of the laws guaranteed by the Fourteenth Amendment. This disposition makes unnecessary any discussion whether such segregation also violates the Due Process Clause of the Fourteenth Amendment.

Because these are class actions, because of the wide applicability of this decision, and because of the great variety of local conditions, the formulation of decrees in these cases presents problems of considerable complexity. On reargument, the consideration of appropriate relief was necessarily subordinated to the primary question—the constitutionality of segregation in public education. We have now announced that such segregation is a denial of the equal protection of the laws. In order that we may have the full assistance of the parties in formulating decrees, the cases will be restored to the docket, and the parties are requested to present further argument on Questions 4 and 5 previously propounded by the Court for the reargument this Term.[22] The Attorney General of the United States is again invited to participate. The Attorneys General of the states requiring or permitting segregation in public education will also be permitted to appear as *amici curiae* upon request to do so by September 15, 1954, and submission of briefs by October 1, 1954. [IT IS SO ORDERED]

E   EMERGENCIES

Emergency situations such as calamities caused by flood, fire or earthquake sometimes alter the application of a rule or require that a different rule be applied. In addition, an emergency may afford a reason for exercising a power of government otherwise dormant. National emergencies such as economic depressions have resulted even in court approval of statutes in partial impairment of the obligations of contracts, as is illustrated by the following case. Note that the emergency here was a force which operated both on the legislature in *adopting* a law, and on the Supreme Court in holding that law to be valid, in spite of Article I, Section 10 of the United States Constitution, which reads: "No State shall . . . pass any . . . Law impairing the Obligation of Contracts. . . ."

HOME BUILDING & LOAN V. BLAISDELL
290 U.S. 398 (1934)

In 1933, Minnesota passed a Mortgage Moratorium law which declared that as a result of the economic emergency, mortgage foreclosure sales might be judicially postponed and periods of redemption of prior sales might be extended to May 1, 1935. Appellees applied to a court for an order extending the time during which they might redeem a lot which they owned but which had been sold at a foreclosure sale. Appellant had purchased the property at the foreclosure sale and contended that the statute was unconstitutional as being repugnant to the contract clause (Article I, § 10) and the due process and equal protection clauses of the Fourteenth Amendment of the Federal Constitution. The statute was sustained by the Supreme Court of Minnesota as an emergency measure although the Minnesota Court admitted that the obligation of a contract had been impaired.

HUGHES, CHIEF JUSTICE: . . . In determining whether the provision for this temporary and conditional relief exceeds the power of the state by reason

---

[22] The questions referred to concerned the nature of the decrees to be formulated by the court to enforce its decision.

of the clause in the Federal Constitution prohibiting impairment of the obligations of contracts, we must consider the relation of emergency to constitutional power, the historical setting of the contract clause, the development of the jurisprudence of this Court in the construction of that clause, and the principles of construction which we may consider to be established.

Emergency does not create power. Emergency does not increase granted power or remove or diminish the restrictions imposed upon power granted or reserved. The Constitution was adopted in a period of grave emergency. Its grants of power to the federal government and its limitations of the power of the States were determined in the light of emergency, and they are not altered by emergency. What power was thus granted and what limitations were thus imposed are questions which have always been, and always will be, the subject of close examination under our constitutional system.

While emergency does not create power, emergency may furnish the occasion for the exercise of power. "Although an emergency may not call into life a power which has never lived, nevertheless emergency may afford a reason for the exertion of a living power already enjoyed" . . . [cases cited]. The constitutional question presented in the light of an emergency is whether the power possessed embraces the particular exercise of it in response to particular conditions. Thus, the war power of the federal government is not created by the emergency of war, but it is a power given to meet that emergency. It is a power to wage war successfully, and thus it permits the harnessing of the entire energies of the people in a supreme co-operative effort to preserve the nation. But even the war power does not remove constitutional limitations safeguarding essential liberties. When the provisions of the Constitution, in grant or restrictions, are specific, so particularized as not to admit of construction, no question is presented. Thus, emergency would not permit a state to have more than two Senators in the Congress, or permit the election of President by a general popular vote without regard to the number of electors to which the States are respectively entitled, or permit the States to "coin money" or to "make anything but gold and silver coin a tender in payment of debts." But, where constitutional grants and limitations of power are set forth in general clauses, which afford a broad outline, the process of construction is essential to fill in the details. That is true of the contract clause. The necessity of construction is not obviated by the fact that the contract clause is associated in the same section with other and more specific prohibitions. . . .

The occasion and general purpose of the contract clause are summed up in the terse statement of Chief Justice Marshall in *Ogden v. Saunders,* 12 Wheat. 213, 354, 355, 6 L. Ed. 606:

The power of changing the relative situation of debtor and creditor, of interfering with contracts, a power which comes home to every man, touches the interest of all, and controls the conduct of every individual in those things which he supposes to be proper for his own exclusive management, had been used to such an excess by the state legislatures, as to break in upon the ordinary intercourse of society, and destroy all confidence between man and man. This mischief had become so great, so alarming, as not only to impair commercial intercourse, and threaten the existence of credit, but to sap the morals of the people, and destroy the sanctity of private faith. To guard against the continuance of the evil, was an object of deep interest with all the truly wise, as well as the virtuous, of this great community, and was one of the important benefits expected from a reform of the government.

But full recognition of the occasion and general purpose of the clause does not suffice to fix its precise scope. . . . To ascertain the scope of the constitutional prohibition, we examine the course of judicial decisions in its application. These put it beyond question that the prohibition is not an absolute one and is not to be read with literal exactness like a mathematical formula. . . . Not only are existing laws read into contracts in order to fix obligations as between the parties, but the reservation of essential attributes of sovereign power is also read into contracts as a postulate of the legal order. The policy of protecting contracts against impairment presupposes the maintenance of a government by virtue of which contractual relations are worth while,—a government which retains adequate authority to secure the peace and good order of society. This principle of harmonizing the constitutional prohibition with the necessary residuum of state power has had progressive recognition in the decisions of this Court. . . .

Undoubtedly, whatever is reserved of state power must be consistent with the fair intent of the constitutional limitation of that power. The reserved power cannot be construed so as to destroy the limitation, nor is the limitation to be construed to destroy the reserved power in its essential aspects. They must be construed in harmony with each other. This principle precludes a construction which would permit the state to adopt as its policy the repudiation of debts or the destruction of contracts or the denial of means to enforce them. But it does not follow that conditions may not arise in which a temporary restraint of enforcement may be consistent with the spirit and purpose of the constitutional provision and thus be found to be within the range of the reserved power of the state to protect the vital interests of the community. It cannot be maintained that the constitutional prohibition should be so construed as to prevent limited and temporary interpositions with respect to the enforcement of contracts if made necessary by a great public calamity such as fire, flood, or earthquake. . . . The reservation of state power appropriate to such extraordinary conditions may be deemed to be as much a part of all contracts as is the reservation of state power to protect the public interest. . . . And, if state power exists to give temporary relief from the enforcement of contracts in the presence of disasters due to physical causes such as fire, flood, or earthquake, that power cannot be said to be nonexistent when the urgent public need demanding such relief is produced by other and economic causes.

Whatever doubt there may have been that the protective power of the state, its police power, may be exercised—without violating the true intent of the provision of the Federal Constitution—in directly preventing the immediate and literal enforcement of contractual obligations by a temporary and conditional restraint, where vital public interests would otherwise suffer, was removed by our decisions relating to the enforcement of provisions of leases during a period of scarcity of housing. . . .

It is manifest from this review of our decisions that there has been a growing appreciation of public needs and of the necessity of finding ground for a rational compromise between individual rights and public welfare. The settlement and consequent contraction of the public domain, the pressure of a constantly increasing density of population, the interrelation of the activities of our people and the complexity of our economic interests, have inevitably led to an increased use of the organization of society in order to protect the very bases of individual opportunity. Where, in earlier days, it was thought that only the concerns of individuals or of classes were involved, and that those of the state itself were touched only remotely, it has later been found that the fundamental interests of the state are directly affected; and that the question is no longer merely that of one party to a contract as against another, but of the use of reasonable means to safeguard the economic structure upon which the good of all depends.

It is no answer to say that this public need was not apprehended a century ago, or to insist that what the provision of the Constitution meant to the vision of that day it must mean to the vision of our time. If by the statement that what the Constitution meant at the time of its adoption it means to-day, it is intended to say that the great clauses of the Constitution must be confined to the interpretation which the framers, with the conditions and outlook of their time, would have placed upon them, the statement carries its own refutation. It was to guard against such a narrow conception that Chief Justice Marshall uttered the memorable warnings: "We must never forget, that it is *a constitution* we are expounding" (*McCulloch v. Maryland,* 4 Wheat. 316, 407, 4 L. Ed. 579); "a constitution intended to endure for ages to come, and, consequently, to be adapted to the various *crises* of human affairs." *Id.* page 415 of 4 Wheat. When we are dealing with the words of the Constitution, said this Court in *Missouri v. Holland,* 252 U.S. 416, 433, . . . "we must realize that they have called into life a being the development of which could not have been foreseen completely by the most gifted of its begetters. . . . The case before us must be considered in the light of our whole experience and not merely in that of what was said a hundred years ago."

Nor is it helpful to attempt to draw a fine distinction between the intended meaning of the words of the Constitution and their intended application. When we consider the contract clause and the decisions which have expounded it in harmony with the essential reserved power of the states to protect the security of their peoples, we find no warrant for the conclusion that the clause has been warped by these decisions from its proper significance or that the founders of our government would have interpreted the clause differently had they had occasion to assume that responsibility in the conditions of the later day. The vast body of law which has been developed was unknown to the fathers, but it is believed to have preserved the essential content and the spirit of the Constitution. With a growing recognition of public needs and the relation of individual right to public security, the court has sought to prevent the perversion of the clause through its use as an instrument to throttle the capacity of the states to protect their fundamental interests. This development is a growth from the seeds which the fathers planted. . . . The principle of this development is, as we have seen, that the reservation of the reasonable exercise of the protective power of the state is read into all contracts. . . .

Applying the criteria established by our decisions, we conclude:

. . . The legislation was addressed to a legitimate end; that is, the legislation was not for the mere advantage of particular individuals but for the protection of a basic interest of society.

. . . We are of the opinion that the Minnesota statute as here applied does not violate the contract clause of the Federal Constitution. Whether the legislation is wise or unwise as a matter of policy is a question with which we are not concerned. . . .

The judgment of the Supreme Court of Minnesota is affirmed. [JUDGMENT AFFIRMED]

No emergency has a more direct impact on the nation as a whole than does war. The repercussions of war and the exercise of emergency war powers have directed the path of executive action, legislation, and judicial decisions even to the extent of denying to citizens their rights to liberty and property.

Toward the beginning of World War II, over 100,000 Japanese, approximately 70,000 of them citizens of the United States from birth, without being charged or indicted for any offense, without any investigation of their loyalty to the United States, were first subjected to a curfew and later removed from their homes in West Coast areas.[23] These people, aliens and citizens alike, were taken into custody by order of the Commanding General of the Western Defense Command and sent to "relocation camps" which were in reality concentration camps, and many of them were detained there for several years. The Japanese-Americans suffered great losses of property

---

[23] See Rostow, The Japanese American Cases—A Disaster, 54 *Yale L.J.* 489 (1945).

—furniture, homes, gardens, and businesses. *Aliens* from Italy and Germany, with whose countries we also were at war, and citizens of Japanese ancestry residing in Hawaii (over 30 percent of the population there) were not "relocated" in this manner. The military ordered and executed the relocation on the West Coast acting under the war powers and pursuant to an executive order of the President and supported by an act of Congress. The white populace of the West had been under great tension from fear of sabotage and an invasion or attack by Japan similar to Pearl Harbor. The military decision to remove the Japanese-Americans from coastal areas was no doubt greatly influenced by this public fear, since there was no known case of sabotage or spying by one of Japanese ancestry and since similar military measures were not undertaken any place else in the country. Several cases resulted challenging the validity of the military action as a discrimination between citizens of Japanese ancestry and those of other ancestry in violation of the Fifth Amendment to the Constitution which states: "No person shall . . . be deprived of life, liberty or property without due process of law. . . ." The decisions generally were in favor of the action of the government as a legitimate exercise of the war power and have been the subject of a great deal of criticism.

In *Hirabayashi v. United States*, 320 U.S. 81 (1943), the Court stated:

Whatever views we may entertain regarding the loyalty to this country of the citizens of Japanese ancestry, we cannot reject as unfounded the judgment of the military authorities and of Congress that there are disloyal members of that population, whose number and strength could not be precisely and quickly ascertained. We cannot say that the war-making branches of the government did not have ground for believing that in a critical hour such persons could not readily be isolated and separately dealt with, and constituted a menace to the national defense and safety, which demanded that prompt and adequate measure be taken to guard against it.

Justice Stone said in the *Hirabayashi* case:

The war power of the national government is "the power to wage war successfully." See Charles Evans Hughes, War Powers under the Constitution, 42 A.B.A. Rep. 232, 238. It extends to every matter and activity so related to war as substantially to affect its conduct and progress. The power is not restricted to the winning of victories in the field and the repulse of enemy forces. It embraces every phase of the national defense, including the protection of war materials and the members of the armed forces from injury and from the dangers which attend the rise, prosecution and progress of war. . . .

Since the Constitution commits to the Executive and to Congress the exercise of the war power in all the vicissitudes and conditions of warfare, it has necessarily given them wide scope for the exercise of judgment and discretion in determining the nature and extent of the threatened injury or

*danger and in the selection of the means for resisting it . . . [cases cited].
Where, as they did here, the conditions call for the exercise of judgment and
discretion and for the choice of means by those branches of the Government
on which the Constitution has placed the responsibility of warmaking, it is
not for any court to sit in review of the wisdom of their action or substitute
its judgment for theirs.*

Justice Stone further indicated the effect of war on the courts when
he held that it justified distinctions between citizens based on race, stating:

*Distinctions between citizens solely because of their ancestry are by their
very nature odious to a free people whose institutions are founded upon the
doctrine of equality. For that reason, legislative classification or discrimination based on race alone has often been held to be a denial of equal protection . . . [cases cited]. We may assume that these considerations would be
controlling here were it not for the fact that the danger of espionage and
sabotage, in time of war and of threatened invasion, calls upon the military
authorities to scrutinize every relevant fact bearing on the loyalty of populations in the danger areas. Because racial discriminations are in most circumstances irrelevant and therefore prohibited, it by no means follows that, in
dealing with the perils of war, Congress and the Executive are wholly precluded from taking into account those facts and circumstances which are
relevant to measures for our national defense and for the successful prosecution of the war, and which may in fact place citizens of one ancestry in a
different category from others. "We must never forget, that it is a constitution
we are expounding, . . . a constitution intended to endure for ages to come,
and, consequently, to be adapted to the various crises of human affairs."*

In *Korematsu v. United States*, 323 U.S. 214 (1944), Justice Jackson,
while dissenting in another case involving the Japanese-Americans, indicated that courts should not interfere with the military in time of war when
he said:

*I should hold that a civil court cannot be made to enforce an order which
violates constitutional limitations even if it is a reasonable exercise of military
authority. The courts can exercise only the judicial power, can apply only
law, and must abide by the Constitution, or they cease to be civil courts and
become instruments of military policy.*

*Of course the existence of military power resting on force, so vagrant, so
centralized, so necessarily heedless of the individual, is an inherent threat to
liberty. But I would not lead people to rely on this court for a review that
seems to me wholly delusive. The military reasonableness of these orders can
only be determined by military superiors. If the people even let command of
the war power fall into irresponsible and unscrupulous hands, the courts wield
no power equal to its restraint. The chief restraint upon those who command
the physical forces of the country, in the future as in the past, must be their*

responsibility to the political judgments of their contemporaries and to the moral judgments of history.

My duties as Justice as I see them do not require me to make a military judgment as to whether General DeWitt's evacuation and detention program was a reasonable military necessity. I do not suggest that the courts should have attempted to interfere with the Army in carrying out its task. But I do not think that they may be asked to execute a military expedient that has no place in law under the Constitution.

The emergency war power extends to activities of the government during so-called periods of peace. Technically, however, a state of war exists until a peace treaty becomes effective.

From the foregoing we have seen that economic and military emergencies may shape the law. Since we seem to live in almost a constant state of emergency, this factor adds uncertainty and instability to the law.

6   CONCLUSION

In this chapter, some of the forces and factors which influence judicial decisions have been discussed. It is not possible to predict with absolute certainty in any case the relative weight to be given them. Each case is peculiar in facts and circumstances and must be viewed in its own environment, and considered individually. Lawyers, in advising clients, must make an educated guess, many times, as to the outcome of a case. It should be readily apparent that in almost all legal disputes victory or defeat may depend on either the facts or the law. Each is variable to some extent. However, it must be recognized that "the authority to exercise judicial discretion is not an arbitrary power of the individual judge, to be exercised when, and as, his caprice, or passion, or partiality may dictate, or forsooth as his vindictiveness or his idiosyncrasies may inspire." [24] A judge may not say that he simply disagrees with a certain accepted rule of law and therefore it will not be used in his court. In many ways, the forces discussed in this chapter have a greater cumulative effect on the total process than on any particular judge in any particular case.

[24] *Smith v. Smith,* 17 N.J. Super. 131 (1951).

COURTS AND LITIGATION

1 THE STATE COURT SYSTEM

Government in the United States is based on a scheme of dual sovereignty, and the judicial branch is an essential element of government at both the state and Federal levels. Both the state and Federal court systems are created and their operations governed from three sources. First of all, constitutions provide the general framework for the court system. Second, the legislature, pursuant to constitutional authority, enacts statutes which add body to the framework. This legislation may provide for various courts, establish their jurisdiction, and deal with such problems as the tenure, selection, and duties of judges. Other legislation may establish the general rules of procedure to be used by these courts. Finally, each court promulgates its own rules of procedure within the statutory bounds set. These rules are detailed and may involve, for example, the form of a summons or the times at which various documents must be filed with the clerk of the court. Thus, a study of the court system for any particular state requires reference to its constitution, such legislation as Civil Practice Acts, and the rules of the various courts. Each state has its own terminology and arrangement for its courts but the chart which follows on page 186 is representative of the court organization of a state with a complex system.

The general jurisdiction trial court is frequently known as the "circuit court," deriving the name from times earlier in our history when the judge "rode the circuit," or in other words traveled from town to town in a certain territory over which his court had jurisdiction, hearing and deciding cases. Some states call the basic trial court the "superior court" while others call it the "district court" or "court of common pleas." In New York it is known as the "Supreme Court." The term "general jurisdiction" means that the court has the power to hear any type of case. The courts below this trial court on the chart are limited in the types of cases which they may hear and thus are referred to as "inferior courts" or courts of limited jurisdiction.

The basic trial courts at one time were divided into two branches, one known as a "court of law" and the other a "court of chancery or equity," but this is no longer the case in most states. The distinction between law and equity is discussed in section 3 of this chapter.

Many states do not have intermediate appellate courts between the trial court and the court of final resort; however, intermediate reviewing courts are usually found in the more heavily populated states. Some states call their court of last resort "Supreme Court of Appeals" or "Court of Appeals."

In states with two levels of reviewing courts, most appeals are taken to the lower of the two courts, and the highest court of the state reviews only very important cases. The lower appellate court will review the findings and rulings of the trial court on questions of fact as well as questions of law. While a party is entitled to one trial and one appeal, he may obtain a second review if the higher reviewing court, in the exercise of its discretion, agrees to such a review. The procedure for requesting a second review is to file what is called a "petition for leave to appeal" in some states and a "petition for a writ of certiorari" in others. In such a review, only questions of law are considered.

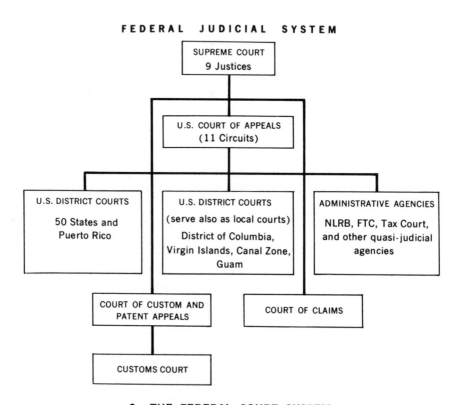

FEDERAL JUDICIAL SYSTEM

2 THE FEDERAL COURT SYSTEM

The United States Constitution, Article III, provides:

Section 1. The judicial Power of the United States, shall be vested in one supreme Court, and in such inferior Courts as the Congress may from time to time ordain and establish. . . .

Section 2. The judicial Power shall extend to all Cases, in Law and Equity, arising under this Constitution, the Laws of the United States, and Treaties made, or which shall be made, under their Authority;—to all Cases affecting Ambassadors, other public Ministers and Consuls;—to all Cases of admiralty and maritime Jurisdiction;—to Controversies to which the United States shall be a Party;—to Controversies between two or more States;—between a State and Citizens of another State; between Citizens of different States;—between Citizens of the same State claiming Lands under Grants of different States, and between a State or the Citizens thereof, and foreign States, Citizens or Subjects.

In all Cases affecting Ambassadors, other public Ministers and Consuls, and those in which a State shall be Party, the supreme Court shall have original Jurisdiction. In all the other Cases before mentioned, the supreme Court shall have appellate Jurisdiction, both as to Law and Fact, with such Exceptions, and under such Regulations as the Congress shall make. . . .

In the foregoing provision, the Constitution defines the original jurisdiction of the Supreme Court (cases which may be initiated in the Supreme Court) and authorizes Congress to establish inferior courts and to determine

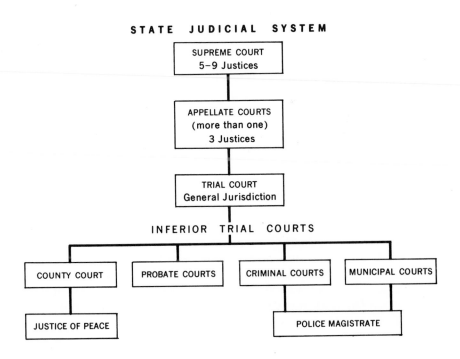

STATE   JUDICIAL   SYSTEM

their jurisdiction. It also indicates the extent of the judicial power and establishes the Federal court system as one that shall have limited jurisdiction.

Pursuant to its constitutional authorization, Congress has enacted legislation which establishes various inferior Federal courts and defines their jurisdiction. The United States Code also contains provisions concerning such matters as appellate procedure and the review of actions by administrative agencies. The Federal Rules of Civil Procedure have been adopted to provide the details concerning the procedures to be followed in litigation in the Federal courts.

Observe that the jurisdiction of the Federal courts is *limited* to only certain types of cases. The two most important of these types by far are those in which a *Federal question* is involved or in which the parties on one side of the litigation are citizens of different states from *all* the parties on the other side of the case. The latter group of cases falls under what is commonly referred to as "diversity jurisdiction." It should be noted that a corporation is a citizen of the state of incorporation *and* of the state in which it has its principal place of business, for purposes of diversity jurisdiction. In addition, access to the Federal courts in both diversity and Federal question cases is limited to those in which a sum of money in excess of $10,000 is involved. There are certain exceptions to this jurisdictional amount requirement, such as civil rights cases and others not directly involving money, but the stated dollar limitation is generally required to obtain access to the Federal system.

It is possible to transfer from the state court system to the Federal court system under three circumstances. First of all, a defendant sued in a state court may have his case removed to the Federal system if it meets the requirements of those cases which could have been brought in the Federal system in the first instance. In other words, if the case involves a Federal question or if there is diversity of citizenship and the requisite amount is involved, the case may be removed by a defendant to the Federal district court. Second, a party may appeal from a decision of the highest court of a state to the Supreme Court of the United States if (a) the case involves the validity of a treaty or statute of the United States and the decision is against its validity, or (b) the case involves the validity of a state statute against the charge that it violates the United States Constitution and the decision is in favor of its validity. Third, a party may seek review of the decision of a highest court of a state by writ of certiorari where a Federal question is involved. In such cases, the Supreme Court has discretion as to whether or not it will review the case, as contrasted with those situations listed above in which the appeal, if properly perfected, is a matter of right. Writs of certiorari are granted only in cases of substantial Federal importance or where there is an obvious conflict between decisions of two or more

Circuit Courts of Appeal in an area of the law which needs clarification. Certiorari may be granted before or after the decision of the Circuit Court of Appeals.

A case which is filed in the Federal court system may be held in abeyance and the litigants directed to try their case in the state court. This is true even if a Federal question is involved under a doctrine known as "abstention." This doctrine is invoked to allow the state to decide state issues prior to the Federal court's deciding Federal issues, especially where the state decision may end the litigation. The doctrine allows Federal courts to eliminate guesswork on the meaning of local laws and is designed to further harmonious relations between state and Federal courts. The state court may decide the Federal question if the parties so desire or it may leave the Federal question to the Federal courts. In the event the state court decides the Federal question, the losing party may appeal to the United States Supreme Court.

Many cases, such as those involving injunctions, are heard by three judges at the district court (trial) level. When a case is heard by three judges, appeal is taken directly to the Supreme Court. However, as is true in those states which have appellate courts, most decisions do not come from three judge courts and are reviewed by a Court of Appeals and not by the Supreme Court. Since litigants are entitled to one review as a matter of right, parties may obtain additional review of decisions only if the Court of Appeals holds a state statute to be unconstitutional or contrary to Federal law or upon the granting of a writ of certiorari by the Supreme Court. In addition, the Supreme Court will review questions of law certified to it for decision by the Court of Appeals. The Federal court system is thus limited in types of cases it will entertain originally and in the types of cases which it will review either by appeal or certiorari. As explained in a prior chapter, there is no Federal common law.

The chart on page 187 illustrates the Federal judicial system, including the administrative agencies.

3   LAW AND EQUITY

Courts having general jurisdiction in the United States have traditionally been divided into courts of law and courts of equity. Some states historically had two separate courts and others simply had one court with one side known as law and the other side known as equity or chancery.

Courts of law were developed early in English jurisprudence to handle cases such as the various forms of trespass, other torts, and breach of contract. These courts were concerned with legal disputes wherein one party was seeking dollar damages from another. Courts of law were not equipped to give remedies such as requiring a person to do or not to do something.

In those situations where courts of law were inadequate to furnish the desired relief, a practice developed of petitioning the King of England for such relief. As the number of such petitions grew, the King delegated his authority in granting or denying the petitions to his Chancellor. The name chancery is derived from this situation. Since the action taken was originally taken by the King, the results were not a matter of right but in each case rested in the grace and favor of the King; or, by modern terminology, the decisions were strictly discretionary.

The concept of equity did not originate in England, however. Aristotle had defined equity to be the "correction of the law, where, by reason of its universality, it is deficient." The purpose of equity has always been to supply defects in the law. When courts of chancery were growing and developing in England, the courts of law strenuously objected, but the need for supplemental legal procedures where courts of law were inadequate assisted the steady growth of equity.

Courts of chancery or equity were firmly entrenched in English jurisprudence by the time the American court system was developed. Those who established our courts recognized the need for resort to natural principles to define and interpret positive law and to remedy its defects and they therefore provided for equity jurisprudence.

In recent years, Federal law and many state laws have attempted to abolish the distinctions between law and equity. These attempts have affected the procedural aspects of the distinction but have not changed its substantive aspects. These attempts have combined the procedures of law and equity into one action known as a "civil action," and in doing so, they have generally used the equitable concepts and adopted them for actions at law. The influence of equity has predominated over law where the procedures have been combined.

Notwithstanding statements that the distinctions between law and equity have been abolished, since the historical substantive distinctions are still important, it is usually necessary to decide whether an action would have been "at law" or "in chancery," and many states require that the pleading so indicate.

Many matters are dependent on whether the action is legal or equitable in nature. For example, cases in chancery, with a few exceptions such as will contests, are not tried before a jury; the court, or in a few states a person appointed by it, known as a "master in chancery," serves as the trier and finder of the facts. Thus, the nature of the action will decide whether a party has a right to a trial by jury.

Equity jurisdiction is used in those cases where the remedy at law is deemed inadequate; that is, where dollar damages are not an adequate remedy, a court of chancery will entertain the case. Such cases as suits for an accounting; cancellation, rescission, or reformation of a contract; injunctions; partition suits; suits to quiet title; and suits for specific performance are litigated in chancery.

Courts of equity use maxims instead of rules of law. Strictly speaking, there are no legal rights in equity, for the decision is to be based on moral rights and natural justice. A court of equity is a court of conscience in which precedent is secondary to natural justice.

Some of the typical maxims of equity are:

1 "Equity will not suffer a right to exist without a remedy."
2 "Equity regards as done that which ought to be done."
3 "Where there is equal equity, the law must prevail."
4 "He who comes into equity must do so with clean hands."
5 "He who seeks equity must do equity."
6 "Equity aids the vigilant."
7 "Equality is equity."

These maxims serve as guides to the chancellor to use in exercising his discretion. For example, the clean hands doctrine (no. 4) prohibits a party who is guilty of misconduct in the matter in litigation from receiving the aid of a court of conscience. Maxim 6 is the equity version of the statute of limitations establishing a concept known as "laches." Thus if, by lapse of time, it would be inequitable to grant relief, this maxim will govern. Maxim 2 is the basis of the remedy of specific performance.

Equity jurisprudence has played an ever-increasing role in our system of jurisprudence, from the time the King of England delegated the decisions in his petitions to the present, and it will continue to do so. The movement toward social justice will require more reliance on the equitable maxims and less reliance on rigid rules of law. This will also contribute to the further decay of the doctrine of stare decisis.

4 JURISDICTION OF COURTS

Jurisdiction refers to the power of a court to hear a case. To have the power to hear a case, the court must have jurisdiction over the subject matter of the case and jurisdiction over the parties to the case. Jurisdiction over the subject matter is present if the case is of the type which the court is authorized to hear. This is not a problem with state courts of general jurisdiction but is involved in cases before the inferior state courts and can be an issue in all Federal cases because, as previously noted, all Federal courts are courts of limited jurisdiction. For example, a Federal court would not have jurisdiction over the subject matter of a breach of contract suit for $5,000 damages between citizens of different states because of lack of the jurisdictional amount. If the amount were $15,000 and the parties were citizens of the same state, the Federal court would still have no power to hear the case because of lack of diversity of citizenship. Similarly, a state probate court would lack the power to hear a murder case.

Jurisdiction over the person of the plaintiff is obtained by his filing the suit. Such action is the voluntary submission to the power of the court. Jurisdiction over the person of the defendant is usually obtained by the service of a summons on him, although in some cases it is obtained by publication of notice and mailing a summons to his last known address. Service of summons on the defendant usually is valid if it is served upon any member of his household above a specified age and another copy addressed to him is mailed to the home. This procedure recognizes the practical difficulties which may exist in finding the defendant and at the same time accomplishes the goal of the summons which is simply to give the defendant fair notice of the suit. For many years, it was felt that a summons could not be properly served beyond the borders of the state in which it was issued. However, this concept has changed and most states now have "long-arm" statutes which provide for the service of process beyond their boundaries.

The following case developed the legal theory which made long-arm statutes possible.

INTERNATIONAL SHOE CO. V. WASHINGTON
326 U.S. 310 (1945)

The State of Washington filed suit against International Shoe Company to collect unemployment compensation taxes it claimed were due because of certain commissions paid to employees of the shoe company who worked in Washington. The suit was initiated by serving a copy of the process on an employee of the company in the state. A notice of suit was also sent to the company by registered mail at its home office.

At the time of this action, International Shoe Company was a Delaware corporation with its principal place of business in Missouri. It had no office in Washington and made no contracts either for sale or purchase of merchandise there. It maintained no stock of merchandise in that state and made no deliveries of goods in intrastate commerce there. During the years from 1937 to 1940, it employed eleven to thirteen salesmen under direct supervision and control of sales managers located in St. Louis. These salesmen resided in Washington; their principal activities were confined to that state; and they were compensated by commissions which totaled over $31,000 per year based upon the amount of their sales. The salesmen only had authority to solicit orders which were accepted or rejected in Missouri and filled by shipment of goods in interstate commerce from places other than Washington. Occasionally they rented rooms for exhibiting samples and these costs were reimbursed by the company. International Shoe contended that the method attempted by Washington to obtain jurisdiction over the person of the company did not meet the procedural requirement of due process of law as set by the Fourteenth Amendment, and hence Washington had no power to sue for the tax. In other words, the shoe company argued that a salesman was not a proper agent of the company to receive personal service of process, since his authority had no connection with its legal activities; that the company itself was not in the state of Washington; and that the notice sent by registered mail was not personally served and had no force or effect outside the borders of the state of Washington. The Supreme Court of Washington held that the activities of International Shoe were sufficient to constitute doing business in that state and to subject the company to suit there. The defendant company appealed to the Supreme Court of the United States, since the application of the Federal Constitution was in issue.

STONE, CHIEF JUSTICE: Historically the jurisdiction of courts to render judgment in personam is grounded on their de facto power over the defendant's person. Hence his presence within the territorial jurisdiction of a court was prerequisite to its rendition of a judgment personally binding him. But now that the capias ad respondendum [1] has given way to personal service of summons or other form of notice, due process requires only that in order to subject a defendant to a judgment in personam, if he be not present within the territory of the forum, he have certain minimum contacts with it such that the maintenance of the suit does not offend "traditional notions of fair play and substantial justice. . . ."

Since the corporate personality is a fiction, although a fiction intended to be acted upon as though it were a fact, it is clear that unlike an individual its "presence" without, as well as within, the state of its origin can be manifested only by activities carried on in its behalf by those who are authorized to act for it. . . . The terms "present" or "presence" are used merely to symbolize those activities of the corporation's agent within the state which courts will deem to be sufficient to satisfy the demands of due process. Those demands may be met by such contacts of the corporation with the state of the forum as make it reasonable, in the context of our federal system of government, to require the corporation to defend the particular suit which is brought there. An "estimate of the inconveniences"

[1] A *capias ad respondendum* is "a judicial writ (usually simply termed a 'capias' . . .) by which actions at law were frequently commenced; and which commands the sheriff to *take* the defendant, and him safely keep, so that he may have his body before the court on a certain day to *answer* the plaintiff in the action. . . ." *Black's Law Dictionary* 262 (4th ed., 1951).

which would result to the corporation from a trial away from its "home" or principal place of business is relevant in this connection.

"Presence" in the state in this sense has never been doubted when the activities of the corporation there have not only been continuous and systematic, but also give rise to the liabilities sued on, even though no consent to be sued or authorization to an agent to accept service of process has been given. . . . Conversely it has been generally recognized that the casual presence of the corporate agent or even his conduct of single or isolated items of activities in a state in the corporation's behalf are not enough to subject it to suit on causes of action unconnected with the activities there. . . . To require the corporation in such circumstances to defend the suit away from its home or other jurisdiction where it carries on more substantial activities has been thought to lay too great and unreasonable a burden on the corporation to comport with due process. . . .

It is evident that the criteria by which we mark the boundary line between those activities which justify the subjection of a corporation to suit, and those which do not, cannot be simply mechanical or quantitative. The test is not merely, as has sometimes been suggested, whether the activity, which the corporation has seen fit to procure through its agents in another state, is a little more or a little less. Whether due process is satisfied must depend rather upon the quality and nature of the activity in relation to the fair and orderly administration of the laws which it was the purpose of the due process clause to insure. That clause does not contemplate that a state may make binding a judgment in personam against an individual or corporate defendant with which the state has no contacts, ties, or relations.

But to the extent that a corporation exercises the privilege of conducting activities within a state, it enjoys the benefits and protection of the laws of that state. The exercise of that privilege may give rise to obligations; and, so far as those obligations arise out of or are connected with the activities within the state, a procedure which requires the corporation to respond to a suit brought to enforce them can, in most instances, hardly be said to be undue. . . .

Applying these standards, the activities carried on in behalf of appellant in the State of Washington were neither irregular nor casual. They were systematic and continuous throughout the years in question. They resulted in a large volume of interstate business, in the course of which appellant received the benefits and protection of the laws of the state, including the right to resort to the courts for the enforcement of its rights. The obligation which is here sued upon arose out of those very activities. It is evident that those operations establish sufficient contacts or ties with the state of the forum to make it reasonable and just according to our traditional conception of fair play and substantial justice to permit the state to enforce the obligations which appellant has incurred there. Hence we cannot say that the maintenance of the present suit in the State of Washington involves an unreasonable or undue procedure. [AFFIRMED]

Subsequent to this decision, states have adopted statutes giving extra-territorial effect to process. Typical statutory provisions are as follows:

Section 16, Illinois Civil Practice Act. Personal service outside State.

(1) *Personal service of summons may be made upon any party outside the State. If upon a citizen or resident of this State or upon a person who has submitted to the jurisdiction of the courts of this State, it shall have the force and effect of personal service of summons within this State; otherwise, it shall have the force and effect of service by publication. . . .*

Section 17. Illinois Civil Practice Act. Act submitting to jurisdiction—Process.

(1) *Any person, whether or not a citizen or resident of this State, who in person or through an agent does any of the acts hereinafter enumerated, thereby submits said person, and, if an individual, his personal representative, to the jurisdiction of the courts of this State as to any cause of action arising from the doing of any of said acts:*

    (a) *The transaction of any business within this State;*

    (b) *The commission of a tortious act within this State;*

    (c) *The ownership, use, or possession of any real estate situated in this State;*

    (d) *Contracting to insure any person, property or risk located within this State at the time of contracting.*

    (e) *With respect to actions of divorce and separate maintenance, the maintenance in this State of a matrimonial domicile at the time the cause of action arose or the commission in this State of any act giving rise to the cause of action.*

(2) *Service of process upon any person who is subject to the jurisdiction of the courts of this State, as provided in this section, may be made by personally serving the summons upon the defendant outside this State, as provided in this Act, with the same force and effect as though summons had been personally served within this State.*

(3) *Only causes of action arising from acts enumerated herein may be asserted against a defendant in an action in which jurisdiction over him is based upon this section.*

The case which follows illustrates that not all activities are within the application of a modern long-arm statute.

SALETKO V. WILLYS MOTORS, INC.
183 N.E.2d 569 (III. 1962)

MURPHY, JUSTICE: In this appeal the principal question is whether the non-resident defendant, Willys Motors, Inc., a Pennsylvania corporation, transacted "any business" within the State of Illinois sufficient to submit defendant "to the jurisdiction of the courts of this state." The trial court decided that it did, and the matter proceeded to a judgment. Defendant appeals.

Plaintiffs filed their complaint in the Circuit Court of Cook County, Illinois. Service of summons was made upon defendant by serving a Toledo office employee of defendant, while he was temporarily in Chicago attending the annual Chicago automobile show, where motor vehicles manufactured by defendant were on display. His duties, responsibilities, and authority were limited to keeping the vehicles on display clean and in good condition, and arranging for the replacement of missing parts. At no time had this employee engaged in any facet of the transaction between plaintiffs and defendant.

Defendant filed its special appearance and motion to quash service of process for lack of jurisdiction over the person of defendant, supported by affidavits setting forth the reasons. After oral argument the motion was overruled, and defendant answered, denied jurisdiction of the court over the person of defendant, and pleaded to the merits of the complaint.

From the allegations of the complaint and defendant's affidavits filed in support of its motion to quash, to which plaintiffs did not file counter-affidavits, it appears that in July, 1958, defendant mailed an invitation from its office at Toledo, Ohio, to plaintiffs in Chicago, to bid for the purchase of surplus automotive parts, including 648 shafts. Plaintiffs, by a letter to defendant at Toledo, made a bid on the shafts of $1.79 each, or a total of $1,159.92. Defendant, by letter, informed plaintiffs that the offer to purchase the shafts was accepted. Under date of August 29, 1958, plaintiffs forwarded to defendant at Toledo plaintiffs' certified check for $1,159.92, together with a letter in which plaintiffs stated that the shafts would be picked up by "our truck the early part of this week."

On September 4, 1958, an employee of defendant telephoned plaintiffs that the number of shafts in stock was only 60 rather than 648. During this telephone conversation, it was agreed that plaintiffs would accept the 60 shafts, and defendant would return the excess balance of the purchase price. Later, on the same day, the 60 shafts were picked up by Truck Transport Company for shipment to Chicago.

On this same day, after the shafts had been turned over to the trucking company and were in transit, plaintiffs telephoned defendant in Toledo that plaintiffs would not accept the 60 shafts and demanded delivery of the 648. Defendant subsequently mailed plaintiffs its check for $1,052.52, being the excess payment. From the record it appears that this check was not accepted by plaintiffs. Plaintiffs' complaint alleges damages of $8,100, which includes $6,940.08 lost profits, because defendant failed to ship the 648 shafts.

As defendant's answer admitted that it owed plaintiffs the sum of $1,052.52, and the case was returned to the trial court to be heard in the regular course of the calendar. Defendant appeals from the judgment on the pleadings, and from the order denying its motion to quash service of process and to dismiss the cause for lack of jurisdiction over the person of defendant.

Defendant asserts that the cause of action, upon which the orders and partial judgment are based, did not arise out of the transaction by defendant or any of its agents of "any business" in Illinois, or the commission of any other act which would submit defendant "personally" to the jurisdiction of the Illinois courts under Section 17 (a) of the Civil Practice Act.

Of the various forms of activity set forth in Section 17(1), by which the defendant might be deemed to have submitted itself to the jurisdiction of the Illinois courts, only subsection (1) (a) is relevant here. Section 17 (1) (a) provides:

> (1) *Any person, whether or not a citizen or resident of this State, who in person or through an agent does any of the acts hereinafter enumerated, thereby submits said person, and, if an individual, his personal representative, to the jurisdiction of the courts of this State as to any cause of action arising from the doing of any of said acts:*
>
> (a) *The transaction of any business within this State.*

Plaintiffs contend that the actions of defendant constituted transaction of business within this state, submitting defendant to its jurisdiction. . . .

Defendant contends that where the contacts of a defendant with Illinois are solely by mail, telephone, or delivery of merchandise to independent carriers outside of Illinois for shipment into this state, the courts have refused to extend *in personam* jurisdiction under Section 17 (1) (a), without a showing of the physical presence of a defendant or its agents in Illinois, in connection with the transaction out of which the cause of action arose. . . .

The performance of jurisdictional acts, by defendant or its agents while physically present in Illinois, is essential for submission to the jurisdiction of the courts of this state under Section 17(1) (a).

Defendant's affidavits show that at the time of the instant transaction defendant did not maintain any office or place of business in Illinois, had no officer, employee, agent or representative residing in or soliciting orders in Illinois. It was not qualified to do business in this state, and no part of the transaction was performed by defendant or any of its agents while physically present in Illinois. The transaction involved a limited correspondence and two telephone calls between Chicago and Toledo. The affidavits indicate that the shafts were delivered, outside of this state, to the trucking company, plaintiffs' agent, for shipment to plaintiff.

The activities of an employee of defendant at the automobile show in Chicago, which were subsequent to and not a part of the instant alleged cause of action, did not constitute the "transaction of any business" within the due process limitations set forth in *International Shoe Co. v. Washington*, 326 U.S. 310, 66 S.Ct. 154. We conclude that this record does not affirmatively show the "transaction of any business" in Illinois sufficient to subject defendant to *in personam* jurisdiction of the courts of this state.

As defendant timely challenged the jurisdiction of the Circuit Court of Cook County over the person of defendant, we are of the opinion that the trial court should have sustained defendant's motion to quash service of process and dismiss the action against defendant.

For the reasons given, the judgment against defendant for the sum of $1,052.52 is reversed and the cause is remanded to the Circuit Court of Cook County with directions to sustain defendant's motion to quash the service of process and to dismiss the action against defendant. [REVERSED AND REMANDED WITH DIRECTIONS]

The foregoing discussion of jurisdiction was in relation to civil suits. In criminal suits, the crime must have been committed within the state for the court to have jurisdiction of the subject matter of the case. Jurisdiction of the person of the defendant is obtained by arrest. In the event of arrest in a state other than that in which the crime was committed, extradition is necessary. This is obtained by the voluntary act of the governor of the state of arrest in turning the prisoner over to the governor of the requesting state. Extradition is thus discretionary with the executive branch of government. However, in those states which have adopted the Uniform Extradition Act, which details extradition proceedings, it is the stated statutory duty of the governor to have arrested and deliver up to the executive authority of any other state of the United States, any person charged in that state with treason, felony, or other crime who has fled from justice and is found in the former state.

5   VENUE

A question similar to jurisdiction refers to the place or court in which the lawsuit should be brought or what is the proper *venue*. While jurisdiction determines if a court has the *power* to hear a case, venue determines whether a court *should* hear the case when any one of several courts might technically have jurisdiction. A typical venue statute provides that suit must be commenced in the county of residence of any defendant who is joined in good faith and with probable cause for the purpose of obtaining a judgment against him and not solely for the purpose of fixing venue in that county, or in the county in which the transaction or some part thereof occurred out of which the cause of action arose. Actions against nonresidents can usually be commenced in any county which has jurisdiction, with jurisdiction being obtained under a long-arm statute. Domestic corporations and foreign corporations authorized to do business in a state are usually considered to be residents of any county in which they have a registered office or are doing business. Foreign corporations not authorized to do business are usually treated as nonresidents. Similar rules usually exist for partnerships, and they are generally considered to be residents of any county in which a partner resides, in which there is a partnership office, or in which the partnership does business. Thus venue statutes provide, as one of two possibilities for the proper forum for a lawsuit, the place of residence of the defendant, and define where this is.

Most venue statutes have special provisions relating to suits involving real estate which require the suit to be brought in the county in which the real estate is located. Special provisions frequently allow suits against insurance companies in the county in which the plaintiff resides.

A defendant may object to the venue for several reasons. First of all, he may complain that the requirements of the venue statute as discussed above are not met. This will not usually be the case because as noted, the statutes are specific and relatively clear. Venue may also be objected to on the ground of prejudice of either the judge or in some cases the probable jury to be selected. The latter objection is frequently made in a criminal trial which has been the subject of substantial publicity. For example, the conviction of Jack Ruby for killing Lee Harvey Oswald was reversed in part because the defendant Ruby could not have a fair trial in Dallas County, Texas, and the court erred in denying his motion for a change of venue. Motions for a change of venue based on the prejudice of the trial judge must usually be supported by affidavit but are granted as a matter of right if in proper form. It must be noted that failure to object to the venue is a waiver, and the trial may proceed if the court where the suit was brought has jurisdiction, in spite of the provisions of the venue statute, or constitutional requirements of due process.

Another ground for a change of venue is the doctrine of *forum non conveniens*. The defendant may attempt to involve this principle, which literally means that the place of trial is not convenient, in cases in which the plaintiff has attempted to have the suit tried in a county which produces juries known for large verdicts. The case which follows illustrates the application of the doctrine of *forum non conveniens*.

GULF OIL CORP. V. GILBERT
330 U.S. 501 (1947)

An explosion occurred in Lynchburg, Virginia, and the plaintiff brought suit for $365,529.77 against the defendant in New York City. The defendant invoked the doctrine of *forum non conveniens,* claiming that the appropriate place for trial was Virginia where the plaintiff lived and the defendant did business, where all events in litigation took place, where most of the witnesses resided, and where both state and Federal courts were available to plaintiff and were able to obtain jurisdiction of the defendant. Plaintiff contended that the amount of damages involved was so large that it would stagger the imagination of a local jury unaccustomed to dealing with such sums. The district court in New York allowed the defendant's motion to dismiss, but the Court of Appeals reversed. The Supreme Court granted certiorari.

I

JACKSON, JUSTICE: It is conceded that the venue statutes of the United States permitted the plaintiff to commence his action in the Southern District of New York and empower that court to entertain it. But that does not settle the question whether it must do so. . . .

This Court, in one form of words or another, has repeatedly reorganized the existence of the power to decline jurisdiction in exceptional circumstances. As formulated by Mr. Justice Brandeis, the rule is:

> *Obviously, the proposition that a court having jurisdiction must exercise it, is not universally true; else the admiralty court could never decline jurisdiction on the ground that the litigation is between foreigners. Nor is it true of courts administering other systems of our law. Courts of equity and of law also occasionally decline, in the interest of justice, to exercise jurisdiction, where the suit is between aliens or nonresidents, or where for kindred reasons the litagation can more appropriately be conducted in a foreign tribunal.* Canada Malting Co. v. Paterson Steamships, Ltd., 285 U.S. 413. . . .

We later expressly said that a state court "may in appropriate cases apply the doctrine of *forum non conveniens."* . . .

In all cases in which the doctrine of *forum non conveniens* comes into play, it presupposes at least two forums in which the defendant is amenable to process; the doctrine furnishes criteria for choice between then.

II

The principle of *forum non conveniens* is simply that a court may resist imposition upon its jurisdiction even when jurisdiction is authorized by the letter of a general venue statute. These statutes are drawn with a necessary generality and usually give a plaintiff a choice of courts, so that he may be quite sure of some place in which to pursue his remedy. But the open door may admit those who seek not simply justice but perhaps justice blended with some harassment. A plaintiff sometimes is under temptation to resort to a strategy of forcing the trial at a most inconvenient place for an adversary, even at some inconvenience to himself.

Many of the states have met misuse of venue by investing courts with a discretion to change the place of trial on various grounds, such as the convenience of witnesses and the ends of justice. The federal law contains no such express criteria to guide the district court in exercising its power. But the problem is a very old one affecting the administration of the courts as well as the rights of litigants, and both in England and in this country the common law worked out techniques and criteria for dealing with it.

Wisely, it has not been attempted to catalogue the circumstances which will justify or require either grant or denial of remedy. The doctrine leaves much to the discretion of the court to which plaintiff resorts, and experience has not shown a judicial tendency to renounce one's own jurisdiction so strong as to result in many abuses.

If the combination and weight of factors requisite to given results are difficult to forecast or state, those to be considered are not difficult to name. An interest to be considered, and the one likely to be most pressed, is the private interest of the litigant. Important considerations are the relative ease of access to sources of proof; availability of compulsory process for attendance of unwilling, and the cost of obtaining attendance of willing, witnesses; possibility of view of premises, if view would be appropriate to the action; and all other practical problems that make trial of a case easy, expeditious and inexpensive. There may also be questions as to the enforceability of a judgment if one is obtained. The court will weigh relative advantages and obstacles to fair trial. It is often said that the plaintiff may not, by choice of an inconvenient forum, "vex," "harass," or "oppress" the defendant by inflicting upon him expense or trouble not necessary to his own right to pursue his remedy. But unless the balance is strongly in favor of the defendant, the plaintiff's choice of forum should rarely be disturbed.

Factors of public interest also have place in applying the doctrine. Administrative difficulties follow for courts when litigation is piled up in congested centers instead of being handled at its origin. Jury duty is a burden that ought not to be imposed upon the people of a community which has no relation to the litigation. In cases which touch the affairs of many persons, there is reason for holding the trial in their view and reach rather than in remote parts of the country where they can learn of it by report only. There is a local interest in having localized controversies decided at home. There is an appropriateness, too, in having the trial of a diversity case in a forum that is at home with the state law that must govern the case, rather than having a court in some other forum untangle problems in conflict of laws, and in law foreign to itself. . . .

III

Turning to the question whether this is one of those rather rare cases where the doctrine should be applied, (in view of the facts) . . . we are convinced that the District Court did not exceed its powers or the bounds of its discretion in dismissing plaintiff's complaint and remitting him to the courts of his own community. The Circuit Court of Appeals took too restrictive a view of the doctrine as approved by this Court. Its judgment is reversed. [REVERSED]

6   CREATION OF LEGAL ISSUES

Most lawsuits are commenced by the plaintiff filing a pleading called a "complaint" with the clerk of the court. The clerk issues a summons which, together with a copy of the complaint, is served on the defendant by leaving it either with him personally or with some member of his family, if the law so provides. The summons notifies the defendant of the date he is required to file his pleading, usually called an "answer," or his appearance in the suit. The defendant's answer will either admit or deny each allegation of the plaintiff's complaint and may contain affirmative defenses which will defeat the plaintiff's claim. The answer may also contain causes of action the defendant has against the plaintiff, called "counterclaims." Upon receipt of the defendant's answer, the plaintiff will, unless the applicable rules of procedure do not so require, file a reply which specifically admits or denies each allegation of the defendant's answer. The factual issues of a lawsuit are thus formed by one party's making an allegation and the other party's either admitting it or denying it. Pleadings give notice of each party's contentions and serve to set the boundary lines of the litigation.

Not all lawsuits involve questions of fact. In many cases the parties may be in complete agreement as to the facts, in which case the issue to be decided is the legal effect of these facts. Such cases involve only questions of law. Questions of law may be raised at several stages of the lawsuit.

First of all, the defendant may, instead of filing an answer, file a pleading, which at common law was called a "general demurrer" but which today is usually called a "motion to dismiss for failure to state a cause of action or a claim for relief." By this pleading the defendant in effect says to the court: "Even if everything the plaintiff says in his complaint is true, he is not entitled to the relief he seeks." For example, in a state where mental cruelty is not a ground for divorce, a divorce complaint which seeks a divorce on the grounds of mental cruelty would be dismissed on the filing of such a motion, and the litigation would end unless the plaintiff would thereafter file an amended complaint properly alleging a ground on which a divorce might be granted.

In addition to a motion to dismiss for failure to state a cause of action, a defendant may also move to dismiss the suit for reasons which as a matter of law prevent the plaintiff from winning his suit. Such matters as a release in bankruptcy, lack of jurisdiction of the court to hear the suit, or expiration of the time limit during which the defendant is subject to suit may be raised by such a motion. These are matters of a technical nature which raise questions of law for the court's decision.

Most states and the Federal courts have procedures where either party may submit the case for final decision by procedures known as "motions for summary judgment" or "motions for judgment on the pleadings." In these hearings, the court examines all papers on file in the case, including affidavits that may have been filled with the motion or in opposition to it, to see if a genuine material issue of fact remains. If there is no such question of fact, the court will then decide the legal question raised by the facts and find for one party or the other.

It should be kept in mind that all the above discussion refers to matters which occur prior to any trial of the case. As the trial itself proceeds, the questions of fact raised by the pleadings may be resolved, leaving only questions of law. If the case is being tried by a jury, a party moves to take the case from the jury by asking the judge to direct a verdict. The court can only direct a verdict if the evidence taken in the light most favorable to the party resisting the motion establishes as a matter of law that the moving party is entitled to a verdict. Either party may make such a motion, although it is usually used by defendants to argue that the plaintiff has failed to prove each allegation of his complaint. Just as a plaintiff must *allege* certain facts or have his complaint dismissed by motion to dismiss, he must have some *proof* of each essential allegation, or lose his case on a motion for a directed verdict.

In cases tried without a jury, either party may move for a finding in his favor. Such a motion will be allowed during the course of the trial if the result is not in doubt. While the judge on such motions weighs the evidence, he may end the trial only if there is no room for a fair difference of opinion as to the result.

Finally, questions of law may be raised after the trial proper is completed by motions seeking such relief as a new trial or a judgment notwithstanding the verdict of the jury. A motion seeking a new trial may be granted if the judge feels that the verdict of the jury is contrary to the manifest weight of the evidence. The court may enter a judgment opposite to that of the verdict of the jury if the judge finds that the verdict is, as a matter of law, erroneous. To reach such a conclusion, the court must find that reasonable men viewing the evidence could not reach the verdict returned. For example, a verdict for the plaintiff may be based on sympathy instead of evidence. Thus, the results of lawsuits may turn on procedural questions of law such as those raised by the pleadings or evidence. These questions of law are the sole province of the court to resolve.

7   DISCOVERY PROCEDURES

During the period that the parties are filing their pleadings and before the trial itself, modern law has provided for procedures commonly referred to as "discovery procedures." These discovery procedures have been designed to take the "sporting aspect" out of litigation and to ensure that the results of lawsuits are based on the merits of the controversy and not on the ability, skill, or cunning of counsel. Historically, an attorney who had no case on the facts or law could win a lawsuit through surprise by keeping silent about a fact or by concealing his true case until the trial. Lawsuits should not be based on the skill or lack thereof of counsel, but on the relative merits of the controversy. Discovery practice is designed to ensure that each side is fully aware of all the facts involved in the case and of the intentions of the parties, prior to trial. One of its avowed purposes is to encourage settlement of suits and to avoid actual trial.

Discovery practices include the taking of the deposition of other parties and witnesses, the serving of written questions to be answered under oath by the opposite party, compulsory physical examinations by doctors chosen by the other party, orders requiring the production of exhibits, documents, maps, photographs, etc., and the serving by one party on another of demands to admit facts under oath. (Some courts, those of Illinois for example, have gone as far as to allow the discovery of the amount of insurance coverage possessed by the defendant in a personal injury case.) The following Federal rule on the scope of inquiry at depositions is illustrative of the modern thinking about discovery procedures.

1954   FEDERAL RULES OF CIVIL PROCEDURE—26 (b)

Scope of Examination . . . the deponent may be examined regarding any matter, not privileged, which is relevant to the subject matter involved in the pending action, whether it relates to the claim or defense of the examining party or to the claim or defense of any other party, including the existence, description, nature, custody, condition and location of any books, documents, or other tangible things and the identity and location of persons having knowledge of relevant facts. It is not ground for objection that the testimony will be inadmissible at the trial if the testimony sought appears reasonably calculated to lead to the discovery of admissible evidence. . . .

8 CONDUCT OF A TRIAL

In addition to questions of law, most lawsuits involve questions of fact. Such cases as automobile negligence actions and criminal proceedings are essentially questions of fact. Suits at law and criminal actions have traditionally been tried before a jury, while suits in equity have been considered too complicated for juries and as a general rule the questions of fact have been found by the master in chancery. It should be noted that juries are sometimes used in chancery cases to serve as the trier of the facts.

For purposes of examining a trial, we shall assume a typical suit for dollar damages either in tort or contract being tried before a jury. As the case is called, the first order of business is to select a jury. Prior to the calling of the case, the clerk of the court will have summoned prospective jurors. Their names will be drawn at random from lists of eligible citizens and twelve of them will be selected or called into the jury box for the conduct of *voir dire* examination. *Voir dire* examination is simply a method by which the court and the attorneys for each party examine the jurors as to their qualifications and ability to hear the case. Each side in the lawsuit may challenge or excuse a juror for cause. In addition, each side will be given a certain number of challenges known as "peremptory challenges" for which no cause need be given. Each side is given an opportunity to examine the jurors and either to accept them or to reject them until his challenges are exhausted. The prospective jurors are sworn to give truthful answers to the questions on *voir dire*. The processes continue until the full jury is selected.

After selecting the jurors to hear the case, the attorneys then make their opening statements. An opening statement is not evidence but is only used to familiarize the jury with the essential facts in the case which each side expects to prove. It is similar to the prologue of a book. In order that the jury may understand the overall picture of the case and the relevancy of each bit of evidence as presented, each side informs the jury of the facts he expects to prove and the witnesses he expects to call to make such proof. After the opening statements are made, the party with the burden of proof, which is usually the plaintiff, presents his evidence. The term "burden of proof" may be used to designate the party who has the burden of coming forward with the evidence in the first instance or it may designate the party with the burden of persuasion. These are usually the same party, typically the plaintiff for the case in chief and the defendant for affirmative defenses.

One special aspect of the burden of proof (persuasion) must be noted. In criminal cases, the state must meet the burden by proving guilt beyond a reasonable doubt. In other words, the scales of justice must be *completely* "out of balance" toward guilt. In most civil cases, the party with the burden of persuasion must prove his contentions by the preponderance or greater weight of the evidence. In terms of the scales of justice, they must be *just* "out of balance" in favor of the plaintiff for him to succeed. In a few civil cases, courts have said that the party with the burden of proof must prove his case by clear and convincing evidence. This is greater than the mere preponderance but less than beyond a reasonable doubt. It is evident that these definitions of burden of proof require very subjective judgment on the part of the jury.

Evidence is normally presented in open court by means of the examination of witnesses and the production of documents and other exhibits. Testimony at a trial is privileged and cannot result in defamation suits. The party calling a witness has a right to examine that witness and ask him questions to establish the facts with which he is familiar about the case. As a general rule, a party calling a witness is not permitted to ask "leading questions." After the party calling the witness has completed his direct examination, the other party is given the opportunity to cross-examine the witness. Matters inquired into on cross-examination are limited to those matters which were raised on direct examination. Cross-examination is an art, and the well-prepared lawyer will usually not ask a question on cross-examination to which he does not already know the answer. After the cross-examination, the party calling the witness again has the opportunity of examining the witness and this examination is called "redirect examination." It is limited to the scope of those matters gone into on cross-examination and is used to clarify matters raised on cross-examination. After redirect examination, the opposing party is allowed re-cross-examination, with the corresponding limitation as to scope of the questions. Witnesses may be asked to identify exhibits. Expert witnesses may be asked to give their opinion, within certain limitations, about the case, and sometimes experts are allowed to answer hypothetical questions. For example, a doctor in a personal injury case may be given all the evidence surrounding the accident and then be asked hypothetically whether such an occurrence might have or could have caused the injury which the plaintiff suffers.

After the party with the burden of proof has presented his evidence, the opposing party usually makes the motion for a directed verdict, as heretofore mentioned. If the motion for directed verdict is overruled, the defendant then presents his evidence. The order of examination of these witnesses is the same as those for the plaintiff. The party calling a witness vouches for his credibility. He is not allowed to impeach witnesses which he has called. After the defendant had presented all his evidence, the original party may bring in rebuttal evidence. When neither party has any additional evidence, the attorneys and the judge retire for a conference to consider the instructions to be given the jury.

The purpose of the jury instructions is to acquaint the jury with the law applicable to the case. As previously stated, the function of the jury is to find the facts and the function of the court is to determine the applicable law. The purpose of the jury instructions is to bring these two together in an orderly manner that will result in a decision. At the conference, each attorney submits to the court instructions which he feels should be given to the jury. The court examines these instructions and confers with the attorneys. He then decides which instructions will be given to the jury. A typical jury instruction follows:

The plaintiff in his complaint has alleged that he was injured as the proximate cause of the negligence of the defendant and that the plaintiff was in exercise of due care and caution for his own safety at the time of the occurrence. If you find from the evidence that the plaintiff was guilty of negligence, which proximately caused his injuries, then your verdict will be for the defendant.

In this instruction, the court is in effect saying that the plaintiff must prove that he was not at fault and if you find that he was at fault your verdict must be for the defendant. Thus the concept of contributory negligence is applied to the facts and the jury is instructed as to the result to be returned if they find certain facts.

After the conference on jury instructions, the attorneys argue the case to the jury. The party with the burden of proof, usually the plaintiff, is given an opportunity to open the argument and to close it. The defendant's attorney is only allowed to argue after the plaintiff's argument and is only allowed to argue once. After the arguments are completed, the court reads the instructions to the jury and the jury retires to deliberate. Upon reaching a verdict the jury returns from the jury room, announces its verdict, and judgment is entered. Thereafter the losing party starts the procedure of posttrial motions and appeals. Any final decision of the court, whether on a motion made before trial, during the trial, or after the trial, or on the court's judgment or decree, may be appealed within certain prescribed time limits. If the appeal is perfected according to law, the right of review is absolute.

9 RULES OF EVIDENCE

In the conduct of a trial, the rules of evidence govern the admissibility of testimony and exhibits, and establish which facts may be presented to the jury and which facts may not. It is a lawyer's problem to be concerned with the specific rules of evidence but an understanding of the areas in which these rules operate will give some insight into the workings of our judicial system.

One of the major rules for excluding evidence is based on what the law calls "privileged communications" or "privilege." Nearly everyone is aware that the Fifth Amendment contains a privilege against compulsory self-incrimination. In addition, communications between husband and wife, doctor and patient, clergy and penitent, and attorney and client are considered privileged by the law in order that these communications can be made without fear of their subsequent use against the parties involved. Fair play requires that an attorney not be required to testify as to matters told him in confidence by his client. The preservation of the home requires that a spouse not be required to testify against the other spouse regarding confidential communications. Some matters are privileged, such as the existence of insurance coverage of a party, because of the great effect that knowledge of the existence of insurance would have on a jury. Matters which are privileged are matters which by the rules of fair play should not be admitted into evidence.

Another basic concept of our judicial system is the right of confrontation, or the right to be confronted by the witnesses against you and to cross-examine them about their allegations or contentions. Cross-examination in open court, as a fundamental right, provides the background for the rule of evidence known as the "hearsay rule." Hearsay is an out-of-court statement which is being offered to prove the truth of the matter contained in the statement. For example, if the issue of the case were whether certain stock had been purchased, the testimony of a witness that his broker had *told* him the stock had been purchased would be hearsay. The statement is offered to prove the purchase of the stock and the *broker* is not available for cross-examination. The lack of cross-examination establishes that hearsay evidence should not be admitted. There are many exceptions to the hearsay rule. For example, if the party *himself* had made the statement, he could hardly object to the fact that he was not able to cross-examine himself and thus we have the exception for admissions against interest by a party to the suit. Testimony at a former trial at which the party was able to cross-examine and subsequent unavailability of the witness create another exception to the hearsay rule. Business entries made in the ordinary course of business constitute still another exception, and may be introduced as evidence of the facts they represent. In a criminal case a dying declaration by the victim of murder is an exception, because the effect of impending death is considered by the courts to give sufficient credibility to the truthfulness of the testimony to eliminate the need for cross-examination. There are many other exceptions to the hearsay rule, but each of them is based on the fact that cross-examination has either been had at a former time or is not required to give a fair trial in the instant case.

There are other rules of evidence, such as the rule requiring that all evidence be relevant to the matter involved in the litigation. If a person is involved in a suit for breach of contract for the sale of goods, wares, or merchandise, the fact that he has been divorced five times should have no effect on the litigation and would not be admissible evidence. It might, if presented, influence some member of the jury who had a particular dislike of divorced persons. In cases where direct testimony as to what happened is not available, evidence of habit or practice is sometimes admitted to show what probably happened, and is considered relevant.

Another rule of evidence concerns the requirement of producing the best evidence available as proof in a lawsuit. The "best evidence rule," as it is commonly referred to, pertains only to written documents. There are many other rules of evidence concerning written documents such as the "parol evidence rule," which prevents the proof of modification or change of a written document by the use of oral evidence. It can be seen from this short examination of these very elementary rules of evidence that they provide the rules of the game, so to speak, to ensure that there is a fair trial and that each party is given ample opportunity to present his contentions and his case without unduly taking advantage of the other party. They were not created to serve as a stumbling block to meritorious litigants or to create unwarranted roadblocks to justice. On the contrary, the rules of evidence were created and should be applied to ensure fair play and to aid in the goal of having controversies determined on their merits.

10   APPELLATE PROCEDURE

Sections 1 and 2 of this chapter discussed the structure of the court system including courts of review. Each state prescribes its own appellate procedure and determines the jurisdiction of its various reviewing courts. While the procedure to be followed in an appeal is essentially a problem for the lawyer, certain aspects of this procedure assist in understanding our judicial system.

Courts of review are concerned with the record of the proceedings below. All the pleadings, testimony, and motions are reduced to a written record, which is filed with the court of review to enable it to study the issues, testimony, and proceedings in order to determine whether prejudicial errors occurred or whether the lower court reached an erroneous result. In addition to the record, each party files a brief (the appellant may file a reply brief on receipt of the appellee's brief) which contains a short description of the nature of the case, the factual situation involved, the points and authorities on which the party relies, and his argument for reversing or affirming the decision of the court below, depending on whether he is an appellant or appellee. The points and authorities contain the statutes and judicial decisions relied upon as precedent in the argument.

In addition to the brief, the reviewing court is often given the benefit of oral argument in deciding the case. The attorneys are allotted a specified amount of time to explain orally to the court their position in the case. This also affords the court of review an opportunity to question the attorneys about the various aspects of the case.

After oral argument, an impression vote is usually taken and the case is assigned to one justice to prepare an opinion. Each justice has a staff of clerks to assist him in the preparation of opinions. The intellectual backgrounds of these clerks have some influence on the decisions. The opinion as prepared by the clerks and the justice may not follow the impression vote. After the opinion is prepared, it will be circulated among the other members of the court. If a majority approve the opinion it is adopted. Those who disagree may prepare a dissenting opinion. Thereafter the opinion is announced and the losing party may ask for a rehearing on points stated in the opinion which he believes to be erroneous. Such rehearings are rarely granted. If the rehearing is denied or none is requested, the decision then becomes final and the mandate of the reviewing court is forwarded to the trial court for appropriate proceedings either by way of enforcement of the decision or new proceedings, if required.

Courts of review are essentially concerned with questions of law. However, a reviewing court may be asked to grant a new trial on the ground that the decision below is contrary to the manifest weight of the evidence found in the record. Thus questions of fact may be examined.

11   ENFORCEMENT OF JUDGMENTS AND DECREES

After a judgment in a court of law or a decree in a court of equity has become final, either because of the decision on appeal or because the losing party failed to perfect his appeal within the proper time, it may become necessary for the successful party to obtain judicial assistance in enforcing the decision of the court. For example, the judgment debtor may not voluntarily pay the amount of the judgment to the judgment creditor.

In such a case the judgment creditor may levy execution on the property of the judgment debtor and cause any property which is not exempt from execution by statute to be sold at public sale and to have the proceeds applied on the judgment. The judgment creditor may also garnishee the wages of the judgment debtor, subject to the amount that is exempt, or attach any property which may be due him. Modern statutes authorize the judgment creditor to question the judgment debtor in open court in order to discover assets that might be applied to the debt. It must be noted that all states provide that a debtor shall be allowed to keep certain items of property and a certain amount of his wages free from his debts. For example, in one state the debtor is allowed to keep the first $5,000 from the sale of his homestead, the first $400 of his personal property and such personal effects as the family Bible and wearing apparel. The same state exempts the first $45 or 85 percent of a judgment debtor's weekly wages from garnishment, whichever is greater. Not only do the exemption laws protect debtors, but the laws of bankruptcy may be used to have a judgment discharged.

Court orders in equity may require assistance of court officers to ensure compliance. Noncompliance with such orders may be punished by arrest and fine, or by jail sentence for contempt of court. The Federal government was compelled to resort to the use of United States Marshals and even the United States Army to enforce some of the decrees in the cases which involved school integration. Fortunately, force is usually unnecessary. The respect for and voluntary or automatic compliance with court orders by our citizens is one of the hallmarks of our "rule-of-law" society which distinguishes it from one in which there is "rule by man."

It should be kept in mind that there is a statute of limitations on the enforcement of a judgment or decree. This statute limits the time (which may vary from state to state) during which the judgment or decree may be enforced by further judicial proceedings.

PART TWO

LAW
AND THE
BUSINESS
ENVIRONMENT

BUSINESS ORGANIZATIONS

1   INTRODUCTION

This chapter is concerned with some of the major legal aspects involved in the selection of the form of business organization under which to operate a business enterprise. Of course the business with substantial capitalization almost of necessity will be a corporation because the partnership form is not capable of bringing together the hundreds or even thousands of investors that a corporation can. However, if a business is to be owned and operated by relatively few persons, the decision as to whether the form of organization should be a partnership or corporation involves a consideration of several factors. The most significant of these are (1) taxation, (2) liability, (3) control, (4) continuity, and (5) legal capacity. "Legal capacity" refers to the capability of the business to sue and be sued in its own name, and to its power to own and dispose of property as well as to enter into contracts in its own name. The five foregoing factors will be discussed in the sections which follow.

It should be kept in mind that a corporation is created by the state's issuing a charter upon the application of certain individuals known as incorporators, whereas a partnership is usually created by an agreement of the parties who are to be the owners and managers, which is a special type of contract called "'Articles of Co-partnership." A partnership is defined by the Uniform Partnership Act as "an association of two or more persons to carry on, as co-owners, a business for profit." Its existence may arise by implication from the conduct of the parties as well as by express contract. The sharing of the net profits of a business enterprise by two persons gives rise to a presumption that a partnership exists between them, except where the share of profits is received by one of them:

1   As a debt.
2   As wages of an employee or rent to a landlord.
3   As an annuity to a widow or representative of a deceased partner.
4   As interest on a loan.
5   As the consideration for the sale of the good will of a business or other property.

2 TAXATION

There are several aspects to the taxation factor of the decision to select one form of organization over another. First of all, a partnership is not subject to the Federal income tax, but a corporation does pay an income tax on its earnings. In addition, shareholders pay an income tax on dividends received so that it is usually stated that corporate earnings are subject to double taxation. The corporate tax rate varies from time to time and currently includes a surtax on earnings above $25,000. In recent years the normal tax rate on income up to $25,000 has varied from 22 to 30 percent, and the tax rate, including the surtax, on amounts over $25,000 has varied from 48 to 52 percent. Thus, corporate income of over $25,000 per year has been subject to roughly a 50 percent tax. The profits paid out as dividends have been taxable income to the individual shareholders at their individual rates, which vary from one person to another depending on the other income they receive.

The fact that a partnership pays no income tax of course does not mean that the profits of the partnership are free of income tax. A partnership files an information return which allocates to each individual partner his proportionate share of profits or losses from operation, dividend income, capital gains or losses, and other items which would affect the income tax owed by a partner. Each partner then reports his share of such items on his individual income tax return, irrespective of whether or not the items have been actually received by him. One of the disadvantages of this scheme of taxation is that partners may be required to pay individual income taxes on profits retained in the business for growth.

Before going further into the tax advantages of the different forms of organization, it is necessary to recognize that there are certain techniques for avoiding in part the double taxation of corporate income. First of all, reasonable salaries paid to corporate officials may be deducted in computing the taxable income of the business. Thus in a closely held corporation in which all or most shareholders are officers or employees, this technique will avoid double taxation. As might be suspected, the Internal Revenue Code disallows a deduction for excessive or unreasonable compensation and contends that such payments are dividends. Therefore the determination of the reasonableness of corporate salaries is an ever-present tax problem in that form of organization.

Second, the capital structure of the corporation may include both common stock and interest-bearing loans from shareholders. For example, assume that a company needs $100,000 of cash to commence business. If $100,000 of stock is issued, there will be no expense to be deducted. However, assume that $50,000 worth of stock is purchased by the owners and $50,000 is loaned to the company by them at 6 percent interest. In this case $3,000 of interest each year is deductible as an expense of the company and thus subject to only one tax as interest income to the owners. Just as in the case of salaries, the Internal Revenue Code has a counteracting rule relating to corporations that are undercapitalized. If the corporation is undercapitalized, interest payments will be treated as dividends, and disallowed as deductible expenses.

The third technique for avoiding double taxation at least in part, is simply not to pay dividends and to accumulate the earnings. After the earnings have been accumulated, the shareholders can sell their stock or have the company dissolved. In either case the difference between the original investment and the amount received is given capital gains treatment. Capital gains are taxed at one-half the taxpayer's normal tax rate, not to exceed 25 percent. Here again, there are tax laws designed to counteract the above technique. There is a special provision for an income tax imposed on "excessive accumulated earnings" in addition to the normal tax. Each year, on the first $100,000 of excessive accumulated earnings, the additional tax is 27½ percent and on all amounts over $100,000 it is 38½ percent.

Finally, there is a special provision in the Internal Revenue Code which allows small closely held business corporations to be treated as partnerships for income tax purposes and thereby to avoid having a tax assessed on the corporate income itself. These corporations, known as "Subchapter S corporations," cannot have over ten shareholders each of whom must elect to be taxed as a partnership, i.e., to have the corporate income allocated to the shareholders annually in computing their income for tax purposes, whether actually paid out or not. Corporations with more than 20 percent of their income from rents, interest, dividends, or royalties do not qualify. There are many technical rules of tax law involved in Subchapter S corporations, but as a rule of thumb, this method of taxation has distinct advantages for a business operating at a loss because the loss is shared and immediately deductible on the returns of the shareholders. It is also advantageous for businesses capable of paying out net profits as earned. In the latter case, the corporate tax is avoided. If net profits must be retained in the business, Subchapter S tax treatment is disadvantageous because income tax is paid on earnings not received, and there is a danger of double taxation to the individual because undistributed earnings which have been taxed once are taxed again in the event of the death of a shareholder. Thus it is evident that the theoretical advantage of using the Subchapter S corporation to avoid double taxation of corporate income must be heavily qualified.

The corporate form of organization has two important tax advantages which have greatly encouraged incorporation by small businesses. First of all, they may establish a qualified pension or profit-sharing plan for their employees including the shareholder employees. Under a qualified plan, the company is entitled to deduct as expenses all payments made to the plan, but the amounts allocated to each employee are not taxable income to the employee at that time. All earnings of the plan are income-tax-free; on retirement the benefits due an employee may be received as a capital gain, or the taxpayer may elect to receive them as an annuity at a time when he has the advantage of increased exemptions and deductions as well as a lower tax rate. Moreover, there are Federal estate tax and income tax savings in the event of death of the employee. Corporations can also adopt deferred compensation plans for their employees and are allowed to deduct the cost of health and accident insurance on employees. All of these special tax advantages are closely regulated to avoid discrimination between owner-employees and other employees.

In evaluating the impact of taxation on a business, an accountant or attorney will look at the projected earnings of the business, the policies to be followed in the distribution of those earnings, and the tax brackets of the individuals involved as owners. Then he will compute the estimated total tax burden under the various forms of organization. This will be considered along with the other factors in making the decision on which form of business organization to use.

3   LIABILITY

Traditionally, it has been said that the investors in a corporation have limited liability but those in a partnership have unlimited liability. As in the case of the usual statements made concernng taxation, this generalization is too broad and needs qualification. To be sure, if one invests in a company listed on the New York Stock Exchange, he will incur no risk greater than his investment and the concept of limited liability certainly applies. However, if the company is a small closely held corporation with limited assets and capital, it will be difficult for the corporation to obtain credit on the strength of its own credit standing alone, and as a practical matter, the shareholders will usually be required to add their own individual liability as security for the debts. For example, if the XYZ Company seeks a loan at a local bank, the bank often will require the owners X, Y, and Z to personally guarantee repayment of the loan. This is not to say that closely held corporations do not have some degree of limited liability. The investors in those types of businesses are protected with limited liability for contract-like obligations (such as taxes) which are imposed as a matter of law and for debts resulting from torts which are committed by company employees while they are about company business.

The Subchapter S corporation is a hybrid business organization for tax purposes, and the law has a similar hybrid for liability purposes. This hybrid is known as a "limited partnership."

The limited partnership is defined by the Uniform Limited Partnership

Act, which has been adopted by most states, as a partnership formed by two or more persons by complying with the provisions of the Act, having as members one or more general partners and one or more limited partners. The limited partners as such are not bound by the obligations of the partnership. It is usually stated that they have liability limited to their contribution. Thus, the limited partnership is a hybrid between the corporation in which all investors have limited liability and a general partnership in which all partners have unlimited liability. A limited partner is in effect loaning money to the business activity for a percentage of the profits rather than a fixed return such as interest. Since creditors ordinarily do not participate in management, neither do limited partners. Participation in management carries with it the liability of a general partner.

Just as the liability aspect of a limited partnership is a cross between a partnership and corporation, so also is the method of creating this type of business organization. A limited partnership, like a general partnership, is created by agreement. But, as in the case of a corporation, the statute prescribes the contents of a certificate similar to a corporate charter which is required to be recorded in order that the public will be fully advised as to the details of the organization. The Uniform Limited Partnership Act requires that the certificate contain the following information: [1]

I. *The name of the partnership,*

II. *The character of the business,*

III. *The location of the principal place of business,*

IV. *The name and place of residence of each member; general and limited partners being respectively designated,*

V. *The term for which the partnership is to exist.*

VI. *The amount of cash and a description of and the agreed value of the other property contributed by each limited partner.*

VII. *The additional contributions, if any, agreed to be made by each limited partner and the times at which or events on the happening of which they shall be made.*

VIII. *The time, if agreed upon, when the contribution of each limited partner is to be returned.*

IX. *The share of the profits or the other compensation by way of income which each limited partner shall receive by reason of his contributions,*

X. *The right, if given, of a limited partner to substitute an assignee as contributor in his place, and the terms and conditions of the substitution,*

XI. *The right, if given, of the partners to admit additional limited partners,*

XII. *The right, if given, of one or more of the limited partners to*

[1] Section 2a.

priority over other limited partners, as to contributions or as to compensation by way of income, and the nature of such priority,

XIII. *The right, if given, of the remaining general partner or partners to continue the business on the death, retirement or insanity of a general partner, and,*

XIV. *The right, if given, of a limited partner to demand and receive property other than cash in return for his contribution.*

There are several restrictions on the rights and activities of a limited partner. His contribution to the firm may be cash or property but not services. His surname may not be used, unless there is a general partner with the same name, or he will incur unlimited liability to unsuspecting general creditors. Finally, as previously noted, he may not participate in management without incurring unlimited liability. The following case concerns some of the usual types of questions raised in litigation involving limited partnerships.

FILESI V. UNITED STATES
352 F.2d 339 (1965)

BOREMAN, JUDGE: The Commissioner of Internal Revenue, asserting that the Jolly Tavern had been operated as a cabaret because dancing had been permitted to the music of a juke box, assessed deficiencies in cabaret excise taxes, penalties and interest in the amount of $46,567.28 against the taxpayer, Alfred Filesi, based on the receipts from the operation of the tavern. . . . Filesi paid $1,000 . . . and brought this action in the District Court to recover that sum. The Government filed a counter claim for the unpaid balance of $45,567.28. . . .

Filesi . . . contended that he was not liable for excise tax for the period from the first quarter of 1954 through the first quarter of 1956 as he was a "limited partner" during this period and did not become a general partner until a written partnership agreement was executed on April 4, 1956. . . .

At the close of all the evidence, the District Court ruled as a matter of law that Filesi was a general partner for the period in dispute. . . . The jury found that there was dancing at the tavern and that the total tax liability for the entire period from 1954 through the third quarter of 1958 should have been $28,854.95 rather than the $46,567.28 assessed by the Commissioner. Judgment was accordingly entered.

The principal errors assigned on appeal relate to rulings of the court: first, that the court erred in ruling as a matter of law and instructing the jury that Filesi was a general partner for the period from the first quarter of 1954 through the first quarter of 1956. . . .

In his testimony Filesi admitted he and Muller were partners but contended he was a "limited partner" and not liable for the tax for the periods before the second quarter of 1956. The facts upon which this contention is based are these. From 1949 when Filesi first became associated with the management of the Jolly Tavern until April 14, 1951, Filesi along with Muller and John Marshall were the only shareholders of a corporation organized to operate the tavern. Marshall wanted out of the business and on April 14, 1951, the corporation was dissolved and Muller assumed to purchase Marshall's interest but to do so Muller borrowed money from an outside source and the loan was subsequently repaid from the profits of the Jolly Tavern before Filesi and Muller received their shares as partners. The effect of this transaction was that Filesi became the purchaser of one half of Marshall's interest. According to Filesi, Muller did not have funds to buy Filesi's interest also so Muller persuaded him to leave his investment in the tavern. In return, Filesi testified, it was orally agreed that he was to manage the business at a stipulated salary and receive fifty percent of all profits but was not to be liable for any losses. The liquor license was transferred to Muller's name and the business was operated under this arrangement until April 4, 1956. On that date Muller and Filesi executed a written partnership agreement under which both were to share gains and losses equally. From April 4, 1956, to April 5, 1957, the tavern was operated under this written agreement. On the latter date the partnership was dissolved and Muller sold his interest to Filesi who has since owned and operated the tavern.

Filesi argues that he was a limited partner from April 14, 1951, to April 4, 1956, and as such he was not liable for any losses of the partnership during this period; that, as the excise tax from the first quarter of 1954 through the first quarter of 1956 would constitute a loss he should not be held accountable for the tax. We cannot agree. It is well settled that to obtain the protections and privileges of limited liability a person must comply with the statutory requirements regulating the formation of limited partnerships or otherwise be held liable as a general partner. . . . [T]he Annotated Code of Maryland specified the acts which must be performed by a person desiring to become a limited partner in the operation of a business within that State. It was clearly shown that Filesi did not comply with these provisions and therefore, he cannot now claim the protection of a limitation of liability. It is clear from the evidence generally and from Filesi's own testimony that he openly and publicly took an active part in the management and control of the business. We think the District Court was correct in holding as a matter of law that Filesi was liable as a general partner for any excise tax properly assessed for the period in dispute.

Even assuming that Filesi was a limited partner his argument is unsound. According to applicable law a limited partner is liable for any losses of the partnership to the extent of his investment in the assets of the business. On this point, however, no evidence was produced to show what Filesi's investment was for the period, although in 1951 it was slightly in excess of $10,000. . . .

[The decision was reversed for other reasons.]

Issues of liability are not restricted to that of the investors in the business or to financial liability alone. Corporation law has developed several instances in which the directors and officers of the corporation will have liability to shareholders or to the corporation for acts or omissions by such directors or officers in their official capacity. Directors are liable to the corporation for losses as a result of fraud or gross negligence in the performance of their duties. However, directors are not liable for losses caused by poor judgment if they acted honestly and within their powers. Statutes frequently impose liability in certain cases on directors. For example, directors who declare a dividend when there is no earned surplus have personal liability for the dividend.

The case below is another example of the kind of liability which may be imposed on a director.

PRECISION EXTRUSIONS, INC. V. STEWART
183 N.E.2d 547 (III. A.C. 1962)

Suit was brought against certain directors of a corporation for allegedly voting to purchase some of the corporation's shares while its assets were less than the sum of its stated capital and surplus accounts, and for voting to purchase the shares while the corporation was insolvent, contrary to the provisions of the Business Corporation Act. The defendants contended that the complaint failed to state a cause of action. The trial court held for plaintiff.

MCCORMICK, JUDGE: There are numerous cases in Illinois and elsewhere discussing the responsibility and liability of the directors of a business corporation. It is generally held that a director of a corporation, though not responsible for errors of judgment, is a fiduciary charged with the duty of caring for the property of the corporation and of managing its affairs honestly and in good faith. If this duty has been so violated as to result in an impairment of its assets or loss of its property he can, without the aid of statute, be compelled to make restitution. Directors are liable to misappropriation of funds where they act ultra vires in authorizing the corporation to purchase its own stock. . . . In *Lyons v. Corder*, 253 Mo. 539, it was held that where a loss results to the corporation because of the disregard of the duties of the directors as prescribed by statute the directors are liable. Ordinarily an action can be brought by the corporation against the directors, or in case of the insolvency of the corporation, by its receiver or assignee. . . .

In *Aiken v. Peabody*, 168 F.2d 615 (7th Cir.), the court held the directors of the corporation would be liable under Illinois law when they authorized a declaration of dividends the payment of which would reduce the "capital stock" of the corporation, providing that they acted in bad faith or were guilty of gross negligence or inattention, and the court further held that, while the case was based upon a statutory violation, the principle was one which had existed at common law. In the present case had the directors authorized the repurchase by the corporation of its own stock under the same circumstance, they could have been held liable at common law. Section 6 of the statute formulates rules with regard to an authorization of the repurchase of its own stock by a corporation, which places a definite duty on the directors. When the directors violate that duty it is not necessary that the statute specifically provide that they can be held responsible. At common law an action against them by the corporation or creditors would lie, since the result of such repurchase would be to illegally withdraw and pay to a stockholder a part of the assets of the corporation. When liability is imposed upon a director of a corporation by statute, his common law liability for misfeasance and negligence in the performance of his duty is not thereby excluded. . . .

The plaintiff further alleges in its complaint that the act of the directors was a violation of section 42 of the Act. Under that section it seems clear that a repurchase by a corporation of shares of its stock at a time when the corporation is insolvent or its net assets are less than its stated capital is a distribution of its assets in part. In *Pace v. Pace Bros. Co.*, 91 Utah 132, 59 P.2d 1 (1936), the court construes a statute which made it a misdemeanor for any director "to divide, withdraw or in any manner, except as provided by law, pay to the stockholders, or any of them, any part of the capital of the corporation." It was held that the statute was violated when the directors authorized the corporation to repurchase its own stock. The court says: "We see no reason why the prohibition against 'paying' to a stockholder a part of the capital does not include buying his stock. . . . Moreover, the phrase 'or any of them' is convincing that it does not contemplate purely a division pro rata, but the prohibition goes to paying any of the capital to any stockholder or stockholders, whether one or more." The court discusses at considerable length similar statutes in other states where the courts have reached the same conclusion. . . . In our opinion the complaint, defective in form as it is, does sufficiently state causes of action. . . .

The orders of the trial court . . . overruling defendant's motion to dismiss plaintiff's . . . complaint, . . . are affirmed. [CASE REMANDED FOR FURTHER PROCEEDINGS]

The Federal Securities Act of 1933 and the Securities Exchange Act of 1934 impose personal liability on directors and others for giving false information in a prospectus and for other acts. Likewise, the antitrust laws impose penalties on individuals who participate in violating them. Thus, directors and officers must be careful to comply with all the laws which govern the corporation or they may incur personal financial or even criminal liability.

Corporations may have criminal liability in addition to civil liability in tort or for breach of contract. However, the fiction of the corporate entity creates some difficult problems insofar as the criminal law is concerned. A corporation can not be imprisoned, although in theory a death penalty of sorts could be imposed simply by the domiciliary state's dissolving it. Corporations act only through agents, and while it is possible to imprison the agents in many instances, this would not be satisfactory punishment for the corporate entity. It is, of course, possible to punish a corporation by imposing a fine. As will be discussed later, such action is one of the enforcement sanctions of the antitrust laws.

Proving the commission of a crime by a corporation is often as difficult as imposing a meaningful penalty. "Crime" is usually defined in terms of intentional commission of some prohibited act, often with the *specific* intent to do so. How can an artificial being with no mind have criminal intent? The law has generally resolved this problem by imputing to the corporation the guilty intent of an agent, if the agent was authorized and acting within the scope of his employment at the time he committed the crime. Many cases have equated "acquiescence" by the company in the wrongful conduct with authority to commit the illegal act.

Modern criminal statutes recognize that a corporation may indeed commit a crime and provide fines in lieu of incarceration for crimes that usually are punished by incarceration. These criminal codes specify those classes of crimes for which the legislature intended corporate liability to exist and call for it only where an agent is acting within the scope of his employment or where the activity is authorized, requested, or performed by the board of directors. It is often a defense to a criminal charge against a corporation that a high managerial agent having supervisory responsibility over the conduct which is the subject matter of the offense exercised due diligence to prevent the commission of the crime.

4   CONTROL

In every business organization, some individual or some group of people will have the power to make decisions or will possess "control" of the business. In a partnership, unless the agreement provides to the contrary, each partner has an equal voice in the firm affairs and has an equal right to possess partnership property for business purposes. Partners are liable for all transactions entered into by any partner in the scope of the partnership business and are similarly liable for any partner's torts committed while he is acting in the course of the firm business. Each partner is in effect both an agent of the partnership and a principal, being capable of creating both contract and tort liability of the firm and his co-partners and being likewise responsible for their acts. There are many technical rules concerning what acts of a partner are within the scope or course of the partnership business. While knowing these is not essential to a general understanding of the concept of control of a partnership, one special rule is worthy of mention. A partner in a trading partnership, i.e., one engaged in the business of buying and selling commodities, has the implied authority to borrow money in the usual course of business and pledge the credit of the firm; but a partner in a nontrading partnership, such as an accounting firm, has no implied power to borrow money. In the latter case, such authority must be actual before the firm will be bound.

In the corporate form of organization, legal problems created by persons in "control" and by those seeking "control" are quite numerous. In the very large corporations, control by management is maintained with a very small percentage of ownership of the stock through the utilization of corporate records and funds to solicit proxies. Management can at corporate expense solicit the right to vote the stock of shareholders who are unable to attend the meetings at which the directors of the company are elected. An outsider must either own sufficient stock to elect the directors or he must solicit proxies at his own expense. Although there are a few proxy fights, the management of the large United States corporation is usually able to maintain control with only a small minority of the actual stock ownership.

In closely held corporations or in corporations with only several hundred shareholders or fewer, a number of techniques are used to gain control without having a majority of the total investment. One technique is to issue classes of stock. In some states there can be nonvoting stock; the group seeking to keep control will buy voting stock while selling nonvoting stock to others. Preferred stock may be used to increase capital without losing control. For example, a group may invest $100,000 in common stock of $1 par value each. Then they will sell another $100,000 of the same common stock with the requirement that for each share of common stock purchased, a $5 share of nonvoting preferred stock must be purchased. Thus, the corporation would raise $700,000 and the $100,000 original investment made by the organizing individuals would have 50% of the voting power. There are other schemes which can be used such as selling some stock to the organizers for 10 cents per share and selling later shares for $1 to outsiders. Another method of gaining and keeping control is to pool the stock of several shareholders into a voting trust so that one person gains the power, by contract, to vote all the shares in the trust. It should be kept in mind that many issues of stocks and bonds are subject to regulation under state securities laws, usually called the "blue-sky" laws, which govern the issue and sale of securities. These laws generally require full disclosure to prospective investors in the business of all material facts concerning it. Also, some states provide for an inquiry into the fairness of the proposed issue by an administrative agency, which has authority to prohibit its sale if minimum standards of fair dealing are not met. In addition, many corporate issues may be subject to requirements imposed by the Federal government in the Securities Act of 1933 and the Securities Exchange Act of 1934.

A major subject of litigation concerns the rights of those who do not possess control in a closely held corporation—the so-called "minority interest." To a very large degree, the owners of the minority interest are subject to the whim or caprice of the majority. The majority may pay themselves high salaries to use up the profits and never declare a dividend. However, the minority interest is not without some rights because the directors and officers stand in a fiduciary relation to the corporation. This relation imposes a duty on directors to act for the best interests of the corporation rather than for themselves individually, as the following case illustrates.

NORTHWESTERN TERRA COTTA CORP. V. WILSON
219 N.E. 2d 860 (Ill. A.C. 1966)

A corporation brought suit against one of its directors to prevent him from voting certain shares of the stock of the corporation which he had purchased from a bank. The corporation claimed that it was interested in purchasing the stock from the bank prior to the time that the director purchased it and that because of his fiduciary relationship, the sale should be transferred to the company. The lower court found for the corporation and the director appealed.

DRICKER, JUDGE: . . . There is a general rule that a director of a corporation owes a duty to the corporation to take no advantage of his position for financial gain in derogation of the corporation's rights. Whether in any case there is a duty upon a corporate official to refrain from purchasing property for himself depends upon whether the corporation has an interest, actual or in expectancy, in the property, or whether the purchase of the property by the officer or director may hinder or defeat the plans and purposes of the corporation in the carrying on or development of the legitimate business for which it was created. Where there is no such duty the director of a corporation may acquire outside interests, although the corporation may be more or less interested. An opportunity may be embraced by a director as his own without accountability to the corporation if the corporation sought without success to obtain it.

The overwhelming evidence in the instant case shows that on November 24, 1964, the plaintiff refused to pay $7 a share for the purchase of its stock and that the highest offer made by the plaintiff to the Bank was only $5. There is no proof that, as alleged in the complaint, defendant "participated in discussions with Hudson, wherein it was agreed that it would be advantageous to plaintiff to purchase said shares" or that the Bank in July 1965 notified Johnson of its willingness to sell 24,000 of its shares to plaintiff at $7 (on June 24, 1965, the agreement for the sale of the stock was entered into between the Bank and the defendant—it was finalized on July 13) or that defendant knew of this purported offer and violated his duty to the corporation by not informing it of this purported offer and by buying some of the stock himself, knowing of such an offer. In his testimony Hudson stated his position to be that he had decided on May 10 that the corporation should pay $7 per share; that he did not communicate this to the Bank; that Fox (the then corporation attorney) advised him that the corporation "should never go out and make an offer to buy the shares."

However, on June 10, 1965, Fox, as attorney for plaintiff, wrote a shareholder in response to a suggestion that plaintiff buy his stock that plaintiff was not presently "redeeming" any of its shares. Defendant was aware of this letter shortly after June 10 having been shown a copy by Earl Johnson.

We find no support for plaintiff's claim that plaintiff was genuinely interested in acquiring its stock at $7 per share prior to the date defendant contracted to purchase the shares in question. At best, after May 10, 1965, it might have considered offers of stockholders who wished to sell their stock (although this is not borne out by its refusal of June 10, 1965) but even this so-called policy was never adopted by the stockholders, Board of Directors or even the Executive Committee.

Plaintiff has cited a number of cases involving a director's usurpation of his corporation's opportunity to purchase shares of stock: We do not consider the corporate opportunity principle to be applicable to the facts of the case before us.

In *Vulcanized Rubber & Plastics Co. v. Scheckter*, 400 Pa. 405, 162 A.2d 400, the corporation sued some of its directors for purchasing some of its own stock in derogation of their fiduciary obligations as directors. The corporation had never adopted a resolution authorizing a purchase. The court held to be erroneous the entry of a temporary injunction enjoining the defendants from voting the shares in question. While in the instant case the corporation had authorized a purchase of 25,493 shares at $4 per share in 1963, of the same number of shares at $4.50 per share in February 1964 and 9,823 shares at $5 in November 1964, there was never any corporate action to purchase any shares at $7 per share. The principle enunciated in *Vulcanized* 162 A.2d at page 404 is applicable here:

. . . [T]he complainant must establish that it is his clear legal right, not doubtful or uncertain, to the specific relief sought; otherwise the preliminary injunction will be dissolved. . . .

Since under all the circumstances of the instant case we do not find that the evidence established a clear legal right, not doubtful or uncertain, to the specific relief sought, the order granting the preliminary injunction is reversed. [REVERSED]

As a result of his fiduciary relationship, contracts made with the corporation by a dominant director or officer may also be challenged. The burden is on the director or majority shareholder to prove good faith and inherent fairness in such transactions when suit is brought. Such suits are known as shareholder's derivative suits and are brought by a shareholder on behalf of the corporation. They generally cannot be commenced until all possible means to solve the problem within the corporate organization have been exhausted.

The basic difficulty of owning a minority interest in a closely held corporation arises from the fact that there is no ready market for the stock in the event the shareholder desires to dispose of it. While the shareholder has the right to attend meetings and vote for directors, he may be constantly outvoted. He has a right to any dividends that are declared but no right to have them declared. He also has a preemptive right, which is to purchase his proportionate share of any new stock issue, but he may not be interested in investing more money when no dividends are being paid. Therefore, as a practical matter, the majority may be able to reduce his percentage of ownership further.

The minority shareholder has a right to inspect the books and records of the company, but at a proper time and place; and the books may not have much meaning to him without having the entries and account balances analyzed by an expert.

Finally, a minority shareholder has the right to his proportionate share of assets on dissolution but he has no right to dissolution, except that he may seek it in a court of equity under circumstances that will cause a court to step in to protect creditors and the corporation.

All corporations are theoretically controlled by the majority of the shareholders who elect the board of directors. (While in small, closely held businesses this theory may be a fact, we have seen that in large corporations management's power to solicit and vote proxies has reduced the theory to a mere technicality. In the latter type of business, almost all shareholders except those who are the management team are in reality "minority" shareholders as far as actual control or rights are concerned.) The board of directors elects the officers and makes policy such as declaring dividends and amending the by-laws. Courts may occasionally step in to find a violation of the fiduciary relationship by directors or officers, but such cases are rare and as a practical matter the minority are at the mercy of the majority. The case which follows illustrates some of the problems of a minority shareholder.

POLIKOFF V. DOLE & CLARK BUILDING CORP.
184 N.E.2d 792 A.C. (Ill. 1962)

ENGLISH, JUDGE: The complaint seeks to set forth a cause of action, on behalf of a minority shareholder, for the liquidation of an Illinois corporation in the exercise by the court of either statutory or inherent equity authority. . . .

The complaint fills fifty pages of the record. In brief, it alleges:

Defendant corporation was organized in 1933 under a plan of reorganization for a defaulted real estate bond issue. The real estate, which is the principal asset of the corporation, consists of a building containing a theater, nine stores, and a 65-room hotel, located at Clark Street and Drummond Place in Chicago.

The stock consists of 942.5 shares of Class A (ineligible for dividends, and having a value on liquidation of $100 per share), and 1015.2 shares of Class B (ineligible for dividends while any Class A shares are outstanding).

Members of defendant Grundman's family own 517.5 shares of Class A (approximately 55%), and 767.7 shares of Class B (approximately 76%).

Plaintiff owns 15 shares of Class A (approximately 1.6%), and 6 shares of Class B (approximately .6%). Her shares represent an investment of $1200 in 1951.

During the years in question (1952–1958), defendant Grundman was president, a director and manager of the property; his son-in-law was secretary and a director; and, since 1958, his daughter has held the third directorship.

During the years 1952 through 1957 the corporation sustained losses averaging $4,935 after making allowances for depreciation. During those years, receipts exceeded expenditures by an average of approximately $4250. For the year 1958 the corporation showed a profit of $1740 after depreciation.

The net worth increased some $16,500 during 1958 to approximately $123,000.

The theater has been closed since April 3, 1958 and has produced no income. For several years prior to that time, the motion picture business in Chicago had been poor and many theaters had closed. There are at least two other motion picture theaters in the vicinity of the corporation's theater.

In 1953 Grundman's wife made a loan of $60,000 to the corporation and was given a mortgage on the real estate. The interest rate is 5% and all payments of interest have been made as they matured. No payment has been made on principal, which was due in 1958 but has been extended to 1963. The mortgage contains a waiver of the right of redemption.

Directors' fees of $300 per year were paid until 1958, when they were eliminated.

Grundman was paid $6000 per year for his services as president of the corporation, manager of the real estate and operating manager of the hotel. It is claimed that this compensation was grossly excessive in view of the financial condition of the corporation. Grundman also took a three-month vacation in 1957 without diminution in compensation.

The corporation spent $60,000 on rehabilitation of the building when it was uncertain whether or not the payments on Mrs. Grundman's mortgage could be maintained. Thus, a foreclosure would inure to the benefit of the Grundman family.

Only about half of the hotel rooms were rented; too little was spent on advertising the hotel; no new tenant was obtained for the theater; Grundman refused to have the corporation operate the theater itself, and failed to communicate with plaintiff concerning a lead to a possible tenant.

Contrary to plaintiff's advice, Grundman has refused to let the corporation sell the real estate. Because of Mrs. Grundman's mortgage, her husband is not in a position to exercise his fiduciary obligations impartially and in the best interest of the corporation.

The corporation's surplus was not used to retire Class A shares during the years in question.

The Grundman family have been buying shares at depressed prices.

Grundman refused to follow suggestions made by plaintiff for the management of the corporation's affairs and he caused the corporation to expend money for attorneys' fees in opposing plaintiff's suit. He and Mrs. Grundman also refused to accept other suggestions of plaintiff calculated to weaken the corporation's mortgage commitment to Mrs. Grundman.

The corporation is in danger of losing its principal asset to Mrs. Grundman through a foreclosure which could be manipulated by those in control of the corporation for their own benefit.

Because of the condition of the corporation there is no reasonable prospect of profitable operation and, therefore, no reasonable prospect of its achieving the principal object for which it was formed—the retirement of its Class A shares.

The prayer of the complaint is primarily for liquidation of the corporation. All its other prayers relate to the details of such a liquidation and are dependent upon it.

The gist of defendants' motion to strike is that the complaint does not allege facts constituting illegal, oppressive, or fraudulent acts on the part of those in control of the corporation, or facts constituting waste or misapplication of corporate assets. . . .

The burden of plaintiff's brief is that Grundman's acts, as outlined, were oppressive and constituted misapplication or waste of corporate assets. The background against which these charges are to be considered is of extreme importance. That background is the routine organization of all corporate entities. As stated by our Supreme Court in words fully as cogent today as when written sixty years ago:

It is, however, fundamental in the law of corporations that the majority of its stockholders shall control the policy of the corporation, and regulate and govern the lawful exercise of its franchise and business. . . . Every one purchasing or subscribing for stock in a corporation impliedly agrees that he will be bound by the acts and proceedings done or sanctioned by a majority of the shareholders, or by the agents of the corporation duly chosen by such majority, within the scope of the powers conferred by the charter. And courts of equity will not undertake to control the policy or business methods of a corporation, although it may be seen that a wiser policy might be adopted, and the business more successful if other methods were pursued. The majority of shares of its stock, or the agents by the holders thereof lawfully chosen, must be permitted to control the business of the corporation in their discretion, when not in violation of its charter, or some public law, or corruptly and fraudulently subversive of the rights and interests of the corporation or of a shareholder. . . .

The Business Corporation Act has given to the courts the power to relieve minority shareholders from oppressive acts of the majority, but the remedy of liquidation is so drastic that it must be invoked with extreme caution. The ends of justice would not be served by too broad an application of the statute, for that would merely eliminate one evil by substituting a greater one—oppression of the majority by the minority. . . .

Almost all aspects of plaintiff's charges relate solely to business decision-making which by our statute is made the responsibility of the board of directors and the officers of a corporation. Whether Grundman spent too much or too little for advertising, or for salaries, or for rehabilitation of the premises, are matters with which the court will not concern itself—at least not in so far as they bear on the question of liquidation. We do not find in the allegations of the complaint sufficient facts to establish oppressive conduct by the management. Nor do we find misapplication or waste of corporate assets.

Along a somewhat similar line, plaintiff argues for liquidation because there is no reasonable expectation of profitable operation. From the facts submitted, we cannot agree. We do not, of course, predict that this will be a profitable enterprise, but, as said in *Central Standard Inc. Co. v. Davis,* 10 Ill. 2d 566, 577, 141 N.E.2d 45, 51: "Time may show that there is no reasonable prospect of profitable operation. The present record does not."

As to the mortgage, the complaint does not allege any facts indicating impropriety in the corporation's borrowing from Mrs. Grundman the money which it needed for rehabilitation of its property. The fact, if it be a fact, that Mr. and Mrs. Grundman have thereby placed themselves in such a position that Grundman might violate his fiduciary obligations to the corporation —that is not enough to justify the relief sought in this complaint. Every corporate director or officer is in a position to betray his position of trust from the moment of his election.

The complaint was properly stricken, and, plaintiff having stood on her pleading, the action was properly dismissed. The order of the Circuit Court is, therefore, affirmed. [AFFIRMED]

5 CONTINUITY AND LEGAL CAPACITY

The legal fiction that creates a corporation brings into life an artificial being separate and apart from the shareholders who own it. It may have perpetual existence and will not be affected by death of a shareholder. Of course, the laws regulating corporations contain provisions concerning their dissolution, merger and consolidation—any of which will end corporate existence—but essentially, perpetual existence is provided for.

On the other hand, a partnership may be dissolved at any time. It may occur by reason of the death of one of the partners. Even if the partnership agreement provides that the partnership will continue for a certain number of years, any partner has the *power* but not the *right* to dissolve the partnership. In other words, liability may attach for wrongful dissolution but dissolution will nevertheless take place if one partner withdraws in violation of his contract. Dissolution is not the equivalent of termination. The latter involves the winding up of the business, while dissolution involves a change in relationship among the partners.

Modern partnership law allows the entry of new partners by agreement among the old partners and contracts among the partners by which the business may continue even though a partner dies or withdraws. These contracts, usually known as "buy and sell agreements," are frequently a part of the articles of co-partnership and provide for payment to a withdrawing partner or to the estate or widow of a deceased partner for his interest in the business. Formulas are frequently used to compute the value of assets other than cash and good will, these forming a part of the agreement. In the case of the death of a partner, the liquidity needed is often provided by the cash proceeds from life insurance which was taken out on the life of the deceased and made payable to the firm. Upon payment of the amount required by the buy and sell agreement to the estate of the deceased, all rights of the deceased end and the surviving partners continue the business. Actually, a new partnership now exists but as a practical matter, business continues as usual at the same place and under the same name. Partnerships of lawyers, doctors, or accountants may thus obtain almost perpetual existence.

In the early law, a corporation was considered a legal entity but a partnership was not. By being a legal entity, it was usually meant that capacity was present to sue and be sued and to hold title to and convey real and personal property in the name of the business instead of the names of the individual owners. Modern statutes on procedure allow suits by and against a partnership in the firm name. They also allow a partnership to own and dispose of real estate and personal property in the firm name.

Actually, a corporation today although a legal entity has more difficulty in gaining access to the courts than does a partnership. Most states by statute require corporations doing business in a state other than that of incorporation to qualify under the local corporation laws. Qualification involves the furnishing of certain information in an initial registration and an annual report as well as the payment of such taxes as franchise taxes and annual license fees. One result of the failure to meet this requirement imposed by states on foreign corporations is illustrated by the following case.

ELI LILLY AND COMPANY V. SAV-ON-DRUGS, INC.
366 U.S. 276 (1961)

BLACK, JUSTICE: The appellant Eli Lilly and Company, an Indiana corporation dealing in pharmaceutical products, brought this action in a New Jersey state court to enjoin the appellee Sav-On-Drugs, Inc., a New Jersey corporation, from selling Lilly's products in New Jersey at prices lower than those fixed in minimum retail price contracts into which Lilly had entered with a number of New Jersey drug retailers. Sav-On had itself signed no such contract but, under the New Jersey Fair Trade Act, prices so established become obligatory upon nonsigning retailers who have notice that the manufacturer has made these contracts with other retailers. Sav-On moved to dismiss this complaint under a New Jersey statute that denies a foreign corporation transacting business in the State the right to bring any action in New Jersey upon any contract made there unless and until it files with the New Jersey Secretary of State a copy of its charter together with a limited amount of information about its operations and obtains from him a certificate authorizing it to do business in the State.

Lilly opposed the motion to dismiss, urging that its business in New Jersey was entirely in interstate commerce and arguing, upon that ground, that the attempt to require it to file the necessary information and obtain a certificate for its New Jersey business was forbidden by the Commerce

Clause of the Federal Constitution. Both parties offered evidence to the Court in the nature of affidavits as to the extent and kind of business done by Lilly with New Jersey companies and people. On this evidence, the trial court made findings of fact and granted Sav-On's motion to dismiss, stating as its ground that "the conclusion is inescapable that the plaintiff [Lilly] was in fact doing business in this State at the time of the acts complained of and was required to, but did not, comply with the provisions of the Corporation Act." On appeal to the Supreme Court of New Jersey, this constitutional attack was renewed and the State Attorney General was permitted to intervene as a party-defendant to defend the validity of the statute. The State Supreme Court then affirmed the judgment upholding the statute, relying entirely upon the opinion of the trial court. We noted probable jurisdiction to consider Lilly's contention that the constitutional question was improperly decided by the state courts.

The record shows that the New Jersey trade in Lilly's pharmaceutical products is carried on through both interstate and intrastate channels. Lilly manufactures these products and sells them in interstate commerce to certain selected New Jersey wholesalers. These wholesalers then sell the products in intrastate commerce to New Jersey hospitals, physicians and retail drugstores, and these retail stores in turn sell them, again in intrastate commerce, to the general public. It is well established that New Jersey cannot require Lilly to get a certificate of authority to do business in the State if its participation in this trade is limited to its wholly interstate sales to New Jersey wholesalers. Under the authority of the so-called "drummer" cases, such as *Robbins v. Shelby County Taxing District*, Lilly is free to send salesmen into New Jersey to promote this interstate trade without interference from regulations imposed by the State. On the other hand, it is equally well settled that if Lilly is engaged in intrastate as well as interstate aspects of the New Jersey drug business, the State can require it to get a certificate of authority to do business. In such a situation, Lilly could not escape state regulation merely because it is also engaged in interstate commerce. We must then look to the record to determine whether Lilly is engaged in intrastate commerce in New Jersey.

The findings of the trial court, based as they are upon uncontroverted evidence presented to it, show clearly that Lilly is conducting an intrastate as well as an interstate business in New Jersey. . . .

We agree with the trial court that "[t]o hold under the facts above recited that plaintiff [Lilly] is not doing business in New Jersey is to completely ignore reality." Eighteen "detailmen," working out of a big office in Newark, New Jersey, with Lilly's name on the door and in the lobby of the building, and with Lilly's district manager and secretary in charge, have been regularly engaged in work for Lilly which relates directly to the intrastate aspects of the sale of Lilly's products. These eighteen "detailmen" have been traveling throughout the State of New Jersey promoting the sales of Lilly's products, not to the wholesalers, Lilly's interstate customers, but to the physicians, hospitals and retailers who buy those products in intrastate commerce from the wholesalers. To this end, they have provided these hospitals, physicians and retailers with up-to-date knowledge of Lilly's products and with free advertising and promotional material designed to encourage the general public to make more intrastate purchases of Lilly's products. And they sometimes even directly participate in the intrastate sales themselves by transmitting orders from the hospitals, physicians and drugstores they service to the New Jersey wholesalers. . . .

Lilly also contends that even if it is engaged in intrastate commerce in New Jersey and can by virtue of that fact be required to get a license to do business in that State, New Jersey cannot properly deny it access to the courts in this case because the suit is one arising out of the interstate aspects of its business. In this regard, Lilly relies upon such cases as *International Textbook Co. v. Pigg,* holding that a State cannot condition the right of a foreign corporation to sue upon a contract for the interstate sale of goods. We do not think that those cases are applicable here, however, for the present suit is not of that kind. Here, Lilly is suing upon a contract entirely separable from any particular interstate sale and the power of the State is consequently not limited by cases involving such contracts. [AFFIRMED]

As was indicated in Chapter 6, a business may be sued in a state with which it has certain minimal contracts under the so-called "long-arm statutes." We therefore have the unique situation that a company may be a defendant but not a plaintiff in a state in which it is a foreign corporation if it has failed "to qualify" when required to do so.

6   CONCLUSION

Persons desiring to form a new business must weigh the foregoing factors and the costs involved and then select a form of organization most suitable to their needs. Any form has disadvantages and the decision often is to select the least objectionable form. Taxation is usually the dominant factor. Not only must new businesses weigh these problems but so also must going businesses when there is a substantial change in circumstance such as a change in tax rates, earnings, or scope of business activity. As a result, the matters discussed in this chapter must be constantly considered and reviewed by closely held businesses.

CHAPTER EIGHT

REGULATION OF COMMERCE

1 INTRODUCTION

The legal environment of business consists primarily of laws regulating and taxing business. Both the legislative and the executive branches of government are actively engaged in the promulgation and execution of laws which control business and the economy as we noted in Chapter 4. Much of this regulation is accomplished by administrative agencies exercising their rule-making, enforcing, and quasi-judicial powers. The determination of the legality of all regulatory activities as well as the application of the rules issued is ultimately a problem for the courts. As a practical matter all branches of government are actively engaged in placing limitations on business activity.

The magnitude of governmental control of business activity becomes apparent upon examination of the requirements which must be met in starting a small business. Let us assume that John Brown desires to open a barbershop in his home town, and examine some of the laws and regulations with which he must comply.

First of all, his shop must be located in an area that is zoned to allow barbershops. The local government, with the assistance of a local zoning board (an administrative agency), will have divided the community into zones and will have limited the areas in which barbershops may be located.

Next, John will have to obtain a state license as a barber. To obtain this license, he will probably be required to pass a test administered by an agency of the state government. Armed with his license and a lease to a shop in a permissible location, he can then turn to his tax problems. Since he will sell certain items of property such as hair oil, he will be required by most states to pay a sales or use tax on such transactions. He must obtain a reporting number from his state department of revenue for this tax, and file periodic returns. Some states have a tax that is imposed on the gross receipts from services, which would require further reporting to the revenue department. Others have a state income tax, which also necessitates the filing of periodic returns. Of course, like everyone else, he will be subject to the Federal income tax. Some municipalities levy taxes on income including that from barbershops.

If John decides to hire some employees to assist him, he will encounter additional legal problems. Depending on the number and earnings of these employees, he may be required to pay the unemployment compensation tax and to have workmen's compensation insurance. In any event, he will be required to deduct the social security tax and to make a monthly or quarterly report of these deductions and his contributed share of the taxes to the Federal government. He also may be subject to minimum wage laws and fair employment practice laws. The last two types of laws will regulate the amount of salary he pays his employees, and his policies and practices with regard to hiring and discharging them. It may be that his employees will decide to bargain collectively with John, thus bringing him within the jurisdiction of administrative agencies concerned with labor-management relations.

The state and local governments may have laws on sanitation which require certain action on John's part such as the sterilization of equipment or the use of certain cleansing techniques. Federal as well as state laws will regulate his selection of customers and prohibit discrimination based on race, color, creed, or national origin. The local government may prohibit business on Sunday or after a certain hour of the day. It even may have laws regulating the type of reading material it is permissible to have in the barbershop for the use of customers.

If John Brown desired to go into the trucking business, instead of barbering, he would encounter a much greater legal problem. He would be required to obtain a certificate of public convenience and necessity from the state government if his activities were intrastate or from the Interstate Commerce Commission if interstate. Obtaining this certificate usually requires approval obtained after an adversary formal hearing upon notice to all interested parties. Competitors are the adversaries. If the certificate is approved, the rates to be charged must also be approved.

This short discussion illustrates some of the regulatory and taxing aspects of government as they relate to business.

The regulatory activities of the state governments are based on the "police power," which has been defined as the power to control persons and property within the jurisdiction of the state for the purpose of promoting the general welfare. The police power of the states was reserved to them by the Constitution and is vested in the legislatures, which have delegated portions of the power to municipalities. The United States has no general police power but it has comparable authority to make laws which are necessary and proper to the exercise of any of the specific enumerated powers granted to it by the states in the Constitution. Thus, actions taken by the Federal government may not be objected to on the ground that they are an exercise of police power, if they are an implementation of a power such as the regulation of commerce. In this area, the exercise of the state police power often conflicts with the exercise of Federal powers.

This chapter will discuss the nature of the power of Federal, state, and local governments to regulate commerce, in general. Subsequent chapters deal with the tax power and single out for specific treatment some of the more important aspects of the legal environment of business, primarily in the areas of government regulation of competition and labor-management relations.

2   FEDERAL POWERS OVER COMMERCE

In Article I, Section 8, the Constitution provides that "Congress shall have Power . . . To regulate Commerce with foreign Nations, and among the several States, and with the Indian Tribes. . . ." The Constitution, while it enumerates the powers of the Federal government, does not define the terms used. Therefore, it was left to the courts to construe this power and to define "commerce." Chief Justice Marshall in *Gibbons v. Ogden*,[1] defining the term, said:

> *Commerce, undoubtedly, is traffic, but it is something more—it is intercourse. . . . The word . . . comprehends . . . a power to regulate navigation. . . . The Constitution . . . comprehend[s] every species of commercial intercourse between the United States and foreign nations. No sort of trade can be carried on between this country and any other, to which this power does not extend. . . .*
>
> *The subject to which the power is next applied, is to commerce, "among the several states." The word "among" means intermingled with. A thing which is among others is intermingled with them. Commerce among the states, cannot stop at the external boundary line of each state, but may be introduced into the interior. It is not intended to say, that these words comprehend that (type of) commerce, which is completely internal, which is carried on between man and man in a state, or between different parts of the same state, and which does not extend to or affect other states. Such a power would be inconvenient, and is certainly unnecessary. Comprehensive as the word "among" is, it may very properly be restricted to that commerce which concerns more states than one. . . . The genius and character of the whole government seem to be, that its action is to be applied to all the external concerns of the nation, and to those internal concerns which affect the states generally; but not to those which are completely within a particular state, which do not affect other states, and with which it is not necessary to interfere, for the purpose of executing some of the general powers of the government. The completely internal commerce of a state, then, may be considered as reserved for the state itself.*
>
> *But in regulating commerce with foreign nations, the power of Congress*

[1] 22 U.S. (9 Wheat.) 1 (1824).

does not stop at the jurisdictional lines of the several states. It would be a very useless power, if it could not pass those lines. The commerce of the United States with foreign nations, is that of the whole United States; every district has a right to participate in it. The deep streams which penetrate our country in every direction, pass through the interior of almost every state in the Union, and furnish the means of exercising this right. If Congress has the power to regulate it, that power must be exercised whenever the subject exists. If it exists within the states, if a foreign voyage may commence or terminate at a port within a state, then the power of Congress may be exercised within a state. . . .

The power of Congress, then, whatever it may be, must be exercised within the territorial jurisdiction of the several states. . . .

We are now arrived at the inquiry—what is this power? It is the power to regulate; that is, to prescribe the rule by which commerce is to be governed. . . . The power over commerce with foreign nations, and among the several states, is vested in Congress as absolutely as it would be in a single government, having in its constitution the same restrictions on the exercise of the power as are found in the Constitution of the United States.

The cases which follow contain examples of the exercise of the power to regulate commerce by the Federal government and the courts' attitude toward these regulations. They, of course, are not exhaustive but are only illustrative of the type of regulation imposed by Congress and Federal administrative agencies. The cases also discuss some of the history of the exercise of the commerce power by the Federal government.

UNITED STATES V. DARBY LUMBER CO.
312 U.S. 100 (1941)

The Darby Lumber Company, a Georgia Corporation, was indicted for criminal violation of the Fair Labor Standards Act of 1938, which then provided for a minimum wage of 25 cents per hour and maximum hours of employment of forty-four hours per week with increased compensation for overtime. The Act also required that certain records concerning the hours of employment per week and wages be kept. The indictment was dismissed when its constitutionality was challenged. The lower court held that the commerce clause did not grant the power to Congress to regulate manufacturing, since that activity cannot be considered interstate commerce. The decision was appealed by the government directly to the Supreme Court.

STONE, JUSTICE: The two principal questions raised by the record in this case are, *first,* whether Congress has constitutional power to prohibit the shipment in interstate commerce of lumber manufactured by employees whose wages are less than a prescribed minimum or whose weekly hours of labor at that wage are greater than a prescribed maximum, and *second,* whether it has power to prohibit the employment of workmen in the production of goods "for interstate commerce" at other than prescribed wages and hours. . . . The Fair Labor Standards Act set up a comprehensive legislative scheme for preventing the shipment in interstate commerce of certain products and commodities produced in the United States under labor conditions as respects wages and hours which fail to exclude from interstate commerce goods produced for the commerce, and to prevent their production for interstate commerce, under conditions detrimental to the maintenance of the minimum standards of living necessary for health and general well-being; and to prevent the use of interstate commerce as the means of competition in the distribution of goods so produced, and as the means of spreading and perpetuating such substandard labor conditions among the workers of the several states. . . .

The effect of the lower court's decision and judgment is thus to deny the power of Congress to prohibit shipment in interstate commerce of lumber produced for interstate commerce under the proscribed substandard labor conditions of wages and hours.

While manufacture is not of itself interstate commerce, the shipment of manufactured goods interstate is such commerce and the prohibition of such shipment by Congress is indubitably a regulation of the commerce. The power to regulate commerce is the power "to prescribe the rule by which commerce is governed." *Gibbons v. Ogden,* 9 Wheat. 1, 196. It extends not only to those regulations which aid, foster and protect the commerce, but embraces those which prohibit it. . . . It is conceded that the power of Congress to prohibit transportation in interstate commerce includes noxious articles, . . . stolen articles, . . . kidnapped persons, . . . and articles such as intoxicating liquor or convict made goods, traffic in which is forbidden or restricted by the laws of the state of destination. . . .

But it is said that the present prohibition falls within the scope of none of these categories; that while the prohibition is nominally a regulation of the commerce its motive or purpose is regulation of wages and hours of persons engaged in manufacture, the control of which has been reserved to the states and upon which Georgia and some of the states of destination have placed no restriction; that the effect of the present statute is not to exclude the proscribed articles from interstate commerce in aid of state regulation . . . , but instead, under the guise of a regulation of interstate commerce, it undertakes to regulate wages and hours within the state contrary to the policy of the state which has elected to leave them unregulated.

The power of Congress over interstate commerce "is complete in itself, may be exercised to its utmost extent, and acknowledges no limitations other than are prescribed in the Constitution." . . . That power can neither be enlarged nor diminished by the exercise or non-exercise of state power. . . . Congress, following its own conception of public policy concerning the restrictions which may appropriately be imposed on interstate commerce, is free to exclude from the commerce articles whose use in the states for which they are destined it may conceive to be injurious to the public health, morals or welfare, even though the state has not sought to regulate their use. . . .

Such regulation is not a forbidden invasion of state power merely because either its motive or its consequence is to restrict the use of articles of commerce within the States of destination; and is not prohibited unless by other constitutional provisions. It is no objection to the assertion of the power to regulate interstate commerce that its exercise is attended by the same incidents which attend the exercise of the police power of the states. . . .

The motive and purpose of the present regulation are plainly to make effective the Congressional conception of public policy that interstate commerce should not be made the instrument of competition in the distribution of goods produced under substandard labor conditions, which competition is injurious to the commerce and to the states from and to which the commerce flows. The motive and purpose of a regulation of interstate commerce are matters for the legislative judgment upon the exercise of which the Constitution places no restriction and over which the courts are given no control. . . . "The judicial cannot prescribe to the legislative department of the government limitations upon the exercise of its acknowledged power." *Veazie Bank v. Fenno,* 8 Wall. 533. Whatever their motive and purpose, regulations of commerce which do not infringe some constitutional prohibition are within the plenary power conferred on Congress by the Commerce Clause. Subject only to that limitation, presently to be considered, we conclude that the prohibition of the shipment interstate of goods produced under the forbidden substandard labor conditions is within the constitutional authority of Congress.

In the more than a century which has elapsed since the decision of *Gibbons v. Ogden,* these principles of constitutional interpretation have been so long and repeatedly recognized by this Court as applicable to the Commerce Clause, that there would be little occasion for repeating them now were it not for the decision of this Court twenty-two years ago in *Hammer v. Dagenhart,* 247 U.S. 251. In that case it was held by a bare majority of the Court over the powerful and now classic dissent of Mr. Justice Holmes setting forth the fundamental issues involved, that Congress was without power to exclude the products of child labor from interstate commerce. The reasoning and conclusion of the Court's opinion there cannot be reconciled with the conclusion which we have reached, that the power of Congress under the Commerce Clause is plenary to exclude any article from interstate commerce subject only to the specific prohibitions of the Constitution.

Hammer v. Dagenhart has not been followed. The distinction on which the decision was rested that Congressional power to prohibit interstate commerce is limited to articles which in themselves have some harmful or deleterious property—a distinction which was novel when made and unsupported by any provision of the Constitution—has long since been abandoned. . . . The thesis of the opinion that the motive of the prohibition or its effect to control in some measure the use or production within the states of the article thus excluded from the commerce can operate to deprive the regulation of its constitutional authority has long since ceased to have force . . . [cases cited]. And finally we have declared "The authority of the federal government over interstate commerce does not differ in extent or character from that retained by the states over intrastate commerce." *United States v. Rock Royal Cooperative,* 307 U.S. 533, 569.

The conclusion is inescapable that *Hammer v. Dagenhart,* was a departure from the principles which have prevailed in the interpretation of the Commerce Clause both before and since the decision and that such vitality, as a precedent, as it then had has long since been exhausted. It should be and now is overruled. . . .

There remains the question whether such restriction on the production of goods for commerce is a permissible exercise of the commerce power. The power of Congress over interstate commerce is not confined to the regulation of commerce among the states. It extends to those activities intrastate which so affect interstate commerce or the exercise of the power of Congress over it as to make regulation of them appropriate means to the attainment of a legitimate end, the exercise of the granted power of Congress to regulate interstate commerce. . . .

While this Court has many times found state regulation of interstate commerce, when uniformity of its regulation is of national concern, to be incompatible with the Commerce Clause even though Congress has not legislated on the subject, the Court has never implied such restraint on state control over matters intrastate not deemed to be regulations of interstate commerce or its instrumentalities even though they affect the commerce. . . . In the absence of Congressional legislation on the subject state laws which are not regulations of the commerce itself or its instrumentalities are not forbidden even though they affect interstate commerce. . . .

But it does not follow that Congress may not by appropriate legislation regulate intrastate activities where they have a substantial effect on interstate commerce. . . . A recent example is the National Labor Relations Act for the regulation of employer and employee relations in industries in which strikes, induced by unfair labor practices named in the Act, tend to disturb or obstruct interstate commerce. . . . But long before the adoption of the National Labor Relations Act this Court had many times held that the power of Congress to regulate interstate commerce extends to the regulation through legislative action of activities intrastate which have a substantial effect on the commerce or the exercise of the Congressional power over it. . . .

Congress, having by the present Act adopted the policy of excluding from interstate commerce all goods produced for the commerce which do not conform to the specified labor standards, it may choose the means reasonably adapted to the attainment of the permitted end, even though they involve control of intrastate activities. Such legislation has often been sustained with respect to powers, other than the commerce power granted to the national government, when the means chosen, although not themselves within the granted power, were nevertheless deemed appropriate aids to the accomplishment of some purpose within an admitted power of the national government . . . [cases cited]. A familiar like exercise of power is the regulation of intrastate transactions which are so commingled with or related to interstate commerce that all must be regulated if the interstate commerce is to be effectively controlled. . . .

The means adopted . . . for the protection of interstate commerce by the suppression of the production of the condemned goods for interstate commerce is so related to the commerce and so affects it as to be within the reach of the commerce power. . . . Congress, to attain its objective in the suppression of nationwide competition in interstate commerce by goods produced under substandard labor conditions, has made no distinction as to the volume or amount of shipments in the commerce or of production for commerce by any particular shipper or producer. It recognized that in present day industry, competition by a small part may affect the whole and that the total effect of the competition of many small producers may be great. . . .

Our conclusion is unaffected by the Tenth amendment. . . . The amendment states but a truism that all is retained which has not been surrendered. There is nothing in the history of its adoption to suggest that it was more than declaratory of the relationship between the national and state governments as it had been established by the Constitution before the amendment or that its purpose was other than to allay fears that the new national government might seek to exercise powers not granted, and that the states might not be able to exercise fully their reserved powers. . . .

From the beginning and for many years the amendment has been construed as not depriving the national government of authority to resort to all means for the exercise of a granted power which are appropriate and plainly adapted to the permitted end. . . . [REVERSED]

In 1942, the Supreme Court again had occasion to consider the scope of the commerce clause in the case which follows involving powers of Congress to regulate agricultural production and consumption of agricultural products. The court reviewed prior decisions and made it clear that questions of the commerce power are not decided by formulas which place reliance on the terms used but are instead based on the effects of the regulated activities on interstate commerce.

WICKARD V. FILBURN
317 U.S. 111 (1942)

Filburn operated a small farm in Montgomery County, Ohio, maintaining a herd of dairy cattle and raising poultry. In the past he had raised a small acreage of winter wheat in order to sell a portion of the crop, feed a part to poultry and livestock on the farm (some of which was sold), use some for flour for home consumption, and keep the rest for seed for the next year. Pursuant to the Agricultural Adjustment Act of 1938, as amended in 1941, Filburn was given notice that a maximum wheat acreage of 11.1 acres and a normal yield of 20.1 bushels of wheat an acre had been set for his farm by the Department of Agriculture for his 1941 wheat crop. Instead of 11.1 acres, however, Filburn sowed 23 acres and from the 11.9 acres of excess harvested 239 bushels of wheat in 1941 which were subject to a penalty of 49 cents a bushel, or $117.11 total due to the government under the Act. Filburn brought suit against the Secretary of Agriculture and others to enjoin enforcement of this marketing penalty, arguing that the scheme was an attempt to regulate production and consumption of wheat, and was beyond the constitutional power of Congress under the commerce clause because such activities were local in character and any effects they had on interstate commerce were at most indirect. The lower court, agreeing with Filburn's position, granted the injunction and Wickard appealed to the Supreme Court.

JACKSON, JUSTICE: . . . At the beginning Chief Justice Marshall described the federal commerce power with a breadth never yet exceeded. *Gibbons v. Ogden,* 9 Wheat. 1, 194, 195, 6 L. Ed. 23. He made emphatic the embracing and penetrating nature of this power by warning that effective restraints on its exercise must proceed from political rather than from judicial processes. . . .

For nearly a century, however, decisions of this Court under the Commerce Clause dealt rarely with questions of what Congress might do in the exercise of its granted power under the Clause and almost entirely with the permissibility of state activity which it was claimed discriminated against or burdened interstate commerce. During this period there was perhaps little occasion for the affirmative exercise of the commerce power, and the influence of the Clause on American life and law was a negative one, resulting almost wholly from its operation as a restraint upon the powers of the states. In discussion and decision the point of reference instead of being what was "necessary and proper" to the exercise by Congress of its granted power, was often some concept of sovereignty thought to be implicit in the status of statehood. Certain activities such as "production," "manufacturing," and "mining" were occasionally said to be within the province of state governments and beyond the power of Congress under the Commerce Clause.

It was not until 1887 with the enactment of the Interstate Commerce Act that the interstate commerce power began to exert positive influence in American law and life. This first important federal resort to the commerce power was followed in 1890 by the Sherman Anti-Trust Act and, thereafter, mainly after 1903, by many others. These statutes ushered in new phases of adjudication, which required the Court to approach the interpretation of the Commerce Clause in the light of an actual exercise by Congress of its power thereunder.

When it first dealt with this new legislation, the Court adhered to its earlier pronouncements, and allowed but little scope to the power of Congress. *United States v. E. C. Knight Co.,* 156 U.S. 1. . . . These earlier pronouncements also played an important part in several of the five cases in which this Court later held that Acts of Congress under the Commerce Clause were in excess of its power.

Even while important opinions in this line of restrictive authority were being written, however, other cases called forth broader interpretations of the Commerce Clause destined to supersede the earlier ones, and to bring about a return to the principles first enunciated by Chief Justice Marshall in *Gibbons v. Ogden, supra.*

Not long after the decision of *United States v. E. C. Knight Co., supra,* Mr. Justice Holmes, in sustaining the exercise of national power over intrastate activity, stated for the Court that "commerce among the states is not a technical legal conception, but a practical one, drawn from the course of business." *Swift & Co. v. United States,* 196 U.S. 375, 398. . . . It was soon demonstrated that the effects of many kinds of intrastate activity upon interstate commerce were such as to make them a proper subject of federal regulation. In some cases sustaining the exercise of federal power over intrastate matters the term "direct" was used for the purpose of stating, rather than of reaching, a result; in others it was treated as synonymous with "substantial' or "material"; and in others it was not used at all. Of late its use has been abandoned in cases dealing with questions of federal power under the Commerce Clause.

In the *Shreveport* rate cases (*Houston, E. & W. T. Ry v. United States*), 234 U.S. 342, . . . the Court held that railroad rates of an admittedly intrastate character and fixed by authority of the state might, nevertheless, be revised by the Federal Government because of the economic effects which they had upon interstate commerce. The opinion of Mr. Justice Hughes found federal intervention constitutionally authorized because of "matters having such a close and substantial relation to interstate traffic that the control is essential or appropriate to the security of that traffic, to the efficiency of the interstate service, and to the maintenance of the conditions under which interstate commerce may be conducted upon fair terms and without molestation or hindrance." 234 U.S. at page 351, 34 Sup. Ct. at page 836, 58 L. Ed. 1341.

The Court's recognition of the relevance of the economic effects in the application of the Commerce Clause exemplified by this statement has made the mechanical application of legal formulas no longer feasible. Once an economic measure of the reach of the power granted to Congress in the Commerce Clause is accepted, questions of federal power cannot be decided simply by finding the activity in question to be "production" nor can consideration of its economic effects be foreclosed by calling them "indirect." The present Chief Justice has said in summary of the present state of the law:

The commerce power is not confined in its exercise to the regulation of commerce among the states. It extends to those activities intrastate which so affect interstate commerce, or the exertion of the power of Congress over it, as to make regulation of them appropriate means to the attainment of a legitimate end, the effective execution of the granted power to regulate interstate commerce. . . . The power of Congress over interstate commerce is plenary and complete in itself, may be exercised to its utmost extent, and acknowledges no limitations other than are prescribed in the Constitution. . . . It follows that no form of state activity can constitutionally thwart the regulatory power granted by the commerce clause to Congress. Hence the reach of that power extends to those intrastate activities which in a substantial way interfere with or obstruct the exercise of the granted power. United States v. Wrightwood Dairy Co., 315 U.S. 110, 119, . . .

The effect of consumption of home-grown wheat on interstate commerce is due to the fact that it constitutes the most variable factor in the disappearance of the wheat crop. Consumption on the farm where grown appears to vary in an amount greater than 20 percent of average production. The total amount of wheat consumed as food varies but relatively little, and use as seed is relatively constant.

The maintenance by government regulation of a price for wheat undoubtedly can be accomplished as effectively by sustaining or increasing the demand as by limiting the supply. The effect of the statute before us is to restrict the amount which may be produced for market and the extent as well to which one may forestall resort to the market by producing to meet his own needs. That appellee's own contribution to the demand for wheat may be trivial by itself is not enough to remove him from the scope of federal regulation where, as here, his contribution, taken together with that of many others similarly situated, is far from trivial. . . .

It is well established by decisions of this Court that the power to regulate commerce includes the power to regulate the prices at which commodities in that commerce are dealt in and practices affecting such prices. One of the primary purposes of the Act in question was to increase the market price of wheat and to that end to limit the volume thereof that could affect the market. It can hardly be denied that a factor of such volume and variability as home-consumed wheat would have a substantial influence on price and market conditions. This may arise because being in marketable condition such wheat overhangs the market and if induced by rising prices tends to flow into the market and check price increases. But if we assume that it is never marketed, it supplies a need of the man who grew it which would otherwise be reflected by purchases in the open market. Home-grown wheat in this sense competes with wheat in commerce. . . .

The conflicts of economic interest between the regulated and those who advantage by it are wisely left under our system to resolution by the Congress under its more flexible and responsible legislative process. Such conflicts rarely lend themselves to judicial determination. And with the wisdom, workability, or fairness, of the plan of regulation we have nothing to do. [REVERSED]

In recent years, the Commerce power has been used in a variety of ways to expand Federal regulation of business. Perhaps the most important piece of legislation recently enacted was the Civil Rights Act of 1964, particularly its provisions pertaining to public accommodations. The purpose of this statute was to obtain equal protection of the laws and equal treatment for all citizens regardless of race, creed, color, or natural origin, but the bill was written and passed as an exercise by Congress of its power to regulate interstate commerce. The case which follows tested the constitutionality of the foregoing legislation.

HEART OF ATLANTA MOTEL, INC. V. UNITED STATES
379 U.S. 241 (1964)

A motel operator in downtown Atlanta, Georgia, sued the United States for a declaratory judgment that the public accommodation provisions of the Federal Civil Rights Statutes of 1964 were unconstitutional. Plaintiff had refused to rent rooms to Negroes. The facts of the case were not in dispute and it was admitted that plaintiff's operations were within the provisions of the Act. Therefore, the sole question before the court was the constitutionality of the Act, which the lower court upheld. The motel operator appealed.

CLARK, JUSTICE: . . . The appellant contends that Congress in passing this Act exceeded its power to regulate commerce under Art. 1, § 8, cl. 3, of the Constitution of the United States. . . .

The appellees counter that the unavailability to Negroes of adequate accommodations interferes significantly with interstate travel, and that Congress, under the Commerce Clause, has power to remove such obstructions and restraints; that the Fifth Amendment does not forbid reasonable regulation and that consequential damage does not constitute a "taking" [of property] within the meaning of that amendment; that the Thirteenth Amendment claim fails because it is entirely frivolous to say that an amendment directed to the abolition of human bondage and the removal of widespread disabilities associated with slavery places discrimination in public accommodations, beyond the reach of both federal and state law. . . .

Section 201 (C) . . . declares that "any inn, hotel, motel or other establishment which provides lodging to transient guests" affects commerce per se. . . .

While the Act as adopted carried no congressional findings the record of its passage through each house is replete with evidence of the burdens that discrimination by race or color places upon interstate commerce. . . . This testimony included the fact that our people have become increasingly mobile with millions of all races traveling from State to State; that Negroes in particular have been the subject of discrimination in transient accommodations, having to travel great distances to secure the same; that often they have been unable to obtain accommodations and have had to call upon friends to put them up overnight, and that these conditions had become so acute as to require the listing of available lodging for Negroes in a special guidebook which was itself "dramatic testimony of the difficulties" Negroes encounter in travel. These exclusionary practices were found to be nationwide, the Under Secretary of Commerce testifying that there is "no question that this discrimination in the North still exists to a large degree" and in the West and Midwest as well. This testimony indicated a qualitative as well as quantitive effect on interstate travel by Negroes. The former was the obvious impairment of the Negro traveler's pleasure and convenience that resulted when he continually was uncertain of finding lodging. As for the latter, there was evidence that this uncertainty stemming from racial discrimination had the effect of discouraging travel on the part of a substantial portion of the Negro community. This was the conclusion not only of the Under Secretary of Commerce but also of the Administrator of the Federal Aviation Agency who wrote the Chairman of the Senate Commerce Committee that it was his "belief that air commerce is adversely affected by the denial to a substantial segment of the traveling public of adequate and desegregated public accommodations." We shall not burden this opinion with further details since the voluminous testimony presents overwhelming evidence that discrimination by hotels and motels impedes interstate travel.

THE POWER OF CONGRESS OVER INTERSTATE TRAVEL

The power of Congress to deal with these obstructions depends on the meaning of the Commerce Clause. . . .

[After reviewing Justice Marshall's decision in *Gibbons v. Ogden*, previously discussed, the court continued:]

In short, the determinative test of the exercise of power by the Congress under the Commerce Clause is simply whether the activity sought to be regulated is "commerce which concerns more than one state" and has a real and substantial relation to the national interest. . . .

"Commerce among the states, we have said, consists of intercourse and traffic between their citizens, and includes the transportation of persons and property." . . .

That Congress was legislating against moral wrongs in many of these areas rendered its enactments no less valid. In framing Title II of this Act Congress was also dealing with what it considered a moral problem. But that fact does not detract from the overwhelming evidence of the disruptive effect that racial discrimination has had on commercial intercourse. It was this burden which empowered Congress to enact appropriate legislation, and, given this basis for the exercise of its power, Congress was not restricted by the fact that the particular obstruction to interstate commerce with which it was dealing was also deemed a moral and social wrong.

It is said that the operation of the motel here is of a purely local character. But, assuming this to be true, "[i]f it is interstate commerce that feels the pinch, it does not matter how local the operation which applies the squeeze." As Chief Justice Stone put it in *United States v. Darby, supra:*

The power of Congress over interstate commerce is not confined to the regulation of commerce among the states. It extends to those activities intrastate which so affect interstate commerce or the exercise of the power of Congress over it as to make regulation of them appropriate means to the attainment of a legitimate end, the exercise of the granted power of Congress to regulate interstate commerce.

Thus the power of Congress to promote interstate commerce also includes the power to regulate the local incidents thereof, including local activities in both the States of origin and destination, which might have a substantial and harmful effect upon that commerce. One need only examine the evidence which we have discussed above to see that Congress may—as it has —prohibit racial discrimination by motels serving travelers, however "local" their operations may appear.

Nor does the Act deprive appellant of liberty or property under the Fifth Amendment. The commerce power invoked here by the Congress is a specific and plenary one authorized by the Constitution itself. The only questions are: (1) whether Congress had a rational basis for finding that racial discrimination by motels affected commerce, and (2) if it had such a basis, whether the means it selected to eliminate that evil are reasonable and appropriate. If they are, appellant has no "right" to select its guests as it sees fit, free from governmental regulation. . . .

We, therefore, conclude that the action of the Congress in the adoption of the Act as applied here to a motel which concededly serves interstate travelers is within the power granted it by the Commerce Clause of the Constitution, as interpreted by this Court for 140 years. It may be argued that Congress could have pursued other methods to eliminate the obstructions it found in interstate commerce caused by racial discrimination. But this is a matter of policy that rests entirely with the Congress not with the courts. How obstructions in commerce may be removed—what means are to be employed—is within the sound and exclusive discretion of the Congress. It is subject only to one *caveat*—that the means chosen by it must be reasonably adapted to the end permitted by the Constitution. We cannot say that its choice here was not so adapted. The Constitution requires no more. [AFFIRMED]

The net effect of the decisions construing the Federal power over commerce has been to make the power illimitable. The Supreme Court's policy of aiding the development of a strong central government and fostering and encouraging regulation of activities which, while local in nature, have some effect on the country as a whole has given the Federal government powers not even dreamed of by the framers of the Constitution. Those in favor of such power laud the Court as being realistic and sensitive to the needs of the country caused by changing conditions. Those opposed harshly criticize the Court's interpretations as aborting the original purpose and true meaning of the Constitution. Despite heated controversy on the matter, the power of the central government over commerce has in fact denied the states much of their so-called "sovereign" authority. The extent to which the sovereign states may control commerce is discussed in the sections which follow.

3   STATE CONTROL OF COMMERCE

The grant of power over commerce to Congress does not contain any provision which expressly excludes the states from exercising authority over commerce. Also, the Supreme Court in *Cooley v. The Board of Wardens of Port of Philadelphia*,[2] held that the nature of the commerce power did not by *implication* prohibit state action and that some state power over commerce

---

[2] 53 U.S. 299 (1851).

is compatible with the Federal power; but that there are certain limitations on the state powers over commerce because of the commerce clause. The decisions of the Court have established three distinct areas of governmental regulation of commerce.

In *Cooley v. The Board, supra,* the Court announced that some areas of regulation were exclusively Federal and others were exclusively local, thus creating two areas on the extremes. The area which is exclusively Federal pertains to those matters where uniformity would be required on a nation-wide basis so that any state regulation is void whether Congress has entered the field or not. In theory, that which is exclusively within the states' power is intrastate commerce, or anything which is not "commerce among the Several states" *as defined by the court.* As previously noted, there are abundant situations which have been described as within the Federal power in recent years, and it is becoming more and more difficult, if not impossible, to find a subject matter which is truly exclusively local.

The third area is between the above two extremes, where joint regulation of interstate commerce by the states and the Federal government is permissible. This middle area can be divided into three subparts. The first concerns those situations in which the Federal government has preempted the field by express language or by comprehensive regulation showing an intent by Congress to exercise exclusive dominion over the subject matter. When a Federal statute has thus preempted the field, *any* state or local law pertaining to the same subject matter is unconstitutional and the state regulation is void. Absent the statute, however, the subject matter involved is of such a nature that state regulation could constitutionally exist. Second, in the area of possible joint activity, there may be some Federal regulation of a subject matter which is not comprehensive enough to preempt the field. Here state regulation is permitted, but when state law is inconsistent or in conflict with the Federal statute, it is unconstitutional and void. In addition, state laws are invalid if they discriminate against interstate commerce or impose an undue burden on it. Third, in the middle area, when no Federal statute exists, state regulation of interstate commerce is permissible, providing, of course, that it is also nondiscriminatory and does not impose an undue burden on interstate commerce. Constitutional limitations such as guarantees of due process, of equal protection of the laws, and of the basic freedoms in the Bill of Rights in addition to other constitutional restraints provide restrictions on both the Federal and state powers to regulate commerce.

While Federal statutes regulating commerce are enacted directly under the commerce clause, state laws are enacted pursuant to either the inherent police power or the taxing power, since the state government does not possess any commerce power as such. The police power has been defined as the power to enact laws protecting and promoting the public health, safety, morals, and general welfare. Conflicts between the state police power or taxing power and the commerce clause have resulted in extensive litigation. In the subsections which follow, the cases will illustrate the foregoing principles and the extent of the use of the police power by states to regulate business activity.

4   THE AREA OF EXCLUSIVE FEDERAL CONTROL

As indicated above, some matters are of such a character that their attempted regulation by states under the police power is unconstitutional. These are usually subjects where national uniformity is essential if there is to be any regulation at all. Frequently, the Federal government has taken no action with regard to a particular activity, but this fact does not necessarily allow the states to legislate on it. The case which follows is illustrative of a situation in which state regulation is not permissible.

SOUTHERN PAC. R.R. V. ARIZONA
325 U.S. 761 (1945)

Arizona enacted a statute which limited the length of passenger trains to fourteen cars and the length of freight trains to seventy cars. It was passed under the police power as a safety measure. The Southern Pacific Railroad challenged the constitutionality of the law under the commerce clause of the Federal Constitution. The Supreme Court of Arizona held the state law constitutional, and Southern Pacific appealed to the United States Supreme Court.

STONE, CHIEF JUSTICE: . . . Although the commerce clause conferred on the national government power to regulate commerce, its possession of the power does not exclude all state power of regulation. It has been recognized that, in the absence of conflicting legislation by Congress, there is a residuum of power in the state to make laws governing matters of local concern which nevertheless in some measure affect interstate commerce or even, to some extent, regulate it. . . . Thus the states may regulate matters which, because of their number and diversity, may never be adequately dealt with by Congress. . . . When the regulation of matters of local concern is local in character and effect, and its impact on the national commerce does not seriously interfere with its operation, and the consequent incentive to deal with them nationally is slight, such regulation has been generally held to be within state authority. . . .

But ever since *Gibbons v. Ogden,* 9 Wheat. 1, the states have not been deemed to have authority to impede substantially the free flow of commerce from state to state, or to regulate those phases of the national commerce which, because of the need of national uniformity, demand that their regulation, if any, be prescribed by a single authority. . . . Whether or not this long recognized distribution of power between the national and the state governments is predicated upon the implications of the commerce clause itself, or upon the presumed intention of Congress, where Congress has not spoken, . . . the result is the same.

In the application of these principles some enactments may be found to be plainly within and others plainly without state power. But between these extremes lies the infinite variety of cases in which regulation of local matters may also operate as a regulation of commerce, in which reconciliation of the conflicting claims of state and national power is to be attained only by some appraisal and accommodation of the competing demands of the state and national interests involved. . . .

For a hundred years it has been accepted constitutional doctrine that the commerce clause, without the aid of Congressional legislation, thus affords some protection from state legislation inimical to the national commerce, and that in such cases, where Congress has not acted, this Court, and not the state legislature, is under the commerce clause the final arbiter of the competing demands of state and national interests. . . .

Congress has undoubted power to redefine the distribution of power over interstate commerce. It may either permit the states to regulate the commerce in a manner which would otherwise not be permissible, . . . or exclude state regulation even of matters of peculiarly local concern. . . .

But in general Congress has left it to the courts to formulate the rules thus interpreting the commerce clause in its application, doubtless because it has appreciated the destructive consequences to the commerce of the nation if their protection were withdrawn, . . . and has been aware that in their application state laws will not be invalidated without the support of relevant factual material which will "afford a sure basis" for an informed judgment. . . . Meanwhile, Congress has accommodated its legislation, as have the states, to these rules as an established feature of our constitutional system. There has thus been left to the states wide scope for the regulation of matters of local state concern, even though it in some measure affects the commerce, provided it does not materially restrict the free flow of commerce across state lines, or interfere with it in matters with respect to which uniformity of regulation is of predominant national concern.

Hence the matters for ultimate determination here are the nature and extent of the burden which the state regulation of interstate trains, adopted as a safety measure, imposes on interstate commerce, and whether the relative weights of the state and national interests involved are such as to make inapplicable the rule, generally observed, that the free flow of interstate commerce and its freedom from local restraints in matters requiring uniformity of regulation are interests safeguarded by the commerce clause from state interference. . . .

The findings show that the operation of long trains, that is trains of more than fourteen passenger and more than seventy freight cars, is standard practice over the main lines of the railroads of the United States, and that, if the length of trains is to be regulated at all, national uniformity in the regulation adopted, such as only Congress can prescribe, is practically indispensable to the operation of an efficient and economical national railway system. . . .

The unchallenged findings leave no doubt that the Arizona Train Limit Law imposes a serious burden on the interstate commerce conducted by appellant. It materially impedes the movement of appellant's interstate trains through that state and interposes a substantial obstruction to the national policy proclaimed by Congress, to promote adequate, economical and efficient railway transportation service. . . . The serious impediment to the free flow of commerce by the local regulation of train lengths and the practical necessity that such regulation, if any, must be prescribed by a single body having a nation-wide authority are apparent. . . .

The principle that, without controlling Congressional action, a state may not regulate interstate commerce so as substantially to affect its flow or deprive it of needed uniformity in its regulation is not to be avoided by "simply invoking the convenient apologetics of the police power." . . .

Here we conclude that the state does go too far. Its regulation of train lengths, admittedly obstructive to interstate train operation, and having a seriously adverse effect on transportation efficiency and economy, passes beyond what is plainly essential for safety since it does not appear that it will lessen rather than increase the danger of accident. Its attempted regulation of the operation of interstate trains cannot establish nation-wide control such as is essential to the maintenance of an efficient transportation system, which Congress alone can prescribe. The state interest cannot be preserved at the expense of the national interest by an enactment which regulates interstate train lengths without securing such control, which is a matter of national concern. To this the interest of the state here asserted is subordinate. . . . Here examination of all the relevant factors makes it plain that the state interest is outweighed by the interest of the nation in an adequate, economical, and efficient railway transportation service, which must prevail. [REVERSED]

In the following case the defendant raised the argument that a regulation by the city of Detroit requiring certain equipment on a ship which operated in interstate commerce was void, because if such requirements were to exist at all, they would have to be uniform nationwide.

HURON PORTLAND CEMENT CO.
V. CITY OF DETROIT, MICHIGAN
362 U.S. 440 (1960)

STEWART, JUSTICE: This appeal from a judgment of the Supreme Court of Michigan draws in question the constitutional validity of certain provisions of Detroit's Smoke Abatement Code as applied to ships owned by the appellant and operated in interstate commerce.

The appellant is a Michigan corporation, engaged in the manufacture and sale of cement. It maintains a fleet of five vessels which it uses to transport cement from its mill in Alpena, Michigan, to distributing plants located in various states bordering the Great Lakes. Two of the ships, the S. S. Crapo and the S. S. Boardman, are equipped with hand-fired Scotch marine boilers. While these vessels are docked for loading and unloading it is necessary, in order to operate deck machinery, to keep the boilers fired and to clean the fires periodically. When the fires are cleaned, the ship's boiler stacks emit smoke which in density and duration exceeds the maximum standards allowable under the Detroit Smoke Abatement Code. Structural alterations would be required in order to insure compliance with the Code.

Criminal proceedings were instituted in the Detroit Recorder's Court against the appellant and its agents for violations of the city law during periods when the vessels were docked at the Port of Detroit. The appellant brought an action in the State Circuit Court to enjoin the city from further prosecuting the pending litigation in the Recorder's Court, and from otherwise enforcing the smoke ordinance against its vessels, "except where the emission of smoke is caused by the improper firing or the improper use of the equipment upon said vessels." The Circuit Court refused to grant relief, and the Supreme Court of Michigan affirmed, 355 Mich. 227. . . .

In support of the claim that the ordinance cannot constitutionally be applied to appellant's ships, two basic arguments are advanced. First, it is asserted that since the vessels and their equipment, including their boilers, have been inspected, approved and licensed to operate in interstate commerce in accordance with a comprehensive system of regulation enacted by Congress, the City of Detroit may not legislate in such a way as, in effect, to impose additional or inconsistent standards. Secondly, the argument is made that even if Congress has not expressly pre-empted the field, the municipal ordinance "materially affects interstate commerce in matters where uniformity is necessary." We have concluded that neither of these contentions can prevail, and that the Federal Contsitution does not prohibit application to the appellant's vessels of the criminal provisions of the Detroit ordinance.

The ordinance was enacted for the manifest purpose of promoting the health and welfare of the city's inhabitants. Legislation designed to free from pollution the very air that people breathe clearly falls within the exercise of even the most traditional concept of what is compendiously known as the police power. In the exercise of that power, the states and their instrumentalities may act, in many areas of interstate commerce and maritime activities, concurrently with the federal government. . . .

The basic limitations upon local legislative power in this area are clear enough. The controlling principles have been reiterated over the years in a host of this Court's decisions. Evenhanded local regulation to effectuate a legitimate local public interest is valid unless pre-empted by federal action . . . or unduly burdensome on maritime activities or interstate commerce. . . .

In determining whether state regulation has been pre-empted by federal action, "the intent to supersede the exercise by the state of its police power as to matters not covered by the Federal legislation is not to be inferred from the mere fact that Congress has seen fit to circumscribe its regulation and to occupy a limited field. In other words, such intent is not to be implied unless the act of Congress, fairly interpreted, is in actual conflict with the law of the state." . . .

In determining whether the state has imposed an undue burden on interstate commerce, it must be borne in mind that the Constitution when "conferring upon Congress the regulation of commerce, . . . never intended to cut the States off from legislating on all subjects relating to the health, life, and safety of their citizens, though the legislation might indirectly affect the commerce of the country. Legislation, in a great variety of ways, may affect commerce and persons engaged in it without constituting a regulation of it, within the meaning of the Constitution." . . . But a state may not impose a burden which materially affects interstate commerce in an area where uniformity of regulation is necessary. . . .

Although verbal generalizations do not of their own motion decide concrete cases, it is nevertheless within the framework of these basic principles that the issues in the present case must be determined. . . .

By contrast, the sole aim of the Detroit ordinance is the elimination of air pollution to protect the health and enhance the cleanliness of the local community. . . . Congressional recognition that the problem of air pollution is peculiarly a matter of state and local concern is manifest. . . .

We conclude that there is no overlap between the scope of the federal ship inspection laws and that of the municipal ordinance here involved. For this reason we cannot find that the federal inspection legislation has pre-empted local action. To hold otherwise would be to ignore the teaching of this Court's decisions which enjoin seeking out conflicts between state and federal regulation where none clearly exists. . . .

The mere possession of a federal license, however, does not immunize a ship from the operation of the normal incidents of local police power, not constituting a direct regulation of commerce. Thus, a federally licensed vessel is not, as such, exempt from local pilotage laws . . . or local quarantine laws . . . safety inspections . . . or the local regulation of wharves and docks. . . . Indeed this court has gone so far as to hold that a state, in the exercise of its police power, may actually seize and pronounce the forfeiture of a vessel "licensed for the coasting trade, under the laws of the United States, while engaged in that trade." *Smith v. Maryland,* 18 How. 71, 74. . . . The present case obviously does not even approach such an extreme, for the Detroit ordinance requires no more than compliance with an orderly and reasonable scheme of community regulation. The ordinance does not exclude a licensed vessel from the Port of Detroit, nor does it destroy the right of free passage. We cannot hold that the local regulation so burdens the federal license as to be constitutionally invalid.

The claim that the Detroit ordinance, quite apart from the effect of federal legislation, imposes as to the appellant's ships an undue burden on interstate commerce needs no extended discussion. State regulation, based on the police power, which does not discriminate against interstate commerce or operate to disrupt its required uniformity, may constitutionally stand. . . .

It has not been suggested that the local ordinance, applicable alike to "any person, firm or corporation" within the city, discriminates against interstate commerce as such. It is a regulation of general application, designed to better the health and welfare of the community. And while the appellant argues that other local governments might impose differing requirements as to air pollution, it has pointed to none. The record contains nothing to suggest the existence of any such competing or conflicting local regulations. . . .

We conclude that no impermissible burden on commerce has been shown. [JUDGMENT AFFIRMED]

5   PREEMPTION OF THE FIELD BY CONGRESS

A matter that is not an exclusively Federal problem may become so as a result of legislation. When Federal laws completely occupy a field, they are said to "preempt" it. In such cases, the state legislatures may not take action under their police powers and the state courts may likewise be excluded from the area, as the following case illustrates.

NORMAN V. LOCAL 4, INTERNATIONAL BHD. OF ELECTRICAL WORKERS
189 N.E.2d 687 (Ill. 1963)

SCHEINEMAN, PRESIDING JUSTICE: This is an appeal from a decree awarding a temporary injunction to plaintiffs, restraining the defendants from doing certain acts set forth in the complaint, and proved on the temporary hearing.

At the beginning of the hearing the defendants noted an objection to the jurisdiction of the court, on the principal ground that the National Labor Relations Board had exclusive jurisdiction of the matters involved.

The hearing proceeded without difficulty, and a considerable amount of stipulation was used to expedite the case. The undisputed facts appear to be these:

Local No. 4, International Brotherhood of Electrical Workers (hereafter referred to as No. 4), and Local No. 525 Teamsters, Chauffeurs, Warehouse-men and Helpers of America (hereafter referred to as No. 525), were both seeking to organize nine operating or technical employees of Radio Station WGNU, Granite City, Illinois, owned and operated by plaintiffs. There is no indication in the record of any jurisdictional dispute. It was simply two rival unions seeking to organize the same group.

Local No. 4 filed a petition with the National Labor Relations Board, but was informed that the Board limits its inquiry to employers doing an annual business of at least $100,000. Plaintiffs do not meet this require-ment, so the defendants voluntarily withdrew their petition. Thereafter, Local No. 525 notified plaintiffs that it represented a majority of the nine affected employees and sought a recognition agreement. When plaintiffs had satis-fied themselves that five of the employees had signed as members of that union, they agreed to the proposal. A union shop agreement was prepared and executed by the parties.

The defendants were informed of this contract, therefore, it might seem the matter was settled. On the contrary, the real trouble arose shortly there-after. Local No. 4 caused letters to be sent to the regular advertisers who had contracted for substantial time on the radio station, announcing a strike, and which contained the following paragraph:

We plan to distribute handbills (of the type enclosed) in front of Companies and Stores who advertise on Radio Station WGNU. Our sole purpose in dis-tributing these handbills is to inform the public of the strike and to request the public not to patronize those who advertise on Radio Station WGNU.

The enclosed handbill read as follows:

PLEASE DO NOT PATRONIZE THIS BUSINESS ESTABLISH-MENT AS LONG AS THEY ADVERTISE ON WGNU AM.

IBEW LOCAL 4
Members on Strike.

The record discloses that two of the four original sympathizers with No. 4 had voluntarily left the employment of plaintiff. There is nothing to disclose the activity of the other two, but there is no evidence that there was any strike, work stoppage, or labor dispute, then existent at the station.

The response to the circular letter was prompt and forceful. Five customers representing a substantial amount of contracted weekly advertising time, canceled their contracts. Others gave notice they would do so upon the first appearance of pickets and handbills.

Thereafter the suit for injunction was filed, hearing held upon notice, and the defendants were restrained from distributing written material or oral matters inducing breach of contract between plaintiffs and advertisers; conveying anything to induce advertisers to breach their contracts; interfering with property rights of plaintiff, especially in contracts with customers; representing that plaintiffs are employing workers not represented by a union when such is not the case; doing any unlawful act to prevent plaintiffs or customers from carrying out lawful contracts or conducting business in a lawful manner.

It is the law of this state that inducing breach of contract is a tortious act for which damages may be recovered, and is a proper subject for injunctive relief. Doubtless the trial court allowed the injunction in reliance on these principles, as the law of this state and many others.

The activities of the defendants are also made illegal under federal law. Parts of Sections 8(b) (4) (i) (ii) (A) and (B) of the National Labor Relations Act declare it is an unfair labor practice for a union or its agents to threaten, coerce, or restrain persons in an industry affecting commerce, with the object of forcing or requiring an employer "to cease doing business with any other person."

The defendants have threatened to distribute handbills designed to induce the public to cease patronizing a business that advertises on Station WGNU. The plain object of this threat is to force these advertisers to cease doing business with plaintiffs' radio station. The circulation of this threat has already procured cancellation of some contracts.

This court is compelled to find that the conduct of the defendants is a prohibited activity under the federal statute above cited. This finding makes it necessary to reverse the decree appealed from, for the following reasons:

When conduct is regulated both by valid federal, as well as state law, conflicts of authority may possibly arise. In that event, it is easy to conclude that the federal authority is, and must be, paramount. This concept is not accepted as sufficient by the United States Supreme Court, which goes further and holds that when federal statutes regulating conduct are enacted, Congress has thereby "preempted" the field.

Under this doctrine the federal authority vested in the National Labor Relations Board is not only paramount, it is *exclusive*. Even when the National Labor Relations Board declines to take or accept jurisdiction, pursuant to its regulations, state authorities remain powerless in the preempted field. An exception is indicated where there is excessive picketing or violence, so that the state may preserve the peace.

Counsel for plaintiffs argue that these principles do not apply in this case because there is no labor dispute involved. This is not the rule as to the type of activity here involved. . . .

For the reasons given the decree is reversed and the cause remanded with directions to dissolve the injunction and dismiss the suit. [REVERSED AND REMANDED]

6 CONFLICTS BETWEEN FEDERAL AND STATE LAWS

Clearly not every Federal law regulating an activity preempts the field and thereby precludes the state from legislating on the same subject. State regulations may exist on the same matter, but may not be in conflict with the Federal ones. Difficult questions as to whether such a conflict exists often are presented to the courts when the validity of a state rule is challenged and there is also a Federal rule in the same area.

The issue of conflicting Federal regulation was raised in the case below.

SWIFT & CO. V. WICKHAM
364 F.2d 241 (1966)

Plaintiffs, packers of frozen stuffed turkeys processed outside New York brought a suit in the Federal district court to have regulations by New York's Commissioner of Agriculture and Markets declared unconstitutional. A Federal statute required only that turkeys be labeled to show the net weight of the stuffed bird. New York's labeling requirements included a showing of the net weight of the unstuffed turkey. New York threatened to stop the sale of the turkeys unless both the stuffed and unstuffed weights were shown. The packers contended that the Federal act preempted the field, or, in the alternative, that the statutes were in conflict and therefore the Federal law was supreme. The lower court dismissed plaintiffs' suit and they appealed.

LUMBARD, CHIEF JUDGE: . . .

FEDERAL PREEMPTION

Appellants contend that the Poultry Products Inspection Act is a "broad comprehensive system of inspection and regulation of poultry and products moving in interstate commerce," that the labeling portions of this legislation are an essential and integral part of the system, and that state laws additionally regulating the labeling of poultry products are therefore pre-empted. In treating this question, we begin with the Supreme Court's caution that, "[F]ederal regulation of a field of commerce should not be deemed preemptive of state regulatory power in the absence of persuasive reasons —either that the nature of the regulated subject matter permits no other conclusion or that Congress has unmistakably so ordained."

The lower court dealt exhaustively with the history and content of the federal Act and concluded that Congress had not preempted more detailed state regulation of the manner in which poultry products are weighed, measured and labeled. We find several reasons for agreeing with this conclusion. First, the principal focus of the federal law was to combat the distribution of adulterated poultry through a uniform scheme of federal inspection. We find no basis for concluding that Congress intended the incidental and less exhaustive labeling provisions to preempt this particular area of state regulation. Second, the Poultry Products Inspection Act's labeling provisions are similar to those in the federal Pure Food, Drug, and Cosmetic Act, which are not preemptive of state regulation. Finally, we find nothing in the nature of the subject matter being regulated—the disclosure of the net weight of poultry products—that requires a uniform national standard. We agree with the district court and with the *amicus* brief of the Department of Justice that the Poultry Products Inspection Act does not preempt state regulation of the area in question.

DIRECT CONFLICT WITH FEDERAL LAW

A more difficult question is whether an irreconcilable conflict has arisen between the Poultry Products Inspection Act and the New York Agriculture and Markets Act, as interpreted. Federal law prohibits the shipment of appellants' turkeys in interstate commerce without an approved label. It is not practicable to thaw the birds after shipment to New York and make a supplemental weighing and labeling in conformance with state law at that time. Since the federal authorities have rejected a label showing the multiple weights required by New York law, and since the state will not permit the sale of stuffed turkeys absent such a label, at least the seeds of conflict are present.

The district court nonetheless held that an irreconcilable conflict had not been established. Starting with the premise that New York would accept a supplemental label showing the multiple weights required, Judge Friendly then noted that nothing in the federal Act indicated that such an additional label was necessarily unlawful. Conceding that construction of the statutory phrase "net weight" was primarily a task for the Administrator, Judge Friendly nevertheless held that the Poultry Division's rejection of the particular labels submitted by Swift and Armour for approval in 1963 did not constitute a broad ruling "that any supplementary labeling of weight in addition to that satisfying the Department would be unlawful." Given this path to reconciliation of the statutory schemes, Judge Friendly concluded that appellants had not discharged their burden of establishing conflict because they had not sought a full-fledged hearing before the Administrator at which the State of New York's interests could be presented and perhaps satisfied.

Appellants' first argument is that, contrary to the assumption of the district court, New York would not permit the multiple weights it requires to be displayed on a supplemental label. Therefore, appellants conclude, even the district court would now hold the New York scheme unlawful because the federal law, as interpreted by the Poultry Division, does not permit the multiple weights to be shown on the principal label which bears the federal markings.

One answer to this contention is that there is insufficient evidence that New York would insist upon enforcing this regulation in the face of federal opposition. But a more fundamental problem with the argument is that it still assumes that the decision of the Poultry Division rejecting appellants' proposed "principal labels" should be accepted as representing the policy of the Department of Agriculture. Like the district court, we cannot accept this assumption in view of the appellants' failure to request a hearing at which the decision of the lower-echelon officials could be more fully explored.

Appellants attack this last aspect of the district court's decision by arguing that the Act gives the right to a hearing to one who "does not accept" the initial administrative ruling and therefore that it is improper to require them to appeal rulings which they "accept." But appellants only accept the Poultry Division's rulings for the purpose of challenging the "contrary" state regulation. While they cannot be compelled to appeal from these rulings, the strong policy against invalidating state regulatory schemes in the absence of a clear showing of irreconcilable conflict with federal law requires that this court not accept the Poultry Division's rulings without a further inquiry into their propriety.

Appellants argue that, for a number of reasons, this is an inappropriate case to require them to pursue additional remedies within the federal agency. We disagree. As the lower court pointed out, uniform and accurate weights and measures are a traditional subject of state regulation. There is nothing in the federal Act or regulations that either requires the rejection of New York's definition of "net weight" or that condemns a labeling scheme that satisfies both current administrative interpretations. The reasons given by the Poultry Division in its letters rejecting appellants' proposed labels do not necessarily indicate that the two administrative positions are in hopeless conflict. In addition, the Deputy Director of the Poultry Division, called as a witness for the plaintiffs, testified that his department has as yet made no attempt to "straighten out any alleged differences" with the New York authorities. We conclude that on this record the two legislative schemes have not been shown to be in irreconcilable conflict.

Accordingly, we affirm the order of the district court. At the same time we suggest that the administrative agencies involved in this controversy should seek to resolve this unsettled situation without delay. [AFFIRMED]

7   THE POLICE POWER OF THE STATES

In those matters which are not exclusively a Federal problem and in which the Federal government has not pre-empted the field, state and local governments may exercise the police power subject to certain well-recognized qualifications. First of all, the regulation must have a relationship to public health, safety, or morals. Second, it must not violate the due-process and equal-protection clauses of the United States Constitution. The objections based on due-process and equal-protection arguments are most frequently used to challenge a tax imposed on interstate commerce but may also be used to challenge a regulating or licensing statute. Third, many state and local laws are challenged on the ground that they violate the Federal Consitution in that they impose an undue or unreasonable burden on interstate commerce. Regulations challenged on this basis usually involve questions as to the extent to which the activity affected is local in nature. Fourth, a state or local law must not discriminate against interstate commerce in favor of intrastate commerce. Fifth, while policy determination is the realm of the state legislature, it may not pass statutes which are unreasonable or arbitrary. Each of these rules will be further illustrated in the subsections below.

In many cases, the motive of the legislative body actually differs from the reason given for the exercise of the police power. For example, a law may be passed to create jobs but a reason such as public safety may be given. The Arizona train length case previously set forth is an example of such a law. Thus, the police power like the "commerce power" is often just a convenient excuse for legislation. In those cases in which the actual reason differs from the stated purpose of a state law, the law is especially susceptible to challenge. It must be remembered that the police power may be used to regulate interstate as well as intrastate commerce without violating the Constitution. When courts review legislation to determine whether there is a valid constitutional objection, they are actually on occasion substituting their judgment for that of the legislative body. Such factors as the need for and desirability of the legislation, while purportedly immaterial, actually may play a substantial role in forming the court's decision.

The cases which follow discuss the meaning of the "police power" and illustrate the usual grounds for challenging laws passed under it.

A   RELATIONSHIP TO PUBLIC HEALTH, SAFETY, OR MORALS

STATE V. GRIMES
190 N.E.2d 588 (Ohio 1963)

Defendants were convicted of violating Ohio's Sunday closing law by operating their businesses on that day, and they appealed, challenging its constitutionality. The Sunday closing law had several exceptions but they did not include the type of business operated by defendants.

CARPENTER, JUSTICE: . . . To be a valid exercise of police power, there must be a substantial relationship to the health, safety and morals of the public.

To justify the state in interposing its authority in behalf of the public over the constitutional rights of the individual, it must appear that the interest of the public generally as distinguished from those of a particular class require such interference and that the means are reasonably necessary for the accomplishment of the desired purpose, and are not unduly oppressive against individuals. . . .

Considering the absolute necessity of maintaining at least a status quo of progress how can we conclude that the regulation is not unreasonable and discriminatory. . . .

". . . This act places an unreasonable and burdensome obligation upon persons engaged in a lawful business, and is an unwarranted exercise of the police power."

Police power is the inherent sovereignty which the people delegate to the legislature for regulation at large to guard the morals, safety, health and good order in accordance with needs.

Section 2, Art. I of the Constitution of Ohio provides: "All political power is inherent in the people. Government is instituted for their equal protections and benefit . . . no special privileges or immunities shall ever be granted."

The police power must be reasonable and necessary to secure the peace, safety, morals and best interests, of the commonwealth.

Such powers must be exercised for the interest of the public in general not unduly oppressive upon individuals. . . .

For the above reasons this court is of the opinion that Section 3773.24 of the Revised Code of Ohio is unconstitutional and void.

Further discussion of the legality of Sunday closing or "blue" laws will be found in Chapter 17.

B DUE PROCESS AND EQUAL PROTECTION

BROOKS V. STATE BD. OF FUNERAL DIRECTORS & EMBALMERS
195 A.2d 728 (Md. 1963)

The state of Maryland by statute prohibited corporations from engaging in the business of funeral directing but excepted therefrom corporations previously licensed and corporations formed to carry on the business by persons who had served in the armed forces during World War II. Brooks formed a corporation after the effective date of the statute and requested a license which was denied. The corporation nevertheless conducted funerals and Brooks' license as an embalmer was suspended for one year. Brooks contended that the statute was unconstitutional under the due process and equal protection clauses of the United States Constitution. The law was passed as a health measure, and its validity was upheld by the lower court. Brooks appealed.

BRUNE, CHIEF JUSTICE: . . . On the question of due process the appellant contends, among other things, that undertaking is essentially a business, rather than a profession, and he challenges the validity of any regulation of the business which prevents its being conducted in corporate form. We are inclined to agree with the appellant's contention that the occupation is a business, rather than a profession.

That undertaking be regarded as a business and not a profession does not of itself solve the problems presented by this case. The occupation is one which bears such a relation to public health as to make it appropriate for regulation through licensing. Requirements as to the subjects upon which applicants for licenses are to be examined show that the business is concerned with matters affecting the public health. This section, after providing that applicants must meet certain requirements, including two years of practical experience as an apprentice, further provides that they "shall be examined as to the proper sanitation and disinfection of the clothing and bedding of persons dying from infectious or contagious diseases and the premises in which they shall have died; [and] as to the laws . . . relative to burials and burial permits and the proper care, preparation for burial or shipment of dead human bodies. . . ."

It is evident, of course, that corporations as such could not be examined on the above matters and that corporations can act only through agents.

The present case arises upon the suspension of the appellant's license as a funeral director, and his corporation is not itself a party to the case. The right or rights which the appellant claims here are seemingly partly individual and partly corporate. He claims as an individual the right to engage in the undertaking business through a corporation and he also seems to seek to assert the right of his corporation to engage in it. The rights of an individual to engage in a lawful business are entitled to protection under the due process and equal protection clauses of the Fourteenth Amendment and by the due process clause, Art. 23, of the State Declaration of Rights.

It is also well established and is not disputed that corporations are entitled to protection under the Due Process and Equal Protection Clauses of the Fourteenth Amendment and under Article 23 of the Declaration of Rights. There may be, however, some important differences between corporations and individuals as to whether rights which an individual may have, actually have been or may be acquired by corporations. A non-existent corporate right could scarcely receive constitutional protection.

The right of individuals to form a corporation to carry on a business is not so extensive as to authorize the formation of corporations for purposes contrary to a statute. Our General Corporation Law provides that corporations may be formed . . . for any one or more lawful purposes. . . . If, . . . a purpose stated in the charter of the Brooks corporation was to conduct the business of funeral director, it is difficult to see how, . . . this could qualify as a "lawful purpose," if Sec. 360 is valid. It follows, we think, that any right of the appellant as an individual to form or cause to be formed a corporation to conduct the business of funeral director can be established only if that prohibition is for some reason invalid. . . . This is a case of a statutory prohibition against a corporation engaging in a specified business, not of an unconstitutional condition imposed upon a right granted by statute to engage in or conduct a business. . . .

The appellant relies heavily upon *Liggett Co. v. Baldridge,* 278 U.S. 105, 49 S.Ct. 57, 73 L.Ed. 204; *Dasch v. Jackson, supra,* and *Schneider v. Duer,* 170 Md. 326, 184 A. 914, to support his contention that the statutory prohibition against new corporations conducting the business of a funeral director and against granting them licenses so to do involve a denial of due process of law. None of these cases seems to us to be controlling here.

Dasch v. Jackson, supra, a licensing case, held invalid unreasonable statutory restrictions upon the right of an *individual* to engage in a lawful, common calling, that of a paperhanger. *Schneider v. Duer, supra,* was a similar case involving the trade of barbering. There was no controversy over the right of a corporation to engage in either the business of paperhanging or that of barbering in spite of a statute prohibiting a corporation from doing so, since no corporation was involved, nor, for that matter, was there any such statute, so far as appears. The right of individuals to work themselves at their respective callings was at issue; not their right to carry on their trades through corporations organized by them.

Liggett Co. v. Baldridge, supra, held invalid, as a denial of due process of law, a Pennsylvania statute requiring that all stockholders in corporations owning drug stores be registered pharmacists. This statute contained an exception in favor of existing corporations authorized to do business in the state, which permitted them to continue to own and conduct drug stores or pharmacies owned and conducted by them when the statute took effect, but they could not own and conduct new drug stores. The Liggett Co. had acquired and wished to operate new drug stores in the state and sought an injunction to prevent enforcement of the statute to keep it from doing so. The Supreme Court, with Justice Holmes and Brandeis dissenting, held the statute void as an undue restriction upon the Liggett Company's business, since the requirement as to ownership of stock bore no reasonable relation to the public health.

The Liggett case has never been expressly overruled, but it has been seriously limited, if not completely undermined. . . .

In *Williamson v. Lee Optical Co.*, 348 U.S. 483, 75 S.Ct. 461, 99 L.Ed. 563, the Supreme Court upheld against challenge under the Due Process Clause of the Fourteenth Amendment a provision of a state statute making it unlawful for an optician to fit or duplicate lenses without a prescription from an ophthalmologist or optometrist. "In practical effect, it means that no optician can fit old glasses into new frames or supply a lens . . . without a prescription." The Supreme Court stated that the statute might "exact a needless, wasteful requirement in many cases," but it thought that the legislature might have concluded that there were enough cases where a prescription was necessary to justify these statutory requirements as to both the fitting and replacement of glasses. . . . The Court stated that "[i]t is enough that there is an evil at hand for correction, and that it might be thought that the particular legislative measure was a rational way to correct it."

Very recently, in *Ferguson v. Skrupa,* 372 U.S. 726, 83 S.Ct. 1028, 10 L.Ed.2d 93, the Supreme Court unanimously sustained a Kansas statute which flatly prohibited the business of debt adjustment, except as an incident to the lawful practice of law. The opinion of the Court referred to its "abandonment of the use of the 'vague contours' of the Due Process Clause to nullify laws which a majority of the Court believed to be economically unwise . . . ," and went on to say: "We refuse to sit as a 'super legislature to weigh the wisdom of legislation,' and we emphatically refuse to go back to the time when courts used the Due Process Clause 'to strike down state laws, regulatory of business and industrial conditions, because they may be unwise, improvident, or out of harmony with a particular school of thought.' " . . . We think that the appellant has failed to show that the exclusion of corporations from the business of funeral directors is not a valid exercise of the police power. That the burden rests upon him to do so hardly needs the citation of authority. The wisdom of such legislation is for the legislature to determine. Our concern is only with its power to adopt it. We think that the legislature can, for the protection of the public health, require that the business of undertaking be conducted only by individuals possessing the qualifications, skills and knowledge specified by Sec. 346. It could accomplish this result in either of these two ways: one by limiting the conducting of the business to such individuals, and the other by permitting not only individuals but also corporations to engage in the business, provided that the actual operations of corporations are carried on by or under the direction of duly licensed individuals. We do not think that the legislature was bound to adopt the second method or, if it had once been adopted, to adhere to it for corporations formed after the legislature determined to abandon it. It may be that the legislature thought that individual responsibility in this field would be promoted by restricting the conduct of the business to individuals or partnerships of which they are members.

The above views relate to the power of the legislature to exclude corporations entirely from conducting the business of funeral directors. This brings us to the question of unreasonableness of the statutory regulation and of discrimination arising from the fact that pre-1937 and World War II servicemen's corporations are permitted to conduct business.

Not every difference amounts to an arbitrary or invidious discrimination. . . . "The prohibition of the Equal Protection Clause goes no further than the invidious discrimination."

We think that the appellant has failed to demonstrate that the provisions in favor of existing corporations as of a past date and of corporations formed to carry on the business of persons serving in the armed forces during World War II constitute invidious discriminations. On the contrary, we deem the preservation of existing investments or values a sufficient basis to warrant separate classification and treatment. . . .

In accordance with our views that Sec. 360 is not unconstitutional as a denial of due process of law under either the Federal or the State Constitution or as a denial of the equal protection of the laws, the order of the Circuit Court will be affirmed. [JUDGMENT AFFIRMED; THE APPELLANT TO PAY THE COSTS]

C   THE PROHIBITION OF UNDUE BURDENS ON INTERSTATE COMMERCE

COMMONWEALTH V. NEW YORK CENT. R.R. CO.
216 N.E.2d 870 (Mass. 1966)

The New York Central Railroad was prosecuted for obstructing a railroad crossing for more than five minutes. Defendant's train had taken seven minutes to pass a crossing but it had not stopped. Defendant contended that the statute was not applicable to moving trains and if applicable, that it was unconstitutional as contravening the commerce clause of the United States Constitution. The defendant was found guilty, and he then appealed.

WILKINS, CHIEF JUSTICE: . . . We have no doubt that the statute is intended to apply to moving trains as well as stationary ones. . . .

There is no violation of art. 1, § 8, of the Constitution of the United States. "The interstate commerce clause did not withdraw from the states the power to legislate with respect to their local concerns, even though such legislation may indirectly and incidentally affect interstate commerce and persons engaged in it."

Nothing in *Southern Pac. Co. v. Arizona ex rel. Sullivan,* 325 U.S. 761, 65 S.Ct. 1515, 89 L.Ed. 1915, persuades us to reverse the court below and to reach a different result. In that case an Arizona statute made it unlawful to operate a passenger train of more than fourteen cars or a freight train of more than seventy cars. The majority opinion recognized that there remained a large area for State regulation: "There has thus been left to the states wide scope for the regulation of matters of local state concern, even though it in some measure affects the commerce, provided it does not materially restrict the free flow of commerce across state lines, or interfere with it in matters with respect to which uniformity of regulation is of predominant national concern. . . ."

It is a far different situation from the consequences of the Arizona statute which is presented by the Massachusetts legislation in the case at bar. The latter is not directed at interstate commerce. Its purpose is "the safety of the public . . . and convenient use of its highways." There is no limitation of speed nor any direct restriction imposed on the length of trains. There is no confusing dislocation of interstate commerce over a distance of more than a thousand miles such that from Los Angeles to El Paso. The Waverly Street crossing is on a branch, and not on a main line. The particular train at this crossing was composed of newly arrived individual cars put together by the defendant at a Framingham classification yard for brief movement to nearby unloading areas. There is nothing to show that such a train could not reasonably be moved over the crossing in five minutes. In short, there is presented a local problem without effect on national or interstate uniformity and in a field where uniformity is not necessary or desirable. This is not a case for voluntary abandonment of municipal regulation. This is a critical moment in the State's right of control over highways at railroad crossings. Rights surrendered now will not be reacquired. Local authorities would be seriously crippled in their duty to preserve the public safety and to keep their highways free of obstructions which they could not control if they should be deprived of the benefit of the reasonable protection of c. 160, § 151. Should this statute be struck down, trains might occupy crossings indefinitely leaving the highways in a continuing state of chaos. [EXCEPTIONS OVERRULED. APPEAL DISMISSED]

MORGAN V. VIRGINIA
328 U.S. 373 (1946)

A Virginia statute required separation of the races in common carriers engaged in both interstate and intrastate commerce. If contiguous seats were occupied by persons of different races, the carrier, its employees, and the passengers involved could be found guilty of a misdemeanor. A Negro was convicted of violating the statute when she refused to change her seat on the request of a bus driver. The defendant contended that the statute was unconstitutional as violating the commerce clause, and the state argued that the statute was a valid exercise of the police power.

REED, JUSTICE: . . . This Court frequently must determine the validity of state statutes that are attacked as unconstitutional interferences with the national power over interstate commerce. This appeal presents that question as to a statute that compels racial segregation of interstate passengers in vehicles moving interstate.

The precise degree of a permissible restriction on state power cannot be fixed generally or indeed not even for one kind of state legislation, such as taxation or health or safety. There is a recognized abstract principle, however, that may be taken as a postulate for testing whether particular state legislation in the absence of action by Congress is beyond state power. This is that the state legislation is invalid if it unduly burdens that commerce in matters where uniformity is necessary—necessary in the constitutional sense of useful in accomplishing a permitted purpose. Where uniformity is essential for the functioning of commerce, a state may not interpose its local regulation. Too true it is that the principle lacks in precision. Although the quality of such a principle is abstract, its application to the facts of a situation created by the attempted enforcement of a statute brings about a specific determination as to whether or not the statute in question is a burden on commerce. Within the broad limits of the principle, the cases turn on their own facts.

In the field of transportation, there have been a series of decisions which hold that where Congress has not acted and although the state statute affects interstate commerce, a state may validly enact legislation which has predominantly only a local influence on the course of commerce. It is equally well settled that, even where Congress has not acted, state legislation or a final court order is invalid which materially affects interstate commerce. Because the Constitution puts the ultimate power to regulate commerce in Congress, rather than the states, the degree of state legislation's interference with that commerce may be weighed by federal courts to determine whether the burden makes the statute unconstitutional. The courts could not invalidate federal legislation for the same reason because Congress, within the limits of the Fifth Amendment, has authority to burden commerce if that seems to it a desirable means of accomplishing a permitted end.

This statute is attacked on the ground that it imposes undue burdens on interstate commerce. It is said by the Court of Appeals to have been passed in the exercise of the state's police power to avoid friction between the races. But this Court pointed out years ago "that a state cannot avoid the operation of this rule by simply invoking the convenient apologetics of the police power." Burdens upon commerce are those actions of a state which directly "impair the usefulness of its facilities for such traffic." That impairment, we think, may arise from other causes than costs or long delays. A burden may arise from a state statute which requires interstate passengers to order their movements on the vehicle in accordance with local rather than national requirements.

On appellant's journey, this statute required that she sit in designated seats in Virginia. Changes in seat designation might be made "at any time" during the journey when "necessary or proper for the comfort and convenience of passengers." This occurred in this instance. Upon such change of designation, the statute authorizes the operator of the vehicle to require, as he did here, "any passenger to change his or her seat as it may be necessary or proper." An interstate passenger must if necessary repeatedly shift seats while moving in Virginia to meet the seating requirements of the changing passenger group. On arrival at the District of Columbia line, the appellant would have had freedom to occupy any available seat and so to the end of her journey.

Interstate passengers traveling via motors between the north and south or the east and west may pass through Virginia on through lines in the day or in the night. The large buses approach the comfort of pullmans and have seats convenient for rest. On such interstate journeys the enforcement of the requirements for reseating would be disturbing.

Appellant's argument, properly we think, includes facts bearing on interstate motor transportation beyond those immediately involved in this journey under the Virginia statutory regulations. To appraise the weight of the burden of the Virginia statute on interstate commerce, related statutes of other states are important to show whether there are cumulative effects which may make local regulation impracticable. Eighteen states, it appears, prohibit racial separation on public carriers. Ten require separation on motor carriers. Of these Alabama applies specifically to interstate passengers with an exception for interstate passengers with through tickets from states without laws on separation of passengers. The language of the other acts, like this Virginia statute before the Court of Appeals' decision in this case, may be said to be susceptible to an interpretation that they do or do not apply to interstate passengers.

In states where separation of races is required in motor vehicles, a method of identification as white or colored must be employed. This may be done by definition. Any ascertainable Negro blood identifies a person as colored for purposes of separation in some states. In the other states which require the separation of the races in motor carriers, apparently no definition generally applicable or made for the purposes of the statute is given. Court definition or further legislative enactments would be required to clarify the line between the races. Obviously there may be changes by legislation in the definition.

The interferences to interstate commerce which arise from state regulation of racial association on interstate vehicles has long been recognized. Such regulation hampers freedom of choice in selecting accommodations. The recent changes in transportation brought about by the coming of automobiles does not seem of great significance in the problem. People of all races travel today more extensively than in 1878 when this Court first passed upon state regulation of racial segregation in commerce. . . . Other federal courts have looked upon racial separation statutes as applied to interstate passengers as burdens upon commerce.

In weighing the factors that enter into our conclusion as to whether this statute so burdens interstate commerce or so infringes the requirements of national uniformity as to be invalid, we are mindful of the fact that conditions vary between northern or western states such as Maine or Montana, with practically no colored population; industrial states such as Illinois, Ohio, New Jersey and Pennsylvania with a small, although appreciable, percentage of colored citizens; and the states of the deep south with percentages of from twenty-five to nearly fifty per cent colored, all with varying densities of the white and colored race in certain localities. Local efforts to promote amicable relations in difficult areas by legislative segregation in interstate transportation emerge from the latter racial distribution. As no state law can reach beyond its own border nor bar transportation of passengers across its boundaries, diverse seating requirements for the races in interstate journeys result. As there is no federal act dealing with the separation of races in interstate transportation, we must decide the validity of this Virginia statute on the challenge it interferes with commerce, as a matter of balance between the exercise of the local police power and the need for national uniformity in the regulations for interstate travel. It seems clear to us that seating arrangements for the different races in interstate motor travel require a single, uniform rule to promote and protect national travel. Consequently, we hold the Virginia statute in controversy invalid.

[REVERSED]

D   THE PROHIBITION OF DISCRIMINATION AGAINST INTERSTATE COMMERCE

OLAN MILLS, INC. V. CITY OF BARRE
194 A.2d 385 (Vt. 1963)

Plaintiff, an Ohio corporation, brought suit to obtain a declaratory judgment that an ordinance requiring the licensing of itinerant photographers was unconstitutional as violating the commerce clause. The ordinance in question required itinerant photographers to file performance bonds and to pay license fees. License fees and bonds were not required of resident photographers. The lower court entered a decree adverse to plaintiff and plaintiff appealed.

SMITH, JUSTICE: . . . The plaintiff has briefed two issues for our consideration:

1 Does the manner in which plaintiff conducts its business in the City of Barre constitute interstate commerce?
2 If plaintiff, Olan Mills, Inc. of Ohio is engaged in interstate commerce, does the Barre City Itinerant Photographer's Ordinance unduly burden that commerce in violation of the commerce clause of the Federal Constitution? . . .

Interstate commerce has been defined by the United States Supreme Court as:

The negotiation of the sales of goods which are in another state, for the purpose of introducing them into the state in which the negotiation is made, is interstate commerce.

The manner in which the plaintiff conducts its business in Barre has been held to be interstate commerce in decisions from other jurisdictions. We think the fact that the plaintiff, Olan Mills, was engaged in interstate commerce is inescapably inferable. . . .

The defendant does not, in its brief, contend that the plaintiff is not engaged in interstate commerce. Defendant contends that the only question presented for decision to this Court is whether its ordinance, as written, is unconstitutional by placing an undue burden upon interstate commerce in its requirement that a license fee be paid for the right to solicit in the City of Barre. . . .

The statutory authority to license and regulate itinerant photographers doing business within a municipality must be exercised without undue and unfair discrimination against such non-residents or the ordinance, so permitting, will be unconstitutional and void. . . .

While it may be that the Barre ordinance was not designed for the purpose of discriminating against the non-resident photographer, it clearly has that effect against one, such as the plaintiff, who is engaged in interstate commerce. . . .

The ordinance . . . requires that the plaintiff, as an itinerant photographer pay a license fee of $10 for one week, $20 for a period of more than one week and less than four weeks, and $75 for a period of more than four weeks. No license fee of any kind is required from resident photographers of Barre, nor are such photographers required to file a performance bond.

While interstate commerce may be required to pay its way, it must be placed on a plane of equality with local trade and commerce.

Such a plane of equality does not exist under the Barre ordinance between the resident photographer, who pays no license fees or regulatory costs, and the itinerant photographer, engaged in interstate commerce, subject to the various fees and costs stated above. The existing ordinance is both unfair and discriminatory. It requires little imagination to foresee that similar ordinances in each of the various municipalities of the state would constitute a burden and barrier on interstate commerce which could not be permitted.

It is the contention of the defendant municipality that because the licensing requirement in the ordinance is directed only to the soliciting of the making and selling of the photographs, such soliciting is local in character and distinct from the interstate commerce aspect of the business of the plaintiff.

If the only thing necessary to sustain a state tax bearing upon interstate commerce were to discover some local incident which might be regarded as separate and distinct from "the transportation or intercourse which is" the commerce itself and then to lay the tax on that incident, all interstate commerce could be subjected to state taxation and without regard to the substantial economic effects of the tax upon the commerce. For the situation is difficult to think of in which some incident of an interstate transaction taking place within a state could not be segregated by an act of mental gymnastics and made the fulcrum of the tax. All interstate commerce takes place within the confines of the states and necessarily involves "incidents" occurring within each state through which it passes or with which it is connected in fact. And there is no known limit to the human mind's capacity to carve out from what is an entire or integral economic process particular phases or incidents, label them as "separate and distinct" or "local," and thus achieve its desired result.

Where an order is solicited by an agent, and the filling of the order and delivery of goods require their transportation from one state to another the solicitation transaction is one of interstate commerce. This contention of the defendant cannot be sustained.

The "Itinerant Photographers" ordinance of the City of Barre being invalid for the reasons indicated, the order must be "Judgment Reversed and Judgment for the Plaintiff."

DEAN MILK CO. V. CITY OF MADISON, WIS.
340 U.S. 349 (1951)

CLARK, JUSTICE: This appeal challenges the constitutional validity of two sections of an ordinance of the City of Madison, Wisconsin, regulating the sale of milk and milk products within the municipality's jurisdiction. One section in issue makes it unlawful to sell any milk as pasteurized unless it has been processed and bottled at an approved pasteurization plant within a radius of five miles from the central square of Madison. . . .

Appellant is an Illinois corporation engaged in distributing milk and milk products in Illinois and Wisconsin. It contended below, as it does here, that . . . the five-mile limit on pasteurization plants . . . violates the Commerce Clause and the Fourteenth Amendment to the Federal Constitution. The Supreme Court of Wisconsin upheld the five-mile limit on pasteurization. . . .

The City of Madison is the county seat of Dane County. Within the county are some 5,600 dairy farms with total raw milk production in excess of 600,000,000 pounds annually and more than ten times the requirements of Madison. Aside from the milk supplied to Madison, fluid milk produced in the county moves in large quantities to Chicago and more distant consuming areas, and the remainder is used in making cheese, butter and other products. At the time of trial the Madison milkshed was not of "Grade A" quality by the standards recommended by the United States Public Health Service, and no milk labeled "Grade A" was distributed in Madison.

The area defined by the ordinance with respect to milk sources encompasses practically all of Dane County and includes some 500 farms which supply milk for Madison. Within the five-mile area for pasteurization are plants of five processors, only three of which are engaged in the general wholesale and retail trade in Madison. Inspection of these farms and plants is scheduled once every thirty days and is performed by two municipal inspectors, one of whom is full-time. The courts below found that the ordinance in question promotes convenient, economical and efficient plant inspection.

Appellant purchases and gathers milk from approximately 950 farms in northern Illinois and southern Wisconsin, none being within twenty-five miles of Madison. Its pasteurization plants are located at Chemung and Huntley, Illinois, about 65 and 85 miles respectively from Madison. Appellant was denied a license to sell its products within Madison solely because its pasteurization plants were more than five miles away.

It is conceded that the milk which appellant seeks to sell in Madison is supplied from farms and processed in plants licensed and inspected by public health authorities of Chicago, and is labeled "Grade A" under the Chicago ordinance which adopts the rating standards recommended by the United States Public Health Service.

Both the Chicago and Madison ordinances, though not the sections of the latter here in issue, are largely patterned after the Model Milk Ordinance of the Public Health Service. However, Madison contends and we assume that in some particulars its ordinance is more rigorous than that of Chicago.

Upon these facts we find it necessary to determine only the issue raised under the Commerce Clause, for we agree with appellant that the ordinance imposes an undue burden on interstate commerce.

This is not an instance in which an enactment falls because of federal legislation which, as a proper exercise of paramount national power over commerce, excludes measures which might otherwise be within the police power of the states. . . . There is no pertinent national regulation by the Congress, and statutes enacted for the District of Columbia indicate that Congress has recognized the appropriateness of local regulation of the sale of fluid milk. D.C.Code, 1940, §§33—301 *et seq.* It is not contended, however, that Congress has authorized the regulation before us.

Nor can there be objection to the avowed purpose of this enactment. We assume that difficulties in sanitary regulation of milk and milk products originating in remote areas may present a situation in which "upon a consideration of all the relevant facts and circumstances it appears that the matter is one which may appropriately be regulated in the interest of the safety, health and well-being of local communities. . . ." *Parker v. Brown,* 1943, 317 U.S. 341. . . . We also assume that since Congress has not spoken to the contrary, the subject matter of the ordinance lies within the sphere of state regulation even though interstate commerce may be affected . . . [cases cited].

But this regulation, like the provision invalidated in *Baldwin v. G. A. F. Selig, Inc., supra,* in practical effect excludes from distribution in Madison wholesome milk produced and pasteurized in Illinois. "The importer . . . may keep his milk or drink it, but sell it he may not." *Id.,* 294 U.S. at page 521, 55 Sup. Ct. at page 500. In thus erecting an economic barrier protecting a major local industry against competition from without the State, Madison plainly discriminates against interstate commerce. This it cannot do, even in the exercise of its unquestioned power to protect the health and safety of its people, if reasonable nondiscriminatory alternatives, adequate to conserve legitimate local interests, are available. . . . A different view, that the ordinance is valid simply because it professes to be a health measure, would mean that the Commerce Clause of itself imposes no limitations on state action other than those laid down by the Due Process Clause, save for the rare instance where a state artlessly discloses an avowed purpose to discriminate against interstate goods. . . . Our issue then is whether the discrimination inherent in the Madison ordinance can be justified in view of the character of the local interests and the available methods of protecting them. . . .

It appears that reasonable and adequate alternatives are available. If the City of Madison prefers to rely upon its own officials for inspection of distant milk sources, such inspection is readily open to it without hardship for it could charge the actual and reasonable cost of such inspection to the importing producers and processors. . . . Moreover, appellee Health Commissioner of Madison testified that as proponent of the local milk ordinance he had submitted the provisions here in controversy and an alternative proposal based on § 11 of the Model Milk Ordinance recommended by the United States Public Health Service. The model provision imposes no geographical limitation on location of milk sources and processing plants but excludes from the municipality milk not produced and pasteurized conformably to standards as high as those enforced by the receiving city. In implementing such an ordinance, the importing city obtains milk ratings based on uniform standards and established by health authorities in the jurisdiction where production and processing occur. The receiving city may determine the extent of enforcement of sanitary standards in the exporting area by verifying the accuracy of safety ratings of specific plants or of the milkshed in the distant jurisdiction through the United States Public Health Service, which routinely and on request spot checks the local ratings. The Commissioner testified that Madison consumers "would be safeguarded adequately" under either proposal and that he had expressed no preference. The milk sanitarian of the Wisconsin State Board of Health testified that the State Health Department recommends the adoption of a provision based on the Model Ordinance. Both officials agreed that a local health officer would be justified in relying upon the evaluation by the Public Health Service of enforcement conditions in remote producing areas.

To permit Madison to adopt a regulation not essential for the protection of local health interests and placing a discriminatory burden on interstate commerce would invite a multiplication of preferential trade areas destructive of the very purpose of the Commerce Clause. Under the circumstances here presented, the regulation must yield to the principle that "one state in its dealings with another may not place itself in a position of economic isolation."

For these reasons we conclude that the judgment below sustaining the five-mile provision as to pasteurization must be reversed.

The Supreme Court of Wisconsin thought it unnecessary to pass upon the validity of the twenty-five-mile limitation, apparently in part for the reason that this issue was made academic by its decision upholding the five-mile section. In view of our conclusion as to the latter provision, a determination of appellant's contention as to the other section is now necessary. As to this issue, therefore, we vacate the judgment below and remand for further proceedings not inconsistent with the principles announced in this opinion. It is so ordered. [JUDGMENT VACATED AND CAUSE REMANDED]

E THE PROHIBITION OF UNREASONABLE, ARBITRARY REGULATION

ROE V. COMMONWEALTH
405 S.W.2d 25 (Ky. 1966)

WILLIAMS, JUDGE: Appellants were arrested April 18, 1965, on their farm in Greenup County, Kentucky, and indicted on a charge of operating a nudist society without a license. At the time of the arrest both appellants, the wife of one, and their children were in the back yard in the nude preparing to begin a church service. This area was visible from the road, and there were at least four cars of "sightseers" parked along the road. Appellants had circulated an application for membership in their "church" and they had solicited people to become members, but no one had joined. A sign warning people of the nudist church had also been posted on the road to the farm. The record indicates that appellants were sincere in their belief that they had been called to establish a new church.

Appellants did not have a license to operate a nudist society nor were the premises surrounded by a 20-foot high wall as is required by KRS 232.020–030.

Appellants demurred to the indictment on the grounds that the statute upon which the indictment is based is violative of their freedom of religion as guaranteed by the Kentucky and United States Constitutions, and also that the statute denies appellants due process of law. This motion and later motions for a directed verdict by appellants were overruled and the case was submitted to a jury which found appellants guilty and fined each of them $1,000. Appellants have now appealed from that conviction.

KRS Chapter 232, reads as follows:

232.010. As used in this chapter, "nudist" means any person who displays any part of his private person naked before persons of the opposite sex, not his husband or wife, at their solicitation or with their consent, for religious or health purposes.
232.020. No person shall own or operate a nudist society unless he first secures a license from the Department of Revenue and pays an annual tax of one thousand dollars.
232.030. No person shall operate a nudist society without first building a wall twenty feet in height, made of brick, stone or cement around the premises on which the society is located.

232.040. Every nudist society shall be inspected by such persons and at such times as may be deemed necessary by the Attorney-General.

232.050. The owner, operator or other person in charge of a nudist society shall keep a register of the names and addresses of all persons who enter the society. The register shall be open to inspection at all times to the proper authorities.

232.990. Any person who violates any of the provisions of this chapter shall be fined not less than one thousand dollars.

We do not reach the contention that the legislation violates freedom of religion for the reason we find it an unreasonable exercise of the police power.

The police power is an indispensable, essential attribute of sovereignty; an inherent power of the state. It is the least limitable of governmental powers, and courts have been unwilling definitely to circumscribe it. The basic standard by which the validity of all exercise of the police power is tested is that it extends only to such measures as are reasonable. It has been said that the *only* limitation upon the exercise of the police power is that such exercise must be reasonable.

. . . The right of the Legislature to declare what is a proper public policy, so as to authorize its being dealt with under the police power, seems to be limited only by the consideration that its action in the matter may not be arbitrary, but must be rested upon some tangible and reasonably clear public purpose to be served, and which has a reasonably substantial tendency to further the interest of the public welfare. . . .

The legislature has seen fit to include nudist societies within the realm of activities which may properly be regulated under the police power. There is no contention they do not fall within that scope. Perhaps they could have been prohibited altogether, but the fact is they were not. The question before us then is whether the statutes regulating them are unreasonable.

. . . Whether the end justifies the means is exclusively for the legislative discretion. Whether the means bear a pertinent and reasonable relation to the end may be looked into by the courts so far only as to determine the fact of pertinency and reasonableness. Only when the means adopted are manifestly unreasonable and oppressive, or bear no logical relation to the object of the legislation, are the courts at liberty to declare the act unconstitutional. . . .

We look to the legislation under consideration. KRS 232.030 requires a masonry wall 20 feet high around the premises on which a nudist society is located. In this case the appellants were attempting to operate a nudist society on their farm. To build a 20-foot masonry wall around the perimeter of the farm would undoubtedly be prohibitive. It seems obvious to us that privacy could be obtained by the exercise of far less stringent measures.

We note in passing that KRS 232.010, construed literally, would define as a nudist a female patient who undergoes an examination by a male physician.

A consideration of the entire legislation pertaining to nudist societies conclusively shows that the regulatory provisions set out therein are so unreasonable as to be prohibitive. The fact that a person seeking to own or operate a nudist society must pay a $1,000 license tax each year and build a 20-foot brick, stone or cement wall around the entire premises, effectively precludes the existence of a nudist society altogether. The legislature did not see fit to prohibit the existence of nudist societies but merely sought to regulate them. Having done so, the regulations should have been reasonable. We feel they were not and, consequently, must declare the act unconstitutional.

For the reasons heretofore stated, the judgment assessing a fine of $1,000 against the appellants is void. [JUDGMENT REVERSED]

CHAPTER NINE

TAXATION OF BUSINESS

1 INTRODUCTION

The taxing power is the power by which government raises revenue to defray its expenses. It is a method of apportioning the cost of government among those who receive its benefits. The purpose of taxation and the purposes and function of government are coextensive, in that the taxing power, in the broad sense, includes all charges and burdens imposed by government upon persons or property for the use and support of government. Government collects revenue from sources other than taxes. Such items as recording fees, filing fees, tolls, and license fees are charges for services or the use of facilities. Such revenues are not taxes in the strict sense of the term.

The taxing system is twofold in operation. The first part is concerned with the levy or imposition of the tax and the determination of the liability. The second is concerned with the collection of the tax. Our primary concern in this chapter is with the first aspect of taxation.

The taxing power can be exercised only for public purposes. A tax is not a contract based on assent but is a statutory liability based on force and authority. A tax is not a debt in the usual sense of the word and the constitutional prohibitions against imprisonment for debt are not applicable.

The theory supporting taxation is that since governmental functions are a necessity, the government has the right to compel persons and property within its jurisdiction to defray the costs of these functions. The payment of taxes gives no right to the taxpayer. The privilege of enjoying the protection and services of government is not based on taxes paid. As a matter of fact, there are many examples which illustrate that those who receive the most from the government pay the fewest taxes.

Taxes are paid by those able to do so, in order that all persons may share in the general benefits resulting from government. Thus property can be taxed without an obvious personal benefit to the property owner.

The power of taxation is in theory exclusively exercised by the legislative branch of the government. The only limitations on the exercise of the taxing power are found in Federal and state constitutions and the political power of the electorate to replace the legislators. Since the power of taxation is a legislative function, statutes dealing with taxation must be complete both as to the method of ascertaining the tax and its collection. The fact that a tax may destroy a business or the value of property is no basis for a judicial determination that the tax is unconstitutional. The court must find that the tax violates some specific provision of the Constitution before the tax can be held invalid. The decision as to the wisdom or propriety of the tax is left to the legislature.

2   CLASSIFICATION OF TAXES

There are many different ways of classifying taxes. Some taxes are referred to as direct taxes as contrasted with indirect taxes. Direct taxes are levied against a person who must bear their burden while the burden of indirect taxes may be passed on by the one paying them to someone else. Another common classification distinguishes specific from ad valorem taxes. A specific tax is fixed by some standard such as weight or measure and only requires a listing of the items to be taxed. For example, taxes on cigarettes are specific. An ad valorem tax is a fixed proportion of the value of the property and requires an appraisal of the property before the tax can be determined. Ad valorem means "according to the value" and an ad valorem tax is levied at a certain rate. For example, an automobile might be taxed at 4 percent of its fair market value. General property taxes on real estate and personal property are the most common examples of ad valorem taxes.

Frequently taxes are classified as general or special. A general tax is levied against all persons or property irrespective of any benefit received, while a special tax or assessment is levied only against those receiving direct benefits. Special assessments to pave streets are typical special taxes while real estate taxes are general.

The most common method of classifying taxes is based on the subject matter on which they are imposed. Taxes are imposed on (1) property, (2) privileges, or (3) persons. Under this method, there are property taxes, excise taxes, and capitation or poll taxes. A property tax is assessed on all property of a certain class within the territory, as of a certain time, and is based on value. Excise taxes are based on the exercise of a privilege, the doing of an act, or the engaging in an occupation. Many state constitutions contain certain limitations on property taxes and other limitations on excise taxes. A considerable amount of litigation has resulted as to whether a particular tax is a property tax or an excise tax to determine if the limitations of that classification have been exceeded. Excise taxes include all taxes not assessed on a person or his property and the term "privilege tax" is synonymous with excise tax. The sales tax and use tax are the most common of the excise taxes.

Capitation or poll taxes are levied upon persons of a certain class such as voters, without regard to property or occupation. The income tax is not a poll tax but an excise tax.

3   FEDERAL TAXATION

The Federal taxing power is a tool of government which is utilized as an aid in policy implementation as well as a means of raising revenue. The taxing power is used to assist governmental attempts to regulate the economy. For example, depreciation allowances have been accelerated in recent years to bolster the economy by making additional cash available for business investment. The periods over which property might be depreciated were varied as an economic tool. Tax laws are also used by the Federal government to equalize competition among different businesses. For example, the gasoline tax is an important part of the equalization of costs between truckers and other forms of transportation. The taxing power has been used to encourage uniform legislation among the states. States were encouraged to adopt inheritance taxes by a Federal law which gave persons an 80 percent credit on the Federal estate tax for death taxes paid to states. It should be noted that since the enactment of the original law, however, the Federal estate tax rates have been increased to such an extent that today only about 10 percent of all death taxes are paid to states. Similar pressure was put on the states by the Unemployment Compensation Act which allows, as a credit against the Federal tax, a certain portion of the tax paid to states. Import taxes imposed by the Federal government are also used as an economic tool. The protection from foreign competition they afforded domestic industries was a significant factor in the development of large manufacturing enterprises in this country. Under the Constitution, states may not impose import taxes [1] and neither the state nor Federal governments may impose direct export taxes.[2] However, note that the taxes on this country's imports are likely to be reciprocated by foreign nations with comparable taxes on imports from America, so that indirectly the Federal import tax policy results in a benefit or burden to American exporting.

The Federal taxing power is also used to implement social policies. For example, the Federal estate tax and the graduated income tax were in part adopted to break up large accumulations of wealth. In addition, the Federal government pays money to the states to encourage certain activities such as education, road building, and slum clearance. Persons in one part of the country may pay for social improvements in another as a direct result of the exercise of the taxing and spending powers of the Federal government. An examination of the implementation policies of the Federal government will reveal that many of them are tied directly to taxation.

Few questions are raised today concerning the *validity* of a federally imposed tax. The Sixteenth Amendment to the Constitution and the broad scope of the Federal taxing power which has been approved by the courts eliminates most such issues. Of course, there is a considerable amount of litigation involving the *interpretation* and *application* of the Federal tax laws

[1] United States Constitution, Art. I, § 10.
[2] United States Constitution, Art. I, §§ 9, 10.

and regulations. One such recent case involved the issue of whether "strike benefits" paid by a union were taxable income to its members.[3] There, the jury held that they constituted a gift. At the state and local levels, serious questions of legality are raised when a tax is sought to be imposed on a business which is operating in interstate commerce. These are discussed in sections which follow.

4   STATE AND LOCAL TAXATION—IN GENERAL

State and local governments impose a variety of taxes on individuals and corporations. These commonly take the form of property taxes, income taxes, sales or use taxes, and license fees. State taxes may range from those on liquor, tobacco, and petroleum products to those on parimutuel betting. The variety and incidence of state taxation will depend on the economy and industry of the state. For example, a tourist state such as Florida may impose a higher tax on room rent receipts of motels and hotels than a non-tourist state does.

Local taxes are imposed by a multitude of municipal corporations in every locality. The boundaries of these municipal corporations overlap, and the local tax bill often is merely the sum total of the tax rates of all these taxing bodies. For example, local taxes may be paid to a (1) school district, (2) park district, (3) fire prevention and protection district, (4) sanitary district, (5) drainage district, (6) city or village, (7) township, (8) county, (9) mental health district, (10) library district, and (11) other public bodies given legislative responsibilities which need funds to carry out their functions. The general property tax is often used to raise money for local government. As the competition for revenue has increased, municipalities have become hard-pressed for sources of revenue. Some have imposed municipal sales or use taxes. Some have attempted and others are contemplating income taxes. Some are raising substantial sums by imposing large license fees on the privilege of doing business. The validity of many of the local revenue-raising schemes remains to be determined. Many of the decisions will depend on the constitutions of the various states, but issues under the Federal Constitution are also present.

Since a large number of businesses conduct interstate operations, complex legal questions arise as to the power of the various states to tax these business activities and the property involved. Taxes imposed on wholly intrastate activities raise no Federal constitutional issues, but there are limitations on the powers of state and local governments to tax interstate activities due to the commerce clause of the Federal Constitution. Courts are frequently faced with the delicate problem of determining the line between the

---

[3] *United States v. Kaiser*, 363 U.S. 299 (1960).

state's power to tax activities occurring within its territorial jurisdiction and its lack of power to burden interstate commercial activity unduly, which, by the Federal Constitution, is within the power of Congress to control. For example, in *State of Minnesota v. Blasius,*[4] a property tax on cattle shipped to a stockyard for sale was approved even though the buyer intended to resell them immediately, because the cattle had come to rest. In this case the court stated:

> *If the interstate movement has not begun, the mere fact that such a movement is contemplated does not withdraw the property from the state's power to tax it. . . . If the interstate movement has begun, it may be regarded as continuing, so as to maintain the immunity of the property from state taxation, despite temporary interruptions due to the necessities of the journey or for the purpose of safety and convenience in the course of the movement. . . .*

> *Where property has come to rest within a state, being held there at the pleasure of the owner, for disposal or use, so that he may dispose of it either within the state, or for shipment elsewhere, as his interest dictates, it is deemed to be a part of the general mass of property within the state and is thus subject to its taxing power.*

> *Here the original shipment was not suspended; it was ended. That shipment was to the South St. Paul Stockyards for sale on that market. That transportation had ceased, and the cattle were sold on that market to Blasius, who became absolute owner and was free to deal with them as he liked. He could sell the cattle within the state or for shipment outside the state. He placed them in pens and cared for them awaiting such disposition as he might see fit to make for his own profit. The tax was assessed on the regular tax day while Blasius thus owned and possessed them. The cattle were not held by him for the purpose of promoting their safe or convenient transit. They were not in transit. Their situs was in Minnesota where they had come to rest. There was no federal right to immunity from the tax.*

Certain general rules can be stated concerning the effect of the commerce clause on state and local taxation. First of all, the states may not impose direct burdens upon interstate commerce; that is, they may not regulate or restrain that which from its nature should be under the control of the one authority and be free from restriction save as it is governed in the manner that the national legislature constitutionally ordains. Thus, the states cannot tax interstate commerce, either by laying the tax upon the business which constitutes such commerce or the privilege of engaging in it, or upon the receipts, as such, derived from it. Similarly, the states may not tax property in transit in interstate commerce.

However, the commerce clause does not prohibit a tax which indirectly affects interstate commerce.

4 290 U.S. 1 (1933).

In *Western Live Stock v. Bureau of Revenue,* 303 U.S. 250 (1938), . . . the United States Supreme Court said:

> *It was not the purpose of the commerce clause to relieve those engaged in interstate commerce from their just share of state tax burden even though it increases the cost of doing the business. "Even interstate business must pay its way," . . . and the bare fact that one is carrying on interstate commerce does not relieve him from many forms of state taxation which add to the cost of his business. . . .*

The law views taxation as a method of distributing the burdens of government among those who benefit from governmental activities. Since interstate businesses receive benefits just as do intrastate businesses, there is no automatic exemption from taxation because of the commerce clause.

There are, however, limitations on the powers of state and local governments to tax interstate commerce. These may be classified as the (1) discrimination, (2) nexus, and (3) apportionment limitations. Nexus is discussed in section 5 of this chapter, and apportionment in section 6.

The discrimination limitation prohibits the tax burden from discriminating against interstate commerce in favor of intrastate commerce. Otherwise, the tax will violate the commerce clause, as the case which follows illustrates.

WEST POINT WHOLESALE GROC. CO. V. CITY OF OPELIKA
354 U.S. 390 (1957)

HARLAN, JUSTICE: This is a suit to recover taxes paid by the appellant to the City of Opelika, Alabama, on the ground that the taxes in question imposed a discriminatory burden on interstate commerce. The state court sustained a demurrer to the complaint, 38 Ala. App. 444, 87 So. 2d 661, rejecting the appellant's federal contention, and we noted probable jurisdiction. 352 U.S. 924. . . .

Section 130(a), of Ordinance No. 101–53 of the City of Opelika, as amended by Ordinance No. 103–53, provides that an annual privilege tax of $250 must be paid by any firm engaged in the wholesale grocery business which delivers, at wholesale, groceries in the City from points without the City. Appellant is a Georgia corporation engaged in the wholesale grocery business in West Point, Georgia. It solicits business in the City of Opelika through salesmen; orders are transmitted to appellant's place of business in Georgia, where they are accepted and the groceries thereupon loaded on trucks and delivered to the City. Appellant has no place of business, office, or inventory in Opelika, its only contact with that City being the solicitation of orders and the delivery of goods.

We held in *Nippert v. City of Richmond,* 327 U.S. 416, . . . and in *Memphis Steam Laundry Cleaner, Inc. v. Stone,* 342 U.S. 389, . . . that a municipality may not impose a flat-sum privilege tax on an interstate enterprise whose only contact with the municipality is the solicitation of orders and the subsequent delivery of goods at the end of an uninterrupted movement in interstate commerce, such a tax having a substantial exclusory effect on interstate commerce. In our opinion the tax here in question falls squarely within the ban of those cases. This is particularly so in that Opelika places no comparable flat-sum tax on local merchants. Wholesale grocers whose deliveries originate in Opelika, instead of paying $250 annually, are taxed a sum graduated according to their gross receipts. Such an Opelika wholesaler would have to gross the sum of $280,000 in sales in one year before his tax would reach the flat $250 amount imposed on all foreign grocers before they may set foot in the City. The Commerce Clause forbids any such discrimination against the free flow of trade over state boundaries.

Since the present tax cannot constitutionally be applied to the appellant, the judgment must be reversed and the case remanded for proceedings not inconsistent with this opinion. [REVERSED]

5   NEXUS

The nexus limitation means that there must be a sufficient contact, connection, tie, or link with the taxing state to support the tax. In other words, there must be sufficient local activities to justify the tax in a constitutional sense. The constitutional requirements are stated in terms of the due process requirements of the Fourteenth Amendment. A business operating in a state directly benefits from its police and fire protection, use of its road and the like. Indirectly it will be able to recruit employees more easily if they have easy access to good schools, parks, and civic centers. If the state gives anything for which it can reasonably expect payment, then the tax has a sufficient nexus. In cases involving property taxes, the term "taxable situs" is used in place of "nexus," but each is concerned with the adequacy of local activities to support the tax. The Braniff Airline case which follows is a typical "nexus" or "situs" case.

BRANIFF AIRWAYS V. NEBRASKA STATE BD. OF EQ. & A.
347 U.S. 590 (1954)

REED, JUSTICE: The question presented by this appeal from the Supreme Court of Nebraska is whether the Constitution bars the State of Nebraska from levying an apportioned ad valorem tax on the flight equipment of appellant, an interstate air carrier. Appellant is not incorporated in Nebraska and does not have its principal place of business or home port registered under the Civil Aeronautics Act, 52 Stat. 977, 49 U.S.C. §§ 401–705, 49

U.S.C.A. §§ 401–705, in that state. Such flight equipment is employed as a part of a system of interstate air commerce operating over fixed routes and landing on and departing from airports within Nebraska on regular schedules. . . . It contends . . . that its flight equipment used in interstate commerce is immune from taxation by Nebraska because it is without situs in that state. . . .

The home port registered with the Civil Aeronautics Authority and the overhaul base for the aircraft in question is the Minneapolis–St. Paul Airport, Minnesota. All of the aircraft not undergoing overhaul fly regular schedules upon a circuit ranging from Minot, North Dakota, to New Orleans, Louisiana, with stops in fourteen states including Minnesota, Nebraska and Oklahoma. . . . The Nebraska stops are of short duration since utilized only for the discharge and loading of passengers, mail, express, and freight, and sometimes refueling. Appellant neither owns nor maintains facilities for repairing, reconditioning, or storing its flight equipment in Nebraska, but rents depot space and hires other services as required.

Required reports filed . . . for 1950 show that about 9% of its revenue and 11½% of the total system tonnage originated in Nebraska and about 9% of its total stops were made in that state. From these figures, using the statutory formula, the Tax Commissioner arrived at a valuation of $118,901 allocable to Nebraska, resulting in a tax of $4,280.44. . . . The Supreme Court of Nebraska held the statute not violative of the Commerce Clause. . . .

The argument upon which appellant depends ultimately, however, is that its aircraft never "attained a taxable situs within Nebraska" from which it argues that the Nebraska tax imposes a burden on interstate commerce. In relying upon the Commerce Clause on this issue and in not specifically claiming protection under the Due Process Clause of the Fourteenth Amendment, appellant names the wrong constitutional clause to support its position. While the question of whether a commodity en route to market is sufficiently settled in a state for purpose of subjection to a property tax has been determined by this Court as a Commerce Clause question, the bare question whether an instrumentality of commerce has tax situs in a state for the purpose of subjection to a property tax is one of due process. However, appellant timely raised and preserved its contention that its property was not taxable because such property had attained no taxable situs in Nebraska. Though inexplicit, we consider the due process issue within the clear intendment of such contention and hold such issue sufficiently presented. . . .

The limitation imposed by the Due Process Clause upon state power to impose taxes upon such instrumentalities was succinctly stated in the *Ott* case: "So far as due process is concerned the only question is whether the tax in practical operation has relation to opportunities, benefits, or protection conferred or afforded by the taxing State." 336 U.S. at page 174. . . . In *Curry v. McCanless*, 307 U.S. 357, . . . the evolution of such restriction on state power was reviewed and the rule stated thusly:

When we speak of the jurisdiction to tax land or chattels as being exclusively in the state where they are physically located, we mean no more than that the benefit and protection of laws enabling the owner to enjoy the fruits of his ownership and the power to reach effectively the interests protected, for the purpose of subjecting them to payment of a tax are so narrowly restricted to the state in whose territory the physical property is located as to set practical limits to taxation by others. Id., 307 U.S. at page 364. . . .

Thus the situs issue devolves into the question of whether eighteen stops per day by appellant's aircraft is sufficient contact with Nebraska to sustain that state's power to levy an apportioned ad valorem tax on such aircraft. We think such regular contact is sufficient to establish Nebraska's power to tax even though the same aircraft do not land every day and even though none of the aircraft is continuously within the state. "The basis of the jurisdiction is the habitual employment of the property within the state." Appellant rents its ground facilities and pays for fuel it purchases in Nebraska. This leaves it in the position of other carriers such as rails, boats and motors that pay for the use of local facilities so as to have the opportunity to exploit the commerce, traffic, and trade that originates in or reaches Nebraska. Approximately one-tenth of appellant's revenue is produced by the pickup and discharge of Nebraska freight and passengers. Nebraska certainly affords protection during such stops and these regular landings are clearly a benefit to appellant. . . . [AFFIRMED]

The concept of what constituted nexus was greatly expanded as well as clarified in two companion cases in 1959. These cases (set forth below) involved state income taxes and apportionment formulas. The concept of apportionment will be discussed further in the next section.

NORTHWESTERN STATES PORTLAND CEMENT CO. V. MINNESOTA
358 U.S. 450 (1959)

CLARK, JUSTICE: These cases concern the constitutionality of state net income tax laws levying taxes on that portion of a foreign corporation's net income earned from and fairly apportioned to business activities within the taxing State when those activities are exclusively in furtherance of interstate commerce. No question is raised in either case as to the reasonableness of the apportionment of net income under the State's formulas nor to the amount of the final assessment made. . . .

The importance of the question in the field of state taxation is indicated by the fact that thirty-five States impose direct net income taxes on corporations. . . .

Although the cases were separately briefed, argued, and submitted, we have, because of the similarity of the tax in each case, consolidated them for the purposes of decision. It is contended that each of the state statutes, as applied, violates both the Due Process and the Commerce Clauses of the United States Constitution. Article 1, § 8, cl. 3; Amend. 14. We conclude that net income from the interstate operations of a foreign corporation may be subjected to state taxation provided the levy is not discriminatory and is properly apportioned to local activities within the taxing State forming sufficient nexus to support the same.

No. 12. *Northwestern States Portland Cement Co. v. State of Minnesota.* This is an appeal from judgments of Minnesota's courts upholding the assessment by the State of income taxes for the years 1933 through 1948 against appellant, an Iowa corporation engaged in the manufacture and sale of cement at its plant in Mason City, Iowa, some forty miles from the Minnesota border. The tax was levied under § 290.03 of the Minnesota statutes, which imposes an annual tax upon the taxable net income of residents and nonresidents alike. One of four classes taxed by the statute is that of "domestic and foreign corporations . . . whose business within this state during the taxable year consists exclusively of foreign commerce, interstate commerce, or both." Minnesota has utilized three ratios in determining the portion of net income taxable under its law. The first is that of the taxpayer's sales assignable to Minnesota during the year to its total sales during that period made everywhere; the second, that of the taxpayer's total tangible property in Minnesota for the year to its total tangible property used in the business that year wherever situated. The third is the taxpayer's total payroll in Minnesota for the year to its total payroll for its entire business in the like period. As we have noted, appellant takes no issue with the fairness of this formula nor of the accuracy of its application here.

Appellant's activities in Minnesota consisted of a regular and systematic course of solicitation of orders for the sale of its products, each order being subject to acceptance, filling and delivery by it from its plant at Mason City. It sold only to eligible dealers, who were lumber and building material supply houses, contractors and ready-mix companies. A list of these eligible dealers was maintained and sales would not be made to those not included thereon. Forty-eight percent of appellant's entire sales were made in this manner to such dealers in Minnesota. For efficient handling of its activity in that State, appellant maintained in Minneapolis a leased sales office equipped with its own furniture and fixtures and under the supervision of an employee-salesman known as "district manager." Two salesmen, including this district manager, and a secretary occupied this three-room office. Two additional salesmen used it as a clearing house. Each employee was paid a straight salary by the appellant direct from Mason City and two cars were furnished by it for the salesmen. Appellant maintained no bank account in Minnesota, owned no real estate there, and warehoused no merchandise in the State. All sales were made on a delivered price basis fixed by the appellant in Mason City and no "pick ups" were permitted at its plant there. The salesmen, however, were authorized to quote Minnesota customers a delivered price. Orders received by the salesmen or at the Minneapolis office were transmitted daily to appellant in Mason City, were approved there, and acknowledged directly to the purchaser with copies to the salesman.

In addition to the solicitation of approved dealers, appellant's salesmen also contacted potential customers and users of cement products, such as builders, contractors, architects, and state, as well as local government purchasing agents. Orders were solicited and received from them, on special forms furnished by appellant, directed to an approved local dealer who in turn would fill them by placing a like order with appellant. Through this system appellant's salesmen would in effect secure orders for local dealers which in turn were filled by appellant in the usual manner. Salesmen would also receive and transmit claims against appellant for loss or damage in any shipments made by it, informing the company of the nature thereof and requesting instructions concerning the same.

No income tax returns were filed with the State by the appellant. The assessments sued upon, aggregating some $102,000, with penalties and interest, were made by the Commissioner of Taxation on the basis of information available to him.

No. 33. *T. V. Williams, Commissioner v. Stockham Valves & Fittings, Inc.* . . . Georgia levies a tax on net incomes "received by every corporation, foreign or domestic, owning property or doing business in this State." The Act defines the latter as including "any activities or transactions" carried on within the State "for the purpose of financial profit or gain" regardless of its connection with interstate commerce. To apportion net income, the Act applies a three-factor ratio based on inventory, wages and gross receipts. Under the Act the State Revenue Commissioner assessed and collected a total of $1,478.31 from respondent for the taxable years 1952, 1954 and 1955, and after claims for refund were denied the respondent filed this suit to recover such payments. It bases its right to recover squarely upon the constitutionality of Georgia's Act under the Commerce and the Due Process Clauses of the Constitution of the United States.

That there is a "need for clearing up the tangled underbrush of past cases" with reference to the taxing power of the States is a concomitant to the negative approach resulting from a case-by-case resolution of "the extremely limited restrictions that the Constitution places upon the states. . . ." *State of Wisconsin v. J. C. Penney Co.,* 1940, 311 U.S. 435, 445. . . . Commerce between the States having grown up like Topsy, the Congress meanwhile not having undertaken to regulate taxation of it, and the States having understandably persisted in their efforts to get some return for the substantial benefits they have afforded it, there is little wonder that there has been no end of cases testing out state tax levies. The result-ing judicial application of constitutional principles to specific state statutes leaves much room for controversy and confusion and little in the way of precise guides to the States in the exercise of their indispensable power of taxation. This Court alone has handed down some three hundred full-dress opinions spread through slightly more than that number of our reports. As was said in *Miller Bros. Co. v. State of Maryland,* 1954, 347 U.S. 340, 344, . . . the decisions have been "not always clear . . . consistent or recon-cilable. A few have been specifically overruled, while others no longer fully represent the present state of the law." From the quagmire there emerge, however, some firm peaks of decision which remain unquestioned.

It has long been established doctrine that the Commerce Clause gives exclusive power to the Congress to regulate interstate commerce, and its failure to act on the subject in the area of taxation nevertheless requires that interstate commerce shall be free from any direct restrictions or impo-sitions by the States. *Gibbons v. Ogden,* 1824, 9 Wheat. 1. . . . In keep-ing therewith a State "cannot impose taxes upon persons passing through the state, or coming into it merely for a temporary purpose" such as itiner-ant drummers. *Robbins v. Taxing District,* 1887, 120 U.S. 489, 493–494. . . . Moreover, it is beyond dispute that a State may not lay a tax on the "privilege" of engaging in interstate commerce, *Spector Motor Service v. O'Connor,* 1951, 340 U.S. 602. . . . Nor may a State impose a tax which discriminates against interstate commerce either by providing a direct com-mercial advantage to local business . . . or by subjecting interstate com-merce to the burden of "multiple taxation." . . . Such impositions have been stricken because the States, under the Commerce Clause, are not al-lowed "one single tax-dollar worth of direct interference with the free flow of commerce." *Freeman v. Hewit,* 1946, 329 U.S. 249, 256. . . .

On the other hand, it has been established since 1918 that a net in-come tax on revenues derived from interstate commerce does not offend constitutional limitations upon state interference with such commerce. The decision of *Peck & Co. v. Lowe,* 247 U.S. 165 38 Sup. Ct. 432, 62 L. Ed. 1049, pointed the way. There the Court held that though true it was that the Constitution provided "No Tax or Duty shall be laid on Articles exported from any State," Art. I, § 9, still a net income tax on the profits derived from such commerce was not "laid on articles in course of exportation or on any-thing which inherently or by the usages of commerce is embraced in exporta-tion or any of its processes. . . . At most, exportation is affected only indirectly and remotely." . . . The first case in this Court applying the doctrine to interstate commerce was that of *United States Glue Co. v. Town of Oak Creek,* 1918, 247 U.S. 321. . . . There the Court distinguished be-tween an invalid direct levy which placed a burden on interstate commerce and a charge by way of net income derived from profits from interstate com-merce. This landmark case and those usually cited as upholding the doctrine there announced, . . . dealt with corporations which were domestic to the taxing State (*United States Glue Co. v. Town of Oak Creek, supra*), or which had "established a 'commercial domicile' " there. . . .

[T]he presence of such a circumstance is not controlling. . . . the entire net income of a corporation, generated by interstate as well as intrastate activities, may be fairly apportioned among the States for tax purposes by formulas utilizing in-state aspects of interstate affairs. In fact, in *Bass, Ratcliff & Gretton* the operations in the taxing State were conducted at a loss, and still the Court allowed part of the over-all net profit of the corporation to be attributed to the State. . . .

Any doubt as to the validity of our position here was entirely dispelled . . . in a unanimous *per curiam* in *West Publishing Co. v. McColgan*, 328 U.S. 823. . . . The case involved the validity of California's tax on the apportioned net income of West Publishing Company, whose business was exclusively interstate. . . . While the statement of the facts in that opinion recites that "The employees were given space in the offices of attorneys in return for the use of plaintiff's books stored in such offices," it is significant to note that West had not qualified to do business in California and the State's statute itself declared that the tax was levied on income derived from interstate commerce within the State, as well as any arising intrastate. The opinion was not grounded on the triviality that office space was given West's soliciters by attorneys in exchange for the chanceful use of what books they may have had on hand for their sales activities. Rather, it recognized that the income taxed arose from a purely interstate operation.

In relying on the foregoing cases for the proposition that a foreign corporation engaged within a state solely in interstate commerce is immune from net income taxation by that state, plaintiff [West Publishing Co.] overlooks the distinction made by the United States Supreme Court between a tax whose subject is the privilege of engaging in interstate commerce and a tax whose subject is the net income from such commerce. It is settled by decisions of the United States Supreme Court that a tax on net income from interstate commerce, as distinguished from a tax on the privilege of engaging in interstate commerce, does not conflict with the commerce clause. . . .

We believe that the rationale of these cases, involving income levies by States, controls the issues here. The taxes are not regulations in any sense of that term. Admittedly they do not discriminate against nor subject either corporation to an undue burden. While it is true that a State may not erect a wall around its borders preventing commerce an entry, it is axiomatic that the founders did not intend to immunize such commerce from carrying its fair share of the costs of the state government in return for the benefits it derives from within the State. The levies are not privilege taxes based on the right to carry on business in the taxing State. The States are left to collect only through ordinary means. The tax, therefore, is "not open to the objection that it compels the company to pay for the privilege of engaging in interstate commerce." . . .

As was said in *State of Wisconsin v. Minnesota Mining & Mfg. Co.*, 1940, 311 U.S. 452, 453, . . . "it is too late in the day to find offense to that [commerce] Clause because a state tax is imposed on corporate net income of an interstate enterprise which is attributable to earnings within the taxing state. . . ."

While the economic wisdom of state net income taxes is one of state policy not for our decisions, one of the "realities" raised by the parties is the possibility of a multiple burden resulting from the exactions in question. The answer is that none is shown to exist here. This is not an unapportioned tax which by its very nature makes interstate commerce bear more than its fair share. As was said in *Central Greyhound Lines of New York v. Mealey*, 1948, 334 U.S. 653, 661, . . . "it is interstate commerce which the State is seeking to reach and . . . the real question [is] whether what the State is exacting is a constitutionally fair demand by the State for that aspect of the interstate commerce to which the State bears a special relation." The apportioned tax is designed to meet this very requirement and "to prevent the levying of such taxes as will discriminate against or prohibit the interstate activities or will place the interstate commerce at a disadvantage relative to local commerce." . . . Logically it is impossible, when the tax is fairly apportioned, to have the same income taxed twice. In practical operation, however, apportionment formulas being what they are, the possibility of the contrary is not foreclosed, especially by levies in domiciliary States. But that question is not before us. . . .

There is nothing to show that multiple taxation is present. We cannot deal in abstractions. In this type of case the taxpayers must show that the formula places a burden upon interstate commerce in a constitutional sense. This they have failed to do. . . .

The taxes here, like that in *West Publishing Co. v. McColgan, supra,* are based only upon the net profits earned in the taxing State. That incidence of the tax affords a valid "constitutional channel" which the States have utilized to "make interstate commerce pay its way." . . . "Taxes may be imposed although their payment may come out of the funds derived from petitioner's interstate business, provided the taxes are so imposed that their burden will be reasonably related to the powers of the State and [are] non-discriminatory." . . .

Nor will the argument that the exactions contravene the Due Process Clause bear scrutiny. The taxes imposed are levied only on that portion of the taxpayer's net income which arises from its activities within the taxing State. These activities form a sufficient "nexus between such a tax and transactions within a state for which the tax is an exaction." . . . It strains reality to say, in terms of our decisions, that each of the corporations here was not sufficiently involved in local events to forge "some definite link, some minimum connection" sufficient to satisfy due process requirements. . . . The record is without conflict that both corporations engage in substantial income-producing activity in the taxing States. In fact in No. 12 almost half of the corporation's income is derived from the taxing State's sales which are shown to be promoted by vigorous and continuous sales campaigns run through a central office located in the State. While in No. 33 the percent of sales is not available, the course of conduct was largely identical. As was said in *State of Wisconsin v. J. C. Penney Co., supra,* the "controlling question is whether the state has given anything for which it can ask return." Since by "the practical operation of [the] tax the state has exerted its power in relation to opportunities which it has given, to protection which it has afforded, to benefits which it has conferred, . . ." it "is free to pursue its own fiscal policies, unembarrassed by the Constitution. . . ." [No. 12—AFFIRMED. No. 33—REVERSED]

After the foregoing decisions, business reacted and encouraged legislation to reduce the burdens of multiple income taxation. The Interstate Income Law, passed by Congress, provides that a tax cannot be imposed on the net income of a person or corporation engaged in interstate business when the only business activity within the state is:

1. *The solicitation of orders by such person, or his representative, in such state for sales of tangible personal property, which orders are sent outside the state for approval or rejection, and, if approved, are filled by shipment or delivery from a point outside the State; or*

2. *the solicitation of orders by such person, or his representative, in such State in the name of or for the benefit of a prospective customer of such person, if orders by such customer to such person to enable such customer to fill orders resulting from such solicitation are orders described in paragraph (1).*

3. *Selling or soliciting sales through one or more independent contractors, whether or not the latter have an office in the taxing state.*

The area of nontaxable activities is obviously quite limited. In addition the act does not grant relief to corporations domiciled in the taxing state or individuals domiciled in the taxing state. For purposes of exception 3, an independent contractor is one who acts on behalf of "more than one principal and who holds himself out as such in the regular course of his business activities."

The state of Louisiana held the Interstate Income Tax Law to be constitutional and the Supreme Court of the United States refused to review this decision. This statute has not ended the clamor for additional laws to reduce the multiple tax burdens on interstate commerce. Some of the reasons for business dissatisfaction with taxation based on nexus and a reasonable apportionment formula are: (1) the major cost in compliance with the record-keeping rules of every state and municipal government (Each is allowed to impose a tax using its own formula.); (2) excessive taxation in the aggregate resulting from various formulas and procedures; (3) erroneous formulas particularly in sales tax apportionment when it is difficult to ascertain the state in which the sale is made; and (4) the need for uniformity in the law to ensure fairness and proper compliance.

To illustrate the complexity of the problem, at least thirty-eight states have corporate income tax laws and sales tax laws, thirty-seven states have capital stock tax laws, and eight states have gross receipts taxes. No two taxing states use identical formulas and there is even a wide variation in the factors included in the various formulas.

Many solutions are being advanced for the difficult problems caused by the "nexus" concept. Some would create a national formula which all taxing bodies would be required to follow. Others would limit the power to tax businesses actually located in the states. Time and the legislative process may provide a solution.

6   APPORTIONMENT

In the foregoing discussion on nexus, it was indicated that income taxes and property taxes usually must be apportioned or allocated by some reasonable formula. The number of formulas which are reasonable is probably infinite and as already noted, the wide range of formulas is one major reason given in support of new legislation. The case which follows illustrates some of the problems concerning apportionment.

FEDERATED DEP'T STORE, INC. V. GEROSA
213 N.E.2d 677 (N.Y. 1965)

BERGAN, JUSTICE: Petitioner is a Delaware corporation with a principal office in Cincinnati, Ohio, and operates 42 retail and specialty stores in 11 States. It owns three large department stores in New York City—an Abraham & Straus store in Brooklyn, the Bloomingdale's store in Manhattan and the one in Queens. Some of the business done in the three New York City stores is interstate. Deliveries are made to customers in New Jersey and Connecticut on sales made in New York.

In conformity with the authorization of section 24-a of the General City Law, Consol. Laws, c. 21, the City of New York has enacted a General Business and Financial Tax Law which imposes an excise tax for the privilege of carrying on business in the city.

But since the city may not impose a tax on the entire interstate business done by a taxpayer . . . , the local law authorizes the Comptroller to prescribe a method of allocation of that portion of the interstate transactions which for local purposes are properly attributable to New York. . . . The Comptroller, with this purpose in view, has laid down a formula of apportionment. . . .

An earlier method of allocation prescribed by the Comptroller was held invalid by this court in 1954. . . . The basis for decision was that the method established a minimum of 33½% in attributing interstate business to city activity. This the court ruled improper, i.e., "and we hold that the comptroller in using such minimum figures acted arbitrarily and out of harmony with the declared legislative purpose of taxing only that part of the interstate receipts which is properly attributable and allocable to the doing of business in the city." . . .

Following this decision the Comptroller undertook to devise a new formula of allocation. He eliminated the absolute minimum which the court had held invalid. He prescribed a rather complicated scheme of allocation which weighs into consideration the total property and total wages within and without the city deemed to have produced the interstate business; the amount of wholly taxable business (that done in intrastate transactions); the amount of wholly untaxed business (that done outside the State), and the allocable business (that done in interstate commerce emanating from the city).

As applied to the petitioner's allocable interstate business emanating from New York City, this formula treats about 45% to 48% of the receipts from that business as taxable in New York in the years 1953 to 1959 which are the subject of the present article 78 proceeding to review the Comptroller's determination.

Petitioner vigorously attacks the formula and suggests that it is both unfair and unconstitutional. But when it is kept in mind that what the formula purports to do is to measure and apportion the share of the interstate business attributable to New York activity, its actual impact on this petitioner seems entirely reasonable. . . .

Any formula purporting to be general in application must use some artificial assumptions. Business enterprises differ greatly, and the activity in New York of a shoe manufacturing enterprise which manufactures in Virginia and sells in New York is different in the apportionment of its activity than a retail sales enterprise which does all the relevant selling in New York and is serviced in some managerial aspects in Ohio. The formula, however, must usually serve different kinds of enterprises. What the formula must offer is not perfection but a "rough approximation" of a just allocation. . . .

Although the petitioner owns many department stores in other States, the contribution which these operations make to the sales of the three New York City stores of merchandise delivered to New Jersey and Connecticut is, so far as the record demonstrates, nil; and while the policy-making and accounting, and other related control procedures pursued in the main office at Cincinnati undoubtedly play some part in the interstate activity of the New York City stores, the part played is not shown to have large significance in a fair allocation of the basic activity which produced the sales.

Thus, when the net result of the application of the formula, complicated though it may be, to the actual operation of the petitioner's activities in New York is that less than half of the allocable business attributed to sales made in New York resulting in out-of-state shipments are regularly attributed to the New York activity, no unfairness is demonstrated. The business of retail sales is a thing closely related to the place where a store is. When sales are made, even to a customer who comes in from New Jersey or Connecticut, an activity in large part traditionally local exists. . . .

The petitioner's attack on the formula of the Comptroller is essentially based on what could happen when it is applied under certain assumed situations, rather than on any unfair or unjust apportionment to the actualities of petitioner's business or to the petitioner's actual experience upon application of the formula. The argument of the city in this court that "the petitioner is not making any direct assertion that the formula has resulted in attributing an excessive share of the interstate receipts to New York City" and that "[i]t limits its attack to the nature of the formula, asserting that it is unusual in nature and contains arbitrary or unreasonable provisions" is not adequately met by petitioner.

The formula by which a percentage of allocation of interstate business to city activity is calculated is laid out in the Comptroller's regulations in this text:

(a) *The Property Factor. A percentage is to be computed on the basis of a fraction.*

The numerator is the value of so much of the property in the City as may be deemed attributable to producing the allocable receipts. It is arrived at by taking such proportion of the property in the City as the allocable receipts bear to the sum of the allocable and the wholly taxable receipts. This eliminates from the property factor the portion of the property within the City attributable to producing wholly taxable receipts.

The denominator is the value of so much of the property within and without the City as may be deemed attributable to producing the allocable receipts. It is arrived at by taking the sum of two figures. The first figure is the amount in the numerator. To this is added such proportion of the value of the property outside the City as the allocable receipts bear to the sum of the allocable and the non-taxable receipts, thus eliminating from the property factor the portion of the property outside of the City attributable to non-taxable receipts.

(b) *The Wages and Salaries Factor. A percentage is computed on the basis of a fraction arrived at by the same method as above, except that wages and salaries constitute the factor rather than property.*

(c) Add the above two percentages, divide by two, and multiply the allocable receipts by the result. Where the resultant average of the percentages exceeds 66⅔%, it shall be reduced to 66⅔% for the purpose of allocation. The product will be the portion of the allocable receipts to be included in the measure of the tax.

Petitioner's main argument for invalidity of this formula suggests that the tax tends to increase as a taxpayer's out-of-state and hence wholly non-taxable receipts increase when the relative amounts of property and wages are constant. If one carries through calculations required by the formula, keeping the property and wages at the same level, this can be seen to be borne out.

The city argues, however, that it would not normally be expected that such an actual situation would occur. In spite of this theoretical possibility under the formula, the city contends that in its application to petitioner's business it falls within the test laid down in *Butler Bros. v. McColgan,* 315 U.S. 501, 506, 62 S.Ct. 701, 86 L.Ed. 991, as a method "fairly calculated" to assign to New York the proportion reasonably attributable to business done there.

By way of illustration the city observes that, if all of the out-of-State property of petitioner were an Ohio store which had $9,000,000 in receipts and the allocable (interstate) receipts of the New York stores were $1,000,000, the formula would assume that one tenth of the property and wages of the Ohio store were devoted to creating the New York allocable receipts. If, with all wages and property unchanged, the Ohio store's receipts were increased to $19,000,000 while the New York allocable receipts remained at $1,000,000, the formula would assume that only one twentieth of the Ohio wages and property had been devoted to creating the New York allocable receipts.

"As a result," argues the city, "the New York City property and wages treated as creating the allocable receipts would become a larger proportion of the total property and wages treated as creating such receipts. . . . In a year when the New York City allocable receipts is a larger proportion of both types of receipts, the share of the Ohio property and wages attributed to the New York allocable receipts is greater. In a year when the New York City allocable receipts remain unchanged but the total of both types of receipts is increased because the Ohio sales have increased, the share of the Ohio property and wages attributable to the New York City allocable receipts necessarily decreases."

Although the formula, which as it has been noted, was written for many different types of businesses, treats the out-of-State property and wages as helping materially to create the New York allocable sales in a business such as petitioner's, the part actually played by the out-of-State activity in the creation of the allocable sales could be quite insignificant. Thus the city contends that the actual application of the formula "is overgenerous to a taxpayer in petitioner's circumstances."

Whether it is overgenerous or not, its application is not demonstrated to be unfair or to represent an unreasonable thrust on the interstate activities of petitioner. There could well be circumstances where the formula, mechanically applied, would operate unfairly and impose too heavy a burden on interstate activities. To some extent the 66⅔% ceiling built into the formula would tend to avoid this.

Theoretical calculations under the formula can be pursued where the influence of out-of-State investment, wages and sales activity would be unfairly thrown out of focus as related to New York transaction to cast too heavy a burden on interstate activity. If such cases actually occur, the Comptroller has the power, and it would be his duty, to make adjustments which would keep the formula within a reasonable attribution to the local business activity in the city, by providing an alternative method of apportionment as article 210 of his published regulations allows. The petitioner has not demonstrated unfairness in the actual impact on it of the tax assessments of which it complains.

The order should be affirmed, with costs.

On occasion, the Courts have approved taxes which are not apportioned. This usually occurs when the taxpayer fails to establish that another state is taxing the same property or activity. In *Northwest Airlines v. Minnesota*, 322 U.S. 292 (1944), the Supreme Court allowed Minnesota as the state of domicile to tax the entire fleet of planes of Northwest Airlines because there was no showing that any of them was permanently outside of Minnesota throughout the taxable year. This decision was modified later in *Standard Oil v. Peck*, 342 U.S. 382 (1952), where the court held that "The rule which permits taxation by two or more states on an apportionment basis precludes taxation of all of the property by the state of the domicile. . . ." Otherwise there would be multiple taxation of interstate operations and the tax would have no relation to the opportunities, benefits, or protection which the taxing state gives those operations.

In 1964, the Supreme Court in *General Motors Corporation v. Washington* [5] (which was a case somewhat similar to Northwest Airlines), approved an *unapportioned* gross receipts tax levied by the State of Washington against General Motors. The Washington tax was measured by General Motors' gross wholesale income and was challenged as a tax on the privilege of engaging in interstate commerce; as inherently discriminatory; as resulting in the imposition of a multiple tax burden; and as a

[5] 377 U.S. 436 (1964).

deprivation of property without due process of law. General Motors had district managers and service representatives in the state but no formal offices. In this case, Justice Clark, speaking for the majority of the court, said in part:

> Because every state has equal rights when taxing the commerce it touches, there exists the danger that such taxes can impose cumulative burdens upon interstate transactions which are not presented to local commerce. Such burdens would destroy interstate commerce and encourage the re-erection of those trade barriers which made the Commerce Clause necessary. And in this connection, we have specifically held that interstate commerce cannot be subjected to the burden of "multiple taxation." Nevertheless, as we have seen, it is well established that taxation measured by gross receipts is constitutionally proper if it is fairly apportioned.
>
> A careful analysis of the cases in this field teaches that the validity of the tax rests upon whether the State is exacting a constitutionally fair demand for that aspect of interstate commerce to which it bears a special relation. . . . In other words, the question is whether the State has exerted its power in proper proportion to appellant's activities within the State and to appellant's consequent enjoyment of the opportunities and protections which the State has afforded. Where, as in the instant case, the taxing State is not the domiciliary State, we look to the taxpayer's business activities within the State, i.e., the local incidents, to determine if the gross receipts from sales therein may be fairly related to those activities. . . . [I]t is admitted that General Motors has entered the State and engaged in activities therein. . . . "The general rule, applicable here, is that a taxpayer claiming immunity from a tax has the burden of establishing his exemption."
>
> The tax that Washington levied . . . is unapportioned and, as we have pointed out, is, therefore, suspect. We must determine whether it is so closely related to the local activities of the corporation as to form "some definite link, some minimum connection, between a state and the person, property or transaction it seeks to tax." On the basis of the facts found by the state court we are not prepared to say that its conclusion was constitutionally impermissible. . . . "Petitioner has not established that such services as were rendered . . . [through intrastate activity] were not decisive factors in establishing and holding this market." Although mere entry into a State does not take from a corporation the right to continue to do an interstate business with tax immunity, it does not follow that the corporation can channel its operations through such a maze of local connections as does General Motors, and take advantage of its gain on domesticity, and still maintain that same degree of immunity.
>
> A more difficult question might arise from appellant's claim of multiple taxation. General Motors claims that some of its products taxed by Washington are manufactured in St. Louis where a license tax, measured by sales

before shipment, is levied. It is also urged that General Motors' Oregon-based activity which concerns Washington sales might afford sufficient incidents for a similar tax by Oregon. The Court touched upon the problem of multiple taxation in Northwest Airlines v. Minnesota, *322 U.S. at 295, but laid it to one side as "not now before us." Thereafter in* Northwestern States Portland Cement Co. v. Minnesota, *supra, 358 U.S. at 463, we held that "[i]n this type of case the taxpayers must show that the formula places a burden upon interstate commerce in a constitutional sense." Appellant has not done this. It has not demonstrated what definite burden, in a constitutional sense, the St. Louis tax places on the identical interstate shipments by which Washington measures its tax. And further, it has not been shown that Oregon levies any tax on appellant's activity bearing on Washington sales. In such cases we have refrained from passing on the question of "multiple taxation," e.g.,* Northwestern States Portland Cement Co. v. Minnesota, *supra, and we adhere to that position.*

Thus it is apparent that states may impose a nondiscriminatory apportioned tax on businesses engaged in interstate commerce where a sufficient nexus exists. Even an unapportioned tax may be imposed on such businesses, unless an undue burden in the constitutional sense is shown to exist.

The variety of taxes levied by local governments creates legal issues other than "nexus" and "apportionment," since each tax has its own peculiarities and technical aspects. Some of these are illustrated in the sections which follow.

7   STATE INCOME TAXES

The first state to establish an income tax was Wisconsin in 1911. Since that time at least thirty-seven additional states have added an income tax. These taxes have immensely increased the accounting and legal difficulties of both individuals and business enterprises. As was discussed in prior sections, states are not only empowered to tax local residents but can also tax persons and businesses earning any income within their borders. Individuals and businesses may be subject to an income tax in several states if income is derived from these states.

Inherent in a variety of state income tax laws is the difficulty of knowing the requirements of each and of compliance therewith. Each state has its own tax forms, which are similar to the Federal Form 1040. One encouraging trend is for many states to tie the figures directly to the Federal return. This simplifies both the reporting and enforcement. Most states provide different forms for residents and nonresidents.

The amount of income which must be earned before a report is required illustrates the divergence in state tax laws. Some states start at $500 and others do not start until $6,000. In addition, personal exemptions vary from $17.50 to $500 for a single person. Some states do not allow deductions but instead tax gross income while others do allow deductions. From the foregoing, it is obvious that compliance by nonresidents and interstate businesses is difficult and imposes costly record-keeping burdens on them.

Income taxes are a major source of revenue for states that impose them, but again, the importance of the tax varies greatly from state to state. In New York, the tax may supply close to half of the total revenue, while in Louisiana, it will supply less than 5 percent.

The income tax will be a continually growing source of revenue. Municipalities are turning to it and states without an income tax are likely to adopt one. The problem of allocation and apportionment for interstate commerce which was discussed in section 5 will continue to grow unless legislation is enacted creating uniformity or exemption. The latter is highly unlikely because of the states' ever-growing need for funds.

8   SALES AND USE TAXES

For many years the sales tax has been an important source of state revenue. However, problems of avoidance arose when one state imposed a sales tax and a neighboring state did not. For example, if the state of Illinois imposed a 4 percent sales tax and the state of Indiana did not, a new car buyer would save $160 on a $4,000 car if he purchased it in Indiana. To plug this gap, the use tax was developed. The case which follows further illustrates attempted sales tax evasion and discusses the constitutionality of a use tax.

GRAY V. OKLAHOMA TAX COMMISSION
379 P.2d 843 (Okl. 1963)

PER CURIAM: This is an appeal from a ruling of the Oklahoma Tax Commission assessing a tax of $161.94, together with interest and penalties, for use tax upon a purchase of a livestock feed in the sum of $8,097.40. The purchase was made in the State of Texas, and the feed was shipped to the ranch of plaintiff in Johnston County, Oklahoma.

Prior to 1957, livestock feed was subject to a sales tax of 2% upon such feed purchased in Oklahoma. See 68 O.S. 1951 §§ 1251 to 1251n. Feed purchased in other states and shipped into the state for consumption was subject to a use tax of 2%. See 68 O.S. 1951 §§ 1310 to 1310i. In 1957 the Legislature of Oklahoma repealed the sales tax on feed purchased in the state. The effect of this repeal, if the contention of the Tax Commission is correct, is that the use tax upon feed purchased in other states is still in effect. The contention of plaintiff is that this 2% levy on out-of-state purchases constitutes a levy on interstate commerce and is therefore unconstitutional.

Use taxes upon interstate shipments have been sustained by the United States Supreme Court where enacted to offset a sales tax within the State, thereby doing away with any differential between out-of-state purchases and those within the State. See *Henneford v. Silas Mason Co.,* 300 U.S. 577, 57 S.Ct. 524, 81 L.Ed. 814.

It is asserted by the Commission that "the tax upon the use after the property is at rest is not so measured or conditioned as to hamper the transaction of interstate commerce or discriminate against them."

The fallacy in this contention is readily apparent. If the use tax were equally applied to all like products, there could be little objection urged. But where it is placed upon a product within the state, it is obvious that the tax is wholly one levied because of the point of origin and for no other reason. We cannot agree with the contention that such a levy is not one burdening interstate commerce.

In the case of *Southeastern, Inc. v. Oklahoma Tax Commission,* 351 P.2d 739 (Okl.), this court said in regard to this very use tax:

The use tax is an excise tax which the State is authorized to exact, in connection with the sales tax, *for the primary purposes, of raising revenue for state purposes, and* is designed to prevent consumers from escaping sales tax by going outside of the state and purchasing property and bringing it into the state for use or consumption. [EMPHASIS ADDED]

This very language demonstrates that such a use tax is a barrier to bringing in goods from without the State. It can be justified, as held in the Southeastern case, as a means for preventing the escape from a sales tax. But here no sales tax exists, and the reasoning of the Southeastern case ceases to apply. Clearly, the language of the court demonstrates that it is actually a levy on interstate commerce and without the justification existing in that case.

We deem the question conclusively settled by the Supreme Court of the United States in *Welton v. Missouri,* 91 U.S. 275, 23 L.Ed. 347, where the court said in discussing the exclusive power of Congress to regulate interstate commerce:

That power was vested in Congress to insure uniformity of commercial regulation against discriminating state legislation. It covers property which is transported as an article of commerce from foreign countries, or among the States, from hostile or interfering state legislation until it has mingled with and become a part of the general property of the country, and protects it even after it has entered a State, from any burdens imposed by reason of its foreign origin. [EMPHASIS ADDED]

Again in *McGoldrick v. Berwind-White Coal Mining Co.,* 309 U.S. 33, 60 S.Ct. 388, 84 L.Ed. 565, it is held that state taxes whose tendency is to prohibit interstate commerce *or place it at a disadvantage as compared or in competition with intrastate commerce, or which discriminates against interstate commerce are unconstitutional.*

We are fortified in the above conclusions by the following authorities. In 11 Am. Jur., Commerce, Sec. 108, at page 96, appears this text:

. . . *Thus, a state is without power, by prohibition, regulation or* taxation, *to impose upon the products of other states, brought therein for sale or use, more onerous public burdens than it imposes upon like products of its own territory, or to discriminate, in the matter of trade regulations, in favor of its citizens and against the citizens of other states or foreign countries.* . . . [EMPHASIS ADDED]

This text is supported by opinions of the Supreme Court holding such a situation violative of the commerce clause of the Constitution.

In the case of *Best & Co. v. Maxwell,* 311 U.S. 454, 61 S.Ct. 334, 85 L.Ed. 275, appears this language in the opinion:

The commerce clause forbids discrimination, whether forthright or ingenious. In each case it is our duty to determine whether the statute under attack, whatever its name may be, will in its practical operation *work discrimination against interstate commerce.* . . . [EMPHASIS ADDED]

Whatever reasoning may be indulged to sustain the statute under consideration, in its final analysis it had but one purpose, to discriminate against products from without the state.

We deem the following quotations from the case of *Baldwin v. G. A. F. Seelig,* 294 U.S. 511, 55 S.Ct. 497, 79 L.Ed. 1032 to be extremely pertinent:

Such a power, if exerted, will set a barrier to traffic between one state and another as effective as if customs duties, equal to the price differential, had been laid upon the thing transported.

. . . .

The Constitution was framed under the dominion of a political philosophy less parochial in range. It was framed upon the theory that the peoples of the several states must sink or swim together, and that in the long run prosperity and salvation are in union and not division.

. . . .

A state tax upon merchandise brought in from another state, or upon its sales, whether in original packages or not, after it has reached its destina-

tion and is in a state of rest, is lawful only when the tax is not discriminating in its incidence against the merchandise because of its origin in another state.

. . . .

Neither the power to tax nor the police power may be used by the state of destination with the aim and effect of establishing an economic barrier against competition with the products of another state or the labor of its residents.

We therefore hold that the application of the use tax to livestock feed purchased outside of Oklahoma is under present conditions unconstitutional and that sections 1310, 1310a to 1310i, inclusive, 68 O.S. 1951, are invalid in so far as they levy a use tax upon goods brought into the state which would not be subject to sales tax if purchased within the state.

The order of the Tax Commission levying assessment herein is hereby vacated and set aside.

As might be suspected, there are many cases involving the collection of sales and use taxes on services and on goods which have moved or are moving in interstate commerce. Insofar as services are concerned, income from a ski tow was taxed in Wisconsin, and a Georgia case held that "slot machine" income is subject to the use tax.

An additional question arises of whether or not a businessman in one state must collect and remit sales and use taxes to all other states in which the goods he has sold may be delivered or used. To what extent must a seller inquire of the domicile of his buyer? Do use taxes extend to service income? These and other questions are involved in the following decisions.

SCRIPTO, INC. V. CARSON
362 U.S. 207 (1960)

CLARK, JUSTICE: Florida, by statute, requires appellant, a Georgia corporation, to be responsible for the collection of a use tax on certain mechanical writing instruments which appellant sells and ships from its place of business in Atlanta to residents of Florida for use and enjoyment there. Upon Scripto's failure to collect the tax, the appellee Comptroller levied a use tax liability of $5,150.66 against it. Appellant then brought this suit to test the validity of the imposition, contending that the requirement of Florida's statute places a burden on interstate commerce and violates the Due Process Clause of the Fourteenth Amendment to the Constitution. It claimed, in effect, that the nature of its operations in Florida does not form a sufficient nexus to subject it to the statute's exactions. Both the trial court and the Supreme Court of Florida held that appellant does have sufficient jurisdictional contacts in Florida and, therefore, must register as a dealer under the statute and collect and remit to the State the use tax imposed on its afore-said sales. 105 So. 2d 775. We noted probable jurisdiction. 361 U.S. 806. . . . We agree with the result reached by Florida's courts.

Appellant operates in Atlanta an advertising specialty division trading under the name of Adgif Company. Through it, appellant is engaged in the business of selling mechanical writing instruments which are adapted to advertising purposes by the placing of printed material thereon. In its Adgif operation, appellant does not (1) own, lease, or maintain any office, dis-tributing house, warehouse or other place of business in Florida, or (2) have any regular employee or agent there. Nor does it own or maintain any bank account or stock of merchandise in the State. Orders for its products are solicited by advertising specialty brokers or, as the Supreme Court of Florida called them, wholesalers or jobbers, who are residents of Florida. At the time of suit, there were 10 such brokers—each having a written contract and a specific territory. The somewhat detailed contract provides, *inter alia*, that all compensation is to be on a commission basis on the sales made, provided they are accepted by appellant; repeat orders, even if not solicited, also carry a commission if the salesman has not become inactive through failure to secure acceptable orders during the previous 60 days. The contract specifically provides that it is the intention of the parties "to create the relationship . . . of independent contractor." Each order is to be signed by the solicitor as a "salesman"; however, he has not authority to make collec-tions or incur debts involving appellant. Each salesman is furnished cata-logs, samples, and advertising material, and is actively engaged in Florida as a representative "of Scripto for the purpose of attracting, soliciting and obtaining Florida customers" for its mechanical advertising specialties. Orders for such products are sent by these salesmen directly to the Atlanta office for acceptance or refusal. If accepted, the sale is consummated there and the salesman is paid his commission directly. No money passes between the purchaser and the salesman—although the latter does occasionally ac-cept a check payable to the appellant, in which event he is required to for-ward it to appellant with the order.

As construed by Florida's highest court, the impost levied by the statute is a tax "on the privilege of using personal property . . . which has come to rest . . . and has become a part of the mass of property" within the State. 105 So. 2d at page 781. It is not a sales tax, but "was developed as a device to complement [such a tax] in order to prevent evasion . . . by the completion of purchases in a nontaxing state and shipment by interstate commerce into a taxing forum." *Id.*, at page 779. The tax is collectible from "dealers" and is to be added to the purchase price of the merchandise "as far as practicable." In the event that a dealer fails to collect the tax, he himself is liable for its payment. The statute has the customary use tax provisions "against duplication of the tax, an allowance to the dealer for making the collection, and a reciprocal credit arrangement which credits against the Florida tax any amount up to the amount of the Florida tax which might have been paid to another state." *Id.*, at page 782. Florida held appellant to be a dealer under its statute. "The application by that Court of its local laws and the facts on which it founded its judgment are of course controlling here." . . .

The question remaining is whether Florida, in the light of appellant's operations there, may collect the State's use tax from it on the basis of property bought from appellant and shipped from its home office to purchasers in Florida for use there.

Florida has well stated the course of this Court's decisions governing such levies, and we need but drive home its clear understanding. There must be, as our Brother Jackson stated in *Miller Bros. Co. v. State of Maryland*, 1954, 347 U.S. 340, 344–345, 74 Sup. Ct. 535, 539, 98 L. Ed. 744, "some definite link, some minimum connection, between a state and the person, property or transaction it seeks to tax." We believe that such a nexus is present here. First, the tax is a nondiscriminatory exaction levied for the use and enjoyment of property which has been purchased by Florida residents and which has actually entered into and become a part of the mass of property in that State. The burden of the tax is placed on the ultimate purchaser in Florida and it is he who enjoys the use of the property, regardless of its source. We note that the appellant is charged with no tax— save when, as here, he fails or refuses to collect it from the Florida customer. Next, as Florida points out, appellant has 10 wholesalers, jobbers, or "salesmen" conducting continuous local solicitation in Florida and forwarding the resulting orders from that State to Atlanta for shipment of the ordered goods. The only incidence of this sales transaction that is nonlocal is the acceptance of the order. True, the "salesmen" are not regular employees of appellant devoting full time to its service, but we conclude that such a fine distinction is without constitutional significance. The formal shift in the contractual tagging of the salesman as "independent" neither results in changing his local function of solicitation nor bears upon its effectiveness in securing a substantial flow of goods into Florida. This is evidenced by the amount assessed against appellant on the statute's 3% basis over a period of but four years. To permit such formal "contractual shifts" to make a constitutional difference would open the gates to a stampede of tax avoidance. . . .

Moreover, we cannot see, from a constitutional standpoint, "that it was important that the agent worked for several principals." Chief Judge Learned Hand, in *Bomze v. Nardis Sportswear*, 2 Cir. 165 F.2d 33, 36. The test is simply the nature and extent of the activities of the appellant in Florida. In short, we conclude that this case is controlled by *General Trading Co.*, *supra*. As was said there:

All these differentiations are without constitutional significance. Of course, no State can tax the privilege of doing interstate business. . . . That is within the protection of the Commerce Clause and subject to the power of Congress. On the other hand, the mere fact that property is used for interstate commerce or has come into an owner's possession as a result of interstate commerce does not diminish the protection which he may draw from a State to the upkeep of which he may be asked to bear his fair share. 322 U.S. at page 338.

Nor do we believe that Florida's requirement that appellant be its tax collector on such orders from its residents changes the situation. As was pointed out in *General Trading Co.,* this is "a familiar and sanctioned device." *Id.* Moreover, we note that Florida reimburses appellant for its service in this regard.

Appellant earnestly contends that *Miller Bros. Co. v. State of Maryland, supra,* is to the contrary. We think not. Miller had no solicitors in Maryland; there was no "exploitation of the consumer market"; no regular, systematic displaying of its products by catalogs, samples or the like. But, on the contrary, the goods on which Maryland sought to force Miller to collect its tax were sold to residents of Maryland when personally present at Miller's store in Delaware. True, there was an "occasional" delivery of such purchases by Miller into Maryland, and it did occasionally mail notices of special sales to former customers; but Marylanders went to Delaware to make purchases—Miller did not go to Maryland for sales. Moreover, it was impossible for Miller to determine that goods sold for cash to a customer over the counter at its store in Delaware were to be used and enjoyed in Maryland. This led the Court to conclude that Miller would be made "more vulnerable to liability for another's tax than to a tax on itself." 347 U.S. at page 346. . . . In view of these considerations, we conclude that the "minimum connections" not present in *Miller* are more than sufficient here.

The judgment is therefore affirmed. [AFFIRMED]

ALSIDE, INC. V. BOWERS
190 N.E.2d 274 (Ohio 1963)

ZIMMERMAN, JUDGE: Appellant, a manufacturer of aluminum building products, is an Ohio Corporation and maintains a plant and offices in Summit County, Ohio. For the purpose of shipping its finished products to its customers outside Ohio and to bring materials to its Ohio plant from other states, appellant leased tractors and trailers from Alside Equipment Company, a Delaware corporation, not licensed to do business in Ohio, and a wholly owned subsidiary of appellant. The equipment company has a statutory agent in Delaware, but its records are kept in Ohio. It was organized to purchase, hold, lease and operate motor vehicle rolling stock. It owned tractors and trailers licensed in Delaware but employed no drivers. Over the audit period involved, the equipment company leased all its motor vehicles to appellant by leases executed in Ohio. A number of such motor vehicles were delivered by the equipment company to appellant in Ohio. Rental payments for such equipment were made by checks signed in Ohio by one of appellant's officers. Such checks were received by the same officer on behalf of the equipment company, he being also an officer of that company. These checks were transmitted to a Delaware bank for deposit to the account of the equipment company. Appellant furnished drivers for the motor vehicles, which vehicles were employed in the manner hereinbefore described. Appellant billed its customers for delivery charges. Consequently, the lease contracts, having been executed in Ohio and the payment for and delivery of such motor trucks having taken place in Ohio, there was a consummation of the leases in Ohio.

Under Section 5739.01(B), Revised Code, rentals of tangible personal property are regarded as sales of such property, and, since the rental transactions herein did not come within the exception of subdivision (E) of that section, they constituted or were equivalent to retail sales and are taxable as such, unless they are removed from taxation by the provision of Section 5739.02(B) (11), Revised Code, which makes the Ohio sales tax inapplicable to "sales not within the taxing power of this state under the constitution of the United States."

Therefore, we are confronted with the problem of whether the sales of the equipment company's motor vehicles to appellant in Ohio, measured by the amount paid as rentals, with transfer of possession and payment in Ohio, are excepted from the Ohio sales tax because appellant used the motor vehicles to transport its products out of Ohio and to import materials from outside Ohio for its use in Ohio.

As already noted, appellant contended that the sales tax as levied here represents a tax on instrumentalities used exclusively in interstate commerce, and that such a tax is prohibited by the commerce clause of the federal Constitution.

Appellee takes the position that since the rental contracts were made in Ohio and that delivery of possession of the motor vehicles and the payment therefor were also Ohio incidents, the use of the vehicles thereafter in carrying on a business which constitutes interstate commerce is not so identified with that commerce as to make the sales immune from the nondiscriminatory Ohio sales tax. Such a tax upon local sales is not regarded as imposing a direct burden on interstate commerce and has no greater or different effect upon that commerce than a general property tax to which all those enjoying the protection of the state may be subjected.

So, where commodities, brought into one state from another by virtue of an agreement consummated in the first state, find lodgment in the first state and are then used by the one to whom they were delivered for carrying on interstate business, they are not thereby removed from taxation by the first state. Upon application of this rule to the present case, the fact that the motor trucks purchased in Ohio were for use in interstate commerce does not except the transactions from the Ohio sales tax.

It is our conclusion that the decision of the Board of Tax Appeals is neither unreasonable nor unlawful, and it is, therefore, affirmed. [DECISION AFFIRMED]

O'BRIEN V. ISAACS
203 N.E.2d 890 (III. 1965)

KLINGBIEL, JUSTICE: Rule 42 of the Illinois Retailers' Occupation Tax Regulation provides in part, "Where Illinois florists receive telegraphic instructions from other florists located outside of Illinois for the delivery of flowers in Illinois, the receiving Illinois florist is liable for tax with respect to any receipts which he may realize from the transaction. . . ." (CCH, Ill. State Tax Reporter, vol. 1, par. 60–147.) This action was brought in the circuit court of Cook County to test the constitutionality of the regulation. The circuit court dismissed the action and the case has been appealed directly to this court because public revenue is involved.

There is no dispute as to the factual description of the transaction covered by the regulation, but there is a wide divergence of opinion as to its legal effect. A customer orders flowers from an out-of-state florist for delivery to an Illinois addressee. The out-of-state florist telegraphs the order to an Illinois florist who delivers flowers from his stock to the Illinois addressee. The customer pays the out-of-state florist for the flowers, the cost of the telegram and frequently a service charge. Payment from the out-of-state florist to the Illinois florist is made through a trade association clearing house.

The plaintiffs are Thomas J. O'Brien, an individual Chicago florist, Allied Florists Association of Illinois, composed of 1500 Illinois florists and 500 out-of-state florists, and Illinois State Florists Association, composed of 400 Illinois florists. The legal analysis they have attributed to the transaction, particularly the activity of the Illinois florist, varies throughout their brief. They first state, "The only local incident which occurs to bring within the possible reach of the Illinois taxing power any phase of the transaction is the Illinois delivery. This is not performed by any agent or employee of the original seller (the out-of-state florist), but by an independent contractor (the Illinois florist)." Next they say, ". . . the Illinois florist doesn't actually 'sell' any goods. . . ." Then they state, "They [the Illinois florists] just deliver goods the title to which passes elsewhere. They are for all practical purposes only bailors [sic]." They finally say that if the Illinois florist has made a sale, it is a sale to the out-of-state florist for the purpose of re-sale.

It is clear that the Illinois florist cannot be called an independent con-tractor, bailee or "one who does not really sell any goods." He has title to the flowers which he transfers to the buyer for a price. This is a sale and the Illinois florist is a seller. The sale is a present sale and whether the contract is unilateral or bilateral, title passes in Illinois.

The only question concerning the transaction is whether the customer or the out-of-state florist is the buyer from the Illinois florist. If the buyer were the out-of-state florist, then the sale would be one for resale and not subject to the retailers' occupation tax. If the buyer is the out-of-state cus-tomer than the transfer of title and possession by the Illinois florist has been for use or consumption within the meaning of the statute.

We conclude that the out-of-state customer is the buyer from the Illinois florist. The out-of-state florist is not a buyer or a seller. The service he renders is similar to that rendered by the commercial airline companies. Airline X will book passage on Airline Y, yet the person for whom passage was booked is a passenger of Airline Y and will fly on Airline Y. This is true although the passenger's order is given to Airline X and payment is made to Airline X.

This brings us to plaintiffs' principal contention that the tax on the transaction in question is an unjust discrimination against interstate com-merce. In *International Harvester Co. v. Department of Treasury*, 322 U.S. 340, 345, 64 S.Ct. 1019, 88 L.Ed. 1313, Indiana had taxed sales by an Indiana seller of Indiana goods to an out-of-state buyer who came into In-diana, took delivery there and transported the goods to another State. The court held that the agreement to sell and delivery in Indiana were adequate to sustain a sales tax by Indiana. In State Tax Commission of *Utah v. Pacific States Cast Iron Pipe Co.*, 372 U.S. 605, 83 S.Ct. 925, 10 L.Ed.2d 8, the court in a short *per curiam* decision reversed a decision of the Utah Supreme Court holding that a tax on a Utah seller of Utah goods sold in Utah and delivered in Utah to an out-of-state buyer for use outside the State unlaw-fully discriminated against interstate commerce. The holding is contained in the single statement, "We reverse its [the Utah Supreme Court's] judg-ment on the authority of *International Harvester Co. v. Department of Treasury* (citation), which holds on facts close to those of this case that a State may levy and collect a sales tax, since the passage of title and de-livery to the purchaser took place within the State." 372 U.S. 605, 606, 83 S.Ct. 925, 10 L.Ed.2d 8, 9.

In the *International Harvester* and *Pacific States Cast Iron Pipe* cases the principal issue was whether the certainty of interstate shipment, that is, the fact that the buyer and seller both know the goods were purchased for use outside the State and were certain to be so used, brought the transaction within the prohibition of the commerce clause of the Federal constitution. Here we have not only an Illinois seller making a sale in this State of goods located in this State, title to which passes in this State and delivery of which is made in this State, but the goods are purchased for use in this State and are used here. We are of the opinion that the tax measured by the proceeds of such a sale does not unlawfully discriminate against interstate commerce.

The judgment of the circuit court of Cook County is affirmed. [JUDGMENT AFFIRMED]

CELINA MUTUAL INS. CO. V. BOWERS
213 N.E.2d 175 (Ohio 1965)

ZIMMERMAN, JUSTICE: In support of their position and the favorable judgments of the Court of Appeals, appellees rely on Section 5725.25, Revised Code, first effective in 1931 and which has remained in substantially the same form ever since. That section, as applicable and pertinent, reads:

The real estate of a domestic insurance company shall be taxed in the place where it is located, the same as the real estate of other persons is taxed, but the tax provided for by sections 5725.01 to 5725.26, inclusive, of the Revised Code, shall be in lieu of all other taxes on the other property and assets of such domestic insurance company and of all other taxes, charges, and excises on such domestic insurance companies. . . . Sections 5725.01 to 5725.26, inclusive, of the Revised Code do not assess any tax on any foreign insurance company or affect any tax on a foreign insurance company under any laws of this state.

Appellant, Tax Commissioner, contends that the interpretation given Section 5725.25, Revised Code, by the Court of Appeals whereby the appellees, domestic insurance companies, are relieved generally from the payment of sales and use taxes renders such statute unconstitutional as offensive to Section 2, Article I of the Constitution of Ohio, and Article XIV of the Constitution of the United States, in that it is made to operate in an unconstitutional and discriminatory manner against foreign insurance companies admitted to do business in Ohio, the effect of such interpretation being to make those companies subject to the Ohio sales and use taxes, whereas domestic insurance companies are freed therefrom.

The so-called Sales Tax Act was first enacted as a temporary measure in 1934 and the Use Tax Act was enacted in 1935. In 1936, the two acts were made permanent.

Applicable Section 5739.02, Revised Code, levies the retail sales tax on each retail sale in this state, and applicable Section 5739.01 (E), Revised Code, as pertinent here, defines "retail sale" in the following language:

(E) *"Retail sale" and "sales at retail" include* all sales *except those in which the purpose of the consumer is:* . . .

(5) *To resell, hold, use, or consume the thing transferred as* evidence *of a contract of insurance.* [EMPHASIS ADDED]

Section 5741.02, Revised Code, levies the use tax upon the storage, use or other consumption of tangible personal property in this state, and subdivision (4) of paragraph (C) of Section 5741.01, Revised Code, in its applicable form, contains the same exception as found in subdivision (5) of paragraph (E) of Section 5739.01, Revised Code.

Incidentally, it may be appropriate to remark that the "use tax" is complementary or supplemental to the "sales tax" and is not designed to duplicate it.

It is now established in Ohio that statutes relating to the exemption or exception from sales or use taxes are to be strictly construed, and one claiming such exemption or exception must affirmatively show his right thereto. *L. A. Wells Constr. Co. v. Bowers,* 164 Ohio St. 357, 358 130 N.E.2d 803, 804.

In the opinion of this court, the enactment of Section 5739.01(E) (5), Revised Code, and Section 5741.01(C) (4), Revised Code, subsequent to the enactment of what is now Section 5725.25, Revised Code, shows a legislative intent to subject the purchase and use of tangible personal property by insurance companies generally to the sales and use taxes except in those instances where the purpose of the consumer (insurance company) is "[t]o resell, hold, use, or consume the thing transferred *as evidence* of a contract of insurance." The manual and manual sheets do not come within the exception.

(5) Moreover, it is to be noted that the "in lieu of" provision of Section 5725.25 refers to "all other taxes on the other property and assets of such domestic insurance company and all other taxes, charges, and excises." In reality, the Ohio sales and use taxes are on *transactions*—the *exercise of a privilege,* viz., the right to acquire and use tangible personal property, and they apply only to the transactions by which that privilege is exercised. As is pointed out in *Young Men's Christian Ass'n v. State,* 265 Ala. 640, 93 So.2d 781, by the language of the use tax statute, "the tax is imposed on the storage, use, or other consumption of the specified property. The tax is not, by the language of the statute, imposed on the property."

A view similar to the one we have expressed was taken by the Connecticut Supreme Court of Errors in the case of *Connecticut Light & Power Co. v. Walsh,* 134 Conn. 295, 57 A.2d 128, 1 A.L.R. 2d 453, where the gist of the holding is that a statutory declaration that a gross-earnings tax imposed on power companies shall be "in lieu of" all other taxes does not free or exempt such companies from the payment of subsequently imposed sales and use taxes on the purchase of materials—tangible personal property—used in their business. Compare *Oxford v. Housing Authority,* 104 Ga.App. 797, 123 S.E.2d 175.

By reason of our stated position, the judgments of the Court of Appeals are reversed, and the decisions of the Board of Tax Appeals are affirmed. [JUDGMENTS REVERSED]

9   PROPERTY TAXES

Property taxes are ad valorem taxes and there is a substantial amount of litigation concerning valuations, procedures of taxing authorities, and the exemptions created by statute. In many areas, attempts are made to assess or value business property on a different basis from other property. Such discrimination is usually unconstitutional. Railroads whose rights of way are subject to tax by every area through which they pass frequently serve as watchdogs over property taxes because they have the staff and knowledge to challenge wrongful procedures and practices. The cases in this section are typical of those which arise throughout the country in regard to ad valorem property taxes.

PEOPLE V. S.B.A. CO.
215 N.E.2d 233 (Ill. 1966)

SOLFISBURG, JUSTICE: This case arises on an application of the county treasurer and ex-officio county collector of Winnebago County for judgment for delinquent taxes assessed for the year 1963, filed in the Winnebago County division of the circuit court of the 17th Judicial Circuit, and for the adjudication of the objections filed and claims for refund of taxes paid under protest on the basis that the property was so excessively overvalued as to amount to constructive fraud.

The defendant, S.B.A. Company, the owner of two pieces of real estate referred to as tract I and tract II, objected to their assessment and sought a refund of taxes paid under protest. After a hearing the trial court reduced the assessments, and ordered a partial refund to the defendant. The collector appeals this order directly to this court because the case involves the revenue.

The two tracts involved are situated in Rockford. Tract I is occupied by a concrete and steel warehouse building built in 1949, containing 47,100 square feet. In 1963 the original assessment of $126,230 was reduced by the board of review to $110,230. It is agreed that assessments in Winnebago County are based on 60% of fair market value, and therefore the final assessment was based upon a full value of approximately $183,700.

An officer of the defendant thought the property was worth $104,000 in 1963 with a reproduction cost of $170,000. William Franzen, a qualified appraiser testified for defendant that in his opinion the full fair cash market value of tract I was $173,500.

As to tract II the property was assessed by the assessor at $48,330 and reduced by the board of review after hearing to $34,500. Defendant's only qualified expert, Franzen, was of the opinion that the fair cash market value of tract II was $43,000. Deputy assessor Wood testified that the reproduction cost of the building on tract II was $110,000 and the fair cash market value was $57,000.

The trial court, after hearing, sustained the defendant's objections on the ground of constructive fraud, found that the assessed value of tract I should be $106,110, and should be $28,700 for tract II, and ordered tax refunds of $137.03 on tract I and $192.91 on tract II.

In summary the difference of opinion as to assessed value and full value are as follows:

	TRACT I	
	ASSESSED VALUE	APPRAISED VALUE
Board of Review	$110,230	$183,700
Trial Court	106,110	177,000
Defendant's Appraiser	104,100	173,500

	TRACT II	
Board of Review	$ 34,500	$ 57,500
Trial Court	28,700	47,800
Defendant's Appraiser	25,800	43,000

The collector's theory is that the court cannot be an assessing officer; that the objectors did not prove actual or constructive fraud by clear and convincing evidence; that the assessed value of property may not be impeached merely because of a difference of opinion as to value between the assessing officer and the court; and that an assessment is not fraudulent merely because it is excessive, if the assessor has acted from proper motives.

The defendant taxpayer argues that the evidence was sufficient to sustain the finding of constructive fraud, and to deny a taxpayer judicial review of his assessment deprives him of due process of law.

We have consistently held that the taxation of property is a legislative rather than a judicial function, and under section 1 of article IX of the Illinois constitution, S.H.A., the courts, in the absence of fraud, have no power to review or determine the value of property fixed for purposes of taxation by the appropriate elected or appointed administrative officers. . . .

We are also unconvinced by the taxpayer's argument that the ordinary. taxpayer is discriminated against in favor of railroads. While review of the Department of Revenue's administrative assessment of railroad property is subject to the provisions of the Administrative Review Act, (*People ex rel. Chicago & No. W. Ry. Co. v. Hulman,* 31 Ill. 2d 166, 201 N.E.2d 103,) the scope of the inquiry available to the railroad is no greater than that available to other taxpayers in a hearing on objections. In both situations we believe that the taxpayer is limited to a judicial inquiry as to whether the assessment is actually or constructively fraudulent.

We must next consider if the facts in the record support the finding of the trial court that the assessments were constructively fraudulent. There is no evidence that the actions of the assessor and board of review were based upon improper motives or procedures or that they were discriminatory. As to tract I the board of review based their assessment on 60% of a cash market value of $183,700, while the taxpayer's appraiser gave an opinion of value of $173,500 making a difference of 5.5%. Even defendant's appraiser recognized the possibility of a 5% difference of opinion between qualified appraisers. The difference of opinion as to tract I clearly is insufficient to justify the action of the trial court in substituting its judgment for that of the administrative authority regardless of the scope of review.

The disparity between the assessment of tract II by the board of review and the opinion of the taxpayer's appraiser is approximately 25%. The testimony of the deputy assessor shows that he followed approved techniques in the appraisal of the property, although the appraisal by the taxpayer's witness may be conceded to be more thorough. It may well be that the record as to tract II would justify a trier of fact in finding that this tract was over-valued, but the trial court does not act as a super board of review. The court must presume, in the absence of contrary evidence, that the assessing officers performed their duty, and the court will not set aside an assessment merely because of a difference of opinion as to value. . . .

There is no evidence in this record of actual fraud or malfeasance, nor is there evidence that the assessment was made in disregard of recognized elements of value, or in violation of any accepted standards or regulations. The most that can be said is that the record discloses an honest difference of opinion between one appraiser and the assessing authorities. This is made evident by the compromise judgment of the trial court.

We adhere to our previous decisions relating to the scope of judicial inquiry in assessment matters and accordingly hold that there is no evidence sufficient to support the trial court's finding of constructive fraud.

GOLDBERG V. BOARD OF REVISION
218 N.E.2d 723 (Ohio 1966)

O'NEILL, JUDGE: The issue before the court is whether the Board of Tax Appeals has properly interpreted and followed the order of this court.

Sarah R. Goldberg owns business property in Cleveland, Ohio. The fair market value of that property was agreed upon by the parties to be $42,600. It is undisputed in the record that the prevailing average ratio of assessed value to fair market value of all real property in Cuyahoga County is approximately 40%.

The board assessed the Goldberg property at 52% of its agreed fair market value. This was undisputed in the record to be the prevailing average ratio of assessed value to fair market value of commercial property in Cuyahoga County. This assessment was based upon the finding of the Board of Tax Appeals, which reads as follows:

(2) *A parcel of residential property is comparable only to other parcels of residential property and a parcel of commercial property is comparable only to other parcels of commercial property.*

This finding denies the taxpayer his state and federal constitutional rights and is directly contra to the law as pronounced by this court in this case in the opinion which resulted in the remand of this case to the Board of Tax Appeals.

Section 2 of Article XII of the Ohio Constitution provides: . . . *"Land and improvements thereon shall be taxed by uniform rule according to value. . . ."*

Section 1 of the Fourteenth Amendment to the Constitution of the United States provides in part that no state "shall . . . deny to any person within its jurisdiction the equal protection of the laws." . . .

"It is clear that under the Ohio law all real property, regardless of its nature or use, may be assessed and taxed only by a uniform rule on the basis of value.

". . . It is and has been the practice in this state for taxation purposes to establish an assessed value of less than actual value. . . . This raises the question of uniformity. Taxation by uniform rule within the requirement of the constitutional provision requires uniformity in the mode of assessment. . . . All property, whether commercial, residential or vacant, must be assessed on the basis of the same uniform percentage of actual value."

It could not be stated in more succinct language.

The decision of the Board of Tax Appeals is, therefore, reversed, the cause is remanded to the Board of Tax Appeals, and the board is ordered to comply with the law as established by this court. [DECISION REVERSED]

CONTINENTAL COFFEE CO. V. BOWERS
189 N.E.2d 901 (Ohio 1963)

MATTHIAS, JUDGE: Two basic questions are raised by this appeal.

First, do the cleaning, blending and roasting of green coffee beans constitute manufacturing within the meaning of the Ohio tax laws? Second, where green coffee is delivered from foreign countries to a coffee processing plant and stored therein for use in such plant, does it retain its character as an import so long as it is in the original package and is it thus immune, under the provisions of Section 10, Article I of the United States Constitution, from state taxation?

First, we will turn our attention to the question as to whether appellant is a manufacturer.

Section 5711.16, Revised Code, provides in part as follows:

A person who purchases, receives, or holds personal property for the purpose of adding to its value by manufacturing, refining, rectifying, or combining different materials with a view of making a gain or profit by so doing is a manufacturer.

Appellant contends, however, that such statutory definition is not dispositive of whether appellant is a manufacturer so far as the federal Constitution is concerned. It is appellant's theory that it is engaged in the business of selling, not manufacturing, coffee. However, the term, "manufacturing," has broad connotations; it is not confined solely to the construction of tangible property but extends to the creation of a usable product. The activities in which any given business engages must be examined to determine whether such business is engaged in manufacturing.

In general it may be said that one is engaged in manufacturing when he takes raw material unfit for human use or consumption and by the use of various processes converts it into a finished product which is fit for such use or consumption. . . .

A consideration of the facts in the instant case clearly indicates that appellant is engaged in manufacturing. Here green coffee beans from a number of foreign countries are delivered directly to appellant's plant. There is no question that at that time the coffee beans in their delivered state are unfit for consumption. These coffee beans are good for only one purpose and that is for consumable coffee after a variety of processes are performed thereon. They have no present commercial value except to the coffee roaster. Before such coffee beans have any general commercial value, they must be cleaned, blended and roasted, and it is only then that they are fit for consumption. In other words, these coffee beans are not a salable, consumable commodity when delivered to appellant; it is only after such coffee beans are cleaned, blended and roasted that the commodity which appellant sells comes into existence.

Thus, the cleaning, blending and roasting of green coffee beans constitute manufacturing.

However, appellant urges that this coffee was still in the original packages in which it was imported and retained its character as an import, exempting it from state taxation, under the terms of Section 10, Article I of the Constitution of the United States, which reads in part as follows:

No State shall, without the Consent of the Congress, lay any Imposts or Duties on Imports or Exports, except what may be absolutely necessary for executing its inspection Laws: and the net Produce of all Duties and Imposts, laid by any State on Imports or Exports, shall be for the Use of the Treasury of the United States; and all such Laws shall be subject to the Revision and Control of the Congress.

In this case there is no question that this coffee was still in the original package at the time the tax was assessed thereon.

So far as taxation is concerned, the "original package doctrine" arose in the case of *Brown v. Maryland,* 25 U.S. 419, 12 Wheat. 419, 6 L.Ed. 678. That case held in essence that the state could not tax property imported for sale so long as the property remained in the original package in the warehouse of the importer. Such doctrine was extended in *Hooven & Allison Co. v. Evatt,* 324 U.S. 652, 65 S.Ct. 870, 89 L.Ed. 1252, to goods imported by a manufacturer for use in his business, which goods retained such character as imports until used for the purpose for which they were imported.

However, the purpose of Section 10, Article I of the United States Constitution, is to prohibit a state from imposing taxes on imports, or rather import taxes, and not to relieve property from state taxation which has become part of the inventory used in business by a manufacturer.

The original package doctrine was modified by the Supreme Court of the United States in *Youngstown Sheet & Tube Co. v. Bowers,* 358 U.S. 534, 79 S.Ct. 383, 3 L.Ed.2d 490 (affirming 166 Ohio St. 122, 140 N.E.2d 313), which held that the imported product loses its character as an import when it is irrevocably committed to use in manufacturing.

In that case, a manufacturer of iron and steel imported iron ore from foreign countries for use in its manufacturing. The ore was stored in piles in ore yards adjacent to the processing plant, and the daily ore needs of the plant were supplied from these ore yards. Similarly, in the case of *United States Plywood Corp. v. City of Algoma,* 358 U.S. 534, 79 S.Ct. 383, 3 L.Ed.2d 490, which was decided together with the Youngstown case, a manufacturer of veneered wood products imported veneers in bundles which were kept in the same form in which received in piles for use as needed in the daily manufacturing process of the plant. The court in those cases said:

*We are therefore confronted with the practical, albeit vexing, problem
of reconciling the competing demands of the constitutional immunity of imports and of the State's power to tax property within its borders. The design
of the constitutional immunity was to prevent "[t]he great importing States
[from laying] a tax on the nonimporting States," to which the imported property is or might ultimately be destined, which would not only discriminate
against them but also "would necessarily produce countervailing measures on
the part of those States whose situation was less favourable to importation."
. . . The constitutional design was then to immunize imports from taxation
by the importing States, and all others through or into which they may pass,
so long as they retain their distinctive character as imports. Hence, that design
is not impinged by the taxation of materials that were imported for use in
manufacturing after all phases of the importation definitely have ended and
the materials have been "put to the use for which they [were] imported"*
(Hooven & Allison Co. v. Evatt, *supra*, 324 *U.S.* at page 657, 65 S.Ct. at page
873 (89 L.Ed. 1252), *for in such a case they have lost their distinctive character as imports and are subject to taxation. . . .*

*The materials here in question were imported to supply, and were essen-
tial to supply, the manufacturer's current operating needs. When, after all
phases of their importation had ended, they were put to that use and indiscriminate portions of the whole were actually being used to supply daily operating needs, they stood in the same relation to the State as like piles of
domestic materials at the same place that were kept for use and used in the
same way. The one was then as fully subject to taxation as the other. In
those circumstances, the tax was not on "imports," nor was it a tax on the
materials because they had been imported. They were therefore subject to
taxation just like domestic property that was kept at the same place in the
same way for the same use. . . .*

The rule which is not applicable to property imported by a manufacturer is that once such property becomes a part of the inventory of the
manufacturer necessary to supply its current operating needs the property
loses its character as an import and is subject to state taxation. In other
words, once an import is irrevocably committed to supply the current operating needs of a manufacturer and is being used to supply its daily operating
needs the status as an import is lost.

Section 5709.01, Revised Code, provides in part that "[a]ll personal
property located and used in business in this state . . . are subject to
taxation."

Personal property is used in business "when stored or kept on hand as
material." Section 5701.08(A), Revised Code.

Clearly, such coffee beans are used in business by appellant. Although
appellant contends that it is engaged in selling coffee, not manufacturing it,
it is readily apparent from the record that this is not the fact. Appellant is

engaged in both the manufacture and sale of coffee. It is not contended that appellant is engaged in the business of selling green coffee. It sells only the finished product.

Therefore, we are left with the qustion as to whether the coffee stored by appellant has retained its character as an import. Is this inventory of green coffee necessary to supply the current operating needs of appellant within the meaning of the Supreme Court decision? If it is, the United States Supreme Court has held that once it is placed in a position to supply the current operating needs of appellant it loses its character as an import and is used in business within the meaning of the Ohio tax statutes.

Here the coffee is stored in the plant in a place immediately adjacent to the manufacturing area. A supply for only three weeks duration is all that is maintained at any given time and from this supply is drawn the daily needs of the plant. This falls exactly within the rule promulgated by the Supreme Court of the United States in the *Youngstown Sheet & Tube* case holding that such material has lost its character as an import.

In other words, coffee stored by an importer-manufacturer of coffee in an amount sufficient only to meet the manufacturer's current operating needs and from which is drawn the amount needed daily in its business, is used in business and thus has lost its character as an import even though it is stored in the original package in which it was imported.

The decision of the Board of Tax Appeals, being neither unreasonable nor unlawful, is affirmed. [DECISION AFFIRMED]

STATE BD. OF TAX COMM'RS V. WRIGHT
215 N.E.2d 57 (Ind. 1966)

WICKENS, JUDGE: One hundred and four cabins used for temporary dwelling purposes during church conferences are located on premises owned by the Wabash Annual Conference of the Free Methodist Church of North America, Inc. Whether these cabins are entitled to be held exempt from property tax, as being used exclusively for religious purposes and owned and actually occupied by the religious conference is the issue here.

All tax exemption is an important topic of public interest. A new and unique inquiry is whether cabins built and/or occupied by church members on church premises for temporary residential purposes during church conferences, should be afforded property tax exemption. A justification for tax exemption is the public benefit. Thus the purpose of exemption, whether under religious or other classification, is to insure that property and funds devoted to one public benefit are not diminished by being diverted through taxation for another public benefit.

Property tax exemption for religious purposes has its historical roots in antiquity. It is more fundamental than mere tradition. From it has probably sprung those features of estate and income tax laws which exempt contributions for religious, charitable and public purposes and also exempt certain organizations. It is possible that the legal concept of a "charity" and its favorable treatment found in the law of trusts has developed therefrom. . . .

The General Assembly has enacted property tax exemption laws, applicable provisions of which read as follows:

The following property shall be exempt from taxation: . . .

Fifth. Every building, or part thereof, used and set apart for educational, literary, scientific, religious or charitable purposes by any institution or by any individual or individuals, association or corporation, provided the same is owned and actually occupied by the institution, individual, association or corporation using it for such purpose or purposes. . . .

Sixth. Every building or part thereof used for religious worship, and the pews and furniture within the same, and also the parsonage belonging thereto and occupied as such, and the land whereon said building or buildings are situate, not exceeding fifteen (15) acres, when owned by a church or religious society, or in trust for its use. Acts 1919, ch. 59, § 5, p. 198, § 64-201 Burns' 1961 Replacement.

These provisions limiting property exempt status also should be noted:

If all or any part, parcel or portion of any tract or lot of land or any buildings or personal property enumerated in the preceding section as exempt from taxation shall be used or occupied for any other purpose or purposes than those recited in said section by reason whereof they are exempted from taxation, such property, part, parcel or portion shall be subject to taxation so long as the same shall not be set aside or used exclusively for some one of the purposes specified in said enumeration. Acts 1919, ch. 59, § 6, p. 198, § 64–202 Burns' 1961 Replacement.

and

When real estate which is exempt from taxation is leased to another whose property is not exempt, and the leasing of which does not make the real estate taxable, the leasehold estate and the appurtenances shall be listed as the property of the lessee thereof, or his assignee, as real estate. Acts 1919, ch. 59, § 33, p. 198, § 64-204 Burns' 1961 Replacement. . . .
While an exemption statute is to be construed strictly against those arguing for nontaxability . . . the interpretation should not be so narrow and literal as to defeat its settled purpose, which in this instance is that of encouraging, fostering and protecting religious and educational institutions.

Courts in other jurisdictions which have statutory "exclusive use" requirements for religious purposes have held personal living quarters to be exempt from taxation especially if incidental and necessary for the effective welfare of the exempt religious institution. . . .

As to the occupancy of the cabins by the Church the trial court held they were constructively occupied by the Church through its members. We are in agreement with this. The only purpose and the only use for the cabins was shown to be religious. We can see no distinction between occupancy of property by a church and occupancy by any other corporate body. The members of the corporate body in fact do the physical occupying, but it is still correct to say the premises are occupied by the corporation. Here we have occupancy by the Church, and it is limited to religious use. The trial court properly held the cabins were necessary and were used exclusively to effectuate the religious purpose and activities of the Church.

The religious exemption provisions are entitled to no less favorable treatment and consideration than the other provisions of the exemption statute. In its most recent opinion construing that statute our Supreme Court held in favor of an exemption where lodge dining facilities were involved.

Any narrowing of the statutory construction might contravene the position of the Supreme Court of the United States elucidated by Mr. Justice Douglas who said in *Zorach v. Clauson* (1952), 343 U.S. 306, 314, 72 S.Ct. 679, 684, 96 L.Ed. 954, 962:

But we find no constitutional requirement which makes it necessary for government to be hostile to religion and to throw its weight against efforts to widen the effective scope of religious influence. . . .

For the reasons given we affirm the decision of the trial court.

10   LICENSE FEES

A license must be obtained by a person before he may engage in many professions, occupations, or businesses. To obtain the license, a fee is usually required. The purpose of the fee is to pay the cost of regulating and supervising the licensed activity. However, many license fees may actually be revenue-producing measures, and the laws requiring the license may be subject to attack for that reason. Some licensing statutes may be challenged because they discriminate against interstate commerce in favor of intrastate commerce.

Many taxes paid by individuals are in reality license fees. For example, the money deposited in parking meters is a license fee to defray the cost of regulating parking and pay for parking spaces. Auto license fees are justified on the same basis. Physicians are required to purchase a license to dispense or prescribe which is a means of regulating the use of narcotics.

In recent years, various taxes similar to license taxes have been used to raise substantial amounts of revenue. Some of these are admission taxes at places of entertainment and taxes on parimutuel betting. The latter taxes have been held valid even where other statutes prohibit gambling since they are revenue measures.

Many cases involving license fees are concerned with whether or not the activity is interstate commerce or intrastate commerce, and with problems of apportionment. Just as in the case of property and income taxes, a license fee is not unconstitutional just because it imposes a burden on interstate commerce, because not all burdens are forbidden—only undue or discriminatory ones.

The case which follows involves the validity of a state license fee as affected by the Federal Soldiers' and Sailors' Civil Relief Act.

CALIFORNIA V. BUZARD
382 U.S. 386 (1966)

BRENNAN, JUSTICE: Section 514 of the Soldiers' and Sailors' Civil Relief Act of 1940, as amended, provides a nonresident serviceman present in a State in compliance with military orders with a broad immunity from that State's personal property and income taxation. Section 514 (2) (b) of the Act further provides that

the term "taxation" shall include but not be limited to licenses, fees, or excises imposed in respect to motor vehicles or the use thereof: Provided, That the license, fee, or excise required by the State, . . . of which the person is a resident or in which he is domiciled has been paid.

The respondent here, Captain Lyman E. Buzard, was a resident and domiciliary of the State of Washington stationed at Castle Air Force Base in California. He had purchased an Oldsmobile while on temporary duty in Alabama, and had obtained Alabama license plates for it by registering it there. On his return, California refused to allow him to drive the car on California highways with the Alabama plates, and, since he had not registered or obtained license tags in his home State, demanded that he register and obtain license plates in California. When he sought to do so, it was insisted that he pay both the registration fee of $8.00 imposed by California's Vehicle Code and the considerably larger "license fee" imposed by its Revenue and Taxation Code. The license fee is calculated at "two (2) percent of the market value of the vehicle," § 10752, and is "imposed . . . in lieu of all taxes according to value levied for State or local purposes on vehicles . . . subject to registration under the Vehicle Code. . . ." § 10758. Captain Buzard refused to pay the 2% fee, and was prosecuted and convicted for violating Vehicle Code § 4000, which provides that "[N]o person shall drive . . . any motor vehicle . . . upon a highway unless it is registered and the appropriate fees have been paid under this Code." The conviction, affirmed by the District Court of Appeal, was reversed by the

Supreme Court of California. We granted certiorari to consider whether § 514 barred California from exacting the 2% tax as a condition of registering and licensing Captain Buzard's car. We conclude that it did, and affirm. . . .

Although little appears in the legislative history to explain the proviso, Congress was clearly concerned that servicemen stationed away from their home State should not drive unregistered or unlicensed motor vehicles. Every State required in 1944, and requires now, that motor vehicles using its highways be registered and bear license plates. Such requirements are designed to facilitate the identification of vehicle owners and the investigation of accidents, thefts, traffic violations and other violations of law. Commonly, if not universally, the statutes imposing the requirements of registration or licensing also prescribe fees which must be paid to authorize state officials to issue the necessary documents and plates. To assure that servicemen comply with the registration and licensing laws of some State, whether of their home State or the host State, we construe the phrase "license, fee, or excise *required by* the State . . ." as equivalent to "license, fee, or excise *of* the State. . . ." Thus read, the phrase merely indicates Congress' recognition that, in one form or another, all States have laws governing the registration and licensing of motor vehicles, and that such laws impose certain taxes as conditions thereof. The serviceman who has not registered his car and obtained license plates under the laws "of" his home State, whatever the reason, may be required by the host State to register and license the car under its laws.

The proviso is to be read, at the least, as assuring that § 514 would not have the effect of permitting servicemen to escape the obligation of registering and licensing their motor vehicles. It has been argued that § 514 (2)(b) also represents a congressional judgment that servicemen should contribute to the costs of highway maintenance, whether at home or where they are stationed, by paying whatever taxes the State of registration may levy for that purpose. We conclude, however, that no such purpose is revealed in the section or its legislative history and that its intent is limited to the purpose of assuring registration. Since at least the 2% tax here involved has been held not essential to that purpose as a matter of State law, we affirm the California Supreme Court's judgment.

It is plain at the outset that California may collect the 2% tax only if it is a "license, fee or excise" on a motor vehicle or its use. The very purpose of § 514 in broadly freeing the nonresident serviceman from the obligation to pay property and income taxes was to relieve him of the burden of supporting the governments of the States where he was present solely in compliance with military orders. The statute operates whether or not the home State imposes or assesses such taxes against him. As we said in *Dameron v. Brodhead,* 345 U.S. 322, 326, 73 S.Ct. 721, 724, 97 L.Ed. 1041, ". . . though the evils of potential multiple taxation may have given rise to this provision, Congress appears to have chosen the broader technique of the statute carefully, freeing servicemen from both income and property taxes imposed by any state by virtue of their presence there as a result of military orders. It saved the sole right of taxation to the state of original residence whether or not that state exercised the right." Motor vehicles were included as personal property covered by the statute. Even if Congress meant to do more by the proviso of § 514(2) (b) than insure that the car would be registered and licensed in one of the two States, it would be inconsistent with the broad purposes of § 514 to read subsection (2) (b) as allowing the host State to impose taxes other than "licenses, fees, or excises" when the "license, fee, or excise" of the home State is not paid.

Although the Revenue and Taxation Code expressly denominates the tax "a license fee," § 10751, there is no persuasive evidence Congress meant state labels to be conclusive; therefore, we must decide as a matter of federal law what "licenses, fees or excises" means in the statute. See *Storaasli v. Minnesota*, 283 U.S. 57, 62, 51 S.Ct. 354, 355, 75 L.Ed. 839. There is nothing in the legislative history to show that Congress intended a tax not essential to assure registration, such as the California "license fee," to fall within the category of "licenses, fees, or excises" host States might impose if home State registration was not effected. While it is true that a few state taxes in effect in 1944, like the California 2% "license fee," were imposed solely for revenue purposes, the great majority of state taxes also served to enforce registration and licensing statutes. No discussion of existing State laws appears in the Committee Reports. There is thus no indication that Congress was aware that any State required that servicemen contribute to the costs of highway maintenance without regard to the relevance of such requirements to the nonrevenue purposes of state motor vehicle laws.

The conclusion that Congress lacked information about the California practice does not preclude a determination that it meant to include such taxes, levied only for revenue, as "licenses, fees, or excises." But in deciding that question in the absence of affirmative indication of congressional meaning, we must consider the overall purposes of § 514 as well as the words of subsection (2) (b). Taxes like the California 2% "license fee" serve primarily a revenue interest, narrower in purpose but no different in kind from taxes raised to defray the general expenses of government. It is from the burden of taxes serving such ends that nonresident servicemen were to be freed, in the main, without regard to whether their home States imposed or sought to collect such taxes from them. *Dameron v. Brodhead, supra*. In recent amendments, Congress has reconfirmed this basic purpose. We do not think that subsection (2) (b) should be read as impinging it. Rather, reading the Act, as we must, "with an eye friendly to those who dropped their affairs to answer their country's call," *Le Maistre v. Leffers,* 333 U.S. 1, 6, 68 S.Ct. 371, 373, 92 L.Ed. 429, we conclude that subsection (2) (b) refers only to those taxes which are essential to the functioning of the host

State's licensing and registration laws in their application to the motor vehicles of nonresident servicemen. Whether the 2% tax is within the reach of the federal immunity is thus not to be tested, as California argues, by whether its inclusion frustrates the administration of California's tax policies. The test, rather, is whether the inclusion would deny the State power to enforce the nonrevenue provisions of state motor vehicle legislation.

Whatever may be the case under the registration and licensing statutes of other States California authorities have made it clear that the California 2% tax is not imposed as a tax essential to the registration and licensing of the serviceman's motor vehicle. Not only did the California Supreme Court regard the statutes as permitting registration without payment of the tax, but the District Court of Appeal, in another case growing out of this controversy, expressly held that "[t]he registration statute has an entirely different purpose from the licenses fee statutes, and it is clearly severable from them." *Buzard v. Justice Court,* 198 Cal.App. 2d 814, 817, 18 Cal. Rptr. 348, 349–350. The California Supreme Court also held, in effect, that invalidity of the "license fee" as applied was a valid defense to prosecution under Vehicle Code § 4000. In these circumstances, and since the record is reasonably to be read as showing that Captain Buzard would have registered his Oldsmobile but for the demand for payment of the 2% tax, the California Supreme Court's reversal of his conviction is affirmed. [AFFIRMED]

11   DEATH TAXES

The Federal government imposes an estate tax on the fair market value of property interests passing as a result of a person's death and also imposes a tax on gifts of property made during a person's lifetime. These are substantial taxes with graduated rates and have encouraged major efforts in preventive law to avoid or minimize these taxes. For example, the tax on a $160,000 net estate is $20,800 and the next increment is taxed at 30%.

States also have death taxes which usually take the form of an inheritance tax. Such a tax differs from an estate tax in that an inheritance tax is imposed on the recipient of property and takes into account the amount of property received and the relationship of the recipient to the deceased, whereas the estate tax is levied on the net taxable value of the property itself irrespective of recipient. Under the inheritance tax arrangement, taxes on bequests to friends would be higher than on the property passed to close relatives.

Each state has its own body of law relative to its inheritance tax. Generally a state may impose an inheritance tax on all real estate or tangible personal property located within the state, and in addition it may tax intangible personal property of its domiciliaries wherever it is located. It is important that each person clearly establish a domicile or several states may try to tax his bank accounts, stocks and bonds, and other intangibles on death. A domicile is a person's home or residence and also the place to which he intends to return when he has gone away from it. College students are usually not domiciled in the university community. People who spend their winters in a warm climate and who may purchase a home for this purpose but also maintain a summer residence in another state create an inheritance tax problem by such action.

The following case is an unusual one in the laws of inheritance taxation. It illustrates some aspects of inheritance taxes but is further significant as a unique demonstration of patriotism.

IN RE ESTATE OF ANDERSEN
218 N.E.2d 486 (Ohio 1965)

SCHNEIDER, CHIEF REFEREE: This case came before the court on exceptions filed by the Tax Commissioner of Ohio to the determination of inheritance tax on the succession in the estate of Martin Andersen, deceased, to the United States Government and in which case the court directed a reference.

The facts are not in dispute.

The decedent Martin Andersen, deceased, in Item VII of his Last Will and Testament provided; "All the rest and residue of my estate I give, devise and bequeath to the United States Government." The value of this bequest appears to be $8622.67 and on April 16, 1964, the court found that this bequest was not subject to Ohio inheritance tax.

On May 20, 1964, the Tax Commissioner of Ohio filed exceptions to this determination, claiming that the court erred in finding that the United States Government is entitled to exemption for inheritance tax purposes. . . .

The issue being the taxability of the United States Government under the provisions of Section 573.02, Revised Code, and the Exemption Section 5731.09, Revised Code, it is asserted by the Tax Commissioner that the United States Government is a corporation under the terms of said Sections.

CONSTRUCTION OF THE STATUTES

If the United States is subject to inheritance tax under the provisions of the succession tax laws of the state of Ohio it would necessarily be based upon the fact that the government of the United States is to be regarded as a "corporation" it being provided in Section 5731.02, Revised Code: "A tax is hereby levied upon the succession to any property passing, in trust or otherwise, [to or] for the use of a person, institution or corporation, in the following cases: . . . ."

Under the Constitution of the United States the preamble states: "We, the people of the United States, in order to form a more perfect union . . . do ordain and establish this Constitution of the United States of America." following which the seven separate articles and amendments are set forth. In Webster's International Dictionary the United States is defined as "a federation of states" and the word federation as is applicable, an "act of uniting to form a sovereign power so that each of the uniting powers retains the management of its own local affairs." A fitting definition would be "it is a representative entity, created by the citizens of all the confederated colonies through their delegated representatives, to form a sovereign power." It is frequently referred to as a government of delegated power (Amendment X Constitution). It is a division of power by compact, hence a federal government.

This entity was formed on the basis of a surrender of powers by the separate colonies rather than a grant of powers as the power granted can in no manner be terminated. Additional power or authority can be given and that which has been given can be modified by amendment. The Constitution is the supreme law of the land (Article VI Constitution). From the above it would indicate that to regard the United States of America as a corporation would be a strained deduction from the existing facts as it is operated under the authority surrendered by the states and the fields in which it operates are exclusive, and that of a sovereign state.

If the entity is supreme it cannot be regarded as a corporation when the word is used in ordinary context, without further modification or enlargement of the term.

In considering the exemptions set forth in Section 5731.09, Revised Code, it is provided that no tax is levied on property "passing to or for the use of the state, or to or for the use of a municipal corporation or other political subdivision thereof for exclusively public purposes. . . ." Giving the words used, their ordinary meaning in Section 5731.02, Revised Code, there exists no legal requirement for the exception provisions relating to the state or a political subdivision thereof, as no tax under the terms used was levied by the provisions of the limited field subject to tax appearing in that Section and the only exemption granted by the words used relates to a municipal corporation. The state of Ohio or any other state or political subdivision thereof is not taxed. The phraseology used is indicative that the legislative purpose was directed and limited to the state of Ohio by the use of the singular form "state" but since no tax was levied on a state the exemption was only expressive of the original intent not to tax.

The United States existed for many years prior to the effective date of the tax imposed on successions and if it had been the purpose of the legislature to tax all successions except as were exempted it could have done so.

In re Estate of McLaughlin, Ohio App., 179 N.E.2d 106, 88 Ohio Law

Abst. 105, the testator bequeathed certain monies to the United States Government and the Court of Appeals affirmed the finding of the Probate Court of Noble County the syllabus being: "Section 5731.02, Revised Code imposes a tax on successions only of a person, institution or corporation, and the United States Government is not a person nor a corporation nor an institution within the purview of this statute."

With this conclusion we concur.

The elected and appointed officials of the United States Government act in a representative capacity and at that point its similarity to a corporate entity ceases and reference to it as a corporation can be distinguished in the cases and references made from the context in which the term was so employed.

The states being the reservoir of all remaining power can levy a succession tax upon the sovereign state, but the legislative authority of the state of Ohio was specific in the levy of the tax and in giving the words used their usual and ordinary meaning, did not subject the sovereign to the tax.

DECISION

The United States Government under the provisions of Section 5731.02, Revised Code, is not subject to Ohio inheritance tax.

CHAPTER TEN

REGULATION OF COMPETITION —INTRODUCTION

1 THE COMMON LAW

An ambitious man purchases grain which is on its way to market, with the object of reselling it at a profit. As a result of this business activity, he is arrested, tried, and convicted for committing an offense against the state. This event did not happen in modern communistic Russia or China, but in medieval England, around 1250 A.D. Early common-law developments were designed to regulate trade by ensuring competition and preventing monopoly. By court decision, such acts as buying fish before the boats came into port or buying food supplies on the way to market were criminal offenses. Also, it was an indictable offense to purchase any goods in the kingdom for the purpose of resale. One objective of these decisions was to eliminate all "middlemen." The producer (or importer, for he was permitted to resell goods purchased outside the kingdom) sold directly to the consumer.

Why were these standards of conduct adopted? The answer is found in an analysis of the economy of the times. During the Middle Ages, most persons made their own clothing and produced their own food. Because of a lack of transportation facilities and the simple economy, trading for commodities usually occurred only at local annual fairs. It would have been relatively easy for a man to obtain a "corner" on a certain type of merchandise at a particular fair and sell at almost any price he desired. Even if one purchased just part of the local supply of a commodity, like wheat, with the intention of reselling it, he would not have done so unless he intended to make a profit from the sale. This practice would artificially increase the price of wheat to consumers and so was declared to be illegal.

Of course, these restrictions on trade gradually were eliminated. Although the underlying policy favoring a free market and opposing monopoly remained and still exists, vast changes caused by the industrial revolution and the expansion of our economy created a need for many persons to be engaged in the distribution of goods, wares, and merchandise. Today, the jobber, wholesaler, and retailer each play an essential part in the distribution of products to consumers. They incur costs and perform valuable services, justifying a reasonable profit for their efforts. It is apparent that there was no need for such a service by a "middleman" at the fair of the Middle Ages. The producer could sell directly to the consumer at a lower price.

The fostering of competition to prevent artificially high prices originated in the common law and is given effect today in the common-law principle that contracts which have as their purpose the restraint of trade are illegal. For example, assume that the ABC Department Store and the XYZ Department Store each agreed not to open a branch in the city where the other was doing business. Either store could disregard this agreement and compete with the other, without being liable for damages for breach of contract. By modern statute, the parties to such an agreement might be liable for breach of public laws enacted to preserve competition. While there are many other types of agreements in restraint of trade, not all contracts which limit competition were or are illegal. For example, a contractual restraint of trade which is partial as to the time and area of its operation, and which is reasonably designed to protect some legitimate interest, will be enforced by the courts and is not a violation of public law. Thus, a purchaser of a bakery business could enforce an agreement by the seller not to open up a competing bakery within a reasonable geographical area and time after the sale. The main purpose of such a clause would not be to restrain trade, but to obtain for the buyer the business for which he was paying.

The weakness in the common-law rule opposing agreements in restraint of trade is that, although the court will not enforce these restraints, the parties to such an agreement can perform if they desire, without interference. This common-law rule does not impose any penalty or criminal sanction on them as do modern enactments of public laws. The early history of the United States saw neither state nor Federal legislation dealing with the effective prevention of monopolistic practices. One of the reasons for this lack of legislation was that the American people at the outset favored a system of *laissez faire,* or noninterference by the government in economic life.

2   LAISSEZ FAIRE [1]

Under the feudal system, almost complete control of political, social, and economic life was in the hands of the church, the guilds, and local manoral lords who owned the land and the little equipment that existed. The great majority of people were serfs tied to the land which they worked for their overlords. The Renaissance marked the collapse of the feudal system and of this type of localized control.

Around the beginning of the sixteenth century, nationalistic states emerged in Europe which were characterized by strong central governments.

[1] Steiner, *Government's Role in Economic Life* 46–50, 64–68 (1953).

A new system of mercantilism, in which the interests of the state were supreme, took the place of the feudal system. These states, in their desire to maintain national political control and to expand their influence by colonization, needed vast military power and hence large quantities of gold and other valuable metals. In this period of mercantilism, the government of the state maintained far-ranging controls over the economic life of the nation. Exporting goods brought in the precious metals desired and was encouraged. Importing, which would send them abroad, was discouraged by high tariffs. Manufacturing, labor, and agriculture were subject to strict regulation by the state, which determined such things as the amount of production by each industry, and each individual's occupation as well as his working hours and wages. A sixteenth-century English law, designed to promote wool manufacturing, provided that on Sundays and holidays, each subject over six years old must wear a woolen cap manufactured in England. For a time, men accepted the notion that the state's welfare was more important than the individual's, and that it was natural for their lives to be controlled socially and economically by the state so that its ends could be served.

The English subjected our colonial forefathers to this system of mercantilism, of an economy strictly regulated by a strong central government. Examples of the regulations they imposed are the Trade Acts, which provided that certain items produced in America, such as tobacco, rice, lumber, iron, and furs, could be exported only to England. Other acts required American imports from and exports to Europe to pass through English merchants in the mother country, who of course exacted profits from these transactions. To protect manufacturers in England, laws prohibited the export of American woolens, even to other American colonies; the export of hats; and the milling of iron and manufacture of products from iron. In the 1760s various other regulatory measures were adopted. Lands west of a certain line could no longer be purchased from the Indians, for their disposition was controlled by the King. Taxes were imposed on imports of wines, silks, sugar, lead, and paint, among other commodities. Because of the type and number of the regulatory laws adopted by the British government it was clear to the colonists that, with apparent disregard of the economic effect on them, Great Britain intended to maintain tight political control of the colonies without representation, to enrich the state's coffers with various taxes, and certainly to promote business and manufacturing interests in England at the expense of the Americans.

The colonists, aroused by this oppression, protested through the first Continental Congress. Their protests were met by restraining acts which virtually wiped out colonial commerce, and by even more intense action by the officials of the Crown to subject them to British control. They followed the path of open revolution to eliminate the economic yoke of mercantilism and to acquire political and economic freedom. They rejected the view that the state was all-important and adopted the view that the individual was supreme. Their prevailing philosophies were that each man had the "inalienable rights" of "life, liberty and the pursuit of happiness"; that government, by natural law, acquired its power only with the consent of the governed; and, that "that government is best which governs least."

These sentiments were not exclusively American. Great philosophers and writers elsewhere voiced the same burning ideas proposing individual freedom, much less power in government, and an economic system of *laissez faire*. In 1776, the year the Declaration of Independence was signed, the book *Wealth of Nations* by the great Scottish economist, Adam Smith, was published. In it he argued generally in favor of *laissez faire*.

The natural effort of every individual to better his own condition, when suffered to exert itself with freedom and security, is so powerful a principle that it is alone, and without any assistance, not only capable of carrying on the society to wealth and prosperity, but of surmounting a hundred impertinent obstructions with which the folly of human laws too often incumbers its operations; though the effect of these obstructions is always more or less either to encroach upon its freedom, or to diminish its security.

Smith reasoned that since national wealth was the total wealth of the individuals within the nation, conditions which produced the greatest individual wealth would result in the greatest national wealth. He proposed that each individual, in an economic system with the maximum possible amount of freedom, would unwittingly contribute to the good and wealth of the country because he would have a natural, selfish motivation to use his talents or property to get the highest return possible. Regulation by the government of production and prices was unnecessary, he stated. In fact, free competition and the natural law of supply and demand would regulate business to the good of a country much more effectively than some high governmental official could. If the demand for a particular product were high for the supply, a resulting higher price and greater profit would induce others to enter the field and increase the supply. The increase in supply would lower the price and profit to a normal one. But, if the supply were large for the demand, a low price would result from competition, and the selfish desire for profits would induce some of the suppliers to turn their efforts and resources to where the fields appeared greener.

Smith, however, did not propose *laissez faire* in its absolute extreme. He advocated free competition, which requires a market free of the control of monopolists as well as free of control by government intervention, so that the natural law of supply and demand will operate to regulate the market. He recognized the danger of monopoly. "People of the same trade seldom meet together, even for merriment and diversion, but the conversation ends in a conspiracy against the public, or in some contrivance to raise prices. It is impossible indeed to prevent such meetings by any law which could be executed, or would be consistent with liberty and justice." He also wrote in *Wealth of Nations,* "Where there is an exclusive corporation, it may perhaps be proper to regulate the price of the first necessary of life. But where there is none, the competition will regulate it much better than any assize."

Because of the experience of political and economic oppression by England, and the growing worldwide philosophy that the individual's freedom was natural, more important than the edification of the state, and that freedom would bring more wealth to the nation than the state could by regulation, the people and leaders of the United States, from the outset, were disposed against governmental interference in economic life and in favor of a system of *laissez faire.* At first, this system worked well. It spurred the industrial development of the nation. But the growth of the American economy was paralleled by the development of government regulation of business and a movement away from *laissez faire.* Changing conditions required new laws.

3   THE DEVELOPMENT OF A NEED FOR REGULATION OF COMPETITION [2]

At the turn of the eighteenth century, the United States had a small, simple economy, with agricultural production being the largest single area producing private income. Most men were self-employed and lived on farms or in small communities. The relatively small amount of manufacturing (roughly about one-eighth of agricultural production) was mainly accomplished by village crafts or household industries. Farmers produced and made almost everything they needed and factories were rare. Goods were sold to a large number of purchasers by a large number of small producers. Nationwide monopolies were impossible because of a lack of transportation and because production was in the hands of so many small producers. The conditions were those on which a philosophy of *laissez faire* is premised and under which such a system works best.

During the nineteenth century the industrial revolution transformed the economy from small to large, from simple to complex, from basically agricultural to mass-production industrial. The economies of mass production brought competition and caused manufacture by village crafts and household industries to disappear. Farmers turned to the production of crops for sale instead of just for their own use. Manufacturing equaled, then surpassed agriculture in production of private income. The country's population greatly expanded, due in part to immigration. The population growth provided both an abundant labor force and an enlarging market. The market was nationwide because of Federal constitutional provisions ensuring free-

2 Kemmerer & Jones, *American Economic History* 312–315, 341–344 (1959).

dom of interstate commerce from unduly burdensome controls and taxation by the states, and because of the development of nationwide rail transportation. High import tariffs protected American producers from foreign competition. The raw materials for manufacture were available in the vast store of natural resources of the country. There were a great number of inventions, both of consumer goods and of machines to produce goods, no doubt spurred by the protection afforded the inventor by the patent laws. The invention and development of the steam engine gave manufacturers a new source of power, making them no longer dependent on water power. The profits of business and the savings of the wealthy provided capital for rapid expansion.

Certainly the human motivating force behind the metamorphosis was the desire for material gain. Profit was the end and the ingredients for the means—a labor force, raw materials, new types of machinery, steam power, transportation, capital, and the market—were all there. But the prize of wealth belonged to the one who could produce a large amount and sell most cheaply. Newly invented machines cut the cost of labor, leading to more production per man-hour. Production skills were broken down into steps, so that men with less skill could be hired to perform only a part of the production process, more efficiently and at a lower wage rate. To enjoy these economies of mass production available in many industries, businessmen invested heavily in plant and equipment, without restraint, so that the capacity to produce outgrew demand. The disadvantages of mass production became apparent. While labor and materials are variable costs, so that a cut in production because of slackening demand results in a corresponding cut in these costs, the fixed costs of depreciation of plant and machinery are incurred regardless of the rate of production. Thus the fixed cost *per unit* of production in a factory operated at one-half capacity is twice the fixed cost *per unit* of production in a factory operated at full capacity. Extreme competition resulted from over-capacity. To protect their large investment in plant and machinery, competing businesses cut prices to obtain more sales in an attempt to operate at full capacity. Stronger, larger companies could operate at a loss until smaller competitors, whose profits were destroyed, were forced out of business. The fierce competition for markets resulted either in the destruction of competitors until one or a few survivors took over the field, or in the combining of competitors to fix prices, divide the market, and control production. Investment bankers, such as J. P. Morgan, were deeply interested in protecting capital invested in many industries from suffering heavy losses, and were influential in bringing peace and accord out of chaos and eliminating competition by some form of monopolistic agreement or combination within given industries.

Toward the end of the nineteenth century monopolistic combinations appeared in various industries, such as cottonseed oil, barbed-wire fence, matches, sugar, and beef, threatening the existence of the small producer as well as the purses of consumers. As we have seen, the policy of the law, from its early development, was in favor of maintaining competition and was opposed to monopoly. However, the remedy afforded by the common-law court decisions was wholly inadequate to deal with the problem which existed because of the vast economic changes which had occurred. While the courts would not enforce contracts in restraint of trade, so that the parties could ignore the contract terms, the parties were also at liberty to abide by such agreements to restrict production, maintain prices, divide territories, and the like. Monopolistic combination already existed in many industries and was an impending threat in many others which were so concentrated that production was mainly in the hands of just a few large corporations. Competition had destroyed itself in these industries. The possibility of the domination by just a few of the economic life of the entire country and all the persons in it became greater and greater. Correspondingly, it became increasingly clear that the policy of governmental noninterference in economic life was no longer workable if the benefits of competition were to be restored and preserved.

Responding to the changing needs of the country which resulted from the changed nature of the economy, state legislatures and, shortly thereafter, Congress enacted the first of the so-called "antitrust" laws.

4   THE MEANING OF ANTITRUST

Technically, in the legal sense, a "trust" involves a fiduciary relationship concerning some property interest. The trustee holds the legal title to the property involved in his name, to manage and preserve for the use and enjoyment of the beneficiary. The antitrust laws obviously were not aimed at trusts which serve legitimate and socially desirable purposes, such as promoting education or caring for spendthrift or incompetent children. A charitable trust in which the trustee has the duty of distributing the income of the trust to deserving students in the form of scholarships ought not to be illegal. Such trusts are not within the scope of the antitrust laws.

In the last part of the nineteenth century, the trust device was used extensively for the purpose of gaining monopolistic control of different types of business. Through it, a group of corporations having the same type of business could unite in following common business policies and eliminating competition among themselves by controlling production, dividing the market, and establishing price levels. Yet the companies could remain individual since no actual merger was necessary. Under this method, all or at least a majority of the stock in each company would be transferred to a certain board, consisting of various members of the top management of the companies, by common agreement of the stockholders involved. In exchange, the stockholders were issued trust certificates naming them as beneficiaries of the trust and entitling them to dividends declared on the stock they had transferred. The board, then, was in a position to control the operation and policy making of all the companies, since it held the stock and could vote for directors of its own choosing in each. Technically, the companies were still separate businesses, but in substance they were united under one guiding hand.

Some of the first statutes attempting to control monopolistic combinations were enacted about the time this trust device was in vogue, hence these laws came to be known as "antitrust laws," although they were aimed at protecting the public from any type of monopoly. Today the term "trust," when not used in the strictly technical sense, has come to be generally applied to any monopolistic combination, whether it be by agreement, merger, holding company, interlocking directorate, or trade association.

Chapters 11, 12, and 13 are concerned with a history of the major legislation enacted in the antitrust field, the roles of the Federal Trade Commission and the Justice Department in antitrust policy creation and enforcement, and some typical contemporary problems presented in business operation and decision making which have resulted from government involvement in regulating competition. However, before examining the *legal* requirements relative to competition, it will be beneficial to examine briefly some of the requirements which must be met for competition to exist in the *economic* sense.

5 THE ECONOMIC INDICES OF COMPETITION

A problem facing the student of any technical field is to understand the terminology used in that field in its proper context. Often ordinary words are employed which have been given highly specialized meanings. The problem is amplified in connection with many of the words used in the antitrust area since terms are used which may have, besides their common meanings, two different technical usages—one in the field of law and another in economics. The definition, from a legal standpoint of the type of "competition" it is public policy to preserve and the "monopoly or price discrimination" it is public policy to prevent, may be substantially different from the economist's use of the same terms in theoretical analysis. Thus, if a business act would not be in accordance with the economist's model of "pure" or "perfect" competition, it would not necessarily endanger competition so as to be prohibited by law. Likewise, if certain business conduct fits the economist's definition of "workable" or "effective" competition, this would not necessarily mean that such acts were legal under antitrust laws, nor would failure to meet the economist's test necessarily involve a violation of law. Clearly, the requirements of law are determined by legislatures, courts, and administrative agencies, not theoreticians in the discipline of economics.

However, the law in this area is concerned with business facts. It must determine the actual or probable effect on the market and consumers of specific business activities. Economic theory is of real assistance to the legal process because it furnishes the tools of analysis and a means of systematically studying a multitude of market facts related to questions of competition and monopoly which are invaluable to courts in deciding antitrust cases.

Some of the more frequently encountered situations and economic concepts in regard to competition and monopoly are discussed in the excerpts from a report to the Attorney General of the United States which are presented below. It must be emphasized that the portions of the report appearing here provide no standards for antitrust liability, but present an *economic* analysis of competition and monopoly.

From   REPORT OF THE ATTORNEY GENERAL'S NATIONAL COMMITTEE
TO STUDY THE ANTITRUST LAWS [3]
317–342 (1955)

ECONOMIC INDICIA OF COMPETITION AND MONOPOLY

. . . .

ECONOMIC BENEFITS OF COMPETITION

Generally speaking, economists support competition for four series of reasons, which are of coordinate importance: (1) because the actual level of prices in competitive markets should in the short run more accurately reflect the influence of demand and of cost, and thus in the long run help guide the flow of capital and other resources toward the most productive possible uses; (2) because the goad of competition provides powerful and pervasive incentives for product innovations and product development, and for long-run cost-reduction, both through improved technology and improved management; these forces make themselves felt in the constant process of product variation, and through the pressures implicit in the fact that competitive conditions offer an open opportunity to new entrants in a particular industry; (3) because competitive conditions in business should lead to an equitable diffusion of the resulting real income among consumers and fac-

---

[3] The committee consisted of practicing attorneys, law professors, and economists, who were all specialists in antitrust or cognate fields. It was established by Attorney General Herbert Brownell, Jr., in 1953 with the commission to render a comprehensive report which he hoped would "provide an important instrument to prepare the way for modernizing and strengthening our laws to preserve American free enterprise against monopoly and unfair competition." After much study, debate, drafting, and redrafting of reports, the committee submitted the final draft of its overall report to the Attorney General on March 31, 1955. The vast bulk of this 393-page document deals with the antitrust laws: their concepts, policies, and enforcement. The one portion of the report which is concerned with the distinguishing earmarks of competition from the standpoint of economic theory rather than the antitrust law is what is presented here.

tors of production; and (4) a view held with somewhat less unanimity than the others, because the more flexible prices of competitive markets should make it easier and cheaper for the economy to adjust to industrial fluctuations, and for the Federal Reserve System and the Government to carry through effective contracyclical programs of stabilization, primarily utilizing methods of monetary and fiscal policy.

ECONOMIC DEFINITIONS OF "MONOPOLY," "COMPETITION," AND "WORKABLE COMPETITION"

1. Generic Concepts of Competition and Monopoly

The essence of full monopoly power resides in being the sole source of a product, so that the buyer must meet the seller's terms or go without. The essence of competition is to free the buyer from this power by access to alternative sources of the product. The same considerations apply where the problem is a buyer's monopoly.* The basic economic aspect of monopoly is the seller's power over the terms on which he trades. All the factors and elements which constitute this idea are summed up by the convenient short-hand reference to monopoly power as power over price or power to exclude competitors. Monopoly power in this sense implies the monopoly seller's relative freedom from pressure to reduce costs, to develop new products, or otherwise to innovate, and to diffuse the benefits among customers.† The existence of monopoly power, lodged in private hands which are free to pursue their own advantage, is generally condemned by economists, aside from the question whether such power is used "reasonably" or "progressively." It is an unsafe power to lodge in private hands, making the monopolist a judge in his own case.

The idea of competition itself, as distinguished from the many variant technical concepts of competition, is not so easy to define. The literature of economics uses a good many concepts of "competition" for various purposes: perfect and imperfect competition, pure competition, monopolistic and workable competition, duopoly, oligopoly, and several others. Competition itself, as a generic concept embracing all its subdivisions, implies two ideas, which have a large common area but are not coextensive.

In the first sense, the word competition denotes only the presence of more than one seller in a market, and identifies a condition of rivalry among them—the self-interested and independent rivalry of two or more private competitors. But there is a second generic sense in which the word and the idea of competition are used, both in law and economics, and especially

---

* In this discussion, unless otherwise indicated, what is said of competition among sellers would apply equally where the restraints on competition exist or develop among buyers, and the pressure of these restraints is felt by sellers.

† This does not imply that the presence of monopoly power in the economic sense constitutes "monopolization" under Section 2 of the Sherman Act.

in the law. In this definition, "competition" is contrasted with "monopoly" with respect to the degree of market power possessed by a seller, or a group of sellers acting in concert. This second meaning of competition can be summed up as identifying a market condition in which the rivalry of sellers, of itself, prevents the existence of the discretionary market power of monopoly over price and output. Whether conditions in a given market are of the kind which tends typically to produce "competitive" or "monopolistic" market results in this latter sense depends in varying degrees upon the structure of that market, upon the way in which it conditions and influences the decisions of businessmen as to price and output, upon the character of market incentives for innovation and cost reduction, and upon actual market behavior. To answer this central question, more evidence is needed than the simple fact that the market contains two or more sellers or buyers. One must consider the number and relative size of buyers and sellers, conditions affecting the entry of new firms and the growth of existing firms, relations among rivals in the process of making market decisions, as well as other market factors.

This second generic meaning of the word "competition" requires further analysis before it can be fully useful, notably on the question of how much market power a seller or group of sellers acting in concert may have in a given market situation without such power becoming "monopoly" power. At this point, we wish merely to distinguish between two common meanings of the word competition, and to make it clear that in this section the word "competition" is used in the second sense stated above.

These generic concepts of "competition" and "monopoly" are used in economics and the law in closely similar ways. Both in economics and in law, these are not concepts of all or none, as are the limiting cases of pure theory. Markets exist in great variety, and they can be classified at many points along a spectrum extending from the complete monopoly of a single seller at one end, to the markets of thousands of small suppliers and purchasers, at the other. Economics attempts to divide market situations into categories for various purposes; and legal criteria under different provisions of the antitrust laws differ substantially in the quantum of restraint on competition they proscribe. In utilizing economic concepts of "competition" and "monopoly" in the analysis of legal problems therefore, the task is twofold: (1) To isolate and define the economic concepts relevant in helping to answer questions posed by the law, and, to the degree to which they may be useful, to adapt them to the different standards established by different statutes, on the one hand; and (2) on the other, to examine the legal standards themselves in the light of economic knowledge in order to evaluate their appropriateness.

In seeking to clarify economic concepts which may be of use to the law in the analysis of market forces, a central preliminary task is to define the circumstances under which competition theoretically becomes "effective" from the economic point of view, in preventing a concern or a group of concerns acting in concert from having "effective" monopoly power. For this purpose, the issues center on "effective" or "workable" competition or its absence.

2. "Workable" or "Effective" Competition

The concept of "workable" or "effective" competition can perhaps best be described as the economists' attempt to identify the conditions which could provide appropriate leads for policy in assuring society the substance of the advantages which competition should provide. It is a kind of economist's "Rule of Reason"—not, of course, to be confused with the legal rule of reason, but analogous to it in the sense that it is also an acknowledgment of the inevitability of the exercise of human judgment and discretion in classifying different forms of economic behavior.

The basic characteristic of effective competition in the economic sense is that no one seller, and no group of sellers acting in concert, has the power to choose its level of profits by giving less and charging more. Where there is workable competition, rival sellers, whether existing competitors or new or potential entrants into the field, would keep this power in check by offering or threatening to offer effective inducements, so long as the profits to be anticipated in the industry are sufficiently attractive in comparison with those in other employment, when all risks and other deterrents are taken into account. The result would be to force the seller who sought to increase his profits above this level by employing a high-price, limited-output monopoly policy either to give it up, or to lose ground to his rivals at a rate sufficient to reduce his profits, thus defeating his policy. In an effectively competitive market, the individual seller cannot control his rivals' offerings, and those offerings set narrow limits on his discretion as to price and production. He must, in the light of his own costs, adjust his offerings to a market scale of prices for offerings of different quality or attractiveness. In the moderately long run, he must accept market prices determined by changes in supply and demand beyond any effect which may be attributable to his own change in price or output. These market conditions inflict penalties on high costs or poor services. To bring this result about, it is necessary that rivals be free in fact to compete by lower prices and better service or products and selling activities, if they can achieve low enough costs to enable them to do so; and that no seller have power to limit this freedom of his rivals, and thus escape the pressures and penalties which effective competition imposes.

The market pressures which effective competition imposes upon each seller derive from the self-interested rivalry of his competitors. The essential character of this rivalry is to promote the competitor's economic interest by offering buyers inducements attractive enough to cause them to deal with him, in free bargaining, and in the face of inducements offered by his rivals.* The inducements consist of quantity, quality, time and place of delivery, incidental services, selling effort and price. The chief enabling condition is efficient operation. The rivalry may take the form of trying to enlarge one's share of the market by offering something more attractive than one's competitors, or to avoid a reduction of one's share of the business by offsetting the superior attractions of rivals' offers. In other words, competition includes both aggressive and defensive tactics.

Competitive rivalry in a given business situation may or may not be capable of developing enough force to deny any one seller or group of sellers acting in concert effective power to control the price they will charge, and other conditions of sale. Whether this condition is achieved normally depends on the character of the market. Active competition, for example, may involve initial moves by one competitor, the responses of the buyers, and the further responses of rival sellers. In some cases, the distinction between effective and ineffective competition may depend in part upon the speed of these responses, both the absolute and relative speed, and the certainty or uncertainty of buyers' responses and rivals' responses. The character of these responses may be affected not only by the aggressiveness and business policies of the rival sellers and buyers, but by their number, relative size and the nature of their expectations.

The market pressures of effective competition can be, and should properly be, quite severe. The firm rendering service inferior to that of its rivals would be seriously handicapped; and a firm maintaining superiority over its rivals has a prospect of increasing its volume of trade progressively at their expense so long as it can maintain this superiority. The penalties of unsuccessful competition may take the form of either a positive shrinkage or a failure to expand, and may be viewed in a short-term or a long-run perspective. It is ordinarily poor business policy, to attempt to squeeze out the utmost profit that can be made in a single year, at least where other firms can enter the field, or where substitute goods or services are at all available. In an effectively competitive market, if one seller is shortsighted enough to attempt this, others will grow at his expense. The law need not concern itself with good managerial practice in this regard since it is sufficiently assured by the market itself, provided the conditions of market rivalry are sufficiently free, active, and healthy.

A. DEFINITION OF "THE MARKET"

In evaluating the market forces which together would characterize effective competition, the rivalry of close substitutes which may, for other purposes, be classified as belonging in other industries has, in varying degree, the

---

* The wording is intentionally chosen to avoid stating or implying that the customers *prefer* to deal with him, or that he offers or tries to offer *superior* inducements, such as *lower* prices. The definition should not be read to imply that A is not competing with B unless he invariably offers a lower price than B's. But he must be free to do so.

same kind of effect as that of competing producers of the same or differen-
tiated products or services classified within the same industry. Technical
advance has often made the rivalry of close substitutes quite effective. But
this general fact says nothing about the effectiveness of competition in any
given market. It emphatically does not mean that public policy can afford to
be indifferent to the elimination of competition within the industry. In the
interest of rivalry that extends to all buyers and all uses, competition among
rivals within the industry is always important.

For purposes of economic analysis, the "market" is the sphere of competitive rivalry within which the crucial transfer of buyers' patronage from
one supplier of goods or services to another can take place freely. The
boundaries of an "industry" or "market" will often be uncertain and controversial, and a definition appropriate in one case may be inappropriate
in another. For our purposes, a market is an economic relationship among
sellers and buyers, whose boundaries are not necessarily defined by geographical area alone, nor by conventional product classifications. To ascertain whether a firm or group of firms acting in concert has monopoly power,
"the market" should include all firms whose production has so immediate
and substantial an effect on the prices and production of the firms in question that the actions of the one group cannot be explained without direct
and constant reference to the other. One should include in a market all
firms whose products are in fact good and directly available substitutes for
one another in sales to some significant group of buyers, and exclude all
others. Where the products of different industries compete directly as alternatives for the same use, the market for that class of products should
include the rival goods supplied by different industries. One should combine
into one market two or more products (or two or more areas) if an appreciable
fall in the price of one product (or in one area) will promptly lead to a
relatively large diversion of purchasers from the other product (or area).
The appropriate market area may be international, national, regional or local.

B. TESTS OF PERFORMANCE

The economist's distinction between "effective monopoly" and "effective
competition" does not turn on whether the industry in question is progressively managed or technologically advanced, nor on its policies with regard
to wages, profits or high- or low-price programs. Effective competition is not
a matter of the motives or policies of businessmen. The ultimate question in
distinguishing "effective monopoly" from "effective competition" is whether
the pressures of the market situation are such as tend of themselves to
bring about the main beneficial effects which constitute the economic reasons why we try to maintain competition in our economy.

The process of adjusting the employment of resources to the pressures
and demands of a workably competitive market is one of the chief means
through which the diffusion of the benefits of competition takes place. In

the long run, effective competition, implying the expansion (or contraction or withdrawal) of existing firms, or the entry of new ones, would reduce (or raise) the profit for a representative firm with respect to any particular product or service towards the point where bringing forth the supply earns no more than could be earned in alternative employments of the capital, labor, and management involved. The long-run tendency of effective competition to equalize the attractiveness of investment throughout the economy operates as among industries, as among the firms in any given industry, and within the business firm itself, which is guided by the relative profitability of the various products which it makes or can make. However, beyond the broadest identification of trends, industrywide profit averages have significance only in measuring the comparative pull of different industries in their competition for capital—that is, the comparative profit and risk prospects of different industries. For firms, not industries, are the units through which economic decisions are made. The constant and often severe —and properly severe—pressure of competition to drive rates of profit throughout the economy towards minimum levels is consistent with continuingly high rates of return for firms with better-than-average location, resources, efficiency or rate of innovation. Where firms produce more than one product, cost allocation may afford only a crude and imperfect guide to the relative profitableness of different products, and business policy may diverge from such indications as it does give. But a considerable check on such divergence may come from the competition of rival firms which differ in their product-mix. And the general force of competition in this direction, even if deferred by imperfect knowledge and foresight, is of unquestioned importance in multi-product industries.

The impact of effective competition on profits throughout the economy, and thus on the flow of capital to alternative uses, is one of its most important functions. However, it is altogether normal in a competitive economy that a given industry or group of firms in an industry, each acting independently, can earn extremely high (or low) profits at any given time, and over considerable periods of time. For such profits are the signals through which a market economy attracts capital and other resources to more productive uses, and drives them out of less productive uses.

For these reasons reduction of costs and moderation of profits, like other tests of "progressive" performance in industry, do not prove the existence, nor their absence the lack, of effective competition. The rate of technical progress, and the level of profit in a firm or an industry, can reflect many forces other than the presence or absence of effective competition. In some cases, in conjunction with other more material facts, they may be considered to furnish collateral or corroborative evidence of the nature and significance of competitive forces in the industry.

In terms of progress, a young industry, or one in process of exploiting recent basic or significant improvement inventions or scientific discoveries, might make a better showing than an older and more mature industry, although the latter might be more competitive. Regardless of whether it is competitive or monopolistic, an industry with declining demand might show a very low rate of profit. On the other hand, a monopolistic industry, with dynamic management and active research, might perform better, for example, in the sense of cost reductions, than a fairly competitive branch of industry which is inferior in these characteristics. Our public policy, however, is founded on the economically sound assumption that competition will on the average result in much more progressiveness and efficiency than monopoly.

C. SUMMARY OF FACTORS BEARING ON IDENTIFICATION OF
WORKABLE COMPETITION

What aspects of the market situation are significant in determining whether or not it is effectively competitive from the economic point of view? The short-hand legal definition of monopoly—"power . . . to raise prices or to exclude competition when it desired to do so" *—focuses directly on the ultimate economic elements of the problem. The economic definition of workable competition concentrates on the effective limits it sets on the power of a seller, or group of sellers acting in concert, over their price. That power cannot normally be retained for long without natural or imposed limitations on the opportunity for entry or growth of rivals. Restriction on the entry of rival firms is an integral part of the economic as it is of the legal definition of monopoly power, for competitive results are often less likely in a market where entry is not reasonably free. The factors listed below are considered some of the more important in summing up the economic aspects of workable competition. They indicate some of the types of information that may be used in determining whether, from an economic standpoint, effective competition exists. Of the 10 factors enumerated, the first 3 are the most general. But all the factors are in varying degrees elements of market situations which bear directly on the presence or absence of effective competition, in the sense in which that term is used in this section, i.e., a seller's power over his own price.

Several members emphasize that the first three factors are not only more general but overwhelmingly more important. Freedom of entry is basic but the ultimate test of freedom of entry is the appearance of new rivals; and independence of action of rivals is also basic but independence is highly correlated with the number of rivals—so the number (and relative size) of firms is especially strategic. The minor and equivocal information provided by the other factors should not obscure this broad verdict of economic analysis.

(1) A Number of Effective Competitive Sellers: The Issue of Relative Size
The number and relative strength of firms necessary to effective competition

---

* *American Tobacco Co. v. United States,* 328 U.S. 781, 811 (1946).

cannot be compressed into a formula. The answer to the question depends also on other factors, including those hereafter discussed, so that a given number of firms might be compatible with effective competition in one industry and not in another. Size in the abstract is meaningless. Whatever significance it has exists only in relation to a particular market. Absolute size, as measured by number of employees, or dollars of assets, or similar formulae, has no significance in determining the presence or absence of workable competition. The interrelation and relative importance in different situations of the various factors bearing on the presence or absence of effective competition have not yet been fully isolated and measured by economics. However, where firms are few in number, special study would usually be needed to determine whether an industry were workably competitive.

For effective competition, in the economic sense, to exist, there should be that degree of self-interested independent rivalry in any given market that exists where there is no one firm or group of firms acting in concert which have effective monopoly power, as heretofore defined. By this we mean that no one firm or group of firms acting in concert could hold for long the power to choose its level of profits by giving less and charging more, or to exclude the entry into the market of alternate sources of supply.

Unless numbers are already large in a given market, a reduction of numbers may involve some reduction of competition, although not necessarily a lessening to the point of "effective" monopoly. Where genuine economies of large scale operations, or other considerations (including the capacity to innovate), permit only very small numbers of sellers, added vigilance is indicated as to other requisites of effective competition.

Effective competition may be affected not only by the total number of sellers; their relative size and strength must also be considered. This does not mean that close equality of size among the various firms is essential for workable competition to exist, but only that the rivalry should not depend entirely upon sellers who are so weak or inefficient as to exist by sufferance. For such firms are not independent, and are not properly counted among the number of effectively competitive sellers. And as the number of independent sellers reaches unity, the market obviously reaches monopoly. The presence in any market of a unit much stronger than the others is a factor to be closely examined for its bearing on the workably competitive character of that market, and on the issue of whether any firm in fact exists only by sufferance, but by itself is not indicative of the absence of workable competition.

Where the number of sellers is large, each one of them faces an impersonal market with a market price which he can take or leave. He can do little to affect total supply or to raise the market price.

When sellers are few, each producing a significant share of total market supply, each seller is aware of the fact that any substantial change in his price or his production will have an appreciable effect upon total market supply and market price, and will tend to elicit responsive changes in the prices and outputs of his rivals. Hence there is a mutual awareness rather than an impersonal market relationship. Where such a market is isolated from competitive pressures, the possibility of successful collusion is greater, to detect it is harder, and its rewards may be more immediate and tempting. Hence there is need for vigilance in scrutinizing such industries, without prejudging whether in fact any type of conspiracy exists. When sellers are few, even in the absence of conspiracy, the market itself may not show many of the characteristics of effective competition, and in fact may not be effectively competitive in the economic sense.

(2) *Opportunity for Entry*   From the economic point of view, relative freedom of opportunity for entry of new rivals is a fundamental requisite for effective competition in the long run. Without this condition, it is idle to expect effective competition. The entry and withdrawal of firms, whether new firms or existing firms from other market areas, or other industries, or other stages of production and marketing, is the basic mechanism of the market for achieving its economic results. The cost of entry into the competitive area should not be impracticably high. This does not imply an absolute criterion for ease of entry in terms of a given number of dollars. Nor does it deny recognition to the fact that as a practical matter, the size of minimum adequate investment capital and other factors may make the entry of new firms into even a competitive industry a relatively slow or hazardous process. But it does mean that under prevailing conditions as to the availability of capital, an attempt by existing firms to raise prices considerably above the competitive norm would make it profitable and practicable for new firms or existing borderline firms to invade the field. In economic terms, this means that conditions of cost for a new firm should not be excessively higher, at least after a reasonable period of initial development, than conditions of cost for an existing member of the industry. In many cases, of course, the new firm may start with the cost advantage of being able to use the most advanced available techniques.

Reasonable opportunity of outsiders with requisite skill to enter the market may appear dispensable, for if there are a sufficient number of competitors, and they compete vigorously, what purpose would be served by additional numbers? But if energetic and imaginative rivals cannot enter, the boldest and most rewarding innovations may be excluded.

New firms entering an industry may not all survive. Some may be weeded out in the competitive struggle, sometimes indeed after making their contribution either to pricing or to business methods. But reasonable opportunity for entry is needed if there is to be assurance of a sufficient number of sellers to maintain effective competition and thus prevent markets from evolving gradually into a state of monopolistic stability. The exclusion of new rivals may be a major impairment of competition in itself, and the power to exclude rivals is usually associated with the power to eliminate rivalry between those already in the industry.

(3) Independence of Rivals   A primary condition of workable competition in an economic sense is that there be genuine independence on the part of the business units in an industry, so that each firm pursues its own individual advantage. In industries with numerous sellers, concerted action is difficult to achieve without relatively visible machinery of cooperation. Where there are only a limited number of sellers, however, concerted action can be subtle and informal, and sometimes difficult to detect. In all industries, it is normal for sellers to try to take the reactions of rivals into account in determining their own competitive policies; where there are few sellers it may be easier to forecast such reactions. This may or may not impair competition, depending on whether or not the initiator of a competitive move can expect to retain an improved market position after his rivals have responded. Fewness of sellers does not necessarily lead to mutual interdependence of policies, but it may do so.

(4) Predatory Preclusive Practices   There should be no predatory preclusive tactics, such that their natural effect would be to enable the user to eliminate rivals without regard to their efficiency, or at least to place them under serious handicaps irrelevant to their efficiency. It should be noted as a practical matter that predatory competition in this sense can usually only be waged where a considerable degree of market power already exists, or where an attempt is being made to use a long purse in order to destroy or coerce rivals. Such conduct is regarded therefore as symptomatic either of monopoly or the intent to monopolize, or both, although it may not be necessary for those possessing market power in high degree to use such methods in order to gain or to keep monopolistic advantages from their position. Conversely, the accusation of "predatory" or "cutthroat" practices often turns out on examination not to stem from the abuse of significant degrees of market power, but from the uncomfortably active pressures of competition itself. Only by examining the facts, including the market, is it possible to answer these important questions, among others: whether the low prices or other alleged predatory acts were temporary and for the purpose of destroying or coercing rivals; or whether they were undertaken to meet competition, or to increase profits under high level production at low-cost, or for some equally proper competitive purpose; whether the profit-seeking interests of the company under attack would have been served by predatory or oppressive tactics; and so forth. These facts bear not on the justification for predatory conduct—there is none—but on the issue of whether such conduct exists.

(5) Rate of Growth of the Industry or Market   The speed with which an industry is growing is not a direct economic indicator of the state of competition within it. An industry may be actually in decline and yet be actively effectively competitive. For example, an industry may decline because the

demand for its products is declining and yet there may still be competitive rivalry for shares of the remaining market. Rate of growth, however, is often important in determining the significance to be attached to other factors, and particularly to numbers and reasonable opportunity for entry.

The rate of growth or expansion of a market can, for example, strongly color the significance to competition of the number and relative size of the firms, and alter the effectiveness of barriers to entry. The expected rate of growth of the industry affects the attitudes and expectations of firms in the industry, the attractiveness of the industry to outside firms, and the possibility of maintaining positions of market power without severe restrictions on entry. In a new and rapidly expanding industry, the opening of new markets and the high rate of technical progress usually characteristic of such situations make for uncertainty as to the most profitable policies. The entrance of new firms, if it takes place, may lead to further unsettlement of industry policies and under these circumstances, firms may grow without imposing losses on their rivals. Insofar as any given number of firms find it possible to have a tight hold on a stable industry, they can hold their position more readily than the same firms in an industry that is open to rapid expansion. If such firms are not disposed to engage in competitive activity, they may, by their passivity, not only discourage the entry of rivals, but of new techniques which might, in turn, permit the industry to reduce costs and to expand. On the other hand, such passivity itself may well prove a substantial incentive to the entry of newcomers who might otherwise be deterred by the prospect of immediate, active stiff competition.

(6) Character of Market Incentives to Competitive Moves   Competition may be effective or ineffective, depending upon how the market is organized and behaves, and according to what incentives there are for independent competitive actions: the hope of gain for the individual seller, and the risk of loss. The strength of these incentives may depend on factors which are in themselves neutral and become important only as they influence incentives. The intervals between a competitive move and the expected response, for example, are not themselves indicia of effective competition or its absence. But they come under study in seeking to determine whether incentives are relatively strong or weak.

In general, and outside of such specialized markets as organized exchanges and others of similar character, effective competition may hinge on the condition that the initiator of a competitive action can expect a gain in volume of business at least for a time. That is, the customers' response to an inducement may be quicker than rivals' responses for at least long enough to provide a pay-out period for the competitive action. The incentive to innovation, to price changes, or to other directly competitive moves is an interval during which an innovator may reasonably expect to have an advantage because his moves cannot be met and neutralized promptly enough by his rivals.

Where these competitive moves are not promptly matched and offset, therefore, or where uncertainty exists as to the pattern of rival responses, an influence exists which, *other things being equal,* provides inducements for effective competitive rivalry. Where uncertainty prevails—perhaps because of the presence of a company which refuses to follow prevailing patterns—sellers may be more likely to conclude that they have a chance to make a gain from a competitive innovation, than if the system of market responses had been securely built up by past habits, agreements, or experience. The mere existence and quick dissemination of information on price changes is not of itself evidence either way. But cooperative efforts by an industry to eliminate uncertainty and promote instant knowledge for everybody of everybody else's price may be a device to curb price cutting. Thus, a conviction that rivals will respond immediately may discourage any independent competitive action.

One circumstance that favors a time interval for gain through innovation or price reductions or other competitive moves is the fact that the initiator of a competitive move may gain business at the expense of all his competitors, thus gaining more than any one of them loses, so that they do not have the same decisive need to retaliate.

While information or continued price rigidities may be some indication of the existence or absence of incentives to competitive moves, such information cannot of itself be determinative from an economic standpoint of either effective monopoly or effective competition. Monopolies may change prices in their own interests, and competitive industries may have periods of stable demand and supply conditions. Price changes, or the absence thereof, must therefore be considered in their market settings in order to evaluate their significance.

(7) Product Differentiation and Product Homogeneity   The definition of the word "market," and that of workable competition itself, both turn on the actual and direct competition a seller confronts from the closely related products of others. An important factor in determining the boundaries of the market is the knowledge of buyers as to the alternatives open to them. If other conditions are equal, it would seem for this reason to follow that the more homogeneous the product of rival sellers, the more easily buyers could switch from the output of one competitor to that of others; and therefore the wider the market and the greater the degree of competition in it.

The effect of product differentiation depends on the market setting in which it is placed. Extreme product differentiation, by tending to insulate the demand for one product against that for rival products, may allow real positions of monopoly to develop. Relatively mild differentiation of products within a market otherwise effectively competitive, however, may be a factor favorable to the intensiveness of competition, including price competition and competition in quality. This will tend to be most forcibly the case if the product differentiation reflects product rivalry, that is, product improve-ment, rather than mere heterogeneity of closely similar products. For product differentiation, especially if it constitutes or embodies a genuine innovation, may be a means whereby the seller can take advantage of the time interval the market allows within which he can expect to gain from a competitive move. Particularly if the situation is such as to justify uncertainty as to the speed and completeness with which rivals will counter the initial move, such a move, in the form of product differentiation, may contribute to the competitiveness of market behavior. This would not be the case if the innovation is fortified by obstacles to imitation by rival producers, or ob-stacles to the sale of cheaper and simpler models. Thus the impact of product differentiation on the effectiveness of competition will, as in the case of all the other factors mentioned, have to be judged in each case in its market setting, and in relation to more central indicia of effective com-petition. It is not, as such, evidence either way.

The fact that product homogeneity is the rule in a given market may be a significant element in determining the kind of market structure needed for effective competition. Product homogeneity may increase the zone of competition. Where the primary factors in the market situation indi-cate little question as to the effectiveness of competition, clearly this result will follow. The active and effective competition on organized exchanges and like markets depends upon product homogeneity within grades. But, in other markets, special inquiry may be required to determine whether product homogeneity tends to reduce any one seller's chance to gain through a competitive move. Where, in such markets, there is substantial product homogeneity, an open reduction of price is almost certain to be met in-stantly although, if not so met, a gain in volume as a result of the move is assured.

(8) Meeting or Matching the Prices of Rivals   The above analysis of the varying effects which product homogeneity and differentiation may have on competition in the economic sense in different market settings has a bear-ing also on the question of meeting or matching the prices of competitors. It is of the essence of effective competition that competitors should try to meet, or offer an equivalent for, any superior inducement which one of them offers. Meeting a rival's inducements is the means whereby competi-tion diffuses the gains of productive efficiency. To forbid a seller to meet his rival's price would involve a *reductio ad absurdum,* so long as the market structure itself is untouched. For example, in the case of homogeneous products, if A only part-way meets B's price, it does A no good—he still cannot sell his goods—and if A more than meets B's price, then B cannot sell his goods, or not until he in turn has more than met A's price. Under these circumstances, in the absence of a change in demand, there is no place where competitive price can level off, and no adjustment permitting a number of competitors to remain in the market in question, unless a seller

is permitted to meet his competitor's price. This is the error in holding that a firm is not competing unless it is exceeding its rival's prices.

However, effective competition also involves freedom to undercut rivals' prices. Thus an inflexible requirement that any existing price may be met, but not undercut, would mean that when demand falls off, or when there is a reduction in cost, the decline in price which would follow under effective competition might be aborted, because it would be to no one's interest to make the first move, since it would be matched forthwith. In many such situations, it would be to everyone's interest not to cut prices.

Effective competition is therefore compatible either with meeting (or matching) the prices of rivals, or with undercutting them. Furthermore, prices uniform as among the respective sellers may under the pressure of falling demand give way to a period of undercutting, after which price again settles down to uniformity at a lower level. Hence these are not two mutually exclusive patterns, and price uniformity as of any given short period is not significant, even when the costs of various sellers are widely different from one another. But a rigid uniformity over periods of changing supply and demand, or a persistent failure by firms to increase or decrease prices when their independent self-interest would seem to dictate such a move, is not usually compatible with workable competition. This is a problem altogether distinct and apart from the legal question of whether a complex and rigid system of price-setting and price-changing can only be explained by an agreement or conspiracy. The legal problem transcends although it includes the economic. But any rule, public or private, which forbade the meeting of prices, or one which forbade the undercutting of prices, would be a rule against workable competition.

A climate more stimulating to effective competition might be introduced into such a market in several possible ways, including: new entry, if large profits were being made; price discrimination; variations in the product or in the other terms of the bargain; a change in the structure of the market, by an increase in the number of sellers; or utilization of other competitive devices such as product, service and customer relations improvement and more effective selling. This should not be interpreted as a general recommendation of a policy of discrimination, but is meant merely to point out some of the available alternatives in situations of this kind. Perhaps something could be accomplished by not preventing—and certainly by forbidding private groups the power to prevent—a reasonable variety and variability in pricing practices.

(9) *Excess Capacity*   "Excess capacity" is a term difficult to define satisfactorily, and even more difficult to identify. The term is commonly used to describe capacity unused during a general depression, as well as "excesses" of capacity which may be generated by investment booms in competitive industries. Both these senses should be distinguished from the excess of capacity confronted by a declining industry. In a period of gen-

erally good business, for a growing or stable business, the existence of unused capacity, which could be utilized at or near prevailing costs, may help to demonstrate the presence of either effective monopoly or effective competition in connection with other facts. If the companies in an industry tend generally to pursue policies of making more money by charging high prices and restricting production, the industry may have chronic excess capacity as a result. The practice of a company purchasing and dismantling unused capacity in this sense—that is, capacity which could be utilized at normal costs—has always and rightly been considered strong evidence of attempt to monopolize. On the other hand, a moderate and varying amount of excess capacity naturally tends to develop from time to time as a result of expansion or in response to the rise and fall of demand in a competitive industry, or incident to competitive efforts of producers to increase their share of the market. And its presence is favorable to the effectiveness of competition, if other criteria of competition are present. It permits producers to handle added business at no great increase in unit cost of production, or even at a decrease in average unit costs, depending upon cost conditions at the time. And, as business approaches conditions in which efficient capacity is fully utilized at high profit, a failure on the part of the industry to expand in response to high levels of demand and profit might suggest the possibility of some restrictive arrangement to prevent the normal response of a competitive market.

(10) Price Discrimination   Some types of price discrimination may stimulate effective competition; others may be evidence of effective monopoly, in the economic sense. Before proceeding to examine the differences among the various types of price discrimination, a word of preliminary warning is in order.

Price discrimination as seen by an economist not only is not necessarily the same as "price discrimination" in the sense followed or applied in decisions under the Robinson-Patman Act, but it may be entirely antithetical. Furthermore, even when a price structure happens to be discriminatory in both senses, this may be evidence of either effectively monopolistic or effectively competitive forces, depending on its setting. Finally, even when price discrimination in an economic sense (whether or not in the sense proscribed under the Robinson-Patman Act) is evidence of departures from conditions of effective competition, it does not necessarily result in or denote violation of law.

Price discrimination, in the economic sense, occurs whenever and to the extent that there are price differences for the same product or service sold by a single seller, and not accounted for by cost differences or by changes in the level of demand; or when two or more buyers of the same goods and services are charged the same price despite differences in the cost of serving them. In order to know when there is or is not price discrimination, in the economic sense, between two or more buyers, it is necessary to know not only the price but also the total costs applicable to each class of transaction under comparison.

From the economic point of view, no particular definition of "price" is required; "price" is simply what the buyer has paid the seller as consideration for the goods and related services he has sought and purchased; nor is any close definition of the "goods" or "products" required except that there be some substantial elements of comparability. "Cost," for analysis of situations contemplated in this section of our Report, means average cost. The idea that the cost of serving a given buyer is less than that of serving other buyers, for no other reason than that this buyer's additional purchases spread the overhead, imputes arbitrarily to a particular buyer the savings of larger volume. And such cost differences as are relevant are those consistently characteristic of the categories of business being compared, not transitory or incidental differences. The actual lower costs of serving one or more buyers can arise from a great variety of circumstances. The product sold to some buyers may be physically somewhat different, in lacking certain appliances or finishing touches or quality. There may be differences in the services which go along with the goods to form the complete package for which consideration is given—such services as delivery, packaging, storage, credit extension, risk of default, handling, clerical attention, sales force attention, and many others. There may for these or other reasons be savings on large quantities sold, or on large volume over some time period (entirely apart from the savings arising from spreading the overhead); but large quantities or volumes, without more, are not necessarily more economical. These are all matters of factual detail.

Because many costs, particularly distribution costs, involve large elements of overhead, it may be difficult or impossible to estimate cost differentials with great precision. This is not to say, however, that the task should not be done, nor that cost differentials should be deemed not to exist, in the absence of precise estimates.

Occasional statements in the economic literature that price discrimination is proof of the existence of monopoly elements have been widely misunderstood, and as misunderstood, repeated by noneconomists. Under pure competition (and *a fortiori* under perfect competition) no price discrimination could exist. Every seller would sell at the going price and would have no power to charge more and no need to take less. But any attempt to infer from this that price discrimination, in the economic sense, is "inherently monopolistic" or presumptively anti-competitive, is implicit acceptance of pure or perfect competition as a workable goal of public policy. We have already shown that the terms "pure" and "perfect" mean merely precise or complete in the theoretical sense, not ideal or desirable. We therefore repudiate pure and perfect competition as direct goals of antitrust policy. We do, however, recognize that under workable competition there should exist substantial pressure driving the price of any given product or service toward uniformity, and toward its cost of production, so that there is a potent incentive for a business firm to maintain satisfactory profits over the long run by innovation in products or processes. The constant efforts of businessmen are and ought to be to get into new and higher-margin markets; and the constant effect of competition is to narrow margins in some markets as compared with others, for the leveling force is not felt with equal speed everywhere at the same time. Some amount of discrimination in the economic sense is therefore an inevitable part of the business scene. It remains to examine the circumstances under which it may be considered evidence of workable competition or of workable monopoly.

A single monopolist firm, or a group of firms exerting monopoly power in concert, would find it most profitable to divide up their customers and exact from each one the maximum that he could be made to pay. Such a scheme of discrimination would require that customers paying lower prices be prevented from reselling to those paying higher prices. The monopolist would need to control the product to point of final use, possibly by contract. If resale were practical, then competition among the customers would cause all the product to move through the lower-priced buyers, discrimination thus tending to disappear.

Price discrimination may also take the form of predatory price cutting in selected areas or on selected products in order to eliminate competitors or to force them to follow a price or other policy. The essence of this conduct is its temporary nature; for it only exists in order that prices may eventually be raised once rivals are removed or coerced. Such predatory price discrimination must, however, be carefully distinguished from vigorous competition, where prices are not cut for such temporary purposes, but in order to permit more efficient firms to earn higher profits at low prices than at high prices, or for some other equally competitive reason.

A milder form of what might be regarded as price discrimination in the economic sense, although not in the Robinson-Patman Act sense, may be practiced by a seller who keeps his prices very low or barely remunerative on products facing competition, while maintaining higher prices and profit margins on other products free from competition or facing less competition. In *United States v. United Shoe Machinery Corp.*,[*] for example, the court considered this type of price discrimination as evidence of monopoly power, but it is significant that it did not attempt to extirpate such discrimination by its decree. Explaining its reasons therefor the court stated: "Some price discrimination, if not too rigid, is inevitable. Some may be justified as resting on patent monopolies. Some price discrimination is economically desirable, if it promotes competition in a market whose several multi-product firms compete."

Price discrimination, in the economic sense, may be practiced by a monopolist or by a group of sellers acting in concert, because they wish

[*] 110 F. Supp. 295 (D. Mass. 1953), *aff'd per curiam* 347 U.S. 521 (1954).

to build up or protect the position of certain customers, and weaken that of others. But price discrimination may serve to promote competition, and it may be relevant evidence that competition exists and is effective. While price discrimination of the type described above is therefore relevant to a determination of whether significant degrees of market power inhere in any individual company or group of companies acting in concert, further exploration is required to determine whether effective competition exists.

It is equally clear that in some cases differences in price not related to difference in cost may promote competition. Thus price discrimination may serve to disrupt or preclude any collusive or otherwise interdependent pricing. The very success of a concerted effort by a group of firms to raise prices above the competitive level by restricting output to less than the competitive level would make it attractive for some or all of the firms to offer better terms to some buyers. There is a tendency for such special bargains to be given more and more widely, as buyers try to play sellers off one against the other; and if the tendency is strong enough to make the special prices become the "regular" prices in the course of time, the discrimination has served to make the market more competitive.

These examples illustrate the diverse ways in which price discrimination in the economic sense appears in our market system. Where price discrimination is sustained, persistent and stable, it may throw light either on collusion in price-formation, or on the presence of market imperfections so fundamental as to constitute evidence of effective monopoly power. For, when price discriminations are sustained and substantial, they may have far-reaching effects at several levels of competition, and lead to significant departures from standards of workable competition. Price discrimination may be a means of making existing markets less effectively competitive.

As has been pointed out several times in the preceding analysis, price discrimination may be the force which can increase the number of effective sellers in a market, or disrupt an otherwise effective system of monopoly pricing. Thus price discrimination is a fact of significance, to be considered in relation to other facts, in determining whether a market is workably competitive.

Several members emphasize that such stable patterns of discrimination in the economic sense not only may throw light on collusion or market imperfections but are conclusive evidence that the market is behaving monopolistically.

3. "Workable" Competition Contrasted With Pure or Perfect Competition

"Workable" or "effective" competition supplies no formula which can substitute for judgment. It suggests leads to data of significance, and a means of organizing the data bearing on the question whether a given market of itself is sufficiently competitive in its structure and behavior to be classified as workably competitive. And it provides some bench-marks or criteria, representing somewhat different points of vantage, for the process of making that judgment.

The criteria it offers are not, of course, the criteria of pure or perfect competition. It may be useful at this point to clarify the role of these concepts in economics, and to distinguish them from the concepts used here.

The concepts of pure and perfect competition are tools of theoretical analysis. They are not intended to and do not constitute a description of reality. As a theoretical model, these ideas give economists means for rigorously exploring the interrelationships of certain specified market forces. And, as previously stated, they define rigidly the theoretical conditions necessary to a form of long-run equilibrium in which prices would equal costs, including the minimum economically necessary supply price of capital. Historically, the concept of perfect competition developed first as a series of conclusions about the cost-price relationships which competitive market pressures tend to produce; and later, as the cost-price results theoretically attributed to competition were more exactly defined, they assumed the character of limits, and economics produced a far more precise formulation of the conditions theoretically necessary to those results. These conditions are: (1) that the products of all the rival sellers in the market are precise substitutes for each other, and that all buyers and sellers have perfect knowledge of the market and complete indifference as to their customers or sources of supply; (2) that the number of sellers is so large that no one seller produces more than a negligible share of market supply; (3) that new firms can enter the industry with the same costs as existing firms; and (4) that all buyers and sellers in the market have mobility. To state these conditions is to make manifest their hypothetical character as tools of analysis, not descriptions of reality. As theoretical models, these concepts have facilitated analysis, and the study of real situations, by directing attention to key forces which lead actual markets to deviate in their results from those that it is believed would emerge under perfectly competitive conditions.

The concepts of pure and perfect competition have also clarified and helped to make more precise certain selected results centering on cost-price equilibrium which economists have long concluded should flow from competition. They have, however, neglected the requirements of competitive innovation in processes and products. They thus served to define, in theoretical terms, optimum conditions in the utilization of resources and the distribution of income, although in facilitating the study of optimal cost-price relations, and the relations between productivity and rewards, they may have, as stated, led some economists to neglect market forces inducing innovation in products and processes. It should be emphasized that pure and perfect competition are wholly theoretical standards, in that they are not intended *as such* to be guides to public policy. Nor should the courts be expected to be able to utilize pure and perfect competition concepts in adjudging any given market situation. They seek to define cost-price relations under conditions of equilibrium toward which certain markets tend to move, although in fact markets can never be expected to reach equilibrium. When taken out of context, the very precision of the theoretical standards of pure and perfect competition can be misleading. Nonetheless, these concepts, used in connection with the study of other factors outside their terms, have helped to orient economists' studies of actual situations, and have contributed, along with other influences, to the elaboration of the theory of workable competition, as an instrument for the direct study of market conditions.

Workable competition differs from pure and perfect competition in several ways. In the first place, the two theories have different purposes. The theory of pure and perfect competition is an instrument of theoretical analysis; the theory of workable competition seeks to provide a method for making necessarily less exact but more practical realistic judgments of actual market situations. Secondly, to the extent that the two theories are concerned with the same broad elements—the definition of the product and market, the number and relative size of sellers, and conditions of entry—the concept of workable competition posits a lesser degree of "perfection." Thus perfect competition would require an extremely large number of sellers. Criteria of workable competition, as is explained above, could be satisfied by a lesser number of sellers, some of whom may well produce significant fractions of total supply, provided they really compete and do not foreclose entry of new competitors. except by reason of their superiority. Pure and perfect competition would require that all sellers produce goods which were identical and that no buyers have preferences among sellers. The concept of workable competition is consistent with considerable product differentiation and recognizes the existence of buyer preference among sellers. As to entry, too, perfect competition contemplates complete freedom of entry by new firms, whereas workable competition is compatible with practical barriers to entry, such as considerable capital and even advertising requirements, and a period of higher costs while production is organized and management trained and shaken down. Thirdly, apart from these factors in market analysis which the two theories share, workable competition goes beyond the theory of perfect competition in certain respects. While the theory of perfect competition examines certain implications of the seller's quest for profit under a limited set of assumptions, the literature of workable competition seeks to identify those aspects of competition which provide market incentives for innovation, including quality innovation as well as cost reduction, and taking directly into account other elements of the market situation which change through time. It is of importance, therefore, in using economic analysis of problems of market organization and behavior for antitrust purposes, that in each case the premises of analysis be made clear, and that economic theories not be applied beyond the limits of their own propositional base. Thus it does not follow that such technical economic terms as "elements of monopoly" or "market imperfections," which imply merely the absence of some of the conditions of pure or perfect competition, are for that reason monopoly situations in the antitrust sense, or even that they lessen the effectiveness of competition.

A few members stress that the "doctrine" of workable competition is only a rough and ready judgment by some economists, each for himself, that a particular industry is performing reasonably well—presumably relative to alternative industrial arrangements which are practically attainable. There are no objective criteria of workable competition, and such criteria as are proferred are at best intuitively reasonable modifications of the rigorous and abstract criteria of perfect competition.

COMPARISON OF LEGAL AND ECONOMIC CONCEPTS OF COMPETITION AND MONOPOLY

It seems clear that although there are some similarities between the legal concept of monopoly and competition and the economic concept of effective monopoly and effective competition, there are striking and substantial dissimilarities as well. Chief common ground is found in those instances where the law requires the examination of market situations both of structure and behavior and the marshaling and analysis of evidence relevant thereto, such as the problems of monopoly, substantial lessening of competition, or with regard to judgment as to the economic effect of practices classed as unreasonable *per se*.

One source of difference is the tendency of economists to examine the results to be expected from given conditions, which conditions may or may not be traceable to any one's actions; while the law deals with activities, or practices or courses of action which may be either directly harmful to competition or may be considered to bring about conditions viewed as probably having tendencies harmful to competition. Other differences arise from the particular language of statutes, and from the fact that, especially in the administration of a criminal statute, the law must give weight to concepts of intent and purposefulness of action, some of which have no counterpart in general economic analysis. Thus it is natural that economic theory has given little attention to the distinction between monopoly and monopolization, which has preoccupied the law under Section 2 of the Sherman Act. Again, the law cannot, save in the most obvious cases, assume that actual behavior in the market-place will in fact correspond to the pattern of competitive behavior that would theoretically be expected in a market of a given structure. The economic analysis of market theory, while it suggests important leads to relevant evidence, does not and cannot relieve the law of the necessity for searching out the evidence as to the kind of competitive behavior that actually occurs in a given instance. The law can learn from generalized studies of normal behavior, but it must always be guided by the established facts in the particular case at issue. The antitrust laws establish criminal guilt or civil responsibility; here as in all other phases of the law, legal responsibility is individual.

One of the interests of economics as a study is to reach conclusions about the respective social performance of different industries, and to draw conclusions as to whether a given market, whether competitive or monopolistic, is doing its social job well or not. The antitrust laws, however, are concerned with undue restraints of competition, with monopolization or attempts to monopolize, and with certain practices deemed especially injurious to competition.

Such conduct cannot be excused by proof it represents "progressive" managerial policy or, if defendant is a monopoly, it has been a good one, has performed acceptable social service, or even benefited the consuming public. Neither the Sherman Act nor economists generally discriminate between "good" or "bad" monopolization or undue restraints of trade; and likewise with violations of the Clayton Act. Though the "progressiveness" of business performance may sometimes be helpful in demonstrating the presence or absence of monopoly or undue restraint, its antitrust relevance has no bearing beyond these issues. However, whether conduct represents "progressive" or "unprogressive" managerial policy, performs an acceptable social service or benefits the consuming public may sometimes be helpful in demonstrating the presence or absence of monopolization or undue restraint of or injury to competition and can offer useful guideposts to antitrust officials in the selection of cases and to courts in the formulation of effective decrees. On the other hand, economic study of the social performance of business can make significant contributions to the antitrust laws in helping to clarify and to improve the theory on the basis of which antitrust statutes are drawn and assisting in long run improvements of this statutory system.

EXTERNAL CONDITIONS

Severe depressions and inflations alike have in the past generated demands that the competitive market be superseded as society's chief institution for determining prices and the scale of production, either in general, or in certain branches of production that are relatively hard hit. In the long run, the preservation of free markets, and the achievement of the social and economic values served by the free market, depend upon maintaining, through appropriate fiscal and monetary policies, a balance between aggregate demand and the output of the economy at sufficiently high and stable levels of employment and of growth. While fiscal and monetary policies are outside the terms of reference of this Committee, we deem it appropriate to call attention to their vital importance as fundamental elements of effective economic policy, closely linked to the problems we have been asked to review.

In periods of violent inflation, price and wage rises themselves become socially destructive, and have in the past caused Governments to resort to price and wage controls and other restrictive arrangements. Equally, in severe and extended depressions Governments have adopted programs for restricting competition either by permitting direct private cartellization or government supervised bodies on the N. R. A. model. They have experimented, too, with various depression-inspired schemes for controlling the world market for rubber, sugar, tin, and other commodities, or have adopted increased tariffs and related barriers to competition. While it is easy to understand these depression-inspired demands to thwart the competitive process, it is clear that such restrictive measures do not cure depressions; they may aggravate them; and their presence may make recovery otherwise stimulated slower and more expensive to achieve. To the extent that they can reduce the burden of depression on certain groups, they shift it to others.

This is not to suggest that various forms of industry cooperation in the past have not accomplished useful purposes, in influencing opinion, helping programs of mobilization or even mitigating inflation's effects. The presence of depression or inflation calls primarily for corrective action by the Federal Reserve System and the Government to balance aggregate demand with supply at levels consistent with full-employment, not measures to reduce competition in particular markets through private regulation by parties with a pecuniary interest in the results.

Other conditions external to the market can vitally affect the setting in which markets function and the effectiveness of competition within them. The organization of the labor market upon which a firm or an industry depends obviously influences its costs and its capacity to increase productivity. While trade-union activities generally, and the laws relating to them, are outside the terms of reference of our Committee, we call attention to their importance as elements which may affect both the competitive potential of a firm or an industry and its ability to innovate through cost reduction.

Similarly, situations of substantial market power have depended in the past, and may now depend, on tariff protection. Equivalent protection against competition is obtained by a variety of state, local, and national laws requiring governmental units to deal only with restricted classes of suppliers. While many such enactments substantially limit competition and create or perpetuate positions of great economic advantage, the bearing of tariffs on the maintenance of high degrees of market power in domestic commerce must, of course, be studied case by case. We recommend that the Department of Justice and the Federal Trade Commission, in carrying out their enforcement and investigatory responsibilities, systematically examine the domestic market effects of tariffs and appropriately transmit their findings to the President, Tariff Commission, or the Congress. We recommend also that tariff legislation expressly recognize the purposes of the antitrust laws as one of the justifications for and objectives of both unilateral and negotiated tariff reductions.

Finally, tax laws of the United States also offer certain incentives for integration and disadvantages for independent growing firms as well as for companies which might otherwise sell off part of their properties to separate enterprises. While recent studies have brought forward relevant and suggestive data, there is need for a systematic review to isolate possible tax changes in the interest of furthering the general antitrust goals. We do not attempt to indicate which features of the tax system would be of greatest importance in such a study. Quite possibly, different tax problems arise in this connection for different industries. We do believe, however, that the tax aspect of the problem is of importance, and that a comprehensive and thorough evaluation of antitrust policy requires further study of its tax elements.

Some members dissent from the suggestion that the Justice Department and the Federal Trade Commission concern themselves with tariffs and that antitrust policy supports tariff reductions. If antitrust violation occurs within or without any tariff structure, it warrants enforcement action. Tariff questions are beyond the scope of this Committee's assignment. They involve disparate considerations of foreign trade, full employment, currency, national defense, "peril points," and the like. Whatever may be the individual views on these issues, they are not referable to the antitrust laws.

CHAPTER ELEVEN

HISTORY OF
ANTITRUST LEGISLATION

1 INTRODUCTION

In the preceding chapter, the indices and benefits of competition from the viewpoint of economic theory were discussed. Also presented were some of the more important factors which gave rise to a need for government intervention in economic life if competition in some form were to be preserved. It is the purpose of this chapter to trace the history of the major developments in the law which came about as a result of that need and a policy generally seeking to preserve competition as being in the public interest.

It should be noted that there are several instances in which the actual *practice* of government apparently contradicts the avowed *general policy* of preserving competition. For example, as will be discussed further in section 6, the Robinson-Patman Act in part sought to preserve small businesses *from* the forces of competition. Also, labor unions and agricultural cooperatives have been exempted from the operation of the antitrust laws. In these segments of the economy the forces of competition may produce more public harm than good. The individual worker and the grower of agricultural products finds himself at the mercy of the market because of near "pure" competition in services or goods of the kind he is selling. He is permitted—even encouraged—by law to combine with other workers or farmers to combat these forces of competition. If business enterprises attempted to control a relevant market by combining in a similar fashion, they clearly would be in violation of the law. Because of the inherent advantages in monopolies the policy favoring competition has not been applied to public utilities. Public power, water, telephone, and transportation companies and other quasi-public businesses are granted exclusive or near exclusive markets by government. Permitting true monopoly power over such necessities would obviously be untenable, so, in lieu of the forces of competition, such industries are subjected to supervision of their rates and policies of operation by government agencies. The patent and copyright laws also represent a departure from a general policy favoring competition. Under the patent laws an inventor is given an exclusive monopoly to produce and sell his invention for seventeen years. Similarly, the copyright laws grant a monopoly to authors in that they have the exclusive right to multiply and sell copies of works resulting from their intellectual production for an initial period of twenty-eight years with one renewal permitted for an additional twenty-eight-year period. These are granted "to promote the Progress of Science and useful Arts." [1] Supposedly, the profit incentive given by these laws will induce the production of more inventions and literary works and in the end provide greater public benefit than unrestrained competition would. From this brief discussion it is clear that "competition" in the abstract can neither be labeled good nor bad. Rather, one must evaluate the societal benefit or detriment which is likely to result from the degree of presence or absence of competition in a specific context. In part, this is why our laws appear to be contradictory. It might be said that both the law and economic theory generally appear to favor "competition." However, because questions concerning competition are so highly complex, the foregoing statement is subject to many qualifications.

2   THE SHERMAN ACT

States enacted the first antitrust laws, toward the end of the nineteenth century. These proved to be largely ineffective in preventing monopolistic practices, for a number of reasons. Among these were the lack of enforcement facilities and the fact that monopolies were really a national problem. The Federal government entered the scene in 1887 with the enactment of the Interstate Commerce Act to control the railroads, where the obvious danger of monopoly had first appeared. This was followed in 1890 by the Sherman Act, which was passed by Congress under its constitutional authority to regulate interstate commerce. Some of the pertinent provisions of this act appear below.

Section 1. *Every contract, combination in the form of trust or otherwise, or conspiracy, in restraint of trade or commerce among the several States, or with foreign nations, is hereby declared to be illegal. . . . Every person who shall make any contract, or engage in any combination or conspiracy hereby declared to be illegal by Sections 1–7 of this title, shall be deemed guilty of a misdemeanor, and, on conviction thereof, shall be punished by fine not exceeding five thousand dollars, or by imprisonment not exceeding one year, or by both said punishments, in the discretion of the court.*[2]

Section 2. *Every person who shall monopolize, or attempt to monopolize, or combine or conspire with any other person or persons, to monopolize any part of the trade or commerce among the several States, or with foreign nations, shall be deemed guilty of a misdemeanor, and, on conviction thereof, shall be punished by fine not exceeding five thousand dollars, or by imprison-*

[1] United States Constitution, Art. I § 8.
[2] 26 Stat. 209 (1890), 15 U.S.C. § 1 (1964).

ment not exceeding one year, or by both said punishments, in the discretion of the court.[3]

The Sherman Act represents an announcement by Congress of a policy favoring the preservation of competition. Congress attempted to enforce this policy by furnishing four separate legal remedies for violations of its provisions. First, as the above quotation from the act indicates, it is a Federal crime punishable by fine or imprisonment or both for any person (or corporation) to contract, combine, or participate in a conspiracy in restraint of trade; or to monopolize or attempt to monopolize or combine or conspire with some other person to monopolize some segment of trade. The original maximum fine for *each violation* of Section 1 or 2 of the Act was $5,000, but the maximum was increased by Congress to $50,000 in 1955.[4] Second, the Sherman Act empowers the Federal government to obtain injunctions which will prevent and restrain violations or continued violations of its provisions. Failure to obey such injunctions subjects the defendant to contempt proceedings. A third remedy affords relief to those persons who have been injured by another's violation of the Act. Such victims are given the right, in a civil action, to collect three times the damages they have suffered, plus court costs and reasonable attorney's fees. Normally the objective of awarding money damages to an individual in a private lawsuit is to place him in the position he would have enjoyed, as nearly as this can be done with money, had his rights not been invaded. The treble damage provision of the Sherman Act, however, employs the remedy of damages as a means of punishing the defendant for his wrongful act in addition to compensating the plaintiff for his actual injury. Finally, any property owned in violation of Section 1 of the Act, which is being transported from one state to another, is made subject to seizure by and forfeiture to the United States. This last remedy has rarely been used.[5]

In *United States v. Aluminum Company of America*[6] Circuit Judge Learned Hand had occasion to comment on the purposes and philosophy of the Sherman Act. In holding that Alcoa was guilty of a violation of Section 2 for having intentionally acquired and maintained control of over 90 percent of the domestic "virgin" ingot market in aluminum, even though Alcoa had not misused such monopoly power to obtain exhorbitant profits, Hand said:

> . . . *Having proved that "Alcoa" had a monopoly of the domestic ingot market, the plaintiff had gone far enough; if it was an excuse, that "Alcoa" had not abused its power, it lay upon "Alcoa" to prove that it had not. But the whole issue is irrelevant anyway, for it is no excuse for "monopolizing" a market that the monopoly has not been used to extract from the consumer*

[3] 26 Stat. 209 (1890), 15 U.S.C. § 2 (1964).
[4] 69 Stat. 282 (1955), 15 U.S.C. §§ 1, 2 (1964).
[5] For an example of a case in which forfeiture of property was involved, see *United States v. Addyston Pipe and Steel Co.*, 175 U.S. 2111 (1899).
[6] 148 F.2d 416 (1945).

*more than a "fair" profit. The Act has wider purposes. Indeed, even though we disregarded all but economic considerations, it would by no means follow that such concentration of producing power is to be desired, when it has not been used extortionately. Many people believe that possession of unchallenged economic power deadens initiative, discourages thrift and depresses energy; that immunity from competition is a narcotic, and rivalry is a stimulant, to industrial progress; that the spur of constant stress is necessary to counteract an inevitable disposition to let well enough alone. Such people believe that competitors, versed in the craft as no consumer can be, will be quick to detect opportunities for saving and new shifts in production, and be eager to profit by them. In any event the mere fact that a producer, having command of the domestic market, has not been able to make more than a "fair" profit, is no evidence that a "fair" profit could not have been made at lower prices. . . .
True, it might have been thought adequate to condemn only those monopolies which could not show that they had exercised the highest possible ingenuity, had adopted every possible economy, had anticipated every conceivable improvement, stimulated every possible demand. No doubt, that would be one way of dealing with the matter, although it would imply constant scrutiny and constant supervision, such as courts are unable to provide. Be that as it may, that was not the way that Congress chose; it did not condone "good trusts" and condemn "bad" ones; it forbade all. Moreover, in so doing, it was not necessarily actuated by economic motives alone. It is possible, because of its indirect social or moral effect, to prefer a system of small producers, each dependent for his success upon his own skill and character, to one in which the great mass of those engaged must accept the direction of a few. These considerations, which we have suggested only as possible purposes of the Act, we think the decisions prove to have been in fact its purposes. . . .*

Continuing, Judge Hand indicated that, besides the economic reasons behind the Sherman Act's proscription of monopoly,

. . . there are others, based upon the belief that great industrial consolidations are inherently undesirable, regardless of their economic results. In the debates in Congress Senator Sherman himself . . . showed that among the purposes of Congress in 1890 was a desire to put an end to great aggregations of capital because of the helplessness of the individual before them. Another aspect of the same notion may be found in the language of Mr. Justice Peckham in United States v. Trans-Missouri Freight Association, supra, 166 U.S. 290, 323. That Congress is still of the same mind appears in the Surplus Property Act of 1944, and the Small Business Mobilization Act. Not only does § 2(d) of the first declare it to be one aim of that statute "to preserve the competitive position of small business concerns," but § 18 is given over to directions designed to "preserve and strengthen" their position. In United States v. Hutcheson, 312 U.S. 219, a later statute in pari materia was considered to throw a cross light, upon the Antitrust Acts, illuminating enough even to override an

earlier ruling of the court. Throughout the history of these statutes it has been constantly assumed that one of their purposes was to perpetuate and preserve, for its own sake and in spite of possible cost, an organization of industry in small units which can effectively compete with each other. We hold that "Alcoa's" monopoly of ingot was of the kind covered by § 2. . . .[7]

3   EARLY INTERPRETATION OF THE SHERMAN ACT

The first decision of the Supreme Court of the United States relating to the Sherman Act was *United States v. E.C. Knight Co.*,[8] which was handed down in 1895. That case involved an attempted prosecution of the Sugar Trust, which the Federal government lost due to a restrictive definition by the Court of what constituted "commerce among the several states" and what therefore was constitutionally subject to regulation by Congress. The Court reasoned in the *Knight* case that manufacturing was not commerce, but rather an activity which should be considered wholly intrastate and beyond the reach of Federal power. (Later, in 1937, the Supreme Court liberalized its view of the scope of the power of Congress to regulate commerce, so that today manufacturing is clearly included within the purview of the act.[9]) Since it was in the manufacturing of various commodities that much of the fact or threat of monopolization existed, the *Knight* case, along with some of the other early decisions of the Supreme Court, "made the Sherman Act a comparatively dead law."[10]

The second decision of the Supreme Court came in 1897, *United States v. Trans-Missouri Freight Association.*[11] In that case, the Court upheld the government's suit to have the Association (which included 18 carriers in its membership) dissolved and the agreement forming it declared null and void. In so doing, the Court had occasion to construe the statute and its scope, and stated as one of the issues, "Is [the Sherman Act] confined to a contract or combination which is only in unreasonable restraint of trade or commerce, or does it include what the language of the act plainly and in terms covers, all contracts of that nature?"[12] In answering the question posed, the court said,

Contracts in restraint of trade have been known and spoken of for hundreds of years both in England and in this country, and the term includes all kinds of those contracts, which in fact restrain or may restrain trade. Some of such contracts have been held void and unenforceable in the courts by reason of their restraint being unreasonable, while others have been held

---

[7] *Id.*
[8] 156 U.S. 1 (1895).
[9] See *NLRB v. Jones and Laughlin Steel Corp.*, 301 U.S. 1 (1937) in Chapter 14, page 547.
[10] Barnes, J., in *Klor's Inc. v. Broadway-Hale Stores*, 255 F.2d 214 (1958).
[11] 166 U.S. 290 (1897).
[12] *Id.*

valid because they were not of that nature. A contract may be in restraint of trade and still be valid at common law. Although valid, it is nevertheless a contract in restraint of trade, and would be so described either at common law or elsewhere. By the simple use of the term "contract in restraint of trade," all contracts of that nature, whether valid or otherwise, would be included, and not alone that kind of contract which was invalid and unenforceable as being in unreasonable restraint of trade. When, therefore, the body of an act pronounces as illegal every contract or combination in restraint of trade or commerce among the several States, etc., the plain and ordinary meaning of such language is not limited to that kind of contract alone which is in unreasonable restraint of trade, but all contracts are included in such language, and no exception or limitation can be added without placing in the act that which has been omitted by Congress.[13]

The Court then considered the question of whether contractual restraints such as those ancillary to a sale of property, long recognized as valid at common law if reasonable in scope, should be excluded from the type of contract prohibited by the Act and reached the conclusion that:

A contract which is the mere accompaniment of the sale of property, and thus entered into for the purpose of enhancing the price at which the vendor sells it, which in effect is collateral to such sale, and where the main purpose of the whole contract is accomplished by such sale, might not be included, within the letter or spirit of the statute in question. But we cannot see how the statute can be limited, as it has been by the courts below, without reading into its text an exception which alters the natural meaning of the language used, and that, too, upon a most material point, and where no sufficient reason is shown for believing that such alteration would make the statute more in accord with the intent of the law-making body that enacted it. . . .[14]

However, the following year, in *United States v. Joint Traffic Association*,[15] the Court retreated somewhat from a strictly literal, all-encompassing construction of the meaning of the Sherman Act. And finally, in the case which follows, the Court gave up the literal approach altogether in announcing the so-called "rule of reason."

STANDARD OIL CO. V. UNITED STATES
221 U.S. 1 (1911)

The United States brought this action for an injunction under the Sherman Antitrust Act to enforce its provisions against seventy-one corporations, including the Standard Oil Companies of New Jersey, California, Indiana,

[13] *Id.*
[14] *Id.*
[15] 171 U.S. 505 (1898).

Iowa, Kansas, Kentucky, Nebraska, New York, and Ohio, and seven individuals, all of whom were engaged in purchasing, shipping, refining and selling petroleum and its products. The government charged that defendants had conspired to restrain the trade and commerce in petroleum among the several states, and claimed that the conspiracy was started around 1870 by three of the individual defendants, John D. Rockefeller, William Rockefeller and Henry M. Flagler, who along with Standard Oil of Ohio and others entered into agreements for the purpose of price fixing, limiting production, and controlling the transportation of oil and its products. It was further alleged that at a later time certain of the defendants turned over the managements of all aspects of their businesses to nine trustees in exchange for trust certificates, which constituted a restraint of trade in violation of the act. Finally it was alleged that in further pursuance of their conspiracy, the individual defendants, operating through Standard Oil Company of New Jersey as a holding corporation, caused that company to acquire a majority of the stocks of various corporations engaged in the oil business and in this fashion managed and controlled the corporations in violation of the act. The trial court found Standard Oil Company of New Jersey, thirty-seven of its corporate subsidiaries, and the seven individuals guilty of forming a combination in restraint of trade, of attempting to monopolize, and of a monopolization under the Sherman Act. The action was dismissed as to the thirty-three other corporations, because they were not proved to be parties to the combination. In its decree the court enjoined the Standard Oil Company of New Jersey from voting stocks or otherwise controlling the thirty-seven subsidiaries, and the individuals and thirty-eight corporations from entering into any similar combination to evade the decree. In addition, all guilty parties were enjoined *from engaging in the petroleum business at all* as long as their illegal combination continued. This appeal to the Supreme Court by the defendants resulted.

WHITE, CHIEF JUSTICE: . . . . There can be no doubt that the sole subject with which the first section [of the Sherman Antitrust Act] deals is restraint of trade as therein contemplated, and that the attempt to monopolize and monopolization is the subject with which the second section is concerned. It is certain that those terms, at least in their rudimentary meaning, took their origin in the common law, and were also familiar in the law of this country prior to and at the time of the adoption of the act in question.

We shall endeavor then, first to seek their meaning, not by indulging in an elaborate and learned analysis of the English law and of the law of this country, but by making a very brief reference to the elementary and indisputable conceptions of both the English and American law on the subject prior to the passage of the Antitrust Act.

a. It is certain that at a very remote period the words "contract in restraint of trade" in England came to refer to some voluntary restraint put by contract by an individual on his right to carry on his trade or calling. Originally all such contracts were considered to be illegal, because it was deemed they were injurious to the public as well as to the individuals who made them. In the interest of the freedom of individuals to contract this doctrine was modified so that it was only when a restraint by contract was so general as to be coterminous with the kingdom that it was treated as void. That is to say, if the restraint was partial in its operation and was otherwise reasonable the contract was held to be valid.

b. Monopolies were defined by Lord Coke as follows:

A monopoly is an institution, or allowance by the king by his grant, commission, or otherwise to any person or persons, bodies politic or corporate, of or for the sole buying, selling, making, working, or using of anything, whereby any person or persons, bodies politic or corporate, are sought to be restrained of any freedom or liberty that they had before, or hindered in their lawful trade. . . .

Let us consider the language of the first and second sections, guided by the principle that where words are employed in a statute which had at the time a well-known meaning at common law or in the law of this country they are presumed to have been used in that sense unless the context compels to the contrary. . . .

As there is no room for dispute that the statute was intended to formulate a rule for the regulation of interstate and foreign commerce, the question is what was the rule which it adopted? . . .

The statute . . . evidenced the intent not to restrain the right to make and enforce contracts, whether resulting from combination or otherwise, which did not unduly restrain interstate or foreign commerce, but to protect that commerce from being restrained by methods, whether old or new, which would constitute an interference that is an undue restraint. . . .

[A]s the contracts or acts embraced in the provision were not expressly defined, since the enumeration addressed itself simply to classes of acts, those classes being broad enough to embrace every conceivable contract or combination which could be made concerning trade or commerce or the subjects of such commerce, and thus caused any act done by any of the enumerated methods anywhere in the whole field of human activity to be illegal if in restraint of trade, it inevitably follows that the provision necessarily called for the exercise of judgment which required that some standard should be resorted to for the purpose of determining whether the prohibitions contained in the statute had or had not in any given case been violated. Thus not specifying but indubitably contemplating and requiring a standard, it follows that it was intended that the standard of reason which had been applied at the common law and in this country dealing with subjects of the character embraced by the statute, was intended to be the measure used for the purpose of determining whether in a given case a particular act had or had not brought about the wrong against which the statute provided.

And a consideration of the text of the second section serves to establish that it was intended to supplement the first and to make sure that by no possible guise could the public policy embodied in the first section be frustrated or evaded. . . .

Undoubtedly, the words "to monopolize" and "monopolize" as used in the section reach every act bringing about the prohibited results. The ambiguity, if any, is involved in determining what is intended by monopolize. But this ambiguity is readily dispelled in the light of the previous history of the law of restrant of trade to which we have referred and the indication which it gives of the practical evolution by which monopoly and the acts which produce the same result as monopoly, that is, an undue restraint of the course of trade, all came to be spoken of as, and to be indeed synonymous with, restraint of trade. In other words, having by the first section forbidden all means of monopolizing trade, that is, unduly restraining it by means of every contract, combination, etc., the second section seeks, if possible, to make the prohibitions of the act all the more complete and perfect by embracing all attempts to reach the end prohibited by the first section, that is, restraints of trade by any attempt to monopolize, or monopolization thereof, even although the acts by which such results are attempted to be brought about or are brought about be not embraced within the general enumeration of the first section. And, of course, when the second section is thus harmonized with and made as it was intended to be the complement of the first, it becomes obvious that the criteria to be resorted to in any given case for the purpose of ascertaining whether violations of the section have been committed, is the rule of reason guided by the established law and by the plain duty to enforce the prohibitions of the act and thus the public policy which its restrictions were obviously enacted to subserve. And it is worthy of observation, as we have previously remarked concerning the common law, that although the statute by the comprehensiveness of the enumerations embodied in both the first and second sections makes it certain that its purpose was to prevent undue restraints of every kind or nature, nevertheless by the omission of any direct prohibition against monopoly in the concrete it indicates a consciousness that the freedom of the individual right to contract when not unduly or improperly exercised was the most efficient means for the prevention of monopoly, since the operation of the centrifugal and centripetal forces resulting from the right to freely contract was the means by which monopoly would be inevitably prevented if no extraneous or sovereign power imposed it and no right to make unlawful contracts having a monopolistic tendency were permitted. In other words that freedom to contract was the essence of freedom from undue restraint of the right to contract. . . .

Our conclusion is that the decree below was right, and should be affirmed, except as to the minor matters concerning which we have indicated the decree should be modified. . . . [Those matters were discussed in portions of the opinion which have been omitted here.]

In the same year in *United States v. American Tobacco Co.,*[16] the Court interpreted its own ruling in the above case and stated:

[*In* Standard Oil] . . . *it was held not that acts which the statute prohibited could be removed from the control of its prohibitions by a finding that they were reasonable, but that the duty to interpret which inevitably arose from the general character of the term restraint of trade required that the words restraint of trade should be given a meaning which would not destroy the individual right to contract and render difficult if not impossible any movement of trade in the channels of interstate commerce—the free movement of which it was the purpose of the statute to protect.*

The rule that contracts or conspiracies in restraint of trade were illegal only if they constituted undue or unreasonable restraints of trade, and that only unreasonable attempts to monopolize were covered by the Sherman Act, obviously gave the courts a great deal of power and discretion. In effect the courts were legislating in each case by determining what activities would be considered reasonable or unreasonable, as a matter of law. At this time in history, one of the Supreme Court's major concerns and emphases centered around the protection of individual constitutional rights, particularly property ownership and freedom of contract. Since the Sherman Act represented an attempt by Congress to make inroads into these two rights, particularly in the case of business activity, it is easy to see how the court in protecting such rights would seek a balance and not give as much sweeping effect to the Sherman Act as would literally have been possible under its broad, general language, even as modified by the rule of reason. Thus for many of its rulings in the antitrust area the court received heavy criticism from some quarters for being too conservative and too pro-business, and of course just for creating its rule of reason on the theory that the court was taking too much power, disregarding the true intent of Congress, and legislating the court's own philosophy instead. On the latter point, the reader is referred to Anthony Lewis's article, "The Changing Role of the Supreme Court of the U.S.A." which appears in Chapter 18 on pages 744–748, particularly page 745, where he writes:

The basic difficulty for the Supreme Court in saying what Congress meant is that so often Congress meant nothing at all. It simply never envisaged the problem before the Court. The Congress that wrote the Sherman Act back in 1890, prohibiting "every contract or combination in restraint of trade"

---

[16] 221 U.S. 106 (1911).

simply gave the Court a blank check to fill in with contemporary legal and economic theory. It is hardly surprising that the Court has had some difficulty deciding what is an antitrust violation, or that the justices have disagreed. . . .

Mr. Lewis in discussing the performance of Congress noted:

When [Congress] comes to a difficult problem, its tendency is to fuzz things over and let the Court resolve the difficulty under the guise of discovering what Congress "intended." I remember the offshore oil legislation, when Congress could have stated right in the statute how far out into the Gulf of Mexico state mineral rights should run. But it was too difficult politically to make that decision, and so Congress asked the Court to do it on the basis of some ambiguous history. At the argument Justice Frankfurter said something about Congress passing the buck. . . .

Although Mr. Lewis's last statements apply specifically to offshore oil legislation, they appear to have general application to much legislation by Congress, including the Sherman Act. Thus, it would seem that the Congress which passed the Sherman Act in 1890 and waited practically a quarter of a century until 1914 to legislate further in the antitrust area should shoulder at least some of the blame placed on the court by its critics for the early antitrust decisions.

4   THE CLAYTON ACT

After it had been in effect for a time, the Sherman Act was criticized as being inadequate. For one thing, the Act did little to prevent practices which *tended* to reduce competition or were *conducive* to creating monopolies. As interpreted with the rule of reason announced in the *Standard Oil* case, it did not apply to situations which were likely to lead to the destruction of competition, but which fell short of an actual monopoly or combination in unreasonable restraint of trade. Also, as was noted previously, the rule of reason and the lack of specificity in the Sherman Act practically required that courts decide each alleged violation on its own merits on a case-by-case basis. It was felt by many that this gave the courts undue power and further that the interpretations which they were placing on the Act in exercising that power made it much less effective in preserving competition than Congress had intended. In addition, at the time, some particular business practices which were common were felt by some to be destructive of competition but had been held outside the purview of the Sherman Act by the Courts.

The foregoing were among the factors underlying the passage of the Clayton Act and the Federal Trade Commission Act in 1914, which both represent major developments in antitrust law. In addition, since rulings of the Supreme Court had subjected organized labor to the provisions of the Sherman Act, one of the purposes of the Clayton Act was to exclude labor along with nonprofit agricultural organizations from the scope of antitrust legislation.

The Clayton Act was more specific than the Sherman Act in declaring certain enumerated practices in commerce to be illegal, which practices might have an adverse effect on competition, but were not themselves contracts, combinations, or conspiracies in restraint of trade, and did not go far enough to constitute actual monopolization or attempts to monopolize. Further, the enumerated practices did not have to actually injure competition to be wrongful; they were outlawed if their effect *might* be to substantially lessen competition, or *tend* to create a monopoly. Thus, the burden of proving a violation was eased and the rule of reason was circumvented to some extent in certain cases. It would be much easier, for example, for a court to find that certain practices *tended* toward monopoly, than to find that they *amounted* to a monopoly. The Clayton Act made it possible to attack many practices in their incipiency which, if continued, eventually could destroy competition or create monopoly. The idea was to remedy these matters before the full harm was done. Some of the more pertinent provisions of the Clayton Act—Section 2 on price discrimination, Section 3 on trying leases, Section 7 on acquisition of the stock of one corporation by another, and Section 8 on interlocking directorates—are summarized below.

Section 2 made it unlawful for a seller to discriminate in the price charged different purchasers of commodities where the effect *might* be to substantially lessen competition or *tend* to create a monopoly in any line of commerce. However, this section specified that price discrimination was lawful if due to differences in the grade, quality, or quantity of the product sold, or differences in cost of transportation. Also, no violation existed if the seller discriminated in price in order to meet competition in good faith. The objective of this section was to put purchasers of goods, wares, or merchandise on the same competitive ground, with the exceptions noted.

Section 3 made it unlawful for a person engaged in commerce to lease or sell commodities (whether patented or unpatented) or to fix a price charged, on the condition that the lessee or purchaser should not use or deal in the commodities of a competitor of the lessor or seller, where the effect *may* be to substantially lessen competition or *tend* to create a monopoly. An example of the type of business activity forbidden by Section 3 of the Clayton Act is found in *International Salt Co., Inc. v. United States*.[17] International Salt leased its patented salt-processing machines to customers who were required by the leases to purchase all salt used in the machines from International Salt Company. The court held that these were unreasonable restraints which might substantially lessen competition, by foreclosing

[17] 332 U.S. 392 (1947).

competitors from a substantial market, and indicated that International Salt could require its lessees to use salt of minimum purity in the machines, but clearly could not require the use of its own brand.

Section 7 prohibited the acquisition, by a corporation engaged in commerce, of all or part of the stock of other such corporations, where the effect *might* be to lessen competition substantially or to *tend* to create a monopoly in any line of commerce. The section was inapplicable to corporations which purchased stock solely for investment and further did not prevent the formation of subsidiary corporations for the actual carrying on of the parent's lawful business, if the effect were not substantially to lessen competition. Also exempted were certain acquisitions by common carriers.

Section 8 of the Clayton Act was aimed at interlocking directorates. It prohibits a person from being a member of the board of directors of two or more corporations at the same time, when one of them has capital, surplus, and undivided profits totaling more than $1,000,000, where elimination of competition by agreement between such corporations would amount to a violation of any of the antitrust laws. Portions of Section 8 which deal exclusively with banks, and Section 10, which deals exclusively with common carriers, are not discussed here. The case which follows is an example of the application of Section 8.

UNITED STATES V. SEARS ROEBUCK & CO.
111 F. Supp. 614 (S.D.N.Y., 1953)

These proceedings were brought by the Government against Sears Roebuck & Co., The B.F. Goodrich Company, and Sidney J. Weinberg, seeking an order under Section 8 of the Clayton Act directing that Weinberg resign from the board of directors of one or both of the corporate defendants. The defendants admitted to the following facts: that Sears and Goodrich are New York corporations, each having capital, surplus, and undivided profits in excess of 1 million dollars; that Weinberg was and had been for many years a director of both companies; that each corporation was engaged in interstate commerce; that the two were competitors at retail in ninety-seven communities in the sale of appliances, hardware, automotive supplies, sporting goods, tires, radios, television sets, and toys; and that for 1951 the total volume of sales of the foregoing items in the ninety-seven communities by Sears was over 65 million dollars compared to total sales of 16 million dollars by Goodrich. This case was one of first impression, involving the first judicial construction of Section 8 since it was passed in 1914, almost forty years earlier.

WEINFELD, DISTRICT JUDGE: . . . The relevant portion of § 8 provides: ". . . No person at the same time shall be a director in any two or more corporations, any one of which has capital, surplus, and undivided profits aggregating more than $1,000,000, engaged in whole or in part in commerce . . . if such corporations are or shall have been theretofore, by virtue of their business and location of operation, competitors, so that the elimination of competition by agreement between them would constitute a violation of any of the provisions of any of the antitrust laws. . . ."

The basic issue presented for decision under the admitted facts is whether Sears and Goodrich are "competitors, so that the elimination of competition by agreement between them would constitute a violation of any of the provisions of any of the antitrust laws." If so, then § 8 forbids Weinberg to be a director of both. The case is one of novel impression involving the first construction of this section of the Clayton Act since its passage in 1914.

Defendants in substance contend that the clause just quoted severely limits the scope of the prohibition upon interlocking directorates; that it requires a finding that a hypothetical merger between the two corporations would violate the antitrust laws before the same director is forbidden them; that plaintiff has not demonstrated that the combined position of the two corporate defendants in the sale of the particular commodities is such that there is a "reasonable probability that they could together substantially restrain trade or create a monopoly" and that, therefore, the plaintiff cannot succeed since a merger would not be violative of the antitrust laws without such a showing. In essence, the defendants would apply the merger test as spelled out in § 7 of the Clayton Act, 15 U.S.C.A. § 18.

The plaintiff urges to the contrary that "a violation of any of the provisions of any of the antitrust laws" is not limited to a merger or acquisition situation; that it includes agreements to fix prices or divide markets; that such agreements are illegal per se; and that, therefore, Sears and Goodrich may not retain in their service the same director since an agreement between them to fix prices or to divide territories would constitute a per se violation of § 1 of the Sherman Act, 15 U.S.C.A. §1.

The Senate and House Reports on the various proposals antecedent to the passage of § 8 of the Clayton Act and the Congressional Debates shed little light on the precise point at issue. However, the broad purposes of Congress are unmistakably clear. Section 8 was but one of a series of measures which finally emerged as the Clayton Act, all intended to strengthen the Sherman Act, which, through the years, had not proved entirely effective. Congress had been aroused by the concentration of control by a few individuals or groups over many gigantic corporations which in the normal course of events should have been in active and unrestrained competition. Instead, and because of such control, the healthy competition of the free enterprise system had been stifled or eliminated. Interlocking directorships on rival corporations had been the instrumentality of defeating the purpose of the antitrust laws. They had tended to suppress competition or to foster joint action against third party competitors. The continued potential threat to the competitive system resulting from these conflicting directorships was the evil aimed at. Viewed against this background, a fair reading of the legislative debates leaves little room for doubt that, in its efforts to strengthen the antitrust laws, what Congress intended by § 8 was to nip in the bud incipient violations of the antitrust laws by removing the opportunity or temptation to such violations through interlocking directorates. The legislation was essentially preventative.

It is in the context of this history that defendants' argument must be evaluated. . . .

Defendants also rely on the asserted necessity for reading § 8 in connection with § 7 of the Clayton Act, 38 Stat. 731, as amended, 64 Stat. 1125, 15 U.S.C.A. § 18, which deals with mergers and interdicts the acquisition by one corporation of the stock or the assets of another where the effect of such acquisition "may be substantially to lessen competition, or to tend to create a monopoly."

Defendants argue, as set forth above, that § 8 does not prohibit defendant Weinberg's directorship on the two Boards, absent a showing that the effect of an assumed consolidation between Sears and Goodrich "may be substantially to lessen competition, or to tend to create a monopoly," as set forth in § 7. The vital distinction between § 7 and § 8, however, is that the latter omits the § 7 test and promulgates its own substantiality standard in the form of the one million dollar size requirement. The omission of "substantially to lessen competition, or to tend to create a monopoly" from § 8 in contradistinction to its inclusion in § 7 and other sections of the same Act may not be deemed inadvertent. Were the defendants' construction to be adopted, it would require the application under § 8 of a test which Congress appears deliberately to have omitted. . . .

Further, the defendants' construction would denude of meaning the phrase *"any* of the provisions of *any* of the antitrust *laws."* [EMPHASIS ADDED] This language is broad enough to cover all methods of violating antitrust legislation. At the time of the passage of § 8, price fixing and division of territory agreements were in common use to effect such violations. Merger or aquisition was not the sole means used to achieve this result. There is no logical basis upon which to infer that the all-inclusive language was intended to exclude the other known methods from the reach of § 8.

Finally, defendants urge that no policy reasons have been advanced to show that the public interest is affected by the dual directorship of the defendant Weinberg on the Boards of the corporate defendants. They say that the government has failed to show that there exists between Sears and Goodrich any agreement fixing prices, restricting territories or otherwise restraining competition between them or that there is a likelihood of any such agreement; further, that no contention is made that the individual defendant's dual directorship has had the effect, or has the potentiality, of restraining competition. But this argument ignores the preventative nature of § 8. The instant case presents a good example of what the section was intended to avert.

The defendants have conceded that they are competitors in the sale of the seven categories of items at retail in commerce as the term is used in the Clayton Act. The sales of the seven items in the 97 communities amounted to $80,000,000 for 1951. The fact that this volume of sales may represent but a small percentage of either or both of the corporate defendants' annual sales, or a fraction of the annual retail sales volume of all distributors in the country of those commodities, does not militate against the undesirability of directorates common to both corporations. Actually, commerce in a particular product, using refrigerators as an example, while perhaps insignificant as related to the corporate defendants' total sales of all their other products or infinitesimal compared to the national retail volume, may, nonetheless, represent the total absorptive capacity of a given community within which they are competitors.

Assume that Sears and Goodrich are selling refrigerators competitively in a town of 30,000 population, the effective and easy means is at hand, through a price fixing agreement or the withdrawal of either Sears or Goodrich from the territory or an agreement not to sell the refrigerators in the same area, to eliminate or lessen competition. While the government does not charge that any such agreement has been made or is contemplated, a director serving in a dual capacity might, if he felt the interest of an interlocking corporation so required, either initiate or support a course of action resulting in price fixing or division of territories or a combination of his competing corporations as against a third competitive corporation. The fact that this has not happened up to the present does not mean that it may not happen hereafter.

In summary, an agreement between Sears and Goodrich which fixed the prices at which they would sell the seven categories of items would eliminate competition, as would an agreement by which they allocated as between themselves the territories in which they would sell those items. Price fixing and territorial division between competitors are per se violation of § 1 of the Sherman Act, 26 Stat. 209, 15 U.S.C.A. § 1, without regard to the amount of commerce affected. No showing of industry domination is required. It is the character of the restraint and not the amount of commerce affected that taints the transactions. . . .

Since Sears and Goodrich are competitors, since a price fixing or division of territory agreement would eliminate competition between them, and since such an agreement would per se violate at least one "of the provisions of . . . the antitrust laws," namely § 1 of the Sherman Act, it follows that § 8 forbids defendant Weinberg to be a director of both corporations.

The government's motion for summary judgment is granted. . . .

Violations of Section 2, 3, 7, and 8 of the original Clayton Act were not made crimes by its provisions, and the Act contained no sanction for forfeiture of property. However, it did provide that the Justice Department might obtain injunctions to prevent violations of it. Those persons who were injured by a violation could obtain injunctive relief in their own behalf and, in addition, were given the right to collect treble the damages they suffered plus court costs and reasonable attorney's fees. Also, the Federal Trade Commission (FTC) was authorized to enforce Sections 2, 3, 7, and 8. If the commission, in a proper hearing before it, determined that a violation existed, it was empowered to issue a cease and desist order, which is, of course, subject to review and to being set aside or enforced by the Circuit Courts of Appeals of the United States.

While persons guilty of acts proscribed by Sections 2, 3, 7, and 8 of the Clayton Act were not subject to a criminal sanction, Section 14 imposed criminal liability on *directors* and *agents* of corporations which violated penal provisions of the antitrust laws (such as those found in Sections 1 and 2 of the Sherman Act), if they had a part in the prohibited activity.

The act expanded the Sherman Act provisions by allowing private individuals to obtain injunctions in cases of *threatened* loss due to violations by another person or corporation of any of the antitrust laws. It also greatly eased the burden of proof which normally must be shouldered by a plaintiff; a final judgment or decree in favor of the United States to the effect that a defendant has violated the antitrust laws was made prima facie evidence of such violation in a suit brought by a person who was injured by it against the same defendant.

5   THE FEDERAL TRADE COMMISSION ACT

As was indicated above, the Federal Trade Commission Act was passed in 1914 as well as the Clayton Act, with the same general reasons behind its passage. The Act established the FTC as one of the so-called "independent" administrative agencies. The five commissioners are appointed by the President, with the advice and consent of the Senate, in staggered terms of seven years each. One of the five is appointed chairman by the President. They are not permitted to engage in any other busines or employment during their terms, and may be removed from office by the President only for inefficiency, neglect of duty, or malfeasance in office. Under this act, the commission was given investigating, prosecuting, legislative, and judicial powers. The Clayton Act itself gave the FTC jurisdiction over cases arising under Sections 2, 3, 7, and 8 of the Act, and the power to enforce their provisions. Presumably, the commission was to be composed of members who were experts in business matters and economics and who by applying their expertise to the specific problems of preserving or restoring competition could resolve them in a better manner than the courts could. In fact, it might be said that by creating the commission Congress was creating competition itself, between the courts and the commission, in the matter of enforcing the laws intended to preserve competition. In addition, the Act enabled the President to appoint persons whom he felt would take a less conservative, more vigorous approach to the problems of enforcing the antitrust laws, so that more progress could be made in this area than under the Sherman Act alone or in the court system alone. However, it should be noted that Congress did not express its complete distrust of the courts (as it did in the case of the enforcement of later labor legislation—the Wagner Act) since actions under the Clayton Act could also be brought by private individuals who were injured by violations thereof in the regular court system or by the Attorney General in the Federal District Courts.

In addition to the foregoing, Section 5 of the Federal Trade Commission Act declared that "unfair methods of competition in commerce" were unlawful, and empowered and directed the commission (exclusively) "to prevent persons, partnerships, or corporations . . . from using unfair methods of competition in commerce." Later this provision was amended to make "unfair methods of competition in commerce *and unfair or deceptive acts or practices in commerce*" unlawful.[18] [EMPHASIS ADDED] It would appear that this section gave the commission a broad, sweeping legislative power—and mandate—to determine what methods, acts, or practices fell within the vague category of being "unfair," and thus unlawful, on a case-by-case basis. Briefly, the procedures established were as follows: The commission would investigate alleged violations of the antitrust laws over which it had jurisdiction. If it felt that an actual violation existed, the commission would hold a hearing in the nature of a judicial proceeding to resolve issues of fact and law. Hearings were required to follow certain procedures, such as giving the one accused of the violation proper notice of the hearing and an opportunity to appear, defend himself, and present evidence in his own behalf. Upon a finding that a violation did in fact exist, the commission was empowered to issue a cease and desist order, which could include all and everything necessary to prevent further violation. As in the case of orders of other administrative agencies, the orders of the commission were made subject to review by the Circuit Courts of Appeals of the United States, so that a defendant could petition that court to set aside the order of the commission, and conversely, if some defendant did not obey the commission's orders, the commission could petition the court for a decree enforcing its order. The following case is one of the first to arise under the Federal Trade Commission Act and Section 5. In it is found an example of one type of "unfair method of competition" and a holding that the granting of broad powers to the commission in Section 5 was not an unconstitutional delegation of legislative and judicial power.

[18] Wheeler-Lee Amendments, 52 Stat. 111 (1938), 15 U.S.C. § 45 (1964).

SEARS, ROEBUCK & CO. V. FTC
258 F. 307 (1919)

BAKER, CIRCUIT JUDGE: This is [a] petition to review an order entered by the respondent, the Federal Trade Commission, against the petitioner, Sears, Roebuck & Co., a corporation, commanding the petitioner to desist from certain unfair methods of competition in commerce.

. . . Respondent's authority over the subject matter of its order is derived from the following provision in [Section 5 of the Federal Trade Commission Act]: "Unfair methods of competition in commerce are hereby declared unlawful." Section 4 (Comp. St § 8836d) is a dictionary of terms used in the act. "Commerce" means interstate or foreign commerce; but the general term, "unfair methods of competition," is nowhere defined specifically, nor is there a schedule of methods that shall be deemed unfair.

In its complaint respondent averred that petitioner is engaged in interstate and foreign commerce, conducting a "mail-order" business; that petitioner for more than two years last past has practiced unfair methods of competition in commerce by false and misleading advertisements and acts, designed to injure and discredit its competitors and to deceive the general public, in the following ways:

(1) By advertising that petitioner, because of large purchases of sugar and quick disposal of stock, is able to sell sugar at a price lower than others offering sugar for sale;

(2) By advertising that petitioner is selling its sugar at a price much lower than that of its competitors and thereby imputing to its competitors the purpose of charging more than a fair price for their sugar;

(3) By selling certain of its merchandise at less than cost on the condition that the customer simultaneously purchase other merchandise at prices which give petitioner a profit on the transaction, without letting the customer know the facts;

(4) By advertising that the quality of merchandise sold by its competitors is inferior to that of similar merchandise sold by petitioner, and that petitioner buys certain of its merchandise in markets not accessible to its competitors, and is therefore able to give better advantages in quality and price than those offered by its competitors.

Petitioner extensively circulated the following advertisements, among others:

We can afford to give this guarantee of a "less than wholesale price" because we are among the largest distributors of sugar wholesale or retail in the world. We sell every year thirty-five million pounds of sugar. And, buying in *such vast quantities, and buying directly from the refineries, we naturally get our sugar for less money than other dealers.*

For instance, every grocer carries granulated sugar in stock, but does he tell you which kind? There are two kinds—granulated cane sugar and granulated beet sugar—and they look exactly alike. Some people prefer the one and some the other. But beet sugar usually costs less than cane sugar, so if you are getting beet sugar you should pay less for it. Do you know which kind you are getting and which you are paying for?

Our teas have a pronounced, yet delicate, tea flavor with an appealing fragrance because we spare neither time nor expenses to get the very best the greatest tea gardens of the world can produce.

First, because of the difficulty of getting in this country the exact character and flavor of certain teas, we do our own importing and critically test every tea. Our representative goes to the various tea-growing countries and makes the selection in person. Then, the greatest care is taken to get only first-crop pickings from upland soil.

Also, by buying direct from the tea gardens, while the crops are being harvested, we are able to have them always perfectly fresh.

It would be natural for you to conclude that all this care in buying and selecting would make our teas very high in price, but in reality, our prices are unusually low for such high quality. Here is a reason: By buying direct from the tea gardens we cut out the middleman's profit.

Over land and sea, from the greatest coffee regions in the world we bring you the choicest of the crop, and make it possible for you to have that fresh, savory, and fragrantly tempting cup of coffee for your breakfast. You see, we buy direct from the best plantations in the world. We get the pick of the crop —upland coffees from rich, healthy soil and growers of unquestioned experience and skill. We buy enormous quantities and pay cash, thus making it possible to offer our customers the very best coffees at very low prices.

Petitioner's sales of sugar during the second half of 1915 amounted to $780,000 on which it lost $196,000. Petitioner used sugar as a "leader" ("You save 2 to 4 cents on every pound"), offering a limited amount at the losing price in connection with a required purchase of other commodities at prices high enough to afford petitioner a satisfactory profit on the transaction as a whole, without letting the customer know that the sugar was being sold on any other basis than that of the other commodities. Petitioner obtained its sugar in the open market from refiners and wholesalers. Competitors got their sugar from the same sources, of the same quality and at the same price. Sugar is a staple in the market. Price concessions upon large purchases are unobtainable. From the facts respecting petitioner's methods of advertising and buying and selling sugar respondent found, and properly so, in our judgment, that petitioner intentionally injured and discredited its competitors by falsely leading the public to believe that the competitors were unfair dealers in sugar and the other commodities which petitioner was offering in connection with sugar.

Petitioner purchased 75 percent of its teas from wholesalers and importers in the United States. The remainder it purchased through its representative Peterson in Japan; but there was no proof that Peterson made or was qualified to make "selections in person" or "first-crop pickings from upland soil." All of petitioner's coffees were purchased from wholesalers and importers in the United States. Respondent found that petitioner's advertisements of teas and coffees were false and designed to deceive the public and injure competitors.

By the order issued on June 24, 1918, petitioner was commanded to desist from:

(1) *Circulating throughout the states and territories of the United States and the District of Columbia catalogues containing advertisements offering the sale of sugar, wherein it is falsely represented to its customers or prospective customers of said defendant or to customers of competitors, or to the people generally, or leads them to believe, that because of large purchasing power and quick-moving stock, defendant is able to sell sugar at a price lower than its competitors.*

(2) *Selling, or offering to sell, sugar below cost through catalogues circulated throughout the states and territories of the United States and the District of Columbia among its customers, prospective customers and customers of its competitors;*

(3) *Circulating throughout the various states and territories of the United States and the District of Columbia, among customers, prospective customers and customers of its competitors, catalogues containing advertisements representing that defendant's competitors do not deal justly, fairly and honestly with their customers;*

(4) *Circulating throughout the various states and territories of the United States and the District of Columbia, among customers, prospective customers or customers of its competitors, catalogues containing advertisements offering for sale its teas, in which said advertisements it falsely stated that the defendant sends a special representative to Japan who personally goes into the tea gardens of said country and personally supervises the picking of such teas;*

(5) *Circulating through the various states and territories of the United States and the District of Columbia, among customers, prospective customers or customers of its competitors, catalogues containing advertisements offering for sale its coffees, in which it falsely stated that the defendant purchases all of its coffees direct from the best plantations in the world.*

. . . Petitioner urges that the declaration of section 5 must be held void for indefiniteness unless the words "unfair methods of competition" be construed to embrace no more than acts which on September 26, 1914, when Congress spoke, were identifiable as acts of unfair trade then condemned by the common law as expressed in prior cases. But the phrase is no more indefinite than "due process of law." The general idea of that phrase as it appears in Constitutions and statutes is quite well known; but we have never encountered what purported to be an all-embracing schedule or found a specific definition that would bar the continuing processes of judicial inclusion and exclusion based upon accumulating experience. If the expression "unfair methods of competition" is too uncertain for use, then under the same condemnation would fall the innumerable statutes which predicated rights and prohibitions upon "unsound mind," "undue influence," "unfaithfulness," "unfair use," "unfit for cultivation," "unreasonable rate," "unjust discrimination," and the like. This statute is remedial, and orders to desist are civil; but even in criminal law convictions are upheld on statutory prohibitions of "rebates or concessions" or of "schemes to defraud," without any schedule of acts or specific definition of forbidden conduct, thus leaving the courts free to condemn new and ingenious ways that were unknown when the statutes were enacted. Why? Because the general ideas of "dishonesty" and "fraud" are so well, widely and uniformly understood that the general term "rebates or concessions" and "schemes to defraud" are sufficiently accurate measures of conduct.

On the face of this statute the legislative intent is apparent. The commissioners are not required to aver and prove that any competitor has been damaged or that any purchaser has been deceived. The commissioners, representing the government as parens patriae, are to exercise their common sense, as informed by their knowledge of the general idea of unfair trade at common law, and stop all those trade practices that have a capacity or a tendency to injure competitors directly or through deception of purchasers, quite irrespective of whether the specific practices in question have yet been denounced in common-law cases. But the restraining order of the commissioners is merely provisional. The trader is entitled to his day in court, and there the same principles and tests that have been applied under the common law or under statutes of the kinds hereinbefore recited are expected by Congress to control. This prima facie reading of legislative intent is confirmed by reference to committee reports and debates in Congress, wherein is disclosed a refusal to limit the commission and the court to a prescribed list of specific acts. . . .

But such a construction of section 5, according to petitioner's urge, brings about an unconstitutional delegation of legislative and judicial power to the commission. Grants of similar authority to administrative officers and bodies have not been found repugnant to the Constitution. . . .

With the increasing complexity of human activities many situations arise where governmental control can be secured only by the "board" or "commission" form of legislation. In such instances Congress declares the public policy, fixes the general principles that are to control, and charges an administrative body with the duty of ascertaining within particular fields from time to time the facts which bring into play the principles established by Congress. Though the action of the Commission in finding the facts and declaring them to be specific offenses of the character embraced within the general definition by Congress may be deemed to be quasi legislative, it is so only in the sense that it converts the actual legislation from a static into a dynamic condition. But the converter is not the electricity. And though the action of the commission in ordering desistance may be counted quasi judicial on account of its form, with respect to power it is not judicial, because a judicial determination is only that which is embodied in a judgment or decree of a court and enforceable by execution or other writ of the court.

In the second paragraph of the order petitioner is commanded to cease selling sugar below cost. We find in the statute no intent on the part of Congress, even if it has the power, to restrain an owner of property from selling it at any price that is acceptable to him or from giving it away. But manifestly in making such a sale or gift the owner may put forward representations and commit acts which have a capacity or a tendency to injure or to discredit competitors and to deceive purchasers as to the real character of the transaction. That paragraph should therefore be modified by adding to it "by means of or in connection with the representations prohibited in the first paragraph of this order, or similar representation."

Sufficient appears in this record and in the presentation of the case to warrant us in expressing the belief that petitioner's business standards were at least as high as those generally prevailing in the commercial world at the times in question, and that the action of the commission is to be taken rather as a general illustration of the better methods required for the future than a specific selection of petitioner for reproof on account of its conduct in the past.

Respondent is directed to modify its order as above stated; and in other respects the petition is denied.

It is obvious that in seeking to remedy problems which came about from practices which were destructive of competition, Congress had in Section 5 of the Clayton Act created new problems. What really were "unfair" methods of competition? In the final analysis, where did the power lie to answer that question, in the court or in the commission itself? In *FTC v. Gratz*,[19] the opinion indicated that the courts, not the commission, had the obligation of ultimately defining "unfair" methods of competition, and stated that those words would not apply "to practices never heretofore regarded as opposed to good morals . . . [or] characterized by deception, bad faith,

[19] 253 U.S. 421 (1920).

fraud, or oppression or [not previously regarded] as against public policy because of their dangerous tendency unduly to hinder competition or create monopoly. The act was certainly not intended to fetter free and fair competition as commonly understood and practiced by honorable opponents in trade." Here we see evidence of a tendency to resist too broad a policy-making and interpretative power in the commission, and to interpret unfair methods in terms of past precedent, rather than current problems and new ingenious devices of those who were unscrupulous. Thus, the earlier decisions appeared to interpret Section 5 a bit narrowly. However, later decisions were more liberal. In *FTC v. Bunte Bros.*,[20] the court stated that "unfair competition was designed by Congress as a flexible concept with evolving content. It touches the greatest variety of unrelated activities. . . ." The case which follows discusses the problem of defining "unfair methods of competition" at some length and contains some of the legislative history pertaining to the final choice by Congress of these words for the Federal Trade Commission Act.

FTC V. R. F. KEPPEL & BRO., INC.
291 U.S. 304 (1934)

After conducting a hearing, the Federal Trade Commission issued a cease and desist order forbidding certain practices engaged in by R. F. Keppel & Bro., Inc., in pursuing the business of manufacturing and distributing penny candy as unfair methods of competition under Section 5 of the Federal Trade Commission Act. On review, the Circuit Court of Appeals set aside the commission's order on the ground that the practices in question were not unfair methods of competition within the meaning of the statute. The FTC then sought and obtained a writ of certiorari from the Supreme Court to review the adverse decree of the Circuit Court of Appeals.

STONE, JUSTICE: . . . The Commission found that respondent, one of numerous candy manufacturers similarly engaged, manufactures, sells, and distributes, in interstate commerce, package assortments of candies known to the trade as "break and take" packages, in competition with manufacturers of assortments known as "straight goods" packages. Both types are assortments of candies in packages in convenient arrangement for sale by the piece at a small price in retail stores in what is known as the penny candy trade. The break and take assortments are so arranged and offered for sale to consumers as to avail of the element of chance as an inducement to the retail purchasers. One assortment, consisting of 120 pieces retailing at 1 cent each, includes four pieces, each having concealed within its wrapper a single cent, so that the purchasers of those particular pieces of candy

[20] 312 U.S. 349 (1941).

receive back the amount of the purchase price and thus obtain the candy without cost. Another contains 60 pieces of candy, each having its retail price marked on a slip of paper concealed within its wrapper; 10 pieces retail at 1 cent each, 10 at 2 cents, and 40 at 3 cents. The price paid for each piece is that named on the price ticket, ascertained only after the purchaser has selected the candy and the wrapper has been removed. A third assortment consists of 200 pieces of candy, a few of which have concealed centers of different colors, the remainder having white centers. The purchasers of the candy found to have colored centers are given prizes, packed with the candy, consisting of other pieces of candy or a package containing lead pencils, penholder and ruler. Each assortment is accompanied by a display card, attractive to children, prepared by respondent for exhibition and use by the dealer in selling the candy, explaining the plan by which either the price or the amount of candy or other merchandise which the purchaser receives is affected by chance. The pieces of candy in the break and take packages are either smaller than those of the competing straight goods packages, which are sold at a comparable price without the aid of any chance feature, or they are of inferior quality. Much of the candy assembled in the break and take packages is sold by retailers, located in the vicinity of schools, to school children.

The Commission found that the use of the break and take package in the retail trade involves the sale or distribution of the candy by lot or chance; that it is a lottery or gambling device which encourages gambling among children; that children, enticed by the element of chance, purchase candy so sold in preference to straight goods candy; and that the competition between the two types of package results in a substantial diversion of trade from the manufacturers of the straight goods package to those distributing the break and take type. It found further that in some states lotteries and gaming devices are penal offenses; that the sale or distribution of candy by lot or chance is against public policy; that many manufacturers of competing candies refuse to engage in the distribution of the break and take type of package because they regard it as a reprehensible encouragement of gambling among children; and that such manufacturers are placed at a disadvantage in competition. The evidence shows that others have reluctantly yielded to the practice in order to avoid loss of trade to their competitors.

The court below held as the respondent argues here, that respondent's practice does not hinder competition or injure its competitors, since they are free to resort to the same sales method; that the practice does not tend to create a monopoly or involve any deception to consumers or the public and hence is not an unfair method of competition within the meaning of the statute.

Upon the record it is not open to question that the practice complained of is a method of competition in interstate commerce and that it is successful in diverting trade from competitors who do not employ it. If the practice is unfair within the meaning of the act, it is equally clear that the present proceeding, aimed at suppressing it, is brought, as section 5 of the act requires, "in the interest of the public." The practice is carried on by forty or more manufacturers. The disposition of a large number of complaints pending before the Commission, similar to that in the present case, awaits the outcome of this suit. Sales of the break and take package by respondent aggregate about $234,000 per year. The proceeding involves more than a mere private controversy. A practice so generally adopted by manufacturers necessarily affects not only competing manufacturers but the far greater number of retailers to whom they sell, and the customers to whom the retailers sell. Thus the effects of the device are felt throughout the penny candy industry. A practice so widespread and so far reaching in its consequences is of public concern if in other respects within the purview of the statute. . . . Hence we pass without further discussion to the decisive question whether the practice itself is one over which the Commission is given jurisdiction because it is unfair.

Although the method of competition adopted by respondent induces children, too young to be capable of exercising an intelligent judgment of the transaction, to purchase an article less desirable in point of quality or quantity than that offered at a comparable price in the straight goods package, we may take it that it does not involve any fraud or deception. It would seem also that competing manufacturers can adopt the break and take device at any time and thus maintain their competitive position. From these premises respondent argues that the practice is beyond the reach of the Commission because it does not fall within any of the classes which this Court has held subject to the Commission's prohibition. . . . But we cannot say that the Commission's jurisdiction extends only to those types of practices which happen to have been litigated before this Court.

Neither the language nor the history of the act suggests that Congress intended to confine the forbidden methods to fixed and unyielding categories. The common law afforded a definition of unfair competition and, before the enactment of the Federal Trade Commission Act, the Sherman Anti-Trust Act (15 U.S.C.A. §§ 1–7, 15 note) had laid its inhibition upon combinations to restrain or monopolize interstate commerce which the courts had construed to include restraints upon competition in interstate commerce. It would not have been a difficult feat of draftsmanship to have restricted the operation of the Trade Commission Act to those methods of competition in interstate commerce which are forbidden at common law or which are likely to grow into violations of the Sherman Act, if that had been the purpose of the legislation.

The act undoubtedly was aimed at all the familiar methods of law violation which prosecutions under the Sherman Act had disclosed. . . . But, as this Court has pointed out it also had a broader purpose. . . .

As proposed by the Senate Committee on Interstate Commerce and as introduced in the Senate, the bill which ultimately became the Federal Trade Commission Act declared "unfair competition" to be unlawful. But it was because the meaning which the common law had given to those words was deemed too narrow that the broader and more flexible phrase "unfair methods of competition" was substituted. Congress, in defining the powers of the Commission, thus advisedly adopted a phrase which, as this Court has said, does not "admit of precise definition, but the meaning and application of which must be arrived at by what this court elsewhere has called the gradual process of judicial inclusion and exclusion."

The argument that a method used by one competitor is not unfair if others may adopt it without any restriction of competition between them was rejected by this Court. . . . A method of competition which casts upon one's competitors the burden of the loss of business unless they will descend to a practice which they are under a powerful moral compulsion not to adopt even though it is not criminal, was thought to involve the kind of unfairness at which the statute was aimed.

The practice in this case presents the same dilemma to competitors, and we can perceive no reason for distinguishing between the element of chance as employed here and the element of deception involved in labeling cotton goods, "Natural Wool," as in the Winsted Case. It is true that the statute does not authorize regulation which has no purpose other than that of relieving merchants from troublesome competition or of censoring the morals of business men. But here the competitive method is shown to exploit consumers, children, who are unable to protect themselves. It employs a device whereby the amount of the return they receive from the expenditure of money is made to depend upon chance. Such devices have met with condemnation throughout the community. Without inquiring whether, as respondent contends, the criminal statutes imposing penalties on gambling, lotteries and the like, fail to reach this particular practice in most or any of the states, it is clear that the practice is of the sort which the common law and criminal statutes have long deemed contrary to public policy. For these reasons a large share of the industry holds out against the device, despite ensuing loss in trade, or bows reluctantly to what it brands unscrupulous. It would seem a gross perversion of the normal meaning of the word, which is the first criterion of statutory construction, to hold that the method is not "unfair." . . .

While this Court has declared that it is for the courts to determine what practices or methods of competition are to be deemed unfair, *Federal Trade Commission v. Gratz, supra,* in passing on that question the determination of the Commission is of weight. It was created with the avowed purpose of lodging the administrative functions committed to it in "a body specially competent to deal with them by reason of information, experience and careful study of the business and economic conditions of the industry affected," and it was organized in such a manner, with respect to the length and expiration of the terms of office of its members, as would "give to them an opportunity to acquire the expertness in dealing with these special questions concerning industry that comes from experience." Report of Senate Committee on Interstate Commerce, No. 597, June 13, 1914, 63d Cong., 2d Sess., pp. 9, 11. . . . If the point were more doubtful than we think it, we should hesitate to reject the conclusion of the Commission, based as it is upon clear, specific and comprehensive findings supported by evidence.

We hold that the Commission correctly concluded that the practice was an unfair method of competition within the meaning of the statute. It is unnecessary to attempt a comprehensive definition of the unfair methods which are banned, even if it were possible to do so. We do not intimate either that the statute does not authorize the prohibition of other and hitherto unknown methods of competition or, on the other hand, that the Commission may prohibit every unethical competitive practice regardless of its particular character or consequences. New or different practices must be considered as they arise in the light of the circumstances in which they are employed. [REVERSED]

6   THE ROBINSON-PATMAN ACT

From 1914 to 1936, there was no major Federal legislation in the antitrust field,[21] but in that year Congress passed the landmark Robinson-Patman Act. Essentially this act replaced Section 2 of the original Clayton Act, dealing with price discrimination. The Robinson-Patman Act has often been referred to as the "Chain Store Act" because the larger chain stores were able to demand—and obtain—from their suppliers large discounts due to the larger quantities of goods they were able to purchase. In turn, the chain stores (particularly in the food industry) cut prices to their retail customers, seeking to drive out small competitors. Quantity discounts were permitted under the original Section 2. Basically the act was designed to ensure equality of treatment to all buyers by a seller, where the result of unequal treatment may be to substantially lessen competition or tend to create a monopoly in any line of commerce. Section 2 of the Clayton Act had not accomplished this end, partly due to the legality of quantity discounts under it, and partly because some buyers were able to obtain indirect benefits, which in the final analysis amounted to giving them a discount or com-

---

[21] The National Industrial Recovery Act of 1933 purported to empower the President to approve "codes of fair competition" for different industries. These codes could contain, among other things, exemptions from the operation of the antitrust laws for business activities which otherwise would be distructive of competition and prohibited. However, the Recovery Act was declared unconstitutional by the Supreme Court in 1935. See *Schechter Poultry Corp. v. United States*, 295 U.S. 495 (1935), in Chapter 4, page 104.

petitive advantage over other buyers from the same seller. The Clayton Act did not deal specifically with such matters. The Robinson-Patman Act made it a crime for a seller to sell at lower prices in one geographical area than elsewhere in the United States in order to eliminate competition or a competitor, or to sell at unreasonably low prices to drive out a competitor. In addition, the Federal Trade Commission was given jurisdiction and authority to eliminate quantity discounts and to forbid brokerage allowances, except to independent brokers. The statute also prohibited promotional allowances, except on an equal basis. A summary of the provisions of Section 2 follows below:

Section 2(a) [22] provides that it shall be unlawful for any person to discriminate in price between different purchasers of commodities of like grade and quality, where any of the purchases involved in such discrimination are in commerce, where such commodities are sold for use or resale within the United States, and where the effect of such discrimination may be substantially to lessen competition or tend to create a monopoly in any line of commerce, or to injure competition with any person who either grants or knowingly receives a benefit of such discrimination, or with customers of either of them. The statute then makes certain exceptions: (1) Price differentials based on differences in the cost of manufacture, sale, or delivery of commodities are permitted, except that the Federal Trade Commission may fix and establish quantity limits as to particular commodities where it finds so few purchasers as to render differentials on account of quantity unjustly discriminatory or promotive of monopoly; (2) persons engaged in selling goods, wares, or merchandise in commerce may select their own customers in bona fide transactions and not in restraint of trade; and (3) price changes may be made in response to changing conditions such as actual or imminent deterioration of perishable goods, obsolescence of seasonal goods, distress sales under court process, or sales in good faith in discontinuance of business in the goods concerned.

Section 2(b) places the burden of showing justification upon the person charged with a violation of this section once there has been proof of discrimination in price; and, unless justification is affirmatively shown, the Commission is authorized to issue an order terminating the discrimination. A seller is permitted to justify a discrimination by showing that his lower price of services or facilities to any purchaser was made in good faith to meet an equally low price of a competitor.

Parts (c), (d), and (e) of Section 2 prohibit various indirect price discriminations by making it unlawful to pay or receive a commission or discount on sales or purchases, except for actual services rendered; to pay a customer for any services or facilities he furnishes in connection with a transaction, unless such payment is available to all customers on equal terms; and to favor one purchaser of a commodity over another by furnish-

[22] 38 Stat. 730 (1914), 49 Stat. 1526 (1936), 15 U.S.C. § 13 (1964).

ing him services or facilities in connection with a sale which are not available to all purchasers on equal terms.

The following case illustrates an application of Section 2 of the Clayton Act, as amended by the Robinson-Patman Act. It raises the questions
of whether a company is guilty of price discrimination under the Act if it
grants its customers discounts which vary with the amount of its product
purchased, and whether it must be proved that policies *actually injure* competition before a violation of the Act is established.

FTC V. MORTON SALT CO.
334 U.S. 37 (1948)

BLACK, JUSTICE: The Federal Trade Commission, after a hearing, found that
the respondent, which manufactures and sells table salt in interstate commerce, had discriminated in price between different purchasers of like grades
and qualities, and concluded that such discriminations were in violation of
§ 2 of the Clayton Act, 38 Stat. 730, as amended by the Robinson-Patman
Act, 49 Stat. 1526, 15 U.S.C. § 13, 15 U.S.C.A. § 13. It accordingly issued
a cease and desist order. 39 F.T.C. 35. Upon petition of the respondent the
Circuit Court of Appeals, with one judge dissenting, set aside the Commission's findings and order, directed the Commission to dismiss its complaint
against respondent, and denied a cross petition of the Commission for enforcement of its order. 7 Cir., 162 F.2d 949. . . .

Respondent manufactures several different brands of table salt and
sells them directly to (1) wholesalers or jobbers, who in turn resell to the
retail trade, and (2) large retailers, including chain store retailers. Respondent sells its finest brand of table salt, known as Blue Label, on what it
terms a standard quantity discount system available to all customers. Under
this system the purchasers pay a delivered price and the cost to both wholesale and retail purchasers of this brand differs according to the quantities
bought. These prices are as follows, after making allowance for rebates and
discounts:

	PER CASE
Less-than-carload purchases	$1.60
Carload purchases	1.50
5,000-case purchases in any consecutive 12 months	1.40
50,000-case purchases in any consecutive 12 months	1.35

Only five companies have ever bought sufficient quantities of respondent's
salt to obtain the $1.35 per case price. These companies could buy in such
quantities because they operate large chains of retail stores in various parts
of the country. As a result of this low price these five companies have been

able to sell Blue Label salt at retail cheaper than wholesale purchasers from respondent could reasonably sell the same brand of salt to independently operated retail stores, many of whom competed with the local outlets of the five chain stores. . . .

First. Respondent's basic contention, which it argues this case hinges upon, is that its "standard quantity discounts, available to all on equal terms, as contrasted for example, to hidden or special rebates, allowances, prices or discounts, are not discriminatory, within the meaning of the Robinson-Patman Act." Theoretically, these discounts are equally available to all, but functionally they are not. For as the record indicates (if reference to it on this point were necessary) no single independent retail grocery store, and probably no single wholesaler, bought as many as 50,000 cases or as much as $50,000 worth of table salt in one year. Furthermore, the record shows that, while certain purchasers were enjoying one or more of respondent's standard quantity discounts, some of their competitors made purchases in such small quantities that they could not qualify for any of respondent's discounts, even those based on carload shipments. The legislative history of the Robinson-Patman Act makes it abundantly clear that Congress considered it to be an evil that a large buyer could secure a competitive advantage over a small buyer solely because of the large buyer's quantity purchasing ability. The Robinson-Patman Act was passed to deprive a large buyer of such advantages except to the extent that a lower price could be justified by reason of a seller's diminished costs due to quantity manufacture, delivery or sale, or by reason of the seller's good faith effort to meet a competitor's equally low price.

Section 2 of the original Clayton Act had included a proviso that nothing contained in it should prevent "discrimination in price . . . on account of differences in the grade, quality, or quantity of the commodity sold, or that makes only due allowance for difference in the cost of selling or transportation. . . ." That section has been construed as permitting quantity discounts, such as those here, without regard to the amount of the seller's actual savings in cost attributable to quantity sales or quantity deliveries. . . . The House Committee Report on the Robinson-Patman Act considered that the Clayton Act's proviso allowing quantity discounts so weakened § 2 "as to render it inadequate, if not almost a nullity." The Committee considered the present Robinson-Patman amendment to § 2 "of great importance." Its purpose was to limit "the use of quantity price differentials to the sphere of actual cost differences. Otherwise," the report continued, "such differentials would become instruments of favor and privilege and weapons of competitive oppression." The Senate Committee reporting the bill emphasized the same purpose, as did the Congressman in charge of the Conference Report when explaining it to the House just before final passage. And it was in furtherance of this avowed purpose—to protect competition from all price differentials except those based in full on cost savings—that § 2(a) of the amendment provided "That nothing herein contained shall prevent differentials which make only due allowance for differences in the cost of manufacture, sale, or delivery resulting from the differing methods or quantities in which such commodities are to such purchasers sold or delivered."

The foregoing references, without regard to others which could be mentioned, establish that respondent's standard quantity discounts are discriminatory within the meaning of the Act, and are prohibited by it whenever they have the defined effect on competition. . . .

Second. The Government interprets the opinion of the Circuit Court of Appeals as having held that in order to establish "discrimination in price" under the Act the burden rested on the Commission to prove that respondent's quantity discount differentials were not justified by its cost savings. Respondent does not so understand the Court of Appeals decision, and furthermore admits that no such burden rests on the Commission. We agree that it does not. First, the general rule of statutory construction that the burden of proving justification or exemption under a special exception to the prohibitions of a statute generally rests on one who claims its benefits, requires that respondent undertake this proof under the proviso of § 2(a). Secondly, § 2(b) of the Act specifically imposes the burden of showing justification upon one who is shown to have discriminated in prices. . . .

Third. It is argued that the findings fail to show that respondent's discriminatory discounts had in fact caused injury to competition. There are specific findings that such injuries had resulted from respondent's discounts although the statute does not require the Commission to find that injury has actually resulted. The statute requires no more than that the effect of the prohibited price discriminations "may be substantially to lessen competition . . . or to injure, destroy, or prevent competition." After a careful consideration of this provision of the Robinson-Patman Act, we have said that "the statute does not require that the discriminations must in fact have harmed competition, but only that there is a reasonable possibility that they 'may' have such an effect." . . . Here the Commission found what would appear to be obvious, that the competitive opportunities of certain merchants were injured when they had to pay respondent substantially more for their goods than their competitors had to pay. The findings are adequate. . . .

The adequacy of the evidence to support the Commission's findings of reasonably possible injury to competition from respondent's price differentials between competing carload and less-than-carload purchasers is singled out for special attacks here. It is suggested that in considering the adequacy of the evidence to show injury to competition respondent's carload discounts and its other quantity discounts should not be treated alike. The argument is that there is an obvious saving to a seller who delivers goods in carload lots. Assuming this to be true, that fact would not tend to disprove injury to the merchant compelled to pay the less-than-carload price.

For a ten-cent carload price differential against a merchant would injure him competitively just as much as a ten-cent differential under any other name. However relevant the separate carload argument might be to the question of justifying a differential by cost savings, it has no relevancy in determining whether the differential works an injury to a competitor. Since Congress has not seen fit to give carload discounts any favored classification we cannot do so. Such discounts, like all others, can be justified by a seller who proves that the full amount of the discount is based on his actual savings in cost. The trouble with this phase of respondent's case is that it has thus far failed to make such proof.

It is also argued that respondent's less-than-carload sales are very small in comparison with the total volume of its business and for that reason we should reject the Commission's finding that the effect of the carload discrimination may substantially lessen competition and may injure competition between purchasers who are granted and those who are denied this discriminatory discount. To support this argument, reference is made to the fact that salt is a small item in most wholesale and retail businesses and in consumers' budgets. For several reasons we cannot accept this contention.

There are many articles in a grocery store that, considered separately, are comparatively small parts of a merchant's stock. Congress intended to protect a merchant from competitive injury attributable to discriminatory prices on any or all goods sold in interstate commerce, whether the particular goods constituted a major or minor portion of his stock. Since a grocery store consists of many comparatively small articles, there is no possible way effectively to protect a grocer from discriminatory prices except by applying the prohibitions of the Act to each individual article in the store.

Furthermore, in enacting the Robinson-Patman Act Congress was especially concerned with protecting small businesses which were unable to buy in quantities, such as the merchants here who purchased in less-than-carload lots. To this end it undertook to strengthen this very phase of the old Clayton Act. The committee reports on the Robinson-Patman Act emphasized a belief that § 2 of the Clayton Act had "been too restrictive in requiring a showing of general injury to competitive conditions. . . ." The new provision, here controlling, was intended to justify a finding of injury to competition by a showing of "injury to the competitor victimized by the discrimination." Since there was evidence sufficient to show that the less-than-carload purchasers might have been handicapped in competing with the more favored carload purchasers by the differential in price established by respondent, the Commission was justified in finding that competition might have thereby been substantially lessened or have been injured within the meaning of the Act. . . .

The judgment of the Circuit Court of Appeals is reversed and the proceedings are remanded to that court to be disposed of in conformity with this opinion. [REVERSED]

On its face, the Robinson-Patman Act purports to have the objective of preserving competition. However, in fact, it represents a withdrawal from that policy. As the *Morton Salt* case illustrates, the Act does not allow a supplier to encourage those who are able to buy his product in very large quantities by giving them price concessions or discounts. The net result is to partially remove the small, individual business from the forces of competition. Insulating such businesses from competition and preserving them may have the effect of rewarding less efficient operations and keeping prices artificially high for the consumer. Thus the objectives of the legislation in the antitrust area are to some extent contradictory. Some of the acts have the purpose of preserving competition. The Robinson-Patman Act has at least as one of its purposes the preservation of small *competitors* at the cost of competition. Fair trade legislation, which is discussed in the following section, has the purpose of removing a manufacturer's brand or trade name products from price competition at the retail level, even though this may be detrimental to the consumer insofar as price is concerned.

7   FAIR TRADE LEGISLATION

In 1937, Congress passed the Miller-Tydings Act [23] which amended Section 1 of the Sherman Act to permit fair trade pricing of certain articles for retail sale and represented a retrenching of the effective application of the Sherman Act and the national policy favoring competition. By the Act, language was added to Section 1 of the Sherman Act to the effect that "nothing herein contained shall render illegal contracts or agreements prescribing minimum prices for the resale" of certain commodities when "contracts or agreements of that description are lawful as applied to intrastate transactions" under local law. In other words, in any state which had passed the requisite enabling fair trade statute, a manufacturer of a brand or trade name product was permitted to enter into a contract with a retailer whereby the retailer agreed to sell that product at no less than the minimum prices specified, without having the agreement constitute a violation of the Sherman Act. If the state in question had no fair trade legislation, any such contract would be unenforceable and would amount to a violation of the Act, as a contract, combination, or conspiracy in restraint of trade. The purpose of such legislation was to permit the states to allow the manufacturer of a brand or trade name product to protect that brand name and the aura of quality carried with it by a higher price. Human psychology being what it is, if the item in question were sold at a cut-rate price in a discount store, presumably the intrinsic worth of the product would also diminish, at least in the mind's eye of the consumer. In *Schwegmann Bros. v. Calvert Distillers*

---

[23] 50 Stat. 693 (1937), 15 U.S.C. § 1 (1964).

Corp.[24] the Supreme Court inquired into the legality of the Louisiana fair trade legislation, which not only permitted a manufacturer to contract to set minimum retail prices for the manufacturer's product, but also made it unfair competition for *anyone* to sell at less than the price agreed, even though the seller was not a party to the contract which fixed the resale price. That is, the contract setting minimum retail prices was made enforceable both against parties to the contract and against nonsigners. In the case in question, Calvert and Seagram each brought suit against Schwegmann Brothers, to prevent the defendants from continuing to sell their products at cut-rate prices. Calvert and Seagram had executed price fixing contracts with over 100 retailers in Louisiana under which the buyers (retailers) promised not to sell at less than prices stated in the plaintiffs' schedules. However, Schwegmann Brothers was not a party to such a contract, so that the plaintiffs were attempting to invoke the nonsigner provisions of the Louisiana statute. The Supreme Court held that if the distributor and retailer want to agree, combine, or conspire to set minimum prices, they can under the Miller-Tydings Act, where the state law permits. However, the court pointed out that under a literal interpretation of the Louisiana statute, if just one retailer signed, all others in the state would be compelled to abide by his contract to observe minimum resale prices under the nonsigner provision. The court, in refusing the injunction, held that the noncontracting group were to be governed by the preexisting law (i.e., the Sherman Act Section 1 forbidding contracts in restraint of trade) and ruled that the Louisiana statute was invalid to the extent of the nonsigner provision it contained.

In 1952, the year following the handing down of the *Schwegmann* case, Congress responded by enacting the McGuire Fair Trade Act [25] which amended subsection (a) of Section 5 of the Federal Trade Commission Act [26] to permit fair trade pricing of articles for retail sale in those states with fair trade laws, without having the same constitute a violation of *any* of the antitrust laws. Pursuant to the McGuire Act, the State of Ohio enacted a fair trade law which was very similar to the Louisiana statute involved in the *Schwegmann* case discussed above, and which was brought into issue in the case which follows.

HUDSON DISTRIBUTORS, INC. V. UPJOHN CO.
377 U.S. 386 (1964)

GOLDBERG, JUSTICE: These appeals raise the question of whether the McGuire Act . . . permits the application and enforcement of the Ohio Fair Trade Act·against appellant in support of appellees' system of retail price main-

[24] 341 U.S. 384 (1951).
[25] 66 Stat. 632 (1952), 15 U.S.C. 45 (a) (1)-(5) (1964).
[26] Section 5 prohibits unfair methods of competition, acts and practices.

tenance. For the reasons stated below, we hold that the Ohio Act, as applied to the facts of these cases, comes within the provisions of the McGuire Act exempting certain resale price systems from the prohibitions of the Sherman Act. . . .

The two appeals, one involving The Upjohn Co., and one involving Eli Lilly & Co., were considered together in the Ohio courts. For simplicity we state only the facts of the Lilly case. Appellant, Hudson Distributors, Inc., owns and operates a retail drug chain in Cleveland, Ohio. Appellee, Eli Lilly & Co., manufactures pharmaceutical products bearing its trademarks and trade names. Lilly sells its products directly to wholesalers and makes no sales to retailers. Hudson purchases Lilly brand products from Regal D.S., Inc., a Michigan wholesaler.

In June 1959, the Ohio Legislature enacted a new Fair Trade Act. . . . Subsequently Lilly sent letters to all Ohio retailers of Lilly products, including Hudson, to notify them of Lilly's intention to establish minimum retail resale prices for its trademarked products pursuant to the new Ohio Act and to invite the retailers to enter into written fair-trade contracts. More than 1,400 Ohio retailers of Lilly products (about 65% of all the retail pharmacists in Ohio) signed fair-trade contracts with Lilly. Hudson, however, refused to enter into a written contract with Lilly and ignored the specified minimum resale prices. Lilly formally notified Hudson that the Ohio Act required Hudson to observe the minimum retail resale prices for Lilly commodities. Hudson, nevertheless, continued to purchase and then to resell Lilly products at less than the stipulated minimum retail resale prices.

Hudson thereupon filed a petition in the Court of Common Pleas for Cuyahoga County, Ohio, for a judgment declaring the Ohio Act invalid under the State Constitution and federal law. Lilly answered and cross-petitioned for enforcement of the Ohio Act against Hudson. The Court of Common Pleas held the Ohio Act unconstitutional under the State Constitution. On appeal, the Court of Appeals for Cuyahoga County, after discussing the federal and state legislation . . . reversed the trial court and entered a judgment declaring that the Ohio Act was "neither in violation of the Constitution of the State of Ohio nor of the Constitution of the United States. . . ." On further appeal, the Supreme Court of Ohio affirmed the judgment of the Court of Appeals. . . .

This Court noted probable jurisdiction. . . .

Hudson contends that the provisions of the Ohio Act under which Lilly established minimum resale prices are not authorized by the McGuire Act. . . . Section 2 of the McGuire Act provides in pertinent part as follows:

Nothing contained in this section or in any of the Antitrust Acts shall render unlawful any contracts or agreements prescribing minimum or stipulated prices. . . . When contracts or agreements of that description are lawful as applied to intrastate transactions under any statute, law, or public policy now or hereafter in effect in any State. . . .

Section 3 of the McGuire Act reads as follows:

Nothing contained in this section or in any of the Antitrust Acts shall render unlawful the exercise or the enforcement of any right or right of action created by any statute, law, or public policy now or hereafter in effect in any State, Territory, or the District of Columbia, which in substance provides that willfully and knowingly advertising, offering for sale, or selling any commodity at less than the price or prices prescribed in such contracts or agreements whether the person so advertising, offering for sale, or selling is or is not a party to such a contract or agreement, is unfair competition and is actionable at the suit of any person damaged thereby.

. . . The Report of the House Committee on Interstate and Foreign Commerce, which accompanied the McGuire Act, declared that:

The primary purpose of the [McGuire] bill is to reaffirm the very same proposition which, in the committee's opinion, the Congress intended to enact into law when it passed the Miller-Tydings Act . . . , to the effect that the application and enforcement of State fair-trade laws—including the nonsigner provisions of such laws—with regard to interstate transactions shall not constitute a violation of the Federal Trade Commission Act or the Sherman Antitrust Act. This reaffirmation is made necessary because of the decision of a divided Supreme Court in Schwegmann Bros. v. Calvert Distillers Corp. *. . .*

This authoritative report evinces the clear intention of Congress that, where sanctioned by a state fair-trade act, a trademark owner such as Lilly could be permitted to enforce, even against a nonsigning retailer such as Hudson, the stipulated minimum prices established by written contracts with other retailers. . . .

The price fixing authorized by the Ohio Fair Trade Act and involving goods moving in interstate commerce would be, absent approval by Congress, clearly illegal under the Sherman Act. . . . "Fixing minimum prices, like other types of price fixing, is illegal per se." *Schwegmann Bros. v. Calvert Distillers Corp., supra.* . . . Congress, however, in the McGuire Act has approved state statutes sanctioning resale price maintenance schemes such as those involved here. Whether it is good policy to permit such laws is a matter for Congress to decide. Where the statutory language and the legislative history clearly indicate the purpose of Congress that purpose must be upheld. We therefore, affirm the judgments of the Supreme Court of Ohio. [AFFIRMED]

8   THE CELLER–KEFAUVER ACT

Just prior to the McGuire Act, in 1950 Congress enacted the Celler-Kefauver Act.[27] This Act amends Section 7 of the Clayton Act so that now Section 7 prohibits the acquisition, by a corporation engaged in commerce, of the stock *or assets* of other such corporations, where the effect may be to lessen competition substantially or tend to create a monopoly *in any line of commerce* in any section of the country. In spite of the original provisions against certain acquisitions of stock in the Clayton Act, Section 7, corporate mergers were on the increase. The Celler-Kefauver Act was motivated by Congress' concern about this and the effect such mergers were having on the competitive situation in many industries and geographical areas. It therefore significantly broadened the scope of Section 7. First of all, the amendment plugged a loophole in that the original Section 7 only prohibited certain acquisitions of *stock* by one corporation of another. Technically, the same end could be accomplished and was permitted under it through an acquisition of *assets*. Therefore, this was also prohibited. Secondly, the original statute prohibited acquisitions "where the effect . . . may be to substantially lessen competition *between the corporation whose stock is so acquired and the corporation making the acquisition, or to restrain such commerce in any section or community.*" [EMPHASIS ADDED] This language led to a somewhat restrictive interpretation of the types of acquisitions which were outlawed. The amendment broadens the prohibition by outlawing acquisitions where the effect may be to lessen competition substantially *in any line of commerce* in any section of the country.

The application of Section 7 of the Clayton Act, as amended by the Celler-Kefauver Act, is discussed and illustrated in Chapter 12 on corporate mergers and acquisitions.

9   STATE REGULATION OF COMPETITION

Most attempts by states to control competition have not had the same impact on business as the Federal regulation. As noted previously, among the reasons for the relative insignificance of the state activity in this area are the interstate nature of many businesses where threat to competition is involved, inadequate enforcement facilities at the state level, and the fact that the Federal government has already dealt with the problem, to a large extent.

However, many states do have legislation which regulates competition to a lesser or greater degree with a lesser or greater degree of effectiveness. Some may only prohibit sales below cost to prevent the use of "loss leaders" to woo customers away from competitors. Others may just prohibit price

---

[27] 64 Stat. 1125 (1950), 15 U.S.C. § 18 (1964).

fixing and restriction of production. Still others may have a fairly comprehensive scheme of regulating competition modeled in part on the Federal laws. The businessman should become familiar with the antitrust laws of the states in which he conducts his operations so that he will seek legal counsel before implementing his plans, when a particular course of action under consideration might involve a violation.

In those states which have adopted the Uniform Deceptive Trade Practices Act, certain activities by business are prohibited as being "deceptive." This is one of the most recent acts drafted and proposed by the National Conference of Commissioners on Uniform State Laws. It has not enjoyed general acceptance to date, having been adopted by only five states, as of this writing.[28] The Uniform Deceptive Trade Practices Act provides that a person who shows he is *likely* to be damaged by certain activities may obtain an injunction, but neither grants money damages to persons injured by violations of its provisions nor imposes criminal penalties. Proof of actual money damage, loss of profits, or intent to deceive is not necessary. Section 2 of the Act states that:

A person engages in a deceptive trade practice when, in the course of his business, vocation or occupation, he:

(1) *passes off goods or services as those of another;*

(2) *causes likelihood of confusion or of misunderstanding as to the source, sponsorship, approval or certification of goods or services;*

(3) *causes likelihood of confusion or of misunderstanding as to affiliation, connection or association with or certification by another;*

(4) *uses deceptive representations or designations of geographic origin in connection with goods or services;*

(5) *represents that goods or services have sponsorship, approval, characteristics, ingredients, uses, benefits or quantities that they do not have or that a person has a sponsorship, approval, status, affiliation or connection that he does not have;*

(6) *represents that goods are original or new if they are deteriorated, altered, reconditioned, reclaimed, used or secondhand;*

(7) *represents that goods or services are a particular standard, quality or grade or that goods are a particular style or model, if they are of another;*

(8) *disparages the goods, services or business of another by false or misleading representation of fact;*

(9) *advertises goods or services with intent not to sell them as advertised;*

(10) *advertises goods or services with intent not to supply reasonably*

---

[28] These are Connecticut, Delaware, Idaho, Illinois, and Oklahoma. A revised act was approved in 1966 by both the National Conference of Commissioners on Uniform Laws and the American Bar Association. The 1966 act was introduced in at least nine other states in their 1967 legislative sessions.

expectable public demand, unless the advertisement discloses a limitation of quantity;

(11) *makes false or misleading statements of fact concerning the reasons for, existence of or amounts of price reductions;*

(12) *engages in any other conduct which similarly creates a likelihood of confusion or of misunderstanding.*

In order to prevail in an action under this Act, a complainant need not prove competition between the parties or actual confusion or misunderstanding.

This Section does not affect unfair trade practices otherwise actionable at common law or under other statutes of this State.

10   CONCLUSION

In this chapter, we have seen how the Federal government responded to a need it saw in the economy and launched a policy generally favoring competition and opposed to monopoly by passing the Sherman Act. As inadequacies appeared in that act, as business shifted its practices and the economy changed, other legislation was needed and passed to effectuate the aforesaid policy. The process might be viewed as a constant struggle or sparring match between business on the one hand, striving for growth, profits, and competitive advantage (utilizing openings afforded by the law even though destructive of competition) and the Federal government on the other hand, trying to defend by shifting its attack with the use of new statutes and enforcement policies, as holes in its prior schemes were found by business. Obviously, the preceding is an oversimplification. There are many complex forces in the economy which affect its degree of competitiveness in any given segment. And, to reemphasize what has already been noted in Section 1, many contradictions exist between the *practice* of government and its *general policy* favoring competition. The face of the sparring partner cannot always be clearly seen. At any rate, the match is far from over.

The two chapters which follow deal with the current application to business activity of the laws discussed in this chapter. Instead of a piecemeal consideration of the separate provisions of each of the antitrust laws, their application is discussed in terms of particular business functions or activities such as pricing policies, growth by merger, and the like. In this manner, it is hoped that the reader will obtain a clearer idea of the main restrictions the antitrust laws place upon the initiation and pursuit of various business policies by himself as well as his competitors.

LEGAL ASPECTS OF
MERGERS AND ACQUISITIONS

1 INTRODUCTION

Obviously it is possible, in spite of our antitrust laws, for a business to become large or to accumulate a substantial amount of economic power. Many American businesses have billions of dollars worth of assets and commensurate annual income. There are, however, restraints on the methods by which business may achieve such economic power. Internal growth is generally regarded as a proper means of expanding total resources and income, but growth by means of acquisition of other companies or by merger may be suspect. In this chapter we are concerned with the legal constraints on expansion by merger or acquisition of other business organizations. In this context, a merger may be accomplished in a number of ways. For example, two (or more) businesses may agree to join together and lose their identity completely by forming an entirely new enterprise, issuing its shares to former owners of the dissolved businesses. Or one business may acquire sufficient share capital in another to effectively control it by electing its board of directors, who will determine its policies. In such a case, the business entities technically have the same separate existence as before, but actual operations may be altered. Sometimes one business simply purchases all the *assets* of another, leaving only one legal entity in existence. Under the last two methods, the stock or assets acquired may be paid for in cash, by some other asset, or very likely, by the capital stock of the acquiring enterprise.

Mergers may be horizontal, vertical, or conglomerate in nature, or some combination of these.

A horizontal merger combines two businesses which formerly competed with each other in a particular line of commerce, leading to greater concentration in that industry. A vertical merger brings together a company which is the *customer* of the other in one of the lines of commerce in which the other is a supplier. Clearly, such a combination ordinarily removes the merged customer from the market as far as other suppliers are concerned. A conglomerate merger is one in which the businesses involved neither compete nor are related as customer and supplier in any given line of commerce. It may have as its purpose the bringing together of several enterprises under a top management which is more trained, able, experienced, and efficient than such businesses could offer if they were operated separately. Diversification may be the objective of a conglomerate merger. Another benefit might be that each enterprise has the capital backing—and power, if needed—of the whole. Sometimes the reduction of corporate income taxes is the motivation underlying a conglomerate merger. A failing business may be acquired by a healthy one in order to write off the losses of the former against the net income of the latter. Income derived from the sale of a long-term investment in a subsidiary may qualify for capital gains treatment.

Any of these types of mergers, however accomplished, can amount to a violation of the Sherman Act as a combination in unreasonable restraint of trade or a monopolization, or attempted monopolization. However, mergers are more apt to run afoul of the amended Section 7 of the Clayton Act which provides essentially, that no corporation engaged in commerce shall acquire any of the stock or assets of another such corporation if the effect may be to substantially lessen competition or to tend to create a monopoly in any line of commerce in any section of the country. The Sherman Act required a finding of actual anticompetitive effects before a violation could be demonstrated. As previously noted, the limited application of the Sherman Act and its resultant incapability to curtail practices which were deemed likely to adversely affect competition, or monopoly in its incipiency, were the main reasons underlying the passage of the Clayton Act. Section 7 of the Clayton Act only requires a finding and conclusion that a given acquisition have a reasonable *probability* of lessening competition or *tendency* toward monopoly. This chapter is limited to a discussion of the legality of mergers under Section 7 of the Clayton Act. Since that section is so much broader than the Sherman Act in its application, it is difficult to conceive of a merger which would violate the Sherman Act without also violating Section 7. As a practical matter, since the burden of proof required to demonstrate a violation of Section 7 is considerably less, it is and will be employed by the Justice Department and FTC when the legality of a merger is challenged, rather than the Sherman Act.

The legal guidelines for determining when a particular combination will or will not be permissible under Section 7 are not clearly drawn, but are unfolding to reveal new mysteries almost constantly. Perhaps definitive guidelines never will be pronounced. Adding to the uncertainty is the nature of the facts which must be established—the relevant product and geographic market which is affected, and the probable *future* detrimental effects the merger in question *will* have on that market, if any. Both determinations must be made on a case-by-case basis. The latter almost requires the use of a crystal ball. The dynamics of the economy as a whole further complicate the issue. We are, therefore, in an area where there are a multitude of unknowns; some exist regarding the law and many regarding each individual case. While the law relating to mergers is far from complete, past cases do serve to warn business when it is treading on dangerous ground and inviting interference by the government. Mr. Frederick M. Rowe, a member of the District of Columbia Bar and an authority on antitrust law, notes the following "peril points" in mergers: [1]

(1) *When an acquisition of a substantial competitor in the same business is made by one of the top-ranking firms, or results in a combination which achieves on the order of 15 per cent of an identifiable market—particularly in a static industry where new entry is rare.*

(2) *When a combination joins a leading customer and a leading supplier so that other suppliers are permanently foreclosed from a substantial market, or other customers are left without an independent source of supply.*

(3) *When the acquiring or the acquired company is the leading factor in its industry, and the other company is among the leaders in a different field.*

(4) *When the acquisition sharply disrupts the pattern of pre-existing competition in the market where the acquired company operates.*

Vulnerability to attack rises with such atmospheric considerations as:

(5) *the acquiring company's history of growth by acquisitions;*

(6) *the pendency of other merger cases in the same industry;*

(7) *the interest of a congressional committee in the troubles of smaller industry members;*

(8) *the presence of a special angle with legal sex appeal inviting a test case.*

Concerning the above "peril points," Mr. Rowe goes on to note: "Needless to say, there is no certainty of suit if any of these conditions are met; conversely, there is no guarantee of safety for mergers falling below the line. Nor are these factors earmarks of illegality. They are merely symptoms which, based on experience, warrant caution—pending further interpretations by court decisions in the future."

2   THE ORIGINAL SECTION 7 OF THE CLAYTON ACT

The case which follows is one of the landmark decisions involving Section 7 of the Clayton Act. Note that the government brought suit in 1949. Thus, the decision was rendered on the basis of the Act as it existed prior to the broadening 1950 amendment. Also note that the government's action was commenced thirty years after the acquisitions in question occurred. This was due at least in part to the fact that almost all authorities, including the

[1] Rowe, Mergers and the Law: New Directions for the Sixties, 47 *A.B.A.J.* 1074, 1076 (Nov., 1961). Used by permission from the American Bar Association and the *American Bar Association Journal*.

FTC, had held the view that the original Section 7 was applicable only to horizontal mergers. In addition the case is significant in that it illustrates these principles: that an acquisition of stock or assets may be perfectly legal at the time, but later may become illegal because it "threatens to ripen into a prohibited effect;" and that proof of a wrongful intent is not required to demonstrate a Section 7 violation.

UNITED STATES V. E. I. DU PONT DE NEMOURS & CO.
353 U.S. 586 (1957)

Du Pont acquired 23% of the stock of General Motors in 1917 to 1919. Subsequently, in 1949, the government brought action charging that this acquisition violated Section 7 of the Clayton Act. The District Court dismissed the action and the government appealed. One of the arguments of du Pont was that Section 7 did not apply, since this was a vertical, not horizontal, combination; that is, du Pont and General Motors were not in competition with each other.

BRENNAN, JUSTICE: The primary issue is whether du Pont's commanding position as General Motors' supplier of automotive finishes and fabrics was achieved on competitive merit alone, or because its acquisition of General Motors' stock, and the consequent close intercompany relationship, led to the insulation of most of the General Motors' market from free competition, with the resultant likelihood, at the time of suit, of the creation of a monopoly of a line of commerce. . . .

Section 7 is designed to arrest in its incipiency not only the substantial lessening of competition from the acquisition by one corporation of the whole or any part of the stock of a competing corporation, but also to arrest in their incipiency restraints or monopolies in a relevant market which, as a reasonable probability, appear at the time of suit likely to result from the acquisition by one corporation of all or any part of the stock of any other corporation. The section is violated whether or not actual restraints or monopolies, or the substantial lessening of competition, have occurred or are intended. Acquisitions solely for investment are excepted, but only if, and so long as, the stock is not used by voting or otherwise to bring about, the substantial lessening of competition.

We are met at the threshold with the argument that § 7, before its amendment in 1950, applied only to an acquisition of the stock of a competing corporation, and not to an acquisition by a supplier corporation of the stock of a customer corporation—in other words, that the statute applied only to horizontal and not to vertical acquisitions. . . .

The first paragraph of § 7, written in the disjunctive, plainly is framed to reach not only the corporate acquisition of stock of a competing corporation, where the effect may be substantially to lessen competition between them, but also the corporate acquisition of stock of any corporation, competitor or not, where the effect may be either (1) to restrain commerce in any section or community, or (2) tend to create a monopoly of any line of commerce. The amended complaint does not allege that the effect of du Pont's acquisition may be to restrain commerce in any section or community but alleges that the effect was ". . . to tend to create a monopoly in particular lines of commerce. . . ."

Appellees argue that there exists no basis for a finding of a probable restraint or monopoly within the meaning of § 7 because the total General Motors market for finishes and fabrics constituted only a negligible percentage of the total market for these materials for all uses, including automotive uses. It is stated in the General Motors brief that in 1947 du Pont's finish sales to General Motors constituted 3.5% of all sales of finishes to industrial users, and that its fabrics sales to General Motors comprised 1.6% of the total market for the type of fabric used by the automobile industry.

Determination of the relevant market is a necessary predicate to a finding of a violation of the Clayton Act because the threatened monopoly must be one which will substantially lessen competition "within the area of effective competition." Substantiality can be determined only in terms of the market affected. The record shows that automotive finishes and fabrics have sufficient peculiar characteristics and uses to constitute them products sufficiently distinct from all other finishes and fabrics to make them a "line of commerce" within the meaning of the Clayton Act. . . . Thus, the bounds of the relevant market for the purpose of this case are not coextensive with the total market for finishes and fabrics, but are coextensive with the automobile industry, the relevant market for automotive finishes and fabrics.

The market affected must be substantial. . . . Moreover, in order to establish a violation of § 7 the Government must prove a likelihood that competition may be "foreclosed in a substantial share of . . . [that market]." Both requirements are satisfied in this case. The substantiality of a relevant market comprising the automobile industry is undisputed. The substantiality of General Motors' share of that market is fully established in the evidence.

General Motors is the colossus of the giant automobile industry. It accounts annually for upwards of two fifths of the total sales of automotive vehicles in the nation.

In 1955 General Motors ranked first in sales and second in assets among all United States industrial corporations and became the first corporation to earn over a billion dollars in annual net income. In 1947 General Motors' total purchases of all products from du Pont were $26,628,274, of which $18,938,229 (71%) represented purchases from du Pont's Finishes Division. . . . Expressed in percentages, du Pont supplied 67% of General

Motors' requirements for finishes in 1946 and 68% in 1947. In fabrics du Pont supplied 52.3% of requirements in 1946, and 38.5% in 1947. Because General Motors accounts for almost one-half of the automobile industry's annual sales, its requirements for automotive finishes and fabrics must represent approximately one-half of the relevant market for these materials. Because the record clearly shows that quantitatively and percentagewise du Pont supplies the largest part of General Motors' requirements, we must conclude that du Pont has a substantial share of the relevant market.

The appellees argue that the Government could not maintain this action in 1949 because § 7 is applicable only to the acquisition of stock and not to the holding or subsequent use of the stock. This argument misconceives the objective toward which § 7 is directed. The Clayton Act was intended to supplement the Sherman Act. Its aim was primarily to arrest apprehended consequences of inter corporate relationships before those relationships could work their evil, which may be at or any time after the acquisition, depending upon the circumstances of the particular case. The Senate declared the objective of the Clayton Act to be as follows:

. . . Broadly stated, the bill, in its treatment of unlawful restraints and monopolies, seeks to prohibit and make unlawful certain trade practices which, as a rule, singly and in themselves, are not covered by the Act of July 2, 1890 [the Sherman Act], or other existing anti-trust acts, and thus, by making these practices illegal, to arrest the creation of trusts, conspiracies, and monopolies in their incipiency and before consummation. . . . S. Rep. No. 698, 63d Cong., 2d Sess. 1. [italics added]

"Incipiency" in this context denotes not the time the stock was acquired, but any time when the acquisition threatens to ripen into a prohibited effect. See Transamerica Corp. v. Board of Governors, 3 Cir., 206 F.2d 163, 166. To accomplish the congressional aim, the Government may proceed at any time that an acquisition may be said with reasonable probability to contain a threat that it may lead to a restraint of commerce or tend to create a monopoly of a line of commerce. Even when the purchase is solely for investment, the plain language of § 7 contemplates an action at any time the stock is used to bring about, or in attempting to bring about, the substantial lessening of competition.

Prior cases under § 7 were brought at or near the time of acquisition. . . . None of these cases holds, or even suggests, that the Government is foreclosed from bringing the action at any time when a threat of the prohibited effects is evident.

Related to this argument is the District Court's conclusion that 30 years of nonrestraint negated "any reasonable probability of such a restraint" at the time of the suit. While it is, of course, true that proof of a mere *possibility* of a prohibited restraint or tendency to monopoly will not establish the statutory requirement that the effect of an acquisition "may be" such restraint or tendency, the basic facts found by the District Court demonstrate the error of its conclusion. . . .

The fact that sticks out in this voluminous record is that the bulk of du Pont's production has always supplied the largest part of the requirements of the one customer in the automobile industry connected to du Pont by a stock interest. The inference is overwhelming that du Pont's commanding position was promoted by its stock interest and was not gained solely on competitive merit.

We agree with the trial court that considerations of price, quality and service were not overlooked by either du Pont or General Motors. Pride in its products and its high financial stake in General Motors' success would naturally lead du Pont to try to supply the best. But the wisdom of this business judgment cannot obscure the fact, plainly revealed by the record, that du Pont purposely employed its stock to pry open the General Motors market to entrench itself as the primary supplier of General Motors' requirements for automotive finishes and fabrics.

Similarly, the fact that all concerned in high executive posts in both companies acted honorably and fairly, each in the honest conviction that his actions were in the best interests of his own company and without any design to overreach anyone, including du Pont's competitors, does not defeat the Government's right to relief. It is not requisite to the proof of a violation of § 7 to show that restraint or monopoly was intended.

The statutory policy of fostering free competition is obviously furthered when no supplier has an advantage over his competitors from an acquisition of his customer's stock likely to have the effects condemned by the statute. We repeat, that the test of a violation of § 7 is whether, at the time of suit, there is a reasonable probability that the acquisition is likely to result in the condemned restraints. The conclusion upon this record is inescapable that such likelihood was proved as to this acquisition. The fire that was kindled in 1917 continues to smolder. It burned briskly to forge the ties that bind the General Motors market to du Pont, and if it has quieted down, it remains hot, and, from past performance, is likely at any time to blaze and make the fusion complete.

The judgment must therefore be reversed and the cause remanded to the District Court for a determination, after further hearing, of the equitable relief necessary and appropriate in the public interest to eliminate the effects of the acquisition offensive to the statute. [REVERSED]

Upon remand, the District Court divested Du Pont of the right to vote its 63 million shares of General Motors stock, prohibited Du Pont from attempting to influence General Motors in any way, and canceled preferential trade arrangements or understandings and requirements contracts between the two companies.[2] Additional relief included a ruling that officers of one of the companies could not henceforth be members of the board of directors of the other.

However, on petition by the government, the Supreme Court of the United States reviewed the District Court's disposition and agreed with the government that partial divestiture by transfer of voting rights would not be an effective remedy. The Supreme Court then directed the District Court to enter a decree requiring the Du Pont company to divest itself *completely* of the General Motors stock, no later than ten years after the decree's effective date.[3]

3   SECTION 7 AS AMENDED—VERTICAL AND HORIZONTAL MERGERS, IN GENERAL

The Du Pont case in the previous section is an example of a vertical merger. The decision which follows below involved a merger which had both vertical and horizontal aspects. It is also significant in that it is one of the first Supreme Court decisions applying Section 7 of the Clayton Act as it read after the 1950 Celler-Kefauver Amendment. It has thus been one of the primary sources relied upon for statements of precedent regarding the interpretation of Section 7. Besides giving thorough consideration to the economic factors which were involved in the merger, the court also inquires into the legislative history of Section 7.

BROWN SHOE CO. V. UNITED STATES
370 U.S. 294 (1962)

In 1956, Brown Shoe Company, Inc., acquired the G. R. Kinney Company, Inc., through an exchange of Kinney for Brown Stock. The government brought suit in the Federal District Court, charging that the merger of Brown (the third largest seller of shoes in the United States by dollar volume) and Kinney (the eighth largest seller among those engaged primarily in selling shoes) constituted a violation of the amended Section 7 of the Clayton Act. The District Court found in favor of the government and, among other things, ordered Brown to divest itself completely of all stock, share capital, assets, or other interests it held in Kinney. Brown Shoe Company appealed directly to the Supreme Court.

[2] 177 F. Supp. 1 (1959)
[3] 366 U.S. 316 (1961).

WARREN, CHIEF JUSTICE: . . . In order fully to understand and appraise . . . [Brown's contentions on appeal], it is necessary to set out in some detail the District Court's findings concerning the nature of the shoe industry and the place of Brown and Kinney within that industry.

THE INDUSTRY

The District Court found that although domestic shoe production was scattered among a large number of manufacturers, a small number of large companies occupied a commanding position. Thus, while the 24 largest manufacturers produced about 35% of the Nation's shoes, the top 4— International, Endicott-Johnson, Brown (including Kinney) and General Shoe —alone produced approximately 23% of the Nation's shoes or 65% of the production of the top 24.

In 1955, domestic production of nonrubber shoes was 509.2 million pairs. . . .

The public buys these shoes through about 70,000 retail outlets, only 22,000 of which, however, derive 50% or more of their gross receipts from the sale of shoes and are classified as "shoe stores" by the Census Bureau. These 22,000 shoe stores were found generally to sell (1) men's shoes only, (2) women's shoes only, (3) women's and children's shoes, or (4) men's, women's, and children's shoes.

The District Court found a "definite trend" among shoe manufacturers to acquire retail outlets. For example, International Shoe Company had no retail outlets in 1945, but by 1956 had acquired 130; General Shoe Company had only 80 retail outlets in 1945 but had 526 by 1956; Shoe Corporation of America, in the same period increased its retail holdings from 301 to 842; Melville Shoe Company from 536 to 947; and Endicott-Johnson from 488 to 540. Brown, itself, with no retail outlets of its own prior to 1951, had acquired 845 such outlets by 1956. Moreover, between 1950 and 1956 nine independent shoe store chains, operating 1,114 retail shoe stores, were found to have become subsidiaries of these large firms and to have ceased their independent operations.

And once the manufacturers acquired retail outlets, the District Court found there was a "definite trend" for the parent-manufacturers to supply an ever increasing percentage of the retail outlets' needs, thereby foreclosing other manufacturers from effectively competing for the retail accounts. Manufacturer-dominated stores were found to be "drying up" the available outlets for independent producers.

Another "definite trend" found to exist in the shoe industry was a decrease in the number of plants manufacturing shoes. And there appears to have been a concomitant decrease in the number of firms manufacturing shoes. In 1947, there were 1,077 independent manufacturers of shoes, but by 1954 their number had decreased about 10% to 970.

BROWN SHOE

Brown Shoe was found not only to have been a participant, but also a moving factor, in these industry trends. Although Brown had experimented several times with operating its own retail outlets, by 1945 it had disposed of them all. However, in 1951, Brown again began to seek retail outlets by acquiring the Nation's largest operator of leased shoe departments, Wohl Shoe Company (Wohl), which operated 250 shoe departments in department stores throughout the United States. Between 1952 and 1955 Brown made a number of smaller acquisitions: Wetherby-Kayser Shoe Company (three retail stores), Barnes & Company (two stores), Reilly Shoe Company (two leased shoe departments), Richardson Shoe Store (one store), and Wohl Shoe Company of Dallas (not connected with Wohl) (leased shoe departments in Dallas). In 1954, Brown made another major acquisition: Regal Shoe Corporation which, at the time, operated one manufacturing plant producing men's shoes and 110 retail outlets.

The acquisition of these corporations was found to lead to increased sales by Brown to the acquired companies. Thus although prior to Brown's acquisition of Wohl in 1951, Wohl bought from Brown only 12.8% of its total purchases of shoes, it subsequently increased its purchases to 21.4% in 1952 and to 32.6% in 1955. Wetherby-Kayser's purchases from Brown increased from 10.4% before acquisition to over 50% after. Regal, which had previously sold no shoes to Wohl and shoes worth only $89,000 to Brown, in 1956 sold shoes worth $265,000 to Wohl and $744,000 to Brown.

During the same period of time, Brown also acquired the stock or assets of seven companies engaged solely in shoe manufacturing. As a result, in 1955, Brown was the fourth largest shoe manufacturer in the country, producing about 25.6 million pairs of shoes or about 4% of the Nation's total footwear production.

KINNEY

Kinney is principally engaged in operating the largest family-style shoe store chain in the United States. At the time of trial, Kinney was found to be operating over 400 such stores in more than 270 cities. These stores were found to make about 1.2% of all national retail shoe sales by dollar volume. Moreover, in 1955 the Kinney stores sold approximately 8 million pairs of nonrubber shoes or about 1.6% of the national pairage sales of such shoes. Of these sales, approximately 1.1 million pairs were of men's shoes or about 1% of the national pairage sales of men's shoes; approximately 4.2 million pairs were of women's shoes or about 1.5% of the national pairage sales of women's shoes; and approximately 2.7 million pairs were of children's shoes or about 2% of the national pairage sales of children's shoes.

In addition to this extensive retail activity, Kinney owned and operated four plants which manufactured men's, women's, and children's shoes and whose combined output was 0.5% of the national shoe production in 1955, making Kinney the twelfth largest shoe manufacturer in the United States.

Kinney stores were found to obtain about 20% of their shoes from Kinney's own manufacturing plants. At the time of the merger, Kinney bought no shoes from Brown; however, in line with Brown's conceded reasons for acquiring Kinney, Brown had, by 1957, become the largest outside supplier of Kinney's shoes, supplying 7.9% of all Kinney's needs.

It is in this setting that the merger was considered and held to violate § 7 of the Clayton Act. . . .

III. LEGISLATIVE HISTORY

This case is one of the first to come before us in which the Government's complaint is based upon allegations that the appellant has violated § 7 of the Clayton Act, as that section was amended in 1950. . . .

As enacted in 1914, § 7 of the original Clayton Act prohibited the acquisition by one corporation of the *stock* of another corporation when such acquisition would result in a substantial lessening of competition *between the acquiring and the acquired* companies, or tend to create a monopoly in any line of commerce. The Act did not, by its explicit terms, or as construed by this Court, bar the acquisition by one corporation of the *assets* of another. Nor did it appear to preclude the acquisition of stock in any corporation other than a direct competitor. . . .

The dominant theme pervading congressional consideration of the 1950 amendments was a fear of what was considered to be a rising tide of economic concentration in the American economy. Apprehension in this regard was bolstered by the publication in 1948 of the Federal Trade Commission's study on corporate mergers. Statistics from this and other current studies were cited as evidence of the danger to the American economy in unchecked corporate expansions through mergers. Other considerations cited in support of the bill were the desirability of retaining "local control" over industry and the protection of small businesses. Throughout the recorded discussion may be found examples of Congress' fear not only of accelerated concentration of economic power on economic grounds, but also of the threat to other values a trend toward concentration was thought to pose.

What were some of the factors, relevant to a judgment as to the validity of a given merger, specifically discussed by Congress in redrafting § 7?

First, there is no doubt that Congress did wish to "plug the loophole" and to include within the coverage of the Act the acquisition of assets no less than the acquisition of stock.

Second, by the deletion of the "acquiring-acquired" language in the original text, it hoped to make plain that § 7 applied not only to mergers between actual competitors, but also to vertical and conglomerate mergers whose effect may tend to lessen competition in any line of commerce in any section of the country.

Third, it is apparent that a keystone in the erection of a barrier to what Congress saw was the rising tide of economic concentration, was its provision of authority for arresting mergers at a time when the trend to a lessening of competition in a line of commerce was still in its incipiency.

Fourth, and closely related to the third, Congress rejected, as inappropriate to the problem it sought to remedy, the application to § 7 cases of the standards for judging the legality of business combinations adopted by the courts in dealing with cases arising under the Sherman Act, and which may have been applied to some early cases arising under original § 7.

Fifth, at the same time that it sought to create an effective tool for preventing all mergers having demonstrable anti-competitive effects, Congress recognized the stimulation to competition that might flow from particular mergers. When concern as to the Act's breadth was expressed, supporters of the amendments indicated that it would not impede, for example, a merger between two small companies to enable the combination to compete more effectively with larger corporations dominating the relevant market, nor a merger between a corporation which is financially healthy and a failing one which no longer can be a vital competitive factor in the market. The deletion of the word "community" in the original Act's description of the relevant geographic market is another illustration of Congress' desire to indicate that its concern was with the adverse effects of a given merger on competition only in an economically significant "section" of the country. Taken as a whole, the legislative history illuminates congressional concern with the protection of *competition,* not *competitors,* and its desire to restrain mergers only to the extent that such combinations may tend to lessen competition.

Sixth, Congress neither adopted nor rejected specifically any particular tests for measuring the relevant markets, either as defined in terms of product or in terms of geographic locus of competition, within which the anti-competitive effects of a merger were to be judged. Nor did it adopt a definition of the word "substantially," whether in quantitative terms of sales or assets or market shares or in designated qualitative terms, by which a merger's effects on competition were to be measured.

Seventh, while providing no definite quantitative or qualitative tests by which enforcement agencies could gauge the effects of a given merger to determine whether it may "substantially" lessen competition or tend toward monopoly, Congress indicated plainly that a merger had to be functionally viewed, in the context of its particular industry. That is, whether the consolidation was to take place in an industry that was fragmented rather than concentrated, that had seen a recent trend toward domination by a few leaders or had remained fairly consistent in its distribution of market shares among the participating companies, that had experienced easy access to markets by suppliers and easy access to suppliers by buyers or had witnessed foreclosure of business, that had witnessed the ready entry of new competition or the erection of barriers to prospective entrants, all were aspects, varying in importance with the merger under consideration, which would properly be taken into account.

Eighth, Congress used the word "*may* be substantially to lessen competition" [EMPHASIS SUPPLIED], to indicate that its concern was with probabilities, not certainties. Statutes existed for dealing with clear-cut menaces to competition; no statute was sought for dealing with ephemeral possibilities. Mergers with a probable anti-competitive effect were to be proscribed by this Act.

It is against this background that we return to the case before us.

IV. THE VERTICAL ASPECTS OF THE MERGER

Economic arrangements between companies standing in a supplier-customer relationship are characterized as "vertical." The primary vice of a vertical merger or other arrangement tying a customer to a supplier is that, by foreclosing the competitors of either party from a segment of the market otherwise open to them, the arrangement may act as a "clog on competition," which "deprive[s] . . . rivals of a fair opportunity to compete." Every extended vertical arrangement by its very nature, for at least a time, denies to competitors of the supplier the opportunity to compete for part or all of the trade of the customer-party to the vertical arrangement. However, the Clayton Act does not render unlawful all such vertical arrangements, but forbids only those whose effect "may be substantially to lessen competition, or to tend to create a monopoly" "in any line of commerce in any section of the country." Thus, as we have previously noted,

[d]etermination of the relevant market is a necessary predicate to a finding of a violation of the Clayton Act because the threatened monopoly must be one which will substantially lessen competition "within the area of effective competition." Substantiality can be determined only in terms of the market affected.

The "area of effective competition" must be determined by reference to a product market (the "line of commerce") and a geographic market (the "section of the country").

THE PRODUCT MARKET

The outer boundaries of a product market are determined by the reasonable interchangeability of use or the cross-elasticity of demand between the product itself and substitutes for it. However, within this broad market, well-defined submarkets may exist which, in themselves, constitute product markets for antitrust purposes. The boundaries of such a submarket may be determined by examining such practical indicia as industry or public recognition of the submarket as a separate economic entity, the product's peculiar characteristics and uses, unique production facilities, distinct customers, distinct prices, sensitivity to price changes, and specialized vendors. Because § 7 of the Clayton Act prohibits any merger which may substantially lessen competition "in *any* line of commerce" [EMPHASIS SUPPLIED], it is necessary to examine the effects of a merger in each such economically significant submarket to determine if there is a reasonable probability that the merger will substantially lessen competition. If such a probability is found to exist, the merger is proscribed.

Applying these considerations to the present case, we conclude that the record supports the District Court's finding that the relevant lines of commerce are men's, women's, and children's shoes. These product lines are recognized by the public; each line is manufactured in separate plants; each has characteristics peculiar to itself rendering it generally noncompetitive with the others; and each is, of course, directed toward a distinct class of customers.

Appellant, however, contends that the District Court's definitions fail to recognize sufficiently "price/quality" and "age/sex" distinctions in shoes. Brown argues that the predominantly medium-priced shoes which it manufactures occupy a product market different from the predominantly low-priced shoes which Kinney sells. But agreement with that argument would be equivalent to holding that medium-priced shoes do not compete with low-priced shoes. We think the District Court properly found the facts to be otherwise. It would be unrealistic to accept Brown's contention that, for example, men's shoes selling below $8.99 are in a different product market from those selling above $9.00.

This is not to say, however, that "price/quality" differences, where they exist, are unimportant in analyzing a merger; they may be of importance in determining the likely effect of a merger. . . . We . . . [further] agree with the District Court's conclusion that in the setting of this case to subdivide the shoe market further on the basis of "age/sex" distinctions would be "impractical" and "unwarranted."

THE GEOGRAPHIC MARKET

We agree with the parties and the District Court that insofar as the vertical aspect of this merger is concerned, the relevant geographic market is the entire Nation. . . .

THE PROBABLE EFFECT OF THE MERGER

Once the area of effective competition affected by a vertical arrangement has been defined, an analysis must be made to determine if the effect of the arrangement "may be substantially to lessen competition, or to tend to create a monopoly" in this market.

Since the diminution of the vigor of competition which may stem from a vertical arrangement results primarily from a foreclosure of a share of the market otherwise open to competitors, an important consideration in determining whether the effect of a vertical arrangement "may be substantially to lessen competition, or to tend to create a monopoly" is the size of the share of the market foreclosed. However, this factor will seldom be determinative. If the share of the market foreclosed is so large that it approaches monopoly proportions, the Clayton Act will, of course, have been violated; but the arrangement will also have run afoul of the Sherman Act. And the legislative history of § 7 indicates clearly that the tests for measuring the legality of any particular economic arrangement under the Clayton Act are to be less stringent than those used in applying the Sherman Act. On the other hand, foreclosure of a *de minimis* share of the market will not tend "substantially to lessen competition."

Between these extremes, in cases such as the one before us, in which the foreclosure is neither of monopoly nor *de minimis* proportions, the percentage of the market foreclosed by the vertical arrangement cannot itself be decisive. In such cases, it becomes necessary to undertake an examination of various economic and historical factors in order to determine whether the arrangement under review is of the type Congress sought to proscribe.

A most important such factor to examine is the very nature and purpose of the arrangement. Congress not only indicated that "the tests of illegality (under § 7) are intended to be similar to those which the courts have applied to interpreting the same language as used in other sections of the Clayton Act," but also chose for § 7 language virtually identical to that of § 3 of the Clayton Act, which had been interpreted by this Court to require an examination of the interdependence of the market share foreclosed by, and the economic purpose of, the vertical arrangement. . . .

The importance which Congress attached to economic purpose is further demonstrated by the Senate and House Reports on H.R. 2734, which evince an intention to preserve the "failing company" doctrine of *International Shoe Co. v. FTC,* 280 U.S. 291. Similarly, Congress foresaw that the merger of two large companies or a large and a small company might violate the Clayton Act while the merger of two small companies might not, although the share of the market foreclosed be identical, if the purpose of the small companies is to enable them in combination to compete with larger corporations dominating the market.

The present merger involved neither small companies nor failing companies. In 1955, the date of this merger, Brown was the fourth largest manufacturer in the shoe industry with sales of approximately 25 million pairs of shoes and assets of over $72,000,000 while Kinney had sales of about 8 million pairs of shoes and assets of about $18,000,000. Not only was Brown one of the leading manufacturers of men's, women's, and children's shoes, but Kinney, with over 350 retail outlets, owned and operated the largest independent chain of family shoe stores in the Nation. Thus, in this industry, no merger between a manufacturer and an independent retailer could involve a larger potential market foreclosure. Moreover, it is apparent both from past behavior of Brown and from the testimony of Brown's President, that Brown would use its ownership of Kinney to force Brown shoes into Kinney stores. Thus, in operation this vertical arrangement would be quite analogous to one involving a tying clause.

Another important factor to consider is the trend toward concentration in the industry. It is true, of course, that the statute prohibits a given merger only if the effect of *that* merger may be substantially to lessen competition. But the very wording of § 7 requires a prognosis of the probable *future* effect of the merger.

The existence of a trend toward vertical integration, which the District Court found, is well substantiated by the record. Moreover, the Court found a tendency of the acquiring manufacturers to become increasingly important sources of supply for their acquired outlets. The necessary corollary of these trends is the foreclosure of independent manufacturers from markets otherwise open to them. And because these trends are not the product of accident but are rather the result of deliberate policies of Brown and other leading shoe manufacturers, account must be taken of these facts in order to predict the probable future consequences of this merger. It is against this background of continuing concentration that the present merger must be viewed.

Brown argues, however, that the shoe industry is at present composed of a large number of manufacturers and retailers, and that the industry is dynamically competitive. But remaining vigor cannot immunize a merger if the trend in that industry is toward oligopoly. It is the probable effect of the merger upon the future as well as the present which the Clayton Act commands the courts and the Commission to examine.

Moreover, as we have remarked above, not only must we consider the probable effects of the merger upon the economics of the particular markets affected but also we must consider its probable effects upon the economic way of life sought to be preserved by Congress. Congress was desirous of preventing the formation of further oligopolies with their attendant adverse effects upon local control of industry and upon small business. Where an industry was composed of numerous independent units, Congress appeared anxious to preserve this structure. The Senate Report, quoting with approval from the Federal Trade Commission's 1948 report on the merger movement, states explicitly that amended § 7 is addressed, *inter alia*, to the following problem:

> *Under the Sherman Act, an acquisition is unlawful if it creates a monopoly or constitutes an attempt to monopolize. Imminent monopoly may appear when one large concern acquires another, but it is unlikely to be perceived in a small acquisition by a large enterprise. As a large concern grows through a series of such small acquisitions, its accretions of power are individually so minute as to make it difficult to use the Sherman Act tests against them. . . .*
>
> *Where several large enterprises are extending their power by successive small acquisitions, the cumulative effect of their purchases may be to convert an industry from one of intense competition among many enterprises to one in which three or four large concerns produce the entire supply.*

The District Court's findings, and the record facts, many of them set forth in Part I of this opinion, convince us that the shoe industry is being subjected to just such a cumulative series of vertical mergers which, if left unchecked, will be likely "substantially to lessen competition."

We reach this conclusion because the trend toward vertical integration in the shoe industry, when combined with Brown's avowed policy of forcing its own shoes upon its retail subsidiaries, may foreclose competition from a substantial share of the markets for men's, women's, and children's shoes, without producing any countervailing competitive, economic, or social advantages.

V. THE HORIZONTAL ASPECTS OF THE MERGER

An economic arrangement between companies performing similar functions in the production or sale of comparable goods or services is characterized as "horizontal." The effect on competition of such an arrangement depends, of course, upon its character and scope. Thus, its validity in the face of the antitrust laws will depend upon such factors as: the relative size and number of the parties to the arrangement; whether it allocates shares of the market among the parties; whether it fixes prices at which the parties will sell their product; or whether it absorbs or insulates competitors. Where the arrangement effects a horizontal merger between companies occupying the same product and geographic market, whatever competition previously may have existed in that market between the parties to the merger is eliminated. Section 7 of the Clayton Act, prior to its amendment, focused upon this aspect of horizontal combinations by proscribing acquisitions which might result in a lessening of competition between the acquiring and the acquired companies. The 1950 amendments made plain Congress' intent that the validity of such combinations was to be gauged on a broader scale: their effect on competition generally in an economically significant market.

Thus, again, the proper definition of the market is a "necessary predicate" to an examination of the competition that may be affected by the horizontal aspects of the merger. . . . [A]ppellant contest[s] the District Court's finding that the merger of the companies' *retail* outlets may tend substantially to lessen competition.

THE PRODUCT MARKET

Shoes are sold in the United States in retail shoe stores and in shoe departments of general stores. These outlets sell: (1) men's shoes, (2) women's shoes, (3) women's or children's shoes, or (4) men's, women's or children's shoes. Prior to the merger, both Brown and Kinney sold their shoes in competition with one another through the enumerated kinds of outlets characteristic of the industry.

In Part IV of this opinion we hold that the District Court correctly defined men's, women's, and children's shoes as the relevant lines of commerce in which to analyze the vertical aspects of the merger. For the reasons there stated we also hold that the same lines of commerce are appropriate for considering the horizontal aspects of the merger.

THE GEOGRAPHIC MARKET

The criteria to be used in determining the appropriate geographic market are essentially similar to those used to determine the relevant product market. Moreover, just as a product submarket may have § 7 significance as the proper "line of commerce," so may a geographic submarket be considered the appropriate "section of the country." Congress prescribed a pragmatic, factual approach to the definition of the relevant market and not a formal, legalistic one. The geographic market selected must, therefore, both "correspond to the commercial realities" of the industry and be economically significant. Thus, although the geographic market in some instances may encompass the entire Nation, under other circumstances it may be as small as a single metropolitan area. The fact that two merging firms have competed directly on the horizontal level in but a fraction of the geographic markets in which either has operated, does not, in itself, place their merger outside the scope of § 7. That section speaks of "any . . . section of the country," and if anticompetitive effects of a merger are probable in "any" significant market, the merger—at least to that extent—is proscribed.

The parties do not dispute the findings of the District Court that the Nation as a whole is the relevant geographic market for measuring the anti-competitive effects of the merger viewed vertically or of the horizontal merger of Brown's and Kinney's manufacturing facilities. As to the retail level, however, they disagree. The District Court found that the effects of this aspect of the merger must be analyzed in every city with a population exceeding 10,000 and its immediate contiguous surrounding territory in which both Brown and Kinney sold shoes at retail through stores they either owned or controlled. By this definition of the geographic market, less than one-half of all the cities in which either Brown or Kinney sold shoes through such outlets are represented. The appellant recognizes that if the District Court's characterization of the relevant market is proper, the number of markets in which both Brown and Kinney have outlets is sufficiently numerous so that the validity of the entire merger is properly judged by testing its effects in those markets. However, it is appellant's contention that the areas of effective competition in shoe retailing were improperly defined by the District Court. It claims that such areas should, in some cases, be defined so as to include only the central business districts of large cities, and in others, so as to encompass the "standard metropolitan areas" within which smaller communities are found. It argues that any test failing to distinguish between these competitive situations is improper.

We believe, however, that the record fully supports the District Court's findings that shoe stores in the outskirts of cities compete effectively with stores in central downtown areas, and that while there is undoubtedly some commercial intercourse between smaller communities within a single "stand-ard metropolitan area," the most intense and important competition in retail sales will be confined to stores within the particular communities in such an area and their immediate environs.

We therefore agree that the District Court properly defined the relevant geographic markets in which to analyze this merger as those cities with a population exceeding 10,000 and their environs in which both Brown and Kinney retailed shoes through their own outlets. Such markets are large enough to include the downtown shops and suburban shopping centers in areas contiguous to the city, which are the important competitive factors, and yet are small enough to exclude stores beyond the immediate environs of the city, which are of little competitive significance.

THE PROBABLE EFFECT OF THE MERGER

. . . Brown objects that the District Court did not examine the competitive picture in each line of commerce and each section of the country it had defined as appropriate. . . .

However, we believe the record is adequate to support the findings of the District Court. While it is true that the court concentrated its attention on the structure of competition in the city in which it sat and as to which detailed evidence was most readily available, it also heard witnesses from no less than 40 other cities in which the parties to the merger operated. . . . We recognize that variations of size, climate and wealth as enumerated by Brown exist in the relevant market. . . . Each competitor within a given market is equally affected by these factors, even though the city in which he does business may differ from St. Louis in size, climate or wealth. . . .

In the case before us, not only was a fair sample used to demonstrate the soundness of the District Court's conclusions, but evidence of record fully substantiates those findings as to each relevant market. An analysis of undisputed statistics of sales of shoes in the cities in which both Brown and Kinney sell shoes at retail, separated into the appropriate lines of commerce, provides a persuasive factual foundation upon which the required prognosis of the merger's effects may be built. . . . They show, for example, that during 1955 in 32 separate cities, ranging in size and location from Topeka, Kansas, to Batavia, New York, and Hobbs, New Mexico, the combined share of Brown and Kinney sales of women's shoes (by unit volume) exceeded 20%. In 31 cities—some the same as those used in measuring the effect of the merger in the women's line—the combined share of children's shoe sales exceeded 20%; in 6 cities their share exceeded 40%. In Dodge City, Kansas, their combined share of the market for women's shoes was over 57%; their share of the children's shoe market in that city was 49%. In the 7 cities in which Brown's and Kinney's combined shares of the market for women's shoes were greatest (ranging from 33% to 57%) each of the parties alone, prior to the merger, had captured substantial portions of these markets (ranging from 13% to 34%); the merger intensified this existing concentration. In 118 separate cities the combined shares of the market of Brown and Kinney in the sale of one of the relevant lines of commerce exceeded 5%. In 47 cities, their share exceeded 5% in all three lines.

The market share which companies may control by merging is one of the most important factors to be considered when determining the probable effects of the combination on effective competition in the relevant market. In an industry as fragmented as shoe retailing, the control of substantial shares of the trade in a city may have important effects on competition. If a 5% control were now approved, we might be required to approve future merger efforts by Brown's competitors seeking similar market shares. The oligopoly Congress sought to avoid would then be furthered and it would be difficult to dissolve the combinations previously approved. Furthermore, in this fragmented industry, even if the combination controls but a small share of a particular market, the fact that this share is held by a large national chain can adversely affect competition. Testimony in the record from numerous independent retailers, based on their actual experience in the market, demonstrates that a strong, national chain of stores can insulate selected outlets from the vagaries of competition in particular locations and that the large chains can set and alter styles in footwear to an extent that renders the independents unable to maintain competitive inventories. A third significant aspect of this merger is that it creates a large national chain which is integrated with a manufacturing operation. The retail outlets of integrated companies, by eliminating wholesalers and by increasing the volume of purchases from the manufacturing division of the enterprise, can market their own brands at prices below those of competing independent retailers. Of course, some of the results of large integrated or chain operations are beneficial to consumers. Their expansion is not rendered unlawful by the mere fact that small independent stores may be adversely affected. It is competition, not competitors, which the Act protects. But we cannot fail to recognize Congress' desire to promote competition through the protection of viable, small, locally owned businesses. Congress appreciated that occasional higher costs and prices might result from the maintenance of fragmented industries and markets. It resolved these competing considerations in favor of decentralization. We must give effect to that decision.

Other factors to be considered in evaluating the probable effects of a merger in the relevant market lend additional support to the District Court's conclusion that this merger may substantially lessen competition. One such factor is the history of tendency toward concentration in the industry. As we have previously pointed out, the shoe industry has, in recent years, been a prime example of such a trend. . . . We cannot avoid the mandate of Congress that tendencies toward concentration in industry are to be curbed in their incipiency, particularly when those tendencies are being accelerated through giant steps striding across a hundred cities at a time. In the light of the trends in this industry we agree with the Government and the court below that this is an appropriate place at which to call a halt.

At the same time appellant has presented no mitigating factors, such as the business failure or the inadequate resources of one of the parties that may have prevented it from maintaining its competitive position, nor a demonstrated need for combination to enable small companies to enter into a more meaningful competition with those dominating the relevant markets. . . . We hold that the District Court was correct in concluding that this merger may tend to lessen competition substantially in the retail sale of men's, women's, and children's shoes in the overwhelming majority of those cities and their environs in which both Brown and Kinney sell through owned or controlled outlets. [AFFIRMED]

As was indicated previously, and as the analysis of the Brown Shoe case illustrates, a determination of the legality or illegality of any given merger under Section 7 requires findings which provide the answers to two questions: (1) What is the relevant market affected by the merger? (2) What are the *likely* or *probable* future anti-competitive effects which will result in that market from the merger?

Defining the "line of commerce" or relevant market which a given merger affects entails a consideration of both the *product* market and the *geographical* market. In the *Du Pont* case, the court narrowed its definition of the relevant product market in question, so that it was not the total market for finishes and fabrics, but *automotive* finishes and *automotive* fabrics. Since it is within the relevant market that the substantiality of future anticompetitive effects of the merger will be measured, it is obvious that a definition by the court which narrows or enlarges the "line of commerce" affected may be critical to its decision as to whether a violation exists or not. Equally important to the outcome may be a determination that the effects are to be measured, nationwide, in only one state, in just one metropolitan area, or in some other geographical area. In the sections which follow the three determinations of fact which must be made before a Section 7 violation can be demonstrated are discussed in more detail.

4   THE PRODUCT MARKET

In the case below the importance of the definition of the product market to the legality of a merger is dramatically illustrated.

REYNOLDS METALS CO. V. FTC
309 F.2d 223 (1962)

In 1956, Reynolds Metals Company acquired the stock and assets of Arrow Brands, Inc., a company which converted aluminum foil and sold it nationally to wholesale florist supply houses for decorative purposes. The FTC instituted a proceeding against Reynolds under Section 7 of the Clayton Act and ordered its divestiture of the stock and assets of Arrow, after finding that the acquisition might "have the effect of substantially lessening competition or tending to create a monopoly in the production and sale of decorative aluminum foil to the florist trade." Reynolds brought this proceeding to have the Commission's order reviewed and set aside by the Circuit Court of Appeals.

BURGER, JUDGE: . . . It is urged on appeal that the Commission erred in its conclusion that the "production and sale of decorative aluminum foil *to the florist trade"* is the "relevant line of commerce" within the meaning of Sec. 7 of the Clayton Act; secondly, that the Commission erred in concluding that Reynolds' acquisition of Arrow violated Sec. 7. . . .

Reynolds is the largest producer of aluminum foil in the world. In 1957 its production capacity of 117 million pounds per year formed 40.5% of the total foil production capacity of all ten foil producers in the United States. The record indicates that the large foil producers such as Reynolds find it both impracticable and unprofitable to accept small orders from small buyers of foil to be used for specific and limited end purposes such as the decoration of flower pots or foodstuffs. Consequently, Reynolds and other major raw foil producers sell in quantity to intermediaries known in the trade as converters, who have come into existence precisely to meet the needs of these small foil markets, which individually do not require a sufficiently large amount of raw foil to purchase it in the minimum quantities sold by the manufacturers. These converters purchase large quantities of foil from the producers in so-called "jumbo" rolls, and after breaking these down and processing them with decorative or other features sought by the end users, sell in limited quantities to the several smaller markets.

Arrow, prior to and since its acquisition by Reynolds in 1956, has been engaged in converting "jumbo" rolls of raw foil into such limited quantities of a specialized kind which are then sold, in decorated form, almost exclusively to the florist trade. While roughly 200 foil converters are active in the United States, only eight (approximately) including Arrow, served the florist industry when this proceeding began. In 1956, these eight firms sold not more than an estimated 1,500,000 pounds of florist foil altogether, of which Arrow accounted for approximately 33%. Several of the firms competing with Arrow in converting foil for the florist industry purchased their plain or raw foil from Reynolds prior to the acquisition. Raw foil costs to an unintegrated florist foil converter, such as Arrow was, account for 70% of the total cost of production.

The remainder of the 200 converters process aluminum foil for all its many other uses, including usage as tape, candy box liners, covers for take-out foodstuffs, condensers and many others. The uses are almost endless. The government concedes that theoretically all 200 converters could supply florist foil, but observes that in fact only the eight firms comprise the domestic *florist* foil converting industry. The record supports this view and we must assume for this discussion that the florist trade is supplied almost exclusively by the eight firms listed. . . . The problem of market definition in the present case centers only on the determination of the "line of commerce," since Reynolds does not disagree with the Commission's finding that the geographical area for measuring the competitive effects of this acquisition is the entire United States. . . .

[I]n a very recent case, *Brown Shoe Co. v. United States,* 370 U.S. 294 (1962), the concepts of interchangeability of use and cross-elasticity of demand underwent certain important qualifications and development. It is now clear that mere potential interchangeability or cross-elasticity may be insufficient to mark the legally pertinent limits of a "relevant line of commerce." The "outer limits" of a general market may be thus determined, but sharply distinct submarkets can exist within these outer limits which may henceforth be the focal point of administrative and judicial inquiry under Section 7. . . .

Analyzing the facts of the present case makes it abundantly clear that under these standards the production and sale of florist foil may rationally be defined by the Commission as comprising the relevant line of commerce in terms of (1) public and industrial recognition of it as a separate economic entity, (2) its distinct customers and (3) its distinct prices. . . .

The record indicates that total annual United States shipments of aluminum foil of all thicknesses below .006 inches averaged close to 200 million pounds in 1956 and 1957, approximately 75% of which was utilized in some form of packaging or wrapping. However, not all foil used for packaging or wrapping is suitable for the particular use which any given market may require. Suitability for use in particular markets is determined first by thickness. While all sheet aluminum below .006 inches is considered foil, the variety of thicknesses employed below that is large and ranges all the way down to .00065 of an inch, which is considered the thinnest sheet which may be practicably and inexpensively produced with the necessary physical characteristics of strength and tear resistance. Between the extremes of .006 and .00065 inches, uses may and do vary in hundreds of ways, from the packaging of dairy products, meat, tobacco and milling products to the decoration of flower pots and ordinary household use.

Reynolds itself has subdivided its packaging sales division for foil into seven marketing groups, each designed to supply foil for different end uses such as the wrapping and packaging of soap, drugs, dairy products, tobacco, textiles and many others. One subdivision is devoted to supplying foil to converters such as Arrow, whose business is largely confined to the purchase of the giant or "jumbo" rolls from Reynolds at .00065 gauge. As noted, the converter's service to its customers consists of reducing the large economy or "jumbo" lots to lesser quantities purchasable by limited markets such as the florist industry, and decorating these smaller quantities by one of the several coloring or embossing techniques.

It is important to note at this point that *decorative* foil appears as a distinct category in overall aluminum foil production. Of the 192,000,000 pounds of domestic converted aluminum foil shipped in 1956, approximately 9.7 million pounds was composed of decorative foil of all kinds. While the record affords us no precise definition of decorative foil, it does reflect that of the 9.7 million pounds, less than 1½ million pounds were shipped to florist outlets by the eight firms including Arrow which supply that particular trade. Florist foil is undoubtedly one type of decorative foil.

The record also affords little affirmative basis for assuming any marked difference between the characteristics of the 1½ million pounds of florist foil and the remainder of the 9.7 million pounds of decorative foil, particularly in view of the variations and tolerances allowed as to weight. All decorative foil, including florist foil, appears to be gauged at approximately the same thickness, .00065 inches. Reynolds further argues that the decorative characteristics of foil sent to the florist is not distinguishable otherwise from foil decorated by similar coloring, laminating or embossing but used, *inter alia*, as cheese wrap, coffee cup covers, suppository wrap, potato wrap and meat interleaving. . . .

[O]n the basis of the *use and quality* of the products displayed on the record, we would have difficulty in affirming the Commission's determination that the florist foil converting industry is a line of commerce distinctly separable from the considerably larger decorative foil industry viewed in the aggregate. Nevertheless we must affirm the Commission on the earlier mentioned bases of (1) distinct pricing and purchaser identity, and (2) indisputable industry and consumer recognition of the florist foil converting industry as a separate economic entity.

First, the identity of purchasers of florist foil is distinct and limited. With insignificant exception, the sole purchasers of florist foil are the nation's 700 wholesale florist outlets and, through these, the 25,000 retail florists throughout the country. Despite a clearly lower price for florist foil, discussed *infra*, other end users of decorative foil have not joined the identifiable mass of florist foil purchasers in noticeable numbers. As already noted, the identity of the florist foil converters who *alone* serve these florist purchasers is clearly limited to eight firms including Arrow, with some minor and as yet undefined competition from a few foreign firms indicated by the record. It is noteworthy that not only the number of firms thus serving the florists has remained fairly constant but up through the 1956 acquisition, now under review, the same individual firms comprised this number.

Secondly, both producer and consumer recognition of the florist foil submarket as a definite economic entity is clearly demonstrated by what appears to have been the election of other decorative foil converters not to serve the florist industry, by the habit and practice of the extensive florist industry itself in purchasing only from florist foil converters like Arrow and not from other decorative foil converters, and again, by the failure of decorative foil users other than florists to purchase the lower priced florist foil.

Pricing forms the final point. Substantial evidence discloses a markedly lower price for florist foil compared with the price of other colored or embossed aluminum foil sold in comparable weight units and gauged at approximately the same thickness. We think price differentials have an important if not decisive bearing in the quest to delimit a submarket. No prudent businessman (the ordinary end user of foil), would purchase colored or embossed foil at prices on this record of $1.15 to $1.22 per unit when another foil converter market offers florist foil, similarly colored or embossed, and of similar gauge and weight, at a cost of only $.75 to $.85 per unit. The fact that prudent businessmen do so supports the inference, drawn in the negative since as we have noted the record lacks affirmative evidence on the point, that florist foil must be distinct and separable from aluminum foil generally or the many users of the latter would have long ago begun to substitute the former at the lower price. Such a difference in price as appears on this record must effectively preclude comparison, and inclusion in the same market, of products as between which the difference exists, at least for purposes of inquiry under Sec. 7 of the Clayton Act.

It appears, therefore, that the florist foil market probably is a distinguishable product market, and therefore the production and sale of decorative aluminum foil to the florist trade is a "line of commerce" within the meaning of Sec. 7.

The effect of the acquisition of Arrow on this line of commerce was therefore justifiably predicated as substantially anti-competitive. While as many as eight or more firms converted foil for the florist industry, we have observed that roughly 33% of this business had been captured by Arrow alone prior to the 1956 transaction tying Arrow into Reynolds. When Arrow was vertically integrated through the Reynolds' acquisition, one minor anti-competitive effect foreseeable was the exclusion of other manufacturers of raw foil (Reynolds' competitors) from selling to approximately 33% of the florist foil converting industry. However, neither the examiner nor the Commission rested their conclusions that Sec. 7 had been violated on this basis, nor should we. The truer picture of anti-competitive effect emerges from even the most cursory consideration of the post-acquisition competitive postures of the eight previously independent florist foil converters *vis a vis* one another. Arrow's assimilation into Reynolds' enormous capital structure and resources gave Arrow an immediate advantage over its competitors who were contending for a share of the market for florist foil. The power of the "deep pocket" or "rich parent" for one of the florist foil suppliers in a competitive group where previously no company was very large and all were relatively small opened the possibility and power to sell at prices approximating cost or below and thus to undercut and ravage the less affluent competition. The Commission is not required to establish that the Reynolds' acquisition of Arrow did in fact have anti-competitive consequences. It is sufficient if the Commission shows the acquisition had the capacity or potentiality to lessen competition. That such a potential emerged from the combination of Reynolds and Arrow was enough to bring it within Sec. 7. But the Commission on substantial evidence has additionally provided us with a finding of *actual* anti-competitive effect, where as an apparent consequence of retroactive price reductions for Arrow foil after the acquisition of florist foil sales of 5 of Arrow's 7 competitors had by 1957 dropped from 14% to 47% below 1955 sales. Arrow's sales over the same period increased by 18.9%.

The necessary probability of anti-competitive effect has thus been shown. In agreeing with the Commission, however, we do not, nor could we intimate, that the mere intrusion of "bigness" into a competitive economic community otherwise populated by commercial "pygmies" will *per se* invoke the Clayton Act. Each factual situation under judicial review has its own atmosphere of economic freedom and viability or lack thereof; occasion may well arise where an acquisition superficially similar to the one here condemned by the Commission may be encouraged as necessary to *preserve* competition, to maintain production levels adequate to meet consumer demand or otherwise to produce "countervailing competitive, economic or social advantages." . . .

Affirmed and order will be enforced.

5   THE GEOGRAPHIC MARKET

While in the *Reynolds* case above, defining the product market was all-important to the finding of a violation of the Clayton Act, in the case which follows, identifying the line of commerce seems somewhat secondary to the determination of the geographical market, which was held to be an area of four counties. Besides illustrating the importance of such determinations in merger cases, the decision is significant as the first one in which the Supreme Court considered the application of the antitrust laws to the commercial banking industry.

UNITED STATES V. PHILADELPHIA NAT'L BANK
374 U.S. 321 (1963)

The United States brought this action under the antitrust laws to enjoin a merger which was planned by two Philadelphia Banks, the Philadelphia National Bank (PNB) and the Girard Trust Corn Exchange Bank (Girard). The District Court gave judgment for the defendants and the government appealed.

BRENNAN, JUSTICE: . . . Commercial banking in this country is primarily unit banking. That is, control of commercial banking is diffused throughout a very large number of independent, local banks—13,460 of them in 1960 —rather than concentrated in a handful of nationwide banks, as, for example, in England and Germany. There are, to be sure, in addition to the independent banks, some 10,000 branch banks; but branching, which is controlled largely by state law—and prohibited altogether by some States—

enables a bank to extend itself only to state lines and often not that far. It is also the case, of course, that many banks place loans and solicit deposits outside their home area. But with these qualifications, it remains true that ours is essentially a decentralized system of community banks. Recent years, however, have witnessed a definite trend toward concentration. Thus, during the decade ending in 1960, the number of commercial banks in the United States declined by 714, despite the chartering of 887 new banks and a very substantial increase in the Nation's credit needs during the period. Of the 1,601 independent banks which thus disappeared, 1,503, with combined total resources of well over $25,000,000,000, disappeared as the result of mergers. . . .

The Philadelphia National Bank and Girard Trust Corn Exchange Bank are, respectively, the second and third largest of the 42 commercial banks with head offices in the Philadelphia metropolitan area, which consists of the City of Philadelphia and its three contiguous counties in Pennsylvania. The home county of both banks is the city itself; Pennsylvania law, however, permits branching into the counties contiguous to the home county, and both banks have offices throughout the four-county area. PNB, a national bank, has assets of over $1,000,000,000, making it (as of 1959) the twenty-first largest bank in the Nation. Girard, a state bank, is a member of the FRS and is insured by the FDIC; it has assets of about $750,000,000. Were the proposed merger to be consummated, the resulting bank would be the largest in the four-county area, with (approximately) 36% of the area banks' total assets, 36% of deposits, and 34% of net loans. It and the second largest (First Pennsylvania Bank and Trust Company, now the largest) would have between them 59% of the total assets, 58% of deposits, and 58% of the net loans, while after the merger the four largest banks in the area would have 78% of total assets, 77% of deposits, and 78% of net loans.

The present size of both PNB and Girard is in part the result of mergers. Indeed, the trend toward concentration is noticeable in the Philadelphia area generally, in which the number of commercial banks has declined from 108 in 1947 to the present 42. Since 1950, PNB has acquired nine formerly independent banks and Girard six; and these acquisitions have accounted for 59% and 85% of the respective banks' asset growth during the period, 63% and 91% of their deposit growth, and 12% and 37% of their loan growth. During this period, the seven largest banks in the area increased their combined share of the area's total commercial bank resources from about 61% to about 90%.

In November 1960 the boards of directors of the two banks approved a proposed agreement for their consolidation under the PNB charter. By the terms of the agreement, PNB's stockholders were to retain their share certificates, which would be deemed to represent an equal number of shares in the consolidated bank, while Girard's stockholders would surrender their shares in exchange for shares in the consolidated bank, receiving 1.2875 such shares for each Girard share. Such a consolidation is authorized, subject to the approval of the Comptroller of the Currency, by 12 U.S.C. (1958 ed., Supp. IV) § 215. But under the Bank Merger Act of 1960, the Comptroller may not give his approval until he has received reports from the other two banking agencies and the Attorney General respecting the probable effects of the proposed transaction on competition. All three reports advised that the proposed merger would have substantial anticompetitive effects in the Philadelphia metropolitan area. However, on February 24, 1961, the Comptroller approved the merger. No opinion was rendered at that time. But as required by § 1828(c), the Comptroller explained the basis for his decision to approve the merger in a statement to be included in his annual report to Congress. As to effect upon competition, he reasoned that "[s]ince there will remain an adequate number of alternative sources of banking service in Philadelphia, and in view of the beneficial effects of this consolidation upon international and national competition it was concluded that the over-all effect upon competition would not be unfavorable." He also stated that the consolidated bank "would be far better able to serve the convenience and needs of its community by being of material assistance to its city and state in their efforts to attract new industry and to retain existing industry." The day after the Comptroller approved the merger, the United States commenced the present action. No steps have been taken to consummate the merger pending the outcome of this litigation. . . . Upon . . . [the] record the District Court held that: (1) the passage of the Bank Merger Act of 1960 did not repeal by implication the antitrust laws insofar as they may apply to bank mergers; (2) § 7 of the Clayton Act is inapplicable to bank mergers because banks are not corporations "subject to the jurisdiction of the Federal Trade Commission"; (3) but assuming that § 7 is applicable, the four-county Philadelphia metropolitan area is not the relevant geographical market because PNB and Girard actively compete with other banks for bank business throughout the greater part of the northeastern United States; (4) but even assuming that § 7 is applicable and that the four-county area is the relevant market, there is no reasonable probability that competition among commercial banks in the area will be substantially lessened as the result of the merger; (5) since the merger does not violate § 7 of the Clayton Act, *a fortiori* it does not violate § 1 of the Sherman Act; (6) the merger will benefit the Philadelphia metropolitan area economically. The District Court also ruled that for the purposes of § 7, commercial banking is a line of commerce; the appellees do not contest this ruling. . . .

We have no difficulty in determining the "line of commerce" (relevant product or services market) and "section of the country" (relevant geographical market) in which to appraise the probable competitive effects of appellees' proposed merger. We agree with the District Court that the cluster of products (various kinds of credit) and services (such as checking accounts and trust administration) denoted by the term "commercial banking," composes a distinct line of commerce. Some commercial banking products or services are so distinctive that they are entirely free of effective competition from products or services of other financial institutions; the checking account is in this category. Others enjoy such cost advantages as to be insulated within a broad range from substitutes furnished by other institutions. For example, commercial banks compete with small-loan companies in the personal-loan market; but the small-loan companies' rates are invariably much higher than the banks' in part, it seems, because the companies' working capital consists in substantial part of bank loans. Finally, there are banking facilities which, although in terms of cost and price they are freely competitive with the facilities provided by other financial institutions, nevertheless enjoy a settled consumer preference, insulating them, to a marked degree, from competition; this seems to be the case with savings deposits. In sum, it is clear that commercial banking is a market "sufficiently inclusive to be meaningful in terms of trade realities."

We part company with the District Court on the determination of the appropriate "section of the country." The proper question to be asked in this case is not where the parties to the merger do business or even where they compete, but where, within the area of competitive overlap, the effect of the merger on competition will be direct and immediate. This depends upon "the geographic structure of supplier-customer relations." Kaysen and Turner, Anti-trust Policy (1959), 102. In banking, as in most service industries, convenience of location is essential to effective competition. Individuals and corporations typically confer the bulk of their patronage on banks in their local community; they find it impractical to conduct their banking business at a distance. The factor of inconvenience localizes banking competition as effectively as high transportation costs in other industries. Therefore, since, as we recently said in a related context, the "area of effective competition in the known line of commerce must be charted by careful selection of the market area in which the seller operates, *and to which the purchaser can practicably turn for supplies.*" [T]he four-county area in which appellees' offices are located would seem to be the relevant geographical market. In fact, the vast bulk of appellees' business originates in the four-county area. Theoretically, we should be concerned with the possibility that bank offices on the perimeter of the area may be in effective competition with bank offices within; actually, this seems to be a factor of little significance.

We recognize that the area in which appellees have their offices does not delineate with perfect accuracy an appropriate "section of the country" in which to appraise the effect of the merger upon competition. Large borrowers and large depositors, the record shows, may find it practical to do a large part of their banking business outside their home community; very small borrowers and depositors may, as a practical matter, be confined to bank offices in their immediate neighborhood; and customers of intermediate size, it would appear, deal with banks within an area intermediate between these extremes. . . . So also, some banking services are evidently more local in nature than others. But that in banking the relevant geographical market is a function of each separate customer's economic scale means simply that a workable compromise must be found; some fair intermediate delineation which avoids the indefensible extremes of drawing the market either so expansively as to make the effect of the merger upon competition seem insignificant, because only the very largest bank customers are taken into account in defining the market, or so narrowly as to place appellees in different markets, because only the smallest customers are considered. We think that the four-County Philadelphia metropolitan area, which state law apparently recognizes as a meaningful banking community in allowing Philadelphia banks to branch within it, and which would seem roughly to delineate the area in which bank customers that are neither very large nor very small find it practical to do their banking business, is a more appropriate "section of the country" in which to appraise the instant merger than any larger or smaller or different area. We are helped to this conclusion by the fact that the three federal banking agencies regard the area in which banks have their offices as an "area of effective competition." Not only did the FDIC and FRB, in the reports they submitted to the Comptroller of the Currency in connection with appellees' application for permission to merge, so hold, but the Comptroller, in his statement approving the merger, agreed: "With respect to the effect upon competition, there are three separate levels and effective areas of competition involved. These are the national level for national accounts, the regional or sectional area, and the local area of the City of Philadelphia and the immediately surrounding area."

Having determined the relevant market, we come to the ultimate question under § 7: whether the effect of the merger "may be substantially to lessen competition" in the relevant market. Clearly, this is not the kind of question which is susceptible of a ready and precise answer in most cases. It requires not merely an appraisal of the immediate impact of the merger upon competition, but a prediction of its impact upon competitive conditions in the future; this is what is meant when it is said that the amended § 7 was intended to arrest anticompetitive tendencies in their "incipiency." Such a prediction is sound only if it is based upon a firm understanding of the structure of the relevant market; yet the relevant economic data are both complex and elusive. And unless businessmen can assess the legal consequences of a merger with some confidence, sound business planning is retarded. So also, we must be alert to the danger of subverting congressional intent by permitting a too-broad economic investigation. And so in any case in which it is possible, without doing violence to the congressional objective embodied in § 7, to simplify the test of illegality, the courts ought to do so in the interest of sound and practical judicial administration. This is such a case.

We noted in *Brown Shoe Co. v. United States* 370 U.S., at 315, that "[t]he dominant theme pervading congressional consideration of the 1950 amendments (to § 7) was a fear of what was considered to be a rising tide of economic concentration in the American economy." This intense congressional concern with the trend toward concentration warrants dispensing, in certain cases, with elaborate proof of market structure, market behavior, or probable anticompetitive effects. Specifically, we think that a merger which produces a firm controlling an undue percentage share of the relevant market, and results in a significant increase in the concentration of firms in that market is so inherently likely to lessen competition substantially that it must be enjoined in the absence of evidence clearly showing that the merger is not likely to have such anticompetitive effects.

Such a test lightens the burden of proving illegality only with respect to mergers whose size makes them inherently suspect in light of Congress' design in § 7 to prevent undue concentration. Furthermore, the test is fully consonant with economic theory. That "[c]ompetition is likely to be greatest when there are many sellers, none of which has any significant market share," is common ground among most economists, and was undoubtedly a premise of congressional reasoning about the antimerger statute.

The merger of appellees will result in a single bank's controlling at least 50% of the commercial banking business in the four-county Philadelphia metropolitan area. Without attempting to specify the smallest market share which would still be considered to threaten undue concentration, we are clear that 30% presents that threat. Further, whereas presently the two largest banks in the area (First Pennsylvania and PNB) control between them approximately 44% of the area's commercial banking business, the two largest after the merger (PNB-Girard and First Pennsylvania) will control 59%. Plainly, we think, this increase of more than 33% in concentration must be regarded as significant. . . .

There is nothing in the record of this case to rebut the inherently anticompetitive tendency manifested by these percentages. There was, to be sure, testimony by bank officers to the effect that competition among banks in Philadelphia was vigorous and would continue to be vigorous after the merger. We think, however, that the District Court's reliance on such evidence was misplaced. This lay evidence on so complex an economic-legal problem as the substantiality of the effect of this merger upon competition was entitled to little weight, in view of the witnesses' failure to give concrete reasons for their conclusions.

Of equally little value, we think, are the assurances offered by appellees' witnesses that customers dissatisfied with the services of the resulting bank may readily turn to the 40 other banks in the Philadelphia area. In every case short of outright monopoly, the disgruntled customer has alternatives; even in tightly oligopolistic markets, there may be small firms operating. A fundamental purpose of amending § 7 was to arrest the trend toward concentration, the *tendency* to monopoly, before the consumer's alternatives disappeared through merger, and that purpose would be ill-served if the law stayed its hand until 10, or 20, or 30 more Philadelphia banks were absorbed. This is not a fanciful eventuality, in view of the strong trend toward mergers evident in the area; and we might note also that entry of new competitors into the banking field is far from easy.

So also, we reject the position that commercial banking, because it is subject to a high degree of governmental regulation, or because it deals in the intangibles of credit and services rather than in the manufacture or sale of tangible commodities, is somehow immune from the anticompetitive effects of undue concentration. Competition among banks exists at every level—price, variety of credit arrangements, convenience of location, attractiveness of physical surroundings, credit information, investment advice, service charges, personal accommodations, advertising, miscellaneous special and extra services—and it is keen; on this appellees' own witnesses were emphatic. There is no reason to think that concentration is less inimical to the free play of competition in banking than in other service industries. . . .

We turn now to three affirmative justifications which appellees offer for the proposed merger. The first is that only through mergers can banks follow their customers to the suburbs and retain their business. This justification does not seem particularly related to the instant merger, but in any event it has no merit. There is an alternative to the merger route; the opening of new branches in the areas to which the customers have moved—so called *de novo* branching. Appellees do not contend that they are unable to expand thus, by opening new offices rather than acquiring existing ones, and surely one premise of an antimerger statute such as § 7 is that corporate growth by internal expansion is socially preferable to growth by acquisition.

Second, it is suggested that the increased lending limit of the resulting bank will enable it to compete with the large out-of-state bank, particularly the New York banks, for very large loans. We reject this application of the concept of "countervailing power." If anticompetitive effects in one market could be justified by procompetitive consequences in another, the logical upshot would be that every firm in an industry could, without violating § 7, embark on a series of mergers that would make it in the end as large as the industry leader. For if all the commercial banks in the Philadelphia area merged into one, it would be smaller than the largest bank in New York City. This is not a case, plainly, where two small firms in a market propose to merge in order to be able to compete more successfully with the leading firms in that market. Nor is it a case in which lack of adequate banking facilities is causing hardships to individuals or businesses in the community. The present two largest banks in Philadelphia have lending limits of $8,000,000 each. The only businesses located in the Philadelphia area which find such limits inadequate are large enough readily to obtain bank credit in other cities.

This brings us to appellees' final contention, that Philadelphia needs a bank larger than it now has in order to bring business to the area and stimulate its economic development. We are clear, however, that a merger the effect of which "may be substantially to lessen competition" is not saved because, on some ultimate reckoning of social or economic debits and credits, it may be deemed beneficial. A value choice of such magnitude is beyond the ordinary limits of judicial competence, and in any event has been made for us already, by Congress when it enacted the amended § 7. Congress determined to preserve our traditionally competitive economy. It therefore proscribed anticompetitive mergers, the benign and the malignant alike, fully aware, we must assume, that some price might have to be paid.

In holding as we do that the merger of appellees would violate § 7 and must therefore be enjoined, we reject appellees' pervasive suggestion that application of the procompetitive policy of § 7 to the banking industry will have dire, although unspecified, consequences for the national economy. Concededly, PNB and Girard are healthy and strong; they are not undercapitalized or overloaned; they have no management problems; the Philadelphia area is not overbanked; ruinous competition is not in the offing. Section 7 does not mandate cutthroat competition in the banking industry, and does not exclude defenses based on dangers to liquidity or solvency, if to avert them a merger is necessary. It does, require, however, that the forces of competition be allowed to operate within the broad framework of governmental regulation of the industry. The fact that banking is a highly regulated industry critical to the Nation's welfare makes the play of competition not less important but more so. At the price of some repetition, we note that if the businessman is denied credit because his banking alternatives have been eliminated by mergers, the whole edifice of an entrepreneurial system is threatened; if the costs of banking services and credit are allowed to become excessive by the absence of competitive pressures, virtually all costs, in our credit economy, will be affected; and unless competition is allowed to fulfill its role as an economic regulator in the banking industry, the result may well be even more governmental regulation. Subject to narrow qualifications, it is surely the case that competition is our fundamental national economic policy, offering as it does the only alternative to the cartelization or governmental regimentation of large portions of the economy. There is no warrant for declining to enforce it in the instant case.

The judgment of the District Court is reversed and the case remanded with direction to enter judgment enjoining the proposed merger. It is so ordered.

6   THE NATURE OF THE ANTICOMPETITIVE EFFECTS PROHIBITED

As already noted, in addition to determining what relevant market is affected by a given merger, the court must also find that within that market the effect of the merger "may be substantially to lessen competition, or to tend to create a monopoly" before a violation of Section 7 of the Clayton Act is established. In the case which follows, the acquisition in question added only 1.3% to the acquiring company's control of the relevant market, aluminum conductor. The definition of what was the relevant market was disputed by the defendant, who sought to have copper conductor included, which would have had the effect of reducing the control acquired much below 1.3%. And, since the defendant produced no copper conductor, such a definition of the line of commerce would have reduced the degree to which the acquisition increased concentration. (The portions of the opinion discussing relevant market have been omitted.)

UNITED STATES V. ALUMINUM CO. OF AMERICA
377 U.S. 271 (1964)

The Aluminum Company of America (Alcoa) acquired the stock and assets of Rome Cable Corporation (Rome) in 1959. The government brought this civil suit for divestiture, arguing that the acquisition's effect might be "substantially to lessen competition or to tend to create a monopoly" in violation of Section 7 of the Clayton Act. The District Court held after trial that there was no violation and dismissed the complaint. The government appealed directly to the Supreme Court.

DOUGLAS, JUSTICE: . . . Taking aluminum conductor as an appropriate "line of commerce" we conclude that the merger violated § 7.

Alcoa is a leader in markets in which economic power is highly concentrated. Prior to the end of World War II it was the sole producer of primary aluminum and the sole fabricator of aluminum conductor. It was held in 1945 to have monopolized the aluminum industry in violation of § 2 of the Sherman Act. See *United States v. Aluminum Co. of America,* 148 F.2d 416. Relief was deferred while the United States disposed of its wartime aluminum facilities under a congressional mandate to establish domestic competition in the aluminum industry. As a result of that policy and further federal financing and assistance, five additional companies entered the primary aluminum field so that by 1960 the primary producers showed the following capacity:

ALUMINUM INGOT CAPACITY EXISTING OR UNDER CONSTRUCTION
AT THE END OF 1960

Short Tons

COMPANY	CAPACITY	% OF U.S. TOTAL
United States Total	2,655,750	100.
Aluminum Company of America	1,025,250	38.6
Reynolds Metals Company	701,000	26.4
Kaiser Aluminum & Chemical Corp.	609,500	23.0
Ormet, Inc.	180,000	6.8
Harvey Aluminum	75,000	2.8
Anaconda Aluminum Company	65,000	2.4

In 1958—the year prior to the merger—Alcoa was the leading producer of aluminum conductor, with 27.8% of the market; in bare aluminum conductor, it also led the industry, with 32.5%. Alcoa plus Kaiser controlled 50% of the aluminum conductor market and, with its three leading competitors, more than 76%. Only nine concerns (including Rome with 1.3%) accounted for 95.7% of the output of aluminum conductor. In the narrow market of insulated aluminum conductor, Alcoa was third with 11.6% and four smaller ones, including Rome, added another 22.8%.

In other words, the line of commerce showed highly concentrated markets, dominated by a few companies but served also by a small, though diminishing, group of independents. Such decentralization as has occurred resulted from the establishment of a few new companies through federal intervention, not from normal, competitive decentralizing forces. . . .

The committee reports on § 7 show, as respects the Celler-Kefauver amendments in 1950, that the objective was to prevent accretions of power which "are individually so minute as to make it difficult to use the Sherman Act test against them." . . .

The acquisition of Rome added, it is said, only 1.3% to Alcoa's control of the aluminum conductor market. But in this setting that seems to us reasonably likely to produce a substantial lessening of competition within the meaning of § 7. It is the basic premise of that law that competition will be most vital "when there are many sellers, none of which has any significant market share." It would seem that the situation in the aluminum industry may be oligopolistic. As that condition develops, the greater is the likelihood that parallel policies of mutual advantage, not competition, will emerge. That tendency may well be thwarted by the presence of small but significant competitors. Though percentage-wise Rome may have seemed small in the year prior to the merger, it ranked ninth among all companies and fourth among independents in the aluminum conductor market; and in the insulated aluminum field it ranked eighth and fourth respectively. Furthermore, in the aluminum conductor market, no more than a dozen companies could account for as much as 1% of industry production in any one of the five years (1955–1959) for which statistics appear in the record. Rome's competition was therefore substantial. The record shows indeed that Rome was an aggressive competitor. It was a pioneer in aluminum insulation and developed one of the most widely used insulated conductors. Rome had a broad line of high-quality copper wire and cable products in addition to its aluminum conductor business, a special aptitude and skill in insulation, and an active and efficient research and sales organization. The effectiveness of its marketing organization is shown by the fact that after the merger Alcoa made Rome the distributor of its entire conductor line. Preservation of Rome, rather than its absorption by one of the giants, will keep it "as an important competitive factor," to use the words of S.Rep. No. 1775, p. 3; U.S. Code Congressional Service 1950, p. 4295. Rome seems to us the prototype of the small independent that Congress aimed to preserve by § 7.

The judgment is reversed and since there must be divestiture, the case is remanded to the District Court for proceedings in conformity with this opinion. [REVERSED AND REMANDED]

In the case which follows, the main issue before the court also was whether the merger in question might tend toward a substantial lessening of competition.

UNITED STATES V. VON'S GROCERY CO.
384 U.S. 270 (1966)

The United States brought an action which charged that the acquisition by Von's Grocery Company of Shopping Bag Food Stores violated Section 7 of the Clayton Act. After the District Court refused the request of the Government for a temporary injunction, Von's immediately took over Shopping Bag's capital stock and assets. Then, after hearing the evidence, the District Court entered judgment for the defendants, ruling as a matter of law that there was "not a reasonable probability" that the acquisition would tend "substantially to lessen competition" or tend to "create a monopoly." The Government appealed.

BLACK, JUSTICE: . . . The record shows the following facts relevant to our decision. The market involved here is the retail grocery market in the Los Angeles area. In 1958 Von's retail sales ranked third in the area and Shopping Bag's ranked sixth. In 1960 their sales together were 7.5% of the total two and one-half billion dollars of retail groceries sold in the Los Angeles market each year. For many years before the merger both companies had enjoyed great success as rapidly growing companies. From 1948 to 1958 the number of Von's stores in the Los Angeles area practically doubled from 14 to 27, while at the same time the number of Shopping Bag's stores jumped from 15 to 34. During that same decade, Von's sales increased fourfold and its share of the market almost doubled while Shopping Bag's sales multiplied seven times and its share of the market tripled. The merger of these two highly successful, expanding and aggressive competitors created the second largest grocery chain in Los Angeles with sales of almost $172,488,000 annually. In addition the findings of the District Court show that the number of owners operating a single store in the Los Angeles retail grocery market decreased from 5,365 in 1950 to 3,818 in 1961. By 1963, three years after the merger, the number of single-store owners had dropped still further to 3,590. During roughly the same period from 1953 to 1962 the number of chains with two or more grocery stores increased from 96 to 150. While the grocery business was being concentrated into the hands of fewer and fewer owners, the small companies were continually being absorbed by the larger firms through mergers. According to an exhibit prepared by one of the Government's expert witnesses, in the period from 1949 to 1958 nine of the top 20 chains acquired 126 stores from their smaller competitors. Figures of a principal defense witness, . . . illustrate the many acquisitions and mergers in the Los Angeles grocery industry from 1953 through 1961 including acquisitions made by Food Giant, Alpha Beta, Fox and Mayfair, all among the 10 leading chains in the area. Moreover, a table prepared by the Federal Trade Commission appearing in the Government's reply brief, but not a part of the record here, shows that acquisitions and mergers in the Los Angeles retail grocery market have continued at a rapid rate since the merger. These facts alone are enough to cause us to conclude contrary to the District Court that the Von's–Shopping Bag merger did violate § 7. Accordingly, we reverse. . . .

Like the Sherman Act in 1890 and the Clayton Act in 1914, the basic purpose of the 1950 Celler-Kefauver Bill was to prevent economic concentration in the American economy by keeping a large number of small competitors in business. In stating the purposes of the bill, both of its sponsors, Representative Celler and Senator Kefauver, emphasized their fear, widely shared by other members of Congress, that this concentration was rapidly driving the small businessman out of the market. The period from 1940 to 1947, which was at the center of attention throughout the hearings and debates on the Celler-Kefauver Bill, had been characterized by a series of mergers between large corporations and their smaller competitors resulting in the steady erosion of the small independent business in our economy. . . .

The facts of this case present exactly the threatening trend toward concentration which Congress wanted to halt. The number of small grocery companies in the Los Angeles retail grocery market had been declining rapidly before the merger and continued to decline rapidly afterwards. This rapid decline in the number of grocery store owners moved hand in hand with a large number of significant absorptions of the small companies by the larger ones. In the midst of this steadfast trend toward concentration, Von's and Shopping Bag, two of the most successful and largest companies in the area, jointly owning 66 grocery stores merged to become the second largest chain in Los Angeles. This merger cannot be defended on the ground that one of the companies was about to fail or that the two had to merge to save themselves from destruction by some larger and more powerful competitor. What we have on the contrary is simply the case of two already powerful companies merging in a way which makes them even more powerful than they were before. If ever such a merger would not violate § 7, certainly it does when it takes place in a market characterized by a long and continuous trend toward fewer and fewer owner-competitors which is exactly the sort of trend which Congress, with power to do so, declared must be arrested.

Appellee's primary argument is that the merger between Von's and Shopping Bag is not prohibited by § 7 because the Los Angeles grocery market was competitive before the merger, has been since, and may continue to be in the future. Even so, § 7 "requires not merely an appraisal of the immediate impact of the merger upon competition, but a prediction of its impact upon competitive conditions in the future; this is what is meant when it is said that the amended § 7 was intended to arrest anticompetitive tendencies in their 'incipiency.' " *United States v. Philadelphia Nat'l Bank,* 374 U.S., at p. 362. It is enough for us that Congress feared that a market marked at the same time by both a continuous decline in the number of small businesses and a large number of mergers would, slowly but inevitably gravitate from a market of many small competitors to one dominated by one or a few giants, and competition would thereby be destroyed. Congress passed the Celler-Kefauver Bill to prevent such a destruction of competition. Our cases since the passage of that bill have faithfully endeavored to enforce this congressional command. We adhere to them now.

Here again as in *United States v. El Paso Gas Co.,* 376 U.S. 651, 662, . . . since appellees "have been on notice of the anti-trust charge from almost the beginning . . . we not only reverse the judgment below but direct the District Court to order divestiture without delay." [REVERSED]

[Two of the Justices issued a strong dissent from the majority opinion above, stating in effect that the court was holding that the existence of certain superficial facts which were unrelated to any actual anticompetitive effects lead to a conclusion that the merger violated Section 7, per se. They argued that there should be demonstrated at least a reasonable probability of a substantial reduction in competition before a merger is outlawed, and that an examination of the economic facts in the relevant market did not establish such a probability in the *Von's Grocery* case. Excerpts from their dissent follow.]

STEWART, JUSTICE, dissenting (joined by JUSTICE HARLAN): . . . The concept of arresting restraints of trade in their "incipiency" was not an innovation of the 1950 amendment. The notion of incipiency was part of the report on the original Clayton Act by the Senate Committee on the Judiciary in 1914, and it was reiterated in the Senate report in 1950. That notion was not left undefined. The legislative history leaves no doubt that the applicable standard for measuring the substantiality of the effect of a merger on competition was that of a "reasonable probability" of lessening competition. The standard was thus more stringent than that of a "mere possibility" on the one hand and more lenient than that of a "certainty" on the other. I cannot agree that the retail grocery business in Los Angeles is in an incipient or any other stage of a trend toward a lessening of competition, or that the effective level of concentration in the industry has increased. Moreover, there is no indication that the present merger, or the trend in this industry as a whole, augurs any danger whatsoever for the small businessman. The Court has substituted bare conjecture for the statutory standard of a reasonable probability that competition may be lessened.

The Court rests its conclusion on the "crucial point" that, in the 11-year period between 1950 and 1961, the number of single-store grocery firms in Los Angeles decreased 29% from 5,365 to 3,818. Such a decline should, of course, be no more than a fact calling for further investigation of the competitive trend in the industry. For the Court, however, that decline is made the end, not the beginning, of the analysis. In the counting-of-heads game played today by the Court, the reduction in the number of single-store operators becomes a yard-stick for automatic disposition of cases under § 7.

I believe that even the most superficial analysis of the record makes plain the fallacy of the Court's syllogism that competition is necessarily reduced when the bare number of competitors has declined. In any meaningful sense, the structure of the Los Angeles grocery market remains unthreatened by concentration. Local competition is vigorous to a fault, not only among chain stores themselves but also between chain stores and single store operators. The continuing population explosion of the Los Angeles area, which has outrun the expansion plans of even the largest chains, offers a surfeit of business opportunity for stores of all sizes. Affiliated with cooperatives that give the smallest store the buying strength of its largest competitor, new stores have taken full advantage of the remarkable ease of entry into the market. And, most important of all, the record simply cries out that the numerical decline in the number of single-store owners is the result of transcending social and technological changes that positively preclude the inference that competition has suffered because of the attrition of competitors.

Section 7 was never intended by Congress for use by the Court as a charter to roll back the supermarket revolution. Yet the Court's opinion is hardly more than a requiem for the so-called "Mom and Pop" grocery stores —the bakery and butcher shops, the vegetable and fish markets—that are now economically and technologically obsolete in many parts of the country. No action by this Court can resurrect the old single-line Los Angeles food stores that have been run over by the automobile or obliterated by the freeway. The transformation of American society since the Second World War has not completely shelved these specialty stores, but it has relegated them to a much less central role in our food economy. Today's dominant enterprise in food retailing is the supermarket. Accessible to the housewife's automobile from a wide radius, it houses under a single roof the entire food requirements of the family. Only through the sort of reactionary philosophy that this Court long ago rejected in the Due Process Clause area can the Court read into the legislative history of § 7 its attempt to make the automobile stand still, to mold the food economy of today into the market pattern of another era.*

The District Court's finding of fact that there was no increase in market concentration before or after the merger is amply supported by the evidence if concentration is gauged by any measure other than that of a census of the number of competing units. Between 1948 and 1958, the market share of Safeway, the leading grocery chain in Los Angeles, declined from 14% to 8%. The combined market shares of the top two chains declined from 21% to 14% over the same period; for the period 1952-1958, the combined shares of the three, four, and five largest firms also declined. It is true that between 1948 and 1958, the combined shares of the top 20 firms in the market increased from 44% to 57%. The crucial fact here, however, is that seven of these top 20 firms in 1958 were not even in existence

* [footnote by Justice Stewart] ". . . Plenty of living American men and women remember an era when virtually all groceries were sold through very small stores none of which had 'any significant market share.' Was this era the high point of competition in food retailing? Many little towns had, in fact, only one place where a given kind of food could be bought. In a typical city neighborhood, defined by the range of a housewife's willingness to lug groceries home on foot, there might be three or four relaxed 'competitors.' If she did not like the price or quality offered by them, she could take her black-string market bag, board a trolley car, and try her luck among the relaxed 'competitors' of some other neighborhood." Ways, A New "Worst" in Antitrust, Fortune, April 1966, pp. 111-112. . . .

In the present case, the District Court found that in the era preceding the rise of the supermarkets, "the area from which the typical store drew most of its customers was limited to a block or two in any direction and if a particular grocery store happened to be the only one in its immediate neighborhood, it had a virtual monopoly of local trade." Thus, the Court's aphorism in *United States v. Philadelphia Nat'l Bank*, 374 U.S. 321, 363—that "[c]ompetition is likely to be greatest when there are many sellers, none of which has any significant market share"—is peculiarly maladroit in the historic context of the retail food industry.

as chains in 1948. Because of the substantial turnover in the membership of the top 20 firms, the increase in market share of the top 20 as a group is hardly a reliable indicator of any tendency toward market concentration.

In addition, statistics in the record for the period 1953–1962 strongly suggest that the retail grocery industry in Los Angeles is less concentrated today than it was a decade ago. During this period, the number of chain store firms in the area rose from 96 to 150, or 56%. That increase occurred overwhelmingly among chains of the very smallest size, those composed of two or three grocery stores. Between 1953 and 1962, the number of such "chains" increased from 56 to 104, or 86%. Although chains of 10 or more stores increased from 10 to 24 during the period, seven of these 24 chains were not even in existence as chains in Los Angeles in 1953.

Yet even these dramatic statistics do not fully reveal the dynamism and vitality of competition in the retail grocery business in Los Angeles during the period. The record shows that at various times during the period 1953–1962, no less than 269 separate chains were doing business in Los Angeles, of which 208 were two- or three-store chains. During that period, therefore, 173 new chains made their appearance in the market area, and 119 chains went out of existence as chain stores. The vast majority of this market turbulence represented turnover in chains of two or three stores; 143 of the 173 new chains born during the period were chains of this size. Testimony in the record shows that, almost without exception, these new chains were the outgrowth of successful one-store operations. There is no indication that comparable turmoil did not equally permeate single-store operations in the area. In fashioning its *per se* rule, based on the net arithmetical decline in the number of single-store operators, the Court completely disregards the obvious procreative vigor of competition in the market as reflected in the turbulent history of entry and exit of competing small chains. . . .

The Court's reliance on the fact that nine of the top 20 chains acquired 120 stores in the Los Angeles area between 1949 and 1958 does not withstand analysis in light of the complete record. Forty percent of these acquisitions, representing 48 stores with gross sales of more than $71,000,-000, were made by Fox, Yor-Way, and McDaniels, which ranked 9th, 11th, and 20th, respectively, according to 1958 sales in the market. Each of these firms subsequently went into bankruptcy as a result of over-expansion, under-capitalization, or inadequate managerial experience. This substantial post-acquisition demise of relatively large chains hardly comports with the Court's tacit portrayal of the inexorable march of the market toward oligopoly. . . .

With regard to the "plight" of the small businessman, the record is unequivocal that his competitive position is strong and secure in the Los Angeles retail grocery industry. The most aggressive competitors against the

larger retail chains are frequently the operators of single stores. The vitality of these independents is directly attributable to the recent and spectac-
ular growth in California of three large cooperative buying organizations.
Membership in these groups is unrestricted; through them, single-store
operators are able to purchase their goods at prices competitive with those
offered by suppliers even to the largest chains. The rise of these cooperative
organizations has introduced a significant new source of countervailing
power against the market power of the chain stores, without in any way
sacrificing the advantages of independent operation. In the face of the
substantial assistance available to independents through membership in
such cooperatives, the Court's implicit equation between the market power
and the market share resulting from the present merger seems completely
invalid. . . .

The harsh standard now applied by the Court to horizontal mergers
may prejudice irrevocably the already difficult choice faced by numerous
successful small and medium-sized businessmen in the myriad smaller markets where the effect of today's decision will be felt, whether to expand by
buying or by building additional facilities. And by foreclosing future sale as
one attractive avenue of eventual market exit, the Court's decision may over
the long run deter new market entry and tend to stifle the very competition
it seeks to foster.

In a single sentence and an omnibus footnote at the close of its opinion, the Court pronounces its work consistent with the line of our decisions
under § 7 since the passage of the 1950 amendment. The sole consistency
that I can find is that in litigation under § 7, the Government always
wins. . . .

The emotional impact of a merger between the third and sixth largest
competitors in a given market, however fragmented, is understandable, but
that impact cannot substitute for the analysis of the effect of the merger on
competition that Congress required by the 1950 amendment. Nothing in
the present record indicates that there is more than an ephemeral possibility
that the effect of this merger may be substantially to lessen competition.
Section 7 clearly takes "reasonable probability" as its standard. That standard has not been met here, and I would therefore affirm the judgment of the
District Court.

7   CONGLOMERATE AND PRODUCT EXTENSION MERGERS

In the *Procter & Gamble* case, infra, the FTC challenged Procter's acquisition
of a company whose product did not directly compete with those of Procter
but was in the same general market category—laundry products. The acquisition could not be labeled horizontal, vertical or conglomerate, according
to the FTC and the Supreme Court. The Court seems to have created a fourth

category called "product extension" mergers. It is yet too early to tell whether or not there will be substantive disinctions between conglomerate and product extension mergers, or whether the latter will be the more suspect of the two and more likely to be challenged. The *Procter* case may well be a landmark decision.

FTC V. PROCTER & GAMBLE CO.
87 S.Ct. 1224 (1967)

DOUGLAS, JUSTICE: This is a proceeding initiated by the Federal Trade Commission charging that respondent, Procter & Gamble Co., had acquired the assets of Clorox Chemical Co. in violation of § 7 of the Clayton Act, as amended. The charge was that Procter's acquisition of Clorox may substantially lessen competition or tend to create a monopoly in the production and sale of household liquid bleaches.

Following evidentiary hearings, the hearing examiner rendered his decision in which he concluded that the acquisition was unlawful and ordered divestiture. On appeal, the Commission reversed, holding that the record as then constituted was inadequate, and remanded to the examiner for additional evidentiary hearings. After the additional hearings, the examiner again held the acquisition unlawful and ordered divestiture. The Commission affirmed the examiner and ordered divestiture. The Court of Appeals for the Sixth Circuit reversed and directed that the Commission's complaint be dismissed. We find that the Commission's findings were amply supported by the evidence, and that the Court of Appeals erred.

As indicated by the Commission in its painstaking and illuminating report, it does not particularly aid analysis to talk of this merger in conventional terms, namely, horizontal or vertical or conglomerate. This merger may most appropriately be described as a "product-extension merger," as the Commission stated. The facts are not disputed, and a summary will demonstrate the correctness of the Commission's decision.

At the time of the merger, Clorox was the leading manufacturer in the heavily concentrated household liquid bleach industry. It is agreed that household liquid bleach is the relevant line of commerce. The product is used in the home as a germicide and disinfectant, and, more importantly, as a whitening agent in washing clothes and fabrics. It is a distinctive product with no close substitutes. Liquid bleach is a low-price, high-turnover consumer product sold mainly through grocery stores and supermarkets. The relevant geographical market is the Nation and a series of regional markets. Because of high shipping costs and low sales price, it is not feasible to ship the product more than 300 miles from its point of manufacture. Most manufacturers are limited to competition within a single region since they have but one plant. Clorox is the only firm selling nationally; it has 13 plants distributed throughout the Nation. Purex, Clorox's closest competitor in size, does not distribute its bleach in the northeast or middle-Atlantic States; in 1957 Purex's bleach was available in less than 50% of the national market.

At the time of the acquisition, Clorox was the leading manufacturer of household liquid bleach, with 48.8% of the national sales—annual sales of slightly less than $40,000,000. Its market share had been steadily increasing for the five years prior to the merger. Its nearest rival was Purex, which manufactures a number of products other than household liquid bleaches, including abrasive cleaners, toilet soap, and detergents. Purex accounted for 15.7% of the household liquid bleach market. The industry is highly concentrated; in 1957 Clorox and Purex accounted for almost 65% of the Nation's household liquid bleach sales, and, together with four other firms, for almost 80%. The remaining 20% was divided among over 200 small producers. Clorox had total assets of $12,000,000; only eight producers had assets in excess of $1,000,000 and very few had assets of more than $75,000.

In light of the territorial limitations on distribution, national figures do not give an accurate picture of Clorox's dominance in the various regions. Thus, Clorox's seven principal competitors did no business in New England, the mid-Atlantic States, or metropolitan New York. Clorox's share of the sales in those areas was 56%, 72% and 64% respectively. Even in regions where its principal competitors were active, Clorox maintained a dominant position. Except in metropolitan Chicago and the west-central States Clorox accounted for at least 29%, and often a much higher percentage, of liquid bleach sales.

Since all liquid bleach is chemically identical, advertising and sales promotion is vital. In 1957 Clorox spent almost $3,700,000 on advertising, imprinting the value of its bleach in the mind of the consumer. In addition, it spent $1,700,000 for other promotional activities. The Commission found that these heavy expenditures went far to explain why Clorox maintained so high a market share despite the fact that its brand, though chemically indistinguishable from rival brands, retailed for a price equal to or, in many instances, higher than its competitors.

Procter is a large, diversified manufacturer of low-price, high-turnover household products sold through grocery, drug, and department stores. Prior to its acquisition of Clorox, it did not produce household liquid bleach. Its 1957 sales were in excess of $1,100,000,000 from which it realized profits of more than $67,000,000; its assets were over $500,000,000. Procter has been marked by rapid growth and diversification. It has successfully developed and introduced a number of new products. Its primary activity is in the general area of soaps, detergents, and cleansers; in 1957, of total domestic sales, more than one-half (over $500,000,000) were in this field. Procter was the dominant factor in this area. It accounted for 54.4% of all packaged detergent sales. The industry is heavily concentrated—Procter and its nearest competitors, Colgate-Palmolive and Lever Brothers, account for 80% of the market.

In the marketing of soaps, detergents and cleansers, as in the marketing of household liquid bleach, advertising and sales promotion are vital. In 1957, Procter was the Nation's largest advertiser, spending more than $80,000,000 on advertising and an additional $47,000,000 on sales promotion. Due to its tremendous volume, Procter receives substantial discounts from the media. As a multi-product producer Procter enjoys substantial advantages in advertising and sales promotion. Thus, it can and does feature several products in its promotions, reducing the printing, mailing, and other costs for each product. It also purchases network programs on behalf of several products, enabling it to give each product network exposure at a fraction of the cost per product that a firm with only one product to advertise would incur.

Prior to the acquisition, Procter was in the course of diversifying into product lines related to its basic detergent-soap-cleanser business. Liquid bleach was a distinct possibility since packaged detergents—Procter's primary product line—and liquid bleach are used complementarily in washing clothes and fabrics, and in general household cleaning. As noted by the Commission:

> *Packaged detergents—Procter's most important product category—and household liquid bleach are used complementarily, not only in the washing of clothes and fabrics, but also in general household cleaning, since liquid bleach is a germicide and disinfectant as well as a whitener. From the consumer's viewpoint, then, packaged detergents and liquid bleach are closely related products. But the area of relatedness between products of Procter and of Clorox is wider. Household cleansing agents in general, like household liquid bleach, are low-cost, high-turnover household consumer goods marketed chiefly through grocery stores and pre-sold to the consumer by the manufacturer through massive advertising and sales promotions. Since products of both parties to the merger are sold to the same customers, at the same stores, and by the same merchandising methods, the possibility arises of significant integration at both the marketing and distribution levels.*

The decision to acquire Clorox was the result of a study conducted by Procter's promotion department designed to determine the advisability of entering the liquid bleach industry. The initial report noted the ascendancy of liquid bleach in the large and expanding household bleach market, and recommended that Procter purchase Clorox rather than enter independently. Since a large investment would be needed to obtain a satisfactory market share, acquisition of the industry's leading firm was attractive, "Taking over the Clorox business . . . could be a way of achieving a dominant position in the liquid bleach market quickly, which would pay out reasonably well."

The initial report predicted that Procter's "sales distribution and manufacturing setup" could increase Clorox's share of the markets in areas where it was low. The final report confirmed the conclusions of the initial report and emphasized that Procter would make more effective use of Clorox's advertising budget and that the merger would facilitate advertising economies. A few months later, Procter acquired the assets of Clorox in the name of a wholly owned subsidiary, the Clorox Company, in exchange for Procter stock.

The Commission found that the acquisition might substantially lessen competition. The findings and reasoning of the Commission need be only briefly summarized. The Commission found that the substitution of Procter with its huge assets and advertising advantages for the already dominant Clorox would dissuade new entrants and discourage active competition from the firms already in the industry due to fear of retaliation by Procter. The Commission thought it relevant that retailers might be induced to give Clorox preferred shelf space since it would be manufactured by Procter, which also produced a number of other products marketed by the retailers. There was also the danger that Procter might underprice Clorox in order to drive out competition, and subsidize the under-pricing with revenue from other products. The Commission carefully reviewed the effect of the acquisition on the structure of the industry, noting that "the practical tendency of the . . . merger . . . is to transform the liquid bleach industry into an arena of big business competition only, with the few small firms falling by the wayside, unable to compete with their giant rivals." Further, the merger would seriously diminish potential competition by eliminating Procter as a potential entrant into the industry. Prior to the merger, the Commission found that Procter was the most likely prospective entrant, and absent the merger would have remained on the periphery, restraining Clorox from exercising its market power. If Procter had actually entered, Clorox's dominant position would have been eroded and the concentration of the industry reduced. The Commission stated that it had not placed reliance on post-acquisition evidence in holding the merger unlawful.

The Court of Appeals said that the Commission's finding of illegality had been based on "treacherous conjecture," mere possibility and suspicion. It dismissed the fact that Clorox controlled almost 50% of the industry, that two firms controlled 65%, and that six firms controlled 80% with the observation that "[t]he fact that in addition to the six . . . producers sharing eighty per cent of the market, there were two hundred smaller producers . . . would not seem to indicate anything unhealthy about the market conditions." It dismissed the finding that Procter, with its huge resources and prowess, would have more leverage than Clorox with the statement that it was Clorox which had the "knowhow" in the industry, and that Clorox's finances were adequate for its purposes. As for the possibility that Procter would use its tremendous advertising budget and volume discounts to push

Clorox, the court found "it difficult to base a finding of illegality on discounts on advertising." It rejected the Commission's finding that the merger eliminated the potential competition of Procter because "there was no reasonable probability that Procter would have entered the household liquid bleach market but for the merger." "There was no evidence tending to prove that Procter ever intended to enter this field on its own." Finally, "there was no evidence that Procter at any time in the past engaged in predatory practices, or that it intended to do so in the future."

The Court of Appeals also heavily relied on post-acquisition "evidence to the effect that the other producers subsequent to the merger were selling more bleach for more money than ever before," that "there [had] been no significant change in Clorox's market share in the four years subsequent to the merger," and concluded that "this evidence certainly does not prove anti-competitive effects of the merger." The Court of Appeals, in our view, misapprehended the standards for its review and the standards applicable in a § 7 proceeding.

Section 7 of the Clayton Act was intended to arrest the anticompetitive effects of market power in their incipiency. The core question is whether a merger may substantially lessen competition, and necessarily requires a prediction of the merger's impact on competition, present and future. The section can deal only with probabilities, not with certainties. And there is certainly no requirement that the anticompetitive power manifest itself in anticompetitive action before § 7 can be called into play. If the enforcement of § 7 turned on the existence of actual anticompetitive practices, the congressional policy of thwarting such practices in their incipiency would be frustrated.

All mergers are within the reach of § 7, and all must be tested by the same standard, whether they are classified as horizontal, vertical, conglomerate * or other. As noted by the Commission this merger is neither horizontal, vertical, nor conglomerate. Since the products of the acquired company are complementary to those of the acquiring company and may be produced with similar facilities, marketed through the same channels and in the same manner, and advertised by the same media, the Commission aptly called this acquisition a "product-extension merger";

By this acquisition . . . Procter has not diversified its interests in the sense of expanding into a substantially different, unfamiliar market or industry. Rather, it has entered a market which adjoins, as it were, those markets in which it is already established, and which is virtually indistinguishable from them insofar as the problems and techniques of marketing the product to the ultimate consumer are concerned. As a high official of Procter put it, commenting on the acquisition of Clorox, "While this is a completely new

---

* [footnote by the Court] A pure conglomerate merger is one in which there are no economic relationships between the acquiring and the acquired firm.

business for us, taking us for the first time into the marketing of a household bleach and disinfectant, we are thoroughly at home in the field of manufacturing and marketing low-priced, rapid turn-over consumer products."

The anticompetitive effects with which this product-extension merger is fraught can easily be seen; (1) the substitution of the powerful acquiring firm for the smaller, but already dominant, firm may substantially reduce the competitive structure of the industry by raising entry barriers and by dissuading the smaller firms from aggressively competing; (2) the acquisition eliminates the potential competition of the acquiring firm.

The liquid bleach industry was already oligopolistic before the acquisition, and price competition was certainly not as vigorous as it would have been if the industry were competitive. Clorox enjoyed a dominant position nationally, and its position approached monopoly proportions in certain areas. The existence of some 200 fringe firms certainly does not belie that fact. Nor does the fact, relied upon by the court below, that after the merger, producers other than Clorox "were selling more bleach for more money than ever before." In the same period, Clorox increased its share from 48.8% to 52%. The interjection of Procter into the market considerably changed the situation. There is every reason to assume that the smaller firms would become more cautious in competing due to their fear of retaliation by Procter. It is probable that Procter would become the price leader and that oligopoly would become more rigid.

The acquisition may also have the tendency of raising the barriers to new entry. The major competitive weapon in the successful marketing of bleach is advertising. Clorox was limited in this area by its relatively small budget and its inability to obtain substantial discounts. By contrast, Procter's budget was much larger; and, although it would not devote its entire budget to advertising Clorox, it could divert a large portion to meet the short-term threat of a new entrant. Procter would be able to use its volume discounts to advantage in advertising Clorox. Thus, a new entrant would be much more reluctant to face the giant Procter than it would have been to face the smaller Clorox.

Possible economies cannot be used as a defense to illegality. Congress was aware that some mergers which lessen competition may also result in economies but it struck the balance in favor of protecting competition.

The Commission also found that the acquisition of Clorox by Procter eliminated Procter as a potential competitor. The Court of Appeals declared that this finding was not supported by evidence because there was no evidence that Procter's management had ever intended to enter the industry independently and that Procter had never attempted to enter. The evidence, however, clearly shows that Procter was the most likely entrant. Procter had recently launched a new abrasive cleaner in an industry similar to the liquid bleach industry, and had wrested leadership from a brand that had enjoyed even a larger market share than had Clorox. Procter was engaged in a vigorous program of diversifying into product lines closely related to its basic products. Liquid bleach was a natural avenue of diversification since it is complementary to Procter's products, is sold to the same customers through the same channels, and is advertised and merchandised in the same manner. Procter had substantial advantages in advertising and sales promotions, which, as we have seen, are vital to the success of liquid bleach. No manufacturer had a patent on the product or its manufacture, necessary information relating to manufacturing methods and processes were readily available, there was no shortage of raw material, and the machinery and equipment required for a plant of efficient capacity were available at reasonable cost. Procter's management was experienced in producing and marketing goods similar to liquid bleach. Procter had considered the possibility of independently entering but decided against it because the acquisition of Clorox would enable Procter to capture a more commanding share of the market.

It is clear that the existence of Procter at the edge of the industry exerted considerable influence on the market. First, the market behavior of the liquid bleach industry was influenced by each firm's predictions of the market behavior of its competitors, actual and potential. Second, the barriers to entry by a firm of Procter's size and with its advantages were not significant. There is no indication that the barriers were so high that the price Procter would have to charge would be above the price that would maximize the profits of the existing firms. Third, the number of potential entrants was not so large that the elimination of one would be insignificant. Few firms would have the temerity to challenge a firm as solidly entrenched as Clorox. Fourth, Procter was found by the Commission to be the most likely entrant. These findings of the Commission were amply supported by the evidence.

The judgment of the Court of Appeals is reversed and remanded with instructions to affirm and enforce the Commission's order. . . .

The issue presented on the appeal of the above case was whether the FTC's finding of a violation of Section 7 of the Clayton Act was supported by substantial evidence. Thus, it gives some notion of what conclusions of fact by the Commission are likely to be deemed by it as indicating that a particular product extension or conglomerate merger is anticompetitive and illegal. However, it is clear that guidelines for the legality of these types of mergers which have been developed by the FTC and the courts are much less complete and understandable than those concerning vertical and horizontal mergers.

CHAPTER THIRTEEN

ANTITRUST ASPECTS OF MARKETING

1 INTRODUCTION

This chapter will deal with some of the more important restrictions imposed by the antitrust laws on marketing policy with regard to day-by-day business operations. To what extent and in what fashion can a manufacturer of goods require that retailers observe minimum resale prices as set by the manufacturer? To what extent is it illegal to charge different prices to different customers for the same product? For example, aside from costs of transportation, is it permissible to differentiate in price beween the purchasers in one region from those in an entirely different region when those in the first do not compete at all with those in the second? These and other questions relating to business operations and antitrust are considered in the sections which follow.

2 RESALE PRICE MAINTENANCE

The purpose of a manufacturer of a brand or trade name product in having his product's retail price be maintained at a minimum established by him was discussed in Chapter 11,[1] where it was indicated that he may wish to create the image of high quality which consumers often relate to high prices. In addition he may desire to protect his regular retail outlets from price-cutting competition with discount houses, which frequently attract customers by offering a few products for sale as "loss-leaders." As was noted, if a state has a fair trade law which permits a manufacturer to contract with retailers to maintain minimum prices for his brand name goods, such contracts are enforceable and are not in violation of the antitrust laws. Even nonsigners may be bound to observe the prices thereby established if the state law so provides.[2] However, while forty-three states have fair trade laws as of this writing, in twenty-two of these the *state* courts held nonsigner provisions unconstitutional, and the Hawaii legislature repealed such a pro-

---

[1] See section 4, Chapter 11, page 379.
[2] See *Hudson Distribs., Inc. v. Upjohn Co.*, 377 U.S. 386 (1964), Chapter 11, page 403.

vision. Obviously, if nonsigners are not bound, a fair trade law will give very little, if any, real protection to a manufacturer. Additional problems manufacturers face in maintaining fair trade programs are the great growth in the number of discount houses which offer quality items at lower prices to profit from volume sales, and the extremely high cost of effective enforcement of fair trade contracts. As a result, many manufacturers have attempted other methods of maintaining minimum retail prices to maintain their product's reputation and good will, or enhanced subjective value in the consumer's mind.

In *United States v. Colgate Co.*[3] the Supreme Court upheld a District Court decision to dismiss an indictment charging Colgate with violating the Sherman Act by entering into an unlawful combination in restraint of trade. The indictment alleged that Colgate had created a combination with wholesale and retail dealers of its products for the purpose of procuring their adherence to minimum resale prices fixed by the defendant. The court summarized the various things that Colgate was charged with doing in order to carry out its purposes with the following language:

> *Distribution among dealers of letters, telegrams, circulars and lists showing uniform prices to be charged; urging them to adhere to such prices and notices, stating that no sales would be made to those who did not; requests, often complied with, for information concerning dealers who had departed from specified prices; investigation and discovery of those not adhering thereto and placing their names upon "suspended lists"; requests to offending dealers for assurances and promises of future adherence to prices, which were often given; uniform refusals to sell to any who failed to give the same; sales to those who did; similar assurances and promises required of, and given by, other dealers followed by sales to them; unrestricted sales to dealers with established accounts who had observed specified prices, etc. . . .*[4]

In affirming the District Court's dismissal of the indictment, the Supreme Court stated:

> *Considering all said in the opinion (notwithstanding some serious doubts) we are unable to accept the construction placed upon it by the Government. We cannot, e.g., wholly disregard the statement that "The retailer, after buying, could, if he chose, give away his purchase, or sell it at any price he saw fit, or not sell it at all; his course in these respects being affected only by the fact that he might by his action incur the displeasure of the manufacturer, who could refuse to make further sales to him, as he had the undoubted right to do." And we must conclude that, as interpreted below, the indictment does not charge Colgate & Company with selling its products to*

---

[3] 250 U.S. 300 (1919).
[4] *Id.* at 303.

dealers under agreements which obligated the latter not to resell except at prices fixed by the company.

The position of the defendant is more nearly in accord with the whole opinion and must be accepted. And as counsel for the Government were careful to state on the argument that this conclusion would require affirmation of the judgment below, an extended discussion of the principles involved is unnecessary.

The purpose of the Sherman Act is to prohibit monopolies, contracts and combinations which probably would unduly interfere with the free exercise of their rights by those engaged, or who wish to engage, in trade and commerce—in a word to preserve the right of freedom to trade. In the absence of any purpose to create or maintain a monopoly, the act does not restrict the long recognized right of trader or manufacturer engaged in an entirely private business, freely to exercise his own independent discretion as to parties with whom he will deal. And, of course, he may announce in advance the circumstances under which he will refuse to sell. "The trader or manufacturer, on the other hand, carries on an entirely private business, and can sell to whom he pleases." . . . "A retail dealer has the unquestioned right to stop dealing with a wholesaler for reasons sufficient to himself, and may do so because he thinks such dealer is acting unfairly in trying to undermine his trade." . . .[5]

The case which follows concerns a scheme of price maintenance very similar to Colgate's. In it the defendant, Parke Davis, argued that its activities were legal under the doctrine of the *Colgate* case.

UNITED STATES V. PARKE DAVIS & CO.
362 U.S. 29 (1960)

Parke Davis had announced the policy that it would sell its products only to those wholesalers and retailers who observed minimum resale prices suggested by the manufacturer. However, retailers in Washington, D.C., and Richmond, Virginia, began advertising and selling Parke Davis vitamins considerably below the suggested minimum retail price. To promote compliance with its price policy, Parke Davis informed the retailers and wholesalers in the area that it would refuse to sell to any *wholesaler* who *supplied* its products to any retailer who did not observe the suggested minimum retail prices. Several retailers continued to sell Parke Davis vitamins at a discount, and, when their names were furnished to the wholesalers, both Parke Davis and the wholesalers refused to fill their orders for *any* of the manufacturer's products. The government brought action for an injunction, which was dismissed by the District Court, and the government appealed.

[5] *Id.* at 306, 307.

BRENNAN, JUSTICE: . . . The District Court held that the Government's proofs did not establish a violation of the Sherman Act because "the actions of [Parke Davis] were properly unilateral and sanctioned by law under the doctrine laid down in the case of *United States v. Colgate & Co.,* 250 U.S. 300. . . .

The *Colgate* case came to this Court on writ of error under the Criminal Appeals Act, 34 Stat. 1246, from a District Court judgment dismissing an indictment for violation of the Sherman Act. The indictment proceeded solely upon the theory of an unlawful combination between Colgate and its wholesale and retail dealers for the purpose and with the effect of procuring adherence on the part of the dealers to resale prices fixed by the company. However, the District Court construed the indictment as not charging a combination by *agreement* between Colgate and its customers to maintain prices. This Court held that it must disregard the allegations of the indictment since the District Court's interpretation of the indictment was binding and that without an allegation of unlawful *agreement* there was no Sherman Act violation charged. The Court said:

The purpose of the Sherman Act is to prohibit monopolies, contracts and combinations which probably would unduly interfere with the free exercise of their rights by those engaged, or who wish to engage, in trade and commerce—in a word to preserve the right of freedom to trade. In the absence of any purpose to create or maintain a monopoly, the act does not restrict the long recognized right of trader or manufacturer engaged in an entirely private business, freely to exercise his own independent discretion as to parties with whom he will deal; and, of course, he may announce in advance the circumstances under which he will refuse to sell. 250 U.S. at page 307. . . .

The Government concedes for the purposes of this case that under the *Colgate* doctrine a manufacturer, having announced a price maintenance policy, may bring about adherence to it by refusing to deal with customers who do not observe that policy. The Government contends, however, that subsequent decisions of this Court compel the holding that what Parke Davis did here by entwining the wholesalers and retailers in a program to promote general compliance with its price maintenance policy went beyond mere customer selection and created combinations or conspiracies to enforce resale price maintenance in violation of §§ 1 and 3 of the Sherman Act. . . . Judicial inquiry is not to stop with a search of the record for evidence of purely contractual arrangements. The Sherman Act forbids combinations of traders to suppress competition. True, there results the same economic effect as is accomplished by a prohibited combination to suppress price competition if each customer, although induced to do so solely by a manufacturer's announced policy, independently decides to observe specified resale prices. So long as *Colgate* is not overruled, this result is tolerated but only when it is the consequence of a mere refusal to sell in the exercise of the manufacturer's right "freely to exercise his own independent discretion as to parties with whom he will deal." [250 U.S. 300] When the manufacturer's actions, as here, go beyond mere announcement of his policy and the simple refusal to deal, and he employs other means which effect adherence to his resale prices, this countervailing consideration is not present and therefore he has put together a combination in violation of the Sherman Act. Thus, whether an unlawful combination or conspiracy is proved is to be judged by what the parties actually did rather than by the words they used. . . .

The program upon which Parke Davis embarked to promote general compliance with its suggested resale prices plainly exceeded the limitations of the *Colgate* doctrine and under *Beech-Nut* and *Bausch & Lomb* effected arrangements which violated the Sherman Act. Parke Davis did not content itself with announcing its policy regarding retail prices and following this with a simple refusal to have business relations with any retailers who disregarded that policy. Instead Parke Davis used the refusal to deal with the wholesalers in order to elicit their willingness to deny Parke Davis products to retailers and thereby help gain the retailers' adherence to its suggested minimum retail prices. The retailers who disregarded the price policy were promptly cut off when Parke Davis supplied the wholesalers with their names. The large retailer who said he would "abide" by the price policy, the multi-unit Peoples Drug chain, was not cut off. In thus involving the wholesalers to stop the flow of Parke Davis products to the retailers, thereby inducing retailers' adherence to its suggested retail prices, Parke Davis created a combination with the retailers and the wholesalers to maintain retail prices and violated the Sherman Act. Although Parke Davis' originally announced wholesalers' policy would not under *Colgate* have violated the Sherman Act if its action thereunder was the simple refusal without more to deal with wholesalers who did not observe the wholesalers' Net Price Selling Schedule, that entire policy was tainted with the "vice of . . . illegality" . . . when Parke Davis used it as the vehicle to gain the wholesalers' participation in the program to effectuate the retailers' adherence to the suggested retail price. [JUDGMENT REVERSED AND CASE REMANDED WITH DIRECTIONS TO ISSUE INJUNCTION]

In the case which follows, a gasoline company owned its retail outlets, but leased most of them, including the one in question. The lessee was required to sell only the oil of the company, Union Oil, and by a consignment agreement contracted to maintain minimum retail prices as set by Union Oil. The legality of the consignment provision was challenged.

SIMPSON V. UNION OIL CO.
377 U.S. 13 (1964)

Simpson was the lessee and operator of one of the retail filling stations owned by Union Oil Company. Union Oil followed the practice of leasing its stations out to dealers such as Simpson on a year-to-year basis, and also requiring the lessees to sign a consignment agreement valid for a one-year period and thereafter until canceled by either party or until termination of the lease. The consignment agreement provided that title to consigned gasoline would remain in Union Oil until sold by Simpson, and all property taxes would be paid by Union Oil. However, under it Simpson was required to carry personal liability and property damage insurance for losses which might arise from his possession of the gasoline and was responsible for all losses of the gasoline itself, except for those due to certain acts of God. Simpson paid all the costs of operating the station, and was compensated by a commission on sales made. Under the portion of the consignment agreement in question, Union Oil set the prices at which Simpson sold the gasoline. During a local "gas war," Simpson sold gasoline at 2 cents below the price set by the company, and because of this, it refused to renew Simpson's lease upon termination. This suit was an action for treble damages, alleging that Union Oil's consignment contract authorizing it to set prices violated the Sherman Act. The District Court granted summary judgment to the company, which was affirmed by the Circuit Court of Appeals. Simpson then appealed to the Supreme Court, which granted certiorari.

DOUGLAS, JUSTICE: . . . If the "consignment" agreement achieves resale price maintenance in violation of the Sherman Act, it and the lease are being used to injure interstate commerce by depriving independent dealers of the exercise of free judgment whether to become consignees at all, or remain consignees, and, in any event, to sell at competitive prices. The fact that a retailer can refuse to deal does not give the supplier immunity if the arrangement is one of those schemes condemned by the antitrust laws.

There is actionable wrong whenever the restraint of trade or monopolistic practice has an impact on the market; and it matters not that the complainant may be only one merchant.

Congress has, by legislative fiat, determined that such prohibited activities are injurious to the public and has provided sanctions allowing private enforcement of the antitrust laws by an aggrieved party. These laws protect the victims of the forbidden practices as well as the public.

The fact that, on failure to renew a lease, another dealer takes Simpson's place and renders the same service to the public is no more an answer here than it was in *Poller v. Columbia Broadcasting System*, 368 U.S. 464, 473. For Congress, not the oil distributor, is the arbiter of the public interest; and

Congress has closely patrolled price fixing whether effected through resale price maintenance agreements or otherwise. The exclusive requirements contracts struck down in *Standard Oil Co. and Standard Stations v. United States*, 337 U.S. 293, were not saved because dealers need not have agreed to them, but could have gone elsewhere. If that were a defense, a supplier could regiment thousands of otherwise competitive dealers in resale price maintenance programs merely by fear of nonrenewal of short-term leases.

We made it clear in *United States v. Parke, Davis & Co.*, 362 U.S. 29, that a supplier may not use coercion on its retail outlets to achieve resale price maintenance. We reiterate that view, adding that it matters not what the coercive device is. *United States v. Colgate*, 250 U.S. 300, . . . was a case where there was assumed to be no agreement to maintain retail prices. Here we have such an agreement; it is used coercively, and, it promises to be equally if not more effective in maintaining gasoline prices than were the Parke, Davis techniques in fixing monopoly prices on drugs.

Consignments perform an important function in trade and commerce, and their integrity has been recognized by many courts, including this one. Yet consignments, though useful in allocating risks between the parties and determining their rights *inter se*, do not necessarily control the rights of others, whether they be creditors or sovereigns. Thus the device has been extensively regulated by the States. Congress, too, has entered parts of the field, establishing by the Act of June 10, 1930, 46 Stat. 531, as amended, 7 U.S.C. § 449a et seq., a pervasive system of control over commission merchants dealing in perishable agricultural commodities.

One who sends a rug or a painting or other work of art to a merchant or a gallery for sale at a minimum price can, of course, hold the consignee to the bargain. A retail merchant may, indeed, have inventory on consignment, the terms of which bind the parties *inter se*. Yet the consignor does not always prevail over creditors in case of bankruptcy, where a recording statute or a "traders act" or a "sign statute" is in effect. The interests of the Government also frequently override agreements that private parties make. Here we have an antitrust policy expressed in Acts of Congress. Accordingly, a consignment, no matter how lawful it might be as a matter of private contract law, must give way before the federal antitrust policy. Thus a consignment is not allowed to be used as a cloak to avoid § 3 of the Clayton Act. Nor does § 1 of the Sherman Act tolerate agreements for retail price maintenance. . . .

Dealers, like Simpson, are independent businessmen; and they have all or most of the indicia of entrepreneurs, except for price fixing. The risk of loss of the gasoline is on them, apart from acts of God. Their return is affected by the rise and fall in the market price, their commissions declining as retail prices drop. Practically the only power they have to be wholly independent businessmen, whose service depends on their own initiative and enterprise, is taken from them by the proviso that they must sell their gasoline at prices fixed by Union Oil. By reason of the lease and "consign-ment" agreement dealers are coercively laced into an arrangement under which their supplier is able to impose noncompetitive prices on thousands of persons whose prices otherwise might be competitive. The evil of this resale price maintenance program, like that of the requirements contracts held illegal by *Standard Oil Co. of California and Standard Stations v. United States,* supra, is its inexorable potentiality for and even certainty in destroy-ing competition in retail sales of gasoline by these nominal "consignees" who are in reality small struggling competitors seeking retail gas customers.

As we have said, an owner of an article may send it to a dealer who may in turn undertake to sell it only at a price determined by the owner. There is nothing illegal about that arrangement. When, however, a "consign-ment" device is used to cover a vast gasoline distribution system, fixing prices through many retail outlets, the antitrust laws prevent calling the "consignment" an agency, for then the end result of *United States v. Socony-Vacuum Oil Co.,* supra, would be avoided merely by clever manipulation of words, not by differences in substance. The present, coercive "consignment" device if successful against challenge under the antitrust laws, furnishes a wooden formula for administering prices on a vast scale.

Reliance is placed on *United States v. General Electric Co.,* 272 U.S. 476, where a consignment arrangement was utilized to market patented articles. Union Oil correctly argues that the consignment in that case somewhat parallels the one in the instant case. The Court in the *General Electric* case did not restrict its ruling to patented articles; it, indeed, said that the use of the consignment device was available to the owners of articles "patented or otherwise." . . . But whatever may be said of the General Electric case on its special facts, involving patents, it is not apposite to the special facts here.

The Court in that case particularly relied on the fact that patent rights have long included licenses "to make, use and vend" the patented article "for any royalty, or upon any condition the performance of which is reason-ably within the reward which the patentee by the grant of the patent is entitled to secure." Congress in establishing the patent system included 35 U.S.C. § 154, which provides in part: "Every patent shall contain a short title of the invention and a grant to the patentee, his heirs or assigns, for the term of seventeen years, of the right *to exclude others from making, using, or selling* the invention throughout the United States, referring to the specifi-cation for the particulars thereof."

"The right to manufacture, the right to sell, and the right to use are each substantive rights, and may be granted or conferred separately by the patentee." Long prior to the General Electric case, price fixing in the market-ing of patented articles had been condoned, provided it did not extend to sales by purchasers of the patented articles.

The patent laws which give a 17-year monopoly on "making, using, or selling the invention" are *in pari materia* with the antitrust laws and modify them *pro tanto*. That was the *ratio decidendi* of the *General Electric* case. We decline the invitation to extend it.

To allow Union Oil to achieve price fixing in this vast distribution system through this "consignment" device would be to make legality for antitrust purposes turn on clever draftsmanship. We refuse to let a matter so vital to a competitive system rest on such easy manipulation.

Hence on the issue of resale price maintenance under the Sherman Act there is nothing left to try, for there was an agreement for resale price maintenance, coercively employed.

The case must be remanded for a hearing on all the other issues in the case, including those raised under the McGuire Act, 66 Stat. 631, 15 U.S.C. § 45, and the damages, if any, suffered. We intimate no views on any other issue; we hold only that resale price maintenance through the present, coercive type of "consignment" agreement is illegal under the antitrust laws, and that petitioner suffered actionable wrong or damage. We reserve the question whether, when all the facts are known, there may be any equities that would warrant only prospective application in damage suits of the rule governing price fixing by the "consignment" device which we announce today. [REVERSED AND REMANDED]

The case which follows involved attempts by General Motors and a majority of its franchised dealers to protect themselves from price-cutting tactics of automobile discount sales houses in the Los Angeles area.

UNITED STATES V. GENERAL MOTORS CORP.
384 U.S. 127 (1966)

The United States brought action for injunction against General Motors and the three associations of the Chevrolet dealers located in the Los Angeles, California, area, to prevent the defendants from continuing an alleged conspiracy in restraint of trade in violation of the Sherman Act. All Chevrolet dealers in the locality belonged to at least one of the associations. The alleged conspiracy came about as a result of an attempt by the vast majority of the dealers and General Motors to prevent a small minority of the franchised dealers from participating with nonfranchised "discount houses" in retail sales of new Chevrolets. These discount houses claimed to the public that they could sell new cars at bargain prices. Although their relationships with franchised dealers were varied, there were two main methods of dealing. First, the discounter might refer his customer directly to the dealer, who would sell at a price previously agreed upon and pay a commission to the discounter, typically around $50, for supplying the customer. Second, the discounter himself might make the sale, with the dealer transferring title to the customer upon receiving an order from the discounter. Under this type of arrangement one dealer charged the discounter $85 more than invoice cost for the car, and the discounter tried to make the best deal he could with the buyer. About 12 of the 85 dealers in the area were in league with the discounters in some similar fashion. The others began to "feel the pinch" because of these discount sales. Many "potential customers received or thought they would receive a more attractive deal from a discounter who obtained his Chevrolets from a distant dealer." The discounters advertised alleged price savings widely. Besides losing sales, the nonparticipating dealers were often obliged to back up new-car warranties and furnish free service to the purchasers through discounters, because of General Motors' requirements concerning these warranties and services. These dealers and the dealers' associations prevailed upon General Motors to do something about bringing those who were doing business with discount houses into line.

General Motors co-operated with the dealers' associations in obtaining the agreement of each dealer to have nothing more to do with discounters and in enforcing said agreement. The District Court gave judgment to the defendants and the Government appealed to the Supreme Court.

Among other things, General Motors argued that its actions were justified as simply enforcing the "location clause" contained in its franchise agreements, by which dealers promised they would not move to or establish "a new or different location, branch sales office, branch service station, or place of business including any used car lot or location without the prior written approval of Chevrolet."

FORTAS, JUSTICE: . . . By mid-January General Motors had elicited from each dealer a promise not to do business with the discounters. But such agreements would require policing—a fact which had been anticipated. General Motors earlier had initiated contacts with firms capable of performing such a function. This plan, unilaterally to police the agreements, was displaced, however, in favor of a joint effort between General Motors, the three defendant associations, and a number of individual dealers.

On December 15, 1960, the three defendant associations had met and appointed a joint committee to study the situation and to keep in touch with Chevrolet's O'Connor. Early in 1961, the three associations agreed jointly to finance the "shopping" of the discounters to assure that no Chevrolet dealer continued to supply them with cars. Each of the associations contributed $5,000, and a professional investigator was hired. He was instructed to try to purchase new Chevrolets from the proscribed outlets, to tape record the transactions, if any, and to gather all the necessary documentary evidence—which the associations would then lay "at the doorstep of Chevrolet." These joint associational activities were both preceded and supplemented by similar "shopping" activities by individual dealers and by defendant Losor Chevrolet Dealers Association.

General Motors collaborated with these policing activities. There is evidence that zone manager O'Connor and a subordinate, Jere Faust, actively solicited the help of individual dealers in uncovering violations. Armed with information of such violations obtained from the dealers or their associations, O'Connor or members of his staff would ask the offending dealer to come in and talk. The dealer was then confronted with the car purchased by the "shopper," the documents of sale, and in most cases a tape recording of the transaction. In every instance, the embarrassed dealer repurchased the car, sometimes at a substantial loss, and promised to stop such sales. At the direction of O'Connor or a subordinate, the checks with which the cars were repurchased were made payable to an attorney acting jointly for the three defendant associations. . . .

By the Spring of 1961, the campaign to eliminate the discounters from commerce in new Chevrolet cars was a success. Sales through the discount outlets seem to have come to a halt. . . .

We have here a classic conspiracy in restraint of trade: joint, collaborative action by dealers, the defendant associations, and General Motors to eliminate a class of competitors by terminating business dealings between them and a minority of Chevrolet dealers and to deprive franchised dealers of their freedom to deal through discounters if they so choose. Against this fact of unlawful combination, the "location clause" is of no avail. Whatever General Motors might or might not lawfully have done to enforce individual Dealer Selling Agreements by action within the borders of those agreements and the relationship which each defines, is beside the point. And, because the action taken constitutes a combination or conspiracy, it is not necessary to consider what might be the legitimate interest of a dealer in securing compliance by others with the "location clause," or the lawfulness of action a dealer might individually take to vindicate this interest.

The District Court decided otherwise. It concluded that the described events did not add up to a combination or conspiracy violative of the antitrust laws. But its conclusion cannot be squared with its own specific findings of fact. These findings include the essentials of a conspiracy within § 1 of the Sherman Act: That in the summer of 1960 the Losor Chevrolet Dealers Association, "through some of its members," complained to General Motors personnel about sales through discounters (Finding 34); that at a Losor meeting in November 1960 the dealers there present agreed to embark on a letter-writing campaign directed at enlisting the aid of General Motors (Finding 35); that in December and January General Motors personnel discussed the matter with every Chevrolet dealer in the Los Angeles area and elicited from each a promise not to do business with the discounters (Finding 39); that representatives of the three associations of

Chevrolet dealers met on December 15, 1960, and created a joint investigating committee (Finding 40); that the three associations then undertook jointly to police the agreements obtained from each of the dealers by General Motors; that the associations supplied information to General Motors for use by it in bringing wayward dealers into line, and that Chevrolet's O'Connor asked the associations to do so (Findings 41 and 42); that as a result of this collaborative effort, a number of Chevrolet dealers were induced to repurchase cars they had sold through discounters and to promise to abjure such sales in the future (Finding 42).

These findings by the trial judge compel the conclusion that a conspiracy to restrain trade was proved. The error of the trial court lies in its failure to apply the correct and established standard for ascertaining the existence of a combination or conspiracy under § 1 of the Sherman Act. The trial court attempted to justify its conclusion on the following reasoning: That each defendant and alleged co-conspirator acted to promote its own self interest; that General Motors, as well as the defendant associations and their members, has a lawful interest in securing compliance with the "location clause" and in thus protecting the franchise system of distributing automobiles—business arrangements which the court deemed lawful and proper; and that in seeking to vindicate these interests the defendants and their alleged co-conspirators entered into no "agreements" among themselves, although they may have engaged in "parallel action."

These factors do not justify the result reached. It is of no consequence, for purposes of determining whether there has been a combination or conspiracy under § 1 of the Sherman Act, that each party acted in its own lawful interest. Nor is it of consequence for this purpose whether the "location clause" and franchise system are lawful or economically desirable. And although we regard as clearly erroneous and irreconcilable with others of its findings the trial court's conclusory "finding" that there had been no "agreement" among the defendants and their alleged co-conspirators, it has long been settled that explicit agreement is not a necessary part of a Sherman Act conspiracy—certainly not where, as here, joint and collaborative action was pervasive in the initiation, execution, and fulfillment of the plan.

Neither individual dealers nor the associations acted independently or separately. The dealers collaborated, through the associations and otherwise, among themselves and with General Motors, both to enlist the aid of General Motors and to enforce dealers' promises to forsake the discounters. The associations explicitly entered into a joint venture to assist General Motors in policing the dealers' promises, and their joint proffer of aid was accepted and utilized by General Motors.

Nor did General Motors confine its activities to the contractual boundaries of its relationships with individual dealers. As the trial court found (Finding 39), General Motors at no time announced that it would terminate the franchise of any dealer who furnished cars to the discounters. The evidence indicates that it had no intention of acting in this unilateral fashion. On the contrary, over-riding corporate policy with respect to proper dealer relations dissuaded General Motors from engaging in this sort of wholly unilateral conduct, the validity of which under the antitrust laws was assumed, without being decided, in *Parke Davis, supra.*

As Parke Davis had done, General Motors sought to elicit from each dealer agreements, substantially interrelated and interdependent, that none of them would do business with the discounters. These agreements were hammered out in meetings between nonconforming dealers and officials of General Motors' Chevrolet Division, and in telephone conversations with other dealers. It was acknowledged from the beginning that substantial unanimity would be essential if the agreements were to be forthcoming. And once the agreements were secured, General Motors both solicited and employed the assistance of its alleged co-conspirators in helping to police them. What resulted was a fabric interwoven by many strands of joint action to eliminate the discounters from participation in the market, to inhibit the free choice of franchised dealers to select their own methods of trade and to provide multilateral surveillance and enforcement. This process for achieving and enforcing the desired objective can by no stretch of the imagination be described as "unilateral" or merely "parallel." . . .

There can be no doubt that the effect of the combination or conspiracy here was to restrain trade and commerce within the meaning of the Sherman Act. Elimination, by joint collaborative action, of discounters from access to the market is a *per se* violation of the Act. . . .

The principle of . . . [law applicable] is that where businessmen concert their actions in order to deprive others of access to merchandise which the latter wish to sell to the public, we need not inquire into the economic motivation underlying their conduct. Exclusion of traders from the market by means of combination or conspiracy is so inconsistent with the free-market principles embodied in the Sherman Act that it is not to be saved by reference to the need for preserving the collaborators' profit margins or their system for distributing automobiles, any more than by reference to the allegedly tortious conduct against which a combination or conspiracy may be directed—as in *Fashion Originators' Guild of America, Inc. v. FTC, supra,* 312 U.S., at 468.

We note, moreover, that inherent in the success of the combination in this case was a substantial restraint upon price competition—a goal unlawful *per se* when sought to be effected by combination or conspiracy. And the *per se* rule applies even when the effect upon prices is indirect.

There is in the record ample evidence that one of the purposes behind the concerted effort to eliminate sales of new Chevrolet cars by discounters was to protect franchised dealers from real or apparent price competition. The discounters advertised price savings. . . . Some purchasers found and others believed that discount prices were lower than those available through the franchised dealers. Certainly, complaints about price competition were prominent in the letters and telegrams with which the individual dealers and salesmen bombarded General Motors in November 1960. (Finding 38.) And although the District Court found to the contrary, there is evidence in the record that General Motors itself was not unconcerned about the effect of discount sales upon general price levels.

The protection of price competition from conspiratorial restraint is an object of special solicitude under the antitrust laws. We cannot respect that solicitude by closing our eyes to the effect upon price competition of the removal from the market, by combination or conspiracy, of a class of traders. Nor do we propose to construe the Sherman Act to prohibit conspiracies to fix prices at which competitors may sell, but to allow conspiracies or combinations to put competitors out of business entirely.

Accordingly, we reverse and remand to the United States District Court for the Southern District of California in order that it may fashion appropriate equitable relief. [REVERSED AND REMANDED]

3   PRICE FIXING AND OTHER CONCERTED ACTIVITIES AMONG COMPETITORS

The Sherman Act's proscription of contracts or combinations in restraint of trade or commerce obviously could apply to agreements among competitors whereby they establish minimum prices for their goods or services. In fact, such were among the first to be held in violation of the Act. But, under the rule of reason, are only some price-fixing arrangements illegal? Suppose very small competitors, who do not control the market, agree to charge certain prices. Or suppose competitors agree to prevent their own destruction by present economic forces and fix prices which will give them no more than a fair return? Must such arrangements result in an *unreasonable* restraint of trade before a violation of the Sherman Act is demonstrated? Such was the position of the defendant in the case which follows.

UNITED STATES V. TRENTON POTTERIES CO.
273 U.S. 392 (1927)

STONE, JUSTICE: Respondents, twenty individuals and twenty-three corporations, were convicted in the district court for southern New York, of violating the Sherman Anti-Trust Law, Act of July 2, 1890, c 647, 26 Stat. 209. The indictment was in two counts. The first charged a combination to fix and maintain uniform prices for the sale of sanitary pottery, in restraint of interstate commerce; the second, a combination to restrain interstate commerce by limiting sales of pottery to a special group known to respondents as "legitimate jobbers." On appeal, the Court of Appeals for the second circuit reversed the judgment of conviction on both counts on the ground that there were errors in the conduct of the trial. . . .

Respondents, engaged in the manufacture or distribution of 82 percent of the vitreous pottery fixtures produced in the United States for use in bathrooms and lavatories, were members of a trade organization known as the Sanitary Potters' Association.

There is no contention here that the verdict was not supported by sufficient evidence that respondents, controlling some 82 percent of the business of manufacturing and distributing to the United States vitreous pottery of the type described, combined to fix prices and to limit sales in interstate commerce to jobbers.

The issues raised here by the government's specification of errors relate only to the decision of the Court of Appeals upon its review of certain rulings of the District Court made in the course of the trial. It is urged that the court below erred in holding in effect (1) that the trial court should have submitted to the jury the question whether the price agreement complained of constituted an unreasonable restraint of trade. . . .

The trial court charged, in submitting the case to the jury, that if it found the agreements or combination complained of, it might return a verdict of guilty without regard to the reasonableness of the prices fixed, or the good intentions of the combining units, whether prices were actually lowered or raised or whether sales were restricted to the special jobbers, since both agreements of themselves were unreasonable restraints. These instructions repeated in various forms applied to both counts of the indictment. The trial court refused various requests to charge that both the agreement to fix prices and the agreement to limit sales to a particular group, if found, did not in themselves constitute violations of law unless it was also found that they unreasonably restrained interstate commerce. In particular the court refused the request to charge the following:

"The essence of the law is injury to the public. It is not every restraint of competition and not every restraint of trade that works an injury to the public; it is only an undue and unreasonable restraint of trade that has such an effect and is deemed to be unlawful."

The court below held specifically that the trial court erred in refusing to charge as requested and held in effect that the charge as given on this branch of the case was erroneous. This determination was based upon the assumption that the charge and refusals could be attributed only to a mistaken view of the trial judge, expressed in the indictment, that the "rule of reason" announced in *Standard Oil Co. v. United States,* 221 U.S. 1, . . . had no application. . . .

This disposition of the matter ignored the fact that the trial judge plainly and variously charged the jury that the combinations alleged in the indictment, if found, were violations of the statute as a matter of law, saying:

> . . . *the law is clear that an agreement on the part of the members of a combination controlling a substantial part of an industry, upon the prices which the members are to charge for their commodity, is in itself an undue and unreasonable restraint of trade and commerce.* . . .

If the charge itself was correctly given and adequately covered the various aspects of the case, the refusal to charge in another correct form or to quote to the jury extracts from opinions of the Court was not error. . . . The question therefore to be considered here is whether the trial judge correctly withdrew from the jury the consideration of the reasonableness of the particular restraints charged.

That only those restraints upon interstate commerce which are unreasonable are prohibited by the Sherman Law was the rule laid down by the opinions of this Court in the *Standard Oil* and *Tobacco* Cases. But it does not follow that agreements to fix or maintain prices are reasonable restraints and therefore permitted by the statute, merely because the prices themselves are reasonable. Reasonableness is not a concept of definite and unchanging content. Its meaning necessarily varies in the different fields of law, because it is used as a convenient summary of the dominant considerations which control in the application of legal doctrines. Our view of what is a reasonable restraint of commerce is controlled by the recognized purpose of the Sherman Law itself. Whether this type of restraint is reasonable or not must be judged in part at least in the light of its effect on competition, for whatever difference of opinion there may be among economists as to the social and economic desirability of an unrestrained competitive system, it cannot be doubted that the Sherman Law and the judicial decisions interpreting it are based upon the assumption that the public interest is best protected from the evils of monopoly and price control by the maintenance of competition. . . .

The aim and result of every price-fixing agreement, if effective, is the elimination of one form of competition. The power to fix prices, whether reasonably exercised or not, involves power to control the market and to fix arbitrary and unreasonable prices. The reasonable price fixed today may through economic and business changes become the unreasonable price of tomorrow. Once established, it may be maintained unchanged because of the absence of competition secured by the agreement for a price reasonable when fixed. Agreements which create such potential power may well be held to be in themselves unreasonable or unlawful restraints, without the necessity of minute inquiry whether a particular price is reasonable or unreasonable as fixed and without placing on the Government in enforcing the Sherman Law the burden of ascertaining from day to day whether it has become unreasonable through the mere variation of economic conditions.

Moreover, in the absence of express legislation requiring it, we should hesitate to adopt a construction making the difference between legal and illegal conduct in the field of business relations depend upon so uncertain a test as whether prices are reasonable—a determination which can be satisfactorily made only after a complete survey of our economic organization and a choice between rival philosophies. . . . Thus viewed, the Sherman Law is not only a prohibition against the infliction of a particular type of public injury. It "is a limitation of rights, . . . which may be pushed to evil consequences and therefore restrained. . . ."

That such was the view of this Court in deciding the *Standard Oil* and *Tobacco* Cases, and that such is the effect of its decisions both before and after those cases, does not seem fairly open to question. Beginning with *United States v. Trans-Missouri Freight Ass'n, supra*, . . . where agreements for establishing reasonable and uniform freight rates by competing lines of railroads were held unlawful, it has since often been decided and always assumed that uniform price-fixing by those controlling in any substantial manner a trade or business in interstate commerce is prohibited by the Sherman Law, despite the reasonableness of the particular prices agreed upon. In *Addyston Pipe & Steel Co. v. United States*, 175 U.S. 211 . . . for fixing prices, this Court quoted with approval the following passage from the lower court's opinion: " . . . the affiants say that, in their opinion, the prices at which pipe has been sold by defendants have been reasonable. We do not think the issue an important one, because, as already stated, we do not think that at common law there is any question of reasonableness open to the courts with reference to such a contract.". . .

That the opinions in the *Standard Oil* and *Tobacco* Cases were not intended to affect this view of the illegality of price-fixing agreements affirmatively appears from the opinion in the *Standard Oil* Case. . . .

And in *Thompson v. Cayser*, 243 U.S. 66, . . . it was specifically pointed out that the *Standard Oil* and *Tobacco* Cases did not overrule the earlier cases. The decisions in . . . [two other cases] were made on the assumption that any agreement for price-fixing, if found, would have been illegal as a matter of law. In *FTC v. Pacific States Paper Trade Ass'n*, 273 U.S. 52, . . . we upheld orders of the Commission forbidding price-fixing and prohibiting the use of agreed price lists by wholesale dealers in interstate commerce, without regard to the reasonableness of the prices.

Cases in both the Federal and State courts have generally proceeded on a like assumption, and in the second circuit the view maintained below that the reasonableness or unreasonableness of the prices fixed must be submitted to the jury has apparently been abandoned. . . . While not necessarily controlling, the decisions of this Court denying the validity of resale price agreements, regardless of the reasonableness of the price, are persuasive. . . .

The charge of the trial court, viewed as a whole, fairly submitted to the jury the question whether a price-fixing agreement as described in the first count was entered into by the respondents. Whether the prices actually agreed upon were reasonable or unreasonable was immaterial in the circumstances charged in the indictment and necessarily found by the verdict. The requested charge which we have quoted, and others of similar tenor, while true as abstract propositions, were inapplicable to the case in hand and rightly refused. [REVERSED]

It is clear from the foregoing that price-setting arrangements among competitors are considered to be unreasonable per se, or in themselves. In other words, an unreasonable contract or combination in restraint of trade is established by simply proving the existence of such an agreement. Other cases have indicated that the per se rule makes such a combination illegal whether the parties to it have control of the market or not, and whether they are trying to raise *or lower* the market price.

Similar contracts to those fixing the price at which the conspirators sell their product have been held unreasonable, per se. Thus agreements to divide up territories among competitors, or to fix the market price of a product or service they are buying, or to limit the supply of a commodity are outlawed without proof of any unreasonable effects. It is clear from these per se rules that the Sherman Act does not, as might erroneously be assumed, apply only where the public at large is injured by conspiracies or monopolistic practices, and is not of sole interest to big business.

The following case illustrates the significance of the Sherman Act to small businessmen in affording them protection from still a different kind of cooperative activity among competitors.

KLOR'S, INC. V. BROADWAY-HALE STORES, INC.
359 U.S. 207 (1959)

BLACK, JUSTICE: Klor's, Inc., operates a retail store on Mission Street, San Francisco, California; Broadway-Hale Stores, Inc., a chain of department stores, operates one of its stores next door. The two stores compete in the sale of radios, television sets, refrigerators and other household appliances. Claiming that Broadway-Hale and 10 national manufacturers and their distributors have conspired to restrain and monopolize commerce in violation of §§ 1 and 2 of the Sherman Act, 26 Stat. 209, as amended, 15 U.S.C. §§ 1, 2, 15 U.S.C.A. §§ 1, 2, Klor's brought this action for treble damages and injunction in the United States District Court.

In support of its claim Klor's made the following allegations: George Klor started an appliance store some years before 1952 and has operated it ever since either individually or as Klor's, Inc. Klor's is as well equipped as Broadway-Hale to handle all brands of appliances. Nevertheless, manu-facturers and distributors of such well-known brands as General Electric, RCA, Admiral, Zenith, Emerson and others have conspired among them-selves and with Broadway-Hale either not to sell to Klor's or to sell to it only at discriminatory prices and highly unfavorable terms. Broadway-Hale has used its "monopolistic" buying power to bring about this situation. The business of manufacturing, distributing and selling household appliances is in interstate commerce. The concerted refusal to deal with Klor's has seri-ously handicapped its ability to compete and has already caused it a great loss of profits, goodwill, reputation and prestige.

The defendants did not dispute these allegations, but sought summary judgment and dismissal of the complaint for failure to state a cause of action. They submitted unchallenged affidavits which showed that there were hundreds of other household appliance retailers, some within a few blocks of Klor's who sold many competing brands of appliances, including those the defendants refused to sell to Klor's. From the allegations of the complaint, and from the affidavits supporting the motion for summary judg-ment, the District Court concluded that the controversy was a "purely private quarrel" between Klor's and Broadway-Hale, which did not amount to a "public wrong proscribed by the [Sherman] Act." On this ground the complaint was dismissed and summary judgment was entered for the de-fendants. The Court of Appeals for the Ninth Circuit affirmed the summary judgment. . . . It stated that "a violation of the Sherman Act requires conduct of defendants by which the public is or conceivably may be ulti-mately injured." . . . It held that here the required public injury was miss-ing since "there was no charge or proof that by any act of defendants the price, quantity, or quality offered the public was affected, nor that there was any intent or purpose to effect a change in, or an influence on, prices, quan-tity, or quality. . . ." The holding, if correct, means that unless the oppor-tunities for customers to buy in a competitive market are reduced, a group of powerful businessmen may act in concert to deprive a single merchant, like Klor's, of the goods he needs to compete effectively. . . .

We think Klor's allegations clearly show one type of trade restraint and public harm the Sherman Act forbids, and that defendants' affidavits pro-vide no defense to the charges. Section 1 of the Sherman Act makes illegal any contract, combination or conspiracy in restraint of trade, and § 2 for-bids any person or combination from monopolizing or attempting to monop-olize any part of interstate commerce. . . .

Group boycotts, or concerted refusals by traders to deal with other traders, have long been held to be in the forbidden category. . . .

Plainly the allegations of this complaint disclose such a boycott. This is not a case of a single trader refusing to deal with another, nor even of a manufacturer and a dealer agreeing to an exclusive distributorship. Alleged in this complaint is a wide combination consisting of manufacturers, distributors and a retailer. This combination takes from Klor's its freedom to buy appliances in an open competitive market and drives it out of business as a dealer in the defendants' products. It deprives the manufacturers and distributors of their freedom to sell to Klor's at the same prices and conditions made available to Broadway-Hale and in some instances forbids them from selling to it on any terms whatsoever. It interferes with the natural flow of interstate commerce. It clearly has, by its "nature" and "character," a "monopolistic tendency." As such it is not to be tolerated merely because the victim is just one merchant whose business is so small that his destruction makes little difference to the economy. Monopoly can as surely thrive by the elimination of such small businessmen, one at a time, as it can by driving them out in large groups. In recognition of this fact the Sherman Act has consistently been read to forbid all contracts and combinations "which 'tend to create a monopoly,' " whether "the tendency is a creeping one" or "one that proceeds at full gallop." . . .

The judgment of the Court of Appeals is reversed and the cause is remanded to the District Court for trial. [REVERSED]

The facts in the preceding case were undisputed. However, there are obvious difficulties which may arise in connection with proving the existence of a contract, combination, or conspiracy among competitors when they indulge in cooperative action to control the market in some fashion. Must an actual oral or written offer and acceptance be established? If the market behavior of competitors is consciously parallel will it be implied that they are conspiring together? The case which follows deals with the nature of the evidence which is required to prove that a conspiracy or contract in restraint of trade does in fact exist.

THEATRE ENTERPRISES V. PARAMOUNT FILM DISTRIB. CORP.
346 U.S. 537 (1954)

The plaintiff, Theatre Enterprises, owned and operated the Crest Theatre, a modern motion picture theatre located in a shopping center in Baltimore, Maryland, six miles from the downtown area. The plaintiff brought this action for treble damages and an injunction against defendant motion picture producers and distributors, claiming that they had conspired in violation of the antitrust laws to restrict first-run motion pictures to the theatres downtown, thereby limiting the Crest to only subsequent runs. The evidence disclosed that although the plaintiff had asked each of the defendants on different occasions for first-run motion pictures, no one would furnish it these but all uniformly limited their showing to the downtown theatres, of which there were eight. The jury returned a verdict for the defendants, and the trial court entered judgment in their favor. The Circuit Court of Appeals affirmed. On appeal to the Supreme Court, the plaintiff contended that, on the evidence, the trial judge should have directed the jury to find that there was an unlawful conspiracy, and that the only determination of fact the jury should have been permitted to make was the amount of damages suffered.

CLARK, JUSTICE: . . . Admittedly there is no direct evidence of illegal agreement between the respondents and no conspiracy is charged as to the independent exhibitors in Baltimore, who account for 63% of first-run exhibitions. The various respondents advanced much the same reasons for denying petitioner's offers. Among other reasons they asserted that day and date first-runs are normally granted only to noncompeting theatres. Since the Crest is in "substantial competition" with the downtown theatres, a day and date arrangement would be economically unfeasible. And even if respondents wished to grant petitioner such a license, no downtown exhibitor would waive his clearance rights over the Crest and agree to a simultaneous showing. As a result, if petitioner were to receive first-runs, the license would have to be an exclusive one. However, an exclusive license would be economically unsound because the Crest is a suburban theatre, located in a small shopping center, and served by limited public transportation facilities; and, with a drawing area of less than one-tenth that of a downtown theatre, it cannot compare with those easily accessible theatres in the power to draw patrons. Hence the downtown theatres offer far greater opportunities for the widespread advertisement and exploitation of newly released features, which is thought necessary to maximize the overall return from subsequent runs as well as first-runs. The respondents, in the light of these conditions, attacked the guaranteed offers of petitioner, one of which occurred during the trial, as not being made in good faith. Respondents Loew's and Warner refused petitioner an exclusive license because they owned the three downtown theatres receiving their first-run product.

The crucial question is whether respondents' conduct toward petitioner stemmed from independent decision or from an agreement, tacit or express. To be sure, business behavior is admissible circumstantial evidence from which the fact finder may infer agreement. But this Court has never held that proof of parallel business behavior conclusively establishes agreement or, phrased differently, that such behavior itself constitutes a Sherman Act offense. Circumstantial evidence of consciously parallel behavior may have made heavy inroads into the traditional judicial attitude toward conspiracy; but "conscious parallelism" has not yet read conspiracy out of the Sherman Act entirely. Realizing this, petitioner attempts to bolster its argument for a directed verdict by urging that the conscious unanimity of action by respondents should be "measured against the background and findings in the Paramount case." In other words, since the same respondents had conspired in the Paramount case to impose a uniform system of runs and clearances without adequate explanation to sustain them as reasonable restraints of trade, use of the same device in the present case should be legally equated to conspiracy. But the Paramount decrees, even if admissible, were only prima facie evidence of a conspiracy covering the area and existing during the period there involved. Alone or in conjunction with the other proof of the petitioner, they would form no basis for a directed verdict. Here each of the respondents had denied the existence of any collaboration and in addition had introduced evidence of the local conditions surrounding the Crest operation which, they contended, precluded it from being a successful first-run house. They also attacked the good faith of the guaranteed offers of the petitioner for first-run pictures and attributed uniform action to individual business judgment motivated by the desire for maximum revenue. This evidence, together with other testimony of an explanatory nature, raised fact issues requiring the trial judge to submit the issue of conspiracy to the jury. . . . [AFFIRMED]

The language in the foregoing case should be compared with that in *American Tobacco Co. v. United States*,[6] where the American, Liggett and Myers, and Reynolds tobacco companies were found guilty of conspiring or combining in an unlawful restraint of trade in controlling both the market and prices of leaf tobacco they purchased and the market and prices of the manufactured cigarettes they sold. On appeal the Supreme Court upheld the convictions, stating in part:

It is not the form of the combination or the particular means used but the result to be achieved that the statute condemns. It is not of importance whether the means used to accomplish the unlawful objective are in themselves lawful or unlawful. Acts done to give effect to the conspiracy may be in themselves wholly innocent acts. Yet, if they are part of the sum of the acts which are relied upon to effectuate the conspiracy which the statute forbids, they come within its prohibition. No formal agreement is necessary to constitute an unlawful conspiracy. Often crimes are a matter of inference deduced from the acts of the person accused and done in pursuance of a criminal purpose. Where the conspiracy is proved, as here, from the evidence of the action taken in concert by the parties to it, it is all the more convincing proof of an intent to exercise the power of exclusion acquired through that conspiracy. The essential combination or conspiracy in violation of the Sherman Act may be found in a course of dealings or other circumstances as well

[6] 328 U.S. 781 (1946).

as in any exchange of words. . . . Where the circumstances are such as to warrant a jury in finding that the conspirators had a unity of purpose or a common design and understanding, or a meeting of minds in an unlawful arrangement, the conclusion that a conspiracy is established is justified. Neither proof nor exertion of the power to exclude nor proof of actual exclusion of existing or potential competitors is essential to sustain a charge of monopolization under the Sherman Act. . . .

4   PRICE DISCRIMINATION

A price discrimination exists whenever a seller charges different buyers different prices for essentially the same commodities where there are no cost differences or the difference is not attributable to changes in the demand. Such a discrimination may or may not be illegal under Section 2 of the Clayton Act as amended by the Robinson-Patman Act. For a summary of the provisions of Section 2, see page 396, Chapter 11.

First, note that Section 2 makes a discrimination in price a violation of the law "where the effect of such discrimination may be substantially to lessen competition or tend to create a monopoly in any line of commerce. . . ." Thus the same types of determination of fact may be required to show a violation as in Section 7 of the Clayton Act concerning mergers, namely those of the relevant market and the probable anticompetitive effects of the discrimination. In addition, a discrimination is outlawed if the effect may be "to injure, destroy or prevent competition with any person who either grants or knowingly receives the benefit of such discrimination, or with customers of either of them. . . ."

As was noted previously, discounts for quantity purchases were permitted under the original act, but became illegal under the Robinson-Patman amendment, unless justified by differences in costs of production or distribution due to different quantities. Even in the latter event, the FTC is empowered to set quantity limits, and as was indicated in the *Morton Salt* case in Chapter 11, page 398, the quantity discounts must be available not only in theory, but also as a practical matter to all purchasers, large and small alike, or a discrimination exists. In such cases any cost justification claimed must be affirmatively established by a defendant.

Of course, one may sell entirely different products at different prices to two different purchasers, because Section 2 only outlaws price discriminations between two different purchasers of "commodities of like grade and quality." In the case which follows, the defendant contended that the discrimination in price being challenged did not fall within the purview of Section 2(a) of the Robinson-Patman Act because of this requirement set by it.

FTC V. THE BORDEN CO.
383 U.S. 637 (1966)

WHITE, JUSTICE: The Borden Company, respondent here, produces and sells evaporated milk under the Borden name, a nationally advertised brand. At the same time Borden packs and markets evaporated milk under various private brands owned by its customers. This milk is physically and chemically identical with the milk it distributes under its own brand but is sold at both the wholesale and retail level at prices regularly below those obtained for the Borden brand milk. The Federal Trade Commission found the milk sold under the Borden and the private labels to be of like grade and quality as required for the applicability of § 2(a) of the Robinson-Patman Act, held the price differential to be discriminatory within the meaning of the section, ascertained the requisite adverse effect on commerce, rejected Borden's claim of cost justification and consequently issued a cease-and-desist order. The Court of Appeals set aside the Commission's order on the sole ground that as a matter of law, the customer label milk was not of the same grade and quality as the milk sold under the Borden brand. Because of the importance of this issue, which bears on the reach and coverage of the Robinson-Patman Act, we granted certiorari. We now reverse the decision of the Court of Appeals and remand the case to that court for the determination of the remaining issues raised by respondent Borden in that court.

The position of Borden and of the Court of Appeals is that the determination of like grade and quality, which is a threshold finding essential to the applicability of § 2(a), may not be based solely on the physical properties of the products without regard to the brand names they bear and the relative public acceptance these brands enjoy—"consideration should be given to all commercially significant distinctions which affect market value, whether they be physical or promotional." . . . Here, because the milk bearing the Borden brand regularly sold at a higher price than did the milk with a buyer's label, the court considered the products to be "commercially" different and hence of different "grade" for the purposes of § 2(a), even though they were physically identical and of equal quality. Although a mere difference in brand would not in itself demonstrate a difference in grade, decided consumer preference for one brand over another, reflected in the willingness to pay a higher price for the well-known brand, was, in the view of the Court of Appeals, sufficient to differentiate chemically identical products and to place the price differential beyond the reach of § 2(a).

We reject this construction of § 2(a), as did both the examiner and the Commission in this case. The Commission's view is that labels do not differentiate products for the purpose of determining grade or quality, even though the one label may have more customer appeal and command a higher price in the marketplace from a substantial segment of the public. That this is the Commission's long-standing interpretation of the present Act, as well as of § 2 of the Clayton Act before its amendment by the Robinson-Patman Act, may be gathered from the Commission's decisions dating back to 1936. These views of the agency are entitled to respect, and represent a more reasonable construction of the statute than that offered by the Court of Appeals.

Obviously there is nothing in the language of the statute indicating that grade, as distinguished from quality, is not to be determined by the characteristics of the product itself, but by consumer preferences, brand acceptability or what customers think of it and are willing to pay for it. Moreover, what legislative history there is concerning this question supports the Commission's construction of the statute rather than that of the Court of Appeals.

During the 1936 hearings on the proposed amendments to § 2 of the Clayton Act, the attention of the Congress was specifically called to the question of the applicability of § 2 to the practice of a manufacturer selling his product under his nationally advertised brand at a different price than he charged when the product was sold under a private label. Because it was feared that the Act would require the elimination of such price differentials, Hearings on H.R. 4995 before the House Committee on the Judiciary, 74th Cong., 2d Sess., p. 355, and because private brands "would thus be put out of business by the nationally advertised brands," it was suggested that the proposed § 2(a) be amended so as to apply only to sales of commodities of "like grade, quality and *brand*." [EMPHASIS ADDED] There was strong objection to the amendment and it was not adopted by the Committee. The rejection of this amendment assumes particular significance since it was pointed out in the hearings that the legality of price differentials between proprietary and private brands was then pending before the Federal Trade Commission in The Goodyear Tire & Rubber Co., 22 F.T.C. 232. By the time the Committee Report was written, the Commission had decided *Goodyear*. The report quoted from the decision and interpreted it as holding that *Goodyear* had violated the Act because "at no time did it offer to its own dealers prices on Goodyear brands of tires which were comparable to prices at which respondent was selling tires of equal or comparable quality to Sears, Roebuck & Co." H.R.Rep. No. 2287, 74th Cong., 2d Sess., p. 4.

During the debates on the bill, Representative Patman, one of the bill's sponsors, was asked about the private label issue. His brief response is wholly consistent with the Commission's interpretation of § 2(a), 80 Cong. Rec. 8115:

MR. TAYLOR OF SOUTH CAROLINA   *There has grown up a practice on the part of manufacturers of making certain brands of goods for particular chain stores. Is there anything in this bill calculated to remedy that situation?*

MR. PATMAN. . . . *I have not time to discuss that feature, but the bill will protect the independents in that way, because they will have to sell to the independents at the same price for the same product where they put the same quality of merchandise in a package, and this will remedy the situation to which the gentleman refers.*

MR. TAYLOR OF SOUTH CAROLINA   *Irrespective of the brand.*

MR. PATMAN   *Yes; so long as it is the same quality. . . .*

The Commission's construction of the statute also appears to us to further the purpose and policy of the Robinson-Patman Act. Subject to specified exceptions and defenses, § 2(a) proscribes unequal treatment of different customers in comparable transactions, but only if there is the requisite effect upon competition, actual or potential. But if the transactions are deemed to involve goods of disparate grade or quality, the section has no application at all and the Commission never reaches either the issue of discrimination or that of anticompetitive impact. We doubt that Congress intended to foreclose these inquiries in situations where a single seller markets the identical product under several different brands, whether his own, his customers or both. Such transactions are too laden with potential discrimination and adverse competitive effect to be excluded from the reach of § 2(a) by permitting a difference in grade to be established by the label alone or by the label and its consumer appeal.

If two products, physically identical but differently branded, are to be deemed of different grade because the seller regularly and successfully markets some quantity of both at different prices, the seller could, as far as § 2(a) is concerned, make either product available to some customers and deny it to others, however discriminatory this might be and however damaging to competition. Those who were offered only one of the two products would be barred from competing for those customers who want or might buy the other. The retailer who was permitted to buy and sell only the more expensive brand would have no chance to sell to those who always buy the cheaper product or to convince others, by experience or otherwise, of the fact which he and all other dealers already know—that the cheaper product is actually identical with that carrying the more expensive label.

The seller, to escape the Act, would have only to succeed in selling some unspecified amount of each product to some unspecified portion of his customers, however large or small the price differential might be. The seller's pricing and branding policy, by being successful, would apparently validate itself by creating a difference in "grade" and thus taking itself beyond the purview of the Act.

Our holding neither ignores the economic realities of the marketplace nor denies that some labels will command a higher price than others, at least from some portion of the public. But it does mean that "the economic factors inherent in brand names and national advertising should not be considered in the jurisdictional inquiry under the statutory 'like grade and quality' test." Report of The Attorney General's National Committee to Study the Antitrust Laws 158 (1955). And it does mean that transactions like those involved in this case may be examined by the Commission under § 2(a). The Commission will determine, subject to judicial review, whether the differential under attack is discriminatory within the meaning of the Act, whether competition may be injured, and whether the differential is cost justified or is defensible as a good-faith effort to meet the price of a competitor. "[T]angible consumer preferences as between branded and unbranded commodities should receive due legal recognition in the more flexible 'injury' and 'cost justification' provisions of the statute." Report of The Attorney General's National Committee to Study the Antitrust Laws 159 (1955). This, we think, is precisely what Congress intended. The arguments for exempting private brand selling from § 2(a) are, therefore, more appropriately addressed to the Congress than to this Court.

The Court of Appeals suggested that the Commission's views of like grade and quality for the purposes of § 2(a) cannot be squared with its rulings in cases where a seller presents the defense under § 2(b) that he is in good faith meeting the equally low price of a competitor. In those cases, it is said, the Commission has given full recognition to the significance of the higher prices commanded by the nationally advertised brand "in holding that a seller who reduces the price of his premium product to the level of his non-premium competitors is not merely meeting competition, but undercutting it.". . .

The Commission, on the other hand, sees no inconsistency between its present decision and its § 2(b) cases. In its view, the issue under § 2(b) of whether a seller's lower price is a good-faith meeting of competition involves considerations different from those presented by the jurisdictional question of "like grade and quality" under § 2(a).

We need not resolve these contrary positions. The issue we have here relates to § 2(a), not to § 2(b), and we think the Commission has resolved it correctly. The § 2(b) cases are not now before us and we do not venture to decide them. The judgment of the Court of Appeals is reversed and the case is remanded for further proceedings consistent with this opinion. It is so ordered. [REVERSED AND REMANDED]

[Justice Stewart felt that "grade and quality" determinations should also take into account commercial attributes, such as the good will of a brand name.]

STEWART, JUSTICE, dissenting (joined by JUSTICE HARLAN): There is nothing intrinsic to the concepts of grade and quality that requires exclusion of the commercial attributes of a product from their definition. The product purchased by a consumer includes not only the chemical components that any competent laboratory can itemize, but also a host of commercial intangibles that distinguish the product in the market place. The premium paid for

Borden brand milk reflects the consumer's awareness, promoted through advertising, that these commercial attributes are part and parcel of the premium product he is purchasing. The record in the present case indicates that wholesale purchasers of Borden's private label brands continued to purchase the premium brand in undiminished quantities. The record also indicates that retail purchasers who bought the premium brand did so with the specific expectation of acquiring a product of premium quality. Contrary to the Court's suggestion, ante, this consumer expectation cannot accurately be characterized as a misapprehension. Borden took extensive precautions to insure that a flawed product did not reach the consumer. None of these precautions was taken for the private brand milk packed by Borden. An important ingredient of the premium brand inheres in the consumer's belief, measured by past satisfaction and the market reputation established by Borden for its products, that tomorrow's can will contain the same premium product as that purchased today. . . .

In a price discrimination case under Section 2 of the amended Clayton Act, when the plaintiff has introduced proof of differential pricing of the same kind of goods by the defendant and proof of the requisite injury to competition which resulted, he has established a prima facie case. Sections 2(a) and 2(b) provide for several instances in which a price discrimination is not violative of the law. However, these are affirmative defenses, since the Act imposes the burden of proving them on the defendant, rather than making it the obligation of the plaintiff to negate their existence.

The first justification for a price discrimination is the cost defense. Section 2(a) provides that nothing "shall prevent differentials which make only due allowance for *differences in the cost of manufacture, sale, or delivery* resulting from the differing methods or quantities in which . . . commodities are . . . sold or delivered." [EMPHASIS ADDED] This would appear to be a significant excuse which would permit cost savings to be passed on to customers. However, according to the Attorney General's Committee "the cost defense has proved largely illusory in practice." [7] Because of the complexities in determining what is "cost" very rarely has this defense been successful in the past. One obvious problem is that of bringing forth acceptable *evidence* of cost. As the Supreme Court noted in *Automatic Canteen Co. v. FTC*, "Proof of a cost justification being what it is, too often no one can ascertain whether a price is cost justified." [8] The Attorney General's Committee notes two other reasons why the cost defense is "illusory." The first of these is ". . . the failure of past adjudications to evolve workable criteria by which the cost defense can attain its intended role." [9] The other

---

[7] Report of the Attorney General's National Committee to Study the Antitrust Laws 171 (1955).
[8] 346 U.S. 61, 79 (1953).
[9] Report of the Attorney General's National Committee to Study the Antitrust Laws 171 (1955).

is "[t]he absence of officially sanctioned accounting standards [which] has provoked needless dispute over easily reconcilable disparities in technique." [10] The Committee concludes that the circumstances are such that "only the most prosperous and patient business firms could afford pursuit of [this] often illusory defense. Pressure builds to gain legal safety by withholding price differentials from more efficient buyers, thus denying to the public the benefits of mass production and economical distribution processes which Congress intended to preserve by enacting the cost proviso in Section 2(a)." [11]

In addition to the foregoing, price differentials due to savings resulting from larger quantity sales may be further limited by the FTC, which is authorized under certain circumstances to "fix and establish quantity limits."

A second affirmative defense is afforded those who discriminate in price due to changing conditions. Section 2(a) also exempts "price changes from time to time where in response to changing conditions affecting the market for or the marketability of the goods concerned, such as but not limited to actual or imminent deterioration of perishable goods, obsolescence of seasonal goods, distress sales under court process or sales in good faith in discontinuance of business in the goods concerned." The Attorney General's Committee recommended a liberal interpretation of this provision "to promote competitors' freedom to react realistically to the spontaneous movements of a dynamic market." [12] However, the extent to which this exemption actually is available to justify changes in pricing due to changes in *market conditions*, apart from the types of changes in *marketability of goods* specifically enumerated is not clear.

A final affirmative defense justifying price discrimination is the good faith meeting of competition. Section 2(b) of the Act permits a defendant to demonstrate that a given price discrimination was not unlawful by "showing that his lower price or the furnishing of services or facilities to any purchaser or purchasers was made in good faith to meet an equally low price of a competitor, or the services or facilities furnished by a competitor."

Under this last defense a seller can meet but clearly is not permitted to undercut the equally low price of a competitor.

In *FTC v. A. E. Staley Mfg. Co.*,[13] the defendant company manufactured corn syrup in Decatur, Illinois, but sold it for list price plus freight from Chicago, Illinois, to the delivery point. Staley was held to be in violation of Section 2(a), even though it argued it should be exempt under Section 2(b), since it was merely meeting the same prices charged by its competitors. The court upheld the Commission's finding that Staley was not meeting

[10] *Id.* at 172, 173.
[11] *Id.* at 173.
[12] *Id.* at 178.
[13] 324 U.S. 746 (1945).

competition in good faith by using the same basing point pricing system as that used by the other competitors, which was unlawful on its face. The Supreme Court also had occasion to consider the application of the "meeting competition" defense to a price discrimination in the case which follows.

<hr />

STANDARD OIL CO. V. FTC
340 U.S. 231 (1951)

<hr />

BURTON, JUSTICE: In this case the Federal Trade Commission challenged the right of the Standard Oil Company, under the Robinson-Patman Act, to sell gasoline to four comparatively large "jobber" customers in Detroit at a less price per gallon than it sold like gasoline to many comparatively small service station customers in the same area. The company's defenses were that (1) the sales involved were not in interstate commerce and (2) its lower price to the jobbers was justified because made to retain them as customers and in good faith to meet an equally low price of a competitor. The Commission, with one member dissenting, ordered the company to cease and desist from making such a price differential. The Court of Appeals slightly modified the order and required its enforcement as modified. . . .

For the reasons hereinafter stated, we agree with the court below that the sales were made in interstate commerce but we agree with petitioner that, under the Act, the lower price to the jobbers was justified if it was made to retain each of them as a customer and in good faith to meet an equally low price of a competitor. . . .

Petitioner presented evidence tending to prove that its tank-car price was made to each "jobber" in order to retain that "jobber" as a customer and in good faith to meet a lawful and equally low price of a competitor. Petitioner sought to show that it succeeded in retaining these customers, although the tank-car price which it offered them merely approached or matched, and did not undercut, the lower prices offered them by several competitors of petitioner. The trial examiner made findings on the point but the Commission declined to do so, saying: "Based on the record in this case the Commission concludes as a matter of law that it is not material whether the discriminations in price granted by the respondent to the said four dealers were made to meet equally low prices of competitors. The Commission further concludes as a matter of law that it is unnecessary for the Commission to determine whether the alleged competitive prices were in fact available or involved gasoline of like grade or quality or of equal public acceptance. Accordingly the Commission does not attempt to find the facts regarding those matters because, even though the lower prices in question may have been made by respondent in good faith to meet the lower prices of competitors, this does not constitute a defense in the face of affirmative proof that the effect of the discrimination was to injure, destroy and prevent competition with the retail stations operated by the said named dealers and with stations operated by their retailer-customers."

The court below affirmed the Commission's position. . . .

The defense relating to the meeting of the price of a competitor appears only in subsection (b). There it is applied to discrimination in services or facilities as well as to discriminations in price, which alone are expressly condemned in subsection (a). In its opinion in the instant case, the Commission recognizes that it is an absolute defense to a charge of price discrimination for a seller to prove, under § 2(a), that its price differential makes only due allowances for differences in cost or for price changes made in response to changing market conditions. Each of these three defenses is introduced by the same phrase "nothing . . . shall prevent," and all are embraced in the same word "justification" in the first sentence of § 2(b). It is natural, therefore, to conclude that each of these defenses is entitled to the same effect, without regard to whether there also appears an affirmative showing of actual or potential injury to competition at the same or a lower level traceable to the price differential made by the seller. The Commission says, however, that the proviso in § 2(b) as to a seller meeting in good faith a lower competitive price is not an absolute defense if an injury to competition may result from such price reduction. We find no basis for such a distinction between the defenses in § 2(a) and (b). . . .

This right of a seller, under § 2(b), to meet in good faith an equally low price of a competitor has been considered here before. Both in *Corn Prod. Ref. Co. v. FTC,* 324 U.S. 726, and in *FTC v. A. E. Staley Mfg. Co.,* 324 U.S. 746, evidence in support of this defense was reviewed at length. While this Court did not sustain the seller's defense in either case, it did unquestionably recognize the relevance of the evidence in support of that defense. The decision in each case was based upon the insufficiency of the seller's evidence to establish its defense, not upon the inadequacy of its defense as a matter of law.

In the *Corn Products* case, *supra,* after recognizing that the seller had allowed differentials in price in favor of certain customers, this Court examined the evidence presented by the seller to show that such differentials were justified because made in good faith to meet equally low prices of a competitor. It then said: "Examination of the *testimony* satisfies us, as it did the court below, that it was *insufficient* to sustain a finding that the lower prices allowed to favored customers were in fact made to meet competition. Hence petitioners *failed to sustain the burden* of showing that the price discriminations were granted for the purpose of meeting competition." [EMPHASIS ADDED]

In the *Staley* case, *supra,* most of the Court's opinion is devoted to the consideration of the evidence introduced in support of the seller's defense under § 2(b). The discussion proceeds upon the assumption, applicable here, that if a competitor's "lower price" is a lawful individual price offered to any of the seller's customers, then the seller is protected, under § 2(b), in making a counteroffer provided the seller proves that its counteroffer is made to meet in good faith its competitor's equally low price. On the record in the *Staley* case, a majority of the Court of Appeals, in fact, declined to accept the findings of the Commission and decided in favor of the accused seller. This Court, on review, reversed that judgment but emphatically recognized the availability of the seller's defense under § 2(b) and the obligation of the Commission to make findings upon issues material to that defense. It said:

> *Congress has left to the Commission the determination of fact in each case whether the person, charged with making discriminatory prices, acted in good faith to meet a competitor's equally low prices. The determination of this fact from the evidence is for the Commission. In the present case, the Commission's finding that respondents' price discriminations were not made to meet a "lower" price and consequently were not in good faith, is amply supported by the record, and we think the Court of Appeals erred in setting aside this portion of the Commission's order to cease and desist. . . .*

All that petitioner asks in the instant case is that its evidence be considered and that findings be made by the Commission as to the sufficiency of that evidence to support petitioner's defense under § 2(b). . . .

We need not now reconcile, in its entirety, the economic theory which underlies the Robinson-Patman Act with that of the Sherman and Clayton Acts.

It is enough to say that Congress did not seek by the Robinson-Patman Act either to abolish competition or so radically to curtail it that a seller would have no substantial right of self-defense against a price paid by a competitor. For example, if a large customer requests his seller to meet a temptingly lower price offered to him by one of his seller's competitors, the seller may well find it essential, as a matter of business survival, to meet that price rather than to lose the customer. It might be that this customer is the seller's only available market for the major portion of the seller's product, and that the loss of this customer would result in forcing a much higher unit cost and higher sales price upon the seller's other customers. There is nothing to show a congressional purpose, in such a situation, to compel the seller to choose only between ruinously cutting its prices to all its customers to match the price offered to one, or refusing to meet the competition and then ruinously raising its prices to its remaining customers to cover increased unit costs. There is, on the other hand, plain language and established practice which permits a seller, through § 2(b), to retain a customer by realistically meeting in good faith the price offered to that customer, without necessarily changing the seller's price to its other customers.

In a case where a seller sustains the burden of proof placed upon it to establish its defense under § 2(b), we find no reason to destroy that defense indirectly, merely because it also appears that the beneficiaries of the seller's price reductions may derive a competitive advantage from them or may, in a natural course of events, reduce their own resale prices to their customers. It must have been obvious to Congress that any price reduction to any dealer may always affect competition at that dealer's level as well as at the dealer's resale level, whether or not the reduction to the dealer is discriminatory. Likewise, it must have been obvious to Congress that any price reductions initiated by a seller's competitor would, if not met by the seller, affect competition at the beneficiary's level or among the beneficiary's customers just as much as if those reductions had been met by the seller. The proviso in § 2(b), as interpreted by the Commission, would not be available when there was or might be an injury to competition at a resale level. So interpreted, the proviso would have such little, if any, applicability as to be practically meaningless. We may, therefore, conclude that Congress meant to permit the natural consequences to follow the seller's action in meeting in good faith a lawful and equally low price of its competitor.

. . . The judgment of the Court of Appeals, accordingly, is reversed and the case is remanded to that court with instructions to remand it to the Federal Trade Commission to make findings in conformity with this opinion. It is so ordered. [REVERSED AND REMANDED]

In the preceding case, the Supreme Court clarified the defense of meeting an equally low price of a competitor by holding that it is available to one charged with selling at discriminatory prices, even if the discrimination might have anticompetitive effects otherwise prohibited. In doing so, however, it raised other questions by occasionally using the word "lawful" in referring to the "equally low prices of competitors" which the defense permits one to meet. Is, then, a seller justified in discriminating in price between his customers because he is meeting an equally low price offered one of them by a competitor *only if the competitor's price is "lawful"*? If a competitor's lower price amounts to a forbidden price discrimination by him in favor of the customer, can a seller meet it in "good faith" if doing so would result in his charging discriminatory prices for his product also? While some Federal court decisions seem to indicate that the defense is available in spite of the fact that the competitor's lower price is not a "lawful" one, some FTC rulings appear to hold otherwise.[14] Because the court did not more clearly define the defense of meeting competition to a price discrimination charge in the *Standard Oil* case, the Attorney General's Committee concluded that

---

[14] For a thorough discussion of the problem, see Johnston and Day, Meeting Competitive Prices? Must They Be Lawful? 52 *Ill. B.J.* 828 (June, 1964).

. . . *serious problems of statutory interpretation today confront tribunals—in Government proceedings or private damage suits—adjudicating the legality of a seller's prices in the light of his "meeting competition" defense. Difficulties cluster around the following complex issues; meeting of a competitor's unlawful prices; sporadic or regular competitive differentials; exact dollar-for-dollar meeting or undercutting and stopping short of a rival's price; reductions to retain old or to compete for new business; the content of the "good faith" concept in the proviso. In fact, not a single seller in a recorded case to date has succeeded in finally justifying a challenged discrimination by recourse to Section 2(b)'s "meeting competition" defense.*[15]

Sections 2(c), (d), and (e) of the Clayton Act as amended by the Robinson-Patman Act proscribe certain hidden or indirect discriminations by sellers in favor of certain buyers.

Section 2(c) prohibits an unearned brokerage or commission related to a sale of goods. Section 2(d) outlaws granting promotional allowances or payments on goods bought for resale, unless they are available to all competing customers. Section 2(e) prohibits the giving of promotional facilities or services on goods bought for resale, unless they are available to all competing customers. Note that the Act does not *expressly* require that any anticompetitive effects be demonstrated to prove a violation of these provisions. Further, it does not *expressly* avail the seller who has committed any of the prohibited acts the three defenses, already discussed, which he has to a charge of out and out *price* discrimination under Section 2(a). Obviously, Sections 2(c), (d), and (e) leave many business practices open to question and many issues regarding their application in doubt. In the case which follows, the legality under Section 2(c) of certain discriminatory brokerage allowances granted by the defendant to some of his customers was brought into issue.

EMPIRE RAYON YARN CO. V. AMERICAN VISCOSE CORP.
364 F.2d 491 (1966)

Empire Rayon Yarn Co. brought action for treble damages against the defendant, American Viscose Corporation, alleging a violation of Sections 2(c), (d), and (e) of the amended Clayton Act, because of American's allowing 5 percent brokerage allowances to certain jobbers but refusing the same privilege to the plaintiff. American was in the business of manufacturing and selling unprocessed rayon yarn, while American's jobbers as well as the plaintiff, Empire, were in the business of buying unprocessed rayon yarn and either reselling it in its original state as received from the manufacturer, or converting and selling it for use in the textile trade.

[15] Report of the Attorney General's National Committee to Study the Antitrust Laws 181 (1955).

An outline of the method of distribution chosen by American was given by its general sales manager, as follows:

Many years ago American established a distribution policy for the sale of viscose rayon yarn by direct sales to consumers of most of the product and sales to two jobbers, the defendants Malina and Gutner, of a small percentage of the product. These two jobbers were able to sell and service smaller units of the textile trade at lower selling costs than American and for that reason American established the jobber relation. These jobbers performed such services as the maintenance of substantial inventories of yarn in their plants as well as in warehouses, maintenance of an experienced selling organization, assumption of all risk of loss and credit, advertising American products, assumption of all risk of price fluctuation and furnishing of technical assistance to users of rayon. For acting as such jobbers American allowed a discount from list price on all viscose rayon yarn resold by the jobbers. On all sales to these jobbers for processing (not for resale) they pay the current price just the same as the plaintiff [Empire] or any other customer.

As the reason for refusing a similar discount to Empire, American's general sales manager stated that American's "offices . . . in the exercise of their own business judgment decided that the volume of yarn sold by the jobbing trade did not, and does not (as of January, 1958) . . . justify the appointment by American of more . . . jobbers." The District Court granted summary judgment to the defendant American. However, on appeal, the Court of Appeals, Second Circuit (three judges) held that the payments in question violated Section 2(c) and reversed, remanding the case to the District Court to ascertain the plaintiff's damages and to enter summary judgment for the plaintiff. The defendant petitioned the Court of Appeals, Second Circuit, for a rehearing before them, *in banc* (nine circuit judges), and the court granted the rehearing.

MOORE, CIRCUIT JUDGE: This opinion supersedes the previous opinion of a panel of this Court wherein that panel reversed an order which had granted defendants' motion for summary judgment. Thereafter defendants petitioned for a rehearing *in banc* which by order dated March 31, 1966 was granted, reconsideration to be had on the record and briefs. Because of the importance of the issue involved, the Court, *sua sponte,* requested the Federal Trade Commission "to submit a brief *amicus curiae* on the issues raised by this case." The Commission filed such brief to which appellants and appellee replied. After due consideration of the briefs filed originally, of the briefs filed in the *in banc* rehearing and of the position taken by the Commission in its *amicus* brief, we unanimously affirm the order granting summary judgment for the defendants and denying the cross motion therefor.

The facts are set forth adequately in the panel opinion, 354 F.2d 182.

Nor need the arguments *pro* and *con* therein stated be repeated. The Court adopts the statutory interpretation set forth in the dissenting opinion, 354 F.2d, pages 188–192. Brief reference, however, should be made to the views of the Federal Trade Commission, the agency which to a considerable extent is charged with the administration of the Robinson-Patman Act.

The issue, as before, is whether the payment by American of a 5% discount from list price to Malina and Gutner, which together with Shawmut had been acting for special factual reasons as jobbers for American, was an illegal brokerage payment within the compass of, and in violation of, Section 2(c).

The Commission has taken the position that upon the facts here presented this 5% discount was not "an unlawful 'brokerage' payment, or allowance or discount in lieu thereof, violative of Section 2(c)" and that these facts "preclude[s] a finding that it constituted a violation of Section 2(c)." The Commission noted that Malina and Gutner were not "dummy" brokers; that they were not powerful buyers able to compel because of economic power the payment of discounts in lieu of brokerage; that American did not utilize brokers in selling its rayon yarn; and that Malina and Gutner did not fall into the buying broker category. The Commission further noted that Malina and Gutner took title and resold to small manufacturers; solicited and obtained their own customers; assumed all risks of loss and credit; operated warehouses; maintained inventories; employed selling organizations; advertised; and furnished technical assistance to their customers. The factual conclusion reached by the Commission was that Malina and Gutner were "independent business men who operated as jobbers at a level of distribution between the manufacturers of the yarn and the processor who found it economically difficult to buy direct"; that they "satisfied an economic need by facilitating the movement of American's rayon yarn to the small units in the textile trade"; and that the 5% discount "bears all the characteristics of a functional discount, the validity of which should be judged under Section 2(a)."

Reliance upon Section 2(c) might well, in the Commission's view, "render all functional discounts illegal *per se*" and prevent the recognition of price differentials at non-competing business levels.

It is our conclusion that if plaintiff has any grievance, it must finds its remedy under Section 2(a) and not as here under Section 2(c), (d) and (e).
[AFFIRMED]

Finally, Section 2 does more than make it illegal to *grant* a price discrimination. Section 2(f) makes it unlawful for any person in commerce "knowingly to *induce* or *receive* a discrimination in price" [EMPHASIS ADDED] which is prohibited by Section 2.

5   TYING CONTRACTS AND EXCLUSIVE DEALINGS

A tying contract is one in which property is sold or leased for use only on condition that the buyer or lessee purchase certain additional products or services from the seller or lessor. An *exclusive dealing*, however, does not necessarily involve more than one product and the terms of its sale. An exclusive dealing may be a requirements contract whereby the buyer agrees to purchase all his business needs of a product supplied by the seller during a certain period of time. The buyer may be a manufacturer who has a reasonably ascertainable need for the raw materials or parts agreed to be supplied, or he may be a retailer who needs goods for resale. An exclusive dealing also is present in a contract whereby a buyer agrees not to purchase an item or items of merchandise from competitors of the seller. Such a contract might take the form of a franchise, in which a dealer agrees to sell only the product manufactured or distributed by the seller—a particular make of automobile, for instance. Either tying contracts or exclusive dealings may be in violation of the antitrust laws.

Perhaps the most obvious basis for the illegality of tying contracts or exclusive dealings is Section 3 of the Clayton Act, as amended by the Robinson-Patman Act, already discussed in Chapter 11, page 380. Under Section 3, an agreement by a buyer or lessee of a commodity not to use or deal in the goods of a competitor of the lessor or seller is outlawed "where the effect . . . may be to substantially lessen competition or tend to create a monopoly in any line of commerce." Taken literally, then, the same issues concerning the *relevant market* and *probable anticompetitive effects* are involved in the determination of a violation of Section 3 of the Clayton Act, as may be in issue in a case arising under Section 7 on mergers, discussed in Chapter 12, or under Section 2 on price discrimination, discussed in Section 4 of this chapter.

In the *International Salt* case, summarized in Chapter 11, page 380, a typical tying contract required the lessees of patented machines to process in them salt purchased from the lessor and no other supplier. There, the probable anticompetitive effects of the contracts in question were sufficient to amount to a violation of Section 3, since the monopoly power of a patent was used to tie in the promise to buy an unpatented item and the amount of business in question was not "insignificant or insubstantial." In *Times-Picayune Publishing Co. v. United States*,[16] the court said, "the essence of illegality in tying agreements is the wielding of monopolistic leverage." It went on to state that when a seller or lessor "enjoys a monopolistic position in the market for the tying product, *or* if a substantial volume of commerce in the 'tied' product is restrained, a tying agreement violates the narrower standards expressed in Section 3 of the Clayton Act because from either factor, the requisite potential lessening of competition is inferred."

16 345 U.S. 594, 608, 611 (1953).

The case which follows is one of the leading decisions involving the legality of exclusive dealings under Section 3.

STANDARD OIL CO. OF CALIFORNIA V. UNITED STATES
337 U.S. 293 (1949)

As of March, 1947, Standard Oil Company of California had entered into exclusive supply or requirements contracts with the operators of 5,937 independent stations in the seven Western states in which it was doing business. These amounted to 16 percent of the total retail gasoline outlets in that area. Several types of contracts were involved, but in all of them, the dealer had undertaken to purchase from Standard Oil either his business requirements of petroleum products, or his business requirements of petroleum products plus tubes, tires, and batteries. They were either to last for a specified period or to run from year to year, being terminable by either party upon giving thirty days' notice in the latter case. In 1947 these independent dealers purchased roughly $58,000,000 worth of gasoline and $8,200,000 worth of other products from Standard. In 1946, Standard sold 6.8 percent of the total sales of gasoline in the area involved through its company-owned service stations, and 6.7 percent of that total to the independent operators under the exclusive dealings contracts. Standard's six leading competitors, who employed similar contracts, sold 42.5 percent of the total sales of gasoline in the area through service stations during the same year. Only 1.6 percent of the stations in the seven-state region sold the gasoline of more than one supplier. The United States brought this action against Standard Oil and its wholly owned subsidiary, Standard Stations, Inc., for an injunction preventing the defendants from enforcing or entering into exclusive supply contracts with any independent dealer, alleging that these contracts violated § 1 of the Sherman Act and § 3 of the Clayton Act. The District Court granted the injunction, and the defendants appealed.

FRANKFURTER, JUSTICE: . . . Since § 3 of the Clayton Act was directed to prohibiting specific practices even though not covered by the broad terms of the Sherman Act, it is appropriate to consider first whether the enjoined contracts fall within the prohibition of the narrower Act. The relevant provisions of § 3 are:

> It shall be unlawful for any person engaged in commerce, in the course of such commerce, to lease or make a sale or contract for sale of goods, wares, merchandise, machinery, supplies, or other commodities, whether patented or unpatented, for use, consumption, or resale within the United States . . . on the condition, agreement, or understanding that the lessee or purchaser

thereof shall not use or deal in the goods . . . of a competitor or competitors of the . . . seller, where the effect of such lease, sale, or contract for sale or such condition, agreement, or understanding may be to substantially lessen competition or tend to create a monopoly in any line of commerce.

Obviously the contracts here at issue would be proscribed if § 3 stopped short of the qualifying clause beginning, "where the effect of such lease, sale, or contract for sale. . . ." If effect is to be given that clause, however, it is by no means obvious, in view of Standard's minority share of the "line of commerce" involved, of the fact that that share has not recently increased, and of the claims of these contracts to economic utility, that the effect of the contracts may be to lessen competition or tend to create a monopoly. It is the qualifying clause, therefore, which must be construed.

The District Court held that the requirement of showing an actual or potential lessening of competition or a tendency to establish monopoly was adequately met by proof that the contracts covered "a substantial number of outlets and a substantial amount of products, whether considered comparatively or not." Given such quantitative substantiality, the substantial lessening of competition—so the court reasoned—is an automatic result, for the very existence of such contracts denies dealers opportunity to deal in the products of competing suppliers and excludes suppliers from access to the outlets controlled by those dealers. . . .

The issue before us, therefore, is whether the requirement of showing that the effect of the agreements "may be to substantially lessen competition" may be met simply by proof that a substantial portion of commerce is affected or whether it must also be demonstrated that competitive activity has actually diminished or probably will diminish. . . .

International Salt Co. v. United States, 332 U.S. 392, . . . at least as to contracts tying the sale of a nonpatented to a patented product, rejected the necessity of demonstrating economic consequences once it has been established that "the volume of business affected" is not "insignificant or insubstantial" and that the effect of the contracts is to "foreclose competitors from [a] substantial market." Upon that basis we affirmed a summary judgment granting an injunction against the leasing of machines for the utilization of salt products on the condition that the lessee use in them only salt supplied by defendant. It was not established that equivalent machines were unobtainable, it was not indicated what proportion of the business of supplying such machines was controlled by defendant, and it was deemed irrelevant that there was no evidence as to the actual effect of the tying clauses upon competition. It is clear, therefore, that unless a distinction is to be drawn for purposes of the applicability of § 3 between requirements contracts and contracts tying the sale of a nonpatented to a patented product, the showing that Standard's requirements contracts affected a gross business of $58,000,000 comprising 6.7% of the total in the area goes far toward supporting the inference that competition has been or probably will be substantially lessened.

In favor of confining the standard laid down by the International Salt case to tying agreements, important economic differences may be noted. Tying agreements serve hardly any purpose beyond the suppression of competition. The justification most often advanced in their defense—the protection of the good will of the manufacturer of the tying device—fails in the usual situation because specification of the type and quality of the product to be used in connection with the tying device is protection enough. In the usual case only the prospect of reducing competition would persuade a seller to adopt such a contract and only his control of the supply of the tying device, whether conferred by patent monopoly or otherwise obtained, could induce a buyer to enter one. The existence of market control of the tying device, therefore, affords a strong foundation for the presumption that it has been or probably will be used to limit competition in the tied product also.

Requirements contracts, on the other hand, may well be of economic advantage to buyers as well as to sellers, and thus indirectly of advantage to the consuming public. In the case of the buyer, they may assure supply, afford protection against rises in price, enable long-term planning on the basis of known costs, and obviate the expense and risk of storage in the quantity necessary for a commodity having a fluctuating demand. From the seller's point of view, requirements contracts may make possible the substantial reduction of selling expenses, give protection against price fluctuations, and—of particular advantage to a newcomer to the field to whom it is important to know what capital expenditures are justified—offer the possibility of a predictable market. They may be useful, moreover, to a seller trying to establish a foothold against the counterattacks of entrenched competitors. Since these advantages of requirements contracts may often be sufficient to account for their use, the coverage by such contracts of a substantial amount of business affords a weaker basis for the inference that competition may be lessened than would similar coverage by tying clauses, especially where use of the latter is combined with market control of the tying device. A patent, moreover, although in fact there may be many competing substitutes for the patented article, is at least prima facie evidence of such control. And so we could not dispose of this case merely by citing *International Salt Co. v. United States,* 332 U.S. 392.

Thus, even though the qualifying clause of § 3 is appended without distinction of terms equally to the prohibition of tying clauses and of requirements contracts, pertinent considerations support, certainly as a matter of economic reasoning, varying standards as to each for the proof necessary to fulfill the conditions of that clause. If this distinction were accepted, various tests of the economic usefulness or restrictive effect of requirements contracts would become relevant. Among them would be evidence that competition has flourished despite use of the contracts, and under this test much of the evidence tendered by appellant in this case would be important. Likewise bearing on whether or not the contracts were being used to suppress competition, would be the conformity of the length of their term to the reasonable requirements of the field of commerce in which they were used. Still another test would be the status of the defendant as a struggling newcomer or an established competitor. Perhaps most important, however, would be the defendant's degree of market control, for the greater the dominance of his position, the stronger the inference that an important factor in attaining and maintaining that position has been the use of requirements contracts to stifle competition rather than to serve legitimate economic needs.

Yet serious difficulties would attend the attempt to apply these tests. We may assume, as did the court below, that no improvement of Standard's competitive position has coincided with the period during which the requirements-contract system of distribution has been in effect. We may assume further that the duration of the contracts is not excessive and that Standard does not by itself dominate the market. But Standard was a major competitor when the present system was adopted, and it is possible that its position would have deteriorated but for the adoption of that system. When it is remembered that all the other major suppliers have also been using requirements contracts, and when it is noted that the relative share of the business which fell to each has remained about the same during the period of their use, it would not be farfetched to infer that their effect has been to enable the established suppliers individually to maintain their own standing and at the same time collectively, even though not collusively, to prevent a late arrival from wresting away more than an insignificant portion of the market. If, indeed, this were a result of the system, it would seem unimportant that a short-run by-product of stability may have been greater efficiency and lower costs, for it is the theory of the antitrust laws that the long-run advantage of the community depends upon the removal of restraints upon competition.

Moreover, to demand that bare inference be supported by evidence as to what would have happened but for the adoption of the practice that was in fact adopted or to require firm predication of an increase of competition as a probable result of ordering the abandonment of the practice, would be a standard of proof if not virtually impossible to meet, at least most ill-suited for ascertainment by courts. Before the system of requirements contracts was instituted, Standard sold gasoline through independent service-station operators as its agents, and it might revert to this system if the judgment below were sustained. Or it might, as opportunity presented itself, add service stations now operated independently to the number managed by its subsidiary, Standard Stations, Inc. From the point of view of maintaining or extending competitive advantage, either of these alternatives would be just as effective as the use of requirements contracts, although of course insofar as they resulted in a tendency to monopoly they might encounter the anti-monopoly provisions of the Sherman Act. As appellant points out, dealers might order petroleum products in quantities sufficient to meet their estimated needs for the period during which requirements contracts are now effective, and even that would foreclose competition to some degree. So long as these diverse ways of restricting competition remain open, therefore, there can be no conclusive proof that the use of requirements contracts has actually reduced competition below the level which it would otherwise have reached or maintained. . . . It seems hardly likely that, having with one hand set up an express prohibition against a practice thought to be beyond the reach of the Sherman Act, Congress meant, with the other hand, to re-establish the necessity of meeting the same tests of detriment to the public interest as that Act had been interpreted as requiring. Yet the economic investigation which appellant would have us require is of the same broad scope as was adumbrated with reference to unreasonable restraints of trade in *Chicago Bd. of Trade v. United States,* 246 U.S. 231. To insist upon such an investment would be to stultify the force of Congress' declaration that requirements contracts are to be prohibited wherever their effect "may be" to substantially lessen competition. . . .

We conclude, therefore, that the qualifying clause of § 3 is satisfied by proof that competition has been foreclosed in a substantial share of the line of commerce affected. It cannot be gainsaid that observance by a dealer of his requirements contract with Standard does effectively foreclose whatever opportunity there might be for competing suppliers to attract his patronage, and it is clear that the affected proportion of retail sales of petroleum products is substantial. In view of the widespread adoption of such contracts by Standard's competitors and the availability of alternative ways of obtaining an assured market, evidence that competitive activity has not actually declined is inconclusive. Standard's use of the contracts creates just such a potential clog on competition as it was the purpose of § 3 to remove wherever, were it to become actual, it would impede a substantial amount of competitive activity.

Since the decree below is sustained by our interpretation of § 3 of the Clayton Act, we need not go on to consider whether it might also be sustained by § 1 of the Sherman Act. . . .

The judgment below is affirmed.

The Attorney General's Committee, discussing the foregoing decision, noted: [17]

[17] Report of the Attorney General's National Committee to Study the Antitrust Laws 142, 143–144 (1955).

While postulating "foreclosure" of competitors from a significant market as the index of illegality, the Court never analyzed the factual arrangements at bar. Without explaining what "foreclosure" meant, the Court assumed rather than demonstrated that Standard's requirements contracts actually "foreclosed" competitors from market access. Hence its affirmance of the District Court's "quantitative substantiality" ruling intimated that exclusive arrangements violated the Clayton Act merely if covering a substantial number of outlets or volume of trade.

Sequels to Standard Stations have, however, retreated from any "quantitative substantiality" criterion. . . .

. . . [S]ubsequent interpretations of Section 3 and the Standard Oil ruling—both in Supreme Court opinions and Federal Trade Commission determinations—have refrained from a strict "quantitative substantiality" test. Rather than subjecting exclusive arrangements to rigid criteria tantamount to per se illegality, they have accorded thorough scrutiny to the specific factual pattern of each case. This inquiry is evidently directed to determine whether the challenged practice menaces competition in the distribution process by actually "foreclosing" competitors from access to a substantial share of the consuming market.

The legality of both tying and exclusive arrangements is thus tested by criteria adapted to their special characteristics in measuring adverse market effects. . . .

Tying arrangements and exclusive dealings may also run afoul of § 1 of the Sherman Act as contracts in unreasonable restraint of trade. In the case below the application of the Sherman Act to tying clauses included in sales or leases of land was in issue.

NORTHERN PACIFIC RY. CO. V. UNITED STATES
356 U.S. 1 (1958)

BLACK, JUSTICE: In 1864 and 1870 Congress granted the predecessor of the Northern Pacific Railway Company approximately forty million acres of land in several Northwestern States and Territories to facilitate its construction of a railroad line from Lake Superior to Puget Sound. In general terms, this grant consisted of every alternate section of land in a belt 20 miles wide on each side of the track through States and 40 miles wide through Territories. The granted lands were of various kinds; some contained great stands of timber, some iron ore or other valuable mineral deposits, some oil or natural gas, while still other sections were useful for agriculture, grazing or industrial purposes. By 1949 the Railroad had sold about 37,000,000 acres of its holdings, but had reserved mineral rights in 6,500,000 of those acres.

Most of the unsold land was leased for one purpose or another. In a large number of its sales contracts and most of its lease agreements the Railroad had inserted "preferential routing" clauses which compelled the grantee or lessee to ship over its lines all commodities produced or manufactured on the land, provided that its rates (and in some instances its service) were equal to those of competing carriers. Since many of the goods produced on the lands subject to these "preferential routing" provisions are shipped from one State to another, the actual and potential amount of interstate commerce affected is substantial. Alternative means of transportation exist for a large portion of these shipments including the facilities of two other major railroad systems.

In 1949 the Government filed suit under § 4 of the Sherman Act seeking a declaration that the defendant's "preferential routing" agreements were unlawful as unreasonable restraints of trade under § 1 of that Act. After various pretrial proceedings the Government moved for summary judgment contending that on the undisputed facts it was entitled, as a matter of law, to the relief demanded. The district judge . . . issued an order enjoining the defendant from enforcing the existing "preferential routing" clauses or from entering into any future agreements containing them. The defendant took a direct appeal to this Court. . . .

The Sherman Act was designed to be a comprehensive charter of economic liberty aimed at preserving free and unfettered competition as the rule of trade. It rests on the premise that the unrestrained interaction of competitive forces will yield the best allocation of our economic resources, the lowest prices, the highest quality and the greatest material progress, while at the same time providing an environment conducive to the preservation of our democratic political and social institutions. But even were that premise open to question, the policy unequivocally laid down by the Act is competition. And to this end it prohibits "Every contract, combination . . . or conspiracy, in restraint of trade or commerce among the several States." Although this prohibition is literally all-encompassing, the courts have construed it as precluding only those contracts or combinations which "unreasonably" restrain competition.

However, there are certain agreements or practices which because of their pernicious effect on competition and lack of any redeeming virtue are conclusively presumed to be unreasonable and therefore illegal without elaborate inquiry as to the precise harm they have caused or the business excuse for their use. This principle of *per se* unreasonableness not only makes the type of restraints which are proscribed by the Sherman Act more certain to the benefit of everyone concerned, but it also avoids the necessity for an incredibly complicated and prolonged economic investigation into the entire history of the industry involved, as well as related industries, in an effort to determine at large whether a particular restraint has been unreasonable—an inquiry so often wholly fruitless when undertaken. Among the practices which the courts have heretofore deemed to be unlawful in and of themselves are price fixing, group boycotts, and tying arrangements.

For our purposes a tying arrangement may be defined as an agreement by a party to sell one product but only on the condition that the buyer also purchases a different (or tied) product, or at least agrees that he will not purchase that product from any other supplier. Where such conditions are successfully exacted competition on the merits with respect to the tied product is inevitably curbed. Indeed "tying agreements serve hardly any purpose beyond the suppression of competition." They deny competitors free access to the market for the tied product, not because the party imposing the tying requirements has a better product or a lower price but because of his power or leverage in another market. At the same time buyers are forced to forego their free choice between competing products. For these reasons "tying agreements fare harshly under the laws forbidding restraints of trade." They are unreasonable in and of themselves whenever a party has sufficient economic power with respect to the tying product to appreciably restrain free competition in the market for the tied product and a "not insubstantial" amount of interstate commerce is affected. Of course where the seller has no control or dominance over the tying product so that it does not represent an effectual weapon to pressure buyers into taking the tied item any restraint of trade attributable to such tying arrangements would obviously be insignificant at most. As a simple example, if one of a dozen food stores in a community were to refuse to sell flour unless the buyer also took sugar it would hardly tend to restrain competition in sugar if its competitors were ready and able to sell flour by itself.

In this case we believe the district judge was clearly correct in entering summary judgment declaring the defendant's "preferential routing" clauses unlawful restraints of trade. We wholly agree that the undisputed facts established beyond any genuine question that the defendant possessed substantial economic power by virtue of its extensive landholdings which it used as leverage to induce large numbers of purchasers and lessees to give it preference, to the exclusion of its competitors, in carrying goods or produce from the land transferred to them. Nor can there be any real doubt that a "not insubstantial" amount of interstate commerce was and is affected by these restrictive provisions.

As was pointed out before, the defendant was initially granted large acreages by Congress in the several Northwestern States through which its lines now run. This land was strategically located in checkerboard fashion amid private holdings and within economic distance of transportation facilities. Not only the testimony of various witnesses but common sense makes it evident that this particular land was often prized by those who purchased or leased it and was frequently essential to their business activities. In disposing of its holdings the defendant entered into contracts of sale or lease covering at least several million acres of land which included "preferential routing" clauses. The very existence of this host of tying arrangements is itself compelling evidence of the defendant's great power, at least where, as here, no other explanation has been offered for the existence of these restraints. The "preferential routing" clauses conferred no benefit on the purchasers or lessees. While they got the land they wanted by yielding their freedom to deal with competing carriers, the defendant makes no claim that it came any cheaper than if the restrictive clauses had been omitted. In fact any such price reduction in return for rail shipments would have quite plainly constituted an unlawful rebate to the shipper. So far as the Railroad was concerned, its purpose obviously was to fence out competitors, to stifle competition. While this may have been exceedingly bene ficial to its business, it is the very type of thing the Sherman Act condemns. In short, we are convinced that the essential prerequisites for treating the defendant's tying arrangements as unreasonable *"per se"* were conclusively established below and that the defendant has offered to prove nothing there or here which would alter this conclusion.

In our view *International Salt Co. v. United States,* 332 U.S. 392, which has been unqualifiedly approved by subsequent decisions, is ample authority for affirming the judgment below. . . . [AFFIRMED]

A third provision in the antitrust laws under which a tying arrangement or exclusive dealing may be found illegal is Section 5 of the Federal Trade Commission Act, which prohibits "unfair methods of competition . . . and unfair or deceptive acts or practices. . . ." In the case which follows, Brown Shoe Company had entered into franchise agreements for the sale of its products, which were exclusive dealing contracts, with over 600 retail stores. These were challenged by the Federal Trade Commission under Section 5. It is interesting to note that this is the same Brown Shoe Company which was involved in the 1962 case already presented in Chapter 12 on page 416. There, the reader will recall, Brown Shoe had attempted to accomplish the same end as here (namely to obtain additional retail outlets which would handle Brown Shoe products exclusively) but by the means of the acquisition of Kinney, a chain of shoe stores. That acquisition was successfully challenged by the Justice Department as a violation of Section 7 of the Clayton Act, and divestiture was ordered. It would appear that the activities of Brown Shoe Company have been under rather close scrutiny by the agencies of the Federal government charged with antitrust enforcement.

FTC V. BROWN SHOE CO.
384 U.S. 316 (1966)

BLACK, JUSTICE: Section 5(a) (6) of the Federal Trade Commission Act empowers and directs the Commission "to prevent persons, partnerships, or corporations . . . from using unfair methods of competition in commerce and unfair or deceptive acts or practices in commerce." Proceeding under the authority of § 5, the Federal Trade Commission filed a complaint against the Brown Shoe Co., Inc., one of the world's largest manufacturers of shoes with total sales of $236,946,078 for the year ending October 31, 1957. The unfair practices charged against Brown revolve around the "Brown Franchise Stores' Program" through which Brown sells its shoes to some 650 retail stores. The complaint alleged that under this plan Brown, a corporation engaged in interstate commerce, had "entered into contracts or franchises with a substantial number of its independent retail shoe store operator customers which require said customers to restrict their purchases of shoes for resale to the Brown lines and which prohibit them from purchasing, stocking or reselling shoes manufactured by competitors of Brown." Brown's customers who entered into these restrictive franchise agreements, so the complaint charged, were given in return special treatment and valuable benefits which were not granted to Brown's customers who did not enter into the agreements. In its answer to the Commission's complaint Brown admitted that approximately 259 of its retail customers had executed written franchise agreements and that over 400 others had entered into its franchise program without execution of the franchise agreement. Also in its answer Brown attached as an exhibit an unexecuted copy of the "Franchise Agreement" which, when executed by Brown's representative and a retail shoe dealer, obligates Brown to give to the dealer but not to other customers certain valuable services, including among others, architectural plans, costly merchandising records, services of a Brown field representative, and a right to participate in group insurance at lower rates than the dealer could obtain individually. In return, according to the franchise agreement set out in Brown's answer, the retailer must make this promise:

In return I will:
1. Concentrate my business within the grades and price lines of shoes representing Brown Shoe Company Franchises of the Brown Division and will have no lines conflicting with Brown Division Brands of the Brown Shoe Company.

Brown's answer further admitted that the operators of "such Brown Franchise Stores in individually varying degrees accept the benefits and perform the obligations contained in such franchise agreements or implicit in such Program," and that Brown refuses to grant these benefits "to dealers who are dropped or voluntarily withdraw from the Brown Franchise Program. . . ." The foregoing admissions of Brown as to the existence and operation of the franchise program were buttressed by many separate detailed fact findings of a trial examiner, one of which findings was that the franchise program effectively foreclosed Brown's competitors from selling to a substantial number of retail shoe dealers. Based on these findings and on Brown's admissions the Commission concluded that the restrictive contract program was an unfair method of competition within the meaning of § 5 and ordered Brown to cease and desist from its use.

On review the Court of Appeals set aside the Commission's order. In doing so the court said:

By passage of the Federal Trade Commission Act, particularly § 5 thereof, we do not believe that Congress meant to prohibit or limit sales programs such as Brown Shoe engaged in in this case. . . . The custom of giving free service to those who will buy their shoes is widespread, and we cannot agree with the Commission that it is an unfair method of competition in commerce.

In addition the Court of Appeals held that there was a "complete failure to prove an exclusive dealing agreement which might be held violative of Section 5 of the Act." We are asked to treat this general conclusionary statement as though the court intended it to be a rejection of the Commission's findings of fact. We cannot do this. Neither this statement of the court nor any other statement in the opinion indicate a purpose to hold that the evidence failed to show an agreement between Brown and more than 650 franchised dealers which restrained the dealers from buying competing lines of shoes from Brown's competitors. Indeed, in view of the crucial admissions in Brown's formal answer to the complaint we cannot attribute to the Court of Appeals a purpose to set aside the Commission's findings that these restrictive agreements existed and that Brown and most of the franchised dealers in varying degrees lived up to their obligations. Thus the question we have for decision is whether the Federal Trade Commission can declare it to be an unfair practice for Brown, the second largest manufacturer of shoes in the Nation, to pay a valuable consideration to hundreds of retail shoe purchasers in order to secure a contractual promise from them that they will deal primarily with Brown and will not purchase conflicting lines of shoes from Brown's competitors. We hold that the Commission has power to find, on the record here, such an anticompetitive practice unfair, subject of course to judicial review.

In holding that the Federal Trade Commission lacked the power to declare Brown's program to be unfair the Court of Appeals was much influenced by and quoted at length from this Court's opinion in *FTC v. Gratz,* 253 U.S. 421. That case, decided shortly after the Federal Trade Commission Act was passed, construed the Act over a strong dissent by Mr. Justice Brandeis as giving the Commission very little power to declare any trade practice unfair. Later cases of this Court, however, have rejected the *Gratz* view and it is now recognized in line with the dissent of Mr. Justice Brandeis in *Gratz* that the Commission has broad powers to declare trade practices unfair. This broad power of the Commission is particularly well established with regard to trade practices which conflict with the basic policies of the Sherman and Clayton Acts even though such practices may not actually violate these laws. The record in this case shows beyond doubt that Brown, the country's second largest manufacturer of shoes, has a program, which requires shoe retailers, unless faithless to their contractual obligations with Brown, substantially to limit their trade with Brown's competitors. This program obviously conflicts with the central policy of both § 1 of the Sherman Act and § 3 of the Clayton Act against contracts which take away freedom of purchasers to buy in an open market. Brown nevertheless contends that the Commission had no power to declare the franchise program unfair without proof that its effect "may be to substantially lessen competition or tend to create a monopoly" which of course would have to be proved if the Government were proceeding against Brown under § 3 of the Clayton Act rather than § 5 of the Federal Trade Commission Act. We reject the argument that proof of this § 3 element must be made for as we pointed out above our cases hold that the Commission has power under § 5 to arrest trade restraints in their incipiency without proof that they amount to an outright violation of § 3 of the Clayton Act or other provisions of the antitrust laws. This power of the Commission was emphatically stated in *FTC v. Motion Picture Advertising Co.*, 344 U.S. 392, at pp. 394–395:

It is . . . clear that the Federal Trade Commission Act was designed to supplement and bolster the Sherman Act and the Clayton Act . . . to stop in their incipiency acts and practices which, when full blown, would violate those Acts . . . as well as to condemn as "unfair methods of competition" existing violations of them.

We hold that the Commission acted well within its authority in declaring the Brown franchise program unfair whether it was completely full blown or not. [REVERSED]

The application of Section 5 of the Federal Trade Commission Act is discussed at greater length in the next section.

6   UNFAIR METHODS OF COMPETITION AND UNFAIR OR DECEPTIVE TRADE PRACTICES

As the 1966 *Brown Shoe* case presented above illustrates, a particular business activity may be prohibited by the Federal Trade Commission if it amounts to an "unfair method of competition" or an "unfair or deceptive act or practice" in violation of Section 5 of the Federal Trade Commission Act. Justice Black's words in that opinion bear repeating here: ". . . the Commission has broad power to declare trade practices unfair. This broad power is particularly well established with regard to trade practices which conflict with the basic *policies* of the Sherman and Clayton Acts *even though such practices may not actually violate these laws.*" [EMPHASIS ADDED] Thus, the Commission may outlaw practices which it feels are injurious to competition, but which do not exactly fall within the categories of activities proscribed by the other antitrust laws. Note that Section 5 does *not* undertake to define what are unfair or deceptive trade practices in commerce, does *not* expressly refer to a "relevant market" or "line of commerce," and does *not* expressly require a finding that a prohibited course of conduct have an adverse effect on competition to be illegal as Sections 2, 3, and 7 of the Clayton Act do (i.e., does not expressly restrict the prohibited trade practices to those whose effect "may be substantially to lessen competition or tend to create a monopoly.")

In the case which follows, the Commission attacked a business arrangement as being unfair under Section 5. The practice in question was not a tying lease or sale within the meaning of Section 3 of the Clayton Act, but did bear some resemblance to tying arrangements.

ATLANTIC REF. CO. V. FTC
381 U.S. 357 (1965)

CLARK, JUSTICE: The Federal Trade Commission has found that an agreement between The Atlantic Refining Company (Atlantic) and The Goodyear Tire & Rubber Company (Goodyear), under which the former "sponsors" the sale of the tires, batteries and accessory products of the latter to its wholesale outlets and its retail service station dealers, is an unfair method of competition in violation of § 5 of the Federal Trade Commission Act. Under the plan Atlantic sponsors the sale of Goodyear products to its wholesale and retail outlets on an overall commission basis. Goodyear is responsible for its sales and sells at its own price to Atlantic wholesalers and dealers for resale; it bears all of the cost of distribution through its warehouses, stores and other supply points and carries on a joint sales promotion program with Atlantic. The latter, however, is primarily responsible for promoting the sale of Goodyear products to its dealers and assisting them in their resale; for this it receives a commission on all sales made to its wholesalers and dealers. The hearing examiner, with the approval of the Commission and the Court of Appeals, enjoined the use of direct methods of coercion on the part of Atlantic toward its dealers in the inauguration and promotion of the plan. Atlantic does not seek review of this phase of the case. However, the Commission considered the coercive practices to be symptomatic of a more fundamental restraint of trade and found the sales-commission plan illegal in itself as "a classic example of the use of economic power in one market . . . to destroy competition in another market. . . ." It prohibited Atlantic from participating in any such commission arrangement. Similarly, it forbade Goodyear from continuing the arrangement with Atlantic or any other oil company. Goodyear and Atlantic filed separate appeals. The Court of Appeals approved the findings of the Commission and affirmed its order. "Appraising the broader aspects of the system (used by Atlantic and Goodyear) as tying arrangement," it agreed with the Commission that it injured "competition in the distribution of tires, batteries and accessories at the manufacturing, wholesale, and retail levels." We granted certiorari. . . .

The Goodyear-Atlantic agreement required Atlantic to assist Goodyear "to the fullest practicable extent in perfecting sales, credit, and merchandising arrangements" with all of Atlantic's outlets. This included announcement to its dealers of its sponsorship of Goodyear products followed by a field representative's call to "suggest . . . the maintenance of adequate stocks of merchandise" and "maintenance of proper identification and advertising" of such merchandise. Atlantic was to instruct its salesmen to urge dealers to "vigorously" represent Goodyear, and to "cooperate with and assist" Goodyear in its "efforts to promote and increase the sale" by Atlantic dealers of Goodyear products. And it was to "maintain adequate dealer training programs in the sales of tires, batteries and accessories." In addition, the companies organized joint sales organization meetings at which plans were made for perfecting the sales plan. One project was a "double teaming" solicitation of Atlantic outlets by representatives of both companies to convert them to Goodyear products. They were to call on the dealers together, take stock orders, furnish initial price lists and project future quotas of purchases of Goodyear products. Goodyear also required that each Atlantic dealer be assigned to a supply point maintained by it, such as a warehouse, Goodyear store, independent dealer or designated Atlantic distributor or retail dealer. Atlantic would not receive any commission on purchases made outside of an assigned supply point. Its commission of 10% on sales to Atlantic dealers and 7.5% on sales to its wholesalers was paid on the basis of a master sheet prepared by Goodyear and furnished Atlantic each month. . . .

Section 5 of the Federal Trade Commission Act declares "[u]nfair methods of competition in commerce, and unfair . . . acts or practices in commerce . . . unlawful." In a broad delegation of power it empowers the Commission, in the first instance, to determine whether a method of competition or the act or practice complained of is unfair. The Congress intentionally left development of the term "unfair" to the Commission rather than attempting to define "the many and variable unfair practices which prevail in commerce. . . ." . . . As the House Report stated, unfair competition could best be prevented "through the action of an administrative body of practical men . . . who will be able to apply the rule enacted by Congress to particular business situations, so as to eradicate evils with the least risk of interfering with legitimate business operations." H.R.Rep. No. 1142, 63d Cong., 2d Sess., 19 (conference report). In thus divining that there is no limit to business ingenuity and legal gymnastics the Congress displayed much foresight. . . . Where the Congress has provided that an administrative agency initially apply a broad statutory term to a particular situation, our function is limited to determining whether the Commission's decision "has 'warrant in the record' and a reasonable basis in law." While the final word is left to the courts, necessarily "we give great weight to the Commission's conclusion. . . ."

Certainly there is "warrant in the record" for the findings of the Commission here. Substantial evidence supports the conclusion that notwithstanding Atlantic's contention that it and its dealers are mutually dependent upon each other, they simply do not bargain as equals. . . .

With this background in mind, we consider whether there was a "reasonable basis in law" for the Commission's ultimate conclusion that the sales-commission plan constituted an unfair method of competition.

At the outset we must stress what we do not find present here. We recognize that the Goodyear-Atlantic contract is not a tying arrangement. . . . As our cases hold, all that is necessary in § 5 proceedings to find a violation is to discover conduct that "runs counter to the public policy declared in the Act." But this is of necessity, and was intended to be, a standard to which the Commission would give substance. In doing so, its use as a guideline of recognized violations of the antitrust laws was, we believe, entirely appropriate. It has long been recognized that there are many unfair methods of competition that do not assume the proportions of antitrust violations. When conduct does bear the characteristics of recognized antitrust violations it becomes suspect, and the Commission may properly look to cases applying those laws for guidance.

Although the Commission relied on such cases here, it expressly rejected a mechanical application of the law of tying arrangements. Rather it looked to the entire record as a basis for its conclusion that the activity of Goodyear and Atlantic impaired competition at three levels of the tires, batteries and accessories industry. It found that wholesalers and manufacturers of competing brands, and even Goodyear wholesalers who were not authorized supply points, were foreclosed from the Atlantic market. In addition, it recognized the obvious fact that Firestone and Goodyear were excluded from selling to Atlantic's dealers in each other's territories. Both of these effects on competition flowed from the contract itself. It also found that the plight of Atlantic wholesalers and retailers was equally clear. They had to compete with other wholesalers and retailers who were free to stock several brands, but they were effectively foreclosed from selling brands other than Goodyear. This restraint is in this respect broader than the one found in *International Salt Co. v. United States,* 332 U.S. 392, where the dealers could stock other salt if they could buy it at lower prices. Here the dealers could buy only at Goodyear's price.

Thus the Commission was warranted in finding that the effect of the plan was *as though* Atlantic had agreed with Goodyear to require its dealers to buy Goodyear products and had done so. It is beyond question that the effect on commerce was not insubstantial. . . .

Goodyear and Atlantic contend that the Commission should have made a far more extensive economic analysis of the competitive effect of the sales-commission plan, examining the entire market in tires, batteries and accessories. But just as the effect of this plan is similar to that of a tie-in, so is it unnecessary to embark upon a full-scale economic analysis of competitive effect. We think it enough that the Commission found that a not insubstantial portion of commerce is affected. . . .

Nor can we say that the Commission erred in refusing to consider evidence of economic justification for the program. While these contracts may well provide Atlantic with an economical method of assuring efficient product distribution among its dealers they also amount to a device that permits suppliers of tires, batteries and accessories, through the use of oil company power, to effectively sew up large markets. Upon considering the destructive effect on commerce that would result from the widespread use of these contracts by major oil companies and suppliers, we conclude that the Commission was clearly justified in refusing the participants an opportunity to offset these evils by a showing of economic benefit to themselves.

The short of it is that Atlantic with Goodyear's encouragement and assistance, has marshaled its full economic power in a continuing campaign to force its dealers and wholesalers to buy Goodyear products. The anticompetitive effects of this program are clear on the record and render unnecessary extensive economic analysis of market percentages or business justifications in determining whether this was a method of competition which Congress has declared unfair and therefore unlawful. . . . [AFFIRMED]

The foregoing case exemplifies the deference the Court displays to the judgment of the Commission when it comes to defining what business practices are "unfair." It is clear that in this area, the Court is very hesitant to substitute its judgment (or to permit the Circuit Courts of Appeal to substitute their judgments) for that of the Commission.

Examples of other business practices which were held to be unfair by the FTC and illegally damaging to competition were presented in Chapter 11. These were: promulgating certain misleading advertising and selling sugar below cost (the *Sears Roebuck & Co.* case on page 387), and selling penny candy to children by a method which involved gambling and a lottery (the *Keppel* case on page 392).

Besides empowering the FTC to issue cease and desist orders restraining unfair trade practices which are *injurious to competition,* Section 5 of the Federal Trade Commission Act also grants it authority to prevent acts or practices which are *deceptive to consumers.* Numerically speaking, the greater percentage of the cases of the Commission involve protecting the consumer from "deceptive" business practices. Typically these involve false or misleading advertising or other misrepresentations of some sort. Often the false advertising attacked is designed to make a prospective purchaser believe he will be getting a "good deal," in terms of price, if he buys the product in question. For example, in *Giant Food Inc. v. FTC*,[18] the defendant was ordered to refrain from advertising its products for sale as follows:

Proctor Steam & Dry Iron #10010 Reg. Price $15.95. Adv. Price $8.47.
Regina Twin Brush Waxer #400 Reg. Price $66.00. Adv. Price $35.47.
Regina Twin Brush Waxer $35.47—Mfg. List $66.00.
Sunbeam Mixmaster $24.88—Manufacturer List Price $37.95.

The Commission ruled that it was deceptive to refer to "regular price" unless the defendant had usually sold the items at that price recently in the regular course of business, and to refer to the "manufacturer's list price," when that list price was not the ordinary and customary retail sales product of the item in the locality. This was in spite of the fact that manufacturers had advertised suggested retail list prices the same as those used by Giant. In ordering enforcement of the Commission's cease and desist order, the Court of Appeals said, "We do not understand the Commission to hold that use of the term 'manufacturer's list price' is unlawful *per se;* rather it is unlawful only if it is not the usual and customary retail price in the area."

The case below also involved a type of price representation as a deceptive practice.

FTC V. MARY CARTER PAINT CO.
382 U.S. 46 (1965)

BRENNAN, JUSTICE: Respondent manufactures and sells paint and related products. The Federal Trade Commission ordered respondent to cease and desist from the use of certain representations found by the Commission to be deceptive and in violation of § 5 of the Federal Trade Commission Act. The representations appeared in advertisements which stated in various ways that for every can of respondent's paint purchased by a buyer, the

---

[18] 322 F.2d 977 (1963), *cert. denied* 376 U.S. 967 (1963).

respondent would give the buyer a "free" can of equal quality and quantity. The Court of Appeals for the Fifth Circuit set aside the Commission's order. We granted certiorari. We reverse.

Although there is some ambiguity in the Commission's opinion, we cannot say that its holding constituted a departure from Commission policy regarding the use of the commercially exploitable word "free." Initial efforts to define the term in decisions were followed by "Guides Against Deceptive Prices." These informed businessmen that they might advertise an article as "free," even though purchase of another article was required, so long as the terms of the offer were clearly stated, the price of the article required to be purchased was not increased, and its quality and quantity were not diminished. With specific reference to two-for-the-price-of-one offers, the Guides required that either the sales price for the two be "the advertiser's usual and customary retail price for the single article in the recent, regular course of his business," or where the advertiser has not previously sold the article, the price for two be the "usual and customary" price for one in the relevant trade areas. These, of course, were guides, not fixed rules as such, and were designed to inform businessmen of the factors which would guide Commission decisions. Although Mary Carter seems to have attempted to tailor its offer to come within their terms, the Commission found that it failed; the offer complied in appearance only.

The gist of the Commission's reasoning is in the hearing examiner's finding, which it adopted, that

. . . *the usual and customary retail price of each can of Mary Carter paint was not, and is not now, the price designated in the advertisement ($6.98) but was, and is now substantially less than such price. The second can of paint was not, and is not now, "free," that is, was not, and is not now, given as a gift of gratuity. The offer is, on the contrary, an offer of two cans of paint for the price advertised as or purporting to be the list price or customary and usual price of one can.*

In sum, the Commission found that Mary Carter had no history of selling single cans of paint; it was marketing twins, and in allocating what is in fact the price of two cans to one can, yet calling one "free," Mary Carter misrepresented. It is true that respondent was not permitted to show that the quality of its paint matched those paints which usually and customarily sell in the $6.98 range, or that purchasers of paint estimate quality by the price they are charged. If both claims were established, it is arguable that any deception was limited to a representation that Mary Carter has a usual and customary price for single cans of paint, when it has no such price. However, it is not for courts to say whether this violates the Act. "[T]he Commission is often in a better position than are courts to determine when a practice is 'deceptive' within the meaning of the Act." There was substantial evidence in the record to support the Commission's finding; its determination that the practice here was deceptive was neither arbitrary nor clearly wrong. The Court of Appeals should have sustained it. . . .

Judgment of Court of Appeals reversed. . . .

Besides involving misleading price representations, deceptive practices may result from fraudulent, false, or misleading advertising or other representations concerning the performance, capability, quality, or character of goods or services being sold. The decision which follows illustrates this kind of representation as well as the limitations on the use of "mock-ups" for purposes of television commercials.

FTC V. COLGATE-PALMOLIVE CO.
380 U.S. 379 (1965)

WARREN, CHIEF JUSTICE: . . . [This] case arises out of an attempt by respondent Colgate-Palmolive Company to prove to the television public that its shaving cream, "Rapid Shave," outshaves them all. Respondent Ted Bates & Company, Inc., an advertising agency, prepared for Colgate three one-minute commercials designed to show that Rapid Shave could soften even the toughness of sandpaper. Each of the commercials contained the same "sandpaper test." The announcer informed the audience that, "To prove RAPID SHAVE'S super-moisturizing power, we put it right from the can onto this tough, dry sandpaper. It was apply . . . soak . . . and off in a stroke." While the announcer was speaking, Rapid Shave was applied to a substance that appeared to be sandpaper, and immediately thereafter a razor was shown shaving the substance clean.

The Federal Trade Commission issued a complaint against respondents Colgate and Bates charging that the commercials were false and deceptive. The evidence before the hearing examiner disclosed that sandpaper of the type depicted in the commercials could not be shaved immediately following the application of Rapid Shave, but required a substantial soaking period of approximately 80 minutes. The evidence also showed that the substance resembling sandpaper was in fact a simulated prop, or "mock-up," made of plexiglass to which sand had been applied. However, the examiner found that Rapid Shave could shave sandpaper, even though not in the short time represented by the commercials, and that if real sandpaper had been used in the commercials the inadequacies of television transmission would have made it appear to viewers to be nothing more than plain, colored paper. The examiner dismissed the complaint because neither misrepresentation —concerning the actual moistening time or the identity of the shaved substance—was in his opinion a material one that would mislead the public.

The Commission, in an opinion dated December 29, 1961, reversed the hearing examiner. It found that since Rapid Shave could not shave sandpaper within the time depicted in the commercials, respondents had misrepresented the product's moisturizing power. Moreover, the Commission found that the undisclosed use of a plexiglass substitute for sandpaper was an additional material misrepresentation that was a deceptive act separate and distinct from the misrepresentation concerning Rapid Shave's underlying qualities. Even if the sandpaper could be shaved just as depicted in the commercials, the Commission found that viewers had been mislead into believing they had seen it done with their own eyes. As a result of these findings the Commission entered a cease-and-desist order against the respondents.

An appeal was taken to the Court of Appeals for the First Circuit. . . . The Court of Appeals . . . found unsatisfactory that portion of the order dealing with simulated props and refused to enforce it.

We granted certiorari, to consider this aspect of the case and do not have before us any question concerning the misrepresentation that Rapid Shave could shave sandpaper immediately after application, that being conceded. . . .

Over the vigorous objection of respondents, the Commission issued its final order on May 7, 1963. Both respondents were ordered to cease and desist from:

Unfairly or deceptively advertising any . . . product by presenting a test, experiment or demonstration that (1) is represented to the public as actual proof of a claim made for the product which is material to inducing its sale, and (2) is not in fact a genuine test, experiment or demonstration being conducted as represented and does not in fact constitute actual proof of the claim, because of the undisclosed use and substitution of a mock-up or prop instead of the product, article, or substance represented to be used therein. . . .

In reviewing the substantive issues in the case, it is well to remember the respective roles of the Commission and the courts in the administration of the Federal Trade Commission Act. When the Commission was created by Congress in 1914, it was directed by § 5 to prevent "[u]nfair methods of competition in commerce." Congress amended the Act in 1938 to extend the Commission's jurisdiction to include "unfair or deceptive acts or practices in commerce"—a significant amendment showing Congress' concern for consumers as well as for competitors. It is important to note the generality of these standards of illegality; the proscriptions in § 5 are flexible, "to be defined with particularity by the myriad of cases from the field of business."

This statutory scheme necessarily gives the Commission an influential role in interpreting § 5 and in applying it to the facts of particular cases arising out of unprecedented situations. Moreover, as an administrative agency which deals continually with cases in the area, the Commission is often in a better position than are courts to determine when a practice is "deceptive" within the meaning of the Act. This Court has frequently stated that the Commission's judgment is to be given great weight by reviewing courts. This admonition is especially true with respect to allegedly deceptive advertising since the finding of a § 5 violation in this field rests so heavily on inference and pragmatic judgment. Nevertheless, while informed judicial determination is dependent upon enlightenment gained from administrative experience, in the last analysis the words "deceptive practices" set forth a legal standard and they must get their final meaning from judicial construction.

We are not concerned in this case with the clear misrepresentation in the commercials concerning the speed with which Rapid Shave could shave sandpaper, since the Court of Appeals upheld the Commission's finding on that matter and the respondents have not challenged the finding here. We granted certiorari to consider the Commission's conclusion that even if an advertiser has himself conducted a test, experiment or demonstration which he honestly believes will prove a certain product claim, he may not convey to television viewers the false impression that they are seeing the test, experiment or demonstration for themselves, when they are not because of the undisclosed use of mock-ups.

We accept the Commission's determination that the commercials involved in this case contained three representations to the public: (1) that sandpaper could be shaved by Rapid Shave; (2) that an experiment had been conducted which verified this claim; and (3) that the viewer was seeing this experiment for himself. Respondents admit that the first two representations were made, but deny that the third was. The Commission, however, found to the contrary, and, since this is a matter of fact resting on an inference that could reasonably be drawn from the commercials themselves, the Commission's finding should be sustained. For the purposes of our review, we can assume that the first two representations were true; the focus of our consideration is on the third which was clearly false. The parties agree that § 5 prohibits the intentional misrepresentation of any fact which would constitute a material factor in a purchaser's decision whether to buy. They differ, however, in their conception of what "facts" constitute a "material factor" in a purchaser's decision to buy. Respondents submit, in effect, that the only material facts are those which deal with the substantive qualities of a product. The Commission on the other hand, submits that the misrepresentation of *any* fact so long as it materially induces a purchaser's decision to buy is a deception prohibited by § 5.

The Commission's interpretation of what is a deceptive practice seems more in line with the decided cases than that of respondents. This Court said in *FTC v. Algoma Lumber Co.*, 291 U.S. 67: "[T]he public is entitled to get what it chooses, though the choice may be dictated by caprice or by fashion or perhaps by ignorance." It has long been considered a deceptive practice to state falsely that a product ordinarily sells for an inflated price but that it is being offered at a special reduced price, even if the offered price represents the actual value of the product and the purchaser is receiving his money's worth. Applying respondents' arguments to these cases, it would appear that so long as buyers paid no more than the product was actually worth and the product contained the qualities advertised, the misstatement of an inflated original price was immaterial.

It has also been held a violation of § 5 for a seller to misrepresent to the public that he is in a certain line of business, even though the misstatement in no way affects the qualities of the product. As was said in *FTC v. Royal Milling Co.*, **288 U.S. 212:**

If consumers or dealers prefer to purchase a given article because it was made by a particular manufacturer or class of manufacturers, they have a right to do so, and this right cannot be satisfied by imposing upon them an exactly similar article, or one equally as good, but having a different origin.

The courts of appeals have applied this reasoning to the merchandising of reprocessed products that are as good as new, without a disclosure that they are in fact reprocessed. And it has also been held that it is a deceptive practice to misappropriate the trade name of another.

Respondents claim that all these cases are irrelevant to our decision because they involve misrepresentations related to the product itself and not merely to the manner in which an advertising message is communicated. This distinction misses the mark for two reasons. In the first place, the present case is not concerned with a mode of communication, but with a misrepresentation that viewers have objective proof of a seller's product claim over and above the seller's word. Secondly, all of the above cases, like the present case, deal with methods designed to get a consumer to purchase a product, not with whether the product, when purchased, will perform up to expectations. We find an especially strong similarity between the present case and those cases in which a seller induces the public to purchase an arguably good product by misrepresenting his line of business, by concealing the fact that the product is reprocessed, or by misappropriating another's trademark. In each the seller has used a misrepresentation to break down what he regards to be an annoying or irrational habit of the buying public—the preference for particular manufacturers or known brands regardless of a product's actual qualities, the prejudice against reprocessed goods, and the desire for verification of a product claim. In each case the seller reasons that when the habit is broken the buyer will be satisfied with the performance of the product he receives. Yet, a misrepresentation has been used to break the habit and, as was stated in Algoma Lumber, a misrepresentation for such an end is not permitted.

We need not limit ourselves to the cases already mentioned because there are other situations which also illustrate the correctness of the Commission's finding in the present case. It is generally accepted that it is a deceptive practice to state falsely that a product has received a testimonial from a respected source. In addition, the Commission has consistently acted to prevent sellers from falsely stated that their product claims have been "certified." We find these situations to be indistinguishable from the present case. We can assume that in each the underlying product claim is true and in each the seller actually conducted an experiment sufficient to prove to himself the truth of the claim. But in each the seller has told the public that it could rely on something other than his word concerning both the truth of the claim and the validity of his experiment. We find it an immaterial difference that in one case the viewer is told to rely on the word of a celebrity or authority he respects, in another on the word of a testing agency, and in the present case on his own perception of an undisclosed simulation.

Respondents again insist that the present case is not like any of the above, but is more like a case in which a celebrity or independent testing agency has in fact submitted a written verification of an experiment actually observed, but, because of the inability of the camera to transmit accurately an impression of the paper on which the testimonial is written, the seller reproduces it on another substance so that it can be seen by the viewing audience. This analogy ignores the finding of the Commission that in the present case the seller misrepresented to the public that it was being given objective proof of a product claim. In respondents' hypothetical the objective proof of the product claim that is offered, the word of the celebrity or agency that the experiment was actually conducted, does exist; while in the case before us the objective proof offered, the viewer's own perception of an actual experiment, does not exist. Thus, in respondents' hypothetical, unlike the present case, the use of the undisclosed mock-up does not conflict with the seller's claim that there is objective proof.

We agree with the Commission, therefore, that the undisclosed use of plexiglass in the present commercials was a material deceptive practice, independent and separate from the other misrepresentation found. We find unpersuasive respondents' other objections to this conclusion. Respondents claim that it will be impractical to inform the viewing public that it is not seeing an actual test, experiment or demonstration, but we think it inconceivable that the ingenious advertising world will be unable, if it so desires, to conform to the Commission's insistence that the public be not misinformed. If, however, it becomes impossible or impractical to show simulated demonstrations on television in a truthful manner, this indicates that television is not a medium that lends itself to this type of commercial, not that the commercial must survive at all costs. Similarly unpersuasive is respondents' objection that the Commission's decision discriminates against sellers whose product claims cannot be "verified" on television without the use of simulations. All methods of advertising do not equally favor every seller. If the inherent limitations of a method do not permit its use in the way a seller desires, the seller cannot by material misrepresentation compensate for those limitations. . . .

Respondents finally object to what they consider to be the absence of an adequate record to sustain the Commission's finding. It is true that in its initial stages the case was concerned more with the misrepresentation about the product's underlying qualities than with the misrepresentation that objective proof was being given. Nevertheless, both misrepresentations were in the case from the beginning, and respondents were never prejudicially misled into believing that the second question was not being considered. Nor was it necessary for the Commission to conduct a survey of the viewing public before it could determine that the commercials had a tendency to mislead, for when the Commission finds deception it is also authorized, within the bounds of reason, to infer that the deception will constitute a material factor in a purchaser's decision to buy. We find the record in this case sufficient to support the Commission's findings.

We turn our attention now to the order issued by the Commission. It has been repeatedly held that the Commission has wide discretion in determining the type of order that is necessary to cope with the unfair practices found, and that Congress has placed the primary responsibility for fashioning orders upon the Commission. For these reasons the courts should not "lightly modify" the Commission's orders. However, this Court has also warned that an order's prohibitions "should be clear and precise in order that they may be understood by those against whom they are directed," and that "[t]he severity of possible penalties prescribed . . . for violations of orders which have become final underlines the necessity for fashioning orders which are, at the outset, sufficiently clear and precise to avoid raising serious questions as to their meaning and application."

The Court of Appeals has criticized the reference in the Commission's order to "test, experiment or demonstration" as not capable of practical interpretation. It could find no difference between the Rapid Shave commercial and a commercial which extolled the goodness of ice cream while giving viewers a picture of a scoop of mashed potatoes appearing to be ice cream. We do not understand this difficulty. In the ice cream case the mashed potato prop is not being used for additional proof of the product claim, while the purpose of the Rapid Shave commercial is to give the viewer objective proof of the claims made. If in the ice cream hypothetical the focus of the commercial becomes the undisclosed potato prop and the viewer is invited, explicitly or by implication, to see for himself the truth of the claims about the ice cream's rich texture and full color, and perhaps compare it to a "rival product," then the commercial has become similar to the one now before us. Clearly, however, a commercial which depicts happy actors delightedly eating ice cream that is in fact mashed potatoes or drinking a product appearing to be coffee but which is in fact some other substance is not covered by the present order.

The crucial terms of the present order—"test, experiment or demonstration . . . represented . . . as actual proof of a claim"—are as specific as the circumstances will permit. If respondents in their subsequent commercials attempt to come as close to the line of misrepresentation as the Commission's order permits, they may without specifically intending to do so cross into the area proscribed by this order. However, it does not seem "unfair to require that one who deliberately goes perilously close to an area of proscribed conduct shall take the risk that he may cross the line." In commercials where the emphasis is on the seller's word, and not on the viewer's own perception, the respondents need not fear that an undisclosed use of props is prohibited by the present order. On the other hand, when the commercial not only makes a claim, but also invites the viewer to rely on his own perception, for demonstrative proof of the claim, the respondents will be aware that the use of undisclosed props in strategic places might be a material deception. We believe that respondents will have no difficulty applying the Commission's order to the vast majority of their contemplated future commercials. If, however, a situation arises in which respondents are sincerely unable to determine whether a proposed course of action would violate the present order, they can, by complying with the Commission's rules, oblige the Commission to give them definite advice as to whether their proposed action, if pursued, would constitute compliance with the order.

Finally, we find no defect in the provision of the order which prohibits respondents from engaging in similar practices with respect to "any product" they advertise. The propriety of a broad order depends upon the specific circumstances of the case, but the courts will not interfere except where the remedy selected has no reasonable relation to the unlawful practices found to exist. In this case the respondents produced three different commercials which employed the same deceptive practice. This we believe gave the Commission a sufficient basis for believing that the respondents would be inclined to use similar commercials with respect to the other products they advertise. We think it reasonable for the Commission to frame its order broadly enough to prevent respondents from engaging in similarly illegal practices in future advertisements. As was said in *FTC v. Ruberoid Co.*, 343 U.S. 470: "[T]he Commission is not limited to prohibiting the illegal practice in the precise form in which it is found to have existed in the past." Having been caught violating the Act, respondents "must expect some fencing in."

The judgment of the Court of Appeals is reversed and the case remanded for the entry of a judgment enforcing the Commission's order. [REVERSED AND REMANDED]

HARLAN, JUSTICE, dissenting (joined by JUSTICE STEWART): Under the limited grant of certiorari in this case, the Court must assume that the advertiser can perform the experiment in question and that the demonstration is as simple to execute as it appears on television. The only question here is what techniques the advertiser may use to convey essential truth to the television viewer. If the claim is true and valid, then the technique for projecting that claim, within broad boundaries, falls purely within the advertiser's art. The warrant to the Federal Trade Commission is to police the verity of the claim itself.

I do not agree that the use of "mock-ups" by the television advertiser is of itself a deceptive trade practice. Further, while there was an independent deceptive element in this commercial, I do not think this record justifies the broad remedial order issued by the Commission. . . .

The faulty prop in the Court's reasoning is that it focuses entirely on what is taking place in the studio rather than on what the viewer is seeing on his screen. That which the viewer sees with his own eyes is not, however, what is taking place in the studio, but an electronic image. If the image he sees on the screen is an accurate reproduction of what he would see with the naked eyes were the experiment performed before him with sandpaper in his home or in the studio, there can hardly be a misrepresentation in any legally significant sense. . . .

Nor can I readily understand how the accurate portrayal of an experiment by means of a mock-up can be considered more deceptive than the use of mashed potatoes to convey the glamorous qualities of a particular ice cream . . . : indeed, to a potato-lover "the smile on the face of the tiger" might come more naturally than if he were actually being served ice cream.

It is commonly known that television presents certain distortions in transmission for which the broadcasting industry must compensate. Thus, a white towel will look a dingy gray over television, but a blue towel will look a sparkling white. On the Court's analysis, an advertiser must achieve accuracy in the studio even though it results in an inaccurate image being projected on the home screen. This led the Court of Appeals to question whether it would be proper for an advertiser to show a product on television that somehow, because of the medium, looks better on the screen than it does in real life. . . .

A perhaps more commonplace example suggests itself: Would it be proper for respondent Colgate, in advertising a laundry detergent, to "demonstrate" the effectiveness of a major competitor's detergent in washing white sheets; and then "before the viewer's eyes," to wash a white (not a blue) sheet with the competitor's detergent? The studio test would accurately show the quality of the product, but the image on the screen would look as though the sheet had been washed with an ineffective detergent. All that has happened here is the converse; a demonstration has been altered in the studio to compensate for the distortions of the television medium, but in this instance in order to present an accurate picture to the television viewer.

In short, it seems to me that the proper legal test in cases of this kind concerns not what goes on in the broadcasting studio, but whether what is shown on the television screen is an accurate representation of the advertised product and of the claims made for it. . . .

Some of the other practices which have been barred as deceptively misleading have involved mislabeling or misbranding a product. For example, lumber dealers have been barred from advertising under names such as "California White Pine" and "Western White Pine" when their products were inferior to genuine "White Pine" even though these terms were accepted and understood in the trade.[19]

Note that the penalty for disobeying a cease and desist order issued by the FTC is a fine of $5,000.00 *per day* for each day the violation continues, if the order has become final (i.e., the business prosecutes no timely appeal or the order is affirmed on appeal). "Consent orders," which are issued with the agreement of a business charged with a violation, have the same legal effect as a final cease and desist order.

7   CONCLUSION

In the last four chapters, an attempt has been made to acquaint the reader with the historical, political, and economic reasons for the antitrust laws, their historical development, and the general nature of the constraints they impose today upon business policy formulation and implementation. No effort has been made to present a thorough and comprehensive guide for business activity in this field of law. The purpose has been more to point up danger areas in business conduct which have been created by the antitrust laws. Obviously, the antitrust laws are fraught with uncertainty. Many of the statutes, as well as the decisions interpreting them, are phrased in generalities and often contain ambiguities, raising more questions than they answer. No set of clear-cut rules has been laid down to mark a safe path. As we have seen, the application of some of these laws requires something of a "crystal ball approach" in that conclusions must be reached as to the probable *future* anticompetitive effects of challenged business activity. And, finally, the fact that the ills sought to be remedied by the antitrust laws are those of an economy which is constantly changing should not be deemphasized as a complicating factor in their application.

[19] 291 U.S. 67 (1934).

CHAPTER FOURTEEN

LABOR LAW

1 INTRODUCTION

This chapter will examine the legal problems which arise as a result of the fact that a business usually employs people to carry on its work. In many ways, people are the most important single factor in the conduct of a business, and in the social sense they are the very reason for its existence. Corporations, being intangible legal entities, must always act through agents and employees. A partnership is essentially an agency relationship among the partners and often employs additional persons to assist in its operation. Most sole proprietorships also employ other persons. It is not surprising, therefore, that a substantial body of law exists to determine the rights and duties of employers with respect to their employees as well as to third parties. This area of the law concerns questions of both contract and tort liability in addition to the complex body of statutory-based law respecting labor-management relations which has developed in our industrial society. All of these matters will be discussed in the sections which follow in this chapter.

2 AGENCY

The law of agency in the narrow sense is concerned with questions of contractual liability when an alleged agent enters into a contract with a third party on behalf of a purported principal. The liability of the principal, the liability of the agent, and the rights of third parties are frequent subjects of agency litigation. While it is not our purpose to explore the substantive law of agency in detail, the general rule is that a principal has liability on all contracts entered into by the agent within the scope of the actual or apparent authority of the agent. Before the person dealing with the agent can hold the principal to the contract, he must prove the existence of this authority of the agent, although such factors as trade custom and emergencies may be used to establish it. The term "apparent authority" or "ostensible authority" refers to situations in which no actual authority exists but in which the law binds the principal as if it did because, by his conduct, he has led third persons to believe that the agent has authority, and to rely on that belief. In *Reusche v. California Pac. Title Ins. Co.,*[1] the court said: Ostensible authority is defined ". . . as such authority . . . as a principal, intentionally or by want of ordinary care, causes or allows a third person to believe the agent to possess." Liability of the principal for the ostensible agent's acts rests on the doctrine of estoppel and its essential elements are representation by the principal, justifiable reliance thereon by the third party and change of position or injury resulting from such reliance.

A principal who puts an agent in a position that enables the agent, while apparently acting within his authority, to commit a fraud upon third persons is subject to liability to such third persons for the fraud. The principal is liable although he is entirely innocent, although he has received no benefit from the transaction, and although the agent acts solely for his own purposes. Liability is based upon the fact that the agent's position facilitates the consummation of the fraud, in that, from the point of view of the third persons, the transaction seems regular on its face and the agent appears to be acting in the ordinary course of the business entrusted to him. The law reasons that in such a case, where one of two innocent parties must suffer, the loss should be accepted by the principal who is responsible for the selection of the agent and for the definition of his authority.

The principal-agent relationship is used to describe the nature of the employment where the employee has power to contract. In those situations where he has no such power, the relationship is usually characterized as master-servant. A principal is liable for the torts of his agent just as a master is liable for the torts of his servant if the agent or servant is acting within the course of his employment or is engaged in work for the employer. This subject is discussed further in Chapter 16 on the law of torts. Essentially, the rule is that both the agent or servant and the principal or master have tort liability if the course-of-employment test is met.

The law of agency also deals with the duties an agent owes his employer, such as the duty of undivided loyalty. Conflict-of-interest questions, which frequently arise, are decided under this principle. The duty of loyalty arises because the agency relationship is a fiduciary one, and any benefits other than those agreed upon, which the agent receives because of his position, actually belong to the principal. Many acts of disloyalty involve so-called "trade secrets." The case which follows illustrates the length to which courts will go in protecting employers from disloyalty by employees relating to business trade secrets.

---

[1] 42 Cal. Rpt. 262 (1965).

ALBERT B. CORD CO. V. S & P MANAGEMENT SERVS., INC.

194 N.E.2d 173 (Ohio C.P. 1963)

LEIS, JUSTICE: . . . The plaintiff, Albert B. Cord Company, Inc., is an Ohio corporation engaged in management consulting. Mr. Albert B. Cord is the president of said corporation.

The defendant, S & P Management Services, Inc., is, likewise, a management consulting business and was organized some time after May 30, 1961. The individual defendants, Mr. Anthony M. Schummer and Mr. J. Paul Pickering, S & P's principal shareholders, were employed by the plaintiff prior to May 30, 1961. Mr. Schummer, an engineer, became a member of plaintiff's staff as a Staff Engineer at or about June 1948. In January 1950, he was promoted to the supervisory staff as Chief Engineer. In this capacity Mr. Schummer was recognized as Assistant General Manager with full power and authority to act in the event anything happened to the General Manager (Mr. Albert Cord), and he had full force and power to perform anything that, in his discretion, he saw fit. Mr. J. Paul Pickering was employed by the plaintiff as its Sales Manager prior to his resignation.

Management consulting firms offer assistance to business concerns in solving various problems in such areas as labor relations, shop operations, wage plans, production, administration, sales promotion and related problems peculiar to modern business. Service is rendered upon a fee basis. One of the chief assets of a management consulting firm is its staff of well-trained engineers, accountants, administrators and salesmen; men who are qualified and trained both technically and through years of experience in all the phases of business activity in production control, sales and sales promotion, administration, accounting and cost control, statistics, engineering, etc. These assets are "human assets" and, as experts, their minds and mentality, and their ability to analyze the problems presented to them, apply their technical knowledge, experience and imagination and recommend a workable remedy to cure the business ailment are of intangible value to the management consulting firm. Another asset of relative and equal importance to the management consulting company is a knowledge of, and access to, companies which are likely to need its services.

In the case at bar Mr. Pickering was the person most relied upon to secure the clientele. He was continually "on the road" making business calls in the midwest—Ohio, Indiana, Michigan, Illinois, Missouri, Pennsylvania and West Virginia. Whenever he made a call he submitted a report to the office for filing in the customer's file (if the call merited such a file). These reports were variously entitled, per the exhibits before the Court as "Survey Authorization," "Sales Report," "Survey Report," "Client Reactivation Sales Report," "Memorandum." The contents of the reports included the name of the person or persons contacted, a summarization of any discussions with the prospective client, including observations of the manner in which he (the salesman) was received, the problems confronting the prospect, if any; information concerning employees, financial data and statistics, affiliation with other companies, contemplated plans of merger or sale, volume of business activity, D & B credit rating of the client or prospect and many other items and facts pertinent and helpful to the plaintiff, for the present and for the future, in ascertaining whether or not the prospect is in need, or will be in need of service and if repeat calls should be made. All this data and these comprehensive reports were accumulated in the plaintiff's confidential file with the hope that at some future time it would or will be available in securing an engagement for the plaintiff. Much time, effort and money was spent by the plaintiff through its sales representatives, under the leadership of Mr. Pickering.

The plaintiff's plan followed a definite pattern, namely:

1 The first sales call, and
2 Follow-up calls (if deemed advantageous.), leading to
3 An initial Survey, followed up by
4 Contract to perform service to cure the "business ill." A natural by-product of these contacts was a building of confidence, a relationship between the plaintiff and its personnel and a healthy atmosphere for a successful tenure if a contract was forthcoming.

This Court recognizes the unique character of this type of business as compared to the type of business which offers a commodity or product, or a common service. The Court also recognizes the fact that repeat business can result from a successful initial engagement. Another element of this business that entered into this Court's consideration is the fact that Cord Company personnel had to work closely with their client's management and personnel. Such close contact can result in relationships of confidence and trust in the personnel of the plaintiff. For this reason the plaintiff, in its contracts, included the following statement:

In order to maintain a professional atmosphere it is our policy to consider your personnel ineligible for employment with our organization, and we require your commitment to similar conditions regarding the employment or engagement of our personnel by your organization.

All of these factors emphasize the unique character of the plaintiff's business service and of its intangible value, a value which cannot be measured accountingwise in money, but which is a valuable asset to the corporation in the nature of good will.

The defendants, Mr. Schummer and Mr. Pickering, were the top men in the plaintiff company. The evidence shows that while other employees had written contracts of employment none were required of Mr. Schummer and Mr. Pickering. Evidence was presented to show that Mr. Cord and the defendants worked closely together and freely interchanged information at all times and, as a result of membership in this "inner circle" the defendants had unlimited access to confidential information contained in the locked files of the Cord Company. The defendants had keys to all the locked confidential files except two drawers which contained private papers of Mr. Cord.

This case is categorized under the topic in law entitled "Trade Secrets." The Restatement of Torts, Section 757, comment (b) (1939) defines a "Trade Secret" as follows:

A trade secret may consist of any formula, pattern, device, or compilation of information which is used in one's business, and which gives him an opportunity to obtain an advantage over competitors who do not know or use it. It may be a formula for a chemical compound, a process of manufacturing, treating or preserving materials, a pattern for a machine or other device, or a list of customers. . . .

A trade secret, therefore, is almost anything and everything useful or advantageous in business activity that is not generally known or easily or immediately ascertainable to members of the trade. . . .

The plaintiff in its Second Amended Petition alleges that the defendants

. . . have solicited on behalf of S & P Management Services, Inc. the following clients or prospective clients of plaintiff, among others, with whom said individual defendants had dealt on behalf of plaintiff during the last three years of their employment by plaintiff and with respect to whom defendants possessed information secured in the course of their confidential employment by plaintiff and regarded as confidential: . . .

The plaintiff then lists twenty-six company names. Included in the list is the Frick-Gallagher Mfg. Co., Wellston, Ohio, a client of the plaintiff and with whom the plaintiff had been negotiating additional service when defendants were plaintiff's employees, which company plaintiff alleges the defendants induced to retain defendant S & P Management Services, Inc., to perform management-consulting service on the basis of information available to Mr. Schummer and Mr. Pickering as a result of their confidential employment by plaintiff.

The Supreme Court of Ohio stated in *Curry v. Marquart,* 133 Ohio St. 77, 11 N.E.2d 868 (1937):

The authorities are quite uniform that disclosures of trade secrets by an employee secured by him in the course of confidential employment will be restrained by the process of injunction, and in numerous instances attempts to

use for himself or for a new employer information relative to the trade or business in which he has been engaged, such as lists of customers regarded as confidential, have been restrained.

In the case of *Soeder v. Soeder*, 82 Ohio App. 71, 77 N.E.2d 474 (1947), the Court held:

Disclosure of secrets secured by an employee in the course of confidential employment, such as lists of customers, will be restrained by injunctive process.

In the 1960 case of *Hance v. Peacock*, Ohio Com.Pl., 169 N.E.2d 564, the Court held:

Lists of customers obtained by defendant while in employ of plaintiff's bottle gas business was confidential information and its use by defendant after defendant terminated his employment with plaintiff and began his own business could be enjoined as unauthorized use of a trade secret.

A court of appeals of California case is very much in point to the matter now before this Court, namely, *Alex Food, Inc. v. Metcalfe*, 137 Cal. App. 2d 415, 290 P.2d 646 (1955):

Independent of an express contract, equity will enjoin the disclosure of confidential knowledge of trade secrets which a former employee learned in the course of his employment. The fact that a defendant was employed by plaintiff for years during which he learned the names, address, and requirements of plaintiff's customers, justifies injunctive relief where the defendant undertook to use such information in unfair competition to the detriment of plaintiff. Such knowledge is a part of the good will of the business and is a trade secret. A list of customers is a trade secret if there is confidential information as to such customers. To act upon it is an improper use of confidential information and amounts to unfair competition.

This Court concludes that the information available to the defendants Mr. Schummer and Mr. Pickering was confidential information and was the property of the plaintiff, secured and paid for by the plaintiff with the aid and assistance of the defendants while they were employed by the plaintiff in a confidential capacity. The defendants were confidential employees intrusted with information, in the regular course of their employment, of such a nature that it was not necessary that there be a written customer list for an injunction to issue. The defendants are men of high intelligence and this Court concludes that their memories are as good as any written list. The information about the clients and prospective clients was available to the defendants up until the day of their termination of employment.

This Court grants the temporary injunction per the plaintiff's motion filed November 27, 1961.

3   STATE REGULATION OF EMPLOYMENT

The creation and operation of the employer-employee relationship is subject to many types of regulation today. State governments regulate this relationship by statutes which control such matters as (1) child labor, (2) hours of work, particularly for women and minors, (3) minimum wages, (4) unemployment compensation, (5) workmen's compensation, (6) safety appliances and conditions of work, (7) factory inspection, (8) wage assignments, and (9) employment agencies. Some of the pressures and social conditions which caused the foregoing kinds of legislation are discussed in the cases and sections which follow. Each statute that regulates employment tends in some fashion to eliminate or reduce the freedom of employers and employees to contract. When these statutes first became abundant, cases were tried challenging the power of government to regulate the employment relationship for social and economic purposes. While today we universally recognize that government possesses the power to enact social legislation, such was not always the case. *West Coast Hotel v. Parrish* [2] was the landmark case upholding minimum wage legislation.

In this decision the court, speaking through Chief Justice Hughes, said in part:

The principle which must control our decision is not in doubt. The constitutional provision invoked is the due process clause of the Fourteenth Amendment governing the states. . . . [T]he violation alleged by those attacking minimum wage regulation for women is deprivation of freedom of contract. It speaks of liberty and prohibits the deprivation of liberty without due process of law. In prohibiting that deprivation, the Constitution does not recognize an absolute and uncontrollable liberty. Liberty in each of its phases has its history and connotation. But the liberty safeguarded is liberty in a social organization which requires the protection of law against the evils which menace the health, safety, morals, and welfare of the people. Liberty under the Constitution is thus necessarily subject to the restraints of due process, and regulation which is reasonable in relation to its subject and is adopted in the interests of the community is due process.

This essential limitation of liberty in general governs freedom of contract in particular. More than twenty-five years ago we set forth the applicable principle in these words. . . .

"But it was recognized in the cases cited, as in many others, that freedom of contract is a qualified, and not an absolute, right. There is no absolute freedom to do as one wills or to contract as one chooses. The guaranty of liberty does not withdraw from legislative supervision that wide department of activity which consists of the making of contracts, or deny to government the power to provide restrictive safeguards. Liberty implies the absence of

[2] 300 U.S. 379 (1936).

arbitrary restraint, not immunity from reasonable regulations and prohibitions imposed in the interests of the community. . . ."

The point that has been strongly stressed that adult employees should be deemed competent to make their own contracts was decisively met nearly forty years ago in Holden v. Hardy, supra, where we pointed out the inequality in the footing of the parties. We said . . . :

"The legislature has also recognized the fact, which the experience of legislators in many states has corroborated, that the proprietors of these establishments and their operatives do not stand upon an equality, and that their interests are, to a certain extent, conflicting. The former naturally desire to obtain as much labor as possible from their employés, while the latter are often induced by the fear of discharge to conform to regulations which their judgment, fairly exercised, would pronounce to be detrimental to their health or strength. In other words, the proprietors lay down the rules, and the laborers are practically constrained to obey them. In such cases self-interest is often an unsafe guide, and the legislature may properly interpose its authority."

And we added that the fact

". . . that both parties are of full age, and competent to contract, does not necessarily deprive the state of the power to interfere, where the parties do not stand upon an equality, or where the public health demands that one party to the contract shall be protected against himself. . . . The state still retains an interest in his welfare, however reckless he may be. The whole is no greater than the sum of all the parts, and when the individual health, safety, and welfare are sacrificed or neglected, the state must suffer. . . ."

There is an additional and compelling consideration which recent economic experience has brought into a strong light. The exploitation of a class of workers who are in an unequal position with respect to bargaining power and are thus relatively defenseless against the denial of a living wage is not only detrimental to their health and well being, but casts a direct burden for their support upon the community.

The foregoing case rather effectively eliminated constitutional objections to social legislation regulating employment. Today, we have statutes covering most aspects of employment which are designed to solve all sorts of problems that employees may face. For example, the hazard of unemployment is reduced by the state unemployment compensation statutes which provide for payments for a stated period to workers who are unemployed through no fault of their own.

Another important risk employees and their families face is death, sickness, or injury. At common law, anyone was liable in money damages for injuries caused to another as a proximate result of negligence, or the lack of exercise of reasonable care. However, the law also provided three defenses known as (1) assumption of risk, (2) contributory negligence, and

(3) the fellow-servant doctrine. An employer could use these to escape liability, even though he were negligent. As a practical matter, the injured worker suffered the loss in most industrial accidents, paying his own medical expenses, losing his wages while recuperating, and frequently losing part or all of the income from his services for life, in the event of permanent physical impairment. For example, assume that employer E knowingly permitted workers to operate dangerous machinery not equipped with any safety devices, even though he realized injury to them was likely. W, a worker, had his arm mangled when it was caught in the gears of one of these machines. Even though E was negligent in permitting this hazardous condition to persist, if W were cognizant of the inherent dangers which existed, he would be unable to recover damages because he knowingly *assumed the risk* of his injury. In addition, if the injury were caused by *contributory negligence* of the employee, as well as the negligence of the employer, the action was defeated. And when injury existed because of the negligence of another employee, the negligent employee rather than the employer was liable because of the *fellow-servant rule.* Legislation to change these common-law principles of negligence, as far as industrial accidents were concerned, was enacted. These statutes provide for employees to receive workmen's compensation.

Most state workmen's compensation statutes provide a system to pay workers or their families in the event the worker is killed or injured or incurs an occupational disease while employed. To be compensable, the death, illness, or injury must arise out of and in the course of the employment. Formal court action is dispensed with and the statutes usually specify the amount to be paid by some formula so that these laws do not contain the uncertainities of personal injury verdicts awarded by juries. For example, in one state a worker who loses a hand will be paid 100 weeks of compensation at $50 per week. When a workmen's compensation statute is adopted, the defenses of contributory negligence, assumption of the risk, and the fellow-servant doctrine are abolished. The right of recovery is given without regard to negligence or fault of either the employer or employee in the traditional sense, being predicated on the employment relationship and the fact that the injury arose out of and in the course of the employment. The social policy underlying these acts is that the cost of on-the-job injuries and accidents should not be borne by the worker but should be treated as part of the cost of production and passed on to the consumers who create the demand for the product or service being furnished.

The traditional test for determining whether an employee is entitled to workmen's compensation is: "Did the injury arise out of and in the course of the employment?" Cases in recent years have tended to expand the coverage and the scope of the employer's liability. Liability has been found to exist for injuries incurred during lunch hour and even for heart attacks and other common diseases where the employee either had a preexisting disease or a physical condition likely to lead to the disease.

4   FEDERAL REGULATION OF EMPLOYMENT

The Federal government also has statutes creating liability of employers for injuries, diseases and death arising out of the course of employment. The statute applicable to most cases under federal law is the Federal Employer's Liability Act (FELA). The case below is indicative of the trend at both the state and federal levels to expand the liability of employers for mishaps befalling their employees.

HOPSON V. TEXACO, INC.
383 U.S. 262 (1966)

PER CURIAM: These actions were brought under the Jones Act . . . to recover damages for injuries sustained by one seaman and for the death of another, as a result of an automobile accident on the Island of Trinidad. Judgment on the jury's verdict was entered in United States District Court in favor of the plaintiffs, but the Court of Appeals reversed. . . . We granted a writ of certiorari and reverse.

The facts are not in dispute. The two seamen were members of the crew of respondent's tanker which was docked at respondent's refinery at Pointe-a-Pierre on the Island of Trinidad. Both fell ill and it was determined that they would be unable to continue the voyage. In order to discharge an incapacitated seaman in a foreign port, federal law requires that he be taken to a United States Consul where arrangements for his return to the United States can be made. The United States Consul's Office was located in Port-of-Spain, some 38 miles distant. Although respondent had a fleet of motor vehicles used for transportation in the immediate vicinity of the refinery and docking areas, its practice was to utilize either of two local taxi companies for journeys to more distant points. The ship's Master procured one of these cabs, which set out for Port-of-Spain with the two ill seamen. En route, the taxi collided with a truck, killing the Master and one of the seamen; the other seaman was seriously injured. The jury found that the taxi driver had been negligent—a finding challenged neither in the Court of Appeals nor here. The Court of Appeals reversed the District Court's determination that respondent is liable to petitioners for this negligence of the taxi operator.

The Jones Act incorporates the standards of the Federal Employers' Liability Act which renders an employer liable for the injuries negligently inflicted on its employees by its "officers, agents, or employees." We noted in *Sinkler v. Missouri Pac. R. Co.*, 356 U.S. 326, . . . that the latter Act was "an avowed departure from the rules of the common law," . . . which, recognizing "[t]he cost of human injury, and inescapable expense of rail-roading," undertook to "adjust that expense equitably between the worker and the carrier." . . . In order to give "an accommodating scope . . . to the word 'agents'" we concluded that "when [a]n . . . employee's injury is caused in whole or in part by the fault of others performing, under contract, operational activities of the employer, such others are 'agents' of the. employer within the meaning of § 1 of FELA." . . .

We think those principles apply with equal force here. These seamen were in the service of the ship and the ill-fated journey to Port-of-Spain was a vital part of the ship's total operations. The ship could not sail with these two men, nor could it lawfully discharge them without taking them to the United States Consul. Indeed, to have abandoned them would have breached the statutory duty to arrange for their return to the United States. Getting these two ill seamen to the United States Consul's office was, therefore, the duty of respondent. And it was respondent—not the seamen—which selected, as it had done many times before, the taxi service. Respondent—the law says—should bear the responsibility for the negligence of the driver which it chose. This is so because, as we said in *Sinkler*, "justice demands that one who gives his labor to the furtherance of the enterprise should be assured that all combining their exertions with him in the common pursuit will conduct themselves in all respects with sufficient care that his safety while doing his part will not be endangered." . . .

[REVERSED]

In recent years, fair employment practices legislation has been introduced and passed by several state legislatures. The purpose of this legislation is to ensure equal job opportunities to all persons, regardless of race, creed, or color. To date, the goals of these laws have not been obtained even in those states which have adopted the statutes, primarily because equal opportunity requires equal background and ability, and compliance with the spirit as well as the letter of the law. Until educational opportunities are equal, it is not likely that job opportunities will be equal. A typical act provides that it is an unfair employment practice for any employer to refuse to hire or otherwise discriminate against any individual because of his race, color, religion, national origin, or ancestry. If employment agencies or labor organizations discriminate against an individual in any way because of one of the foregoing reasons, they are also guilty of an unfair employment practice. Such acts establish an administrative body, generally known as the Fair Employment Practices Commission, which is given the power to promulgate rules and regulations to effectuate the purposes of the act and hear and decide charges of violations filed by complainants. If conciliation fails and the commission after a formal hearing sustains the charge, it is empowered to issue an order requiring the person charged to cease and desist from the unfair employment practice complained of. The commission may also take such other action as is necessary to eliminate the effect of the original unfair act.

The Federal government has been very active, too, in other matters concerning employment. First of all, it plays a major role in labor-management relations. Also, Federal statutes such as the Fair Labor Standards Act and the Civil Rights Act of 1964 contain significant provisions regulating employment.

The Fair Labor Standards Act contains provisions relating to minimum wages, hours of work, overtime pay, and other matters for employees who engage in work which is in or affects interstate or foreign commerce. It also requires the keeping of adequate records which will reflect whether or not the employer is complying with the Act.

The coverage of the Fair Labor Standards Act has been constantly broadened to include new categories of workers and the minimum wage has been steadily increased as well. The overtime provisions have also been expanded to cover, for example, residential construction where the contractor's gross volume is over $350,000. While there are still some exempt businesses such as small retail establishments, their number is decreasing and the trend is to require the minimum wage for all, with time and a half for overtime. Each business must examine its operations to determine whether it is covered or whether it comes under any of the exceptions. The case which follows illustrates typical litigation concerning the scope of the Fair Labor Standards Act.

WIRTZ V. FIRST STATE ABSTRACT AND INS. CO.
362 F.2d 83 (1966)

HUNTER, JUDGE: The Secretary of Labor, as plaintiff, brought this action to enjoin defendant, First State Abstract and Insurance Company, from violating the minimum wage, overtime and record keeping provisions of the Fair Labor Standards Act (29 U.S.C. § 201 et seq.), and to restrain defendant from continuing to withhold unpaid minimum wages and overtime compensation due certain of its employees who were engaged in preparing insurance policies, applications, reports and other documents intended for interstate transmission in connection with the transaction of business for out-of-state insurance companies.

The defendant admitted noncompliance with the Act's requirements, but claimed that these employees were not subject to the Act. The District Court found that only to the extent the defendant's employees deal with and handle policies transmitted in interstate commerce from the insurers to the insureds through the medium of defendant's agency are the employees engaged in interstate commerce and covered by the Act; held that plaintiff failed to make a case for an award of back pay to any employee and declined to issue any injunction. Both plaintiff and defendant have appealed from those portions of the judgment they deem adverse to them.

The facts are relatively undisputed. Defendant is a wholly owned subsidiary corporation of the First State Bank of Lonoke, Arkansas, where it is engaged in a single office in performing title abstract work and in conducting insurance transactions for eleven nationwide insurance companies whose branch offices or agencies are located in Little Rock, Arkansas, and whose home offices are located outside the State of Arkansas. Defendant's insurance activities, which will be described more fully later, generally consist of the writing and selling of fire, of casualty, and of automobile liability insurance of these nationwide insurance companies, and in placing with them applications for Workmen's Compensation and other forms of business liability insurance. It is these insurance activities which are in question here, and it is not contended that any phase of the abstract operation is covered by the Fair Labor Standards Act.

Policies of fire, of casualty, and of automobile liability insurance of the nationwide insurance companies are written by defendant's employees and sold directly to the purchaser. In connection with these particular transactions an employee of defendant interviews the prospective purchaser, prepares a detailed application for insurance on printed forms provided by the particular insurance company from its out-of-state office or its out-of-state printer, collects the premium, and prepares a separate "daily report" to advise the involved insurance company of the risk to which it is bound. Following each such sale copies of the application, the policy and the daily report are forwarded to the appropriate branch office in Little Rock which in turn forwards these documents to the home or regional office located outside of the state.

Workmen's Compensation policies and certain other forms of business liability insurance policies are written at the out-of-state home offices of the insurance companies, after receipt of and consideration of detailed applications which are prepared by certain of defendant's employees at defendant's Lonoke, Arkansas office. When one of these policies is written and approved, the out-of-state home office transmits it directly to defendant's office for delivery to the insured.

Each month on an average defendant sells or places, by one of the above described methods, 120 policies at a monthly dollar volume of $6,500 to $7,000 in initial premiums. At the end of each month certain of defendant's employees prepare for each of the insurance companies a detailed "account current" report based on entries made throughout the month, showing each policy issued, total premiums collected, premiums returned on cancelled policies and commissions due defendant. These reports, together with a check for the sums collected less defendant's commissions and refunded premiums, are forwarded to the respective insurance companies' Little Rock offices which in turn forward them to the appropriate office of the insurance company located outside the state of Arkansas.

At the present time the business of First State Abstract and Insurance Company, both insurance and abstract, is performed by two employees. During one transitional period defendant had three employees. A total of four present or past employees are involved in this action.

Norene Hicks, employed from October, 1961, to September, 1962, and her replacement, Helen Caperton, employed from September, 1962, to July, 1963, regularly performed the insurance activities above described, including writing and typing insurance policies, preparing applications, daily reports and other statements; posting and compiling the "account current" reports for each insurance company; preparing checks; sending statements, collecting and posting payments and making deposits. In addition to the initial premiums collected on new policies these two employees processed collections of recurring premiums on a daily basis. Mrs. Caperton was paid 50¢ an hour for the first two weeks, and 75¢ an hour for the rest of her employment. Mrs. Hicks was paid $1.00 an hour. These two employees apparently performed no overtime work.

Employee Eunice Brown had been in charge of defendant's office since 1961. In addition to her office management duties she regularly performed the same duties as did Hicks and Caperton, including the writing and typing of policies, applications, reports, statements, waiting on customers, and the posting and maintaining necessary accounts pertaining to the insurance transactions. She has regularly worked a 5½ to 6 day a week schedule (44–48 hours) for a salary of $350.00 a month without additional compensation for hours over 40 per week.

Employee Judy High does mostly abstract work but upon occasion she has, among other things, waited on insurance customers and has typed letters for forwarding to the Little Rock office of the various insurance companies. Mrs. Caperton when asked the frequency with which Judy High assisted in the insurance operation replied that usually some time during each day Miss High "would do something, maybe post checks that come in, take collections from insureds who came in to pay." . . . "[O]ccasionally if she was caught up in abstracts (the principal work) she would help us in insurance." Mrs. Hicks testified Miss High would take in insurance collections and sometimes if Mrs. Hicks made an error in the insurance Miss High would help her check to find the error. Miss High described her work as mainly abstracting but that she did insurance when it was necessary and when she could help and there was some overflow. She testified she had typed policies, had taken in collections, entered the premiums on the account current and had written checks for the insurance companies. While unable to specify exactly how frequently she had done these things she related that it had been more often since Mrs. Caperton had left (July, 1963) since there was only Mrs. Brown and herself in the office. She also had performed work in connection with the receipt of mail and over-the-counter payments, "sometime during every week" and in connection therewith would fill in the deposit book and pull the statement from the accounts receivable and mark it paid. Even when Mrs. Brown was present Miss High waited on customers and if they wanted to pay an insurance premium Miss High would take the money. If the customer wanted an insurance policy Miss High would either refer the customer to Mrs. Brown, or, upon occasion, take the information regarding the insurance the purchaser desired, and being unable to figure the policies, would give the information to Mrs. Brown. Miss High has performed these insurance duties right up to the present time. Miss High was paid 50¢ an hour from November, 1961, to March, 1962, 75¢ an hour from March, 1962, to March, 1964, and thereafter was paid at the rate of $1.00 an hour.

The principal issue before us on this appeal is whether the four mentioned employees of the defendant were engaged in interstate commerce or in the production of goods for interstate commerce within the meaning of the Fair Labor Standards Act.

In *United States v. South-Eastern Underwriters Ass'n,* 322 U.S. 533, the Supreme Court, through Mr. Justice Black, declared that an insurance company which conducts a substantial part of its business transactions across state lines is "engaged in commerce among the several states" and subject to regulation by Congress under the Commerce Clause. We believe it clear that defendant's insurance business, conducted as we have described it above, is an engagement in interstate commerce and not an isolated, local activity.

The question of whether certain employees of a business such as the one before us are "engaged in commerce," as that term is used in Sections 206 and 207 of the Act, requires, however, that we focus on the activities of the employees and not on the business of the employer. It is the activities of the individual employees, not those of the employer, that are the controlling factor. Practical considerations, not technical conceptions, are to be used in making the determination, and in furtherance of the purpose of the Act a liberal construction is to be given to the language contained therein. . . . "While Congress obviously has not extended coverage under the Act to all activities affecting commerce, as it might do if it so chose, this does not and, as indicated by the Supreme Court in the *Overstreet* opinion, should not narrowly circumscribe the meaning of the phrase 'engaged in commerce' or detract in any way from the statutory definition as to the meaning of commerce itself. Such definition is not to be given a strained and narrow construction. Transportation, transmission or communication among the several states are literally within the Act's coverage."

Employees whose activities are so directly and vitally related to interstate commerce as to be in practice and legal contemplation a part thereof, are to be considered as engaged in interstate commerce, and may, therefore, be within the provisions of the Fair Labor Standards Act.

We are persuaded that the described work and activities of the four mentioned employees are such as to result in each of them being engaged in interstate commerce within the intent of the Fair Labor Standards Act. All of these employees' work which relates to defendant's insurance business contributes so directly, materially and vitally to interstate commerce as to be a part thereof. In practical effect these employees in the manner and to the degree stated are transacting business in interstate commerce for nationwide insurance companies by soliciting insurance sales, processing insurance applications, preparing or typing policies, collecting premiums, and compiling and checking essential reports and statements, all for forwarding to out-of-state home offices by way of the Little Rock Offices; and by, in return, receiving from out-of-state locations insurance policy forms and other insurance materials and communications. All of this constitutes transmission and communication between the states within the meaning and literal terms of the statute.

In the *South-Eastern Underwriters Ass'n* case, *supra*, it is recognized that the interrelationship, interdependence and integration of activities between home offices and local agents engaged in soliciting prospects, utilizing policy forms sent from home offices and making regular reports to their companies by mail, telephone or telegraph are practical aspects of the insurance companies' method of doing business. The nationwide business of such insurance companies places them in interstate commerce activities. The employees or persons who actually do that work, whether they be located in the branch office of the particular insurance company or employed in an office such as that of the defendant, are doing essential and vital work which, when practically viewed, must be considered as interstate activity. Through their work and activities they serve as the fingers of the branch office, transmitting the results of their activities to the branch office for the purpose of and where they are ultimately forwarded to the home office located in another state. The branch office is but a convenient intermediate step in the process of getting them to their final destination.

Although defendant contended and the trial court held that Miss High's insurance activities were not sufficiently substantial to bring her within the scope of the Act such a conclusion based on the undisputed facts we have mentioned is clearly erroneous. Her described insurance activities, some of which were on a daily basis, were not inconsequential, sporadic, or isolated. Rather, they were as regular and continuous as the needs of her employment required.

Since we have reached the conclusion that all four employees are engaged in interstate commerce and are within the coverage of the Act it is unnecessary to consider whether they are engaged in the production of goods for interstate commerce.

The District Court found that employee Eunice Brown was excepted from the minimum wage and overtime provisions by virtue of Section 13(a)(1) of the Act, which exempts those employees who are employed in a bona fide administrative capacity as that term is defined by regulations of the Administrator. Pursuant thereto the Administrator issued appropriate regulations which, among other conditions, exempted only those of specified minimum salary. The District Court mistakenly found that the minimum salary for this exemption was $75.00 per week from 1961 to September, 1963, although the actual salary required for the exemption was $95.00 per week during this period and was raised to $100.00 per week, effective September 30, 1963. Mrs. Brown received a salary of $350.00 per month. She therefore did not meet the requirements of this exemption at any time in her employment.

Although the District Court found that to the extent defendant's employees deal with and handle insurance policies they are engaged in interstate commerce, it ruled that plaintiff failed to make a case for an award of back pay to any employee because plaintiff did not specifically show during any particular work week the actual amount of time so spent by the particular employee.

An employer who has not kept the records required by Section 11(c) of the Act cannot be heard to complain that there is no evidence of the precise amount of time worked in interstate commerce, including overtime so worked. It is sufficient if the plaintiff produces evidence to show the amount and extent of that work as a matter of fact and reasonable inference. If defendant had kept the employee work records which the Act required it to keep, the information necessary to show when and for what periods of time each employee performed work in interstate commerce would have been available to plaintiff. It was the absence of such records that prevented plaintiff from making this showing.

Plaintiff has shown that the four employees worked on interstate as well as intrastate business; that the two classes of work were commingled in defendant's business operations and that defendant did not attempt to distinguish between the two in the payment of wages. Under such circumstances plaintiff has made a prima facie showing that those employees are entitled to the protection of the Act. There is strong authority for the proposition that if an employee's duties are partly interstate and partly intrastate, his entire compensation must conform to the provisions of the Act. It is the rule that when employment is in interstate commerce or in producing goods for interstate commerce the burden is on the employer to show the segregation if he claims it. In the instant case there has been no attempt on the part of defendant to segregate the interstate work from the intrastate work or to keep any records of the time spent by the employees in either type of work. Under such circumstances the entire pay of the employees must be in accordance with the Act. . . .

We reverse as to the appeal by the Secretary of Labor; affirm as to the appeal by defendant; and remand this cause for appropriate findings and for an order restraining defendant from withholding the back wages which are due Eunice Brown, including overtime; from withholding the back wages which are due Norene Hicks, Judy High, and Helen Caperton, in violation of the Act and to reconsider the prayer for injunctive relief.

LABOR–MANAGEMENT RELATIONS

5   THE HISTORY OF THE UNION MOVEMENT [3]

In the colonial period, there was a great shortage of labor in America. This was due in part to the low cost of land, which made it easy for a person to acquire a farm and work it for himself. Those who worked for someone else were mainly members of the family, apprentices, indentured servants (including a great many convicts), and Negro slaves. The hours of labor for these people were long, generally from sunrise to sunset. After the Revolutionary War, this shortage still prevailed. Most of the able-bodied men were engaged in agriculture and those who were not so occupied were mainly self-employed craftsmen.

During the nineteenth century, the population grew (partially because of a large number of immigrants) and the labor force increased, becoming overplentiful. This growth accompanied the dramatic change in the economy from basically agrarian to mass-production industrial. By the end of the century, instead of farming or working for themselves, most men were wage earners, dependent upon their employer and his business for a livelihood. In many instances newly developed machines made it possible to break down production steps and replace unskilled workmen altogether, or substitute unskilled workmen for the skilled. The change in the economy and methods of production brought about far-reaching changes in the relationship of laborer to employer. Independent craftsmen who produced goods which they sold directly to the consumer became rare or nonexistent. The employer and employee no longer worked together but seemingly had conflicting interests. Instead of being a master craftsman working alongside his journeymen, an employer furnished the capital for the business, became more involved in management and selling, and no longer belonged to the same social sphere.

A major problem in the distribution of finished goods and merchandise was brought about by great increases in productive capacity. Instead of marketing finished products himself, the factory owner was forced to look to middlemen to perform this function. Consumers naturally sought lower

[3] Kemmerer & Jones, *American Economic History* 23–27, 212–226, 398–418, 567–585 (1959).

prices from competing retailers, who in turn sought lower prices from competing middlemen, who also sought lower prices from competing manufacturers. This cutthroat competition, while distinctly beneficial from the customer's point of view, was distinctly disadvantageous from the wage earner's standpoint. The answer to the manufacturer was to produce more for less. To meet prices which had been forced down by overcapacity and to protect and make some profit on his capital invested in plant and machinery, the factory owner had to reduce his costs and naturally sought to reduce the cost of labor. This was done in a number of ways: simply reducing the hourly wage or piece rate paid to present employees; employing women, children, or convicts who were available at a lower wage; or increasing the output per man-hour by utilizing machines developed through technological advances. Of course, faced with these economic pressures, employers were not prone to raise their costs to make working conditions more comfortable and enjoyable, or even to eliminate hazardous and unhealthful conditions which existed in many factories. This economic situation naturally led to attempts on the part of workingmen to organize and defend themselves. As individuals they were in a very weak bargaining position because of their oversupply. United, their ever-increasing number would give them strength, especially in a democracy, for their votes outnumbered those of the employers by far.

It should be noted that the labor movement did make some progress in the nineteenth century. The hours of work per day were shorter, although they still averaged eleven around 1860; in some industries such as steel, they remained at twelve a day, six days a week, until well into the twentieth century. Increased production brought increased wealth, and wages in terms of their purchasing power rose. But a greater percentage of this wealth was being retained by the owners of businesses. This caused resentment by the workers, since in their eyes they were largely responsible for the production of the business. In addition, working in a factory was degrading. The dignity of labor declined. The social gap between workman and owner widened greatly, and within the wage-earner class skilled workmen lost ground economically and socially compared to the unskilled.

For more than one hundred years, until the latter part of the nineteenth century, the attempts by laborers to organize resulted in no strong, lasting unions. During this period, membership in unions resulted in some wage increases. However, during periodic depressions, times of unemployment and falling prices, wages were lowered to cut costs and nonunion workers were hired by employers. Previous members of unions abandoned their organizations because they were willing to work at any price to escape privation and hunger, and their unions had no funds for relief during bad times. Organizations were wiped out by this understandable lack of loyalty by workmen and consequent drop in membership. As a result, the union movement showed little progress during this period.

The pattern began to change from one of failure to success with the appearance of unions on the national scale. Among the first of the national unions were the Railway Brotherhoods, starting with the Engineers, who were organized in 1854, and followed by the Conductors, Firemen, and Trainmen. The Knights of Labor was organized in 1869 as a secret society at first. Anyone who worked could become a member. For a time, this union was of importance, but it disintegrated, among other reasons, because of internal dissension between skilled and unskilled workers, loss of prestige in the workingmen's eyes due to a number of strike failures, and loss of public support from occasional violence in strikes. The American Federation of Labor began in 1886 as a loose association of twenty-five almost independent national unions organized along trade lines, such as carpenters, miners, iron molders, and cigar makers. The national union concerned itself with problems which were general in nature, and avoided unskilled labor, useless strikes, and violence. After its founding, it attracted many of the skilled members from the Knights of Labor. The Industrial Workers of the World, one of the most notorious labor unions, was organized in 1905 by two socialists and indulged in strikes, physical force, and sabotage to better the lot of the unskilled. The IWW had as its ultimate aim the socialistic goal of placing the direction and control of industry in the hands of laborers by direct, violent means, and seriously damaged the cause of labor in the eyes of the public. Its demise occurred during World War I as a result of internal conflict and its inherent unpatriotic qualities.

World War I brought prosperity which enhanced union expansion, so that by 1920, the AFL numbered 4 million members. However, for a number of reasons, total union membership dropped back to about 3.5 million during the 1920s. The attempt to organize workers in the steel industry and the steel strike of 1919–1920 failed, losing prestige for labor and the hope of organizing mass-production industries for some time to come. The general public became alarmed for fear of influence by Communists and other radical left-wing elements in the labor movement. Management actively combated union activity by fighting organization or by improving working conditions so that union membership seemed unnecessary to laborers. The Federal government's attitude during this period was generally antiunion, influenced no doubt by business pressures, public reaction, and a sentiment that subversive radicals had too much to do with labor.

The Great Depression caused a further setback to unions and membership dropped to less than 3 million. However, the election of Franklin D. Roosevelt with his New Deal program, including the Wagner Act discussed in Section 7, resulted in a governmental climate favoring union growth, so that by 1939 union membership increased by three-fold to 9 million. Because of the influence of certain strong craft unions of skilled laborers, which were concerned with the prospect of losing control to the industrial unions of essentially unskilled laborers, the AFL in 1935 stood opposed to encouraging further organization of workers in mass-production industries. As a result, eight former AFL unions with a membership of 1 million, including the United Mine Workers, formed a separate organization which was to become the Congress of Industrial Organizations, and set about organizing such industries as steel, oil, automobile, and rubber.

World War II brought an end to the unemployment which had existed despite the New Deal and further stimulated union growth, so that by 1946 the total union membership reached 15 million, 7.2 million of these belonging to the AFL and 6 million to the CIO. After World War II, unions flexed their muscles in a series of crippling strikes which were felt by the whole nation. The obvious control that unions had gained over the economy and their great power in getting their own way resulted in a loss of support for organized labor from the general public. It became apparent that too much power in the hands of the leaders of large unions would result in exploitation just as *laissez faire* had resulted in business combination and monopoly inimicable to the public interest. Since the need for control of big labor was demonstrated to be as essential as the need for control of big business, in 1947 Congress passed the Taft-Hartley Labor Management Relations Act, which still is the law essentially as enacted originally. In 1956, the rift between the AFL and the CIO was mended and the two giant unions merged, having a total membership of around 15 million. One factor causing merger no doubt was a desire to become more effective politically. Unions had been unable to procure the repeal of the Taft-Hartley Act and had not acquired any significant legislation favoring labor at the expense of management since the days of the New Deal.

Throughout their history, the prime goals of unions generally have been related to bettering labor's economic position and providing economic security for members. Labor organizations have more or less continuously placed pressures on the owners of capital to reduce the hours of employment and increase the amount of wages paid employees, so that wage earners would obtain a larger proportionate share of the fruits of their work and would have more leisure time for the enjoyment of these increased benefits. Other economic goals of unions have included payments to the unemployed during periods of recession or depression and some form of pension payments to elderly, retired members. Another objective of organized labor was to improve working conditions by eliminating hazardous and unhealthy situations and to shift the losses incurred in industrial accidents from the injured employee to the employer. The latter was accomplished with the adoption of workmen's compensation statutes previously discussed.

Unions have used political and economic pressures as weapons to achieve their objectives. They have exerted political pressure by placing their case before the general public in an attempt to gain sympathetic support. And, as was noted, the voting power of the union members themselves could not be ignored by politicians. Unions have exerted economic pressure through strikes (which also made the public aware of their complaints) and through boycotts.

Employers have combated union action with their own political and economic pressures. They, too, have formed organizations and have sought general public support of their point of view through the medium of the newspapers, to which they generally have had better access than the unions. The main economic weapons which employers have used have been related to their bargaining superiority. With an overabundance of labor, employers maintained an open shop and refused to hire union members. So-called "yellow-dog contracts" have been used, in which the worker agrees when he is hired that he will not join a union, and can be fired in the event that he does. To locate union members and organizers, employers shared their information by circulating "black lists," and utilized employees who were "labor spies" in their own plants. If labor trouble were brewing, an employer could take the initiative by using the device of a "lock-out," or, in other words, closing his factory and stopping production for a time. This permitted the owner to choose the time of inactivity and made the workers aware of the importance of their jobs to them, since they would earn and receive no wages during the period of shutdown. Unions without relief funds could be destroyed by loss of members during a lock-out. If the unionized employees of a business went out on strike, the employer could fire and replace them with nonunion laborers or "scabs." Often the use of "scabs" to take the place of strikers would lead to retaliation by the union members in the form of violence which resulted in damage to property, injury to persons, and sometimes death.

The common law placed a very powerful weapon in the hands of employers whose workers were on strike—the court injunction. An injunction is an order of a court of equity directing the defendant to do or refrain from doing certain specific acts. Its issuance is largely within the discretion of the court, but generally an injunction will lie where irreparable damage to the plaintiff or his property is likely and the law offers no adequate remedy. If the defendant persists in committing the enjoined acts, he is subject to fine and imprisonment for contempt of court. Toward the end of the nineteenth century, courts became increasingly liberal in granting injunctive relief to employers whose workers were on strike. Of course, where actual violence by the strikers was resulting in loss of property and life and was likely to continue, courts were very sympathetic to the employer. The right of workers to strike included the right to leave their jobs in protest and peacefully voice their complaints and grievances but did not extend to actual force, violence, and destruction, which were illegal. Some courts took the view that such a thing as peaceful picketing did not exist, that *all* picketing was likely to result in violence and destruction, and issued injunctions forbidding picketing even where no physical force had been used by the strikers. Other courts favored factory owners even more by hold-ing that any *strike* could be enjoined because it was certain to cause irrep-arable damage.

It is easy to see from the foregoing that the bargaining position of the employer was vastly superior to that of his workers. In the absence of statu-tory restriction, the employer was free to hire and fire whom he pleased and discriminate against union members. He could import nonunion help during a strike and generally had the court injunction available as a weapon. Thus, the unions had as secondary goals the enactment of remedial statutes which would neutralize the bargaining position of employers. Only by doing this could the unions make effective use of their main weapons—the strike and the boycott—and attain their primary economic goals. Unions sought a closed shop, legislation prohibiting discrimination against their mem-bers, the outlawing of yellow-dog contracts and the use of scab labor, and, of course, statutes prohibiting the use of court injunctions in labor disputes. The sections which follow reflect the extent to which unions have been suc-cessful in attaining many of their economic and political objectives.

6   LABOR LAWS PRIOR TO 1935

Prior to the twentieth century, there were no Federal statutes dealing di-rectly with labor-management relations. The law was developed in the indi-vidual cases and was based essentially on contract principles rather than on economic or social policies.

The first Federal statute of any importance was the Clayton Act, passed in 1914. It simply contained a provision establishing that the antitrust laws did not apply to labor unions, as had been attempted in certain cases under the Sherman Antitrust Act. The Sherman Act, discussed in Chapter 11, was aimed at business combinations, but in practice was sometimes applied to the labor movement. In *Loewe v. Lawler,*[4] it was contended that the Sher-man Act did not apply to unions but the court, ruling that it did, said:

> The records of Congress show that several efforts were made to exempt, by legislation, organizations of farmers and laborers from the operation of the act, and that all these efforts failed, so that the act remained as we have it before us.
>
> In an early case the United States filed a bill under the Sherman Act in the circuit court for the eastern district of Louisiana, averring the existence of "a gigantic and widespread combination of the members of a multitude of separate organizations for the purpose of restraining the commerce among the several states and with foreign countries," and it was contended that the

[4] 208 U.S. 274 (1907).

statute did not refer to combinations of laborers. But the court, granting the injunction, said:

I think the congressional debates show that the statute had its origin in the evils of massed capital; but, when the Congress came to formulating the prohibition, which is the yardstick for measuring the complainant's right to the injunction, it expressed it in these words: "Every contract or combination in the form of trust, or otherwise in restraint of trade or commerce among the several states or with foreign nations, is hereby declared to be illegal." The subject had so broadened in the minds of the legislators that the source of the evil was not regarded as material, and the evil in its entirety is dealt with. They made the interdiction include combinations of labor as well as of capital; in fact, all combinations in restraint of commerce, without reference to the character of the persons who entered into them. It is true this statute has not been much expounded by judges, but, as it seems to me, its meaning, as far as relates to the sort of combinations to which it is to apply, is manifest, and that it includes combinations which are composed of laborers acting in the interest of laborers.

It is the successful effort of the combination of the defendants to intimidate and overawe others who were at work in conducting or carrying on the commerce of the country, in which the court finds their error and their violation of the statute. One of the intended results of their combined action was the forced stagnation of all the commerce which flowed through New Orleans. This intent and combined action are none the less unlawful because they included in their scope the paralysis of all other business within the city as well. . . .

The Clayton Act provision followed.

In 1926, Congress adopted the Railway Labor Act, which had as an avowed purpose the encouragement of collective bargaining in railroads to the end that labor disputes would not interrupt transportation. It provided machinery for settling disputes, both major and minor. The Act was later extended to airlines and is applicable to both air and rail transportation today.

In 1932, The Norris–La Guardia Act, sometimes referred to as the Anti-injunction Statute, was passed by Congress. The Clayton Act had not provided sufficient protection for labor and attempts were still being made to prevent union growth in the courts through injunctions. The Norris–La Guardia Act attempted to encourage collective bargaining by limiting the use of injunctions in Federal courts in labor disputes. It also declared contracts forbidding union membership to be unenforceable as contrary to public policy. While it prevented the use of the injunction to stop the organization of a union, its negative approach did not supply the impetus for a tremendous growth of unions and union power. Union development was further hampered by the depression and the overabundant labor supply.

7 THE WAGNER ACT

The labor movement received its greatest stimulus with the adoption in 1935 of the National Labor Relations Act (Wagner Act). This statute did for all business engaged in interstate commerce what the Railway Labor Act had done for transportation. Its purpose was to diminish the causes of labor disputes which burdened or obstructed interstate commerce by encouraging the union movement and collective bargaining. The Act created the NLRB and protected the rights of workers to organize and bargain collectively by defining certain practices as unfair labor practices and creating certain remedies for unions and their members. Principally the Act accomplished its purpose in two sections of the statute.

Section 7 provides: "Employees shall have the right to self organization, to form, join, or assist labor organizations, to bargain collectively through representatives of their own choosing, and to engage in concerted activities for the purpose of collective bargaining or other mutual aid or protection."

The rights granted by Section 7 were secured against employer interference by Section 8, which describes and prohibits five practices defined to be unfair to labor:

1 Interference with efforts of employees to form, join, or assist labor organizations, or to engage in concerted activities for mutual aid or protection. Section 8(a)(1).

2 Domination of a labor organization. This outlawed the company formed or assisted labor union. Section 8(a)(2).

3 Discrimination in hire or tenure of employees for reason of union affiliation. Section 8(a)(3).

4 Discrimination against employees for filing charges or giving testimony under the Act. Section 8(a)(4).

5 Refusal to bargain collectively with a duly designated representative of the employees. Section 8(a)(5).

Unions and employees are entitled to cease and desist orders, injunctions and awards for damages if unfair labor practices are committed.

In *NLRB v. Jones & Laughlin Steel Corp.*,[5] the Supreme Court held that the Wagner Act was constitutional and applicable to manufacturing enterprises. Its constitutionality was affirmed as a valid exercise of power by Congress under the commerce clause. Chief Justice Hughes, speaking for the court, reviewed the scheme of the Wagner Act and stated:

The first section sets forth findings with respect to the injury to commerce resulting from the denial by employers of the right of employees to organize and from the refusal of employers to accept the procedure of collective bar-

[5] 301 U.S. 1 (1937).

gaining. There follows a declaration that it is the policy of the United States to eliminate these causes of obstruction to the free flow of commerce. The Act then defines the terms it uses, including the terms "commerce" and "affecting commerce." § 2. It creates the National Labor Relations Board and prescribes its organization. §§ 3–6. It sets forth the right of employees to self-organization and to bargain collectively through representatives of their own choosing. § 7. It defines "unfair labor practices." § 8. It lays down rules as to the representation of employees for the purpose of collective bargaining. § 9. The Board is empowered to prevent the described unfair labor practices affecting commerce and the Act prescribes the procedure to that end. The Board is authorized to petition designated courts to secure the enforcement of its orders. The findings of the Board as to the facts, if supported by evidence, are to be conclusive. If either party on application to the court shows that additional evidence is material and that there were reasonable grounds for the failure to adduce such evidence in the hearings before the Board, the court may order the additional evidence to be taken. Any person aggrieved by a final order of the Board may obtain a review in the designated courts with the same procedure as in the case of an application by the Board for the enforcement of its order. § 10. The Board has broad powers of investigation. § 11. Interference with members of the Board or its agents in the performance of their duties is punishable by fine and imprisonment. § 12. Nothing in the Act is to be construed to interfere with the right to strike. § 13. . . .

In discussing the right of employees to bargain collectively, the Chief Justice said:

That is a fundamental right. Employees have as clear a right to organize and select their representatives for lawful purposes as the respondent has to organize its business and select its own officers and agents. Discrimination and coercion to prevent the free exercise of the right of employees to self-organization and representation is a proper subject for condemnation by competent legislative authority. Long ago we stated the reason for labor organizations. We said that they were organized out of the necessities of the situation; that a single employee was helpless in dealing with an employer; that he was dependent ordinarily on his daily wage for the maintenance of himself and family; that if the employer refused to pay him the wages that he thought fair, he was nevertheless unable to leave the employ and resist arbitrary and unfair treatment; that union was essential to give laborers opportunity to deal on an equality with their employer. . . . We reiterated these views when we had under consideration the Railway Labor Act of 1926. Fully recognizing the legality of collective action on the part of employees in order to safeguard their proper interests, we said that Congress was not required to ignore this right but could safeguard it. Congress could seek to make appropriate collective action of employees an instrument of peace rather than of strife. We said that such collective action would be a mockery if representation were made futile by interference with freedom of choice. Hence the prohibition by Congress of interference with the selection of representatives for the purpose of negotiation and conference between employers and employees, "instead of being an invasion of the constitutional right of either, was based on the recognition of the rights of both." . . .

The Act was also challenged under the due process clause and for being one sided in its application since there was no provision relating to unfair labor practices by unions. Chief Justice Hughes disposed of these arguments by saying:

The Act does not compel agreements between employers and employees. It does not compel any agreement whatever. It does not prevent the employer "from refusing to make a collective contract and hiring individuals on whatever terms" the employer "may by unilateral action determine." The Act expressly provides in § 9 (a) that any individual employee or a group of employees shall have the right at any time to present grievances to their employer. The theory of the Act is that free opportunity for negotiation with accredited representatives of employees is likely to promote industrial peace and may bring about the adjustments and agreements which the Act in itself does not attempt to compel. . . . The Act does not interfere with the normal exercise of the right of the employer to select its employees or to discharge them. The employer may not, under cover of that right, intimidate or coerce its employees with respect to their self-organization and representation, and, on the other hand, the Board is not entitled to make its authority a pretext for interference with the right of discharge when that right is exercised for other reasons than such intimidation and coercion. The true purpose is the subject of investigation with full opportunity to show the facts. It would seem that when employers freely recognize the right of their employees to their own organizations and their unrestricted right of representation there will be much less occasion for controversy in respect to the free and appropriate exercise of the right of selection and discharge.

The Act has been criticized as one-sided in its application; that it subjects the employer to supervision and restraint and leaves untouched the abuses for which employees may be responsible; that it fails to provide a more comprehensive plan,—with better assurances of fairness to both sides and with increased chances of success in bringing about, if not compelling, equitable solutions of industrial disputes affecting interstate commerce. But we are dealing with the power of Congress, not with a particular policy or with the extent to which policy should go. We have frequently said that the legislative authority, exerted within its proper field, need not embrace all the evils within its reach. The Constitution does not forbid "cautious advance, step by step," in dealing with the evils which are exhibited in activities within the range of legislative power. . . . The question in such cases is whether the legislature, in what it does prescribe, has gone beyond constitutional limits. . . .

Through the years, the Supreme Court has reviewed numerous NLRB decisions concerning unfair labor practices by employers. Most decisions are resolved against employers, if the union can show that the activity could result in an unfair labor practice. An examination of two kinds of employer activity—bestowal of economic benefits on employees, and the discharge of employees for breaking company rules—will be helpful in illustrating the type of employer conduct which may be held in violation of the Wagner Act.

When a company bestows unrequested economic benefits on its workers, it is immediately suspect of an unfair labor practice. This occurred in *Medo Photo Supply v. NLRB*,[6] where a union had been certified as the bargaining agent and union representatives had contacted the company relative to a new contract. A meeting was scheduled for June 9th but on June 7th, a committee of employees speaking for a majority approached the employer and suggested that, if they could get certain wage increases on their own, they would abandon the union. At first the employer refused, not wanting to negotiate with the employees over the head of the union. But he reconsidered on June 9th, granted the wage increase, and was told by the employees that they ". . . felt that they did not need the union, and we would rather stay out." The employer refused to meet with the union representatives, saying the employees no longer wanted the union and there was nothing to discuss.

Chief Justice Stone, speaking for a majority of the Court, held that Medo violated Sections 8(a)(1) and 8(a)(5) of the Wagner Act. The employees were still members of the union when they asked for the wage increase and were in no position to bargain for themselves. The promise to quit the union was conditional on the employer's promise to increase wages. The employees could have revoked the union's authority at any time before talking to the employer, but not the other way around.

At present, the NLRB has a rule that once it has certified a union following a representation election, the employer must bargain with this union for one year after such certification, even though he can prove that *all* his employees have rejected the union. However, the employer may ask for a new election after the one-year period has passed.

Not all cases involving the bestowing of benefits are so clear-cut as the *Medo Photo* case. For example, in *NLRB v. Katz*,[7] the union for Katz's technical employees notified the employer of its desire to bargain out merit increases, general wage levels and increases, and a sick-leave proposal. During the course of the negotiations, the company unilaterally announced a change in sick-leave policy, granted numerous merit increases, and instituted a new system of wage increases which were to be automatic, all with no strings attached. Katz was held guilty of the unfair labor practice of

---

[6] 321 U.S. 678 (1944).
[7] 369 U.S. 736 (1962).

refusing to bargain collectively. The grants by the employer to the employ-ees were greater than offers which had been made to and rejected by the union at the bargaining table, and showed the bad faith in the negotiations. The Court said, " . . . an employer is not required to lead with his best offer and he is free to bargain, but even after an impasse is reached, the employer has no license to grant wage increases greater than those offered to the union at the bargaining table."

The case which follows is another example of an unfair labor practice based on the conferring of benefits.

NLRB V. EXCHANGE PARTS CO.
375 U.S. 405 (1964)

HARLAN, JUSTICE: . . . This case presents a question concerning the limita-tions which § 8(a)(1) of the National Labor Relations Act, . . . places on the right of an employer to confer economic benefits on his employees shortly before a representation election. The precise issue is whether that section prohibits the conferral of such benefits, without more, where the employer's purpose is to affect the outcome of the election. . . .

The respondent, Exchange Parts Company, is engaged in the business of rebuilding automobile parts in Fort Worth, Texas. Prior to November 1959 its employees were not represented by a union. On November 9, 1959, the International Brotherhood of Boilermakers, Iron Shipbuilders, Black-smiths, Forgers and Helpers, AFL-CIO, advised Exchange Parts that the union was conducting an organizational campaign at the plant and that a majority of the employees had designated the union as their bargaining representative. On November 16 the union petitioned the Labor Board for a representation election. The Board conducted a hearing on December 29, and on February 19, 1960, issued an order directing that an election be held. The election was held on March 18, 1960.

At two meetings on November 4 and 5, 1959, C. V. McDonald, the Vice-President and General Manager of Exchange Parts, announced to the employees that their "floating holiday" in 1959 would fall on December 26 and that there would be an additional "floating holiday" in 1960. On Feb-ruary 25, six days after the Board issued its election order, Exchange Parts held a dinner for employees at which Vice-President McDonald told the employees that they could decide whether the extra day of vacation in 1960 would be a "floating holiday" or would be taken on their birthdays. The employees voted for the latter. McDonald also referred to the forthcoming representation election as one in which in the words of the trial examiner, the employees would "determine whether . . . [they] wished to hand over their right to speak and act for themselves." He stated that the union had distorted some of the facts and pointed out the benefits obtained by the employees without a union. He urged all the employees to vote in the election.

On March 4 Exchange Parts sent its employees a letter which spoke of "the *Empty Promises* of the Union" and "the *fact* that *it is the Company that puts things in your envelope. . . .*" After mentioning a number of benefits, the letter said: "The Union can't put any of those things in your envelope—*only the Company can do that.*" Further on, the letter stated: " . . . [I]t didn't take a Union to get any of those things and . . . it won't take a Union to get additional improvements in the future." Accompanying the letter was a detailed statement of the benefits granted by the company since 1949 and an estimate of the monetary value of such benefits to the employees, included in the statement of benefits for 1960 were the birthday holiday, a new system for computing overtime during holiday weeks which had the effect of increasing wages for those weeks, and a new vacation schedule which enables employees to extend their vacations by sandwiching them between two weekends. Although Exchange Parts asserts that the policy behind the latter two benefits was established earlier, it is clear that the letter of March 4 was the first general announcement of the changes to the employees. In the ensuing election the union lost.

The Board, affirming the findings of the trial examiner, found that the announcement of the birthday holiday and the grant and announcement of overtime and vacation benefits were arranged by Exchange Parts with the intention of inducing the employees to vote against the union. It found that this conduct violated § 8(a)(1) of the National Labor Relations Act and issued an appropriate order. On the Board's petition for enforcement of the order, the Court of Appeals rejected the finding that the announcement of the birthday holiday was timed to influence the outcome of the election. . . . However, noting that "the benefits were put into effect unconditionally on a permanent basis, and no one has suggested that there was any implication the benefits would be withdrawn if the workers voted for the union," . . . the court denied enforcement of the Board's order. It believed that it was not an unfair labor practice under § 8(a)(1) for an employer to grant benefits to its employees in these circumstances.

Section 8(a)(1) makes it an unfair labor practice for an employer "to interfere with, restrain, or coerce employees in the exercise of the rights guaranteed in section 7." Section 7 provides:

Employees shall have the right to self-organization, to form, join, or assist labor organizations, to bargain collectively through representatives of their own choosing, and to engage in other concerted activities for the purpose of collective bargaining or other mutual aid or protection, and shall also have the right to refrain from any or all of such activities except to the extent that such right may be affected by an agreement requiring membership in a labor

organization as a condition of employment as authorized in section 8(a)
(3). . . .

We think the Court of Appeals was mistaken in concluding that the conferral of employee benefits while a representation election is pending, for the purpose of inducing employees to vote against the union, does not "interfere with" the protected right to organize.

The broad purpose of § 8(a)(1) is to establish "the right of employees to organize for mutual aid without employer interference." We have no doubt that it prohibits not only intrusive threats and promises but also conduct immediately favorable to employees which is undertaken with the express purpose of impinging upon their freedom of choice for or against unionization and is reasonably calculated to have that effect. In *Medo Photo Supply Corp. v. NLRB,* 321 U.S. 678, this Court said: "The action of employees with respect to the choice of their bargaining agents may be induced by favors bestowed by the employer as well as by his threats or domination." Although in that case there was already a designated bargaining agent and the offer of "favors" was in response to a suggestion of the employees that they would leave the union if favors were bestowed, the principles which dictated the result there are fully applicable here. The danger inherent in well-timed increases in benefits is the suggestion of a fist inside the velvet glove. Employees are not likely to miss the inference that the source of benefits now conferred is also the source from which future benefits must flow and which may dry up if it is not obliged. The danger may be diminished if, as in this case, the benefits are conferred permanently and unconditionally. But the absence of conditions or threats pertaining to the particular benefits conferred would be of controlling significance only if it could be presumed that no question of additional benefits or renegotiation of existing benefits would arise in the future; and, of course, no such presumption is tenable. . . .

We cannot agree with the Court of Appeals that enforcement of the Board's order will have the "ironic" result of "discouraging benefits for labor." . . . The beneficence of an employer is likely to be ephemeral if prompted by a threat of unionization which is subsequently removed. Insulating the right of collective organization from calculated good will of this sort deprives employees of little that has lasting value. [REVERSED]

Another area of employer activities that can amount to unfair labor practices is that of discharging employees for breaking company rules. Many problems have arisen over the nonsolicitation rules of companies and the discharges that have resulted from a worker's soliciting others for union membership. The first of these to be decided by the Supreme Court was

Republic Aviation Corp. v. NLRB.[8] Republic had adopted a plant policy long before any union activity began that read: "Soliciting of any type cannot be permitted in the factory or offices." One employee persisted, after being warned of the rule, in soliciting union membership in the plant and was subsequently discharged for infraction of the rule. This action was taken without discrimination by Republic against *union* activity. Three other employees were discharged for wearing UAW-CIO union steward buttons after being asked to remove the insignia. Republic claimed the union was not the duly designated representative of the employees, that the insignia represented an acknowledgment of the authority of the stewards to represent the employees, and it might thus infringe on Republic's policy of strict neutrality in union matters.

The NLRB ruled, and the Supreme Court agreed, that the enforcement of the no-solicitation rule violated Section 8(a)(1) of the Wagner Act, as it interfered with, restrained, and coerced employees in their rights under Section 7 and discriminated against the discharged employee under Section 8(a)(3). The Board directed reinstatement of the four discharged employees with back pay and also the recission of " . . . the rule against solicitation in so far as it prohibits union activity and solicitation on company property during the employees' own time."

Another rule frequently used in industry is that a worker may not leave work without permission. In *NLRB v. Washington Aluminum Co.,*[9] the employer discharged seven employees for violating this rule. The employees on a particularly cold day had walked off the job from an uninsulated machine shop which on that day had no heat. On other occasions protests had been made about the poor heat. The employees claimed to have acted as a group in protest against unfit working conditions, hoping that their concerted action would cause the employer to heat the shop properly. The employer justified the discharge action by claiming the men left work without permission.

The NLRB ruled that the action of the employees was protected concerted activity under Section 7 of the Wagner Act as amended and that their discharge amounted to an unfair labor practice under Section 8(a)(1). The Supreme Court agreed in a unanimous decision that employees do not

> . . . *necessarily lose their right to engage in concerted activities under Section 7 merely because they do not present a specific demand upon their employer to remedy a condition which they find objectionable. The language of Section 7 is broad enough to protect concerted activities whether they take place before, after, or at the same time such a demand is made. . . . Having no bargaining representative and no established procedure . . . the men took the most direct course to let the company know they wanted a warmer place in which to work.*

Actions by employers which may constitute unfair labor practices are

[8] 324 U.S. 793 (1945).
[9] 370 U.S. 9 (1962).

too numerous to mention. The intent of the employer will often be determinative of the issue. If the activity complained of does and is designed to inhibit collective bargaining by employees in any way, a violation will probably be determined to exist. The extent to which the Wagner Act, as amended, requires employer cooperation with unions is illustrated by the following case.

NLRB V. ACME INDUSTRIAL CO.
385 U.S. 432 (1967)

STEWART, JUSTICE: . . . In this case we deal with the obligation to furnish information that allows a union to decide whether to process a grievance.

In April 1953, at the conclusion of a strike, the respondent entered into a collective bargaining agreement with the union which was the certified representative of its employees. The agreement contained two sections relevant to this case. Article I, § 3, provided, "It is the Company's general policy not to sub-contract work which is normally performed by employees in the bargaining unit where this will cause the layoff of employees or prevent the recall of employees who would normally perform this work. . . ." In Art. VI, § 10, the respondent agreed that "[i]n the event the equipment of the plant . . . is hereafter moved to another location of the Company, employees working in the plant . . . who are subject to reduction in classification or layoff as a result thereof may transfer to the new location with full rights and seniority, unless there is then in existence at the new location a collective bargaining agreement covering . . . employees at such location." A grievance procedure culminating in compulsory and binding arbitration was also incorporated into the collective agreement.

The present controversy began in January 1964, when the union discovered that certain machinery was being removed from the respondent's plant. When asked by union representatives about his movement, the respondent's foremen replied that there had been no violation of the collective agreement and that the company, therefore, was not obliged to answer any questions regarding the machinery. After this rebuff, the union filed 11 grievances charging the respondent with violations of the above quoted clauses of the collective agreement. The president of the union then wrote a letter to the respondent, requesting "the following information at the earliest possible date:"

1. *The approximate dates when each piece of equipment was moved out of the plant.*
2. *The place to which each piece of equipment was moved and whether such place is a facility which is operated or controlled by the Company.*
3. *The number of machines or equipment that was moved out of the plant.*

4. *What was the reason or purpose of moving the equipment out of the plant.*
5. *Is this equipment used for production elsewhere.*

The company replied by letter that it had no duty to furnish this information since no layoffs or reductions in job classification had occurred within five days (the time limitation set by the contract for filing grievances) prior to the union's formal request for information.

This refusal prompted the union to file unfair labor practice charges with the Board. A complaint was issued, and the Board, overruling its trial examiner, held the respondent had violated § 8(a)(5) of the Act by refusing to bargain in good faith. Accordingly, it issued a cease-and-desist order. The Board found that the information requested was "necessary in order to enable the Union to evaluate intelligently the grievances filed" and pointed out that the agreement contained no "clause by which the Union waives its statutory right to such information."

The Court of Appeals for the Seventh Circuit refused to enforce the Board's order. It did not question the relevance of the information nor the finding that the union had not expressly waived its right to the information. The court ruled, however, that the existence of a provision for binding arbitration of differences concerning the meaning and application of the agreement foreclosed the Board from exercising its statutory power. . . .

There can be no question of the general obligation of an employer to provide information that is needed by the bargaining representative for the proper performance of its duties. Similarly, the duty to bargain unquestionably extends beyond the period of contract negotiations and applies to labor-management relations during the term of an agreement. The only real issue in this case, therefore, is whether the Board must await an arbitrator's determination of the relevance of the requested information before it can enforce the union's statutory rights under § 8(a)(5). . . .

But even if the policy of the *Steelworkers* Cases were thought to apply with the same vigor to the Board as to the courts, that policy would not require the Board to abstain here. When it [NLRB] ordered the employer to furnish the requested information to the union, the Board was not making a binding construction of the labor contract. It was only acting upon the probability that the desired information was relevant, and that it would be of use to the union in carrying out its statutory duties and responsibilities. This discovery-type standard decided nothing about the merits of the union's contractual claim. When the respondent furnishes the requested information, it may appear that no subcontracting or work transfer has occurred, and, accordingly, that the grievances filed are without merit. On the other hand, even if it appears that such activities have taken place, an arbitrator might uphold the respondent's contention that no breach of the agreement occurred because no employees were laid off or reduced in grade within five days prior to the filing of any grievance. Such conclusions would clearly not be precluded by the Board's threshold determination concerning the potential relevance of the requested information. Thus, the assertion of jurisdiction by the Board in this case in no way threatens the power which the parties have given the arbitrator to make binding interpretations of the labor agreement.

Far from intruding upon the preserve of the arbitrator, the Board's action was in aid of the arbitral process. Arbitration can function properly only if the grievance procedures leading to it can sift out unmeritorious claims. For if all claims originally initiated as grievances had to be processed through to arbitration, the system would be woefully overburdened. Yet, that is precisely what the respondent's restrictive view would require. It would force the union to take a grievance all the way through to arbitration without providing the opportunity to evaluate the merits of the claim. The expense of arbitration might be placed upon the union only for it to learn that the machines had been relegated to the junk heap. Nothing in federal labor law requires such a result.

We hold that the Board's order in this case was consistent both with the express terms of the Labor Act and with the national labor policy favoring arbitration which our decisions have discerned as underlying that law. Accordingly, we reverse the judgment and remand the case to the Court of Appeals wtih directions to enforce the Board's order. [REVERSED AND REMANDED]

8   THE TAFT–HARTLEY ACT

The Wagner Act provided the open door for the rapid growth of the union movement. From 1935 to the end of World War II the power and influence of unions grew by leaps and bounds. Where prior to the Wagner Act the employers had the greater advantage in bargaining power, by 1946 many persons felt the pendulum had shifted and the unions with their power of nationwide crippling strikes had the greater bargaining power. It may be stated that the general desire of government has been for equality of bargaining power between labor and management so that fair and equitable employment contracts are agreed upon. The individual employee did not have equality with the large corporation which could discharge him and hire someone else. On the other hand, one company or one industry did not necessarily have equal bargaining power with a union which represented all employees in an industry.

As an attempt to balance the scale, the Labor Management Relations Act of 1947 (the Taft-Hartley Act) was enacted to amend the Wagner Act. It provided that certain practices by unions were also unfair labor practices. Perhaps its most important provisions provided for an 80-day cooling-off period in strikes which imperil the national health or safety. The Act also created a Federal Mediation and Conciliation Service to assist in the settlement of labor disputes. In addition, unions became subject to suit and the closed shop was outlawed.

The purposes of the Taft-Hartley Act were to ensure the full flow of commerce by eliminating practices of unions which burden commerce and to provide procedures for avoiding disputes which jeopardize the public health, safety, or interest. It recognized that both parties to collective bargaining need protection from wrongful interference by the other and that employees sometimes need protection from the union itself. Finally, the Taft-Hartley Act recognized the need for protection of the public in labor disputes which affect commerce.

In adding the other side of the coin to the field of unfair labor practices, the Congress eliminated one of the objections to the Wagner Act raised in the *Jones & Laughlin* case discussed on page 547. The following is a list of the acts by unions which are unfair labor practices as specified in Section 8(b) of the Taft-Hartley Act, as amended by the Landrum-Griffin Act (Section 9) in 1959:

1 Restraining or coercing employers or an employee to join a union.
2 Causing or attempting to cause the employer to discriminate against an employee who is not a union member, unless he is not a member because of failure to pay dues.
3 Refusing to bargain with an employer.
4 Striking, picketing, and engaging in secondary boycotts for illegal purposes.
5 Charging new members excessive or discriminating initiation fees under union shop agreements.
6 Causing an employer to pay for work not performed (feather bedding).
7 Picketing for purposes of requiring collective bargaining where the union is not currently certified as representing the employees, or where the correct procedure for becoming certified is not followed.
8 Executing "hot cargo" contracts.

The Landrum-Griffin Amendment also added the unfair labor practice for *management* to enter into hot cargo contracts. A hot cargo contract is an agreement which provides that a company will not accept delivery of goods from another company whose employees are on strike or are unfair to labor. The cargo is in effect made "hot" because of the strike at the shipping company or because of some unfair labor practice committed by it.

Employers had complained that the Wagner Act violated the employer's right of free speech. To meet this objection, Congress added Section 8(c), which reads as follows: "(c) The expressing of any views, argument, or opinion, or the dissemination thereof, whether in written, printed, graphic, or visual form, shall not constitute or be evidence of an unfair labor practice under any of the provisions of this Act, if such expression contains no threat of reprisal or force or promise of benefit."

Section 206 of the Taft-Hartley Act provides for the eighty-day "cooling-off period" after certain procedures have been followed. Section 206 begins, "Whenever in the opinion of the President of the United States, a threatened or actual strike or lockout affecting an entire industry or substantial part thereof engaged in trade, commerce, transportation, transmission, or communication among the several states or with foreign nations, or engaged in the production of goods for commerce, will, if permitted to occur or to continue, imperil the national health or safety, he may appoint a board. . . ." Thus the procedure starts with the President, recognizing the emergency characteristics of a strike, appointing a board of inquiry to obtain facts about the strike. The board then makes a study of the strike and reports back to the President. If the board finds that the national health is indeed affected by the strike, then the President, through the Attorney General, goes to the Federal District Court for an injunction ordering the union to suspend the strike (or company to suspend the lockout) for eighty days. During the eighty-day period, the Federal Mediation Service works with the two parties to try to achieve an agreement. If during this time the reconciliation effort fails, the presidential board holds new hearings and receives the company's final offer. The members of the union are then allowed to vote on this final proposal by the company. If they vote for the new proposal, the dispute is over and work continues as usual. If they vote against the proposal, the workers may again be called out on strike. At this point, the strike may continue indefinitely until the disagreement causing it is resolved by collective bargaining, or unless there is additional legislation by Congress to solve the problem. Experience has shown that many disputes are settled during the eighty-day period. The injunction provided for in the Taft-Hartley Act may not be used for all strikes but is limited to "national emergency" strikes. These must involve national defense or key industries, or must have a substantial effect on the economy.

9   THE LANDRUM–GRIFFIN ACT

In the early 1950s corruption in labor unions was revealed in testimony before Congressional investigating committees. This corruption included embezzlement from union treasuries, engaging in juice loans, and converting union resources to the personal interests of union officials. Violence at union meetings was commonplace and the administrative procedures of some unions could hardly be called "democratic." It was also established that some union officials had extensive criminal records and others were members of the Communist party.

During the 1950s, several pieces of proposed legislation to correct these abuses were considered by Congress. In 1959, the Labor-Management Reporting and Disclosure Act (Landrum-Griffin Act) was passed and was signed into law by President Eisenhower. The Act was passed under the Commerce Power and contained the following statement in Section 2(b) as to the reasons for the statute:

The Congress . . . finds, from recent investigations in the labor and management fields, that there have been a number of instances of breach of trust, corruption, disregard of the rights of individual employees, and other failures to observe high standards of responsibility and ethical conduct which require further and supplementary legislation that will afford necessary protection of the rights and interests of employees and the public generally as they relate to the activities of labor organizations, employers, labor relations consultants, and their officers and representatives.

Title 1 of the Act has been called the "Bill of Rights" of union members. These provisions give union members the following rights:

1 To nominate candidates, to vote in elections, to attend membership meetings, and to have a voice in business transactions, subject to reasonable union rules and regulations.
2 To have free expression in union meetings, business discussions, and conventions subject to reasonable rules and regulations.
3 To vote on an increase of dues or fees.
4 To sue and testify against the union.
5 To receive written, specific charges; to be given a reasonable time for defense; and to be accorded a full and fair hearing before any disciplinary action is taken by the union against them.
6 To be given a copy of the collective bargaining agreement that they work under, upon request.

An exception to provision 5 above is made in the case of disciplinary action for nonpayment of dues. The rights and remedies granted to union members by the statute are in addition to any other rights that the members may have under other laws or under union constitutions and by-laws. In the event that the foregoing rights are violated, the statute allows union members to bring civil action for relief, including injunction, in the United States District Court where the violation occurred or where the principal office of the union is located. In one case decided under the "Bill of Rights," it was held that the expulsion of union members for advocating "right-to-work" laws was forbidden under the free-speech rule.

The Landrum-Griffin Act also contains several provisions relating to the Secretary of Labor and reports which he may require of unions. The purpose of these reports is to reveal practices detrimental to union members. For example, each union must adopt a constitution and by-laws and file them with the Secretary of Labor together with the following information:

1 The name and address of the union office and the place where records are kept
2 The names and titles of officers
3 The amount of initiation fees required
4 The amount of dues charged
5 A detailed statement of procedures for (*a*) qualification for office, (*b*) levying fees, (*c*) insurance plans, (*d*) disbursement of funds, (*e*) audits, (*f*) selection of officers, (*g*) removal of officers, (*h*) determining bargaining demands, (*i*) fines, (*j*) approval of contracts, (*k*) calling strikes, and (*l*) issuance of work permits

In addition, yearly financial reports must be filed which indicate:

1 Assets and liabilities
2 Receipts and sources of funds
3 Salaries of officers
4 Loans to members greater than $250
5 Loans to business enterprises
6 Other disbursements

The Act also requires reports on trusteeships. A trusteeship is a method of supervision or control whereby a labor union suspends the autonomy otherwise available to a subordinate body under its constitution and by-laws. In this report the union must state the names and addresses of subordinate organizations, the date of establishing trusteeship, and the reasons for establishing the trusteeship.

In addition to the foregoing reports, union employees and officials must file a yearly report with the Secretary of Labor containing information on possible areas of conflict of interest such as holdings of stock in companies with which the union has dealings, and payments personally received from employers. Employers must file yearly reports with the Secretary containing information concerning payments made to unions or union officials. An employer must also report on payments made to consultants whom he engages to deal with unions. Reports made to the Secretary of Labor become public information. Records supporting the reports must be kept for five years, and the Secretary of Labor is given broad powers to investigate the reports filed with him. He is empowered to delegate this power to a commission, such as the Bureau of Labor-Management Reports, if he desires.

The Landrum-Griffin Act provides for an elaborate system of regulation of internal union activities. It will be seen that most of these regulations cover activities that are supposed to be revealed in the reports. They cover union election procedures, management of union funds, trusteeships, and union personnel. The Secretary is given power to investigate alleged violations of any of the regulations and may institute criminal proceedings through the Attorney General.

The Act requires that elections be held at minimum regular intervals to promote democracy. National unions must hold elections at least every five years, locals every three years, and intermediate bodies every four years. Elections must be by secret ballot of members, or of delegates who were chosen by secret ballot of members.

The Act also states that every candidate for union office must have access to membership lists. The union must provide adequate safeguards to ensure a fair election and every candidate is given the right to post observers at the polls and counting place. This provision is enforceable by civil action instituted by candidates. All candidates must have equal opportunity to run for office without penalty or punishment by the organization or any member thereof, subject to reasonable rules. Union funds may not be used by any candidate in his campaign. The Secretary of Labor may provide for an election to remove a candidate from office if the union constitution does not provide adequate procedures for removal of officers guilty of misconduct. A court may declare an election void if the preponderance of evidence shows a violation that may have affected it. The Act also recognizes the fiduciary responsibility of officers of unions. All exculpatory clauses in union constitutions are void as against public policy. A member of a union may sue for funds mishandled by union officers after he has exhausted union proceedings and he will be repaid the cost of bringing suit.

The Act also makes embezzlement of union funds a Federal crime. The penalty is imprisonment for up to five years or a fine up to $10,000 or both. Every union employee who handles funds must be bonded. No union may lend more than $2,000 to a union employee or official. Any person who wilfully violates either of these two provisions is subject to imprisonment for one year or a fine of up to $10,000, or both. Unions are not permitted to pay the fines imposed on their officers or employees who are convicted of violating the Act. However, the propriety of payments to cover legal fees in lawsuits is judged on an individual basis.

Landrum-Griffin also added to the list of unfair labor practices by unions. It restricted blackmail picketing, hot cargo agreements, and secondary boycotts. These matters are discussed further in Section 12.

10   THE CIVIL RIGHTS ACT OF 1964

The provisions of the Civil Rights Act of 1964 which affect labor law are applicable to employers with twenty-five or more employees, labor unions with twenty-five or more members, all labor unions which operate a hiring hall, and employment agencies. They are not applicable to governmental units, corporations wholly owned by the United States government, Indian tribes, and private membership clubs. Exemptions are also provided for religious corporations, associations, or societies with respect to the employment of individuals of a particular religion to perform work connected with the carrying on of their religious activities, and educational institutions with respect to the employment of persons connected with the educational activities of the institutions.

One of the major purposes of the Act is to eliminate job discrimination based on race, color, religion, sex, or national origin. Discrimination for any of these reasons is a violation of the law, except that:

1 Employers, employment agencies, and labor unions, can discriminate on the basis of religion, sex, or national origin in those certain instances where the above categories are bona fide occupational qualifications.

2 Employers who are working under government security programs can deny employment to individuals because of their inability to obtain security clearance. (This may be unconstitutional.)

3 Employers can deny employment to individuals who are members of the Communist party of the United States or of any other organization which is required to register as a Communist action or Communist-front organization. (This is probably unconstitutional.)

4 Employers can establish different standards, compensation, terms, or conditions of employment if they are applied pursuant to a bona fide seniority or merit system.

The types of employer action in which discrimination is prohibited include discharge; refusal to hire; compensation; and terms, conditions or privileges of employment. Additionally, employers are not permitted to segregate or classify employees on any of these bases where the result tends to affect employee status or opportunity adversely. The act also prevents employers who have or share control of apprenticeship or training programs from discriminating in the admissions to or operations of such programs.

Employment *agencies* are prohibited from either *failing to refer* or from *actually referring* an individual for employment on the basis of race, color, religion, sex, or national origin. This provision is in marked contrast to that binding *employers* where it is unlawful only to fail or refuse to hire on discriminatory grounds—the affirmative act of hiring for a discriminatory reason is apparently not illegal. For example, assume that a contractor with a government contract, in order to improve his compliance reports, seeks a qualified Negro engineer and requests an employment agency to refer such an individual. The agency complies with the request and a Negro is referred and hired. Unless a white applicant was discriminated against, the employer probably did not commit an unlawful practice; but the employment agency, by referring an individual on the basis of his color, unquestionably did commit an unlawful practice under the Act.

Note that, regarding general hiring, referrals, advertising, and admissions to apprenticeship programs, the Act allows discrimination on the basis of religion, sex, or national origin only where these considerations are bona fide occupational qualifications. The omission of *race* and *color* from this exception must mean the Congress does not feel that these two factors are ever bona fide occupational qualifications.

Additional exemptions exist with respect to laws creating preferential treatment for veterans, and to hiring on the basis of professionally developed ability tests. This last exclusion resulted from the case which follows.

MOTOROLA, INC. V. ILLINOIS FAIR EMPLOYMENT PRACTICES COMM'N
215 N.E.2d 286 (III. 1966)

SCHAEFFER, JUSTICE: The Illinois Fair Employment Practices Commission found that the plaintiff, Motorola, Inc., falsely recorded the examination grade of a Negro applicant [Myart] for employment in order to avoid hiring him. The circuit court of Cook County affirmed the Commission's ruling that the plaintiff had committed an unfair employment practice, and this administrative review action comes here . . . because the plaintiff challenges . . . the sufficiency of the evidence. . . .

The hearing examiner heard conflicting evidence concerning both Myart's qualifications for the position of analyzer and phaser and whether Myart informed Motorola of all of his experience and education. The examiner resolved these issues in favor of Myart. Motorola required a score of six on Test No. 10 as a prerequisite to further consideration of an applicant, and a witness for Motorola testified that he recorded Myart's score of four on his application form. Myart's actual test paper was never produced, however, and the examiner found that if it had been produced, it would have been adverse to Motorola's contention that Myart scored four. Although the issue had neither been raised by the pleadings nor discussed by the parties, the examiner also found that the general ability test did not "lend itself to equal opportunity to qualify for the hitherto culturally deprived and the disadvantaged groups." He cited in support of this conclusion certain books and articles which had not been offered in evidence. The examiner ordered Motorola to cease and desist from denying equal employment opportunity to qualified applicants, to cease using the general ability test, to revise its employment application form, and to offer Myart employment as an analyzer and phaser. Motorola sought review of the examiner's decision before the Commission.

The Commission permitted both sides to present new evidence, much of which was directed to the question whether the general ability test was inherently discriminatory against Negroes and other minority groups. Eventually, however, the Commission ruled that this question was not involved in the proceedings before it because Myart had passed the test and because the issue had not been raised by Myart's complaint. The Commission's final decision made the following findings of fact, which are the only findings before us for review:

1. *That the Complainant passed General Ability Test No. 10 on July 15, 1963, when given to him by Respondent.*
2. *That the Respondent marked the Complainant's application form with a failing score for General Ability Test No. 10.*
3. *That the intent of the Respondent in incorrectly marking the Complainant's application was to discriminate against Complainant on account of his race.*
4. *That by reason of this discrimination based on race, the Respondent refused to process further the Complainant's application for employment in the Respondent's hiring procedure.*

The Commission ordered Motorola to cease and desist from denying equal employment opportunity to any qualified applicant because of his race. . . .

Although the [circuit] court noted that it would not have made the findings that the Commission did had it been the trier of fact, it held that those findings were supported by competent evidence from which reasonable men could draw an inference of discrimination. It therefore affirmed the Commission's findings and its cease-and-desist order. . . .

Deference is unquestionably due the factual determinations of an agency charged with the primary responsibility for adjudication in a specialized area. The wisdom of this principle of judicial review is emphasized when the agency's area of competence involves the subtleties of conduct often present in cases of racial discrimination. As the New York Court of Appeals observed, "One intent on violating the Law Against Discrimination cannot be expected to declare or announce his purpose. Far more likely is it that he will pursue his discriminatory practices in ways that are devious, by methods subtle and elusive. . . ." We agree with the circuit court that the Commission must be allowed reasonable latitude in drawing inferences of discrimination from competent circumstantial evidence.

The Commission's findings in this case, however, make the decisive issue not one of motive but one of fact. If Motorola falsely recorded Myart's test score, that action would leave little doubt that an unfair employment practice had been committed. Conversely, if Myart failed the test, the record would not establish an unfair employment practice with respect to him. He would have been refused employment for a reason applicable to all who fared as he did on the examination. The possibility that he might have become a victim of discrimination at a later stage in the hiring process would not, in that circumstance, be significant. We . . . turn to the evidence that led the Commission to its findings on that issue.

The Commission's order recites that evidence was introduced which showed that at the time Myart applied for employment, Negroes were excluded from consideration for the position that he sought. There is no direct testimony in the record on this question. The Commission apparently relied for its statement upon inferences drawn from the testimony of Walter J. Ducey, Executive Director of the Commission, as to a conversation with an officer of Motorola, and upon portions of the testimony of Motorola's personnel director. Although other inferences could have been drawn, it was possible to infer from this testimony that at the time of Myart's application, Motorola was not hiring Negroes in production line jobs in that part of its work which involved production for civilian consumption, and that the first two Negroes to be employed as analyzers and phasers were hired during the week before the hearing commenced. The Commission apparently drew these inferences. While a background of prior discrimination could be taken into account in appraising other evidence, it was not, in itself, sufficient to justify the findings of the Commission.

The key finding of the Commision is that Myart passed test No. 10, but that Motorola marked his application form with a failing score in order to discriminate against him on account of his race. In addition to the evidence of prior discrimination relied upon by the Commission, this finding is based upon the fact that on two occasions, once before and once after he took the test at Motorola, Myart had passed the test, and upon the adverse inference which the Commission drew from Motorola's failure to produce the actual test taken by Myart.

Walter J. Ducey testified that on September 19, 1963, he gave Myart the same examination that he had taken at Motorola in July, and that Myart scored seven. . . . Before the Commission, the Personnel Services Manager of Montgomery Ward testified that the records of Montgomery Ward showed that Myart had taken the test there on October 2, 1962, and that he had scored six. The Commission cited this fact as further evidence that Myart passed the test at Motorola.

While a sufficient demonstration of Myart's ability to pass the test would be admissible as tending to show that he had in fact passed it, expert testimony in this case, coupled with the examiner's refusal to admit evidence as to the circumstances under which the last test was taken, minimizes the probative worth of the evidence on which the Commission relied. Dr. Phillip A. Shurrager, Chairman of the Psychology and Education Department at the Illinois Institute of Technology, testified that he and his wife developed the general ability examination that Myart took. He said that when the test was given to applicants for industrial positions, the mean score was eight; he added that 68 per cent of the population would pass the test when a score of six was required. He further testified that a person would ordinarily improve his score on successive examinations and that a person who had scored a four initially might be expected to score two or three points higher when he took the test again. If this testimony was correct, Myart's performance on the examination given by Ducey was at least as consistent with the contention that he had failed the examination at Motorola as with the contention that he had passed.

Because of the tendency to improve on successive examinations, Myart's performance on the examination at Montgomery Ward might initially seem more significant than his performance on the third examination that he took. Again, however, expert testimony casts doubt on the significance of Myart's passing score. Benjamin S. Bloom, Professor of Education at the University of Chicago, . . . testified on direct examination, "This is . . . one of the shortest aptitude tests in the field. . . . If you repeated this test several times there would be considerable variation from time to time, and much depends upon the accidents of circumstances." Variation within a range of two or three points on even a short examination would hardly seem improbable to a reasonable, nonexpert fact-finder. This expert testimony indicated that Myart's performance on the other examinations was not inconsistent with his allegedly unsatisfactory performance at Motorola.

Another expert, Robert L. French, of Science Research Associates, was called by Myart before the Commission. He testified that while he would not attempt to predict with certainty what any individual might do, he found it difficult to understand that a person with Myart's background could not score six points on the test. In view of the fact that Myart at no time scored better than seven points, French's testimony does not go far toward establishing that Myart passed the test at Motorola.

The actual test taken by Myart was not introduced in evidence. . . . At no time during the investigation of the charge or at the hearing before the examiner did either Myart or the Commission specifically request that Myart's examination paper be produced. . . .

At the hearing before the Commission Motorola introduced evidence to show what had happened to Myart's test paper. Jerry Hoelscher, an employment interviewer, had testified before the hearing examiner that he had conducted Myart's interview, and that he transposed Myart's score of four from the test paper onto his application form at the time of the interview. . . .

At the hearing before the Commission, Motorola called Suzanne LaBuda, a receptionist at its Franklin Park employment office. She testified that she was working as a receptionist on the day Myart applied, and she described in detail the manner in which she administered and graded the applicants' general ability tests. She said that after grading the examinations she attached them to the application forms and left them for the employment interviewer. On cross-examination, she testified that the examination papers were retained at the Franklin Park plant for two months and then sent to the Personnel Testing Center.

After Miss LaBuda's testimony, the planitiff called Raymond A. Orth, Manager of the Personnel Testing Center. He testified that when examination papers are received at the testing center they are checked to determine whether they were properly graded. The scores are then recorded on a score sheet, which is sent to the Data Processing Center. The test papers themselves are destroyed, because 20,000 applicants take the test every year and Motorola does not have the space to store that number of examinations.

Robert Brauch, Motorola's Manager of Data Processing, testified that the information contained on the score sheet that his department receives from the testing center is recorded on IBM cards. He produced the card on which Leon Myart's score was recorded, and it was introduced in evidence. Brauch testified that the score that appeared there, in the form of holes punched in the card, was four.

It appears from this testimony that Myart's test paper was destroyed about two months after he applied for employment. When it was destroyed, Motorola was not a party to any formal proceedings, but it had notice that Myart's complaint had been filed and was under investigation by the Commission. The destruction of the test under these circumstances could reasonably be considered by the Commission as evidence adverse to Motorola's contention that Myart had failed to pass the test. But the possibility remained that the test might have been destroyed innocently. . . .

There are other relevant considerations. If Myart's test score was falsely recorded because he was a Negro, at least two of the plaintiffs' employees must have participated in that dishonest act. Either the receptionist or the employment interviewer would have recorded the false score that appeared on the application form, and someone in either the Personnel Testing Center or the Data Processing Center would, after the re-grading of the test, have caused the same dishonest score to appear on an IBM card. These employees were not cross-examined concerning their attitude toward Negroes, the company's hiring policies, or the instructions they had received from their superiors. The evidence concerning the alleged background of discrimination at Motorola came from the Personnel Director and from the Vice-President in Charge of Human Relations. Thus, if Myart's score was falsely recorded, that action seems to have been the product of an extensive conspiracy within the plaintiff's organization.

The advantage of implementing a policy of discrimination by conspiring to grade examinations falsely is that a company is able to present what seems to be objective evidence of an applicant's disqualification and thereby avoid an inquiry into its good faith. A disadvantage is that the practice is likely to be exposed whenever a receptionist, employment interviewer, worker in the testing center, or data processing technician becomes disaffected with his employer. The practice could also be exposed if an outsider who possesses the general ability test becomes suspicious enough to introduce a Negro applicant primed to answer the requisite number of questions correctly. When all the evidence in this case is considered, some suspicion might reasonably remain that the plaintiff had falsely recorded Myart's test score. Under the Fair Employment Practices Act, however, that suspicion is not enough. The act provides that "A determination sustaining a complaint shall be based upon a preponderance of the evidence." On the record in this case, we are of the opinion that the alleged unfair employment practice was not established by a preponderance of the evidence. The judgment of the circuit court of Cook County is therefore reversed. [JUDG-MENT REVERSED]

Original enforcement of those provisions of the Civil Rights Act outlined above is in the hands of a special Federal administrative agency known as the Equal Employment Opportunity Commission. Its powers are largely restricted to conducting investigations and to moral persuasion. In the course of its investigations, the Commission has broad authority to examine and copy evidence, require the production of documentary evidence, hold hearings, and subpoena and examine witnesses under oath. Upon finding reasonable cause, any member of the Commission may individually file unlawful employment practice charges; but the Commission has no power to issue cease and desist orders or make binding determinations against respondents. Faced with what it considers to be an unlawful employment practice, its authority to resolve the matter is restricted to the sphere of conciliation and persuasion in informal efforts to achieve voluntary compliance.

If it is unsuccessful in its efforts, the Commission can merely so advise the aggrieved person. The Commission itself cannot institute a civil action for enforcement. Its authority to commence civil proceedings is limited to two narrow cases: it may institute legal action to compel compliance with a *prior court order* in the case of a defaulting employer, employment agency, or labor union; and it may obtain a court order requiring recalcitrant respondents to produce records or to appear as witnesses or otherwise to cooperate with the Commission in the exercise of its investigatory powers.

Ancillary powers of the Commission include promulgating record-keeping and report-making requirements, controlling the posting of required notices, establishing procedural regulations, furnishing those persons covered by the Act with technical assistance, cooperating with and utilizing state and other agencies, and making appropriate studies.

While it appears that the power of the Commission is substantially limited to that of moral persuasion, it must be kept in mind that Commission *members* have the right to file charges, and can advise and counsel individuals to institute civil actions which the Commission itself cannot bring. Moreover, while the Commission itself cannot commence civil actions, the Attorney General, in proper cases, may either intervene in actions brought by individuals, or himself institute proceedings. The Commission is expressly authorized to refer matters with recommendations for action and otherwise advise and assist the Attorney General in such suits.

The Congressional intent of preserving the vitality of local fair employment laws finds its expression in the enforcement procedures. Section 706 (b) of the Act provides that where the unlawful practice alleged, if true, is violative of a state or local law, no charge may be filed with the Commission until sixty days after the proceedings have been commenced under that law. Similarly, when a charge is filed by a Commission member where a local law provides relief, the Commission must notify the appropriate officials and defer all action until the local authority has had, in general, at least sixty days to resolve the matter. In either case, the sixty-day waiting requirement is dispensed with if the local proceeding is terminated before that time.

The Federal enforcement procedure can be summarized as follows:

1   Proceedings are commenced by the filing of a written charge by either an individual claiming to be aggrieved or a member of the Commission.
2   The Commission must furnish respondent with a copy of the charge —which cannot be made public—and make an investigation.
3   If the Commission determines there is reasonable cause to believe the charge is true, it endeavors to eliminate the alleged unlawful practices by informal methods of conference, conciliation and persuasion.
4   If the Commission is unable to obtain voluntary compliance within thirty days after the charge was filed (this period may be expanded to sixty days) the Commission so notifies the aggrieved.
5   Within thirty days after being so notified, the aggrieved may commence a civil action against respondent in a District Court. In the court's discretion, the Attorney General may intervene upon certification that the case is of general public importance.
6   The court may grant injunctive relief or order affirmative remedial action only if it finds that respondent intentionally engaged in an unlawful employment practice. The court may further award attorney's fees as part of the costs to any prevailing party other than the Commission or the United States; both, however, may be held liable for costs including attorney's fees. Appeals are taken, as usual, to United States courts of appeals.
7   In the event that a respondent fails to comply with a court order, the Commission may commence proceedings to compel such com-

pliance. The courts retain their usual civil contempt powers but respondents are entitled to jury trials for criminal contempt charges based on conduct outside the court room.

As indicated above, the Attorney General may, upon certification of the general public importance of a civil action brought by an aggrieved person, intervene in it. But beyond this power of intervention, the Attorney General may himself initiate a civil action where he "has reasonable cause to believe that any person or group of persons is engaged in a pattern or practice of resistance to the full enjoyment of any of the rights secured by . . . [the Act], and that the pattern or practice is of such a nature and intended to deny the full exercise of the rights . . . [therein] described. . . ." In such a case, there is no requirement that any charges have been filed by an aggrieved person; neither need the state nor Commission machinery be utilized before the action is instituted directly in a district court and given preferential treatment.

11   MEDIATION AND ARBITRATION

The Federal statutes place a duty on both employers and unions to bargain with each other. This mutual obligation to bargain collectively is a duty to meet at reasonable times and confer in good faith with respect to the negotiation of an agreement, on wages, hours, and other terms and conditions of employment. However, this obligation to *confer* does not compel either party to *agree* to a proposal by the other, or require them to make any concessions to each other. Thus, the Federal acts do not prevent disagreements or disputes between management and labor from arising.

Labor disputes may arise over either the terms to be included in a proposed collective-bargaining agreement, or the interpretation and application of a collective-bargaining agreement currently in force. Frequently the management and the union are able to resolve their differences in the bargaining process by themselves. Sometimes a dispute is settled by conciliation or mediation, where, by mutual agreement, a neutral third party is called upon to assist the employer and the union in their deliberations and help them find a solution which is acceptable to both. A mediator does not make a decision which is binding on the parties but helps them in reaching their agreement. Another method of settling a dispute is by arbitration, where the employer and the union select a third party to make a decision for them. If arbitration is employed, the parties present evidence and arguments to the arbitrator and agree in advance to accept his decision as final and binding on each. If arbitration is not used and agreement cannot be reached, a strike may result. Then, when the public interest is involved, the dispute may be resolved, at least temporarily, by government intervention and force, such as the invoking of the Taft-Hartley Act by obtaining an injunction forbidding the strike for the statutory 80-day cooling-off period.

Frequently collective-bargaining agreements between employers and unions contain a provision that disputes over the interpretation of the agreement will be submitted to an arbitrator when other efforts have failed. In *Textile Workers Union v. Lincoln Mills of Alabama* [10] the parties had entered into this type of agreement, but the employer had denied several grievances of union employees concerning work loads and assignments and had refused a union request for arbitration. In an action by the union to compel arbitration, the Supreme Court held in favor of the union, ruling that a collective-bargaining agreement is equally binding on both parties, and that specific performance of an arbitration provision will lie. This was in spite of the Norris–La Guardia (anti-injunction) Act, since forced arbitration was not one of the abuses of injunctions against which that act was aimed. The decision which follows illustrates the effect of such an agreement to arbitrate, in a case where the employer refused arbitration because the terms of the collective-bargaining agreement were so clear that they were beyond dispute as to their meaning, and there was therefore nothing for an arbitrator to decide.

UNITED STEELWORKERS OF AMERICA V. AMERICAN MFG. CO.
363 U.S. 564 (1960)

Opinion of the Court by DOUGLAS, JUSTICE; announced by BRENNAN, JUSTICE: This suit was brought by petitioner union in the District Court to compel arbitration of a "grievance" that petitioner, acting for one Sparks, a union member, had filed with the respondent, Spark's employer. The employer defended on the ground (1) that Sparks is estopped from making his claim because he had a few days previously settled a workmen's compensation claim against the company on the basis that he was permanently partially disabled, (2) that Sparks is not physically able to do the work, and (3) that this type of dispute is not arbitrable under the collective bargaining agreement in question.

The agreement provided that during its term there would be "no strike," unless the employer refused to abide by a decision of the arbitrator. The agreement sets out a detailed grievance procedure with a provision for arbitration (regarded as the standard form) of all disputes between the parties "as to the meaning, interpretation and application of the provisions of this agreement."

The agreement reserves to the management power to suspend or discharge any employee "for cause." It also contains a provision that the

[10] 353 U.S. 449 (1957).

employer will employ and promote employees on the principle of seniority "where ability and efficiency are equal." Sparks left his work due to an injury and while off work brought an action for compensation benefits. The case was settled, Sparks' physician expressing the opinion that the injury had made him 25% "permanently partially disabled." That was on September 9. Two weeks later the union filed a grievance which charged that Sparks was entitled to return to his job by virtue of the seniority provision of the collective bargaining agreement. Respondent refused to arbitrate and this action was brought. The District Court held that Sparks, having accepted the settlement on the basis of permanent partial disability, was estopped to claim any seniority or employment rights and granted the motion for summary judgment. The Court of Appeals affirmed . . . for different reasons. After reviewing the evidence it held that the grievance is "a frivolous, patently baseless one, not subject to arbitration under the collective bargaining agreement." . . . The case is here on a writ of certiorari. . . .

Section 203(d) of the Labor Management Relations Act, 1947, 61 Stat. 154, 29 U.S.C. § 173(d), . . . states, "Final adjustment by a method agreed upon by the parties is hereby declared to be the desirable method for settlement of grievance disputes arising over the application or interpretation of an existing collective-bargaining agreement. . . ." That policy can be effectuated only if the means chosen by the parties for settlement of their differences under a collective bargaining agreement is given full play.

A state decision that held to the contrary announced a principle that could only have a crippling effect on grievance arbitration. The case was *International Ass'n of Machinists v. Cutler-Hammer, Inc.*, 271 App. Div. 917, 67 N.Y.S.2d 317. . . . It held that "If the meaning of the provision of the contract sought to be arbitrated is beyond dispute, there cannot be anything to arbitrate and the contract cannot be said to provide for arbitration." . . . The lower courts in the instant case had a like preoccupation with ordinary contract law. The collective agreement requires arbitration of claims that courts might be unwilling to entertain. In the context of the plant or industry the grievance may assume proportions of which judges are ignorant. Yet, the agreement is to submit all grievances to arbitration, not merely those that a court may deem to be meritorious. There is no exception in the "no strike" clause and none therefore should be read into the grievance clause, since one is the *quid pro quo* for the other. The question is not whether in the mind of the court there is equity in the claim. Arbitration is a stabilizing influence only as it serves as a vehicle for handling any and all disputes that arise under the agreement.

The collective agreement calls for the submission of grievances in the categories which it describes, irrespective of whether a court may deem them to be meritorious. In our role of developing a meaningful body of law to govern the interpretation and enforcement of collective bargaining agreements, we think special heed should be given to the context in which collective bargaining agreements are negotiated and the purpose which they are intended to serve. . . . The function of the court is very limited when the parties have agreed to submit all questions of contract interpretation to the arbitrator. It is confined to ascertaining whether the party seeking arbitration is making a claim which on its face is governed by the contract. Whether the moving party is right or wrong is a question of contract interpretation for the arbitrator. In these circumstances the moving party should not be deprived of the arbitrator's judgment, when it was his judgment and all that it connotes that was bargained for.

The courts, therefore, have no business weighing the merits of the grievance, considering whether there is equity in a particular claim, or determining whether there is particular language in the written instrument which will support the claim. The agreement is to submit all grievances to arbitration, not merely those which the court will deem meritorious. The processing of even frivolous claims may have therapeutic values of which those who are not a part of the plant environment may be quite unaware.

The union claimed in this case that the company had violated a specific provision of the contract. The company took the position that it had not violated that clause. There was, therefore, a dispute between the parties as to "the meaning, interpretation and application" of the collective bargaining agreement. Arbitration should have been ordered. When the judiciary undertakes to determine the merits of a grievance under the guise of interpreting the grievance procedure of collective bargaining agreements, it usurps a function which under that regime is entrusted to the arbitration tribunal. [REVERSED]

12   THE NLRB

There are no fewer than eight Federal administrative agencies concerned with labor-management relations. Among the most important of these is the NLRB, with its twenty-eight regional offices. The NLRB was established by the Wagner Act in 1935 to administer the provisions of that Act. It determines which union will represent the employees of a given business as their bargaining agent, by supervising elections among the workers for that purpose. Its other main function is to investigate, hear, and decide complaints of alleged unfair labor practices. The early actions of the NLRB were criticized by employers for being too prejudiced in favor of labor. Union supporters, of course, lauded the stand of the Board as being exactly what was needed to place labor on an equal bargaining plane with management. The NLRB no doubt contributed a great deal to the growth and power of unions. While the membership and some of the policies of the NLRB have changed in the years since its creation, it is still the subject of criticism and debate. The author of the article which follows argues that the Board has not met its responsibility to carry out the will and object of Congress as expressed in labor legislation enacted after the Wagner Act.

IS THE LABOR BOARD BIASED? [11]
Henry L. Browne [12]

It is a matter of common knowledge that a critical problem exists in collective bargaining and labor disputes affected with a national interest.

The National Labor Relations Board, as the chief administrator of our labor policy, can advance the efficacy of free collective bargaining. It may be seriously questioned, however, in the light of disturbing Labor Board decisions unsettling the balance of power between labor and management, that the Board has fulfilled this responsibility.

This is not to suggest that, in our complex, highly industrialized society, the rash of current labor disputes can be attributed to Board decisional doctrine alone, for many causes have contributed.

For example, recent years have witnessed a rapid growth and expansion of defense industries, and disputes in this area have a direct impact on public interest.

Moreover, the causes giving rise to labor strife have multiplied, because subjects once considered outside the realm of collective bargaining —such as pensions, profit sharing, bonuses, insurance plans, subcontracting and plant removal, to name but a few—have now found their way onto the bargaining table and have created new sources of division and disagreement. Furthermore, the dynamic nature of labor relations inherently generates a greater national interest in the peaceful settlement of labor disputes than disputes of a commercial nature.

However complex the issues, any study in depth of the root causes of labor strife necessitates a full and fair appraisal of Labor Board doctrine as a point of departure. While the Board's jurisdiction does not extend to all industry—the railroad and airline industries being exempted—the decisions of the Board cannot be considered in isolation or in a vacuum. Each decision has a pervasive and irresistible impact on all bargaining and becomes a part of the whole.

Experience demonstrates that patterns and attitudes of bargaining developed in one segment of our labor economy interlock with the entire industrial complex. The Labor Board must, therefore, share responsibility for the over-all results of our labor policy, good or bad.

At the outset, we must start with the proposition that all responsible citizenry hope for the survival of free collective bargaining, for that is in-

[11] Reprinted from *U.S. News & World Report* 72 (Nov. 28, 1966), published at Washington.
[12] Mr. Browne has had extensive experience in the field of labor law as a private practitioner, as an attorney for the NLRB, and as co-chairman of an American Bar Association panel that deals with Federal agencies on labor law.

digenous to a free and democratic society. One of our first labor statutes, the Norris–La Guardia Act of 1932, was to promote freedom in bargaining between labor and management, with, to quote its leading proponent, Senator Robert Wagner, "the Government occupying a neutral position— lending its extraordinary power neither to those who would have labor unorganized nor to those who would organize it."

This, indeed, has been the scheme behind all comprehensive labor lgeislation in recent times: the Wagner Act of 1935, the Taft-Hartley Act of 1947 and the Landrum-Griffin Act of 1959. The design, said the Supreme Court was to encourage "the making of voluntary labor agreements."

Commensurate with this liberty, and so that collective bargaining could remain free and function in the national interest, Congress set up a statutory cantilever, so to speak, for management and labor to have substantial equality in bargaining power.

It was the judgment of our legislators that a balance of power would result in an assimilation of the legitimate interests of all parties, while excessive power would lead to industrial strife and labor agreements not in the public interest. Senator Taft, in the debates leading to the Taft-Hartley Act, put it this way:

"Unreasonable power leads to the exercise of power to accomplish ends which are not reasonable" and, where there is a balance of power, "neither side feels that it can make an unreasonable demand and get away with it."

This truth is evident today. Experience teaches us that excessive power inevitably leads to a demonstration of power and to industrial conflict, but equality of bargaining power inevitably reduces conflict and leads to an accommodation of the public interest.

Given a labor policy of free collective bargaining and legislation providing for the statutory framework within which management and labor can meet on an equal footing, the National Labor Relations Board was established by Congress to fulfill our national labor policy.

The duty of the Board under the law was to carry out the will of Congress and give it direction; to be guided, as the Supreme Court said in *Mastro Plastics,* not by "a single sentence or member of a sentence but by the provisions of the whole law and to its object and policy."

The question we must ask ourselves is whether the Board has met this responsibility. We submit it has not.

It may be recalled that the Landrum-Griffin Act, the last piece of comprehensive labor legislation passed by Congress, was for the purpose of eliminating union abuses created by excessive union power.

Congress legislated to restrict "blackmail picketing" where a union picketed to compel recognition as bargaining agent, although it did not represent a majority of the employes; it sought to prevent "hot cargo agreements," labor contracts by which unions force a promise from one employer not to do business with another employer whom the union deems "unfair"; and it attempted to eliminate secondary-boycott practices which had allowed unions to strike or otherwise assert economic pressure on neutral secondary employers with impunity.

The scheme of the legislation was to restore the balance between management and labor. But this hope was not accomplished. Shortly after the passage of the Act, and with the advent of a different National Administration in 1961, the complexion of the Board members changed, and new appointees constituted a Board majority. Since that time, an examination of Board decisions involving key provisions of the Act appears to demonstrate that the Board has disregarded congressional policy. Indeed, within three years after the passage of the Act, Senator Griffin (Republican, of Michigan) then Congressman and chief architect of the Act, decried the Board's "strained and tortured reasoning" and declared that "the pattern of recent decisions by the NLRB gives rise to a serious concern that policies laid down by Congress in the Taft-Hartley and Landrum-Griffin Acts are being distorted and frustrated, to say the very least."

Let us now examine some of these decisions, decisions unfortunately which create new immunities for unions in the exercise of excessive power and have upset the preconditions Congress believed essential to industrial peace and settlements in the national interest.

The first indication of prevailing Board doctrine concerning critical provisions of the Landrum-Griffin Act occurred in 1961 in the *Calumet Contractors Association* case.

As mentioned, one of the prime purposes of the legislation was to circumscribe "blackmail picketing" intended to force an employer to bargain with a union that did not represent a majority of employes, or where another union was certified. The Board, however, engrafted an exception on the prohibition and announced the principle that if a union, although not representing a majority, picketed an employer for alleged "substandard" working conditions, the picketing would be immune from the interdiction of the Act.

The decision, the author of the Act declared, did not "support the intent of Congress" and protected picketing which was "directly contrary to the spirit and the letter of the law."

Shortly thereafter, the Board relaxed the restraints on secondary boycotts.

Legislative history reflects a pattern of increasing congressional concern to protect neutral employers against being enmeshed in labor disputes of others. In keeping with this policy, it had been the rule under the *Washington Coca Cola* doctrine that "common situs picketing" at a construction site which had the effect of stopping work of neutral contractors was illegal if the primary contractor with whom the union had a dispute had a place of business within the area which the union might picket. Unions had made an unsuccessful effort in the 1959 Congress to legalize such picketing, but the new Board in *Plauche Electric Company* reversed the old rule and, in effect, legislated that which Congress had rejected.

Prevailing Board doctrine was highlighted on Feb. 20, 1962, when the Board majority reopened and redecided four cases which had already been decided a year earlier. New members by then having been appointed and not having participated in the earlier decisions, they reopened the cases assertedly "to avoid the criticism" that they were not "adequately interpreted" the first time, an assertion hardly borne out by the record of study and consideration previously given to the issues involved.

Nevertheless, the new Board majority then proceeded to reverse two of the four cases outright in favor of unions and diluted the remaining two by allowing broad exceptions to the statutory prohibitions against recognition picketing.

These decisions extended to unions, according to Congressman Griffin, an "astounding invitation to circumvent the law."

The decisions, it may be added, also placed the imprimatur of the Government on the exercise of unjustified raw power to obtain recognition, and encouraged a disregard of the peaceful election procedures set out in the law to determine questions of representation.

The pattern enunciated by the Board in the earlier decisions has been but the prologue to other decisions which have consistently relaxed the legal restraint on the exercise of union power.

Since then, the already emasculated provision on recognition picketing was further diluted by reducing its coverage to exclude picketing by a union which may have lost its majority, and it applied the restriction, if at all, to a union which was seeking to force an employer's "initial acceptance" of the union as bargaining representative, a distinction not found in the language of the Act.

The new direction of the Board appears in other areas also. The Board has determined that bargaining units of employes may be established when they appear to be based on the ability of unions to organize rather than on other relevant criteria, a means by which the success of unionization can almost be assured. A public officer, for example, can always win in a district gerrymandered to include only his own supporters. Past precedents have been disregarded in establishing bargaining units for insurance agents, for chain stores and department stores.

The Board has limited employer "free-speech discussions" with employes, although the discussions contain no "threat of reprisal or promise of benefit" as the Act would otherwise seem to permit.

The Board has required employers to bargain with unions even though they may not truly represent the employes, indeed where employes may have rejected the union in an election.

As "proof" of union majority, the Board relies on union authorization cards, often secured by misrepresentation and pressures. The practice is still followed by the Board, although roundly condemned by a number of federal courts which have had occasion to review Board action.

One court observed, for example, that the Board does not give as "pervasive effect to union unfair-labor practices in consideration of union cards as it imposes on the company."

Another federal court commented that the Board's practice in requiring bargaining without an election was "strong medicine" and a palliative which the Board should not so easily apply, since it imposed on employes a bargaining representative not of their own choosing, contrary to the purposes and policy of the Act.

And still another federal court declared, with respect to the Board's tendency to find a union majority by reliance upon reliable authorization cards, "that the cards partake too strongly 'of the fine-print' clauses in contracts" and that it was not necessary for the Board to "condone chicanery" in order to effectuate the policies of the Act.

In spite of court reversals and critical language of the courts, the Board still adheres to the new doctrines. It is able to do so because it considers itself not bound by the decisions of courts of appeal and because, under the provisions of the Act, the Board is given wide latitude in making its findings of fact and in fashioning remedies. The courts defer to the so-called expertise of the Board.

The pattern of advancing union power reappears in the doctrine of "codetermination," an intrusion into fields which had always been regarded as subject to exclusive management decision.

Before 1961, it was held that the employer's duty to bargain concerned only the consequences of a management decision affecting employes' working conditions, but that there was no duty to bargain on the management decision itself.

The Board, however, in 1962 established the doctrine that the law required an employer to bargain about the decision itself. This principle was first established in cases involving subcontracting. And, since that time, the Board has expanded the theory to encompass management decisions to automate operations, to close a plant and cease business because of economic conditions, to terminate the sole remaining operation in a particular area after a loss of business, and to sell all or part of a business.

Moreover, once the union has been selected as a bargaining representative, the Board appears now to give it a permanency not contemplated by the Act.

The Board, in still another new doctrine, overruled a precedent of some 17 years' standing and severely restricted the employer's right to challenge a union's representation status, even though the employer may have had good-faith doubt as to the union's continuing majority. This notwithstanding what appears to be clear provisions of the Act in section 9(c) (1) (B), which were enacted to give relief to employers against union claims for recognition when they have reasonable grounds for believing that a union making a claim is not the choice of the employes.

These reversals and modifications of previous Board decisions—many of them of long precedent—give us pause, since it appears that in every case, without exception, the new doctrine has resulted in the increase of union power and corresponding diminution of an employer's ability to resist such power.

It is of serious concern, because, as the court of appeals observed in *Fleetwood Trailer Company,* it is "difficult to approve the Board's cavalier use of precedent when it desires to follow it, and disregard of it when it wishes to achieve a different result."

These new doctrines, there can be little doubt, have undoubtedly contributed to the tilting of the power balance in favor of organized labor.

One now discerns a disturbing tendency by the Board to dictate the bargain for the parties. Our labor laws, the Supreme Court declared in the *Jones & Laughlin Steel Corp.* case, do not "compel agreements" between employers and employes. The Act itself states that the duty to bargain does not compel "either party to agree" or to "require the making of a concession."

Recent cases appear to illustrate, however, that the Board may consider refusals of employers to agree to union proposals or to make concessions the basis for finding unfair labor practices. This is what the Board held in the *General Electric* case, when it found that "a 'fair and firm offer' to the unions without holding anything back for later trading or compromising" was an unfair labor practice.

More recently, in the *Roanoke Iron* case, a Board majority ordered that an employer incorporate a checkoff clause into its labor contract with the union. Within the same area, the Board has undertaken to interpret labor contracts, finding unfair labor practices if an employer allegedly misinterpreted the contract even when the issue is covered by arbitration. The contract is thus construed by the Board, not the parties, and would appear to directly contravene the freedom in bargaining which our labor legislation seeks to promote. With respect to this, in the *C & C Plywood* case, the federal court reversed the Board with this admonition:

"It seems to us that what the Board has done under the guise of remedying unfair labor practices is an attempt to bestow . . . benefits which it believes the union should have obtained but failed to obtain . . . as a result of collective bargaining with the company."

Here again, Board decisional doctrine has enhanced the over-all power of unions, weakened management's authority, and unsettled the balance legislated by Congress.

Board decisions, moreover, have not been confined to the relationship of the union vis-a-vis the employer. They also include union control over members and increased union domination so that the exercise of its power cannot be diluted by dissidents. Thus, Board decisions now permit union fines for employes who exceed union-prescribed production quotas, or if the employe voluntarily chooses to cross a picket line or seeks to decertify the union. In the matter of strikes and lockouts, that critical phase of a bargaining situation where an impasse has been reached and the assertion of economic power by one party against the other is most effective, the Board has circumscribed even the limited right of employers to lock out, in contrast to the unlimited right of the union to strike, in negotiations.

While the Board has, in some cases, been reversed on appeal, Board decisions, nevertheless, are demonstrative of the Board's proclivity to upset the equality in the bargaining relationship which Congress sought to achieve.

For example, in the *American Ship Bldg. Co.* case, the Board held an employer guilty of an unfair labor practice when it locked out to enhance its bargaining position after an impasse in negotiations.

Reversing, the Supreme Court said that the Board "construes its functions too expansively" and that its decision was "fundamentally inconsistent with the structure of the Act."

In the *John Brown* case, one of five retail food operators of a multi-employer bargaining unit was struck, in keeping with a right long ago recognized by the Supreme Court in *Buffalo Linen Supply*. The other employers locked out to prevent the union's whipsawing tactic, a tactic employed to divide the employers and to destroy the integrity of the bargaining unit. But the Board held the lockout was illegal. The court of appeals, reversing, noted that it was not "common sense" for the Board to require employers to "aid and abet the success of a whipsaw strike."

In *Hawaiian Meat* and *Abbott Publishing Co.*, the Board held it was illegal for an employer to subcontract out work to maintain customer business during a strike. In reversing, the court called it a "startling doctrine" for the Board "to tell companies and employers faced with extinction because of a strike that, before they can make economic business decisions to contract out work in order to continue operations, they must first consult the union that caused the threat of extinction."

Despite jurisdictional pronouncements, however, the Board seems bent on whittling away the lockout powers of employers, finding subtle distinctions in differing factual circumstances.

In *David Friedland Painting Co.*, an employer in the construction business who operated in the territorial jurisdiction of one local union locked out employes in another area who were members of a sister local that was on strike against an employer association where the employer also performed work. The Board held the lockout unlawful and said that the fact that the employer had an economic interest in the outcome was insufficient justification for a lockout.

In contrast, in *TV & Radio Artists,* decided about two months later, the Board rationale accommodated the union conduct where the "shoe was on the other foot." In approving an otherwise illegal hot-cargo agreement affecting other unions, the Board said that the union's desire to protect the wage standards of union members working for other employers justified the union action.

The two rationalizations simply are not consistent.

What is the conclusion we draw from the Board's new decisional doctrines? The Board, we submit, has fallen before the temptation to rewrite policies of the body of our national labor law rather than only to interpret it. Our basic labor policies are determined by Congress, to be interpreted and applied by the administrative tribunal "in accordance with its design and purpose."

Congress has established the policy that equality of bargaining power is a condition for collective bargaining to function in the national interest, and it has legislated to that end.

It must be conceded, we believe, that the weight of Board decisions since the passage of the Landrum-Griffin Act, the reversals in precedent and the construction of critical provisions of the law have been on the side of organized labor.

Board decisions, we submit, have thwarted the policy and have upset the equality Congress provided as a condition precedent for collective bargaining to serve in the national interest.

To criticisms of Board decisions, the answer by Board spokesmen that Board decisions are subject to review and can be reversed when inappropriate begs the fundamental issue, because the Board, not the courts, is the tribunal set up to administer our national labor policy.

The Board has been given wide latitude under the Act in making its findings of fact and in fashioning remedies and, while courts may disagree with Board decisions, they are most reluctant to interfere where Board decisions may have support in the record and are not clearly erroneous.

Today, as a result, free collective bargaining is on trial, and the Board, as the chief administrator of our national labor policy, cannot escape the consequences.

Early in 1962, the writer asserted, in an article in "The American Bar Association Journal," that "the present National Labor Relations Board has relied on its own policy rather than congressional policy in interpreting the law." He asserted that our labor statutes were enacted to achieve a balance, but a serious question arises whether our new labor laws, as interpreted, have now miscarried and have resulted in an imbalance in power which may jeopardize free collective bargaining as an instrument of our national labor policy and its workability in the national interest.

Are the consequences of Board decisions now being felt? Have the "chickens come home to roost"? Have the decisions of the Board contributed to industrial strife and strikes against the public welfare? . . .

Amidst the outcry, indignation and demands for remedial legislation, many will suggest that, whatever the cause, the cure lies in such remedies as compulsory arbitration, or "cooling off" periods, or the application of antitrust laws to labor organizations, or to increasing the "arsenal of weapons" available to the Chief Executive.

But we would submit that an area for correction in both the cause and the cure may well lie in the Board's reversal of a policy that has upset the balance of power so essential to make collective bargaining work in the public interest, thereby giving our labor statutes a chance to work as Congress originally intended.

If equality is restored, free collective bargaining may yet be made to work in the national interest without federal controls imposed on a free bargaining process that all—the public, labor and management, and the Congress alike—would abjure. [Copyright 1966 U.S. News & World Report, Inc.]

13   CONTEMPORARY PROBLEMS

One economic problem that probably will always be present to some degree is unemployment. Labor and management offer different reasons for its existence as well as different solutions. Some businessmen may contend that the answer lies in larger profits for business, because increased profits mean more capital for investment and thus more jobs. Increased profits could result from changed fiscal policy as well as other factors.

Labor has offered a solution of shortening the work week from the present 40 hours to 35 hours (eventually to 32 hours), while keeping the weekly wage at its present level, thus increasing the hourly wage. This would be accompanied by a raise in pay for overtime from time and a half to double time. Labor argues that this action would encourage management to hire additional employees to keep production at its present level, instead of working present employees overtime and paying the wage premium.

Other solutions to the economic problems of the country offered by labor are reduction of individual income taxes (in the lower- and middle-income brackets); increases in spending by government on public works to create jobs; and the extension of certain extra benefits to the laboring man, such as unemployment compensation. In addition, the AFL-CIO is seeking less government control of labor's activity in labor-management relations, stating that unless the government actually has taken control of an industry it should have no power to prevent strikes. At the same time, unions are pressing for continued governmental protection of labor's bargaining position. Some unions are steadfastly opposed to any moves by business toward automation and the replacing of men with machines to cut production costs.

Many collective-bargaining disputes are centered on the effects of automation on the labor force, labor arguing that the use of such methods will put many more out of jobs and reduce the domestic market for goods. Business counters that technological development in the past has not only resulted in more skilled jobs, but also was one of the most significant factors in making this country and its citizens relatively more wealthy than all others in the world, because of our consequent ability to produce more goods more cheaply.

Business may suggest that unions be made subject to the antitrust laws while unions request new laws to aid union growth. As our economy becomes more dependent on transportation and communication, demands are made to have compulsory arbitration in the event of strikes in these industries. Change and agitation for change are inherent in labor laws. Government seeks to balance the costs of labor and its productivity as a part of our controlled economy. Labor problems have a direct effect on all. In the article which follows, the author discusses the role which law plays in labor-management relations.

THE ROLE OF LAW IN LABOR RELATIONS [13]
By Francis Bergan [14]

The role law plays in labor relations in essential respects is similar to the role it plays in the vast complex of other relations in the modern community; and what it is able to do to promote good labor relations rests in great measure on the techniques and experience drawn from other areas of legal action. Mainly a legal system seeks to promote public order to the end that men and women can go about their affairs without undue interference from the disruptive outbreak of conflicts of interests which always exist in any vital society.

A good legal system approaches this problem in two ways: (a) it formulates rules and procedures by which controversies can be avoided; (b) when controversies occur, it provides the machinery and techniques by which they can be settled by the intervention of public power often, and traditionally, by enforceable judgments of the courts. The growth of law has been a response to specific needs of the community—often slowly responsive to them—but always evoked by recognized disruptive tendencies which needed regulation and adjudication. . . .

If we look away for the moment from the vast controversies and com-

---

[13] 49 *A.B.A.J.* 652 (July, 1963). Used by permission from the American Bar Association and the *American Bar Association Journal.*
[14] The author is Presiding Justice of the Supreme Court of New York, Appellate Division, Third Department.

petitions which stir the international community, in which the force of law is in so elementary a state as to be almost nonexistent in a prevailing international anarchy, we see within the nation that the most significant and fateful area of controversy in our times is in the field of labor relations.

The disruption of normal co-operation between labor and management, which is the indispensable condition of industrial and commercial health, has destructive consequences of far-reaching importance. The disruption is not only harmful to the people immediately involved and to the community at large, in the sense that all uncontained domestic controversy is harmful to the community, but in industrial controversy direct economic harm follows to numbers of people not involved in the issues of the immediate disputants. The strike, the lockout, the boycott are able to spread their dire consequences in concentric circles, in greater or smaller measure, to affect adversely the lives and welfare of very large numbers of people.

The magnitude and significance of these far-reaching consequences impose on the whole legal profession, on the practicing lawyers who have experience in labor law, on the administrators who deal with industrial controversy, on the specialists in the law schools, as well as on the legislators and the judges, a duty to discover and develop legal techniques by which labor controversies may be avoided or be minimized by fair and adequate adjustment.

We have yet to find techniques which are fully adequate to the purpose, but there is no challenge to the domestic law which is more important to the general welfare. Its solution requires, and should have, the constructive thought and the imaginative and creative response of the best minds and experience in our profession. We are under the strongest professional obligation to formulate and perfect workable legal concepts for the use of the community. Experience and patience and creative imagination may and can make them possible. The problem is at once more difficult to solve and more important to the community than the quarrels of barons over land tenures which evoked the laws of real property, or the business controversies which brought the laws of commercial usage.

For one thing, the usual experience of the law has been that when people have a controversy, get into a lawsuit and one or the other side wins, it is a matter of indifference what their future relations will be. But in a labor controversy two things must be achieved: the immediate argument must be settled and the parties must again be brought into a relation of co-operation. A permanent divorce of the parties to a labor controversy is inadmissible; no matter how bitter the point in controversy, the only possible permanent resolution of it is that the parties must come together again.

Every attempted legal adjudication of an industrial controversy must be made with this in mind, and traditionally we lawyers are not used to this kind of a necessity; of fighting with the ultimate objective of getting the parties again into co-operative harmony. Yet labor wants management to resume business and management wants labor to resume work after the quarrel is over, and essentially this is between them a relationship that cannot be terminated and must continue.

Dean Shulman in an address in 1949 on "The Role of Arbitration in Collective Bargaining," referring to collective bargaining agreements, noted: "Though cast in an adversary position, both (parties) are dependent on their common enterprise. . . . They meet in their contract negotiations to fix the terms and conditions of their collaboration in the future." And Archibald Cox, a noted authority on labor law, has observed: "The parties to collective agreements share a degree of mutual interdependence which we seldom associate with simple contracts. Sooner or later an employer and his employees must strike some kind of a bargain. The costs of disagreement are heavy."

Ideas in law are slow-growing plants. Most of the legal concepts which have been found useful have been forged by lawyers and judges by the adaptation and recasting of older concepts or by transferring techniques from one field to another in a progressive and constructive absorption. This lawyer-method has been of large significance in labor relations. Two of the most useful techniques in avoiding industrial controversy and in adjudicating it have been the contract and arbitration. A great deal of federal and state legislation has been aimed at promoting favorable conditions for the negotiation of contracts and a bargaining process toward the formulation of terms agreed upon in a "collective" sense, which involves some enlargement and development of the lawyer's traditional concept of what a "contract" is.

Yet the contract has been of enormous advantage both to labor and management and it is difficult to conceive of successful labor relations in a modern free state without the successful application of the legal theory of "contract" to these complex relations. As an alternative one can think readily only of direct government intervention to lay down by public power the terms of a relationship which must necessarily continue.

The other legal concept useful in labor controversies has been arbitration; a system of private adjudication, running parallel to the publicly supported adjudications provided by the courts, which historically has been used and seems useful in many kinds of controversies, especially in commercial disputes. The policy of the National War Labor Board during World War II gave large encouragement to arbitration in the settlement of labor controversies.

Experience in labor relations demonstrates these are two highly useful instruments when a basic contract relationship has been evolved. But both these instruments rest on agreement. It is evident that a still unsolved problem of the law of labor relations is what happens when there is no agreement; when the contract that has been operative expires; when a contract covers some of the relations, but a dispute arises beyond the scope of the contract; or when no contractual relationship at all has been formulated. These are areas of vast potential damage to the parties and to the community.

This gap in labor relations law should be, ultimately will be, filled in by the creative contribution of our profession to this field of law. Nothing is clearer, however, than the fact that mere naked prohibition by law against strikes, picketing and boycotts is not a solution for labor controversies. To the extent that modern prohibitions on strikes by law have succeeded at all, they have been suspensions of short duration intended to encourage collective bargaining—a "cooling-off" process designed to gain time and to encourage a solution. Picketing has been restrained in very limited and very special areas often related to an operative collective bargaining agreement.

The absolute prohibitions of strikes by modern penal statutes, as for example the statute directed against strikes by public employees, have failed in their purpose. In practice they are unenforceable by the common processes of the criminal law; those processes are unsuited to that purpose. Even when governments are employers, disputes between labor and management look to ultimate co-operative living and working together. A penal law is not a sensible way to get this result.

Beyond this, it is quite clear that the right to strike and to peaceful picketing are rights widely accepted in the modern democratic community as essential instruments in keeping a fair balance between management and labor and that without some form of power residuum on labor's side negotiation is often futile.

Yet it is obvious that no disciplined and well-run community can allow strikes for long periods to break down and disrupt its life and that in situations of vastly destructive controversy the public law of the community must intervene. A strike which breaks down vital health, food, water, sanitation or transportation service and throttles the very life of the community will not in the nature of things be long endured. By one means or another, often by improvisations, it will be settled.

What solution can we lawyers offer for labor relations which break down and in which there is no enforceable contract? It is at this critical juncture that the alternative seems to be either some form of compulsory arbitration or the making of an arrangement, resembling a contract, binding on the parties.

Both of these ideas run strongly counter to the usual theories of free "contract," but with some modification and adaptation of the contract theory, it seems possibly that the process in labor relations could be carried on somewhat further than has been done thus far.

For example, we lawyers have developed in legal theory a relationship known as a "constructive contract" in which the parties are regarded in law as having made the contract which they ought to have made. And while there is a certain retributive element for a "wrong" in this concept, as indeed there is in so many common-law concepts, it may well have possibilities in the field of labor relations.

If it be constantly borne in mind that the parties to a labor negotiation must agree and that ultimate agreement is always implicit throughout the bargaining process, the law might well construe their relation as though they had actually agreed to a sensible solution measured by some objective standard. This is a new step, but actually not a very long one.

As an example, when the point in dispute is a wage rate, fixed two years ago by agreement which has terminated, the present cost-of-living index in ratio to its standing when the agreement was made could be projected into a constructive contract between the parties, if after reasonable effort they were unable to agree. This kind of "contract" might be neither fair nor practicable between parties who would never agree, but it may have possibilities of usefulness among parties who will and inevitably must agree substantially along the lines of the suggested constructive contract.

It is obvious that no legal concept or new idea can succeed in this area without general acceptance by both labor and industry. The contract concept has been successful because it has been found useful and has been widely accepted by both sides. The arbitration mechanism has succeeded because it has been found similarly useful.

No matter how good in theory the legal idea we lawyers may offer to labor and to industry, a general belief that they are good must exist before they will be accepted. This is quite a different thing from the popularity of any single result. It may well be that one side or the other might dislike a particular solution—this is the common reaction in litigation generally—but regard the general system of solution as being basically sound and acceptable. The vast usefulness of the theory of contract in labor relations gives some hope of its extension to areas where there has been a failure to reach agreement. The criteria to be applied must be objective and fairly ascertainable. The cost-of-living index might be one such criterion; the average wage of similar employment and the tendency of wage changes in the industry over several recent years could be another; the profit in the business fairly allocable to labor could be a third. There should be many more.

The submission to arbitration always, in legal theory, rests on a prior agreement to use it rather than the public method of adjudication. Yet if the constructive-contract theory is acceptable in labor relations, its most useful application may possibly be a constructive contract to arbitrate future controverted issues arising from the labor relationship, with the requirement in this kind of a submission that the arbitrators base their award on objective economic criteria, such as the cost-of-living index.

The advantage of arbitration over an automatic constructive contract, spelling out by objective standards the terms of the relationship, is that it would have greater flexibility, be less mechanistic and afford an important forum in which both sides could be fully heard on the ultimate solution. Because both sides want to and must ultimately agree, this kind of arbitration, a little short of "compulsory" in the sense in which that term has usually been employed, may provide one suitable avenue for development of the law of labor relations.

These, of course, are not full-blown solutions. They are, rather, intimations that we lawyers have not yet exhausted the possibilities of adaptation and development of our traditional experience in the field of labor relationships. It is, indeed, here that the most pressing and fateful needs for legal solutions lie. It is a challenge to our experience in adjudication and in the more important process by which disputes are avoided. And a dynamic professional purpose to solve it would offer hope to the well-being of labor, to industry and to the vast community of which we all are a part.

PART THREE

LAW AND SOCIETY

CHAPTER FIFTEEN

PROPERTY

1 THE NATURE OF PROPERTY

Perhaps no legal concept has been as important in American history and to our cultural and economic development as that of property. As one might expect, the vast majority of statutes and decisions rendered by both the courts and administrative agencies deal in some way with issues involving the ultimate determination of property rights. The term "property" is difficult to define. Its meaning is often indistinguishably tied to other terms such as government, contract, tort, right, or value.

The concept of property is frequently described in terms of ownership, title to and possession of corporeal objects. Ownership has to do with the extent of a person's rights in property and is usually synonymous with title. Title itself is a confusing term because it is frequently associated with a document of title such as that to an automobile. Because of this, people frequently think of title in terms of a document labeled "title." Yet a person usually has "title" to the clothes he wears and to his other property without a document of title. Possession is a term often indicative of physical control or dominion. However, in legal contemplation, possession must be defined in terms of the assistance that the law affords a person in controlling property. For example, it is easy to physically possess a book, but impossible to physically possess a 1,000-acre tract of land. However, one may be in legal possession of a 1,000-acre tract because of sanctions provided by law to keep others out.

A portion of a discussion concerned with the nature of property by Dean Roscoe Pound, one of this country's most eminent legal philosophers, is presented here.[1]

If we examine the law of property analytically we may see three grades or stages in the power or capacity which men have of influencing the acts of others with respect to corporeal objects. One is a mere condition of fact, a mere physical holding of or physical control over the thing without any other element whatever. The Roman jurists called this natural possession. We call it custody. Writers on analytical jurisprudence regard it as an element of

---

[1] Pound, *An Introduction to the Philosophy of Law* 124 (1922). Used by permission from the Yale University Press.

possession. But this natural possession is something that may exist independently of law or of the state, as in the so-called pedis possessio of American mining law, where, before law or state authority had been extended to the public domain in the mining country, the miners recognized the claim of one who was actually digging to dig without molestation at that spot. The mere having of an object in one's actual grasp gives an advantage. But it may be only an advantage depending on one's strength or on recognition of and respect for his personality by his fellow men. It is not a legal advantage except as the law protects personality. It is the physical person of the one in natural possession which is secured, not his relation to the thing held. Analytically the next grade or stage is what the Romanist calls juristic possession as distinguished from natural possession. This is a legal development of the extra-legal idea of custody. Where custody or the ability to reproduce a condition of custody is coupled with the mental element of intention to hold for one's own purposes, the legal order confers on one who so holds a capacity protected and maintained by law so to hold, and a claim to have the thing restored to his immediate physical control should he be deprived of it. As the Romanist puts it, in the case of natural possession the law secures the relation of the physical person to the object; in juristic possession the law secures the relation of the will to the object. In the highest grade of proprietary relation, ownership, the law goes much further and secures to men the exclusive or ultimate enjoyment or control of objects far beyond their capacity either to hold in custody or to possess—that is, beyond what they could hold by physical force and beyond what they could actually hold even by the help of the state. Natural possession is a conception of pure fact in no degree dependent upon law. The legally significant thing is the interest of the natural possessor in his personality. Possession or juristic possession is a conception of fact and law, existing as a pure relation of fact, independent of legal origin but protected and maintained by law without regard to interference with personality. Ownership is a purely legal conception having its origin in and depending on the law.

In general the historical development of the law of property follows the line thus indicated by analysis. In the most primitive social control only natural possession is recognized, and interference with natural possession is not distinguished from interference with the person or injury to the honor of the one whose physical contact with the physical object is meddled with. In the earlier legal social control the all-important thing is seisin, or possession. This is a juristic possession, a conception both of fact and of law. Such institutions as tortious conveyance by the person seised in the common law are numerous in an early stage of legal development. They show that primarily the law protected the relation to an object of one who had possession of it. Indeed the idea of dominium, or ownership as we now understand it, was first worked out thoroughly in Roman law, and other systems got their idea of it, as distinguished from seisin, from the Roman books. . . .

Ownership, the third grade of power described by Pound, encompasses, besides the right to possess corporeal objects, the right to dispose of them in various ways, the right to use and enjoy them, the right to change their nature, and probably the right to destroy them. Pound makes it clear that these rights are creatures of the law which are backed by legal sanctions. Thus, without law, property is nonexistent. While the tendency of most people is to think of property as the thing owned itself, this approach is inaccurate. More correctly, it consists of a bundle of legal rights, such as those listed above, with respect to a thing. This concept of property views it as a series of legal relationships between the owner and all other persons, in which the owner has many rights, and the others, each individually, owe him many duties which are often negative in character. Ownership is further defined by a series of limitations imposed by law on the owner and often carries with it duties owed by the owner to other persons who enjoy the correlative rights. The nature of some of these restrictions and duties is discussed in section 7. Viewed in this manner, technically all property is intangible, consisting of specific legal rights and duties, but may exist *with regard to* a physical, tangible object. Nevertheless, it is generally accepted in legal terminology to refer to the property rights associated with corporeal things as being tangible property.

The reader is familiar with some of the more common rights which are attendant with ownership. Clearly, the owner of farm land generally has the right to sow crops on it, harvest them, sell them and keep the proceeds for his own use. (Unless, of course, he has contracted that right away by leasing the land to a tenant.) Also, the owner of a farm has the right, as a rule, to sell it and then use the proceeds of sale as he sees fit. And, by a properly executed will, he can, subject to some limitations, dispose of the farm on his death as he wishes. Fundamental to the concept of property are the rights to exclude others from its possession and use. Besides the foregoing, ownership may carry with it other rights which are not nearly so obvious. The cases which follow in this section are merely illustrative of the complex nature of the "bundle of rights" which is property. They indicate some of the meanings of ownership, and its significance and extent.

IN RE FORSSTROM
38 P.2d 878 (Ariz. 1934)

LOCKWOOD, JUSTICE: . . . The question is solely one of law, and the facts may be briefly stated as follows: The main tracks of the Southern Pacific Railroad cross North Stone Avenue near an intersection of Sixth Street at the present grade of said Avenue. The authorities of the City of Tucson, believing that such grade crossing is a menace and hazard to public travel on the street determined to abolish it by the construction of an underpass or subway below the tracks. . . . [If this is done] ingress and egress to the premises of the abutting property owners will be made more difficult. . . .

We come then to the question as to whether the proposed action of the City of Tucson, in so far as it affects petitioners at all, is a "taking" [of property]. . . .

In order that we may understand the better what is meant by a "taking" of property, we should have a clear knowledge of what property really is. The word is used at different times to express many varying ideas. Sometimes it is taken in common parlance to denote a physical object, as where one says an automobile or a horse is his property. On careful consideration, however, it is plain that "property" in the true and legal sense does not mean a physical object itself, but certain rights over the object. A piece of land in an unexplored and uninhabited region which belongs to no one does not necessarily undergo any physical change merely by reason of its later becoming the property of any person. A wild animal may be exactly the same physically before and after it is captured, but, when it is running free in the forest, no one would speak of it as property. We must therefore look beyond the physical object itself for the true definition of property. Many courts and writers have attempted to define it, using different words, but meaning in essence the same thing. One of the great writers on jurisprudence says:

> *Property is entirely the creature of the law. . . . There is no form, or color, or visible trace, by which it is possible to express the relation which constitutes property. It belongs not to physics, but to metaphysics; it is altogether a creature of the mind. Bentham: Works (Ed. 1843) Vol. 1, p. 308.*

[Others have said:]

> *. . . Property itself, in a legal sense, is nothing more than the "exclusive right of possession, enjoying and disposing of a thing.". . .*

> *Property, in its broader and more appropriate sense, is not alone the chattel or the land itself, but the right to freely possess, use, and alienate the same; and many things are considered property which have no tangible existence, but which are necessary to the satisfactory use and enjoyment of that which is tangible. . . .*

> *It is used in the constitution in a comprehensive and unlimited sense, and so it must be construed. . . . It need not be any physical or tangible property which is subject to a tangible invasion. . . . The right to light and air, and access is equally property. . . .*

It would follow from these definitions and explanations of the meaning of the term "property" that since it consists, not in tangible things themselves, but in certain rights in and appurtenant to them, it would logically follow that, when a person is deprived of any of these rights, he is to that extent deprived of his property, and that it is taken in the true sense, although his title and possession of the physical object remains undisturbed. Any substantial interference, therefore, with rights over a physical object which destroys or lessens its value, or by which the use and enjoyment thereof by its owner is in any substantial degree abridged or destroyed, is both in law and in fact a "taking" of property. It is apparently only of recent years that the meaning of the word "taking" when used in regard to eminent domain has been properly understood by the majority of the courts, although it would seem obvious that a careful analysis of the true nature of "property" would have shown it long since. . . .

[In one of the leading cases it was said:]

From the very nature of these rights of user and of exclusion, it is evident that they cannot be materially abridged without, ipso facto, taking the owner's property. If the right of indefinite user is an essential element of absolute property or complete ownership, whatever physical interference annuls this right takes "property"—although the owner may still have left to him valuable rights (in the article) of a more limited and circumscribed nature. He has not the same property that he formerly had. Then, he had an unlimited right; now, he has only a limited right. His absolute ownership has been reduced to a qualified ownership. Restricting A's unlimited right of using one hundred acres of land to a limited right of using the same land, may work a far greater injury to A than to take from him the title in fee simple to one acre, leaving him the unrestricted right of using the remaining ninety-nine acres. Nobody doubts that the latter transaction would constitute a "taking" of property. Why not the former? . . .

[In another case, the court stated:]

Property in land must be considered, for many purposes, not as an absolute, unrestricted dominion, but as an aggregation of qualified privileges, the limits of which are prescribed by the equality of rights, and the correlation of rights and obligations necessary for the highest enjoyment of land by the entire community of proprietors. . . .

. . . [T]he changing of the street grade which lessens the enjoyment of the easement of ingress and egress is within the true meaning of the constitutional provision a taking of property. . . .

SOUTHWEST WEATHER RESEARCH V. ROUNSAVILLE
320 S.W.2d 211 (Tex. Civ. App. 1958) [2]

PER CURIAM: This is an appeal from an injunction issued by the Eighty-third District Court, Jeff Davis County, Texas, which said injunction commands

[2] Affirmed, 327 S.W.2d 417 (1959).

the appellants "to refrain from seeding the clouds by artificial nucleation or otherwise and from in any other manner or way interfering with the clouds and the natural conditions of the air, sky, atmosphere and air space over plaintiff's lands and in the area of plaintiffs' lands to in any manner, degree or way affect, control or modify the weather conditions on or about said lands. . . ."

Appellees are ranchmen residing in West Texas counties, and appellants are owners and operators of certain airplanes, and equipment generally used in what they call a "weather modification program" and those who contracted and arranged for their services.

It is not disputed that appellants did operate their airplanes at various times over portions of lands belonging to the appellees, for the purpose of and while engaged in what is commonly called "cloud seeding." Appellants do not deny having done this, and testified through the president of the company that the operation would continue unless restrained. He stated, "We seeded the clouds to attempt to suppress the hail." The controversy is really over appellants' right to seed clouds or otherwise modify weather conditions over appellees' property. . . .

We have carefully considered the voluminous record and exhibits that were admitted in evidence, and have concluded that the trial court had ample evidence on which to base his findings and with which to justify the issuance of the injunction. . . .

Appellants maintain that appellees have no right to prevent them from flying over appellees' lands; that no one owns the clouds unless it be the state, and that the trial court was without legal right to restrain appellants from pursuing a lawful occupation; also that the injunction is too broad in its terms. . . .

Appellees urge here that the owner of land also owns in connection therewith certain so-called "natural rights," and cites us the following quotation in which Chief Justice Nelson Phillips states:

Property in a thing consists not merely in its ownership and possession, but in the unrestricted right of use, enjoyment and disposal. Anything which destroys any of these elements of property, to that extent destroys the property itself. The substantial value of property lies in its use. If the right of use be denied, the value of the property is annihilated and ownership is rendered a barren right. . . .

The very essence of American constitutions is that the material rights of no man shall be subject to the mere will of another.

In Volume 34, *Marquette Law Review*, at page 275, this is said:

Considering the property right of every man to the use and enjoyment of his land, and considering the profound effect which natural rainfall has upon the realization of this right, it would appear that the benefits of natural rainfall should come within the scope of judicial protection, and a duty should be imposed on adjoining landowners not to interfere therewith.

In the Stanford Law Review, November 1948, Volume 1, in an article entitled, "Who Owns the Clouds?", the following statements occur:

The landowner does have rights in the water in clouds, however, the basis for these rights is the common law doctrine of natural rights. Literally, the term "natural rights" is well chosen; these rights protect the landowner's use of his land in its natural condition. . . .

All forms of natural precipitation should be elements of the natural condition of the land. Precipitation, like air, oxygen, sunlight, and the soil itself, is an essential to many reasonable uses of the land. The plant and animal life on the land are both ultimately dependent upon rainfall. To the extent that rain is important to the use of land, the landowner should be entitled to the natural rainfall.

In California Law Review, December 1957, Volume 45, No. 5, in an article, "Weather Modification," are found the following statements:

What are the rights of the landowner or public today to natural rainfall? It has been suggested that the right to receive rainfall is one of those "natural rights" which is inherent in the full use of land from the fact of its natural contact with moisture in the air. . . .

Any use of such air or space by others which is injurious to his land, or which constitutes an actual interference with his possession or his beneficial use thereof would be a tresspass for which he would have remedy.

Appellees call our attention to various authorities that hold that although the old *ad coelum* doctrine has given way to the reality of present day conditions, an unreasonable and improper use of the air space over the owner's land can constitute a trespass. Other cases . . . apparently hold that the landowner, while not owning or controlling the entire air space over his property, is entitled to protection against improper or unreasonable use thereof or entrance thereon. . . .

We believe that under our system of government the landowner is entitled to such precipitation as nature deigns to bestow. We believe that the landowner is entitled, therefore and thereby, to such rainfall as may come from clouds over his own property that nature in her caprice may provide. It follows, therefore, that this enjoyment of or entitlement to the benefits of nature should be protected by the courts if interfered with improperly and unlawfully. [ORDER GRANTING INJUNCTION AFFIRMED]

STATE HIGHWAY DEP'T V. BRANCH
152 S.E.2d 372 (Ga. 1966)

This case is an equitable action brought by a property owner and a lessee of his property as individuals and as members of a class of persons similarly situated to enjoin the State Highway Department and certain named state officials from removing certain outdoor signs on petitioner's property adjoining a United States Interstate Highway, which the defendants have threatened to do under the authority of the Georgia Outdoor Advertising Control Act of 1964 (Ga.L. 1964, p. 128, Sec. 12 et seq.). The petitioners allege that (1) their property is not subject to the Act and (2) the law (Secs. 12 and 13 (c), supra) under which the State officials intend to act is unconstitutional, null, and void in violation of Article I, Section X, of the State Constitution and the Fifth and Fourteenth Amendments of the United States Constitution, by attempting to exercise the power of eminent domain without provision for the payment of just and adequate compensation, without due process of law, and impairing the obligations of contracts. The prayers are for equitable relief and the declaration that Sections 12 and 13(c) of Ga.L. 1964, p. 128, be declared unconstitutional and void. General and special demurrers were filed thereto, and after a hearing certain of the general demurrers were overruled. The appeal is from this ruling.

DUCKWORTH, JUSTICE: The enactment of the so-called Outdoor Advertising Control Act (Ga.L. 1964, p. 128) was purely a legislative exercise in futility. Its sole purpose is to dictate, control and limit uses of private property for public purpose, without a semblance of provision for first paying for such taking or damaging. Anyone able and willing to read the Fifth Amendment (Code § 1-805), which provides "nor shall private property be taken for public use, without just compensation," the Fourteenth Amendment (Code § 1-815) which provides, "nor shall any State deprive any person of life, liberty, or property, without due process," and our own State Constitution, Art. I, Sec. III, Par. I, which provides that "[p]rivate property shall not be taken, or damaged, for public purposes, without just and adequate compensation being first paid," would know beyond possible doubt that the 1964 Act is a bold and brazen violation of each of these constitutional clauses.

Decisions of this court leave no room for reasonable doubt that the Constitutions stand as a bar to any invasion of those constitutional rights. It is inexcusable in light of these constitutional protections of private property and decisions of this court showing that legislation seeking to do so would be stricken down, to enact the 1964 Act which is thus foredoomed.

As pointed out in the brief of appellees, the Congress, which is not noted for observing constitutional safeguards of private property, amended the federal statute—in conformity to which the Georgia act was enacted—so as to cause it to provide that "just compensation" be paid for the removal of advertisements forbidden by the Act, and provides for the federal government to pay 75% of such costs. 23 U.S.C.A. § 131(g). By the 1964 Act, the Georgia legislature attempted to destroy private property, although as amended, the federal law requires the federal government to pay three-fourths of the damage suffered by the property owners. Georgia courts, to their eternal credit, have never allowed taking or damaging private property without first paying therefor, and this court stands ready to strike down this legislative attempt to do so.

We believe this matter is important enough to justify the following observations. Private property is the antithesis of Socialism or Communism. Indeed, it is an insuperable barrier to the establishment of either collective system of government. Too often, as in this case, the desire of the average citizen to secure the blessings of a good thing like beautification of our highways, and their safety, blinds them to a consideration of the property owner's right to be saved from harm by even the government. The thought-less, the irresponsible, and the misguided will likely say that this court has blocked the effort to beautify and render our highways safer. But the actual truth is that we have only protected constitutional rights by condemning the unconstitutional method to attain such desirable ends, and to empha-size that there is a perfect constitutional way which must be employed for that purpose. Those whose ox is not being gored by this Act might be impatient and complain of this decision, but if this court yielded to them and sanctioned this violation of the Constitution we would thereby set a precedent whereby tomorrow when the critics are having their own ox gored, we would be bound to refuse them any protection. Our decisions are not just good for today but they are equally valid tomorrow.

We have gone to the heart of this case and decided the constitutional issue without being side-tracked by trivial incidental issues, thus putting an end to this case. For the reasons above stated, the 1964 Act is uncon-stitutional, and the judgment below is affirmed.

Judgment affirmed.

All the Justices concur.

PITTSBURGH ATHLETIC CO. V. KQV BROADCASTING CO.
24 F. Supp. 490 (1938)

SCHOONMAKER, DISTRICT JUDGE: This is an action in equity in which plaintiffs ask for a preliminary injunction to restrain defendant from broadcasting play-by-play reports and descriptions of baseball games played by the "Pirates," a professional baseball team owned by Pittsburgh Athletic Com-pany, both at its home baseball park in Pittsburgh, known as "Forbes Field," and at baseball parks in other cities. . . .

The essential facts are not in dispute. The question at issue is pri-

marily a question of law. Is the defendant within its legal rights in the practices thus pursued by it? The essential facts of the case may be briefly
summarized as follows:

The plaintiff Pittsburgh Athletic Company owns a professional baseball team known as the "Pirates," and is a member of an association known
as the "National League." With the several teams of the members of the
League, the "Pirates" play baseball both at its home field and at the home
fields of the other members of the League in various cities. The home games
are played at a baseball park known as "Forbes Field" which is enclosed
by high fences and structures so that the public are admitted only to the
Park to witness the games at Forbes Field by the payment of an admission
ticket, which provides that the holder of the admission ticket agrees not to
give out any news of the game while it is in progress.

The Pittsburgh Athletic Company has granted by written contract for
a valuable consideration, to General Mills, Inc., the exclusive right to broadcast, play-by-play, descriptions or accounts of the games played by the
"Pirates" at this and other fields. The National Broadcasting Company, also
for a valuable consideration, has contracted with General Mills, Inc., to
broadcast by radio over stations KDKA and WWSW, play-by-play descriptions of these games. The Socony-Vacuum Oil Company has purchased for
a valuable consideration a half interest in the contract of the General Mills,
Inc.

The defendant operates at Pittsburgh a radio broadcasting station
known as KQV, from which it has in the past broadcast by radio play-by-
play descriptions of the games played by the "Pirates" at Pittsburgh, and
asserts its intention to continue in so doing. The defendant secures the
information which it broadcasts from its own paid observers whom it stations at vantage points outside Forbes Field on premises leased by defendant. These vantage points are so located that the defendant's observers can
see over the enclosures the games as they are played in Forbes Field.

On this state of facts, we are of the opinion that the plaintiffs have
presented a case which entitles them under the law to a preliminary injunction.

It is perfectly clear that the exclusive right to broadcast play-by-play
descriptions of the games played by the "Pirates" at their home field rests
in the plaintiffs, General Mills, Inc., and the Socony-Vacuum Oil Company
under the contract with the Pittsburgh Athletic Company. That is a property
right of the plaintiffs with which defendant is interfering when it broadcasts
the play-by-play description of the ball games obtained by the observers on
the outside of the enclosure.

The plaintiffs and the defendant are using baseball news as material
for profit. The Athletic Company has, at great expense, acquired and maintains a baseball park, pays the players who participate in the game, and
have, as we view it, a legitimate right to capitalize on the news value of

their games by selling exclusive broadcasting rights to companies which value them as affording advertising mediums for their merchandise. This right the defendant interferes with when it uses its broadcasting facilities for giving out the identical news obtained by its paid observers stationed at points outside Forbes Field for the purpose of securing information which it cannot otherwise acquire. This, in our judgment, amounts to unfair competition, and is a violation of the property rights of the plaintiffs. For it is our opinion that the Pittsburgh Athletic Company, by reason of its creation of the game, its control of the park, and its restriction of the dissemination of news therefrom, has a property right in such news, and the right to control the use thereof for a reasonable time following the games.

The communication of news of the ball games by the Pittsburgh Athletic Company, or by its licensed news agencies, is not a general publication and does not destroy that right. This view is supported by the so-called "ticker cases."

On the unfair competition feature of the case, we rest our opinion on the case of *International News Serv. v. Associated Press*, 248 U.S. 215. In that case the court enjoined the International News Service from copying news from bulletin boards and early editions of Associated Press newspapers, and selling such news so long as it had commercial value to the Associated Press. The Supreme Court said:

. . . *Regarding the news, therefore, as but the material out of which both parties are seeking to make profits at the same time and in the same field, we hardly can fail to recognize that for this purpose, and as between them, it must be regarded as quasi property, irrespective of the rights of either as against the public.*

In order to sustain the jurisdiction of equity over the controversy, we need not affirm any general and absolute property in the news as such. The rule that a court of equity concerns itself only in the protection of property rights treats any civil right of a pecuniary nature as a property right; and the right to acquire property by honest labor or the conduct of a lawful business is as much entitled to protection as the right to guard property already acquired. . . .

. . . *The right of the purchaser of a single newspaper to spread knowledge of its contents gratuitously, for any legitimate purpose not unreasonably interfering with the complainant's right to make merchandise of it, may be admitted; but to transmit that news for commercial use, in competition with complainant—which is what defendant has done and seeks to justify—is a very different matter. . . .*

In *Twentieth Century Sporting Club, Inc., v. Transradio Press Serv., Inc.*, 165 Misc. 71, 300 N.Y.S. 159, the New York Supreme Court applied the principles of unfair competition to a broadcast of the Louis-Farr fight and entered an injunction.

In *Associated Press v. KVOS, Inc.*, 9 Cir., 80 F.2d 575, a preliminary injunction was granted to restrain Station KVOS from appropriating and broadcasting news gathered by the Associated Press on the ground that the broadcasting station was in competition with the Associated Press in the business of publication of news for profit.

Defendant contends it is not unfairly competing with any of the plaintiffs because it obtains no compensation from a sponsor or otherwise from its baseball broadcasts. It concedes, however, that KQV seeks by its broadcast of news of baseball games to cultivate the good will of the public for its radio station. The fact that no revenue is obtained directly from the broadcast is not controlling, as these broadcasts are undoubtedly designed to aid in obtaining advertising business.

Defendant seeks to justify its action on the ground that the information it receives from its observers stationed on its own property without trespassing on plaintiffs' property, may be lawfully broadcast by it. We cannot follow defendant's counsel in this contention for the reasons above stated. The cases cited by them we have carefully studied and are unable to accept as authority. . . .

CONCLUSIONS OF LAW

1 This Court has jurisdiction of this cause by reason of diversity of citizenship and the amount in controversy.

2 The right, title and interest in and to the baseball games played within the parks of members of the National League, including Pittsburgh, including the property right in, and the sole right, of disseminating or publishing or selling, or licensing the right to disseminate, news, reports, descriptions, or accounts of games played in such parks, during the playing thereof, is vested exclusively in such members.

3 The actions and threatened actions of the defendant constitute a direct and irreparable interference with, and an appropriation of, the plaintiffs' normal and legitimate business; and said action is calculated to, and does, result in the unjust enrichment of the defendant at the expense of the plaintiffs and each of them.

4 The defendant's unauthorized broadcasts of information concerning games played by the Pittsburgh team constitute unfair competition with the plaintiffs and each of them.

5 The defendant wrongfully deprives the plaintiffs and each of them of the just benefits of their labors and expenditures in respect of the baseball games and the public dissemination of news thereof as alleged in the complaint; and the action, threatened action and practice of the defendant constitute a fraud on the public.

6   The actions and threatened actions of the defendant herein alleged constitute a wrongful interference with the contractual rights and obligations of the parties.

7   The defendant's action as herein described constitutes a violation of the Communications Act of 1934, 47 U.S.C.A. § 151 et seq.

8   The plaintiffs have no adequate remedy at law.

9   The plaintiffs are entitled to and are hereby granted a preliminary injunction. [INJUNCTION GRANTED]

Property is usually classified, according to the nature of the subject matter which is owned, as real or personal property and as tangible or intangible property. Real property is land or any interest in land and includes things permanently attached thereto, such as timber and buildings, which are called fixtures. Personal property encompasses chattels or things such as livestock, an automobile, clothing, or a television set. These and real property are referred to as tangible property because the subject matter of the ownership has physical existence (even though as noted above the bundle of rights which is in reality the "property" is intangible). Personal property also includes intangible property such as stocks, bonds, accounts receivable, and patent rights. Frequently intangible property is associated with a document such as a stock certificate. The document itself is not the property interest, or rights owned, but merely evidence of them. Even if the document is destroyed the property may still exist. A good example of intangible personal property was given in the *Pittsburgh Athletic Co.* case above.

The terms real and personal in describing property originated because of early English common law procedures in which certain suits were described as "real" because they were brought to recover possession of the *res* or thing itself. Other suits were designated "personal" because they could be brought against the person of the defendant only for the remedy of money damages, rather than possession of the property. Thus, one can personally own both land and chattels. Likewise, some items of personal property are just as real in the sense of having tangible existence as real property is. Some people argue that a third category may exist called mixed property, or a chattel-real, because of the nature of the suit which is brought to enforce the rights involved. This distinction would appear to have decreasing significance today, and, for all practical purposes, all property rights not involving real estate can be classified generally as personal property. As a matter of fact, the reasons for distinguishing between these two classes of property are gradually disappearing. For example, the rights of relatives or a surviving spouse to property on the death of the owner often have differed depending on whether the property was real or personal. However, movements have been under way to abolish this distinction and some states have done so in their statutes governing the descent and distribution of property.

2   IMPORTANCE OF THE LEGAL CONCEPT OF PROPERTY

The entire social, political, and economic structure of a nation or state to a large degree both depends upon and is reflected in its laws governing ownership of property. The nature of the recognized rights of private individuals in property and the extent to which they are given sanction by the appropriate agencies of the government determine such things as: the nature of the social order, which may range from one in which the rights of the individual are highly valued and held supreme, to one in which these are always sacrificed for the benefit of the state or group; the form of the economic system, which may range all the way from laissez faire to some form of socialist-communistic; and, as shaped by the foregoing, the freedom of individuals in the society generally to act as they please without interference from the state. Clearly the ability to obtain and wield economic power is closely intertwined with political control. As society's attitudes and needs change, so to some degree does the law of property. Dean Roscoe Pound illustrates the spirit of "recent ethics, recent philosophy and recent political thought," by discussing several "noteworthy changes in the law." [3] Quoted here is one of Pound's illustrations dealing with changes in the law of property:

First among these we may note limitations on the use of property, attempts to prevent anti-social exercise of the incidents of ownership. At this point judicial decision has been the agency of progress. This is no time or place for details. I need only refer to the gradual but steady change of front in our case law with respect to the so-called spite fence, and to the establishment in American case law of doctrines with respect to percolating water and to surface water, in which a principle of reasonable use has superseded the old and narrow idea that the owner of the surface might do as he pleased. In this growing tendency of the law to impose limitations on the use of property, especially limitations designed to prevent what the French call "abusive exercise of rights," there is a suggestive parallel between the period of legal development on which we have entered and the earlier period of liberalization which I have called the stage of equity or natural law. Equity sought to prevent the unconscientious exercise of legal rights; today we seek to prevent the anti-social exercise of them. Equity imposed moral limitations; the law of today is imposing social limitations. It is endeavoring to delimit the individual

[3] Pound, *The Spirit of the Common Law* 185, 186 (1921), Beacon Press paperback edition. Used by permission from Marshall Jones Co.

interest better with respect to social interests and to confine the legal right to the bounds of the interest so delimited. More and more the tendency is to hold that what the law should secure is satisfaction of the owner's reasonable wants with respect to the property—that is those which consist with the like wants of his neighbors and the interests of society.

Changes in American law such as the one above indicate that, in the twentieth century, it has entered into a new stage of development which Pound calls "a stage of socialization of law." Explaining his meaning for this term, Pound continues: [4]

For in contrast with the nineteenth century it [law] appears to put the emphasis upon social interests; upon the demands or claims or desires involved in social life rather than upon the qualities of the abstract man in vacuo or upon the freedom of will of the isolated individual. . . . Let us put the new point of view in terms of engineering; let us speak of a change from a political or ethical idealistic interpretation to an engineering interpretation. Let us think of the problem of the end of law in terms of a great task or great series of tasks of social engineering. Let us say that the change consists in thinking not of an abstract harmonizing of human wills but of a concrete securing or realizing of human interests. From an earthly standpoint the central tragedy of existence is that there are not enough of the material goods of existence, as it were, to go round; that while individual claims and wants and desires are infinite, the material means of satisfying them are finite; that while, in common phrase, we all want the earth, there are many of us but there is only one earth. Thus we may think of the task of the legal order as one of precluding friction and eliminating waste; as one of conserving the goods of existence in order to make them go as far as possible, and of precluding friction and eliminating waste in the human use and enjoyment of them, so that where each may not have all that he claims, he may at least have all that is possible. Put in this way, we are seeking to secure as much of human claims and desires—that is as much of the whole scheme of interests—as possible, with the least sacrifice of such interests."

In applying his "engineering interpretation" to the change in law concerning the growth of limitations on the use of property, Pound states: [5]

. . . To the nineteenth-century way of thinking the question was simply one of the right of the owner and of the right of his neighbor. Within his physical boundaries the dominion of each was complete. So long as he kept within them and what he did within them was consistent with an equally absolute dominion of the neighbor within his boundaries, the law was to keep

4 *Id.* at 195, 196.
5 *Id.* at 196–198.

its hands off. For the end of law was taken to be a maximum of self-assertion by each, limited only by the possibility of a like self-assertion by all. If, therefore, he built a fence eight feet high cutting off light and air from his neighbor and painted the fence on the side toward his neighbor in stripes of hideous colors, this was consistent with his neighbor's doing the same; it was an exercise of his incidental jus utendi, *and the mere circumstance that he did it out of unmixed malice was quite immaterial since it in no way infringed the liberty or invaded the property of the neighbor. But suppose we think of law not negatively as a system of hands off while individuals assert themselves freely, but positively as a social institution existing for social ends. Thinking thus, what claims or demands or wants of society are involved in such a controversy? There is an individual interest of substance on the part of each. Each asserts a claim to use, enjoy and get the benefit of the land of which the law recognizes him as the owner. Also the one asserts an individual interest of personality, a claim to exert his will and exercise his faculties freely and hence to employ them in such building operations upon his land as he thinks proper. What shall society say to these claims? If we think in terms of social interests and of giving effect to individual claims to the extent that they coincide with or may be identified with a social interest, we shall say that there is a social interest in the security of acquisitions, on which our economic order rests, and a social interest in the individual life. But that security of acquisitions is satisfied by use of property for the satisfaction of wants of the owner which are consistent with social life; or at least it is not seriously impaired by so limiting it in order to give effect to other wants which are consistent with social life. And the individual life, in which there is a social interest, is a moral and social life. Hence the social interest does not extend to exercise of individual faculties for anti-social purposes of gratifying malice. The moment we put the matter in terms of social life rather than of abstract individual will, we come to the result to which the law has been coming more and more of late throughout the world.*

All societies recognize property rights to some degree—even primitive ones where a man's ownership may be restricted to his hut, dog or chicken, or property created by his own labor. In this country, property is the reason for business activity, the means of economic life, the measure of wealth and frequently the measure of success and status. Property rights also exist in Communistic states where individuals are permitted to own clothing, furniture or other consumer items, but generally may not own or control capital goods or property used for purposes of production. In the article which follows, the author compares and contrasts American law concerning property rights with that of Communistic states, noting the economic successes and shortcomings which have resulted from each system of ownership and the reasons therefor.

MARXISM, SENATOR SHERMAN, AND OUR ECONOMIC SYSTEM [6]
Robert W. Bergstrom [7]

Marxism and state socialism have now been tested in many nations as laboratories, and without exception they have failed. On the other hand, the system of supervised, umpired competition into which the American economy has evolved has produced a gross national product without parallel. The importance of the antitrust laws to this system cannot be exaggerated; they undergird this system of production and distribution and enable it to function. Nonetheless, other statutes, which conflict with the economic theory upon which the antitrust laws are based, erode the distinctions which make the United States' economic system superior to those of eastern Europe. Tax laws, labor laws, and other statutes discussed hereinafter cannot just be treated individually as specialties to be served by expert craftsmen; the intermeshing of these laws to shape our economic system, and hence our destiny, must also be studied.

Russia's central planning system has broken down. After Khrushchev reported in 1961 that, of 100,000 construction projects, most were two or three years late, a year's moratorium was imposed on new building. Housing construction was delayed because no factory had been built to make the baths for bathrooms. The manufacture of tires went out of phase with the manufacture of autos. Industries purported to fulfill their plans by making useless, unwanted articles. The cumbersome industrial system only continued to work because of the clandestine free-market activities of the Fixer who had "blat"—influence and contacts—and would furnish the necessary machine tools or bearings, in complex barter transactions, before the machinery ground to a stop. In the first half of 1966 the Soviet Union's chronic failures in farm production forced it to contract for the purchase of 336 million bushels of wheat and flour over the next three years from Canada at a cost of 800 million dollars. The only country in the Communist bloc which fulfills its agricultural plans is Poland, where most farms are privately owned and operated.

The Hungarian economy is stagnating. By 1959 all but 4 per cent of agricultural land was under state control, but despite substantial investment productivity dropped below previous levels. In contrast, the 1½ acre household plots on state cooperative farms, occupying 14 per cent of the arable land, produced 22 per cent of the farm output. In Budapest 100,000 persons are on the waiting list for an apartment. The government intends to decentralize the economy, make profit rather than gross production the

---

6 55 *Ill. B.J.* 748 (1967). Many of the author's footnotes have been omitted. Used by permission from Mr. Robert W. Bergstrom and the *Illinois Bar Journal*.
7 Mr. Bergstrom, a member of the Illinois Bar, is an expert on antitrust and has been active both as member and chairman of committees of the Chicago, Illinois and American Bar Associations dealing with various aspects of this area of law.

measure of success, and allow prices to be determined by demand instead of by arbitrary decree.

Czechoslovakia has announced the inauguration, as of January 1, 1967, of a "socialist market economy" to extricate itself from the economic strait-jacket which has throttled one of Europe's most productive nations. Threatened by inflation and a growing deficit in foreign trade, Jugoslavia has led the trend to individual enterprise. Private workshops having a maximum of three employees are permitted, and there are now 150,000 of them. Unprofitable enterprises are finding it increasingly difficult to borrow money from state banks and 100 or more plants have been shut down and 20,000 unproductive workers laid off. Rent subsidies are being ended, on the theory that the worker must experience the true cost of his standard of living.

By the end of 1966, 700 industrial enterprises in Russia were operating under the new profit motive and supply-and-demand thesis associated with Professor Liberman, and after two months of 1967 there were 2500 factories operating under the reformed procedures. . . . China has recovered her economic poise since the disastrous days of the Great Leap Forward not because socialist principle was upheld, but because Peking permitted a heretical lapse into capitalism, and peasants were allowed to organize their own private bits of business in the hitherto rigidly regimented People's Communes.

These failures of socialism's central planning and distribution, compared with the marked successes of private enterprise economies such as those of the United States, West Germany, the European Economic Community, Japan, South Korea, and Formosa, must necessarily influence all thinking persons. A doctrine has little intellectual appeal when practical laboratory experimentation has shown it to be a stupid way to manage a country. The reason for this superiority of umpired competition over state socialism is copy-book economics; but it may well be worth repeating here.

In a truly free enterprise economy the three basic resources of labor, materials, and capital or savings, are settled automatically into those areas of production in which they are most needed by means of the composite of the individual decisions and silent votes of millions of consumers. If consumers want five million television sets made for sale this year as compared with two million last year and they want only four million pairs of shoes this year as compared with eight million pairs last year, the prices of television sets go up and the prices of shoes fall because of the lesser demand. Shoe manufacturers cut back the amount of labor and capital they devote to the industry, and on the other hand old and new television manufacturers devote additional capital to creating the machinery necessary for turning out the additional production. They can obtain this money in the financial market from savers because the increased demand reflected in the higher prices promises the investor a better return on his capital. Hence all of the millions of individual decisions not to buy as many shoes and to withdraw savings from the shoe market and not to put one's labor into making shoes are combined with the hopes for additional reward of the new investors in television set production and the job-changing decisions of workmen who shift to the better paid jobs in order to make those television sets.

In contrast, in state socialism a commissar must set production quotas in each industry, without the guide as to demand in a pricing system from the millions of silent voters, without the persuasion of the automatic ebb and flow of capital into the productive arenas in which it is most needed; and no matter how devoted he may be to the public interest, he winds up with four million unneeded pairs of shoes, and the consumers lack three million television sets.

Marx, eyeing the cartels of nineteenth-century Europe, could not believe that the forces of competition would be allowed freedom to allocate production and distribution. The combination of large amounts of capital in joint stock companies, he wrote, *"is equivalent to the abolition of capitalist production within the capitalist system of production*—a glaring anomaly which already at first sight appears as a mere transitional stage to a new form of [socialist] production." His collaborator Friedrich Engels added:

Since Marx wrote the above, new forms of industry have been developed, by which the joint stock company has been raised to the second and third power. The time-honored freedom of competition is at an end and must itself admit its scandalous bankruptcy. It is bankrupt because, in every country, the magnates in any particular branch of industry unite in view of regulating production. . . . And thus it came about that, in some branches, in which the level obtained by the process of production admitted of it, the entire production of the branch was concentrated in one single vast joint stock company under homogeneous management. In these branches, therefore, competition is replaced by monopoly, and the future expropriation by the whole society, the nation, has been most happily prepared.

Marx and Engels failed to foresee that government would enter the economic arena as an umpire, to require that competitive prices, instead of unbridled power, dictate the allocation of capital, labor, and materials —in the United States by way of the Sherman and Clayton Acts. . . .

The antitrust laws epitomize the free enterprise philosophy—that allowing free flow of capital, labor, and materials in accordance with the voted demands of consumers expressed in competitive prices will create the maximum and best production of desired items, maximal satisfaction of wants, and maximum individual freedom. However they are hedged about with exemptions, and with restraints upon trade created by public and private bodies—so much so that the antitrust laws are an oasis of free competition in an environment of monopoly and central controls. By distorting demand and supply, these restraints divert resources from their most efficient productive use. Thereby they drag us down toward the level of the controlled economies whose failure we have already examined.

Combinations to fix the price of labor are exempted from the antitrust laws. The use of monopoly power to fix labor rates and to limit entrance into an industry impairs the free flow of labor into developing industries which would normally outbid others, and it causes wasteful expenditures upon capital assets to replace overpriced monopoly labor in circumstances where unemployed labor cannot be utilized and is therefore lost forever as a productive asset.

The free market application of labor to the most productive arena is further diminished by minimum wage laws, which require the unskilled and non-unionized worker to set a minimum price for his labor. By taking out of the market those jobs where the worker's productivity entitles him to less than this amount, the demand for labor is reduced, total productivity of the nation is decreased, and unemployment—with its total wastage of the unconsumed labor—is increased.

The minimum prices of agricultural commodities are in large measure set by central control instead of the free market, and agricultural cooperatives are exempted from the antitrust laws. In Illinois, once a farmer has signed a long-term marketing agreement with a cooperative, he will be inhibited by summary injunction, obtainable upon affidavit, and by liquidated damages from selling to anyone else; and prospective purchasers will be restrained from buying from him and held liable in damages for making any offer to purchase.

Imperfections in our tax structure and in government subsidies cause plant mis-locations and mis-investments by not permitting the vote of economic forces, through the price structure, to dictate the investment. Because municipal bonds are free of federal taxes, their interest rate is lower. Approximately thirty states now permit public bodies to sell bonds for the purpose of acquiring sites, or equipping buildings, for lease to private companies. Private companies are thus induced to found industries in states which lend them tax-exempt status, instead of the plant locations which would give them the most economical access to materials, power, labor, and markets. Over a billion dollars of such industrial development bonds are outstanding. And capital from investors who would otherwise invest it more profitably in more productive facilities flows into such bonds for the sake of the income tax saving involved.

The two nuclear generators to be built by Tennessee Valley Authority in northern Alabama for $247 million, together with the industry which will be attracted to the area by the available power, are being placed in Alabama through central planning. In a free-market economy, where the location would have been determined by utilities bidding for the funds in the open financial market, with the interest rate determined in a market appraising alternative investment opportunities, and without the aid of a subsidy of 48% of income in the form of exemption from income taxes, the economic place for this industrial complex might have turned out to be Illinois, or New York, or California.

The same distortion of economic decisions results from the federal government's loans at a subsidized 2% interest rate to rural electric co-operatives which they may then relend as equipment loans to industries to induce them to locate in the cooperative's area. A manufacturer planning to build a tape factory in Paterson, New Jersey, was offered a $450,000 equipment loan by a Pennsylvania cooperative if it would build in that area instead.

The present income tax laws impair the efficiency of this umpired competitive machine. The progressive rate structure discourages additional production by diminishing the marginal return for additional effort. The desirability of diverting income to units taxable at lower rates (or of assigning expenses to a highly-taxed unit) causes business investment decisions which are not those of optimum productivity for the economy. Because the present steep progressive rates might well, if strictly enforced, cause a radical loss in the productivity of society, the exempt base is enlarged by tax loopholes which themselves direct investment in ways which are not necessarily the best. When gains from risk-investments are taxed progressively at a higher rate than the rate for deductibility of the loss in the event of failure, risk-taking by small entrepreneurs is discouraged, and they are influenced toward stability as employees of large corporations, whether this is desirable for the economy or not.

Expert craftsmanship on the part of lawyers in these fields is not enough. The antitruster disputing words of art like "quantitative substantiality," the tax attorney shorthanding a problem as a "Clifford trust," the labor lawyer defining a "labor dispute"—these are not dealing with a specialist's narrow domain; they are shaping a society, and they have the responsibility of leadership. The Secretary of Health, Education and Welfare said about such responsibility:

If anything significant is to be accomplished, leaders must understand the social institutions and processes through which action is carried out. And in a society as complex as ours, that is no mean achievement. . . .

Nothing should be allowed to impair the effectiveness and independence of our specialized leadership groups. But such fragmented leadership does create certain problems. One of them is that it isn't anybody's business to think about the big problems that cut across specialties—the largest questions facing our society. . . .

Very few of our most prominent people take a really large view of the leadership assignment. Most of them are simply tending the machinery of that part of the society to which they belong. The machinery may be a great *corporation or a great government agency or a great law practice or a great university. . . .*

One does not blame them, of course. They do not see themselves as leaders of the society at large, and they have plenty to do handling their own specialized roles.

Yet it is doubtful that we can any longer afford such widespread inattention to the largest questions facing us.*

It is necessary, therefore, for businessmen, labor leaders, legislators, and attorneys, to look at our laws in the large, and to discern the conflicts in policy and objective between our antitrust laws, on the one hand, and tax, labor, agricultural, and subsidy laws on the other hand. It is submitted that the record of testing in the world's laboratories justifies the philosophy of individual freedom, decision, and responsibility embodied in the antitrust laws, and that the laws in these other fields should be amended to make them more consistent with this philosophy.

3   METHODS OF ACQUIRING PROPERTY

Both real and personal property can be acquired by transfer from the former owner to a new owner. This may be accomplished during the lifetime of the transferor by a sale, lease, or gift. A transfer may also be effected upon the death of the transferor, by reason of a properly executed and attested will. In the event an owner of property dies intestate, that is, without having a valid will which disposes of the property in question, the property is transferred to his heirs or next of kin according to the statute of descent and distribution of the appropriate state or states. Joint tenancy is sometimes used as a substitute for a will. Real property and, in many states, personal property which is co-owned by two or more persons in joint tenancy becomes the absolute property of the survivor of the owners. The foregoing methods will be discussed further in the two sections which follow.

Transfer of real and personal property can come about in a number of other ways. Judgment creditors may avail themselves of various procedures to obtain payment, such as garnishing the wages of the debtor, attaching his bank account, or levying execution on the nonexempt property of the debtor and having the sheriff sell it at a judicial sale and use the proceeds to pay the judgment debt. Similarly, the sheriff may sell real property for back taxes, the buyer getting a tax deed. Also, in the event of bankruptcy, the trustee in bankruptcy takes title to all of the nonexempt property in the

---

* [footnote by Bergstrom] John W. Gardner, "The Antileadership Vaccine," *Princeton Alumni Weekly*, June 7, 1966, pp. 24–28 (reprinted from the 1965 Annual Report of the Carnegie Corporation of New York). As the Hon. W. W. Butterworth, U.S. Ambassador to Canada, observed to the American Bar Association on August 9, 1966, these conclusions would have seemed self-evident to a Greek of the Age of Pericles or a colleague of Leonardo da Vinci.

bankrupt's estate for the purpose of using it to pay the expenses of bankruptcy and the creditors with provable claims, to the extent possible, in accordance with the Federal bankruptcy law.

One may involuntarily transfer property to another simply by failing to bring suit within the maximum time period allowed by the statute of limitations, thereby losing his right to recover possession of the property he claims as his. In such a case, the transferee is said to have acquired title by adverse possession. The possession must have been exclusive, open and notorious, adverse to the rights of the true owner, under claim of right or color of title, and continuous for the statutory period. The amount of time required varies somewhat from state to state, but in the case of land it is frequently twenty years. One may not obtain title by adverse possession of public lands owned by the state or the United States government.

In addition to the above, title to personal property may be acquired in a number of other ways. First, one may become the owner of personal property by original possession. For example, fish or wild animals belong to the one who captures them and reduces them to his possession and control. Property which was formerly owned by someone, but has been abandoned by him belongs to the first person to take possession of it again. By contrast, property which is misplaced or lost by its owner still belongs to him. However, as against everyone but him, the owner of the realty where the property was *misplaced* has the right to its possession as a general rule. And, ordinarily, the finder of *lost* property has the right to its possession against all but the true owner. These common-law principles can be and in some cases have been modified by statute. Whether any personal property one discovers has been abandoned, lost, or misplaced is a question of fact to be determined from all the circumstances, including exactly where it was found. It would be significant to know whether the property had been in a trash can, on a bench, or on the ground in reaching a conclusion. Of course, once this has been done, the rights of the finder in the property are determined.

One may add to personal property by his labor or by attaching other materials to it, or both. In such a case, it is generally held that the owner of the raw material or the larger unit of property becomes the owner of the whole by *accession*. "Fungible goods" are goods which are accounted for by weight or measure, such as grain or beer, rather than by individual unit, such as furniture or automobiles. The same kind of fungible goods of two or more persons may be mixed together for purposes such as storage. Then, by confusion, each of the former owners becomes a co-owner of an undivided fractional share in the whole mass, proportionate to the amount he contributed. When one wrongfully causes confusion of his property with that of another, the latter becomes the owner of the whole mass, unless the wrongdoer can clearly establish the amount which he added. Finally, title to personal property may be transferred to the owner of real estate to which it is permanently attached with the intent that it be so. The personal property by such attachment becomes a fixture and a part of the realty. Personal property may be physically attached to land and not become an actual part of it, however. The question of whether an attached item is a fixture or not is largely a question of intention of the one attaching it. The degree of physical attachment and whether the personal property is capable of being removed without substantial damage to the realty are factors which are considered in determining this intention. For example, when a contractor pours a concrete foundation for a building, it generally would become a part of the land and the property of the owner thereof. Machinery brought onto land for temporary use by one other than the owner of the land and attached merely by the force of gravity would most likely not become a fixture and would not be the property of the owner of the realty. Similarly, "trade fixtures," such as a soda fountain in a drugstore, usually do not become part of the land.

Because of the distinctive nature of real property, title to it can be acquired in several other ways than those previously mentioned. Many of the titles to land in this country were first obtained by *original entry* and patent from the United States government. Homesteaders acquired title in this fashion to a limited amount of acreage by complying with the requirements of the law. Also, when a river or stream by the slow and gradual process of cutting and filling adds deposits to land whose border is the river or stream, the owner generally obtains title to the land added by *accretion*. Finally, because the growth and development of society at large may vitally depend upon the right of government to obtain real property for public purposes such as highways, electric plants, schools, and the like, the state and Federal governments have the power to acquire land by condemnation, called the power of *eminent domain*. Whenever there is a taking by government of private property, both state and Federal constitutions require that fair and just compensation be given the former owner. This point was illustrated in *State Highway Department v. Branch* on page 600. The propriety of the condemnation of certain land may be challenged by the private owner of it on the ground that the intended purpose for the use of the land is not a public one.

4   THE CONTRACT AS A METHOD OF TRANSFERRING OR CREATING PROPERTY

As was indicated above, one of the methods of transferring both personal and real property is by a sale, which is the result of a contract between the buyer and the seller. Also, instead of transferring the ownership of property, the right to possession and use and enjoyment of it in a certain manner and for a certain time period may be created by a contract called a lease. Enforceable contractual promises may constitute property themselves. For example, in a contract of sale, the buyer's promise to pay is an account receivable of the seller, which is intangible personal property. Generally, such property may be sold and assigned by the creditor to a third party, who then obtains the right to payment of the debt.

The purpose of contract law is to provide the machinery whereby persons can create legal rights and impose legal duties on themselves by their own agreement. The whole force of organized society, exerted by the courts and the appropriate executive agencies, stands behind a valid contract, just as it does behind criminal and tort duties which are imposed on individuals by the law itself. Whenever a contract is breached, the injured party can obtain money damages equivalent to the economic loss which he can prove he suffered because of the breach. If the breach is serious enough, he may be permitted to rescind or cancel the contract. It would be grossly unjust to enforce the promise of the injured party in favor of the one guilty of the breach if the injured party did not obtain substantially what he had bargained for. In some circumstances, the remedy of an injured party may be a decree of specific performance, or order of a court of equity commanding the defendant actually to perform the bargain as he agreed. In this connection, see Section 3, Chapter 6. It should be emphasized that one is not entitled to specific performance as a right but that the decision to grant this remedy lies within the discretion of the court of equity. Contracts for the sale of land, however, are usually specifically enforceable because each parcel of real estate is unique. Failure of a defendant to obey a decree of specific performance may result in his being held in contempt of court and fined or imprisoned or both.

The law prescribes certain requirements for a valid contract. First, there must be an agreement between the parties which is manifested by their words or conduct or a combination of both. In arriving at their mutual understanding, the parties may engage in bickering and in making preliminary suggestions or invitations to the other party to make an offer. When one of them makes a firm proposal which includes the major terms, that is, a promise of what he will do and what he demands from the other party in return, he is said to have made an offer, and is called the "offeror." The one to whom an offer is made is the "offeree," and acquires the legal power of acceptance. In other words, as long as the offer is open, the offeree can by his own act alone comply with the demands of the offeror and accept the offer in the manner requested, thereby creating a contract. If the offeror requests that the offeree actually perform in a certain manner in order to accept, the offer is said to be unilateral, and no contract results until the offeree has substantially performed. For example, a promise to pay $10 if the offeree mows the offeror's lawn would be unilateral. Neither the offeror nor the offeree in such a case is assured of the existence of a contract until the offeree has mowed substantially all of the lawn. Since the offer may be terminated before that happens, the disadvantages to unilateral offers are obvious. Frequently, the offeror would prefer to have the binding *agreement* of the other party to perform in a certain manner, and will request in his offer that the offeree simply promise to perform in a given manner. This is known as a bilateral offer, and requires that the offeree indicate his assent to its terms to create a contract. After he has accepted, the offeree is legally bound to perform as he has promised and the offeror is legally bound to perform as he has promised. In this case, there is an exchange of a promise for a promise.

Note, then, that it is not necessary for either of the parties to have actually performed in order to have a binding contract, but just that each undertakes to perform in a given manner in the future. The whole purpose of contract law is to make promises enforceable.

Besides stating the important terms and identifying the parties, a proposition must unequivocally indicate the intent to be contractually bound to those terms, if they are accepted, in order to be an offer. Clearly, any communication which falls short of these requirements creates no power of acceptance, and any attempted acceptance may in fact be an offer. The major issue in the case below was whether a particular statement made by the agent of one of the parties was sufficient to constitute an offer.

MCGINN V. AMERICAN BANK STATIONERY CO.
195 A.2d 615 (C.A. Md. 1963)

SYBERT, JUDGE: The plaintiff below appeals from a decree granting a motion for a summary judgment in favor of the defendants. The appellant had filed an equity suit against the appellees, American Bank Stationery Company and its president, J. Wilford Sheridan, to enforce an alleged contract to sell 100 shares of the corporation's treasury stock at $50.00 per share.

Appellant claims that a contract arose in the following manner. In June 1960 the board of directors of the corporation passed a resolution authorizing the sale of stock "to such persons as may be selected by the President." At a subsequent meeting of all the salesmen of the corporation, including the appellant, a company official stated that treasury stock was being made available for sale to them, and that if they desired to purchase some, they should make a written request to the president. The salesmen were informed that if the requests exceeded the number of shares which the company intended to sell, then the stock would be prorated on the basis of the amount requested.

The appellant subsequently wrote the appellee Sheridan stating that he would like to buy 100 shares at $50.00 each. At a later conference with

Sheridan, according to the appellant's own testimony, Sheridan did not indicate whether the corporation would sell "100 shares or any amount." Thereafter the appellant was told that 100 shares would not be made available to him, apparently because of the large number of subscriptions, but that he could buy a lesser amount if he so desired. He never requested fewer shares. Later the appellant asked Sheridan when he could expect to get the stock and was told that the corporation did not need money at that time but that the appellant would be informed when it did. No note or memorandum of the alleged contract was ever signed. Appellant never tendered payment in any amount because, to use his own words, "how could I, not knowing how much stock I was going to get or when?" The appellees' principal defense was that the evidence disclosed no contract.

We think the summary judgment was properly granted. The pleadings and the testimony of the appellant show that there was no genuine dispute as to any material fact and that the appellees were entitled to judgment as a matter of law. In order to create a valid contract there must be both an offer and an acceptance. The appellant contends that the statement made at the meeting of the salesmen, that stock would be made available for sale to them, was an offer and his written request for 100 shares was an acceptance thereof. However, we agree with the Chancellor that the statements made at the meeting constituted only an invitation to submit offers, and that the appellant's response requesting 100 shares was merely an offer to buy, which was never accepted. There was never any meeting of minds as to the number of shares to be sold to the appellant. "A contract, to be final, must extend to all the terms which the parties intend to introduce, and material terms cannot be left for future settlement. Until actual completion of the bargain either party is at liberty to withdraw his consent and put an end to the negotiations." *Peoples Drug Stores v. Fenton Realty Corp.*, 191 Md. 489, 494, 62 A.2d 273, 276 (1948). [JUDGMENT FOR APPELLEES, DEFENDANTS BELOW, AFFIRMED]

An offer cannot be accepted until the offeree obtains knowledge of it in the manner intended by the offeror. Even if a valid offer was created, it may terminate in a number of ways before an acceptance can become effective, which results in no contract. An offer will terminate upon the death or the insanity of either the offeror or offeree. Also, if the offer indicates the time period it is to remain open, it will automatically expire at the end of the time stated. Even if no period is mentioned, all offers terminate by lapse after a reasonable time has expired. It is a question of fact dependent upon all the circumstances as to what period of time is reasonable in each individual case. None of the foregoing methods of termination of an offer requires that any notice be given to the offeror.

An offer also expires if the offeree turns it down, by what is called rejection. A counteroffer amounts to a rejection by implication. If the offeree expressly indicates that he is still contemplating the offer, there is no implication of rejection, however.

When the offeree repeats the terms in an attempted acceptance and changes one of them, either intentionally or by mistake, he makes a counteroffer and rejects the offer. An exception to this rule exists in the case of an offer to sell goods, wares, or merchandise. The Uniform Commercial Code provides that any attempted acceptance is an acceptance, even if it does appear to change the offer. The contract thereby formed is on the terms expressed in the original offer, except where the contract is between merchants and the change is a minor one. In this case, the change is incorporated into the contract, unless the offeror objects to it within a reasonable time after receiving the acceptance. A rejection is effective when the offeror learns of it.

Finally, an offer may be revoked by the offeror as long as he takes the necessary steps before an acceptance has become effective. This is true even if the offeror has previously indicated that the offer will be open longer. Such a promise is merely gratuitous and is not binding. Of course, an offeror can contract to keep the offer open for a given period in exchange for some consideration from the offeree. This is an option contract, and makes the offer irrevocable. Usually the consideration given is a sum of money. Here, too, the Code makes an exception if the offer involves a sale of goods, wares, or merchandise and is being made by a merchant. The merchant's written promise to keep his offer open is binding on him, without consideration being given to support it, for any period up to a maximum of three months. A revocation becomes effective as soon as the offeree learns of it, or learns of facts which imply it. It is also effective if written and placed where it would usually be available to the offeree, such as delivered to his residence, whether he reads it or not. Of course, offers, rejections, and revocations may all be communicated through the medium of the mails, by telegrams, by special messenger, or the like.

Like an offer, an acceptance must be unequivocal. It must show an intent to be bound by the terms stated in the offer. If there is more than one offer open, it must be clear which one is being accepted. Many of the legal problems involved in resolving the issue of whether there is an agreement between the parties or not boil down to determining *what various communications are* (that is, are they worded so as to be offers, rejections, or what?) and *when they become effective*. If an offer is in existence and it is accepted before it is terminated by one of the methods described above, there is a contract. Otherwise there is none. The case which follows concerns the time an acceptance becomes effective when the parties are communicating by mail.

MORRISON V. THOELKE
155 So. 2d 889 (Fla. 1963)

The plaintiffs (appellees) owned certain land. On November 26, 1957, the defendants (appellants) mailed to the plaintiffs an executed contract for the purchase of the land. On November 27, 1957, the plaintiffs executed the contract also and mailed it to the defendants' attorney. After the contract was mailed, but before it was received, the plaintiffs called the defendants' attorney and repudiated the execution and the contract. However, the defendants caused the contract to be recorded. The plaintiffs then brought suit to quiet title, requesting that defendants be enjoined from making any claim for the sale of the land under the contract, arguing that their acceptance had been withdrawn before it had become legally effective. The defendants counterclaimed, seeking specific performance of the contract. The lower court entered summary judgment for the plaintiffs, and the defendants appealed.

ALLEN, ACTING CHIEF JUDGE: . . . Turning to the principal point raised in this appeal, we are confronted with a question apparently of first impression in this jurisdiction. The question is whether a contract is complete and binding when a letter of acceptance is mailed, thus barring repudiation prior to receipt. Appellants, of course, argue that posting the acceptance creates the contract; appellees contend that only receipt of the acceptance bars repudiation. . . .

As is abundantly clear from the quoted material excerpted from appellees' cases, the decision in each is predicated on an assumption, correct or incorrect, that the basis of the rule they reject was invalidated by changed postal regulations. The opinions cited by appellees each proceed on the theory that the "deposited acceptance" rule was based on a theory that the depositor lost control of his acceptance when it was deposited and that this fact rendered the acceptance complete upon deposit. To the extent that "loss of control" was the significant element in the "deposited acceptance" rule, the logic of appellees' cases is impeccable. On the other hand, if the rule is, in fact, not based on the "loss of control" element, the fact that this element has been altered may in no way affect the validity of the rule. Determination of the question presented in this appeal cannot then be had merely by adoption or rejection of the logic of appellees' cases. Rather, the source and justification of the "deposited acceptance" rule must be found and appellees' argument considered in light of this finding. Should the proffered justification for the rule be other than the "loss of control" theory, adoption or rejection of the rule must be based on considerations other than those relied upon in appellees' cases. . . .

The "meeting of the minds" justification advanced in Adams v. Lindsell is repeated in the first of two leading American cases on point. In Mactier's Adm'rs v. Frith, New York, 1830, 6 Wendell 103, 21 Am. Dec. 262, the offeree died while an acceptance was in the post. Since, if a "meeting of the minds" was essential to the contract, the contract could have been completed only during the offeree's lifetime, the court found it necessary to determine the effective date of acceptance. They deemed the posting of the assent sufficient and wrote:

> All the authorities state a contract or an agreement (which is the same thing) to be aggregatio mentium. Why should not this meeting of the minds, which makes the contract, also indicate the moment when it becomes obligatory? I might rather ask, is it not and must it not be the moment when it does become obligatory? If the party making the offer is not bound until he knows of this meeting of minds, for the same reason the party accepting the offer ought not to be bound when his acceptance is received, because he does not know of the meeting of the minds, for the offer may have been withdrawn before his acceptance was received. If more than a concurrence of minds upon a distinct proposition is required to make an obligatory contract, the definition of what constitutes a contract is not correct. Instead of being the meeting of the minds of the contracting parties, it should be a knowledge of this meeting. It was said of the argument that if concurrence of minds alone would make a valid contract, one might be constructed out of mere volitions and uncommunicated wishes; I think such a result would not follow. The law does not regard bare volitions and pure mental abstractions. When it speaks of the operations of the mind, it means such as have been made manifest by overt acts; when it speaks of the meeting of minds, it refers to such a meeting as has been made known by proper acts, and when thus made known it is effective, although the parties who may claim the benefit of, or be bound by a contract thus made, may for a season remain ignorant of its being made.

However, the court went beyond this justification and proceeded to consider what facts constituted acceptance.

> What shall constitute an acceptance will depend, in a great measure, upon circumstances. The mere determination of the mind, unacted on, can never be an acceptance. Where the offer is by letter, the usual mode of acceptance is the sending of a letter announcing a consent to accept; where it is made by messenger, a determination to accept returned through him, or sent by another, would seem to be all the law requires, if the contract may be consummated without writing. There are other modes which are equally conclusive upon the parties; keeping silence, under certain circumstances, is an assent to a proposition; anything that shall amount to a manifestation of a formed determination to accept, communicated or put in the proper way to be communicated to the party making the offer, would doubtless complete the contract; but a letter written would not be an acceptance so long as it

remained in the possession of and under the control of the writer. *An accept-ance is the distinct act of one party to the contract as much as the offer is of the other; the knowledge by the party making the offer, of the determination of the party receiving it, is not an ingredient of an acceptance. It is not com-pounded of an assent by one party to the terms offered, and a knowledge of that assent by the other.* [EMPHASIS ADDED]

Thus, the element of loss of control was introduced, not as a primary legal requisite to the existence of a contract but as a factual matter affect-ing the sufficiency of the manifestation of assent. . . .

The unjustified significance placed on the "loss of control" in the cases relied upon by appellee follows from two errors. The first error is failure to distinguish between relinquishment of control as a factual element of mani-fest intent, which it is, and as *the* legal predicate for completion of contract, which it is not. The second error lies in confusing the "right" to recall mail with the "power" to recall mail. Under current postal regulations, the sender has the "power" to regain a letter, but this does not necessarily give him the "right" to repudiate acceptance. The existence of the latter right is a matter of contract law and is determinable by reference to factors which include, but are not limited to the existence of the power to recall mail. In short, the power to recall mail is a factor, among many others, which may be signifi-cant in determining when an acceptance is effective, but the right to effec-tively withdraw and repudiate an acceptance must be dependent upon the initial determination of when that acceptance is effective and irrevo-cable. . . .

The justification for the "deposited acceptance" rule proceeds from the uncontested premise of Adams v. Lindsell that there must be, both in practical and conceptual terms, a point in time when a contract is complete. In the formulation of contracts *inter praesentes* this point is readily reached upon expressions of assent instantaneously communicated. In the formation of contracts *inter absentes* by post, however, delay in communication prevents concurrent knowledge of assents and some point must be chosen as legally significant. . . .

In support of the rule proponents urge its sanction in tradition and practice. They argue that in the average case the offeree receives an offer and, depositing an acceptance in the post, begins and should be allowed to begin reliance on the contract. They point out that the offeror has, after all, communicated his assent to the terms by extending the offer and has him-self chosen the medium of communication. Depreciating the alleged risk to the offeror, proponents argue that having made an offer by post the offeror is seldom injured by a slight delay in knowing it was accepted, whereas the offeree, under any other rule, would have to await both the transmission of the acceptance and notification of its receipt before being able to rely on the contract he unequivocally accepted. Finally, proponents point out that the offeror can always expressly condition the contract on his receipt of an acceptance and, should he fail to do so, the law should not afford him this advantage.

Opponents of the rule argue as forcefully that all of the disadvantages of delay or loss in communication which would potentially harm the offeree are equally harmful to the offeror. Why, they ask, should the offeror be bound by an acceptance of which he has no knowledge? Arguing specific cases, opponents of the rule point to the inequity of forbidding the offeror to withdraw his offer after the acceptance was posted but before he had any knowledge that the offer was accepted; they argue that to forbid the offeree to withdraw his acceptance, as in the instant case, scant hours after it was posted but days before the offeror knew of it, is unjust and indefensible. Too, the opponents argue, the offeree can always prevent the revocation of an offer by providing consideration, by buying an option.

In short, both advocates and critics muster persuasive argument. As Corbin indicated, there must be a choice made, and such choice may, by the nature of things, seem unjust in some cases. Weighing the arguments with reference not to specific cases but toward a rule of general application and recognizing the general and traditional acceptance of the rule as well as the modern changes in effective long-distance communication, it would seem that the balance tips, whether heavily or near imperceptively, to continue adherence to the "Rule in Adams v. Lindsell." This rule, although not entirely compatible with ordered, consistent and sometimes artificial principles of contract advanced by some theorists, is, in our view, in accord with the practical considerations and essential concepts of contract law. Outmoded precedents may, on occasion, be discarded and the function of justice should not be the perpetuation of error, but, by the same token, traditional rules and concepts should not be abandoned save on compelling ground. . . .

In the instant case, an unqualified offer was accepted and the acceptance made manifest. Later the offerees sought to repudiate their initial assent. Had there been a delay in their determination to repudiate permitting the letter to be delivered to appellant, no question as to the invalidity of the repudiation would have been entertained. As it were, the repudiation antedated receipt of the letter. However, adopting the view that the acceptance was effective when the letter of acceptance was deposited in the mails, the repudiation was equally invalid and cannot alone, support the summary decree for appellees.

The summary decree is reversed and the case remanded for further proceedings.

Another prerequisite to the formation of a contract besides the agreement is that of consideration. Actually, consideration is not a separate element, but rather a minimum standard which the terms of the offer an acceptance must meet. From the terms it must appear that each party has incurred a detriment in exchange for the other party's doing so also. Thus, there are three aspects to the standard. The first is the concept of a *detriment*. A detriment consists of giving up a legal right *or* of promising to give up a legal right—of doing or promising to do something the promisor is not legally bound to do. Frequently the detriment to one of the parties benefits the other, but a third party who is not one of those entering into the contract may benefit from it, as in the case where a man takes out life insurance payable to his wife. Second is the requirement that the detriments incurred are exchanged for each other. This goes to the motivation of the parties. The reason that each has for giving up or promising to give up a part of his legal rights is to *bargain* for the other's detriment. This necessitates that there be a present exchange. The third aspect of consideration is sometimes called the requirement of *mutuality. Each* party, not just one of them, incurs a detriment or the terms of the agreement do not meet the minimum standard and are unenforceable. If both of the parties are not bound, then neither is. Thus, if one of the parties can cancel a purported contract at his unrestricted option, the other can ignore the agreement if he chooses.

After reaching an agreement, the parties sometimes decide to modify it later. Generally each must furnish new consideration for the modification to be binding. Otherwise there is no present exchange of detriments. The one who does increase his duties cannot be bargaining for the detriment of the other, since it has already been incurred. The Code, however, removes agreements to modify existing contracts for the sale of goods from the rule and makes them binding without the necessity of having new consideration. In cases other than a sale of goods, if each party gives up just *some* new legal right, no matter how insignificant, the modification is binding, since the value of consideration is not regarded as being important. This latter rule preserves freedom of contract by permitting the parties to weigh values themselves and preventing the courts from interfering and substituting their judgment for that of those entering into the contract. It makes the existence of contract duties much more predictable. In one situation, however, value does become important. To discharge a liquidated money debt by paying money, a debtor must pay in full. This is called the "lesser sum rule." Of course, the creditor can make a gift of the debt or its balance to the debtor, but a donative rather than a bargaining intent on his part must be demonstrated, and there must be constructive or symbolic delivery to the debtor. In settling an unliquidated claim, that is, one which is uncertain in amount, consideration is present even if the amount agreed upon by the parties later appears to be greater or lesser than the actual amount of the claim. A good example of an unliquidated debt is a claim which arises out of the commission of a tort. If the parties agree on a settlement out of court, consideration is present. Each is in reality giving up the right to sue and have the amount established by a judicial proceeding. In the following case, the offer was made by a check and the acceptance was the act of having it certified. The main issue concerns the application of the lesser-sum rule.

NARDINE V. KRAFT CHEESE CO.
52 N.E.2d 634 (Ind. App. 1944)

FLANAGAN, JUDGE: For several years prior to August 24, 1941, the appellant, Lattie Nardine, a resident of Vincennes, Indiana, had operated a grocery in Lexington, Kentucky, under the name of Standard Market. During that time she had been an open account customer of appellee. In July 1941 she purchased from appellee 515¾ pounds of longhorn cheese. After a short time a dispute developed as to this cheese. Appellant said it was spoiled when received and that appellee should take it back. Appellee said that appellant spoiled it trying to force cure it and therefore it could not be returned. This dispute continued until after appellant closed her business on August 24, 1941.

Thereafter letters were exchanged between the parties concerning settlement of appellant's account, whereby it developed that there were other differences as to items in the account. About October 1, 1941, appellee's Lexington manager went to Vincennes to discuss the account with appellant but they were unable to agree as to the amount appellant owed. The dispute concerning the shipment of longhorn cheese above referred to was continued at that conference.

On October 30, 1941, appellant wrote appellee the following letter:

Enclosed please find check in the amount of One Hundred Forty Six Dollars and one cent ($146.01) which according to our records pays my account in full.

You will notice that I have taken a 10¢ per lb. deduction on the 515¾ lb. bad longhorn cheese, that I received from you. We are still at quite a loss on this cheese, as we really had to sacrifice it to get rid of it.

In regard to the balance on your statement of overcharges and deductions, I wish to advise that I find it impossible to check upon this as they are so old. I feel that if the deductions were not in order, that I should have been notified at the time they were taken from the checks. As you told me, these were left over from before the time you took over this account.

We are sorry to have had to make the above deductions, but I really feel that it is a just one. It has been a pleasure to do business with the Kraft Cheese Company at Lexington, and I want to thank you for all past favors.

With best regards to you, I remain,

Enclosed with the letter was a check for $146.01, marked, "This pays my account in full to date." After receiving the letter and check appellee mailed the check to the Vincennes bank on which it was drawn for certification. The bank certified the check and returned it to appellee who still retains it.

Thereafter appellee brought this action against appellant seeking to recover on account for the balance it claimed due after deducting the sum of $146.01. Appellant answered among other things that there had been an accord and satisfaction. Trial resulted in judgment for appellee to the sum of $87.88 and this appeal followed. The sufficiency of the evidence is properly challenged.

When the holder of a check has it certified by the bank on which it is drawn, the drawer is discharged and the debt becomes that of the bank. . . . If it was tendered in full payment of a claim which was unliquidated or concerning which a bona fide dispute existed, the acceptance of the check discharged the debt. . . .

Appellee says that there was no dispute because the trial court found that the longhorn cheese which appellant claims was spoiled when it arrived was in fact spoiled by appellant in trying to force cure it. The trial court could, and undoubtedly did, find that appellant spoiled the cheese. But in determining whether there was an accord and satisfaction we are not concerned with the question as to who was right and who was wrong in an existing dispute. We are concerned only with the question as to whether a good faith dispute existed at the time the check was tendered in full payment. The evidence on this question by both parties was all to the effect that such a dispute did exist.

It is true as appellee contends that the question of accord and satisfaction is ordinarily a question of fact, but where the controlling facts requisite to show accord and satisfaction are undisputed the question becomes one of law. . . .

Our conclusion is that the facts in this case show an accord and satisfaction of the claim sued upon. [JUDGMENT FOR APPELLANT (NARDINE)]

Even though the parties to a contract have arrived at an agreement and adequate consideration is present in the terms, one of them may be able to escape the duties he has undertaken because of special circumstances. Such a contract is called voidable because that party is given the right to rescind or disaffirm it. The party with this right can, if he chooses, enforce the contract. Among such contracts are those made by a minor. A minor lacks contractual capacity and can avoid by giving back what he has remaining of the consideration he received under the contract, if anything. The adult who contracts with a minor is bound, however. The minor must exercise his option to avoid within a reasonable time after he reaches the age of majority. In addition, one who is induced to contract by fraudulent misrepresentations of material fact made by another with the intent to deceive (or recklessly) is given a right to rescind provided he suffered damage as a result of relying on the misrepresentations. Fraud is also a tort, so the injured party may affirm the contract and recover money damages if he chooses. In the event he elects rescission, he must return everything he received or its equivalent (not just what he has left) as is the case with most types of voidable contracts other than minors' contracts. Unintentional misrepresentation has the same elements as fraud, except that the injured party does not have to establish that the misstatements involved were intentionally made. It also makes voidable a contract entered into with the guilty party in reliance on the misrepresentation. Duress, which involves the use of physical force or threats that reasonably cause fear to the injured party in order to obtain a contractual promise, is another ground for rescission. Duress, like fraud, is a tort. Generally if one of the parties enters into a contract under a misapprehension of material fact not due to misrepresentations by the other, he is bound anyway. In other words, normally unilateral mistake is no basis for disaffirming. However, bilateral or mutual mistake of material fact, where both of the parties to a contract have entered into it under a mistaken assumption, makes it voidable at the option of the one who is injured by the mistake. The following case involves this last type of voidable contract.

SLOAN V. STANDARD OIL CO.
203 N.E.2d 237 (Ohio 1964)

HERBERT, JUSTICE: James C. Sloan, appellee herein, filed a petition in the Court of Common Pleas of Marion County, alleging two causes of action. The first cause of action seeks to cancel a release executed between plaintiff and defendant, The Standard Oil Company, appellant herein, as the result of an automobile-truck collision between plaintiff and an employee of defendant, acting within the scope of his employment. The second cause of action seeks to recover damages for personal injuries alleged to have been sustained as a result of the collision. Plaintiff, while stopped at a trafficway intersection, was struck in the rear of his automobile by a pick-up truck driven by such employee of defendant.

Judgment on the first cause of action heard by the court was entered for the plaintiff, holding that a mutual mistake of a material fact existed between the parties to the release at the time of its execution, and that, therefore, the release was invalid and not a bar to plaintiff's second cause of action. . . .

The second cause of action was tried by a jury, resulting in a judgment for the plaintiff, damages being assessed at $8,500.

Upon appeal to the Court of Appeals for Marion County, the judgment of the trial court on the two causes of action was affirmed.

The cause is now before this court upon the allowance of a motion of defendant to certify the record. . . .

Defendant presents one issue to this court for determination: Whether the setting aside of the release was contrary to law. No controversy exists between the parties as to the jury's finding of liability or its assessment of damages.

Defendant places great emphasis on the case of *O'Donnel v. Langdon* (1960), 170 Ohio St. 528, 166 N.E.2d 756. Research indicates that this court has had little occasion to consider the legal principles applicable to releases for personal injuries, despite the fact that an overwhelming number of sister states have been so concerned. It is the opinion of this court that an analysis of this area of the law is needed in Ohio. As a consequence, the O'Donnel decision is hereby overruled.

Can equity grant relief where parties executed a release while operating under a mistake of fact? Equity from its inception has had jurisdiction to concern itself with mistakes. The equitable remedy of cancellation or rescission of contracts and other instruments has long been available as a method of granting relief from the consequences of any mistake of fact which is a material element of the transaction. . . .

A general statement of the rule applicable to releases and personal injuries, as followed in other jurisdictions, is as follows:

*A release may be avoided where the releasor can show that it was executed by mutual mistake, as between himself and the releasee, of a past or present fact, material to the release . . . as where there was a mutual mistake as to the nature, extent, or degree of gravity of the releasor's injury, unless it further appears that the parties intended that claims for all injuries, whether known or unknown at the time of the execution of the release, be relinquished. [*emphasis added*] 76 C.J.S. Release § 25, p. 645. . . .*

Because rescission or cancellation of the release is sought, the spirit of equity is given great emphasis in the application of the above rule. It is required that the release must be fairly and knowingly made. Each case is said to depend on its own facts. It is apparent that the strict terms of the release are not, in many instances, controlling; the releasee cannot circumvent the powers of equity to correct mistakes.

As stated in *Casey v. Proctor* 59 Cal. 2d 97 (1963), 28 Cal. Rptr. 307, 378 P.2d 579:

The essence of the rule is that the wording of the release is not conclusive; it is a question of fact whether the parties to a release actually intended to discharge such liability.

The dispositive inquiry in each case is what did the parties intend? If the facts indicate that the parties intended that all claims for all injuries would be relinquished, the release is not subject to rescission or cancellation in a court of equity.

Certain factors have been judicially recognized as aids whereby the intent of the parties at the time the release was executed may be determined. Stated favorably to the party seeking rescission or cancellation, these factors are: The absence of bargaining and negotiating leading to settlement; the releasee is clearly liable; absence of discussion concerning personal injuries; the contention that the injuries were in fact unknown at the time the release was executed is reasonable; an inadequate amount of consideration received compared with the risk of the existence of unknown injuries; haste by the releasee in securing the release and the terms of the release exclude the injuries alleged.

Because intent is a question of fact, it is necessary in each case to examine all the circumstances surrounding the execution of the release.

In the instant case, plaintiff's automobile, while stopped at a traffic-way intersection, was struck in the rear by a truck driven by an employee of the defendant. Plaintiff testified that he experienced a sudden jerk of the head backwards and a sensation of pain during this jerk, and that a soreness existed in his neck and shoulders for a week to ten days following the accident. Plaintiff and the driver examined the damage to the two vehicles, and the driver advised plaintiff to send a bill for any damage to defendant. Plaintiff returned home after completing his business and took some medication to ward off a headache. The day after the accident, the defendant informed plaintiff to have the damage repaired and to forward the bill. Defendant's office manager, Floyd Arthur, testified that he had no knowledge of any injury to plaintiff other than the stiffness in the neck, as related to Arthur by the employee-driver. Plaintiff expended $20.19 to repair his car and forwarded the bill to defendant. Plaintiff telephoned defendant some time in February, inquiring when defendant was going to pay the bill. On March 4, 1962, Arthur brought a check for $20.19 drawn upon defendant's account and a general release to plaintiff's place of employment. Plaintiff admits reading and signing the release and the acceptance of defendant's check. Approximately six months after the accident, plaintiff felt a tingling sensation in the fingers of his left hand. This sensation grew progressively worse, and plaintiff, some 12 months after the accident, was operated on for a ruptured cervical disc.

Upon this statement of facts, the trial court found:

> . . . at the time this document, designated a release, was prepared, submitted and signed, there existed a mutual mistake of material fact, namely, that plaintiff had [not] sustained personal injuries as a result of this collision and that but for such mistake of a material fact this document would not have

*been prepared and submitted by defendant and would not have been signed
by plaintiff. . . .*

*The court . . . finds that at no time were the damages of plaintiff for
personal injuries considered by the parties or comprehended as within the
terms of the document designated a release. . . .*

This court reaches the same conclusion. Applying the previously stated
factors to determine the intent of the parties, it is evident that there was
no negotiation prior to settlement and no discussion of personal injuries,
the amount of consideration given was the exact amount of property damage, and neither party was aware as to the nature, or degree of gravity of
the releasor's injury.

Therefore, this court finds that the parties were mutually mistaken as
to a material fact. There is clear and convincing evidence to support this
conclusion, and the judgment of the Court of Appeals is affirmed. [JUDGMENT
AFFIRMED]

An agreement which is illegal is void. Generally, the court will not enforce such an agreement for either of the parties. A contract may be illegal
because its object is prohibited by statute, or is against the public policy
of a statute or a public policy determined by judicial decision. Wagering or
gambling contracts are illegal as a rule. Also, one who charges a natural
person interest on a loan in excess of that permitted by statute is guilty of
usury. The remedy for usury varies from state to state, and ranges from
forfeiture of excessive interest to forfeiture of all interest to forfeiture of
both principal and interest. Small loan companies may be excepted from the
general rule and permitted to charge higher rates of interest under special
laws because of the high risk involved in their lending. Also, if a sale of
goods is involved, and not a loan, generally the seller can add a carrying
or finance charge and not be guilty of usury. A minority view treats a finance
charge as interest and subjects it to the usury rules. Sometimes, a contracting party will attempt to insert a term in a contract which purports to
relieve him of any liability to the other party for tort injuries caused the
latter, even if due to the fault of the former. Such terms are called exculpatory clauses, and are void if the party seeking to be relieved has a superior
bargaining position because of the essential character of the service or
product he deals in. Thus, railroads or trucking lines or other common
carriers are not permitted to use such a device to escape liability. In Chapter 10 it was noted that contracts in restraint of trade are illegal and void,
but that, under some circumstances, certain types of restraints are enforceable. The following case involves a restraint in a contract of employment
under which the employer sought injunctive relief, arguing that the agreement in issue fell under the exception to the general rule.

BELTONE ELECTRONICS CORP. V. SMITH
194 N.E.2d 21 (III. App. 1963)

BURKE, PRESIDING JUSTICE: Victor G. Smith appeals from the order for a temporary injunction restraining him, a former employee, from disclosing or using at any time, any secret or confidential information or knowledge attained or acquired by him while employed by Beltone Electronics Corporation and from directly or indirectly performing at any time on or before February 1, 1964, any services for or continuing or accepting employment by or association in any capacity with Zenith Radio Corporation. The Chancellor rejected the recommendations of a Master in Chancery that the application for preliminary injunction be denied.

On May 13, 1957, defendant was hired by Beltone as chief industrial engineer. His initial task was to set up an industrial engineering department and assume responsibility for production control. At the time defendant ceased employment with Beltone he was manager of manufacturing. Smith's duties were largely administrative. He was not an inventor, designer or chemist. When Smith joined Beltone he signed an employment agreement with his employer which states that Smith, "shall not disclose or use at any time, either during or subsequent to his employment by Employer, any secret or confidential information or knowledge obtained or acquired by Employee while in Employer's employment; . . . that he will not, at any time within one (1) year subsequent to the termination of his employment with Employer, however occurring, directly or indirectly perform any service or be employed by, or become associated in any capacity with, any person, firm or corporation engaged in the manufacture or sale of hearing aids or hearing aid accessories or audiometers or be engaged on his own behalf in the manufacture or sale of any such products; . . . that for a violation by Employee of any of the covenants of this Agreement, Employer may have an injunction restraining Employee therefrom." The agreement was not limited as to its geographic scope.

The defendant, in the fall of 1961, began putting out "feelers," answering advertisements and mailing out resumes. He had interviews with Zenith Corporation in December 1962 and was employed by it on January 8, 1963. His position with Zenith Corporation was that of director of hearing aid production. Defendant left Beltone on February 1, 1963. Prior to his termination of employment with Beltone he was warned against taking employment with a competitor. He commenced to work for Zenith on February 18, 1963. An announcement of his retention by Zenith appeared in the Chicago press on February 26, 1963 and shortly thereafter the instant complaint was filed.

The 1931 case of Parish v. Schwartz, 344 III. 563, 176 N.E. 757, 78 A.L.R. 1032, has spelled out the general Illinois rule with respect to enforcement of restrictive covenants in employment contracts. Where a covenant places restrictions upon a party not to engage in subsequent competitive employment or in a competitive line of trade, these restrictions must be reasonably related to safeguarding the employer without putting unreasonable restraints upon trade. An employee, after severing connections with his employer may compete with the former employer in his new position unless restricted by contract. While limitations may be placed upon an employee's freedom of action these limitations must conform to a test of reasonableness which will be stricter in the case of employment contracts.

The Restatement of Contracts, Secs. 313 to 315, 1932, states a test for the validity of post-employment restraints. Such restraining covenants are reasonable if (1) the restraint is no greater than that required for the protection of the employer, (2) they do not impose undue hardship on the employee, and (3) these are not injurious to the public. . . . It does not appear that the activities of the defendant while performing his duties for the plaintiff were such as to require a covenant which would prevent him from obtaining subsequent employment with a competitor for a period of 1 year. From the nature of Smith's work at Beltone and his non-technical position, the restraint upon his engaging in any other employment within 1 year would not be likely to produce corresponding benefits for the plaintiff. The covenant in prohibiting defendant's employment by anyone engaged in the manufacture or sale of hearing aids by anyone in any place goes farther than necessary to protect the plaintiff. Defendant by the covenant cannot be employed in a non-hearing aid capacity by firms employed in the manufacture or sale of other products as well as hearing aids. . . .

The case of World Wide Pharmacal Dist. Co. v. Kolkey, 5 Ill.App.2d 201, 125 N.E.2d 309, relied upon by plaintiff, is not applicable to the facts at hand. The defendant there acquired an intimate knowledge of the methods and procedures used in the plaintiff's business, including the formula in the manufacture of a product. He also secretly organized a corporation and began distribution of the product. In the Kolkey case the former employee was engaged in unfair competition. The defendant in the case at bar had no such secret information nor was his conduct reprehensible. He was not using knowledge of any trade secret to benefit his new employer.

The business of plaintiff is highly competitive. The burden of business risks, inherent in its operation, however, cannot be allocated to the employee by placing such wide restrictions upon his right to future employment. . . .
[ORDER REVERSED]

Although generally oral contracts are enforceable, the Statute of Frauds makes certain types of oral contracts unenforceable by either party unless and until sufficient written evidence of them is presented. No matter how many witnesses can be produced and no matter how convincing their testimony might be concerning the existence of these kinds of contracts, the court will not enforce them. The minimum evidence required by the law is a writing which sets forth the important terms of the agreement, identifies the parties to it, and is signed by the party whom one seeks to enforce the contract against. Although the types of contracts which must be evidenced by a writing differ from state to state, the various statutes almost universally include these four types: first, any contract to sell real estate or any interest in land; second, contracts by which one guarantees the payment of another person's debt and the guarantor does not stand to materially benefit from doing so (this provision does not include primary promises to pay money, but only secondary ones to pay if the principal debtor does not); third, contracts which cannot possibly be performed in accordance with their terms within a period of one year from the time they are made, except that if one of the parties has performed his part of the bargain fully, he can enforce the agreement against the other without written proof of it; and fourth, certain contracts for the sale of personal property which the Uniform Commercial Code controls. The Code provides for three different categories of sales of personal property which must be evidenced by a writing: contracts to sell tangible personal property (goods, wares and merchandise) where the value is $500 or over; contracts to sell investment securities (stocks and bonds) of any value; and contracts to sell intangible personal property other than investment securities (accounts receivable, notes, checks, patent rights, good will, and the like) where the value is $5,000 or over. The Code also provides certain exceptions to contracts which fall into these categories. First, if either the seller or buyer performs partially, he can enforce the agreement to the extent of his part performance. Also, if one of the parties admits the oral contract in his pleadings when being sued, he cannot use the Statute of Frauds as a defense. In addition, if the contract is between merchants, one of them can create enough evidence to enforce it by sending a written confirmation to the other, if the latter does not speak out and deny the oral agreement within ten days after he receives the confirmation. And finally, contracts to sell specially manufactured goods, which are not readily marketable in the ordinary course of the business of the seller, are enforceable even if oral and for $500 or over.

If a party does not perform his contract he still may not have liability for a breach. While changing circumstances which merely result in additional hardship to one of the parties do not excuse him, those which make performance impossible do provide an excuse for not performing his contract obligations. For example, if a person who is contractually bound to perform personal services dies, his estate as well as the surviving contracting party are excused. Note here, however, that death does not have this effect in other types of contracts. The law may change and render an agreement impossible to enforce because its object has become illegal. Also, destruction of some subject matter without which the agreement cannot be performed furnishes an excuse. If a painter has contracted to paint a certain house, and that house burns down before he can perform, obviously impossibility exists. Some cases have excused a party from his contract where extreme hardship existed, but technically no true impossibility did. Such decisions probably provide an equitable result, but lend unpredictability to the law. For examples of two cases in which impossibility was an issue, see Section 5A, Chapter 5 starting on page 155. As is also noted there, the Uniform Commercial Code liberalizes the law in this area by excusing a seller of goods from his contract, if it has become "impracticable" to perform. He is required, however, to allocate existing supplies or production among his regular customers pro rata. The customers are not bound to accept only part of the goods their contract calls for, but are entitled to their share, if they want it.

In some instances, the court will impose a duty on one party to pay for the reasonable value of a benefit he has received from another, in order to achieve justice, even though the parties do not have a contract. The duty imposed is very much like a contract debt and is said to arise out of quasi-contract. The case which follows discusses this remedy.

ANDERSON V. COPELAND
378 P.2d 1007 (Okla. 1963)

PER CURIAM: This is an appeal from the District Court of Cotton County. The parties will be referred to in this Court as they appeared in the court below.

Plaintiff, Jack Copeland, doing business as Copeland Equipment Company, brought this action against defendant, Walter Anderson, to recover for the rental value of a tractor owned by plaintiff which was in defendant's possession for approximately two weeks.

The facts giving rise to this claim were for the most part undisputed. Defendant orally agreed to purchase a used tractor from plaintiff for the sum of $475.00. For eleven days thereafter defendant attempted to borrow money to cover the purchase price but was unable to, and so advised plaintiff. Plaintiff asked defendant to return the tractor, which was done within a few days. The only dispute appears to be in that defendant says the sale was conditioned on defendant's ability to borrow money to pay for it, while plaintiff says the sale was final and without conditions. In any event, both parties agree that the sale contract was rescinded when plaintiff asked that the tractor be returned.

The case was tried to a jury which returned a verdict for plaintiff in the amount of $50.00. Defendant's motion for new trial was overruled and he appeals.

It appears from the facts that the parties instead of attempting to enforce such rights as they may have had under the sale contract, rescinded it. The parties were then in the same position as before the agreement was made, except that defendant had had the use of plaintiff's tractor without paying for it. Under those circumstances the law would imply a contract for defendant would be unjustly enriched.

In the first paragraph of the syllabus in *Pigee v. Mercy Hosp.*, 199 Okla. 411, 186 P.2d 817, we held:

> *Contracts implied by law, or more properly quasi or constructive contracts, are a class of obligations which are imposed or created by law without regard to the assent of the party bound, on the ground that they are dictated by reason and justice, and may be enforced by an action ex contractu.*

Defendant contends that there cannot exist at the same time an express contract and an implied contract between the same parties covering the same subject matter. This statement of law is not applicable in the instant case for the reason that the subject matter of the express contract was a sale, whereas the subject matter of the contract implied in law was a rental. The case of *Berry v. Barbour*, 279 P.2d 355 (Okla.), is somewhat similar. In that case a contractor was employed to make improvements and repairs of the owner's building. During the owner's absence in Europe, the roof of the building was partially destroyed by fire without the fault of the contractor who made necessary repairs of the fire damage, without knowledge of the owner. We held that a quasi contract arose obligating the owner to reimburse the contractor for the reasonable cost of material and labor furnished.

Defendant further contends that the trial court's instructions to the jury were erroneous. The instruction requested by defendant, however, covered contracts implied in fact. Such instruction was not applicable. In *First Nat'l Bank v. Matlock*, 99 Okl. 150, 226 P.328, 36 A.L.R. 1088, we distinguished between contracts implied in fact and contracts implied in law. In the former the intention of the parties is ascertained and enforced. We believe that the instruction to the jury in the instant case sufficiently covered the law to be applied to the facts. There was ample evidence in the case to support the verdict of the jury and the trial court's judgment rendered thereon. [AFFIRMED]

When a person transfers property to another by a contract, the seller can only convey such title as he himself has, as a general rule. Thus, even a good-faith purchaser of goods from a thief obtains no title as against the true owner. Of course, if the owner reclaims such goods, the buyer has a remedy against the seller for breach of the seller's warranty that he had title. Also, one who buys real estate which has been mortgaged takes subject to the equity of the mortgagee, if the mortgage has been properly recorded at the office of the county recorder of deeds. In a similar way, the purchaser of goods or other items of personal property which are the collateral for a debt secured by a properly perfected security device may be subject to the lien of the secured party. But a good-faith purchaser of goods from one who has voidable title to them obtains good title. Suppose S is induced to sell goods on credit by B's fraudulent misrepresentations concerning B's ability to pay for them. S can rescind as against B and recover the goods. But, if B sells the goods to G, a good-faith purchaser, G can keep them free and clear of any claims of S.

Just as land and tangible personal property can be sold, so can intangible personal property, including contract rights themselves. When contract rights are transferred, the transferor is called an assignor and the transferee is called an assignee.

Generally even if the obligor objects, the assignment can be made anyway, and the obligor then becomes legally bound to perform for the assignee. Personal contract rights, however, such as those to the services of the obligor, cannot be assigned without his consent. Clearly, money debts are not personal and are usually assignable. The rights the assignee gets are those of the assignor—no better, no worse. In other words, if the obligor has any defense or right of set off which he can use against the assignor, he can also use it to escape or diminish liability to the assignee. For example, suppose D owes C $50 for goods which C delivered to D. If C assigns the right to payment to X, D must now pay X, unless he pays C in good faith before learning of the assignment. If the goods C delivered contained hidden defects and C breached his implied warranty that the goods were merchantable, D can rescind against C upon discovering the defects and will not have to pay C. Therefore, in this case X will not be able to collect from D either, even if X purchased the contract rights in good faith and had nothing whatever to do with the defects.

A different rule applies where the contract right transferred is commercial paper, or a negotiable instrument such as a promissory note, check or other draft, which meets the requirements of Article 3 of the Uniform Commercial Code. A holder in due course of such an instrument is not subject to the personal defenses the obligor may have against the original payee, and therefore actually may get better rights than his transferor had. A holder in due course, briefly, is one to whom the instrument has been properly negotiated (by delivery if bearer paper or by indorsement and delivery if order paper) and who has paid value for it in good faith before it has become overdue. Personal defenses frequently are those which are related to the consideration underlying a contract and would include such things as breach of contract, fraud in the inducement, and lack of consideration (as when a negotiable instrument is given as a gift). Assume that in the hypothetical given above D had given his $50 *check* to C, instead of just a simple contractual promise to pay in exchange for the goods, and C negotiated the check to X. If X qualifies as a holder in due course, he will have a legal right to recover the full amount of the check from D, free of D's defense, even if D stops payment on the check before it is cashed. D's defense is a personal one, and he is left with recourse against C only. Note that even a holder in due course of a draft or note cannot recover from the obligor who has a real defense, such as the fact that his signature was forged. The main object of these rules is to provide a special type of contract which can take the place of money, and will be, as nearly as possible, as acceptable to creditors as cash. Clearly, the ability of a contract to act as a medium of exchange like money depends upon its acceptability in commerce as such, and equally as clearly, the simple contract which carries with it all defenses would not be satisfactory to most creditors. A negotiable contract which is used in lieu of cash is needed for such purposes as convenience, safety, and to obtain credit.

5   TRANSFER OF PROPERTY BY GIFT

One method of transferring property is by making a gift of it to another, which is a voluntary transfer without any consideration or compensation therefor. It should be noted that a *promise* to make a gift is not enforceable, since it lacks the necessary consideration. However, once a gift has been executed, it is final and cannot be revoked by the donor. In order to have a valid gift, three elements are essential. First, there must be an intention to give on the part of the donor (as contrasted with an intention to bargain, to lend or the like). Second, there must be an acceptance of the gift on the part of the donee. And, finally, there must be a delivery of the subject matter of the gift. Delivery may be conditional on the happening of an event, in which case, if the event does not occur, the gift is incomplete and the subject matter can be reclaimed by the donor. An engagement ring, for example, is given on the condition of marriage, and if the nuptials do not take place, the donor is entitled to recover the ring, perhaps to use it again later with better success. However, if the donor prevents the condition from occurring, as by standing up the bride at the church, he cannot reclaim the diamond (it being something in the nature of a consolation prize, in this instance). A gift of personal property causa mortis, or in anticipation of death where the apprehension of such is reasonably present, vests title in the donee immediately, subject to the condition subsequent that failure of the donor to die revokes the gift. Gifts without this condition are termed gifts "inter vivos."

Sometimes it is troublesome to find the requisite intent to give, since an alleged donor may have intended only to constitute the person to whom property was delivered as his agent or bailee. In resolving this issue, the court considers such things as the relationship between the parties, the value of the alleged gift in comparison with the donor's remaining property, the actions of the donor concerning the property after the gift is alleged to have been made, and the like. The weight of authority holds that if a gift is beneficial, acceptance of the gift will be presumed. If the gift is being made of goods which are capable of manual delivery, such as a book or watch, then manual delivery generally should take place. However, symbolic or constructive delivery may be made where the subject matter of the gift is incapable of manual delivery. It is generally held that a symbolic delivery is one where something is handed over in place of the actual thing itself, while a constructive delivery is the handing over of the means to gain possession or control of the thing, such as a key or a passbook. In order to be effective, delivery must completely divest the donor of dominion and control over the thing given. In one unusual case, it was held that a father effectively delivered a gift of buried treasure to his daughter, by taking her into the garden and pointing out the various places where it had been buried. In that case, the donor was extremely ill, and barely physically capable of even going into the garden and revealing the locations of the property being given.

6   TRANSFER OF PROPERTY UPON DEATH

One method of transferring property is by a validly executed will which takes effect at the death of the testator. Wills may include, besides a disposition of property, the naming of a personal representative to handle the estate, the designation of a guardian for minor children, or a revocation of former wills. A gift by will of personal property is called a bequest or legacy; a gift of realty is a devise. Generally, a will is ambulatory during the lifetime of the testator and therefore can be revoked until he dies. A will usually must be in writing and signed by the testator or by some person in his presence and at his direction. In addition, it must be attested by two or more credible witnesses, who subscribe their names to the will. The testator must either sign or acknowledge the instrument as being his in the presence of the witnesses. Some states require that there be a minimum of three witnesses.

Every person of the requisite age who is of sound mind and memory has the power to pass property by will. In one state, the minimum age to execute a valid will is set at eighteen, even though the age of majority for purposes of entering into binding contracts is set, for males, at twenty-one. To have testamentary capacity, one does not have to be absolutely of sound mind and memory in every respect, but must at the time of executing the will have had sufficient mental capacity to comprehend and remember who are the natural objects of his bounty, to comprehend the kind and character of his property and the particular business in which he is engaged, and to make a disposition of his property according to some plan formed in his mind. He must have capacity, not actual knowledge of these matters. Old age, feeble health, or both, though combined with a defective memory, will not constitute lack of the testamentary capacity required to make a valid will. Mere eccentricity does not constitute unsoundness of mind.

When one dies without leaving a will, or intestate, in effect the state makes one for him. Every state has a statute of descent and distribution which provides rules for determining the manner in which a deceased person's property is to be distributed if he has not validly disposed of it himself by his will. In one state, for example, if a person dies with a surviving spouse and children, the spouse inherits one-third of both his real and personal property and the children inherit two-thirds. If he leaves just children surviving, they take all, and likewise if he is survived just by his spouse and no children, she takes all. In the latter eventuality, some states provide that the decedent's parents and brothers and sisters share with the spouse in some of his property. Statutes of descent and distribution provide further for a proper distribution under various fact situations, such as when a person dies without spouse, children or other descendants, brothers, sisters, parents, and so on. Finally, if no relatives qualify as heirs, the property escheats to the state.

Land or personal property held in the joint tenancy form of co-ownership passes to the surviving owner or owners upon the death of other joint tenants, and not to the deceased person's heirs. In contrast, property held by two or more persons in co-ownership as tenants in common passes to the heirs of a co-owner upon his death, according to either his will or the statute of descent and distribution where he has no applicable will. In both of these forms of tenancy, each owner has an undivided interest in the whole. Many states by statute do not favor joint tenancies, and hold that they, with their attribute of right of survivorship, can be created only by language very clearly negating a tenancy in common. In such states, it is desirable to use the exact wording prescribed by the applicable statute if a joint tenancy is intended.

7   THE EXTENT OF RIGHTS OF OWNERSHIP

In the early common law, it was often indicated that the owner of land had rights that extended from the bowels of the earth up to the heavens. In this view, one who owned a square lot really had space in the form of an inverted pyramid with its tip at the center of the earth, and its base of infinite area somewhere beyond the galaxies. Of course, giving an owner absolute dominion of the air space, in theory, presented no particular practical problems in a time when airplane travel, let alone interplanetary space travel, was both impossible and unheard of. As technology has made air travel possible and even an economic necessity, the law has changed the property rights of the owner of land to the air space above it, cutting them back from the previous theoretical absolute rights to permit the ordinary and reasonable use of the air which does not unduly interfere with the use of his land by the owner.

As Dean Pound indicated on page 607, the twentieth century has brought about changes in the philosophy of the law of property from a viewpoint which seemed to protect the owner of property in doing whatever he pleased with it, regardless of the effect on others, to one limiting the rights of ownership where necessary to protect overriding social interests. The rights of owners are restricted in many instances, and similarly limited is the freedom of contract. As we have seen previously, the antitrust laws significantly limit what one may do with his property. So do tax laws and many labor laws. In addition, one's rights in his own property are limited by the rights others, who are not owners, may have in it. Sometimes these rights are created by statute, such as zoning ordinances which restrict the use of land. They may exist because of court decisions declaring certain uses of land to be private nuisances which unduly interfere with the use and enjoyment of neighboring lands by their owners. Rights of way across land may exist in favor of other persons. These are called easements. For example, a neighbor may have the right to use a private road across your land to get to his own. The telephone company may have an easement which permits it to string wires across land, in the air space of the owner, without being guilty of trespass. Similarly, sewer lines or pipe lines underneath land may be permissible because the owners thereof have an easement. Such rights may be conveyed by the grant of the owner of the land in which the easement exists. They may be taken from him involuntarily by exercise of the power of eminent domain. Easements may also be created by prescription, which is similar to obtaining title to property by adverse possession, simply by use of another's land in the required manner for the necessary statutory time period, which varies from state to state. The two cases which follow illustrate the rights which one may have in the property of another.

DUNBAR V. O'BRIEN
220 N.W. 278 (Neb. 1928)

ROSE, JUSTICE: This is a suit in equity to abate a private nuisance and to protect an easement. Ruth F. Dunbar, plaintiff, owns a lot fronting south on First avenue in Nebraska City. Joseph O'Brien, defendant, owns the adjoining lot on the west. The west wall or the eaves of the house in which plaintiff resides with her family are on the west line of her lot. The east wall of defendant's house is perhaps eight feet farther west. Neither party disputes the title to the lot of the other. The petition contains pleas that defendant piled old lumber and other debris close to the west wall of plaintiff's house in front of her basement windows, thus shutting out light and air, annoying her and damaging her in her property rights; that in committing the wrongs alleged defendant was prompted by malice with intent to annoy and punish plaintiff without serving any useful purpose of his own; that he maintained the nuisance described months after he was requested by plaintiff to abate it.

It is also alleged in the petition that, by prescription or adverse user for more than the statutory period of 10 years, plaintiff and her predecessors in title acquired an easement consisting of the right to enter and use a strip of ground west of her house for the purpose of washing windows, of placing and removing screens, of painting and of making needed repairs; that a fence prevents access from the rear; that defendant forbade access for any purpose and closed her front passageway by a lattice between the houses.

The relief sought by plaintiff is an injunction abating the nuisances and preventing defendant from interfering with her right to exercise her easement.

The answer of defendant contained general denials of facts relating to nuisances and easements; admitted that he erected a lattice extending from the east side of his house to his east lot line; alleged that plaintiff's basement windows were placed in the west wall of her foundation in September, 1925, and that her workmen then trespassed upon his lot, leaving thereon piles of broken rock and other rubbish which he was required to remove, and that consequently he forbade further trespassing; that any use of his lot by plaintiff or former owners of her lot was by his permission and not by the exercise of any right claimed by them.

The answer contains also a cross-petition alleging that plaintiff collects rain-water from the roof of her house and discharges it in a volume on defendant's lot, thus injuring the foundation of his house and damaging his fruit and vegetable cave. He prays for the dismissal of plaintiff's suit and for an injunction preventing her from trespassing on his lot and from discharging rain-water thereon. . . .

Upon a trial of the issues the district court denied an injunction to prevent defendant from interfering with the passage of light and air through the windows in plaintiff's basement; enjoined interference with an easement consisting of the right of plaintiff to use the strip of ground under her west eaves for the purposes of washing windows, placing and removing screens, painting and making necessary repairs; denied an injunction restraining plaintiff from discharging rain-water from the roof of her house upon defendant's lot. Plaintiff appealed and defendant took a cross-appeal.

Was plaintiff entitled to an injunction to prevent defendant from shutting off the light and air from her basement? The trial court found and the evidence showed that defendant unnecessarily piled old lumber and other debris close to the west wall of plaintiff's basement in front of her windows. The work necessary for this annoyance required defendant to move lumber and other materials from the rear of his lot to plaintiff's windows. If the pile was not intended for a continuing nuisance, the additional work of removing it was necessary and all without any benefit to himself. For several months he shut out light and air from plaintiff's basement after he was requested to remove the obstructions. He allowed the debris to remain there until after this suit was brought. The relief based on this nuisance seems to have been denied by the trial court on the ground that defendant removed the obstructions before the case was tried. The proper inference from the evidential facts is that defendant acted through malice and used his property to annoy and punish his neighbor without serving any useful or aesthetic purpose of his own. The fundamental liberty to own and control property implies the duty of the owner to respect the equal rights of others. Contrary to a majority of former opinions of the courts, the modern view, based on reason and justice, is that the owner of property is not permitted to use it for the sole purpose of inflicting malicious injury upon his neighbor. Referring to the majority rule in cases where the courts declined to interfere with malicious structures, the Supreme Court of Alabama said:

> The doctrine of these cases, based on the alleged right of the owner of land to use it according to his malicious fancy, and without any advantage to himself or his land, for the sole purpose of injuring his neighbor in the lawful and beneficial use of his adjoining property, has been carried to such an extent as in many cases to be justly characterized as "odious." And hence statutes have been passed in a number of states abrogating the principle on account of the unjust and injurious effects resulting from its enforcement. The authority of precedents, however, must often yield to the force of reason, and to the paramount demands of justice as well as the decencies of civilized society, and the law ought to speak with a voice responsive to these demands. We have examined the decisions and the reasoning of the various courts upon this question; and, unfettered by any precedents of our own, we are led to the deliberate conclusions that the majority view, as above stated, is founded upon a vicious fallacy, and is violative of sound legal principle as well as of common justice. Norton v. Randolph, 176 Ala. 386, 58 So. 285.

This is in harmony with the Michigan rule, which has been stated as follows:

> A fence erected maliciously, and with no other purpose than to shut out the light and air from a neighbor's windows, is a nuisance. Flaherty v. Moran, 81 Mich. 52, 45 N.W. 381.

Referring to the maxim meaning, "So use your own as not to injure another's property," the Supreme Court of North Carolina said:

> The ancient maxim, . . . "Sic utere tuo ut alienum non laedas," is not founded in any human statute, but in that sentiment expressed by Him who taught good will toward men, and said, "Love thy neighbor as thyself."

Freely translated, it enjoins that every person, in the use of his own property, should avoid injury to his neighbor as much as possible. No one ought to have the legal right to make a malicious use of his property for no benefit to himself, but merely to injure his fellow man. To hold otherwise makes the law an engine of oppression with which to destroy the peace and comfort of a neighbor, as well as to damage his property for no useful purpose, but solely to gratify a wicked and debasing passion. Barger v. Baringer, 151 N.C. 440, 66 S.E. 442. . . .

In the present instance there is nothing in the evidence to prove a justification for the creation or maintenance of the obstruction in front of plaintiff's windows. When this suit was brought plaintiff was entitled to an injunction abating the nuisance. Defendant, by his wrongful conduct, caused plaintiff to resort to the district court for equitable relief. Whether the right to an injunction was defeated by the removal of the debris depends on the good faith of defendant. He was prompted by malice in the first instance, and there is nothing in his pleadings or proof to show that he will not repeat his annoyance, if the litigation ends without any restraint upon his future conduct. On this phase of the case the circumstances disclosed by the evidence on the issues indicate error in the order denying equitable relief.

Did plaintiff prove the existence of an easement permitting access to the west wall of her house and the use of a strip of ground for the purpose indicated?

In *Omaha & R. V. R. Co. v. Richards,* 38 Neb. 847, 57 N.W. 739, the court held:

An easement in real estate may be acquired by open, notorious, peaceable, uninterrupted, adverse possession for the statutory period of ten years.

In the present case there is evidence tending to prove the following facts: Plaintiff's house was standing in its present location as early as 1898. For more than 10 years continuously thereafter owners or occupants of plaintiff's lot had access from the front of defendant's lot and used a narrow strip on the east side of it for the purposes of painting, and washing windows. This use was open, notorious and peaceable without permission of the owners, and after 1925 was first interrupted by defendant, who purchased his lot in 1912 and went into possession in 1913. The easement was continuously exercised by plaintiff and former owners or occupants of her house. On the contrary there is testimony tending to prove that there was no path in the passageway claimed by plaintiff; that owners of defendant's lot did not have notice at any time that a portion of his lot was used adversely by plaintiff and former owners or occupants of her lot; that any such use was permissive, and not adverse. While the evidence on this issue is conflicting to some extent, the preponderance seems to be in favor of plaintiff, whose easement was acquired before defendant purchased his lot, and not subsequently lost. Defendant testified in effect that the husband of plaintiff requested permission for workmen to make repairs on the west side of her house, but this did not amount to an abandonment of the easement or to an admission that it had no existence. A courteous request by a neighbor for such permission, directed to the owner of the fee, did not necessarily disprove an existing right to enter without it. It is clear that the necessary use of the passageway for plaintiff's purposes would not wear a path. After the easement was legally acquired, notice of its continuous use was unnecessary. In the decree below the trial court confined the easement to the ground under the eaves. The evidence shows that stepladders were used, and they seem to be necessary. Their use obviously requires more ground than that covered by the eaves. The width of the easement is determined by necessity, and not by convenience. The former use of a strip to the extent of three feet in width seems to be reasonable and should be protected. The easement does not give plaintiff any right to the fee or to annoy defendant or to litter or injure his lot or to enter his premises for any purpose other than to wash windows, to insert and remove screens, to paint, and to make necessary repairs. For these purposes a passageway two feet wide at the east end of the lattice constructed by defendant will be a proper access and protect plaintiff's easement and will be required.

In so far as the decree below denies an injunction to prevent plaintiff from discharging rain-water on defendant's lot it seems to be correct, and to that extent is affirmed. Otherwise, the judgment of the district court is reversed and the cause remanded for the purposes of a supplemental decree conforming to the views herein expressed, the costs in both courts to be paid by defendant. [JUDGMENT ACCORDINGLY]

STREETT V. MARSHALL
291 S.W. 494 (Mo. 1927)

RAGLAND, JUSTICE: This is an action to perpetually enjoin the defendants from using their premises, known as 5297 Washington boulevard, in the city of St. Louis, as a "funeral home."

Washington boulevard is 70 feet in width. Its length between Lake avenue and Union boulevard is approximately 1,000 feet. On both sides of this portion of the street are residences which are located on lots having a frontage of from 40 to 141 feet, and which cost originally from $15,000 to $20,000. All of these houses, except the one which is the subject of this controversy, are occupied by their owners as family residences. . . .

The funeral services held in defendants' parlors are of the usual character, lasting from 30 minutes to an hour. . . . Many, perhaps the majority, of the funerals conducted by defendants as undertakers are at the homes where the deaths occur. Those held at their "funeral home" between the time they opened the place and the trial of this cause, a period of a little over six months, averaged one a month. How many bodies were brought there with respect to which no funeral services were held does not appear. . . .

The plaintiffs, twenty-four in number, are the several owners and occupants of homes located on both sides of Washington boulevard, between Lake avenue and Union boulevard, and at distances from defendants' "funeral home" which range from 15 feet to 500 feet. Ten or twelve of them testified as witnesses. . . .

They all said that the maintenance and operation of the "funeral home" in their midst brought sadness and depression to them and the members of their families, and that such depression, in certain designated individual cases, had been accompanied with extreme nervousness. None, however, was able to say that his or her health had been directly affected. Plaintiffs also called a number of physicians who testified, in substance, that such an undertaking establishment as that conducted by defendants would have a decidedly depressing effect upon the nervous system of person(s) of nervous temperament, particularly women and children, who lived in its immediate vicinity, and that such depression would be deleterious to health. . . .

Plaintiffs further offered an abundance of expert testimony, practically uncontradicted, tending to show that the continuance of the "funeral home" would depreciate the values of their property from 40 to 50 per cent.

Defendants' evidence tended to show that an undertaking establishment and its activities do not in any respect affect adversely the health of the average normal individual who lives near it; that no sickly zones surround undertaking shops; that from time immemorial men and women have lived within their immediate environment, and lived the vigor of health, even joyously, until the full measure of life's span had been accomplished. Nor did defendants' experts agree with those who testified for plaintiffs. One of them was of the opinion that the living observer of a passing funeral would, or might, be buoyed up by the thought that another, and not he, was on the way to the cemetery. Another was of the opinion that a person suffering from nervousness or depression might be benefited by being stationed at some point of vantage where he could view passing funeral processions. . . .

The trial court held in effect that defendants' "funeral home," because of its location in a strictly residential district, constituted a nuisance, and enjoined its further maintenance at that place. . . .

Appellants' "funeral home" is not an undertaking establishment in the full sense of those terms. It can be more accurately characterized as a mortuary chapel; a place devoted to the reception of the dead and the performance of funeral rites. No contagion and no noxious odors or offensive gases emanate from the place. But the dead are taken there and laid out to be viewed by sorrowing kindred and friends who from time to time come and go; and funerals are held there at recurring intervals, and with them comes the hearse carrying the dead, followed by processions of mourners. These constant reminders of death are the things complained of in this case; the mortuary itself; and the visible activities which take place in connection with it. Respondents say that the immediateness, both as to time and place, with which they suggest death, keep them and their families living, in a very real sense, in the constant presence of the dead, whereby they are greatly saddened and depressed.

Buttressed by the testimony of their experts, as well as the results of everyday experience and observation, as they conceive them, appellants insist that the ills of which respondents complain are simply fanciful or imaginary; that the worry and uneasiness which they do manifest grow out of the fear that their property may suffer some depreciation. . . .

[A]ppellants argue that an undertaking establishment where only bodies which have been embalmed are received, thus eliminating all question of communicating disease or fouling the air with noxious or offensive odors and gases, cannot be held to be a nuisance, although conducted in an exclusively residential neighborhood. In other words, in order for such an establishment to constitute a nuisance, its character must be such as to directly affect the health or grossly offend the physical senses. This position is without support in the decided cases. While it is true that in many, if not all of them, the charge was made that the establishment complained of would communicate contagion, and would emit noxious gases and offensive smells, such charge was almost universally found to be without substantial support in the evidence. A careful reading of the cases will disclose that what has been stressed, and in the last analysis made the basis of injunctive relief, is this: Constant reminders of death, such as an undertaking establishment and the activities connected with it give rise to, impair in a substantial way the comfort, repose, and enjoyment of the homes which are subjected to them. . . .

The evidence fully warranted the chancellor's finding that the use which the defendants are making of their property grievously impinges upon the rights of plaintiffs to the undisturbed enjoyment of their homes. No amount of skill or tact can wholly eliminate from the undertaking business its constant reminders of death, the one thing from which the normal individual instinctively flees, whatever his religion or philosophy of life. To be compelled to live in a continuing atmosphere of death is intolerable. While the undertaking business is not only lawful but indispensable, there is no justification or excuse for its seeking out and establishing itself in localities devoted exclusively to homes, where it not only materially detracts from the comfort and happiness of those who dwell there, but ruinously depreciates the values of their real estate as well.

The judgment of the circuit court is affirmed.

Besides being restricted in how his property can be used, in some instances an owner is limited as to how he can dispose of it. A classic example of this is the right which most states give a surviving spouse to renounce a will of his or her deceased spouse and take a certain minimum amount of the decedent's property. In one state, the spouse is entitled to at least one-third if there are also children surviving the decedent, or to one-half if there are no children, regardless of the provisions in the decedent's will. There is no similar rule for the benefit of children or parents of a decedent. If they are "cut out" of his estate, their only hope is to contest the validity of the will, and have a share of the property pass to them intestate under the statute of descent and distribution.

THE LAW OF TORTS

1 THE NATURE AND EXTENT OF TORT LITIGATION

A tort is a wrong other than a breach of contract committed against a person or his property for which the law gives a right to recover damages. It differs from a crime, which is a wrong against society, although the same act may be both a wrong against a person and against society, as for example, an assault.

Tort liability is predicated on the premises that in a civilized society one person will not intentionally injure another or his property, and that all persons will exercise reasonable care and caution in their activities. The first premise has resulted in a group of torts usually labeled intentional torts. These would include assault and battery, false imprisonment, libel, slander, trespass to real property, and conversion of personal property. The second premise has established the general field of tort liability known as negligence. The field of negligence is frequently further broken into degrees depending on the extent of carelessness involved and the extent of the duty owed. Each of these premises creates liability for wrongful conduct because of fault. Our legal system in effect says: "If you are at fault and cause injury to another or his property, you shall compensate him for his loss or damages with money."

Tort liability is imposed on masters for the torts of their agents or servants acting within the scope of their employment. This includes both intentional and unintentional torts but does not include torts committed by an agent or servant on a frolic of his own or while detoured from the scope of his employment. Employers are held liable for the torts of their employees primarily because of the "deep pocket" theory or simply because of the likelihood that the employer has more ability to pay for the wrong. Society therefore imposes tort liability on employers as a cost of doing business.

Tort claims are the single largest source of litigation in this country. Some of our cities, such as Chicago, have over 50,000 tort cases pending at all times and the great majority of these have arisen as a result of automobile collisions. The correlation between tort litigation and the premiums charged by the casualty insurance industry is obvious. Every person driving or owning an automobile is aware of the cost of insuring against potential tort liability.

In addition to automobile accident cases, business is involved in a large number of tort cases arising out of the sale of a product which has caused an injury. Product liability cases may involve injuries caused by deleterious food or a defective drug. Cases too may concern cosmetics which cause injury to the skin or even cigarettes which cause cancer. In many ways, cases involving product liability have a contractual basis because of the sale of the defective goods, but the fact that suits are for dollar damages for *injuries* caused by products ties this area of the law to torts. The trends in product liability discussed in section 4 will indicate, however, that liability here is not necessarily based on fault.

The law of torts is also significant for businessmen because torts can be committed by employees for which the employer will have liability. This matter is discussed further in section 6 of this chapter.

2   PROBLEMS OF TORT LITIGATION

There are many problems inherent in our system of tort litigation and liability based on fault. First of all, the sheer number of automobiles and auto accidents has created congestion in the courts so that the trial may be several years after the occurrence. Witnesses die or move away or their memories lapse so that the testimony at the trial can hardly be described as accurate. Plaintiffs may tire of waiting because of the need for funds and may be forced to settle a case for less than their actual damages. For many other reasons, delayed justice is no justice at all. Justice requires easy and prompt access to courts which the congestion due to the large number of cases makes impossible.

Second, the nature of tort litigation has resulted in a contingent fee system for compensating attorneys. The contingent fee system means that the attorney is paid a percentage of the recovery or settlement. Usual contingent fees are 25 percent if the case is settled before trial, 33⅓ percent if a trial is held, and 40 to 50 percent if the case is appealed. Contingent fees eliminate the risk of high attorney's fees if the case is lost, but may create some undesirable side effects in many cases. For example, if the injuries are very substantial and liability is easily established, the fees of the attorney may be unfair and unreasonable. Assume a $240,000 verdict is given for the loss of two legs by a plaintiff. It is difficult to see how the $80,000 fee could have been earned. In addition, the chance of earning large fees has encouraged "ambulance chasing" of potentially big cases, especially in large cities. Referrals by doctors, ambulance drivers, undertakers, special investigators, and others who have direct contact with victims are not uncommon, although the organized bar has attempted to prevent these practices. As a direct result of contingent fees and congested courts, some lawyers have been advancing money to clients for current expenses. Such practices have tended to concentrate personal injury litigation in a relatively few lawyers or law firms. This has further added to court congestion and encouraged the lawyer to settle cases below the actual damage in order to get the client "off the payroll."

Another problem for society inherent in tort litigation is the growing cost of liability insurance. Personal injury verdicts have gone up substantially in recent years so that the cost of liability insurance has risen considerably and many insurance companies have become insolvent due to the number and extent of recoveries against their insureds. The cost of liability insurance has risen to the extent that many auto owners cannot realistically afford to pay the premiums.

Many of the foregoing problems have resulted in proposals and suggestions to change many aspects of tort litigation. Some of the problems and proposed changes are discussed in the following article.

THE UNREALITY OF ACCIDENT LITIGATION: A PLEA

FOR A NEW APPROACH [1]

James Marshall

Recently the judges of the New York Supreme Court appeared before the City Planning Commission to appeal for more courthouse space because there were judges without chambers, special referees without hearing rooms and a library spread into the corridors. What they failed to say was that a large part of the cases brought to trial and an even larger proportion of the cases on the docket are motor vehicle accident cases, which in this day and age should rarely be litigated. They are based on inaccurate testimony, antiquated concepts of liability and the distortion necessarily incident to the combat of litigation. If such cases were removed from the courts there would be smaller dockets, fewer cases tried, a need for fewer court clerks, judges and courthouse space. . . .

If a case comes to trial—and only a small proportion does—he [the injured victim] must "show either that the intention was unlawful or that the defendant was at fault; for if the injury was unavoidable and the conduct of the defendant was free from blame, he will not be liable." This judicial opinion written in 1850 defines the essence of the "fault liability" principle that still governs most personal injury litigation in today's courts. One further condition is that the plaintiff himself must be blameless. The question of fault is generally decided by a jury after several witnesses testify. Out of the conflicting stories they are to determine what did happen.

---

[1] 50 *A.B.A.J.* 713 (Aug. 1964). Used by permission from the American Bar Association and the *American Bar Association Journal.*

Are the trial procedures and theory of fault liability derived from pre-automotive centuries appropriate to our age and culture?

A recent report on automobile accidents compiled for the World Health Organization suggests that it may not be humanly possible to determine what happened, for the average "development time" of an automobile accident is estimated at "probably less than ten seconds." Furthermore, as this report (J. D. Norman, *Road Traffic Accidents*) says, "Road accidents do not usually have a single 'cause'," and "each individual accident is likely to have several causative factors. . . . The search for single causes of accidents is therefore likely to prove unproductive." Who can fairly say, then, that the preponderance of evidence supports a finding that one person or one factor caused the accident? Yet the search continues in our courts to find who was at fault during those crucial ten seconds. . . .

[S]cience has been able to show us . . . that the observations which are the essence of eye-witness and earwitness testimony are so conditioned by the witness himself as to have little probative value. . . . Variations in the accuracy of residual observations such as those of distance and motion we know to be great. Yet these are precisely the observations for which we generally rely upon eyewitness testimony in an automobile accident case.

[A] motor vehicle accident . . . is . . . in the course of litigation refracted indefinitely through the lenses of experience by the witness, by his hearers—judge and jury—and by the jurors deliberating among themselves. We may never know what happened during those ten seconds in which the accident occurred, and we may from his testimony learn more about the witness than about what he witnessed. Litigation, despite the proclaimed purpose of the law, is not a quest for truth, but rather a bitter contest in which winner takes all, and this very process further distorts the report of an objective situation such as an accident.

These refractions continue during the later stages of recollection and articulation, as well as during the initial perception and interpretation. In the course of recollection, inevitable distortions occur and the great lapse of time in many jurisdictions between the incident and the trial tends to increase this. The selectivity of recall becomes more pronounced with time and with "taking sides." We know that there is a "curve of forgetting" that is scoop-shaped, like the track of a ski jump. Both the rapidity of the initial drop and the rate of the subsequent gradual decline depend upon the conditions under which the observation was made, the intensity with which it was "learned," and the emotional context. Most observations that make no new demands on the observer will be readily forgotten. More of what is "overlearned," that is, learned with intensity, will be retained for a short while, but after that the curve of forgetting becomes almost a vertical line as the "overlearned" is almost entirely forgotten. This is exemplified by the efforts of a student cramming for examinations. The next morning he may remember enough to pass the course, but a week later he remembers little or nothing of what he overlearned.

Experiments have also shown that shock, fright or pain may enhance the vividness of a recollection and its duration, but will reduce its accuracy. These emotional effects are usually in play during a traumatic experience like an automobile accident.

Acknowledging that memory may be imperfect, the law permits "refreshment" of the witness's recollection. . . .

We refer here to the refreshment that takes place inside the courtroom, although we cannot ignore the likelihood that at least as much refreshing goes on outside it. One report noted that "The distinction between coaching witnesses and preparing a case for trial is unfortunately too fine to be universally observed." But our concern, and the problem for the jury, is how to test "the vagaries of sound and honest minds." In the words of a veteran courtroom observer, "The great body of testimony is subjectively accurate, but objectively false."

When a witness is on the stand he inevitably tends to identify his interest with that of the party for whom he is testifying. Adversary proceedings intensify this identification. If the witness's side wins, he shares in society's endorsement; if his side loses, he too is rejected. When "his side" wins, the witness gets a sense of satisfaction, he feels rewarded, it was worth while for him to have testified. As Dr. William A. White observed long ago, "An unprejudiced individual does not exist."

This identification will work hand in glove with past experience to suggest to the witness ways in which to fill the gaps in his recollection. If a witness is not certain whether or not he heard the siren as he saw the fire engine racing down the street, he may "bet" on the basis of what he has learned through experience with sirens and engines that he did in fact hear it. He will not necessarily do this consciously, with intention to deceive. He simply may not want to appear to be a liar or be made to seem foolish on cross-examination. But it is precisely these departures from the norm, such as failure to sound a siren or horn, that may connote legal fault and are at the heart of a negligence case.

The vagaries of recollection are further modified by those of articulation. The use of words creates ambiguities. It creates a compulsion for the narrator to fill in gaps and obscures the varying degrees of certainty with which facts are recalled. As Hutchins and Slesinger pointed out, when a witness reports that "It was raining and I wore my rubbers," we do not know whether he recalls both of these facts or infers one from the other or has inferred both from a third recollection such as the fact that he was carrying his umbrella. Language has been described as a rigidifying process creating "slippage between the abstraction as it functions in behavior and the abstraction as it is named."

"There is a basic tendency to treat whatever is perceived as both concrete and absolute despite its abstract and nonabsolute nature." Not only does the use of language obscure gradations of clarity, but the continued retelling will eliminate any uncertainty the narrator may have had. When he has repeated his story a number of times, as witnesses do before and during a trial, he becomes increasingly committed to it, more certain of its correctness and, perhaps, more anxious that he may contradict himself.

Beyond the unreliability of evidence and the unsuitability of the fault principle in accident cases, a further defect in the present system is lack of speed and consistency in the results, attributed by many to our reliance on the jury. As former Presiding Justice David W. Peck of New York wrote, "Jury trials in civil cases are only a matter of habit and history—ours is the only country in the world which any longer attempts to handle civil litigation within the jury frame, and coincidentally it is the only country which has court delay. . . ."

In Western Europe trial by jury is provided only in criminal cases, and in Great Britain it is specified in civil cases only when fraud, defamation or other nonphysical injury is alleged. The high esteem for trial by jury in our country again stems from the fact that our Constitution was framed at precisely that point in the development of English law when reliance on the jury was at its apex. Blackstone, the basic text of American law students for more than a century, praised the right to a jury trial as "the most transcendent privilege which any subject can enjoy" and viewed such a trial as "the best criterion for investigating the truth of facts that was ever established in any country."

At that time the jury in England was being strengthened as a bar to the corruption of judges and, even more so, to the subversion of the law by the monarchy. That was just one step in the evolution of the English legal tradition, one point in time out of a thousand years. Because it also happened to be the point at which we grafted onto our form of government many of the devices that symbolized anti-authoritarianism in England, these devices have become ends in themselves and are often viewed as above criticism. Thus while in England, from which it came, the civil jury trial has been greatly modified, we have continued to regard it as essential, as an essential right which may be waived by both litigants but which they cannot be forced to forgo.

From the mangled and contradictory accounts of witnesses the jury must make two decisions: (1) Was the defendant liable? and (2) If so, what damages should the plaintiff get? The first question is defined in terms of fault, as it was defined in England in the eighteenth century. This element of our Puritan heritage was intended to have a punitive effect on the wrongdoer and thus a deterrent effect on others. Its punitive function is illuminated by the rule of contributory negligence that excuses the defendant from liability if the plaintiff too was at fault to any extent. There is evidence, however, that in many cases contributory negligence is not viewed by the jury as a bar to recovery but as an element to be balanced in determining the amount of damages.

Although the liability issue is punitive, the damages to be awarded are compensatory, scaled to the plaintiff's injuries rather than to the degree of wrong done by the defendant. "The rule of damages is a practical instrumentality for the administration of justice," a Massachusetts court wrote in 1908 in deciding a suit brought against the Old Colony Street Railway Company. "The principle on which it is founded is compensation. Its object is to afford the equivalent in money for the actual loss caused by the wrong of another."

Yet in 1958 it could be said that "As recently as a decade ago there was no well-developed law of damages for personal injuries." Appellate courts are reluctant to overturn jury verdicts unless the award, according to the rule stated by Chancellor Kent in 1812 and still applied today, "be so excessive as to strike mankind, at first blush, as being beyond all measure unreasonable and outrageous, and as such, manifestly show the jury to have been actuated by passion, partiality, prejudice, or corruption." Beyond this, the jury has free rein.

Damages for the same injury will vary greatly. They will vary according to the person injured, as is appropriate in terms of his income, lost earning power and life expectancy. But they will also vary with the personality and skill of his attorney, with the size and wealth of the community in which the suit is brought and even sometimes with the season of the year.

Juries are asked to calculate awards in terms of such tangibles as lost wages, loss of anticipated earning power and the cost of medical services. They are also allowed to place a price tag on the plaintiff's pain and suffering caused by the injury so that he may be "made whole again," fully compensated in dollars for the financial and other impacts of the injury. In general, the larger the total award, the larger will be the percentage awarded for pain and suffering. Such factors give considerable rein to the attitudes of jurors and, by the very variances in the awards they make possible for similar injuries, necessarily result in injustice. We also know that juries, although they are not supposed to, often include in their award the fees for the attorney and taxes on the award—even though such awards are not taxable. There is no way to assure observance of the law by juries, or even consistent evasion of the legal principles. . . .

The likelihood that the defendant is insured also helps to increase the sum awarded. Jurors will be freer with the funds of an insurance company than with those of an individual, even though they will eventually pay in higher premiums for their generosity. There is no safeguard against this assumption and its impact for it has been found that telling the jury not to consider insurance serves only to emphasize that consideration.

In a few states automobile liability insurance is compulsory; in many others it is voluntary but extremely widespread. Most states have other mechanisms to maximize the likelihood that the motor vehicle owner will be a solvent defendant, so it is not unreasonable for juries to assume that the damages will be paid. In many states evidence is not permitted as to whether the defendant is insured—although it is permissible to question prospective jurors about whether they or members of their families are employed by an insurance company—and with the increasing incidence of insurance, juries have felt free to return substantial awards against defendants of modest income.

The prevalence of insurance has also affected the punitive function of liability, bringing us one step farther from the punitive concept and closer to the compensatory. Not only does the plaintiff often benefit from the jury's sympathy regardless of fault, but the defendant is scarcely punished when the judgment awarded against him is paid out of the pocket of his insurance company. He may ultimately have to pay a higher premium, but by then the chastisement has been greatly mitigated.

Studies have shown that juries may proportion their award to the degree of defendant's negligence as well as to the extent of plaintiff's injuries. Even if the jury disobeys instructions and does increase the damages to penalize a flagrantly negligent defendant, the insured defendant rarely feels the lash. On the other hand, if defendant's negligence is slight and it appears that the plaintiff too has contributed to causing the injury, the jury will still find the defendant at fault if the plaintiff has been injured seriously and they feel he should be compensated. So insurance has minimized the effectiveness of the theory of fault liability. . . .

Since we know that the rules of evidence with regard to eyewitness testimony are based on psychologically false assumptions, that the legal process is abused through the hostile adversary proceedings of the trial in which victory rather than discovering the truth is the object, that such abuses cannot fail to diminish general respect for the law and that damages rarely punish the wrongdoer or adequately compensate the victim, we may conclude that the courtroom is not the proper place for providing "justice" for the victims of millions of automobile accidents each year.

Even now, only a fraction of all personal injury suits are actually disposed of in the courtroom. It has been extrapolated from recent court records that in New York City only 77,000 of the 193,000 claims even reached the courts. The rest were either abandoned or settled during preliminary negotiations. Of the 77,000 only 7,000 went to trial and only 2,500 all the way to verdict. Thus jury awards were made in 3.4 per cent of all those personal injury cases, usually many years after the accident.

Perhaps we are now at a level of political sophistication that will permit us to question whether a civil jury trial, especially one that is conducted according to defective rules of evidence and liability, and ineffective rules of damages, is in fact serving the social goal that we call "justice." In recent years some judges have begun this scrutiny. The late Judge Jerome

Frank of the Court of Appeals for the Second Circuit was one of the most outspoken critics of this system, and Judge Charles Clark of the same bench observed more recently that "The jury is too fine, as well as too clumsy and expensive an instrument . . . it just isn't the correct way to achieve sound policy for the victims of this industrial age and our modern civilization."

The pressures against change are considerable. Beyond the sheer weight of tradition there would also be opposition from attorneys, insurance companies, political appointees to the courts, and those who appoint them and other beneficiaries of the present system. But in recognition of the defects of this system, its delays, inequities and costliness, some enlightened legislatures have begun to explore alternatives.

Foremost among these is the possibility of a compensation plan analogous to some of those already in effect elsewhere and to the workmen's compensation programs now in effect in every state of the Union. Such a plan would eliminate the requirement that the victim prove fault, it would eliminate belated trials to hear unreliable evidence and it would more explicitly and consistently reflect the consensus of the community that the victim of an automobile accident should be compensated to the extent of his injuries. . . .

The virtues of a compensation plan for automobile accident injuries should encourage us to try to work out some financial guidelines. Such accidents, like the motor vehicle itself, have become part of everyday life. . . . Whether we be drivers, riders in automobiles or buses, or pedestrians, there is not one of us in the United States today who is not a possible victim of an automotive accident. It is a more universal risk than an industrial accident or an impecunious old age. It is a risk that concerns us all throughout our lives.

Several halfway measures have also been suggested, such as enacting compulsory accident and liability insurance, abandoning the doctrine of contributory negligence as a bar to recovery, eliminating the jury from such cases or having automobile accident cases argued before an administrative board rather than in the courtroom. But these do not go to the heart of the matter, which is that the automobile is a necessity and the automobile accident an inevitability, that such accidents cannot be accurately witnessed and testified to and often that they are not the "fault" of anyone. Furthermore, this contentious litigation based on necessarily inaccurate, though not necessarily perjured, evidence demeans the judicial process. Few of those injured are promptly and adequately compensated; and finally, the more circuitous the devices for transferring payment to the injured, the higher the total cost to the entire public will be. A plan addressed to these considerations would not necessarily reduce the number of automobile accidents, but it would unburden the courts, elevate the law and do greater "justice" for the thousands of victims of our machine age. . . .

TRENDS IN TORT LITIGATION

3   TRENDS IN NEGLIGENCE SUITS

A person seeking damages for tort liability based upon negligence is usually required to establish that he was injured (1) without fault of his own (2) by conduct of the defendant which was the proximate cause of his injuries and (3) which was contrary to a duty owed to the injured party. This duty is usually expressed in terms of the degree of care and caution which the wrongdoer was bound to exercise for the other party by reason of the situation and their relationship. For example, an owner of property would owe a higher standard of care and caution to a business visitor than to a trespasser. Therefore, conduct which might be considered negligent to a business visitor might not be so to a trespasser. Negligence, then, is based on a violation of a duty owed which is the proximate cause of an injury to another. The case which follows illustrates the type of situation in which the issue is whether or not certain conduct or omissions constitute negligence.

MICK V. KROGER CO.
218 N.E.2d 654 (Ill. 1966)

Plaintiff sued for personal injuries received when she fell while leaving defendant's grocery store. Defendant had failed to assist plaintiff in carrying out her large bag of groceries, and she fell outside the store and broke her foot. Plaintiff was awarded $4,000 and defendant appealed contending that there was no evidence of negligence on its part.

MORAN, JUSTICE: . . . Negligent conduct consists in the failure to exercise the care that a reasonable man of ordinary prudence would exercise in order to guard against any reasonably foreseeable, unreasonable risks of harm which flow or might flow from his conduct. The essential element of negligence is the exposure of another person to an unreasonable risk of harm.

In fact, the very concept of due care contains within it the implication of due care under certain circumstances, one of which is the presence of a reasonably foreseeable, unreasonable risk of harm. Once it has been established that a duty to exercise due care exists, the question what constitutes due care under particular circumstances remains and must be determined by an analysis of all the facts. Thus, the determination of due care is essentially factual.

Generally, questions of due care including the question of unreasonable risk, are for the jury to determine. Once a determination is made, a verdict will be set aside only if the verdict is against the manifest weight of the evidence or if reasonable minds would not differ as to the presence of due care under the circumstances. The mere fact that a jury could have reached a different conclusion or that a judge disagrees with the verdict does not suffice.

Questions of negligence, due care and proximate cause are ordinarily questions of fact for a jury to decide. The right of trial by jury is recognized in the Magna Charta, our Declaration of Independence and both our State and Federal constitutions. It is a fundamental right in our democratic judicial system. Questions which are composed of such qualities sufficient to cause reasonable men to arrive at different results should never be determined as matters of law. The debatable quality of issues such as negligence and proximate cause, the fact that fair-minded men might reach different conclusions, emphasize the appropriateness and necessity of leaving such questions to a fact-finding body. The jury is the tribunal under our legal system to decide that type of issue. To withdraw such questions from the jury is to usurp its function.

In support of its first contention, the defendant alleges that the allegations of negligence in the complaint are "at most allegations of a deviation from a customary practice of this particular store . . ." and that "proof of a deviation from customary practice is not negligence and cannot in itself sustain a recovery." However, a deviation from customary practice is sufficient to furnish an evidentiary basis for a finding of negligence by a jury whenever there is some evidence in the record from which a jury could infer that the deviation may have resulted in an unreasonable risk of harm to the plaintiff.

There was evidence that the bag of groceries which Mrs. Mick carried from the store was twelve inches in width and eighteen inches in height, that it was "big" and heavy, "and that the top of the bag reached her chin when she carried it." Mrs. Mick testified that the bag "was too heavy for me to carry," that she told the checkout boy that "I don't know if I can manage it," that she normally did not carry "heavy ones like that," but that the store personnel carried them, and that she fell because "the bag weighted me down." In addition, there was evidence that the store personnel would normally help customers when there were large packages similar in size to the one which Mrs. Mick carried from the store. Her testimony was corroborated by the store manager. . . .

The evidence concerning custom, as the plaintiff's brief so well indicates, is competent in that the customs of a business constitute a part of the circumstances which are to be taken into consideration by a jury in determining due care.

In a series of cases, our courts have held that evidence tending to show a general custom and usual manner of conducting a business is competent, and the degree of care required of the defendant should be determined in view of the general practice of those rightfully upon the premises. . . .

The Kroger Company owed to Mrs. Mick, an invitee on its premise, the duty to exercise reasonable care under the circumstances. From the evidence taken as a whole, a jury could and did find that the failure to provide a carry-out service for Mrs. Mick constituted an unreasonable risk of harm and a breach of its duty to exercise reasonable care for her protection as a customer. In this day and age, shoppers generally frequent the modern, self-service supermarkets, where they are furnished with a large cart which they wheel through the store and in which they place large amounts of groceries. It is not unreasonable for a jury to find, under some circumstances, that it would be the duty of a store to furnish assistance to its customers in carrying out their groceries, especially where it has been the custom and practice to do so. Indeed, courtesy, politeness, and proper consideration for a customer's needs are inducements for a customer's trading in a particular store.

This is not to say that the Kroger Company should insure the safety of its customers, but only that, from all the evidence presented in this case, a jury could find that there was an unreasonable risk of harm and a failure to provide reasonable protection against the harm. A jury also could and did find that the negligence of the Kroger Company was the proximate cause of Mrs. Mick's injuries. All of these questions are essentially factual and within the proper scope of a jury. Their findings should be disregarded only if "the verdict of the jury is manifestly and palpably against the weight of the evidence. . . ." [AFFIRMED]

As has been discussed, there are a variety of tort duties owed and various degrees of negligence or misconduct. These may be summarized as follows:

THEORY OF FAULT	DUTY	DEGREE OF FAULT FOR LIABILITY
1. Slight negligence	To use extreme or high degree of care	Failure to use extreme or high degree of care
2. Ordinary negligence	To use ordinary care	Failure to use ordinary care
3. Willful and wanton misconduct	To use slight care	Actions with a conscious disregard for the safety of others (gross recklessness)
4. Intentional tort	Not to intentionally injure another	Actions with intent to harm
5. Strict liability	Not to injure	None

The following case has attracted nationwide attention as being at the extreme in imposing liability or a theory of fault. Note the remoteness of connection between the conduct and the injury, and the questionable foreseeability of risk on the part of the defendant. Could the defendant have reasonably been expected to prevent this injury?

GALLICK V. BALTIMORE & OHIO R.R. CO.
372 U.S. 108 (1963)

Plaintiff sued his employer railroad under the Federal Employer's Liability Act alleging that the railroad was negligent in allowing a stagnant pool of water that attracted vermin and insects to remain on its property. Plaintiff was bitten by an insect. The bite became infected and plaintiff ultimately lost both of his legs. The jury found that the railroad was negligent and awarded plaintiff damages. The state Appellate court reversed, holding that there was no liability as a matter of law and that there was insufficient evidence of negligence to submit the issue to the jury. The state Supreme Court declined to review the case but the Supreme Court of the United States granted certiorari.

WHITE, JUSTICE: . . . The Court of Appeals . . . emphasized . . . that there was no "direct evidence that the existence of the unidentified bug at the time and place had any connection with the stagnant and infested pool," or had become infected by the pool with the substance that caused petitioner's infection, evidence which would negative the alternative possibility that the insect had emanated from "the nearly putrid mouth of the Cuyahoga River, or from weeds, or unsanitary places situated on property not owned or controlled by the railroad." The Court of Appeals therefore deemed the evidence merely "a series of guesses and speculations . . . too tenuous . . . a chain of causation . . . to support a conclusion of liability." "[W]e have a chain of possibilities that the negligence of the defendant might have shared in subjecting the plaintiff to damage and injury, but proof of a legal causal connection between the negligence and the damage falls short of that required for the consideration of a jury." Accordingly, it reversed the judgment of the Court of Common Pleas and entered final judgment for respondent.

I

We think that the Court of Appeals improperly invaded the function and province of the jury in this Federal Employers' Liability Act case. According to the Court of Appeals, the break in the causal chain that turned it into a mere "series of guesses and speculations" was the want of evidence from which the jury could properly conclude that respondent's fetid pool had had something to do with the insect that bit petitioner. The only question was whether or not the insect was from or had been attracted by the pool.

We hold that the record shows sufficient evidence to warrant the jury's conclusion that petitioner's injuries were caused by the acts or omissions of respondent.

As the Court of Appeals stated, "insects were seen on, over and about this stagnant pool." According to petitioner's undisputed testimony, he stood near the pool for about a half a minute; then he started to walk away and was bitten on the leg after he took a few steps, perhaps one or two seconds later. Petitioner also testified, on cross-examination, that he had at times seen insects of about the same size as that which bit him crawling over the dead rats and pigeons in the stagnant pool. And on cross-examination by respondent two medical witnesses testified that stagnant, rat-infested pools breed and attract insects. Moreover, the jury specifically found that the pool accumulated and attracted bugs and vermin.

The Court of Appeals erred in demanding either "direct evidence that the existence of the unidentified bug at the time and place had any connection with the stagnant and infested pool" or else more substantial circumstantial evidence than that adduced here "that the pool created conditions and influences which helped to incubate or furnish an environment for the bug . . . or that the insect, having traveled from other areas, became contaminated or infected by the pool." Under the ruling cases in this Court the evidence present was sufficient to raise an issue for the jury's determination as to whether the insect emanated from the pool.

In *Tennant v. Peoria & P.U.R. Co.*, 321 U.S. 29, one of the leading cases, the Court granted certiorari "because of important problems as to petitioner's right to a jury determination of the issue of causation." There was no direct evidence of how the decedent was killed. There was evidence that the respondent railroad had been negligent or careless in failing to ring a warning bell before moving an engine, and evidence that the victim was killed by being run over by a train. The question of how the victim met his death was susceptible to various answers, all somewhat conjectural because of the want of direct evidence, some of which supported petitioner's claims and others respondent's. The Court of Appeals set aside a jury verdict for petitioner for failure of the evidence to make out proximate cause, but this Court reversed:

It is not the function of a court to search the record for conflicting circumstantial evidence in order to take the case away from the jury on a theory that the proof gives equal support to inconsistent and uncertain inferences. The focal point of judicial review is the reasonableness of the particular inference or conclusion drawn by the jury. It is the jury, not the court, which is the fact-finding body. It weighs the contradictory evidence and inferences, judges the credibility of witnesses, receives expert instructions, and draws the ultimate conclusion as to the facts. The very essence of its function is to select from among conflicting inferences and conclusions that which it con-

siders most reasonable. That conclusion, whether it relates to negligence, causation or any other factual matter, cannot be ignored. Courts are not free to reweigh the evidence and set aside the jury verdict merely because the jury could have drawn different inferences or conclusions or because judges feel that other results are more reasonable. . . .

Under this statute the test of a jury case is simply whether the proofs justify with reason the conclusion that employer negligence played any part . . . in producing the injury. . . . It does not matter that, from the evidence, the jury may also with reason, on grounds of probability, attribute the result to other causes. . . . Judicial appraisal of the proofs to determine whether a jury question is presented is narrowly limited to the single inquiry whether, with reason, the conclusion may be drawn that negligence of the employer played any part at all in the injury or death. Judges are to fix their sights primarily to make that appraisal and, if that test is met, are bound to find that a case for the jury is made out whether or not the evidence allows the jury a choice of other probabilities.

The facts before the jury fall within this standard and the Court of Appeals therefore erred in refusing to accept the jury's verdict.

II

Although we have concluded that the jury could properly find that there was a causal relationship between the railroad's negligence and petitioner's injuries, that does not end the case. Respondent makes the further argument that the judgment under review may be sustained on the alternative ground, not accepted by the Court of Appeals, that the injury was not reasonably foreseeable, and that therefore there was no negligence.

We agree with respondent that reasonable foreseeability of harm is an essential ingredient of Federal Employers' Liability Act negligence, but this requirement has been satisfied in the present case by the jury's findings . . . of negligence in maintaining the filthy pool of water. The jury had been instructed that negligence is the failure to observe that degree of care which people of ordinary prudence and sagacity would use under same or similar circumstances; and that defendant's duty was measured by what a reasonably prudent person would anticipate as resulting from a particular condition—"defendant's duties are measured by what is reasonably foreseeable under like circumstances"—by what "in the light of the facts then known, should or could reasonably have been anticipated." Thus when the jury found these facts: petitioner was bitten by an insect; the insect bite caused illness or disease and led to petitioner's present physical condition; the stagnant pool attracted bugs and vermin and was responsible for the insect bite and the injuries to petitioner; and respondent knew that the accumulation of the pool of water would attract bugs and vermin to the area—it is clear that the jury concluded that respondent should have realized the increased likelihood of an insect's biting petitioner while he was working in the vicinity of the pool. . . .

The Court of Appeals erred in depriving petitioner of the judgment entered upon the special verdict of the jury. The judgment of the Ohio Court of Appeals is reversed and the case is remanded for further proceedings not inconsistent with this opinion. [REVERSED]

HARLAN, JUSTICE, dissenting: Heartrending as the petitioner's accident has turned out to be, I think this case should not have been brought here. It involves no unsettled questions of federal law calling for decision by this Court, nor, in any acceptable sense, a departure by the state courts from legal principles already decided requiring this Court's intervention. The case thus does not qualify for review. . . . The case has necessarily required an inordinate amount of time, which the Court can ill afford In the present state of its docket.

Reaching the merits, however, I would affirm the judgment below. I cannot say that the view of the record taken by the state courts, in holding that the evidence on the issue of causation was insufficient to make a case for the jury, was an arbitrary or unreasonable one. The opinion of the Ohio Court of Appeals evinces a conscientious effort to follow this Court's decisions under the Federal Employers' Liability Act. . . . On this score the Court's reversal seems to me no more than an exercise in second-guessing the state court's estimate of the record.

From another standpoint this case does have significance. It affords a particularly dramatic example of the inadequacy of ordinary negligence law to meet the social obligations of modern industrial society. The cure for that, however, lies with the legislature and not with the courts.

4   TRENDS IN PRODUCT LIABILITY

There is a substantial body of rules of law concerning product liability. These rules of law vary a great deal from state to state. Liability for injury caused by a product may be based on a theory of negligence or it may be contractual in nature arising from: (1) a breach of an express warranty about the goods, (2) a breach of an implied warranty that the goods are of merchantable quality (reasonably fit for their ordinary and intended purpose), or (3) a breach of an implied warranty of fitness for a particular purpose. The theories predicated upon breach of warranty have a statutory basis in the Uniform Commercial Code. Such cases were originally tortious in nature but today are often considered to be based on breach of contract because the statutes authorizing the suits are a part of the contract law of sales.

Cases concerning product liability involve retailers as well as manu-facturers, packers, or growers of products. Liability may be imposed with-out fault in the traditional tort sense because of the contract theories. For example, a grocer who sells a can of beans containing cockroaches is not negligent because he has no reasonable way of ascertaining the contents of the can which he sells. Yet he has liability for the defect because he breaches his implied warranty that the goods are of merchantable quality. This product liability arises from contract. Questions immediately arise as to whether or not a person other than the one purchasing the product can sue for injuries and whether or not suit can be brought against a party by one who has no contract with him. For example, is it legally permissible for a member of the purchaser's family to sue the retailer who sold the defective goods which caused him injury or for the purchaser at retail of such goods to sue the manufacturer? These problems involve "privity of contract" and whether or not "privity" is required.

The trend is toward strict liability for injuries caused by products which are sold by a businessman in the ordinary course of business, regardless of whether he was at fault or negligent, and regardless of whether the injured party who is suing was a party to the contract of sale. The cases which fol-low are merely illustrative of the thousands brought annually to establish liability because of a defective product.

LONZRICK V. REPUBLIC STEEL CORP.
205 N.E.2d 92 (Ohio 1965)

SKEEL, JUSTICE: This appeal comes to this court from a judgment entered for the defendant by the Court of Common Pleas of Cuyahoga County. The action is one for money only. The plaintiff alleges in his petition that he suffered certain personal injuries when "steel bar joist" manufactured by the defendant, which had been placed in a building, collapsed and fell down upon him. The plaintiff was a construction worker employed by a *sub-contractor*, the Valley Steel Erectors, Inc. The joists were purchased from the defendant by the *general contractor*. The cause of action, as stated by the plaintiff, is based on a claim of a breach of the duty imposed by law on the defendant to furnish *merchantable* joist to the general contractor. *No claim of privity between the plaintiff and defendant is stated in the petition,* and under the facts stated no such claim could be made.

We are, therefore, confronted with the question whether the petition states a cause of action.

This question requires a survey of the rapidly changing theory of "product liability." The earlier rule, requiring privity between buyer and seller as a basis for creating liability under an express warranty grew out of the proposition that no such obligation was created until a promise was separately made upon the request of the buyer. Such a warranty was said to be collateral in character and enforceable by an action in tort. As then understood, a breach of such a promise did not breach the contract of sale, and, without such a collateral promise, the doctrine of *caveat emptor* applied. The transition of product liability from caveat emptor to strict tort liability, regardless of privity, where the manufacturer or dealer induces the sale under the law of express warranty, is set out in the case of *Rogers v. Toni Home Permanent Co.,* 105 Ohio App. 53, 139 N.E.2d 871, which statement of the law we hereby adopt without quoting at length.

An implied warranty is one imposed by law which under the Uniform Commercial Code dealing with sales, . . . writes into an agreement of sale certain obligations imposed upon the seller by law and requires the seller to be responsible for certain qualities to be possessed by the goods sold unless clearly negated by the sales contract. This statute does not deal with the rights of third persons not parties to the sale who come into possession of the goods and use them in the manner intended by the manufacturer and are thereby injured by reason of the faulty condition of the goods latent in character due to improper manufacture or the use of faulty materials. The rule, as developed by the cases, was clearly stated by the Supreme Court of West Virginia in the case of *Peters v. Johnson, Jackson & Co.* (1902). . . .

The theory of liability of the manufacturer or producer of chattels to the ultimate consumer without privity for negligence in producing the property, which negligence proximately caused injury or damage to the ultimate consumer while in the proper use of the property, is now almost universally accepted. Only the difficulty of proving negligence in the manufacturing process prevents such remedy from giving adequate relief to the ultimate consumer injured as a proximate result of the lack of care in producing the good purchased. However, with the right to pursue the manufacturer for damages due to dangers created by the negligent manufacture of his product, based on negligence, it was to be expected that the law would expand carrying the responsibility of a manufacturer for the negligent or careless manufacture of his goods, which carelessness created a danger to the consumer when using them in a proper manner, even further and find (as is true as to all persons whose negligence proximately causes injuries to others) grounds for enforcing strict tort liability against the producer whose negligence or lack of reasonable care in producing the goods is the direct cause of injury to the consumer. The source of such an obligation, when recognized, is created by law and has no dependence whatever on contractual relations between the parties. The soundness of this result is established by the weight of authority in recent decisions by many of the courts of last resort in the several states.

In the case of *Randy Knitwear, Inc., v. American Cyanamid Co.,* the plaintiff claimed a breach of an express warranty by the defendant (resin manufacturer) for damages resulting from the use of its product which is used by textile manufacturers to prevent shrinking of fabrics. The plaintiff purchased fabrics from mills licensed by the defendant to treat and sell them under the defendant's label and with the guaranty that the clothes would not shrink when they were "Cyana" finished. The defendant had advertised that the use of its product would make the goods so treated shrinkproof. After the issues were joined a motion for summary judgment was filed on the basis that there was no privity between the plaintiff and defendant. The court denied the motion, holding that substantial fact issues precluded summary judgment for defendant notwithstanding lack of privity between it and the garment dealer (plaintiff). The court said on page 12 of 11 N.Y.2d, page 367 of 226 N.Y.S.2d, page 402 of 181 N.E.2d:

The world of merchandising is, in brief, no longer a world of direct contract; it is, rather, a world of advertising and, when representations expressed and disseminated in the mass communications media and on labels (attached to the goods themselves) prove false and the user or consumer is damaged by reason of his reliance on those representations, it is difficult to justify the manufacturer's denial of liability on the sole ground of the absence of technical privity. . . .

From the foregoing authorities it is clear that one who is injured as a result of the use of a defective chattel may look to the producer for redress. Privity is not a necessary element of such an action. Such liability is imposed by rule of law as pronounced by the highest judicial authority. The world of merchandising is no longer a world of direct contract. Goods are produced to be used by ultimate purchasers, and the representations of the manufacturer through and by the production thereof for use in the channels of commerce, at least, impliedly intend to induce their use in the justifiable belief that, when used as intended, there will be no danger of injury to others. . . .

There are, therefore, three methods by which one who suffers injury or damage in using a chattel delivered by the manufacturer or the vendor in a defective condition may proceed to seek redress against the manufacturer:

1 Where the ultimate purchaser stands in a *contractual relation* with the producer or vendor, an action (if justified by the facts) for breach of express or implied warranty may be maintained as provided by the Uniform Commercial Code.
2 By an action charging *negligence* in producing the chattel . . . *regardless of privity.*
3 By an action seeking to enforce *strict tort liability without privity.* . . .

In the case now before us, the plaintiff states facts which show that he had no contractual relations with the defendant and that he bases his claim on "strict tort liability." While the words "implied warranty" are used, they are intended to mean and describe the duty and representation of a producer of chattels to the buying public that his goods may be used for the purposes intended without danger to the purchaser from latent defects making their use dangerous to the user. The use of the word "warranty" is probably improper; however, the courts, in describing causes of action for strict tort liability in product cases, seem to have continued to use it for want of a better word, not intending it to mean anything more than the manufacturer putting his goods into the stream of commerce, thereby representing that they are of merchantable quality, unless a different intention is clearly expressed.

For the foregoing reasons, the judgment of the Court of Common Pleas sustaining the defendant's demurrer and entering judgment for the defendant is reversed, and the cause is remanded with instructions to overrule the demurrer and for further proceedings. [JUDGMENT REVERSED]

SUNDET V. OLIN MATHIESON CHEM. CORP.
139 N.W.2d 368 (Neb. 1966)

SMITH, JUSTICE: While plaintiff was firing his rifle which contained in its chamber a cartridge allegedly manufactured by defendant, an explosion of the rifle injured him. This action for breach of warranty was dismissed by the district court on motion of defendant at the close of plaintiff's evidence-in-chief. We affirm the judgment on the ground of insufficient evidence that any defective condition of the cartridge existed at the time the cartridge case left defendant's control.

Shortly before the accident plaintiff purchased from a retailer twenty .264-caliber cartridges in an unsealed box. Both the box and the rims of the cartridge cases indicated manufacture by defendant. The explosion occurred on April 21, 1961, while the first cartridge was being used.

Plaintiff may have purchased cartridges with cases which someone else had reloaded. There were grayish discolorations on several cases and plier or vise marks on two bullets. Plaintiff, who repaired firearms and sold equipment for reloading cartridge cases, testified that in the reloading process the neck of a case is crimped against a bullet. Defendant manufactured a product for the box on September 8, 1960, but it knew neither the date of shipment nor the place of delivery. The retailer did not testify. The condition of the product at the time it left defendant's control or the treatment which the product received up to the time of purchase by plaintiff is unknown.

If there was a defect in the cartridge, the defect must be found from these facts and a stipulation excluding the parts and assembly of plaintiff's rifle from the legal cause of injury; but it is necessary for us to consider the sufficiency of the evidence on this point.

In a products liability case against a manufacturer the plaintiff must show that the offending condition existed when the product left defendant's control.

We find no basis for a reasonable inference that defendant manufactured these cartridges. The unsealed box contained earmarks of reloaded cases, and without additional evidence a trier of the facts cannot infer reasonably that defendant was in the business of reloading spent cases. Even if we assume that plaintiff purchased cartridges with unused cases, a reasonable conclusion cannot be drawn that any defect at the time of the retail sale represented a preexistent condition of defendant's making. The evidence is insufficient to carry the issue of warranty to a jury, and the district court correctly dismissed the action. [JUDGMENT AFFIRMED]

FOLEY V. WEAVER DRUGS, INC.
177 S.2d 221 (Fla. 1965)

ROBERTS, JUSTICE: The record shows that on October 17, 1959, James S. Foley purchased from Weaver Drugs, Inc., the respondent here, at one of its retail stores, a bottle of Revlon reducing pills, better known as "Thin Down," for use by his wife, Rose M. Foley. The pills were packed in a glass bottle which closed with a screw-on top. The day after the purchase Mrs. Foley attempted to open the bottle by unscrewing the top when the bottle broke, fragmented, and one piece thereof lacerated her right wrist.

Predicated upon these facts the Foleys instituted an action against Revlon, Inc., the manufacturer, *and Weaver Drugs, Inc., the retail-seller,* [EMPHASIS SUPPLIED] setting forth the facts and their respective damages, and alleging causes of action for negligence and for breach of implied warranty of fitness and merchantability against each defendant.

Weaver Drugs, Inc., moved to dismiss and strike from the complaint every theory of action against it. . . . At the pre-trial conference the court struck all allegations relating to implied warranty as against the defendant Weaver Drugs, Inc., the effect of which was to hold that neither of the plaintiffs had a cause of action against the retailer based on an implied warranty.

A motion for summary judgment filed by the defendant Revlon, Inc., was denied.

On appeal by plaintiffs to the District Court of Appeal, Third District, the court affirmed, without opinion, the actions of the trial court with respect to the defendant Weaver Drugs, Inc., thereby holding, in effect, that neither of the plaintiffs had a cause of action against the defendant retailer for breach of an implied warranty of fitness and merchantability, and also holding, in effect, that they were not entitled to damages on the theory of negligence; but the action of the appellate court in this respect is not complained of in the instant proceeding.

As noted above, the plaintiffs have invoked this court's "conflict jurisdiction" to review the adverse decision of the appellate court, alleging that it directly conflicts with a decision of the District Court of Appeal, Second District, in *Canada Dry Bottling Co., Inc. v. Shaw*, 118 So. 2d 840 (Fla. App. 1960). In that case the injured party purchased a bottle of Canada Dry soda from a retail grocer, Food Fair, and took it home. Shortly thereafter, while attempting to open the bottle on a wall opener in the usual manner, it broke and injured her hand. She filed suit against both the bottler, Canada Dry, and the retailer, Food Fair, on the theory of breach of implied warranty of fitness. A jury verdict and judgment against both defendants was appealed and was affirmed by the appellate court. The rationale of the appellate court's decision was that the strict liability of the retailer for breach of an implied warranty of wholesomeness and fitness applicable to products sold for human consumption, sold by him should be extended to include the bottle, as well as its contents, in a case of this kind. . . .

The court said that it would not, at that time, extend the doctrine of implied warranty to all containers of food, but that "in this case the bottle and its contents are so closely related that it is difficult—if not impossible —to draw a distinction."

It is clear that the decision in the instant case, holding that the plaintiffs had no cause of action against the retailer for breach of an implied warranty of fitness and merchantability, is in direct conflict with the Canada Dry case, insofar as the plaintiff husband, who was in privity with the retailer, is concerned. Thus, we have jurisdiction to determine the question of the implied warranty liability, in general, of a retail-seller of a product sold in a container for injury caused by the container.

This exact question has not heretofore been presented to this court. . . . [O]ther than in the case of foodstuffs, we know of no decision of this court imposing liability upon a retail seller of a product upon the theory of implied warranty, except under established common law principles. . . .

The rationale of our decisions extending to the retail-seller of food products the absolute liability imposed upon the manufacturer of such products, upon the theory of an implied warranty of fitness and wholesomeness, is that neither the retail-purchaser nor the retail-seller can discover that a particular item of food enclosed in a sealed container is defective; that the retail-seller is in a superior position to that of the consumer since he is experienced in buying from the manufacturers, is acquainted with the products and the manufacturers and relies upon the reputation of the manufacturers in stocking such food items; so that, in this area of wholesome food which is of vital concern to the public, the retailer should be held to the same liability as the manufacturer as a matter of public policy. . . . It was pointed out, in a specially concurring opinion, that in many cases the manufacturer of a food product was located in a foreign country beyond the reach of the consumer, that the retailer has a right of indemnity against the manufacturer if compelled to pay damages to a consumer because of the wholesomeness of the food product, and the retailer "can avoid placing himself in a position wherein he could not, in turn, sue the manufacturer by electing to purchase only from responsible manufacturers within the jurisdiction of the courts in which he might enter suit." (45 So. 2d at p. 673).

Assuming for the purpose of this argument that the reducing pills, being for human consumption, would fall within the same category as food-stuffs, insofar as the retailer's liability upon an implied warranty is concerned, the question then becomes: Does public policy dictate that the retailer be held to the same liability for the merchantability and fitness of the container of food products as is imposed upon him for the food products themselves? We confess that we can see no more reason for holding the retailer liable for a defect in a container of foodstuffs (when such defect is unrelated to and has no deleterious effect upon the food product itself) than for a defect in or the non-merchantability of the container of other non-food products which he sells at retail. The public interest in having a non-defective, merchantable container would seem to be the same, regardless of whether it encloses a food product or any other product.

We are not persuaded that considerations of public policy require us to extend to food containers the "implied warranty" liability of retailers as to the food contained therein; on the contrary, we are of the opinion that it would be unreasonably burdensome to extend liability in this respect. . . .

Accordingly, the Third District Court of Appeal was eminently correct in affirming the judgment of the trial court in the instant case insofar as it could be construed as holding that the complaint failed to state a cause of action, upon the theory of breach of implied warranty, against the defendant retailer, Weaver Drugs, Inc. This being so, it is unnecessary to decide whether the plaintiff-wife's suit would have been barred, had a cause of action existed, because of her lack of privity with the defendant, Weaver Drugs, Inc.

. . . For the reasons stated, the decision . . . of the appellate court in the instant case is approved, so the decision under review will not be disturbed and the writ is discharged.

The holding in the above case would seem to be contrary to the provisions of the Uniform Commercial Code and the trend of other recent decisions.

5   TRENDS IN BUSINESS TORTS

In recent years, several torts have arisen or grown in importance which may be classified under the heading "business torts." Such wrongful conduct as interfering with a business relationship, invading one's right of privacy, or violating a statute such as the Sherman Antitrust Act comes under this general category. The right of a victim of a violation of the Antitrust laws to collect treble damages was discussed in Chapters 11 to 13. Similar statutes may create liability for wrongful business conduct in other areas. For example, tort liability may be imposed and damages awarded a person denied equal privileges in using public accommodations under the Civil Rights Act of 1964.

Cases involving other kinds of torts, such as trespass or conversion of property, are common, and the legal principles involved are usually not considered to be complex. However, cases concerned with the invasion of the right of privacy or interference with a contract present complex questions of policy which require a balancing of conflicting objectives. The cases which follow are typical of those which arise in this area of business torts.

SPAHN V. JULIAN MESSNER, INC.
221 N.E.2d 543 (N.Y. 1966)

KEATING, JUSTICE: To the knowing and the novice alike, the name Warren Spahn brings to mind one of professional baseball's great left-handed pitchers.

Each year, millions of people attend various ball parks throughout the country, hoping to root their team on to victory. National network systems transmit the games into homes and offices and huge sums are expended by advertisers for the attention of audiences attracted to the sport. Each Fall at World Series time, commerce and political programs equally are brought close to a standstill while a large part of the national attention is otherwise diverted.

The size of the audience attracted to each game, whether in person or by transmission, is the profession's bread and butter. The individual player's income will frequently be a direct reflection of his popularity and ability to attract an audience. Professional privacy is thus the very antithesis of the player's need and goal.

With this background, the plaintiff, Warren Spahn, seeks an injunction and damages for the defendants' unauthorized publication of a fictitious biography of his life.

The action is predicated on section 51 of the Civil Rights Law, Consol. Laws, c. 6, which authorizes the double remedy where a person's "name, portrait or picture is used within this state for advertising or for the purposes of trade" without that person's written consent. Its enactment may be traced directly to this court's opinion in *Robertson v. Rochester Folding Box Co.*, wherein we denied the existence of a legal right to privacy in New York but said that "The legislative body could very well interfere and arbitrarily provide that no one should be permitted for his own selfish purpose to use the picture or the name of another for advertising purposes without his consent." In *Rhodes v. Sperry & Hutchinson Co.*, the statute enacted as a result of *Robertson* was held constitutional against claims that it deprived persons of liberty and property without due process of law and that it impaired the obligations of contract.

Over the years since the statute's enactment in 1903, its social desirability and remedial nature have led to its being given a liberal construction consonant with its over-all purpose. But at the same time, ever mindful that the written word or picture is involved, courts have engrafted exceptions and restrictions onto the statute to avoid any conflict with the free dissemination of thoughts, ideas, newsworthy events, and matters of public interest.

One of the clearest exceptions to the statutory prohibition is the rule that a public figure, whether he be such by choice or involuntarily, is subject to the often searching beam of publicity and that, in balance with the legitimate public interest, the law affords his privacy little protection.

But it is erroneous to confuse privacy with "personality" or to assume that privacy, though lost for a certain time or in a certain context, goes forever unprotected. Thus it may be appropriate to say that the plaintiff here, Warren Spahn, is a public personality and that, insofar as his professional career is involved, he is substantially without a right to privacy. That is not to say, however, that his "personality" may be fictionalized and that, as fictionalized, it may be exploited for the defendants' commercial benefit through the medium of an unauthorized biography.

The factual reporting of newsworthy persons and events is in the public interest and is protected. The fictitious is not. . . .

The plaintiff's status as a public figure makes him newsworthy and thus places his biography outside the protection afforded by the statute. But the plaintiff does not seek an injunction and damages for the unauthorized publication of his biography. He seeks only to restrain the publication of that which *purports to be his biography.*

In the present case, the findings of fact go far beyond the establishment of minor errors in an otherwise accurate biography. They establish "dramatization, imagined dialogue, manipulated chronologies, and fictionalization of events." In the language of Justice Markowitz, who presided at the trial, "the record unequivocally establishes that the book publicizes areas of Warren Spahn's personal and private life, albeit inaccurate and distorted, and consists of a host, a preponderant percentage, of factual errors, distortions and fanciful passages." A sufficient number of specific instances of falsification are set forth in that opinion to make repetition here unnecessary.

It is urged upon us that application of the statute to the publication of a substantially fictitious biography will run afoul of the freedoms of speech and the press guaranteed by the First and Fourteenth Amendments to the Federal Constitution. The point is urged on the basis of the Supreme Court's opinion in *New York Times Co. v. Sullivan,* 376 U.S. 254. We think it has no application.

The question posed in *New York Times Co. v. Sullivan, supra* was stated by Mr. Justice Brennan as "the extent to which the constitutional protections for speech and press limit a State's power to award damages in a libel action brought by a *public official* against critics of his *official conduct*" (p. 256). [EMPHASIS ADDED] Moreover, Justice Brennan said (p. 270), ". . . we consider this case against the background of a profound national commitment to the principle that debate on public issues should be uninhibited, robust, and wide-open, and that it may well include vehement, caustic, and sometimes unpleasantly sharp attacks on government and public officials." The court thus held that "the Constitution delimits a State's power to award damages for libel in actions brought by *public officials* against critics of their official conduct" (p. 283). [EMPHASIS ADDED]

The present case deals neither with public officials nor official conduct. The free speech which is encouraged and essential to the operation of a healthy government is something quite different from an individual's attempt to enjoin the publication of a fictitious biography of him. No public interest is served by protecting the dissemination of the latter. We perceive no constitutional infirmities in this respect.

We thus conclude that the defendant's publication of a fictitious biography of the plaintiff constitutes an unauthorized exploitation of his personality for purposes of trade and that it is proscribed by section 51 of the Civil Rights Law.

The order appealed from should be affirmed.

HERRON V. STATE FARM MUT. INS. CO.
363 P.2d 310 (Cal. 1961)

GIBSON, JUSTICE: Plaintiffs' attorneys at law brought this action against Mr. and Mrs. Donald Halverson for breach of contract and against State Farm Mutual Insurance Company and its agent, Anthony Caruso, for intentional interference with contractual relations. The Halversons were not served, and a demurrer of State Farm and Caruso (who will be referred to as defendants) was sustained without leave to amend. Plaintiffs have appealed from the ensuing judgment.

The following is a summary of plaintiffs' allegations: The Halversons entered into a contingent fee contract with plaintiffs concerning claims reasonably worth $60,000 for personal injuries sustained in an automobile accident caused by the negligence of a person insured by State Farm. Plaintiffs were to advance all expenses necessary for the preparation of the case and for court costs and were to receive one-third of the amount of the recovery remaining after deduction of the costs. No settlement was to be made without the consent of plaintiffs and the Halversons, and in the event there was no recovery plaintiffs were to receive nothing for their services or for costs advanced. Plaintiffs notified defendants of the agreement immediately after its execution, and they proceeded to hire private investigators, photographers, and a draftsman, make an investigation, and incur expenses in the amount of $1,250. Defendants, by telling the Halversons that they did not need an attorney and that a satisfactory settlement would be made, induced them to breach the contingent fee contract and to discharge plaintiffs and deprive them of the benefits of the contract and the expenses incurred for investigation and preparation. Defendants assisted the Halversons in preparing letters which informed plaintiffs of their dismissal. The conduct of defendants was maliciously designed to injure plaintiffs' rights and lawful business, and it violated the rules of the National Conference Committee on Adjusters of which State Farm or its agents are members. The rules provide, in part, that an insurance company will not deal directly with any claimant represented by an attorney without the consent of the attorney and will not advise the claimant to refrain from seeking legal advice or retaining counsel to protect his interest. As a result of the conduct of defendants, plaintiffs suffered the loss of the expenses incurred in investigation and preparation and did not receive their one-third contingent fee.

Plaintiffs prayed for judgment against defendants for $20,000 or one-third of the judgment or settlement recovered by the Halversons, whichever is the lesser, and, in addition, for $25,000 punitive damages.

An action will lie for the intentional interference by a third person with a contractual relationship either by unlawful means or by means otherwise lawful when there is a lack of sufficient justification. . . . There is no valid reason why this rule should not be applied to an attorney's contingent fee contract. Such an agreement is a legal and valid contract entitled to the protection of the law, and an attorney who is wrongfully discharged is generally entitled to the same amount of compensation as if he had completed the contemplated services. . . . While a client is permitted to discharge his attorney without cause, this is allowed not because the attorney's interest in performing his services and obtaining his fee is unworthy of protection but because of the importance of the client's interest in the successful prosecution of his cause of action. . . . An attorney's interest in his contingent fee agreement is greater than that of a party to a contract terminable at will, as to which it has been held that an intentional and unjustifiable interference is actionable. . . .

Whether an intentional interference by a third party is justifiable depends upon a balancing of the importance, social and private, of the objective advanced by the interference against the importance of the interest interfered with, considering all circumstances including the nature of the actor's conduct and the relationship between the parties. . . . Justification is an affirmative defense and may not be considered as supporting the trial court's action in sustaining a demurrer unless it appears on the face of the complaint. . . . The only allegation relied upon by defendants as showing justification is that State Farm had issued an automobile public liability insurance policy to the person whose negligence caused the injuries to the Halversons. In our opinion this allegation does not establish justification.

The conduct of an insurance company in inducing an injured person to repudiate his contract with an attorney may be detrimental not only to the interests of the attorney but also to the interests of the client since, as we have seen, the client, in addition to being deprived of the aid and advice of his attorney, may also be liable for the full contract fee. Defendants argue that the policy of the law is to encourage settlement, that an insurance company has a legal duty to effect a settlement of a claim against its insured in an appropriate case . . . and that furtherance of the actor's own economic interests will justify an intentional interference with a contractual relationship in some circumstances where his interests are threatened by the contract. However, these considerations standing alone cannot justify inducing the Halversons to repudiate the contract to deprive plaintiffs of its benefits. So far as appears from the complaint, no cause for the dismissal of plaintiffs existed, no efforts were made to negotiate with them, and there is no indication that State Farm could not have protected its interests and obtained a satisfactory settlement without interfering with the contract.

The judgment is reversed with directions to overrule the demurrer.

6   TRENDS IN VICARIOUS LIABILITY

The rule that an employer is liable for the torts of his employees which are committed while they are acting within the scope of their employment was previously stated in Chapter 14. This concept of vicarious liability is an expanding one. In the 20th century juries and courts have tended to enlarge the definition of scope of employment and thus have increased the total risk of businesses. This is especially true since the automobile and truck have come to play a major role in the conduct of business. While the agent or servant at fault also has liability, most recoveries are from the employer. The cases which follow indicate the possible extent of an employer's liability.

RILEY V. STANDARD OIL CO.
132 N.E. 97 (N.Y. 1921)

ANDREWS, JUSTICE: Driving directly towards his master's mill; his master's truck loaded with his master's goods for which his master had sent him; his only purpose to deliver them as his master had commanded; with no independent object of his own in mind; Million, a chauffeur employed by the defendant, ran over the plaintiff, negligently, as the jury have said with some evidence to support their finding. Therefore, the complaint should not have been dismissed unless we can say as a matter of law that at the moment of the accident this chauffeur was not engaged in the defendant's business. We reach no such conclusion.

There could be no debate on this subject were not the essential facts obscured or modified by other circumstances. It appears, however, that the chauffeur had been ordered to go from the mill to the freight yards of the Long Island railroad, about two and one-half miles away, obtain there some barrels of paint and return at once. After the truck was loaded, Million discovered some waste pieces of wood. He threw them on the truck and on leaving the yards turned, not toward the mill, but in the opposite direction. Four blocks away was the house of a sister, and there he left the wood. This errand served no purpose of the defendant nor did the defendant have knowledge of or consent to the act of the chauffeur. Million then started to return to the mill. His course would lead him back past the entrance to the yards. Before he reached this entrance and when he had gone but a short distance from his sister's house, the accident occurred.

A master is liable for the result of a servant's negligence when the servant is acting in his business; when he still is engaged in the course of his employment. It is not the rule itself but its application that ever causes a doubt. The servant may be acting for himself. He may be engaged in an independent errand of his own. He may abandon his master's service permanently or temporarily. While still doing his master's work he may be also serving a purpose of his own. He may be performing his master's work but in a forbidden manner. Many other conditions may arise.

No formula can be stated that will enable us to solve the problem whether at a particular moment a particular servant is engaged in his master's business. We recognize that the precise facts before the court will vary the result. We realize that differences of degree may produce unlike effects. But whatever the facts, the answer depends upon a consideration of what the servant was doing, and why, when, where and how he was doing it.

A servant may be "going on a frolic of his own, without being at all on his master's business." He may be so distant from the proper scene of his labor, or he may have left his work for such a length of time as to evidence a relinquishment of his employment. Or the circumstances may have a more doubtful meaning. That the servant is where he would not be had he obeyed his master's orders in itself is immaterial except as it may tend to show a permanent or a temporary abandonment of his master's service. Should there be such a temporary abandonment the master again becomes liable for the servant's acts when the latter once more begins to act in his business. Such a re-entry is not effected merely by the mental attitude of the servant. There must be that attitude coupled with a reasonable connection in time and space with the work in which he should be engaged. No hard and fast rule on the subject either of space or time can be applied. It cannot be said of a servant in charge of his master's vehicle who temporarily abandons his line of travel for a purpose of his own that he again becomes a servant only when he reaches a point on his route which he necessarily would have passed had he obeyed his orders. He may choose a different way back. Doubtless this circumstance may be considered in connection with other facts involved. It is not controlling.

We are not called upon to decide whether the defendant might not have been responsible had this accident occurred while Million was on his way to his sister's house. That would depend on whether this trip is to be regarded as a new and independent journey on his own business, distinct from that of his master or as a mere deviation from the general route from the mill and back. Considering the short distance and the little time involved, considering that the truck when it left the yards was loaded with the defendant's goods for delivery to its mill and that it was the general purpose of Million to return there it is quite possible a question of fact would be presented to be decided by a jury. At least, however with the wood delivered, with the journey back to the mill begun, at some point in the route Million again engaged in the defendant's business. That point, in view of all circumstances, we think he had reached.

The judgment of the Appellate Division must be modified in so far as it directs the dismissal of the complaint and in so far as it fails to direct a new trial and as so modified affirmed, with costs to abide the event.

MCLAUGHLIN, JUSTICE, dissenting: . . . This court is about to reverse the Appellate Division upon the ground that Million having left his sister's residence, and started back towards the yard, had as matter of law reached a point in the route when he again engaged in the defendant's business. I am unable to see how this conclusion can be reached as matter of law. Nor do I think that the facts would justify a finding to this effect. The uncontradicted facts show, as it seems to me, that Million, at the place where and time when the accident occurred, was not acting for defendant. His act at and immediately prior to the accident was not a mere deviation from his duty or an irregular method of its performance. He was doing an independent act of his own and outside of the service for which he had been employed. When he started from the yard to deliver the wood to his sister's residence, he broke the connection between himself and his master, temporarily terminated the employment, and did not re-enter the same until he had again reached the yard. The return from his sister's residence to the yard was just as much a part of his personal errand as was going to her residence. I cannot believe that the liability of the defendant here is to be determined by the way in which the truck was headed. Rights of property do not rest upon such a slender thread. . . .

FIOCCO V. CARVER
137 N.E. 309 (N.Y. 1922)

CARDOZO, JUSTICE: The defendants, engaged in business in the city of New York, sent a truckload of merchandise from Manhattan to Staten Island. The duty of the driver when he had made delivery of the load was to bring the truck back to the garage at Twenty-third street and Eleventh avenue on the west side of the city. Instead of doing that, he went, as he tells us, to Hamilton street on the east side, to visit his mother. A neighborhood carnival was in progress in the street. A crowd of boys, dressed in fantastic costumes, as Indians, Uncle Sam, cowboys, and the like, were parties to the frolic. They asked the driver for a ride, and in response to the request, he made a tour of the district, going from Hamilton street to Catherine, then through other streets, and back again to Catherine. At this point he stopped in front of a pool room, and left his truck for a moment to say a word to a friend. It is here that the plaintiff, a child of eleven years, arrived upon the scene. The merrymakers were still crowding about the truck. The plaintiff with a playmate tried to join them. While he was climbing up the side, the driver came back and three times ordered him to get off. As the third order was given, the plaintiff started to come down, but before he could reach the ground, the truck, as he tells us, was started without warning, and his foot was drawn into a wheel. The driver gives a different story, insisting that the boy ran after the moving truck and climbed on the side when it was impossible to see him. All the witnesses agree that the truck as it left Catherine street was still carrying the boys. The driver adds that his purpose then was to go back to the garage. Upon these facts a jury has been permitted to find that he was in the course of his employment. The ruling was upheld at the Appellate Division by the divided court.

We think the judgment may not stand.

The plaintiff argues that the jury, if it discredited the driver's narrative of the accident, was free to discredit his testimony that there had been a departure from the course of duty. With this out of the case, there is left the conceded fact that a truck belonging to the defendant was in the custody of the defendant's servant. We are reminded that this without more sustains a presumption that the custodian was using it in the course of his employment. But the difficulty with the argument is that in this case there *is* more, though credit be accorded to the plaintiff's witnesses exclusively. The presumption disappears when the surrounding circumstances are such that its recognition is unreasonable. We draw the inference of regularity, in default of evidence rebutting it, presuming, until otherwise advised, that the servant will discharge his duty. We refuse to rest upon presumption, and put the plaintiff to his proof, when the departure from regularity is so obvious that charity can no longer infer an adherence to the course of duty. . . .

We turn, then, to the driver's testimony to see whether anything there, whether read by itself or in conjunction with the plaintiff's narrative, gives support for the conclusion that the truck was engaged at the moment of the accident in the business of the master. All that we can find there, when we view it most favorably to the plaintiff, is a suggestion that after a temporary excursion in streets remote from the homeward journey, the servant had at last made up his mind to put an end to his wanderings and return to the garage. He was still far away from the point at which he had first strayed from the path of duty, but his thoughts were homeward bound. Is this enough, in view of all the circumstances to terminate the temporary abandonment and put him back into the sphere of service? We have refused to limit ourselves by tests that are merely mechanical or formal. Location in time and space are circumstances that may guide the judgment, but will not be suffered to control it, divorced from other circumstances that may characterize the intent of the transaction. The dominant purpose must be proved to be the performance of the master's business. Till then there can be no resumption of a relation which had been broken and suspended.

We think the servant's purpose to return to the garage was insufficient to bring him back within the ambit of his duty. He was indisputably beyond the ambit while making the tour of the neighborhood which ended when he stopped at Catherine street upon a visit to a pool room. Neither the tour nor the stop was incidental to his service. Duty was resumed, if at all, when ending the tour, he had embarked upon his homeward journey. It was in the very act of starting that the injury was done. The plaintiff had climbed upon the truck while it was at rest in front of the pool room, still engaged upon an errand unrelated to the business. The negligence complained of is the setting of the truck in motion without giving the intruder an opportunity to reach the ground. The self-same act that was the cause of the disaster is supposed to have ended the abandonment and re-established a relation which till then had been suspended. Act and disaster would alike have been avoided if the relation had not been broken. Even then, however, the delinquent servant did not purge himself of wrong. The field of duty once forsaken, is not to be re-entered by acts evincing a divided loyalty and thus continuing the offense. . . .

The judgment of the Appellate Division and that of the Trial Term should be reversed, and the complaint dismissed, with costs in all courts.

MAPLE V. TENNESSEE GAS TRANSMISSION
201 N.E.2d 299 (Ohio C.A. 1963)

BROWN, JUDGE: The plaintiff, while attempting to turn his car on a roadway adjacent to the defendant company's pumping station in icy weather, became stuck in the ditch adjacent to defendant company's driveway. Plaintiff walked onto the defendant's premises, talked with Stewart, one of the defendant company's employees, and told Stewart his problem. Stewart and he went in Stewart's car to one of the garages on the company's property intending to get a truck with which to pull plaintiff's car from the ditch.

While plaintiff and Stewart were attempting to open the garage door Stewart's driverless car proceeded forward pinning plaintiff to the garage doors and seriously injuring him.

The jury returned a verdict for the plaintiff, upon which judgment was rendered.

The fifth assignment of error questions whether the factual situation as demonstrated by the evidence, giving that evidence a construction most favorable to the plaintiff, gives rise to a jury question as to whether Mr. Stewart, defendant's agent, was acting in the course and scope of his agency at the time of the accident.

There was evidence that Stewart, the defendant's employee, was in charge of the pumping station generally in the absence of the superintendent, and that the superintendent was absent on this occasion. There was evidence that the plaintiff's car in the ditch was partly blocking one of the driveways by means of which entrance to and exit from the defendant company's plant was obtained. From this and other evidence in the record, we may presume that Stewart reasonably may have concluded that the defendant company had some interest, or would derive some benefit directly or indirectly from rendering assistance in this emergency. We can not say on this evidence as a matter of law that Stewart at the time of the accident was beyond the scope of his employment. Stewart was acting in an area in which he had some implied authority to exercise discretion in determining whether his rendering help in this emergency was in his company's interest.

We note the following well stated comment in 35 American Jurisprudence, Section 550, Page 981:

. . . *Whether any particular act is within the authority which has been impliedly conferred upon the employee is one which the courts have found oftentimes to be difficult of solution. In this respect, the decisions hold that where authority to act for another has been conferred without special limita-tion, it carries with it, by implication, authority to do all things that may be necessary to its execution; and where the authorization involves the exercise of the discretion of the employee, the use of such discretion is a part of the thing authorized and, where exercised, becomes, as to third persons, the dis-cretion and act of the employer. . . .*

Doubt as to whether or not a servant is acting within the course and scope of his authority when injuring another will be resolved against the master in an action to hold the latter liable for the act, at least to the extent of requiring the question to be submitted to the jury. Assigned error number five is therefore not well taken. [JUDGMENT AFFIRMED]

THE BILL OF RIGHTS AND BUSINESS

1 INTRODUCTION

Perhaps no part of the United States Constitution is so well known or held so sacred as the so-called "Bill of Rights," which consists of the first ten amendments to the Constitution. Most of us are acquainted to some degree with the freedoms of speech, press, religion, and assembly. Usually we do not think of these matters in a business context but more as dealing with personal rights of individuals in a free society. There are, however, very important aspects of these freedoms which relate to economic opportunity and business activity. Of course, many decisions have been handed down which relate to the meaning, interpretation, and application of the Bill of Rights in matters not involving business, but we are not concerned with those in this chapter.

The principles of the first ten amendments to the United States Constitution are generally made binding on the states by the Fourteenth Amendment. Thus the concepts discussed herein are applicable at all levels of government. This chapter will illustrate some of the areas of business activity and types of legal problems which involve these fundamental freedoms.

2 FREEDOM OF RELIGION

Freedom of religion becomes a business issue frequently as a result of legislative enactment of Sunday closing legislation.

Since the time of the Roman empire, Christians have considered Sunday to be a day of rest. Those of the Jewish faith worship from sundown Friday to sundown Saturday. Atheists and agnostics presumably have no day of worship. It is, therefore, not surprising that controversy and litigation result when legislative bodies at either the state or local level attempt to prohibit activities, such as conducting a business at designated times, for religious purposes.

Many states and some municipalities by statute prohibit business activity on Sunday with certain specified exceptions. These statutes, usually referred to as "Blue Laws," may limit an activity to a specified time or may prohibit it altogether. The motives behind such laws are at least in part religious but many have economic justification. For example, car dealers may want to close at least one day a week to reduce overhead, etc., but will not dare do so if their competitors are open for business. A "Blue Law" prohibiting the sale of autos on Sundays at least has some economic justification. In addition, these laws have been justified as improving the state of health and well-being of citizens by giving a day of rest.

Sunday closing laws are attacked for a variety of reasons including the constitutional ones that they violate the guarantee of freedom of religion, the prohibition against taking property without due process of law, and the prohibition against denying people equal protection under the laws. The current attitude of the Supreme Court toward these laws is illustrated by the following case.

TWO GUYS, INC. V. MCGINLEY
366 U.S. 582 (1961)

WARREN, CHIEF JUSTICE: The primary questions presented in this case are whether a Pennsylvania statute enacted in 1959 which makes unlawful the Sunday retail sale of certain commodities, imposing a fine of up to one hundred dollars for the first offense, is violative of the constitutional guarantees of equal protection of the laws and religious freedom. . . .

This statute, with certain exceptions, generally forbids all worldly employment, business and sports on Sunday. Works of charity and necessity are excepted, as is the delivery of milk and necessaries before 9 a.m. and after 5 p.m. Two recent amendments also except wholesome recreation (defined as golf, tennis, boating, swimming, bowling, basketball, picnicking, shooting at inanimate targets and similar activities) and work in connection with the rendering of service by a public utility. Violations of this section carry a penalty of four dollars. Appellant . . . sought an injunction . . . to restrain the District Attorney from enforcing this statute against it, alleging that the statute was unconstitutional for the reasons stated above. . . .

Among the other activities prohibited on Sunday by these Pennsylvania statutes are selling of motor vehicles and trailers, operation of pool rooms or billiard rooms, conduct of boxing or wrestling matches, harness racing, pawnbrokering, contests for retrieving dogs, catching of fish in the Delaware River by use of a net, and extension education in public school buildings. The Sunday exhibition of motion pictures is permitted only after 2 p.m., and then only if the voters in each municipality approve; however, religious motion pictures may be shown by churches at any time providing they are shown within church property and no admission price is charged.

Baseball, football and polo receive similar treatment except the permitted hours are between 1 p.m. and 7 p.m. Public concerts, of music or high order though not necessarily sacred, may only be performed after noon.

The off-the-premises sale of alcoholic beverages on Sunday is disallowed; but private clubs may sell alcoholic beverages to their members on Sunday, as may hotel restaurants between 1 p.m. and 10 p.m. in first and second-class Pennsylvania cities if the voters in those cities so choose. Municipalities and third-class Pennsylvania cities have statutory authority to restrain desecrations of the Sabbath day; one statutory section simply empowers various judicial officers to punish persons who profane the Lord's day. Barbering and beauty culture work on Sunday subjects the actor to license revocation. Male prisoners may not perform manual labor on Sunday and bakery employees are not permitted to commence working on Sunday before 6 p.m.

The statutes generally proscribe hunting and shooting on Sunday but make an exception for the removal of furbearing animals from traps. Sunday fishing from public lands or in public waters is permitted, but not on private property without the consent of the owner. Also banned is the training of dogs except with the permission of the owner upon whose land the activity is undertaken.

The court below . . . denied appellant the injunctive relief sought, dismissing appellant's constitutional objections that the 1959 statute was a law respecting an establishment of religion, that the statute preferred one religion over others and that the classifications drawn by the statute were violative of equal protection of the law. . . .

Appellant contends that the Pennsylvania Sunday Closing Law is one respecting an establishment of religion because it commemorates the Resurrection, obliges everyone to honor this basic doctrine of the major Christian denominations by abstaining from work and encourages Christian religious worship. . . .

To prove its argument, appellant relies on the language of the present laws in question, on the prior history of this legislation and on various statements of the Pennsylvania courts in interpreting the statutes. We agree that an inquiry into these matters is relevant.

The court below found that the connection between religion and the original Pennsylvania Sunday closing statutes was obvious and indisputable. This is clearly demonstrated by the first Pennsylvania Sunday law, enacted in 1682. There were re-enactments several years later, and again in 1700, which once more stated the purposes of preventing "Looseness, Irreligion, and Atheism," and of better permitting on Sunday the reading of the scriptures at home or the frequenting of meetings of religious worship. In 1705, some changes appeared. The preamble of the statute remained religious and the stated purposes of bible reading and religious worship continued. However, some of the exceptions still present in the 1939 statute first appeared, but a specific ban on the drinking of alcoholic beverages in public houses was enacted. The most apparent forerunner of the 1939 statute was passed in 1779. The preamble stated only that the purpose was "for the due observation of the Lord's day." No mention was made of bible reading or religious worship and the specific Sunday prohibition concerning alcoholic beverages was omitted. . . .

The present statutory sections still contain some traces of the early religious influence. The 1939 statute refers to Sunday as "the Lord's day"; but it is included in the general section entitled, "Offenses Against Public Policy, Economy and Health." Title 18 Purdon's Pa. Stat. Ann § 4651 uses the term "Sabbath Day" and refers to the other days of the week as "secular days." But almost every other statutory section simply uses the word, "Sunday," and contains no language with religious connotation. It would seem that those traces that have remained are simply the result of legislative oversight in failing to remove them. Section 4651 was re-enacted in 1959 and happened to retain the religious language; many other statutory sections, passed both before and after this date, omit it. Certain political subdivisions are authorized to restrain "desecrations of the Sabbath day," and there is a jurisdictional section authorizing the punishment of persons who "profane the Lord's day." But many of the activities historically considered to be profane—e.g., the consumption of alcoholic beverages—are now no longer totally prohibited. There is a general immunity for religious motion pictures and some of the recently exempted activities are permitted only during Sunday afternoons.

On the other hand, we find that the 1939 statute was recently amended to permit all healthful and recreational exercises and activities on Sunday. This is not consistent with aiding church attendance; in fact, it might be deemed inconsistent. And the statutory section, § 4699.10, the constitutionality of which is immediately before us, was promoted principally by the representatives of labor and business interests. Those Pennsylvania legislators who favored the bill specifically disavowed any religious purpose for its enactment but stated instead that economics required its passage.

As early as 1848, the Pennsylvania Supreme Court vociferously disclaimed that the purpose of Sunday closing was religious:

All agree that to the well-being of society, periods of rest are absolutely necessary. To be productive of the required advantage these periods must recur at stated intervals, so that the mass of which the community is composed, may enjoy a respite from labour at the same time. They may be established by common consent, or, as is conceded, the legislative power of the state may, without impropriety, interfere to fix the time of their stated return and enforce obedience to the direction. When this happens, some one day must be selected, and it has been said the round of the week presents none which, being preferred, might not be regarded as favouring some one of the numerous religious sects into which mankind are divided. In a Christian community, where a very large majority of the people celebrate the first day of the week as their chosen period of rest from labour, it is not surprising that that day should have received the legislative sanction: and as it is also devoted to religious observances, we are prepared to estimate the reason why the statute should speak of it as the Lord's day, and denominate the infraction of its legalized rest, a profanation. Yet this does not change the character of the enactment. It is still, essentially, but a civil regulation made for the government of man as a member of society, *and obedience to it may properly be enforced by penal sanctions.* Sprecht v. Commonwealth, 8 *Pa.* 312, 323. [EMPHASIS ADDED]

Concededly, there were a number of cases decided after Specht which used language strongly supporting appellant's position. But, these cases, the last of which was decided more than thirty years ago, did not squarely decide a constitutional contention. More persuasively, in the only recent appellate case dealing with the constitutionality of the 1939 statute, the Pennsylvania Superior Court affirmed an opinion which specifically relied on the language and reasoning of Specht. *Commonwealth v. Bauder,* 188 Pa. Super. 424, 145 A.2d 915, affirming 14 Pa.D. & C.R.2d 571.

Having carefully examined the entirety of the present legislation, the relevant judicial characterizations and, particularly, the legislative history leading to the passage of the 1959 Act immediately before us, we hold that neither the statute's purpose nor its effect is religious. See *McGowan v. Maryland, supra,* 81 S.Ct. at page 1107. Moreover, for the same reasons stated in *McGowan v. State of Maryland, supra,* 81 S.Ct. at page 1105, we reject appellant's contention that the State has other means at its disposal to accomplish its secular purpose that would not even remotely or incidentally give state aid to religion.

Accordingly, the decision is affirmed. [AFFIRMED]

Excerpts from a case decided with the one above add further enlightenment on Sunday closing laws. In *Brownfield v. Brown,*[1] Chief Justice Warren in the majority opinion noted:

The statute at bar does not make unlawful any religious practices of appellants; the Sunday law simply regulates a secular activity and, as applied to appellants, operates so as to make the practice of their religious beliefs more expensive. Furthermore, the law's effect does not inconvenience all members of the Orthodox Jewish faith but only those who believe it necessary to work on Sunday. And even these are not faced with as serious a choice as forsaking their religious practices or subjecting themselves to criminal prosecution. Fully recognizing that the alternatives open to appellants and others similarly situ-

[1] 366 U.S. 599 (1961).

ated—retaining their present occupations and incurring economic disadvantage or engaging in some other commercial activity which does not call for either Saturday or Sunday labor—may well result in some financial sacrifice in order to observe their religious beliefs, still the option is wholly different than when the legislation attempts to make a religious practice itself unlawful.

To strike down, without the most critical scrutiny, legislation which imposes only an indirect burden on the exercise of religion, i.e., legislation which does not make unlawful the religious practice itself, would radically restrict the operating latitude of the legislature. Statutes which tax income and limit the amount which may be deducted for religious contributions impose an indirect economic burden on the observance of the religion of the citizen whose religion requires him to donate a greater amount to his church; statutes which require the courts to be closed on Saturday and Sunday impose a similar indirect burden on the observance of the religion of the trial lawyer whose religion requires him to rest on a weekday. The list of legislation of this nature is nearly limitless.

Needless to say, when entering the area of religious freedom, we must be fully cognizant of the particular protection that the Constitution has accorded it. Abhorrence of religious persecution and intolerance is a basic part of our heritage. But we are a cosmopolitan nation made up of people of almost every conceivable religious preference. These denominations number almost three hundred. Year Book of American Churches for 1958, 257 et seq. Consequently, it cannot be expected, much less required, that legislators enact no law regulating conduct that may in some way result in an economic disadvantage to some religious sects and not to others because of the special practices of the various religions. We do not believe that such an effect is an absolute test for determining whether the legislation violates the freedom of religion protected by the First Amendment.

In a separate concurring opinion, Justice Frankfurter, noting that there were many nonreligious reasons for Sunday closing, stated:

It cannot be fairly denied that the institution of Sunday as a time whose occupations and atmosphere differ from those of other days of the week has now been a portion of the American cultural scene since well before the Constitution; that for many millions of people life has a hebdomadal rhythm in which this day, with all its particular associations, is the recurrent note of repose. Cultural history establishes not a few practices and prohibitions religious in origin which are retained as secular institutions and ways long after their religious sanctions and justifications are gone. In light of these considerations, can it reasonably be said that no substantial nonecclesiastical purpose relevant to a well-ordered social life exists for Sunday restrictions?

It is urged, however, that if a day of rest were the legislative purpose, statutes to secure it would take some other form than the prohibition of activity on Sunday. Such statutes, it is argued, would provide for one day's *labor stoppage in seven, leaving the choice of the day to the individual; or, alternatively, would fix a common day of rest on some other day—Monday or Tuesday. But, in all fairness, certainly, it would be impossible to call unreasonable a legislative finding that these suggested alternatives were unsatisfactory. A provision for one day's closing per week, at the option of every particular enterpriser, might be disruptive of families whose members are employed by different enterprises. Enforcement might be more difficult, both because violation would be less easily discovered and because such a law would not be seconded, as is Sunday legislation, by the community's moral temper. More important, one-day-a-week laws do not accomplish all that is accomplished by Sunday laws. They provide only a periodic physical rest, not that atmosphere of entire community repose which Sunday has traditionally brought and which, a legislature might reasonably believe, is necessary to the welfare of those who for many generations have been accustomed to its recuperative effects.*

The same considerations might also be deemed to justify the choice of Sunday as the single common day when labor ceases. For to many who do not regard it sacramentally, Sunday is nevertheless a day of special, long-established associations, whose particular temper makes it a haven that no other day could provide. The will of a majority of the community, reflected in the legislative process during scores of years, presumably prefers to take its leisure on Sunday. The spirit of any people expresses in goodly measure the heritage which links it to its past. Disruption of this heritage by a regulation which, like the unnatural labors of Claudius's shipwrights, does not divide the Sunday from the week, might prove a measure ill-designed to secure the desirable community repose for which Sunday legislation is designed. At all events, Maryland, Massachusetts and Pennsylvania, like thirty-one other States with similar regulations, could reasonably so find. Certainly, from failure to make a substitution for Sunday in securing a socially desirable day of surcease from subjection to labor and routine a purpose cannot be derived to establish or promote religion.

The foregoing opinions were not without dissent. Moreover, legislatures are constantly faced with proposals to change or alter existing laws. The Sunday closing decisions illustrate one aspect of the relationship between the Bill of Rights and economic endeavor.

3 FREEDOM OF SPEECH AND THE PRESS

In our early legal history and into the early portion of this century, the freedoms of speech and the press were an issue in cases involving picketing, especially by unions. The right to picket peacefully for a lawful purpose is well recognized today. Courts may limit the number of pickets in order to preserve order and promote safety but the right to express opinions in a picket line cannot be denied. Currently, the issues involving these freedoms are best illustrated by the cases dealing with *obscenity*. A substantial amount of litigation as well as attempted regulation of business activity is involved with newspapers, magazines, moving pictures, or other means of communication which contain material that is considered by some to be obscene. Regulations frequently take the form of censorship or call for criminal prosecution as an indirect form of censorship. Attempts to prohibit the sale of literature may violate the right of "freedom of the press" and attempts to prohibit verbal communication, such as in a movie, run into the additional obstacle of possibly violating "freedom of speech."

The word "obscene" has had a variety of meanings and perhaps is not capable of exact definition. It has its roots in two Latin words: *ob*, "on account of" and *caenum*, "filth." *Webster's New Collegiate Dictionary* defines obscene as "foul" or "disgusting."

Our laws dealing with obscenity may be traced to an 1857 English Statute known as "Lord Campbell's Act." This act gave magistrates the power to order the destruction of books and prints if, in their opinion, publication of them would amount to a misdemeanor which was proper to be prosecuted as such. In 1868, the Lord Chief Justice Cochbum in the case of *The Queen v. Hicklin* stated: "I think the test of obscenity is this, whether the tendency of the matter charged as obscene is to deprave and corrupt those whose minds are open to such immoral influences, and into whose hands publications of this sort may fall." Note that this rule did not examine the whole manuscript and used the persons who were susceptible to influence as the criterion.

In 1873, Congress passed a statute relating to the sending of obscene literature through the mails. This statute, known as the Comstock Act, provided: ". . . no obscene, lewd, or lascivious book, pamphlet, picture, print, or other publication of indecent character shall be carried in the mails." Prosecutions under this statute were successful if the publication would have a tendency to suggest impure and libidinous thoughts depraving and corrupting morals. Freedom of the press and speech were not violated, as the protection of the First Amendment did not extend to obscene literature. For example, a book on venereal disease was obscene when sold to minors.

The twentieth century has seen drastic changes in the legal attitude toward obscenity. In 1913, Judge Learned Hand noted that "contemporary society should not 'be required to' reduce its treatment of sex to the standard of a child's library in the supposed interest of a salacious few." In 1930, Judge Augustus N. Hand in reviewing a book entitled *The Sex Side of Life*, stated: ". . . the pamphlet is intended to be given to parents and then to their children, and thus is not distributed to children indiscriminately. . . . [A]rticles dealing with sex may arouse lust under some circumstances, but the law did not prohibit everything that might arouse sex impulses." In 1934,

Judge Hand expanded the possible publication of materials when he announced the "dominant effect" test in a case involving the book "Ulysses." He stated:

> . . . [W]e believe that the proper test of whether a given book is obscene is its dominant effect. In applying this test, relevancy of the objectionable parts to the theme, the established reputation of the work in the estimation of approved critics if the book is modern, and the verdict of the past, if it is ancient, are persuasive pieces of evidence; for works of art are not likely to sustain a high position with no better warrant for their existence than their obscene content.[2]

After World War II, many cases arose involving obscenity and the extent to which pornographic literature should be permitted to be available. These cases established that some publications or other items may properly be sold to adults but not to children. In discussing the protection of the First Amendment, the court in *Roth v. United States*[3] said: "All ideas having even the slightest redeeming social importance . . . have the full protection of the guarantees. . . . But implicit in the history of the First Amendment is the rejection of obscenity as utterly without redeeming social importance. . . . We hold that obscenity is not within the area of constitutionally protected speech or press." The court then stated the test of obscenity to be: ". . . whether to the average person, applying contemporary community standards the dominant theme of the material taken as a whole appeals to prurient interest."

Courts in reviewing matters alleged to be obscene use the following rules:

1   The dominant theme of the material *considered as a whole* must be obscene; it is not enough if it is obscene in parts.
2   Its obscenity must be judged by its prurient appeal to the *average normal adult,* and not by its prurient appeal to the susceptible or immature.
3   The obscenity of the material must be judged in light of *contemporary community standards.*
4   To be obscene it must *appeal to prurient interests.*

The application of the foregoing rules has resulted in constitutional protection of books and movies that many people find morally objectionable. These persons often believe that court decisions protecting such publications and communications are contributing to the general moral decay of the country. Others feel that such decisions contribute to the free expression of ideas and the advancement of society. The cases which follow illustrate some current problems involving obscenity.

2 72 F.2d 705 (1934).
3 354 U.S. 476 (1957).

PEOPLE V. BRUCE
202 N.E.2d 497 (Ill. 1964)

PER CURIAM: By an earlier opinion filed June 18, 1964, this court affirmed the judgment of the circuit court of Cook County entered upon a jury verdict finding the defendant herein guilty of giving an obscene performance violative of section 11-20 of the Criminal Code of 1961. On June 22, 1964, the Supreme Court of the United States decided *Jacobellis v. Ohio,* 378 U.S. 184, in which a movie allegedly obscene was held not to be so. On July 7, 1964, the original opinion of this court was vacated, and reargument ordered in the light of Jacobellis.

The performance here consisted of a 55-minute monologue upon numerous socially controversial subjects interspersed with such unrelated topics as the meeting of a psychotic rapist and a nymphomaniac who have both escaped from their respective institutions, defendant's intimacies with three married women, and a supposed conversation with a gas station attendant in a rest room which concludes with the suggestion that the defendant and attendant both put on contraceptives and take a picture. . . .

The entire performance was originally held by us to be characterized by its continual reference, by words and acts, to sexual intercourse or sexual organs in terms which ordinary adult individuals find thoroughly disgusting and revolting as well as patently offensive; that, as is evident from these brief summaries, it went beyond customary limits of candor, a fact which becomes even more apparent when the entire monologue is considered.

Our original opinion recognized defendant's right to satirize society's attitudes on contemporary social problems and to express his ideas, however bizarre, as long as the method used in doing so was not so objectionable as to render the entire performance obscene. Affirmance of the conviction was predicated upon the rule originally laid down in *American Civil Liberties Union v. City of Chicago,* 3 Ill. 2d 334, 121 N.E.2d 585, that the obscene portions of the material must be balanced against its affirmative values to determine which predominates. We rejected defendant's argument that *Roth v. United States,* 354 U.S. 476, struck down this balancing test and held that material, no matter how objectionable the method of its presentation, was constitutionally privileged unless it was utterly without redeeming social importance. It is apparent from the opinions of a majority of the court in Jacobellis that the "balancing test" rule of *American Civil Liberties Union* is no longer a constitutionally acceptable method of determining whether material is obscene, and it is there made clear that material having *any* social importance is constitutionally protected.

While we would not have thought that constitutional guarantees necessitate the subjection of society to the gradual deterioration of its moral fabric which this type of presentation promotes, we must concede that some of the topics commented on by defendant are of social importance. Under *Jacobellis* the entire performance is thereby immunized, and we are constrained to hold that the judgment of the circuit court of Cook County must be reversed and defendant discharged. [JUDGMENT REVERSED]

Obscenity is not the only area in which freedom of speech and press play a role in business decisions or the political process. For example, the State of Alabama had a statute which made it a crime to publish an editorial on election day urging people to vote a certain way. This statute was challenged in *Mills v. State of Alabama*,[4] on ground that it violated the first amendment. Justice Black in addressing himself to this issue stated:

> The First Amendment, which applies to the States through the Fourteenth, prohibits laws "abridging the freedom of speech, or of the press. . . ."
>
> Whatever differences may exist about interpretations of the First Amendment, there is practically universal agreement that a major purpose of that Amendment was to protect the free discussion of governmental affairs. This of course includes discussions of candidates, structures and forms of government, the manner in which government is operated or should be operated, and all such matters relating to political processes. The Constitution specifically selected the press, which includes not only newspapers, books, and magazines, but also humble leaflets and circulars, to play an important role in the discussion of public affairs. Thus the press serves and was designed to serve as a powerful antidote to any abuses of power by governmental officials and as a constitutionally chosen means for keeping officials elected by the people responsible to all the people whom they were selected to serve. Suppression of the right of the press to praise or criticize governmental agents and to clamor and contend for or against change, which is all that this editorial did, muzzles one of the very agencies the Framers of our Constitution thoughtfully and deliberately selected to improve our society and keep it free. The Alabama Corrupt Practices Act by providing criminal penalties for publishing editorials such as the one here silences the press at a time when it can be most effective. It is difficult to conceive of a more obvious and flagrant abridgment of the constitutionally guaranteed freedom of the press.
>
> Admitting that the state law restricted a newspaper editor's freedom to publish editorials on election day, the Alabama Supreme Court nevertheless sustained the constitutionality of the law on the ground that the restrictions on the press were only "reasonable restrictions" or at least "within the field of reasonableness." The Court reached this conclusion because it thought the law imposed only a minor limitation on the press—restricting it only on

4 384 U.S. 214 (1966).

election days—and because the court thought the law served a good purpose. It said:

"It is a salutary legislative enactment that protects the public from confusive last-minute charges and countercharges and the distribution of propaganda in an effort to influence voters on an election day; when as a practical matter, because of lack of time, such matters cannot be answered or their truth determined until after the election is over." *This argument, even if it were relevant to the constitutionality of the law, has a fatal flaw. The state statute leaves people free to hurl their campaign charges up to the last minute of the day before election. The law held valid by the Alabama Supreme Court then goes on to make it a crime to answer those "last-minute" charges on election day, the only time they can be effectively answered. Because the law prevents any adequate reply to these charges, it is wholly ineffective in protecting the electorate "from confusive last-minute charges and countercharges." We hold that no test of reasonableness can save a state law from invalidation as a violation of the First Amendment when that law makes it a crime for a newspaper editor to do no more than urge people to vote one way or another in a publicly held election.*

The judgment of the Supreme Court of Alabama is reversed and the case is remanded for further proceedings not inconsistent with this opinion.

4   THE FOURTH, FIFTH, AND SIXTH AMENDMENTS

The criminal law is generally not regarded as significant to the study of the legal environment of business. However, in recent years, the crime wave which has swept the country has imposed substantial losses on business and has drastically increased the cost of doing business due to increased insurance costs and losses of inventory. Crimes of violence have made many areas unsafe and have greatly boosted the cost of government, with a resulting rise in taxes. The criminal law in many ways typifies the moral climate of business activity and serves as a focal point for comparing the interests of society with the interests of individuals. Therefore, a look at some aspects of criminal laws and trends in criminal decisions is important to the student of the law of business.

Three of the first ten amendments play a major role in shaping our criminal law. The relevant portions of these amendments are:

Amendment IV

The right of the people to be secure in their persons, houses, papers and effects, against unreasonable searches and seizures, shall not be violated, and no warrants shall issue, but upon probable cause, supported by oath or affirmation, and particularly describing the place to be searched, and the persons or things to be seized.

Amendment V

. . . No person shall be compelled in any criminal case to be a witness against himself, nor be deprived of life, liberty, or property without due process of law. . . .

Amendment VI

In all criminal prosecutions the accused shall enjoy the right . . . to be informed of the nature and cause of the accusation; . . . and to have the Assistance of Counsel for his defence.

These three amendments establish, respectively, the rights of individuals with regard to search and seizure, self-incrimination, and defense counsel when accused of a crime. Each of these amendments, as applied to criminal cases, has been the subject of many judicial decisions.

In recent years in opinions which were sharply divided (usually five to four), the Supreme Court has applied the above constitutional protections very strictly and has given maximum protection to the accused. These decisions have been widely criticized and many people feel that criminals are being overly protected at the expense of the rest of society. Confessed rapists and murderers have been set free because of technical procedural errors and, as a result, discontent with the judiciary has swelled. Many believe that the police and law enforcement officials have been unreasonably hampered by these cases. Some of the harshest criticism has been found in the dissenting opinions such as those in the case below.

ESCOBEDO V. ILLINOIS
378 U.S. 478 (1964)

GOLDBERG, JUSTICE: The critical question in this case is whether, under the circumstances, the refusal by the police to honor petitioner's request to consult with his lawyer during the course of an interrogation constitutes a denial of "the Assistance of Counsel" in violation of the Sixth Amendment to the Constitution as "made obligatory upon the States by the Fourteenth Amendment," . . . and thereby renders inadmissible in a state criminal trial any incriminating statement elicited by the police during the interrogation.

On the night of January 19, 1960, petitioner's brother-in-law was fatally shot. At 2:30 a.m. that morning, petitioner was arrested without a warrant and interrogated. Petitioner made no statement to the police and was released at 5 p.m. that afternoon pursuant to a state court writ of habeas corpus obtained by Mr. Warren Wolfson, a lawyer who had been retained by petitioner.

On January 30, Benedict DiGerlando, who was then in police custody and who was later indicted for the murder along with petitioner, told the police that petitioner had fired the fatal shots. Between 8 and 9 p.m. that evening, petitioner and his sister, the widow of the deceased, were arrested and taken to police headquarters. En route to the police station, the police "had handcuffed the defendant behind his back," and "one of the arresting officers told defendant that DiGerlando had named him as the one who shot" the deceased. Petitioner testified, without contradiction, that the "detectives said they had us pretty well, up pretty tight, and we might as well admit to this crime," and that he replied, "I am sorry but I would like to have advice from my lawyer." A police officer testified that although petitioner was not formally charged "he was in custody" and "couldn't walk out the door."

Shortly after petitioner reached police headquarters, his retained lawyer arrived. The lawyer described the ensuing events in the following terms:

On that day I received a phone call (from "the mother of another defendant") and pursuant to that phone call I went to the Detective Bureau at 11th and State. The first person I talked to was the Sergeant on duty at the Bureau Desk, Sergeant Pidgeon. I asked Sergeant Pidgeon for permission to speak to my client, Danny Escobedo. . . . Sergeant Pidgeon made a call to the Bureau lockup and informed me that the boy had been taken from the lockup to the Homicide Bureau. This was between 9:30 and 10:00 in the evening. Before I went anywhere, he called the Homicide Bureau and told them there was an attorney waiting to see Escobedo. He told me I could not see him. Then I went upstairs to the Homicide Bureau. There were several Homicide Detectives around and I talked to them. I identified myself as Escobedo's attorney and asked permission to see him. They said I could not. . . . The police officer told me to see Chief Flynn who was on duty. I identified myself to Chief Flynn and asked permission to see my client. He said I could not. . . . I think it was approximately 11:00 o'clock. He said I couldn't see him because they hadn't completed questioning. . . . [F]or a second or two I spotted him in an office in the Homicide Bureau. The door was open and I could see through the office. . . . I waved to him and he waved back and then the door was closed, by one of the officers at Homicide. There were four or five officers milling around the Homicide Detail that night. As to whether I talked to Captain Flynn any later that day, I waited around for another hour or two and went back again and renewed by [sic] request to see my client. He again told me I could not. . . . I filed an official complaint with Commissioner Phelan of the Chicago Police Department. I had a conversation with every police officer I could find. I was told at Homicide that I couldn't see him and I would have to get a writ of habeas corpus. I left the Homicide Bureau and from the Detective Bureau at 11th and State at approximately 1:00 A. M. (Sunday morning). I had no opportunity to talk to my client that

night. I quoted to Captain Flynn the Section of the Criminal Code which
allows an attorney the right to see his client.

Petitioner testified that during the course of the interrogation he repeatedly asked to speak to his lawyer and that the police said that his lawyer "didn't want to see" him. The testimony of the police officers confirmed these accounts in substantial detail.

Notwithstanding repeated requests by each, petitioner and his retained lawyer were afforded no opportunity to consult during the course of the entire interrogation. At one point, as previously noted, petitioner and his attorney came into each other's view for a few moments but the attorney was quickly ushered away. Petitioner testified "that he heard a detective telling the attorney that the latter would not be allowed to talk to [him] 'until they were done' " and that he heard the attorney being refused permission to remain in the adjoining room. A police officer testified that he had told the lawyer that he could not see petitioner until "we were through interrogating" him.

There is testimony by the police that during the interrogation, petitioner, a 22-year-old of Mexican extraction with no record of previous experience with the police, "was handcuffed" in a standing position and that he "was nervous, he had circles under his eyes and he was upset" and was "agitated because he had not slept well in over a week."

It is undisputed that during the course of the interrogation Officer Montejano, who "grew up" in petitioner's neighborhood, who knew the family, and who uses "Spanish language in [his] police work," conferred alone with petitioner "for about a quarter of an hour. . . ." Petitioner testified that the officer said to him "in Spanish that my sister and I could go home if I pinned it on Benedict DiGerlando," that "he would see to it that we would go home and be held only as witnesses, if anything, if we had made a statement against DiGerlando . . . , that we would be able to go home that night." Petitioner testified that he made the statement in issue because of this assurance. Officer Montejano denied offering any such assurance.

A police officer testified that during the interrogation the following occurred:

I informed him of what DiGerlando told me and when I did, he told me
that DiGerlando was [lying] and I said, "Would you care to tell DiGerlando
that?" And he said, "yes, I will." So, I brought . . . Escobedo in and he
confronted DiGerlando and he told him that he was lying and said, "I didn't
shoot Manuel, you did it."

In this way, petitioner, for the first time admitted to some knowledge of the crime. After that he made additional statements further implicating himself in the murder plot. At this point an Assistant State's Attorney, Theodore J. Cooper, was summoned "to take" a statement. Mr. Cooper, an experienced lawyer who was assigned to the Homicide Division to take "statements from some defendants and some prisoners that they had in custody," "took" petitioner's statement by asking carefully framed questions apparently designed to assure the admissibility into evidence of the resulting answers. Mr. Cooper testified that he did not advise petitioner of his constitutional rights, and it is undisputed that no one during the course of the interrogation so advised him.

Petitioner moved both before and during trial to suppress the incriminating statement, but the motions were denied. Petitioner was convicted of murder and he appealed the conviction.

. . . We granted a writ of certiorari. . . . We . . . reverse the judgment of conviction.

In *Massiah v. United States,* 377 U.S. 201, this Court observed that "a Constitution which guarantees a defendant the aid of counsel at . . . trial could surely vouchsafe no less to an indicted defendant under interrogation by the police in a completely extrajudicial proceeding. Anything less . . . might deny a defendant 'effective representation by counsel at the only stage when legal aid and advice would help him.' "

The interrogation here was conducted before petitioner was formally indicted. But in the context of this case, that fact should make no difference. When petitioner requested, and was denied, an opportunity to consult with his lawyer, the investigation had ceased to be a general investigation of "an unsolved crime." Petitioner had become the accused, and the purpose of the interrogation was to "get him" to confess his guilt despite his constitutional right not to do so. At the time of his arrest and throughout the course of the interrogation, the police told petitioner that they had convincing evidence that he had fired the fatal shots. Without informing him of his absolute right to remain silent in the face of this accusation, the police urged him to make a statement. As this Court observed many years ago:

> It cannot be doubted that, placed in the position in which the accused was when the statement was made to him that the other suspected person had charged him with a crime, the result was to produce upon his mind the fear that, if he remained silent, it would be considered an admission of guilt, and therefore render certain his being committed for trial as the guilty person, and it cannot be conceived that the converse impression would not also have naturally arisen that, by denying, there was hope of removing the suspicion from himself. Bram v. United States, 168 U.S. 532.

Petitioner, a layman, was undoubtedly unaware that under Illinois law an admission of "mere" complicity in the murder plot was legally as damaging as an admission of firing of the fatal shots. The "guiding hand of counsel" was essential to advise petitioner of his rights in this delicate situation. This was the "stage when legal aid and advice" were most critical to petitioner. It was a stage surely as critical as was the arraignment in *Hamilton v. Alabama,* 368 U.S. 52, and the preliminary hearing in *White v. Maryland,* 373 U.S. 59. What happened at this interrogation could certainly "affect the whole trial," since rights "may be as irretrievably lost, if not then and there asserted, as they are when an accused represented by counsel waives a right for strategic purposes." Ibid. It would exalt form over substance to make the right to counsel, under these circumstances, depend on whether at the time of the interrogation, the authorities had secured a formal indictment. Petitioner had, for all practical purposes, already been charged with murder.

The New York Court of Appeals, . . . has recently recognized that, under circumstances such as those here, no meaningful distinction can be drawn between interrogation of an accused before and after formal indictment. In *People v. Donovan,* 13 N.Y.2d 148, 193 N.E.2d 628, that court, in an opinion by Judge Fuld, held that a "confession taken from a defendant, during a period of detention (prior to indictment), after his attorney had requested and been denied access to him" could not be used against him in a criminal trial. The court observed that it "would be highly incongruous if our system of justice permitted the district attorney, the lawyer representing the State, to extract a confession from the accused while his own lawyer, seeking to speak with him was kept from him by the police."

In *Gideon v. Wainwright,* 372 U.S. 335, we held that every person accused of a crime, whether state or federal, is entitled to a lawyer at trial. The rule sought by the State here, however, would make the trial no more than an appeal from the interrogation; and the "right to use counsel at the formal trial [would be] a very hollow thing [if], for all practical purposes, the conviction is already assured by pretrial examination." "One can imagine a cynical prosecutor saying: 'Let them have the most illustrious counsel, now. They can't escape the noose. There is nothing that counsel can do for them at trial.' "

It is argued that if the right to counsel is afforded prior to indictment, the number of confessions obtained by the police will diminish significantly, because most confessions are obtained during the period between arrest and indictment, and "any lawyer worth his salt will tell the suspect in no uncertain terms to make no statement to police under any circumstances." This argument, of course, cuts two ways. The fact that many confessions are obtained during this period points up its critical nature as a "stage when legal aid and advice" are surely needed. The right to counsel would indeed be hollow if it began at a period when few confessions were obtained. There is necessarily a direct relationship between the importance of a stage to the police in their quest for a confession and the criticalness of that stage to the accused in his need for legal advice. Our Constitution, unlike some others, strikes the balance in favor of the right of the accused to be advised by his lawyer of his privilege against self-incrimination.

We have learned the lesson of history, ancient and modern, that a system of criminal law enforcement which comes to depend on the "confession" will, in the long run, be less reliable and more subject to abuses than a system which depends on extrinsic evidence independently secured through skillful investigation. As Dean Wigmore so wisely said:

[A]ny system of administration which permits the prosecution to trust habitually to compulsory self-disclosure as a source of proof must itself suffer morally thereby. *The inclination develops to rely mainly upon such evidence, and to be satisfied with an incomplete investigation of the other sources. The exercise of the power to extract answers begets a forgetfulness of the just limitations of that power. The simple and peaceful process of questioning breeds a readiness to resort to bullying and to physical force and torture. If there is a right to an answer, there soon seems to be a right to the expected answer,—that is, to a confession of guilt. Thus the legitimate use grows into the unjust abuse; ultimately, the innocent are jeopardized by the encroachments of a bad system. Such seems to have been the course of experience in those legal systems where the privilege was not recognized.*

This Court also has recognized that "history amply shows that confessions have often been extorted to save law enforcement officials the trouble and effort of obtaining valid and independent evidence. . . ."

We have also learned the companion lesson of history that no system of criminal justice can, or should, survive if it comes to depend for its continued effectiveness on the citizens' abdication through unawareness of their constitutional rights. No system worth preserving should have to *fear* that if an accused is permitted to consult with a lawyer, he will become aware of, and exercise, these rights. If the exercise of constitutional rights will thwart the effectiveness of a system of law enforcement, then there is something very wrong with that system.

We hold, therefore, that where, as here, the investigation is no longer a general inquiry into an unsolved crime but has begun to focus on a particular suspect, the suspect has been taken into police custody, the police carry out a process of interrogations that lends itself to eliciting incriminating statements, the suspect has requested and been denied an opportunity to consult with his lawyer, and the police have not effectively warned him of his absolute constitutional right to remain silent, the accused has been denied "the Assistance of Counsel" in violation of the Sixth Amendment to the Constitution as "made obligatory upon the States by the Fourteenth Amendment," and that no statement elicited by the police during the interrogation may be used against him at a criminal trial. . . .

Nothing we have said today affects the powers of the police to investigate "an unsolved crime," by gathering information from witnesses and by other "proper investigative efforts." We hold only that when the process shifts from investigatory to accusatory—when its focus is on the accused and its purpose is to elicit a confession—our adversary system begins to operate, and, under the circumstances here, the accused must be permitted to consult with his lawyer.

The judgment of the Illinois Supreme Court is reversed and the case remanded for proceedings not inconsistent with this opinion. [REVERSED AND REMANDED]

STEWART, JUSTICE, dissenting: Under our system of criminal justice the institution of formal, meaningful judicial proceedings, by way of indictment, information, or arraignment, marks the point at which a criminal investigation has ended and adversary litigative proceedings have commenced. It is at this point that the constitutional guarantees attach which pertain to a criminal trial. Among those guarantees are the right to a speedy trial, the right of confrontation, and the right to trial by jury. Another is the guarantee of the assistance of counsel.

The confession which the Court today holds inadmissible was a voluntary one. It was given during the course of a perfectly legitimate police investigation of an unsolved murder. The Court says that what happened during this investigation "affected" the trial. I had always supposed that the whole purpose of a police investigation of a murder was to "affect" the trial of the murderer, and that it would be only an incompetent, unsuccessful, or corrupt investigation which would not do so. The Court further says that the Illinois police officers did not advise the petitioner of his "constitutional rights" before he confessed to the murder. This Court has never held that the Constitution requires the police to give any "advice" under circumstances such as these.

Supported by no stronger authority than its own rhetoric, the Court today converts a routine police investigation of an unsolved murder into a distorted analogue of a judicial trial. It imports into this investigation constitutional concepts historically applicable only after the onset of formal prosecutorial proceedings. By doing so, I think the Court perverts those precious constitutional guarantees, and frustrates the vital interests of society in preserving the legitimate and proper function of honest and purposeful police investigation.

Like my Brother CLARK, I cannot escape the logic of my Brother WHITE'S conclusions as to the extraordinary implications which emanate from the Court's opinion in this case, and I share their views as to the untold and highly unfortunate impact today's decision may have upon the fair administration of criminal justice. I can only hope we have completely misunderstood what the Court has said.

WHITE, JUSTICE, dissenting (joined by JUSTICE CLARK and JUSTICE STEWART): In *Massiah v. United States,* 377 U.S. 201, the Court held that as of the date of the indictment the prosecution is disentitled to secure admissions from the accused. The Court now moves that date back to the time when the prosecution begins to "focus" on the accused. Although the opinion purports to be limited to the facts of this case, it would be naive to think that the new constitutional right announced will depend upon whether the accused has retained his own counsel, or has asked to consult with counsel in the course of interrogation. At the very least the Court holds that once the accused becomes a suspect and, presumably, is arrested, any admission made to the police thereafter is inadmissible in evidence unless the accused has waived his right to counsel. The decision is thus another major step in the direction of the goal which the Court seemingly has in mind—to bar from evidence all admissions obtained from an individual suspected of crime, whether involuntarily made or not. It does of course put us one step "ahead" of the English judges who have had the good sense to leave the matter a discretionary one with the trial court. I reject this step and the invitation to go farther which the Court has now issued.

By abandoning the voluntary-involuntary test for admissibility of confessions, the Court seems driven by the notion that it is uncivilized law enforcement to use an accused's own admissions against him at his trial. It attempts to find a home for this new and nebulous rule of due process by attaching it to the right to counsel guaranteed in the federal system by the Sixth Amendment and binding upon the States by virtue of the due process guarantee of the Fourteenth Amendment. . . . The right to counsel now not only entitles the accused to counsel's advice and aid in preparing for trial but stands as an impenetrable barrier to any interrogation once the accused has become a suspect. From that very moment apparently his right to counsel attaches, a rule wholly unworkable and impossible to administer unless police cars are equipped with public defenders and undercover agents and police informants have defense counsel at their side. I would not abandon the Court's prior cases defining with some care and analyses the circumstances requiring the presence or aid of counsel and substitute the amorphous and wholly unworkable principle that counsel is constitutionally required whenever he would or could be helpful. . . . These cases dealt with the requirement of counsel at proceedings in which definable rights could be won or lost, not with stages where probative evidence might be obtained. Under this new approach one might just as well argue that a potential defendant is constitutionally entitled to a lawyer before, not after, he commits a crime, since it is then that crucial incriminating evidence is put within the reach of the government by the would be accused. Until now there simply has been no right guaranteed by the Federal Constitution to be free from the use at trial of a voluntary admission made prior to indictment.

It is incongruous to assume that the provision for counsel in the Sixth Amendment was meant to amend or supersede the self-incrimination provision of the Fifth Amendment, which is now applicable to the States. That amendment addresses itself to the very issue of incriminating admissions of an accused and resolves it by proscribing only compelled statements. Neither the Framers, the constitutional language, a century of decisions of this Court nor Professor Wigmore provide an iota of support for the idea that an accused has an absolute constitutional right not to answer even in the absence of compulsion—the constitutional right not to incriminate himself by making voluntary disclosures.

Today's decision cannot be squared with other provisions of the Constitution which, in my view, define the system of criminal justice this Court is empowered to administer. The Fourth Amendment permits upon probable cause even compulsory searches of the suspect and his possessions and the use of the fruits of the search at trial, all in the absence of counsel. The Fifth Amendment and state constitutional provisions authorize, indeed require, inquisitorial grand jury proceedings at which, a potential defendant in the absence of counsel, is shielded against no more than compulsory incrimination. A grand jury witness, who may be a suspect, is interrogated and his answers, at least until today, are admissible in evidence at trial. And these provisions have been thought of as constitutional safeguards to persons suspected of an offense. Furthermore, until now, the Constitution has permitted the accused to be fingerprinted and to be identified in a line-up or in the courtroom itself.

The Court chooses to ignore these matters and to rely on the virtues and morality of a system of criminal law enforcement which does not depend on the "confession." No such judgment is to be found in the Constitution. It might be appropriate for a legislature to provide that a suspect should not be consulted during a criminal investigation; that an accused never be called before a grand jury to answer, even if he wants to, what may well be incriminating questions; and that no person, whether he be a suspect, guilty criminal or innocent bystander should be put to the ordeal of responding to orderly noncompulsory inquiry by the State. But this is not the system our Constitution requires. The only "inquisitions" the Constitution forbids are those which compel incrimination. Escobedo's statements were not compelled and the Court does not hold that they were.

This new American judge's rule, which is to be applied in both federal and state courts, is perhaps thought to be a necessary safeguard against the possibility of extorted confessions. To this extent it reflects a deep seated distrust of law enforcement officers everywhere, unsupported by relevant data or current material based upon our own experience. Obviously law enforcement officers can make mistakes and exceed their authority, as today's decision shows that even judges can do, but I have somewhat more faith than the Court evidently has in the ability and desire of prosecutors and of the power of the appellate courts to discern and correct such violations of the law.

The Court may be concerned with a narrower matter; the unknowing defendant who responds to police questioning because he mistakenly believes that he must and that his admissions will not be used against him. But this worry hardly calls for the broadside the Court has now fired. The failure to inform an accused that he need not answer and that his answers may be used against him is very relevant indeed to whether the disclosures are compelled. Cases in this Court, to say the least, have never placed a premium on ignorance of constitutional rights. If an accused is told he must answer and did not know better, it would be very doubtful that the resulting admissions could be used against him. When the accused has not been informed of his rights at all the Court characteristically and properly looks very closely at the surrounding circumstances. I would continue to do so. But, in this case Danny Escobedo knew full well that he need not answer and knew full well that his lawyer had advised him not to answer.

I do not suggest for a moment that law enforcement will be destroyed by the rule announced today. The need for peace and order is too insistent for that. But it will be crippled and its task made a great deal more difficult, all in my opinion, for unsound, unstated reasons, which can find no home in any of the provisions of the Constitution.

Regardless of personal opinion as to the correctness of the decision above and those which follow below, their effect on society and on the environment in which business is conducted is patent. Law enforcement must adjust to these rulings for, unless the law is changed, they are precedents which will be controlling in future criminal investigations and prosecutions.

The three cases which follow are typical of the decisions concerning search and seizure, self-incrimination, and the right to counsel.

FAHY V. CONNECTICUT
375 U.S. 85 (1963)

WARREN, CHIEF JUSTICE: Petitioner waived trial by jury and was convicted in a Connecticut state court of wilfully injuring a public building in violation of Connecticut General Statutes § 53-45(a). Specifically, petitioner and his codefendant Arnold were found guilty of having painted swastikas on a Norwalk, Connecticut, synagogue. At the trial of the case, a can of black paint and a paint brush were admitted into evidence over petitioner's objection. On appeal, the Connecticut Supreme Court of Errors held that the paint and brush had been obtained by means of an illegal search and seizure. . . . However, the court affirmed petitioner's conviction because it found the admission of the unconstitutionally obtained evidence to have been harmless error.

On the facts of this case, it is not now necessary for us to decide whether the erroneous admission of evidence obtained by an illegal search and seizure can ever be subject to the normal rules of "harmless error" under the federal standard of what constitutes harmless error. We find that the erroneous admission of this unconstitutionally obtained evidence at this petitioner's trial was prejudicial; therefore, the error was not harmless, and the conviction must be reversed. We are not concerned here with whether there was sufficient evidence on which the petitioner could have been convicted without the evidence complained of. The question is whether there is a reasonable possibility that the evidence complained of might have contributed to the conviction. To decide this question, it is necessary to review the facts of the case and the evidence adduced at trial.

On February 1, 1960, beween the hours of 4 and 5 a.m., swastikas were painted with black paint on the steps and walls of a Norwalk synagogue. At about 4:40 a.m., Officer Lindwall of the Norwalk police saw an automobile being operated without lights about a block from the synagogue. Upon stopping the car, Lindwall found that Fahy was driving and Arnold was a passenger. Lindwall questioned Fahy and Arnold about their reason for being out at that hour, and they told him they had been to a diner for coffee and were going home. Lindwall also checked the car and found a can of black paint and a paint brush under the front seat. Having no reason to do otherwise, Lindwall released Fahy and Arnold. He followed the car to Fahy's home. Later the same morning, Lindwall learned of the painting of the swastikas. Thereupon, he went to Fahy's home and—without having applied for or obtained an arrest or search warrant—entered the garage under the house and removed from Fahy's car the can of paint and the brush. About two hours later, Lindwall returned to the Fahy home, this time in the company of two other Norwalk policemen. Pursuant to a valid arrest warrant, the officers arrested Fahy and Arnold.

At trial, the court admitted the paint and brush into evidence over petitioner's objection. We assume, as did the Connecticut Supreme Court of Errors, that doing so was error because this evidence was obtained by an illegal search and seizure and was thus inadmissible under the rule of *Mapp v. Ohio.* Examining the effect of this evidence upon the other evidence adduced at trial and upon the conduct of the defense, we find inescapable the conclusion that the trial court's error was prejudicial and cannot be called harmless.

Obviously, the tangible evidence of the paint and brush was itself incriminating. In addition, it was used to corroborate the testimony of Officer Lindwall as to the presence of petitioner near the scene of the crime at about the time it was committed and as to the presence of a can of paint and a brush in petitioner's car at that time. When Officer Lindwall testified at trial concerning that incident, the following transpired:

Q. *Will you tell the court what you found in the car?*

. . . .

A. *Checking on the passengers' side, under the front seat I found a small jar of paint and a paint brush.*

Q. *Are you able to identify this object I show you?*

A. *Yes.*

Q. *What is it?*

A. *A jar of paint I found in the motor vehicle.*

. . . .

Q. *I show you this object and ask you if you can identify that.*

A. *Yes, sir.*

Q. *What is it?*

A. *A paint brush.*

Q. *Where did you first see this paint brush?*

A. *Under the front seat of Mr. Fahy's car.*

The brush and paint were offered into evidence and were received over petitioner's objection. The trial court found: "13. The police found the same can of black paint and the brush in the car which defendants had been operating when stopped by Officer Lindwall earlier in the morning." It can be inferred from this that the admission of the illegally seized evidence made Lindwall's testimony far more damaging than it would otherwise have been.

In addition, the illegally obtained evidence was used as the basis of opinion testimony to the effect that the paint and brush matched the markings on the synagogue, thus forging another link between the accused and the crime charged. At trial, Norwalk Police Officer Tigano testified that he had examined the markings on the synagogue and had determined that they were put on with black paint. He further testified that he had examined the contents of the can illegally seized from Fahy's car and had determined that it contained black paint. Even more damaging was Tigano's testimony that he had taken the illegally seized brush to the synagogue "to measure the width of the paintings of the swastikas." Over objection, Tigano then testified that the brush "fitted the same as the paint brush in some drawings of the lines and some it did not due to the fact that the paint dripped." Thus the trial court found: "14. The two-inch paint brush matched the markings made with black paint upon the synagogue." In relation to this testimony, the prejudicial effect of admitting the illegally obtained evidence is obvious.

Other incriminating evidence admitted at trial concerned admissions petitioner made when he was arrested and a full confession made at the police station later. Testifying at trial, Norwalk Police Lieutenant Virgulak recounted what took place when Fahy, who was just waking up at the time, was arrested:

> I told him I [sic, he] was under arrest for painting swastikas on the synagogue. He said, 'Oh, that?' and he appeared to lay back in bed.
>
> . . . .
>
> Q. Did you have any further conversation with Fahy before you reached the police station that you remember?
> A. I asked him what the reason was for painting the swastikas and he said it was only a prank and I asked him why and he said for kicks.

At the police station, there was further questioning, and Fahy told Lieutenant Virgulak that he, Fahy, would take the responsibility for painting the swastikas. In addition, some hours after the arrest Arnold was asked to give a statement of the events, and he complied, dictating a complete confession of two typewritten pages. After this confession was admitted against Arnold at trial, Lieutenant Virgulak testified that he had read the confession to Fahy and:

> Q. After you finished reading it, will you tell us whether or not he (Fahy) made any comment?
> A. I asked him what his version was and he said the story was as I had it from Mr. Arnold. I asked him if he would like to give a written statement and he declined.

The record does not show whether Fahy knew that the police had seized the paint and brush before he made his admissions at the time of arrest and en route to the police station. In oral argument, however, counsel for the State told the Court that Fahy "probably" had been told of the search and seizure by then. Of course, the full confession was more damaging to the defendants, and unquestionably the defendants knew the police had obtained the paint and brush by the time they confessed. But the defendants were not allowed to pursue the illegal search and seizure inquiry at trial, because, at the time of trial, the exclusionary rule was not applied in Connecticut state courts. Thus petitioner was unable to claim at trial that the illegally seized evidence induced his admissions and confession. Petitioner has told the Court that he would so claim were he allowed to challenge the search and seizure as illegal at a new trial. And we think that such a line of inquiry is permissible. As the Court has noted in the past: "The essence of a provision forbidding the acquisition of evidence in a certain way is that not merely evidence so acquired shall not be used before the Court but that it shall not be used at all." Thus petitioner should have had a chance to show that his admissions were induced by being confronted with the illegally seized evidence.

Nor can we ignore the cumulative prejudicial effect of this evidence upon the conduct of the defense at trial. It was only after admission of the paint and brush and only after their subsequent use to corroborate other state's evidence and only after introduction of the confession that the defendants took the stand, admitted their acts, and tried to establish that the nature of those acts was not within the scope of the felony statute under which the defendants had been charged. We do not mean to suggest that petitioner has presented any valid claim based on the privilege against self-incrimination. We merely note this course of events as another indication of the prejudicial effect of the erroneously admitted evidence.

From the foregoing it clearly appears that the erroneous admission of the illegally obtained evidence was prejudicial to petitioner and hence it cannot be called harmless error. Therefore, the conviction is reversed, and the cause is remanded for proceedings not inconsistent with this opinion. It is so ordered. [REVERSED AND REMANDED]

MALLOY V. HOGAN
378 U.S. 1 (1964)

BRENNAN, JUSTICE: In this case we are asked to reconsider prior decisions holding that the privilege against self-incrimation is not safeguarded against state action by the Fourteenth Amendment.

The petitioner was arrested during a gambling raid in 1959 by Hartford, Connecticut, police. He pleaded guilty to the crime of pool selling, a misdemeanor, and was sentenced to one year in jail and fined $500. The sentence was ordered to be suspended after 90 days, at which time he was to be placed on probation for two years. About 16 months after his guilty plea, petitioner was ordered to testify before a referee appointed by the Superior Court of Hartford County to conduct an inquiry into alleged gambling and other criminal activities in the county. The petitioner was asked a number of questions related to events surrounding his arrest and conviction. He refused to answer any question "on the grounds it may tend to incriminate me." The Superior Court adjudged him in contempt, and committed him to prison until he was willing to answer the questions. Petitioner's application for a writ of habeas corpus was denied by the Superior Court, and the Connecticut Supreme Court of Errors affirmed. The latter court held that the Fifth Amendment's privilege against self-incrimination was not available to a witness in a state proceeding, that the Fourteenth Amendment extended no privilege to him, and that the petitioner had not properly invoked the privilege available under the Connecticut Constitution. We granted certiorari. We reverse. We hold that the Fourteenth Amendment guaranteed the petitioner the protection of the Fifth Amendment's privilege against self-incrimination, and that under the applicable federal standard, the Connecticut Supreme Court of Errors erred in holding that the privilege was not properly invoked.

The extent to which the Fourteenth Amendment prevents state invasion of rights enumerated in the first eight Amendments has been considered in numerous cases in this Court since the Amendment's adoption in 1868. . . .

Gitlow v. New York, 268 U.S. 652, initiated a series of decisions which today hold immune from state invasion every First Amendment protection for the cherished rights of mind and spirit—the freedoms of speech, press, religion, assembly, association, and petition for redress of grievances. . . .

In 1961, . . . it was taken as settled that ". . . the Fourth Amendment's right of privacy has been declared enforceable against the States through the Due Process Clause of the Fourteenth. . . . [O]nly last Term . . . it was held that provision of counsel in all criminal cases was "a fundamental right, essential to a fair trial," and thus was made obligatory on the States by the Fourteenth Amendment.

We hold today that the Fifth Amendment's exception from compulsory self-incrimination is also protected by the Fourteenth Amendment against abridgment by the States. We discuss first the decisions which forbid the use of coerced confessions in state criminal prosecutions.

Brown v. Mississippi, 297 U.S. 278, was the first case in which the Court held that the Due Process Clause prohibited the States from using the accused's coerced confessions against him. . . . The admissibility of a confession in a state criminal prosecution is tested by the same standard applied in federal prosecutions. . . .

The marked shift to the federal standard in state cases began with *Lisenba v. California,* 314 U.S. 219, where the Court spoke of the accused's "free choice to admit, to deny, or to refuse to answer." The shift reflects recognition that the American system of criminal prosecution is accusatorial, not inquisitorial, and that the Fifth Amendment privilege is its essential mainstay. Governments, state and federal, are thus constitutionally compelled to establish guilt by evidence independently and freely secured, and may not by coercion prove a charge against an accused out of his own mouth. Since the Fourteenth Amendment prohibits the States from inducing a person to confess through "sympathy falsely aroused," or other like inducement far short of "compulsion by torture," it follows *a fortiori* that it also forbids the States to resort to imprisonment, as here, to compel him to answer questions that might incriminate him. The Fourteenth Amendment secures against state invasion the same privilege that the Fifth Amendment guarantees against federal infringement—the right of a person to remain silent unless he chooses to speak in the unfettered exercise of his own will, and to suffer no penalty for such silence. . . .

This conclusion is fortified by our recent decision in *Mapp v. Ohio.* . . . We said in Mapp:

We find that, as to the Federal Government the Fourth and Fifth Amendments and, as to the States, the freedom from unconscionable invasions of privacy and the freedom from convictions based upon coerced confessions do enjoy an "intimate relation" in their perpetuation of "principles of humanity and civil liberty [secured] . . . only after years of struggle.". . . The philosophy of each Amendment and of each freedom is complementary to, although not dependent upon, that of the other in its sphere of influence—the very least that together they assure in either sphere is that no man is to be convicted on unconstitutional evidence. . . .
[REVERSED]

5   THE FOURTEENTH AMENDMENT

As was noted in section 1 of this chapter, the Fourteenth Amendment is generally considered to make the constitutional guarantees of the Bill of Rights applicable to the states. The Fourteenth Amendment is quite general in its language and to the extent relevant here provides: "No State shall make or enforce any law which shall abridge the privileges or immunities of citizens of the United States; nor shall any State deprive any person of life, liberty or property, without due process of law, nor deny to any person within its jurisdiction the equal protection of the laws."

The above constitutional provisions are being used by courts to change basic principles of private law in such areas as contracts and rights of ownership of real property. This section will illustrate some of the changes which have resulted from application of the policies of the Fourteenth Amendment. Most of these decisions have substantial significance to business and their volume is staggering. The cases which follow are typical of the myriads which are litigated.

ROBINSON V. FLORIDA
378 U.S. 153 (1964)

BLACK, JUSTICE: A criminal information filed in a Florida state court charged that these eighteen appellants had violated § 509.141 of the Florida Statutes, F.S.A. by remaining in a restaurant after the manager had requested them to leave. The material facts are not in dispute and show: Shell's City Restaurant, which is one of nineteen departments in Shell's Department Store in Miami, had, at the time of appellants' arrest, a policy of refusing to serve Negroes. Appellants, Negroes and whites, went as a group into the restaurant and seated themselves at tables. In accordance with the restaurant's policy, the manager told appellants they would not be served. The manager called the police and, accompanied by one policeman, went to each table, again told appellants they would not be served, and requested them to leave. They refused. The police officers then advised them to leave, and when appellants persisted in their refusal the police placed them all under arrest.

At the trial, the Shell's City management explained that, while Negroes were welcomed as customers in the store's other departments, serving Negroes in the restaurant would be "very detrimental to our business" because of the objections of white customers. After these facts had been brought out during the examination of the State's witnesses, appellants moved for a directed verdict on the ground that their arrest, prosecution, and conviction by the State on this evidence would amount to state discrimination against them on account of color, thereby violating the Fourteenth Amendment's guarantee of equal protection of the laws. This motion was denied. The appellants calling no witnesses, the trial court stayed the adjudication of guilt and the imposition of sentence and placed appellants on probation. . . . [T]he Supreme Court of Florida affirmed. . . . The case is properly here on appeal. . . .

In this case we do not reach the broad question whether the Fourteenth Amendment of its own force forbids a State to arrest and prosecute those who, having been asked to leave a restaurant because of their color, refuse to do so. For here there are additional circumstances which, we think, call for reversal because of our holding in *Peterson v. City of Greenville*, 373 U.S. 244. The petitioners in Peterson were convicted of trespass in violation of a city ordinance after they had seated themselves at a lunch counter and remained there over the manager's protest. At that time, however, there existed another Greenville ordinance which made it unlawful for restaurants to serve meals to white persons and colored persons in the same room or at the same table or counter. In Peterson the city argued that the manager's refusal to serve Negroes was based on his own personal preference, which did not amount to "state action" forbidden by the Fourteenth Amendment. But we held that the case must be decided on the basis of what the ordinance required people to do, not on the basis of what the manager wanted to do. We said:

When a state agency passes a law compelling persons to discriminate against other persons because of race, and the State's criminal processes are employed in a way which enforces the discrimination mandated by that law, such a palpable violation of the Fourteenth Amendment cannot be saved by attempting to separate the mental urges of the discriminators.

In the present case, when appellants were arrested and tried the Florida Board of Health had in effect a regulation, adopted under "authority of the Florida Legislature" and applicable to restaurants, which provided that "where colored persons are employed or accommodated" separate toilet and lavatory rooms must be provided. A month before petitioners were arrested, the State of Florida had issued a "Food and Drink Services" manual, based on state regulations. The manual said that as a "basic requirement,"

Separate facilities shall be provided for each sex and for each race whether employed or served in the establishment.

While these Florida regulations do not directly and expressly forbid restaurants to serve both white and colored people together, they certainly embody a state policy putting burdens upon any restaurant which serves both races, burdens bound to discourage the serving of the two races together. Of course, state action, of the kind that falls within the proscription of the Equal Protection Clause of the Fourteenth Amendment, may be brought about through the State's administrative and regulatory agencies just as through its legislature. Here as in *Peterson v. City of Greenville, supra,* we conclude that the State through its regulations has become involved to such a significant extent in bringing about restaurant segregation that appellants' trespass convictions must be held to reflect that state policy and therefore to violate the Fourteenth Amendment.

The judgment of the Supreme Court of Florida is reversed and the case is remanded for further proceedings not inconsistent with this opinion.

It is so ordered.

The application of the Fifth Amendment privilege against self-incrimination to corporations creates difficult legal problems. Assuming that a corporation cannot plead the Fifth Amendment, the question often arises of whether or not a corporate official may plead it when he himself might be incriminated by giving testimony relating to activities of the corporation in which he was involved. To allow him to do so might effectively extend the privilege to the corporation; but failure to do so would deny him the constitutional privilege. Insofar as corporate business records are concerned, it seems that the official may be required to produce them but may not be required to testify concerning them if the privilege against self-incrimination is asserted by him. Thus, the protection of the Fifth Amendment does not extend to corporations but does to their officers. It should be kept in mind that corporations have been held to be "citizens" for most purposes, including the rights to due process and equal protection of the laws, and that the situations in which constitutional guarantees are not extended to corporations are relatively few.

THE APPLICATION OF THE BILL OF RIGHTS TO STATES

NAACP V. BUTTON
371 U.S. 415 (1963)

The National Association for the Advancement of Colored People brought suit against the Attorney General of Virginia and others for a declaration that a Virginia statute calling for the licensing and regulating of attorneys was unconstitutional. The statute prohibited any arrangement by which prospective litigants were advised to seek assistance of particular attorneys and made it a crime for a person to advise another that his legal rights have been infringed upon. It was also a crime to refer a person to a particular attorney or group of attorneys such as the legal staff of the Virginia conference of NAACP for assistance. The statute allegedly violated freedoms of the First Amendment protected against state action by the Fourteenth Amendment.

The lower courts held for the State, affirming its right to regulate the legal profession and to prevent solicitation of legal business.

BRENNAN, JUSTICE: We reverse the judgment of the Virginia Supreme Court of Appeals. We hold that the activities of the NAACP, its affiliates and legal staff shown on this record are modes of expression and association protected by the First and Fourteenth Amendments which Virginia may not prohibit, under its power to regulate the legal profession, as improper solicitation of legal business violative of Chapter 33 and the Canons of Professional Ethics.

We meet at the outset the contention that "solicitation" is wholly outside the area of freedoms protected by the First Amendment. To this contention there are two answers. The first is that a State cannot foreclose the exercise of constitutional rights by mere labels. The second is that abstract discussion is not the only species of communication which the Constitution protects; the First Amendment also protects vigorous advocacy, certainly of lawful ends, against governmental intrusion. In the context of NAACP objectives, litigation is not a technique of resolving private differences; it is a means for achieving the lawful objectives of equality of treatment by all government, federal, state and local, for the members of the Negro community in this country. It is thus a form of political expression. Groups which find themselves unable to achieve their objectives through the ballot frequently turn to the courts. Just as it was true of the opponents of New Deal legislation during the 1930's, for example, no less is it true of the Negro minority today. And under the conditions of modern government, litigation may well be the sole practicable avenue open to a minority to petition for redress of grievances.

We need not, in order to find constitutional protection for the kind of cooperative, organizational activity disclosed by this record, whereby Negroes seek through lawful means to achieve legitimate political ends, subsume such activity under a narrow, literal conception of freedom of speech, petition or assembly. For there is no longer any doubt that the First and Fourteenth Amendments protect certain forms of orderly group activity. Thus we have affirmed the right "to engage in association for the advancement of beliefs and ideas." We have deemed privileged, under certain circumstances, the efforts of a union official to organize workers. We have said that the Sherman Act does not apply to certain concerted activities of railroads "at least insofar as those activities comprised mere solicitation of governmental action with respect to the passage and enforcement of laws" because "such a construction of the Sherman Act would raise important constitutional questions," specifically, First Amendment questions. And we have refused to countenance compelled disclosure of a person's political associations in language closely applicable to the instant case:

Our form of government is built on the premise that every citizen shall have the right to engage in political expression and association. This right was enshrined in the First Amendment of the Bill of Rights. Exercise of these basic freedoms in America has traditionally been through the media of political associations. Any interference with the freedom of a party is simultaneously an interference with the freedom of its adherents. All political ideas cannot and should not be channeled into the programs of our two major parties. History has amply proved the virtue of political activity by minority, dissident groups. . . .

The NAACP is not a conventional political party; but the litigation it assists, while serving to vindicate the legal rights of members of the American Negro community, at the same time and perhaps more importantly, makes possible the distinctive contribution of a minority group to the ideas and beliefs of our society. For such a group, association for litigation may be the most effective form of political association. . . .

We conclude that under Chapter 33, as authoritatively construed by the Supreme Court of Appeals, a person who advises another that his legal rights have been infringed and refers him to a particular attorney or group of attorneys (for example, to the Virginia Conference's legal staff) for the assistance has committed a crime, as has the attorney who knowingly renders assistance under such circumstances. There thus inheres in the statute the gravest danger of smothering all discussion looking to the eventual institution of litigation on behalf of the rights of members of an unpopular minority.

It is apparent, therefore, that Chapter 33 as construed limits First Amendment freedoms. As this Court said in *Thomas v. Collins*, 323 U.S. 516, 537, " 'Free trade in ideas' means free trade in the opportunity to persuade to action, not merely to describe facts." Thomas was convicted for delivering a speech in connection with an impending union election under National Labor Relations Board auspices, without having first registered as a "labor organizer." He urged workers to exercise their rights under the National Labor Relations Act and join the union he represented. This Court held that the registration requirement as applied to his activities was constitutionally invalid. In the instant case, members of the NAACP urged Negroes aggrieved by the allegedly unconstitutional segregation of public schools in Virginia to exercise their legal rights and to retain members of the Association's legal staff. Like Thomas, the Association and its members were advocating lawful means of vindicating legal rights.

We hold that Chapter 33 as construed violates the Fourteenth Amendment by unduly inhibiting protected freedoms of expression and association. . . . However, the State's attempt to equate the activities of the NAACP and its lawyers with common-law barratry, maintenance and champerty, and to outlaw them accordingly, cannot obscure the serious encroachment worked by Chapter 33 upon protected freedoms of expression. The decisions of this Court have consistently held that only a compelling state interest in the regulation of a subject within the State's constitutional power to regulate can justify limiting First Amendment freedoms. Thus it is no answer to the constitutional claims asserted by petitioners to say, as the Virginia Supreme Court of Appeals has said, that the purpose of these regulations was merely to insure high professional standards and not to curtail free expression. For a State may not, under the guise of prohibiting professional misconduct, ignore constitutional rights.

However valid may be Virginia's interest in regulating the traditionally illegal practices of barratry, maintenance and champerty, that interest does not justify the prohibition of the NAACP activities disclosed by this record. Malicious intent was of the essence of the common-law offenses of fomenting or stirring up litigation. And whatever may be or may have been true of suits against government in other countries, the exercise in our own, as in this case, of First Amendment rights to enforce constitutional rights through litigation, as a matter of law, cannot be deemed malicious. Even more modern, subtler regulations of unprofessional conduct or interference with professional relations, not involving malice, would not touch the activities at bar; regulations which reflect hostility to stirring up litigation have been aimed chiefly at those who urge recourse to the courts for private gain, serving no public interest. Hostility still exists to stirring up private litigation where it promotes the use of legal machinery to oppress: as, for example, to sow discord in a family; to expose infirmities in land titles, as by hunting up claims of adverse possession; to harass large companies through a multiplicity of small claims; or to oppress debtors as by seeking out unsatisfied judgments. For a member of the bar to participate, directly or through intermediaries, in such misuses of the legal process is conduct traditionally condemned as injurious to the public. And beyond this, for a lawyer to attempt to reap gain by urging another to engage in private litigation has also been condemned; that seems to be the import of Canon 28, which the Virginia Supreme Court of Appeals had adopted as one of its Rules.

Objection to the intervention of a lay intermediary, who may control litigation or otherwise interfere with the rendering of legal services in a confidential relationship, also derives from the element of pecuniary gain. Fearful of dangers thought to arise from that element, the courts of several States have sustained regulations aimed at these activities. We intimate no view one way or the other as to the merits of those decisions with respect to the particular arrangements against which they are directed. It is enough that the superficial resemblance in form between those arrangements and that at bar cannot obscure the vital fact that here the entire arrangement employs constitutionally privileged means of expression to secure constitutionally guaranteed civil rights. There has been no showing of a serious danger here of professionally reprehensible conflicts of interest which rules against solicitation frequently seek to prevent. This is so partly because no monetary stakes are involved, and so there is no danger that the attorney will desert or subvert the paramount interests of his client to enrich himself or an outside sponsor. And the aims and interests of NAACP have not been shown to conflict with those of its members and nonmember Negro Litigants; compare *NAACP v. Alabama ex rel. Patterson*, 357 U.S. 449, 459, where we said:

> [*The NAACP*] *and its members are in every practical sense identical. The Association, which provides in its constitution that "[a]ny person who is in accordance with (its) principles and policies . . ." may become a member, is but the medium through which its individual members seek to make more effective the expression of their own views.*

Resort to the courts to seek vindication of constitutional rights is a different matter from the oppressive, malicious, or avaricious use of the legal process for purely private gain. Lawsuits attacking racial discrimination, at least in Virginia, are neither very profitable nor very popular. They are not an object of general competition among Virginia lawyers; the problem is rather one of an apparent dearth of lawyers who are willing to undertake such litigation. There has been neither claim nor proof that any assisted Negro litigants have desired, but have been prevented from retaining, the services of other counsel. We realize that an NAACP lawyer must derive personal satisfaction from participation in litigation on behalf of Negro rights, else he would hardly be inclined to participate at the risk of financial sacrifice. But this would not seem to be the kind of interest or motive which induces criminal conduct.

We conclude that although the petitioner has amply shown that its activities fall within the First Amendment's protections, the State has failed to advance any substantial regulatory interest, in the form of substantive evils flowing from petitioner's activities, which can justify the broad prohibitions which it has imposed. Nothing that this record shows as to the nature and purpose of NAACP activities permits an inference of any injurious intervention in or control of litigation which would constitutionally authorize the application of Chapter 33 to those activities. . . . [REVERSED]

EVANS V. NEWTON
382 U.S. 296 (1966)

DOUGLAS, JUSTICE: In 1911 United States Senator Augustus O. Bacon executed a will that devised to the Mayor and Council of the City of Macon, Georgia, a tract of land which, after the death of the Senator's wife and daughters, was to be used as "a park and pleasure ground" for white people only, the Senator stating in the will that while he had only the kindest feeling for the Negroes he was of the opinion that "in their social relations the two races (white and negro) should be forever separate." The will provided that the park should be under the control of a Board of Managers of seven persons, all of whom were to be white. The city kept the park segregated for some years but in time let Negroes use it, taking the position that the park was a public facility which it could not constitutionally manage and maintain on a segregated basis.

Thereupon, individual members of the Board of Managers of the park brought this suit in the state court against the City of Macon and the trustees of certain residuary beneficiaries of Senator Bacon's estate, asking that the city be removed as trustee and that the court appoint new trustees, to whom title to the park would be transferred. The city answered, alleging it could not legally enforce racial segregation in the park. The other defendants admitted the allegation and requested that the city be removed as trustee.

Several Negro citizens of Macon intervened, alleging that the racial limitation was contrary to the laws and public policy of the United States, and asking that the court refuse to appoint private trustees. Thereafter the city resigned as trustee and amended its answer accordingly. Moreover, other heirs of Senator Bacon intervened and they and the defendants other than the city asked for reversion of the trust property to the Bacon estate in the event that the prayer of the petition were denied.

The Georgia court accepted the resignation of the city as trustee and appointed three individuals as new trustees, finding it unnecessary to pass on the other claims of the heirs. On appeal by the Negro intervenors, the

Supreme Court of Georgia affirmed, holding that Senator Bacon had the right to give and bequeath his property to a limited class, that charitable trusts are subject to supervision of a court of equity, and that the power to appoint new trustees so that the purpose of the trust would not fail was clear. The case is here on a writ of certiorari.

There are two complementary principles to be reconciled in this case. One is the right of the individual to pick his own associates so as to express his preferences and dislikes, and to fashion his private life by joining such clubs and groups as he chooses. The other is the constitutional ban in the Equal Protection Clause of the Fourteenth Amendment against state-sponsored racial inequality, which of course bars a city from acting as trustee under a private will that serves the racial segregation cause. A private golf club, however, restricted to either Negro or white membership is one expression of freedom of association. But a municipal golf course that serves only one race is state activity indicating a preference on a matter as to which the State must be neutral. What is "private" action and what is "state" action is not always easy to determine. Conduct that is formally "private" may become so entwined with governmental policies or so impregnated with a governmental character as to become subject to the constitutional limitations placed upon state action. The action of a city in serving as trustee of property under a private will serving the segregated cause is an obvious example. A town may be privately owned and managed, but that does not necessarily allow the company to treat it as if it were wholly in the private sector. Thus we held in *Marsh v. Alabama,* 326 U.S. 501, that the exercise of constitutionally protected rights on the public streets of a company town could not be denied by the owner. A State is not justified, we said, in "permitting a corporation to govern a community of citizens so as to restrict their fundamental liberties. . . ." We have also held that where a State delegates an aspect of the elective process to private groups, they become subject to the same restraints as the State. That is to say, when private individuals or groups are endowed by the State with powers or functions governmental in nature, they become agencies or instrumentalities of the State and subject to its constitutional limitations.

Yet generalizations do not decide concrete cases. Only by sifting can we determine whether the reach of the Fourteenth Amendment extends to a particular case. The range of government activities is broad and varied, and the fact that government has engaged in a particular activity does not necessarily mean that an individual entrepreneur or manager of the same kind of undertaking suffers the same constitutional inhibitions. While a State may not segregate public schools so as to exclude one or more religious groups, those sects may maintain their own parochial educational systems.

If a testator wanted to leave a school or center for the use of one race only and in no way implicated the State in the supervision, control, or management of that facility, we assume *arguendo* that no constitutional difficulty would be encountered.

This park, however, is in a different posture. For years it was an integral part of the City of Macon's activities. From the pleadings we assume it was swept, manicured, watered, patrolled, and maintained by the city as a public facility for whites only, as well as granted tax exemption under Ga. Code Ann. § 92-201. The momentum it acquired as a public facility is certainly not dissipated *ipso facto* by the appointment of "private" trustees. So far as this record shows, there has been no change in municipal maintenance and concern over this facility. Whether these public characteristics will in time be dissipated is wholly conjectural. If the municipality remains entwined in the management or control of the park, it remains subject to the restraints of the Fourteenth Amendment just as the private utility in *Public Utils. Comm'n v. Pollak*, 343 U.S. 451, remained subject to the Fifth Amendment because of the surveillance which federal agencies had over its affairs. We only hold that where the tradition of municipal control had become firmly established, we cannot take judicial notice that the mere substitution of trustees instantly transferred this park from the public to the private sector.

This conclusion is buttressed by the nature of the service rendered the community by a park. The service rendered even by a private park of this character is municipal in nature. It is open to every white person, there being no selective element other than race. Golf clubs, social centers, luncheon clubs, schools such as Tuskegee was at least in origin, and other like organizations in the private sector are often racially oriented. A park on the other hand, is more like a fire department or police department that traditionally serves the community. Mass recreation through the use of parks is plainly in the public domain; . . . and state courts that aid private parties to perform that public function on a segregated basis implicate the State in conduct proscribed by the Fourteenth Amendment. Like the streets of the company town in *Marsh v. Alabama, supra,* the elective process of *Terry v. Adams, supra,* and the transit system of *Public Utils. Comm'n v. Pollak, supra,* the predominant character and purpose of this park is municipal.

Under the circumstances of this case, we cannot but conclude that the public character of this park requires that it be treated as a public institution subject to the command of the Fourteenth Amendment, regardless of who now has title under state law. We may fairly assume that had the Georgia courts been of the view that even in private hands the park may not be operated for the public on a segregated basis, the resignation would not have been approved and private trustees appointed. We put the matter that way because on this record we cannot say that the transfer of title *per se* disentangled the park from segregation under the municipal regime that long controlled it.

Since the judgment below gives effect to that purpose, it must be and is

Reversed.

[The foregoing decision was not unanimous.]

BLACK, JUSTICE, dissenting: The State Supreme Court's interpretation of the scope and effect of this Georgia decree should be binding upon us unless the State Supreme Court has somehow lost its power to control and limit the scope and effect of Georgia trial court decrees relating to Georgia wills creating Georgia trusts of Georgia property. A holding that ignores this state power would be so destructive of our state judicial systems that it could find no support, I think, in our Federal Constitution or in any of this Court's prior decisions. For myself, I therefore accept the decision of the Georgia Supreme Court as holding only what it declared it held, namely, that the trial court committed no error under Georgia law in accepting the City of Macon's resignation as trustee and in appointing successor trustees to execute the Bacon trust.

I am not sure that the Court is passing at all on the only two questions the Georgia Supreme Court decided in approving the city's resignation as trustee and the appointment of successors. If the Court is holding that a State is without these powers, it is certainly a drastic departure from settled constitutional doctrine and a vastly important one which, I cannot refrain from saying, deserves a clearer explication than it is given. Ambiguity cannot, however, conceal the revolutionary nature of such a holding, if this is the Court's holding, not successfully obscure the tremendous lopping off of power heretofore uniformly conceded by all to belong to the States. This ambiguous and confusing disposition of such highly important questions is particularly disturbing to me because the Court's discussion of the constitutional status of the park comes in the nature of an advisory opinion on federal constitutional questions the Georgia Supreme Court did not decide.

HARLAN, JUSTICE, also dissenting: This decision, in my opinion, is more the product of human impulses, which I fully share, than of solid constitutional thinking. It is made at the sacrifice of long-established and still wise procedural and substantive constitutional principle. I must respectfully dissent. . . .

On the merits, which I reach only because the Court has done so, I do not think that the Fourteenth Amendment permits this Court in effect to frustrate the terms of Senator Bacon's will, now that the City of Macon is no longer connected so far as the record shows, with the administration of Baconsfield. If the majority is in doubt that such is the case, it should remand for findings on that issue and not reverse.

The Equal Protection Clause reaches only discriminations that are the product of capricious state action; it does not touch discriminations whose origins and effectuation arise solely out of individual predilections, prejudices, and acts. . . .

Quite evidently uneasy with its first ground of decision, the majority advances another which ultimately emerges as the real holding. This ground derives from what is asserted to be the "public character" of Baconsfield and the "municipal . . . nature of its services. . . ." The cases cited by the majority do not support this novel state action theory. . . .

More serious than the absence of any firm doctrinal support for this theory of state action are its potentialities for the future. Its failing as a principle of decision in the realm of Fourteenth Amendment concerns can be shown by comparing—among other examples that might be drawn from the still unfolding sweep of governmental functions—the "public function" of privately established schools with that of privately owned parks. Like parks, the purpose schools serve is important to the public. Like parks, schools may be available to almost anyone of one race or religion but to no others. Like parks, there are normally alternatives for those shut out but there may also be inconveniences and disadvantages caused by the restriction. Like parks, the extent of school intimacy varies greatly depending on the size and character of the institution.

For all the resemblance, the majority assumes that its decision leaves unaffected the traditional view that the Fourteenth Amendment does not compel private schools to adapt their admission policies to its requirements, but that such matters are left to the States acting within constitutional bounds. I find it difficult, however, to avoid the conclusion that this decision opens the door to reversal of these basic constitutional concepts, and, at least in logic, jeopardizes the existence of denominationally restricted schools while making of every college entrance rejection letter a potential Fourteenth Amendment question.

While this process of analogy might be spun out to reach privately owned orphanages, libraries, garbage collection companies, detective agencies, and a host of other functions commonly regarded as nongovernmental though paralleling fields of governmental activity, the example of schools is, I think, sufficient to indicate the pervasive potentialities of this "public function" theory of state action. It substitutes for the comparatively clear and concrete tests of state action a catch-phrase approach as vague and amorphous as it is far-reaching. It dispenses with the sound and careful principles of past decisions in this realm. And it carries the seeds of transferring to federal authority vast areas of concerns whose regulation has wisely been left by the Constitution to the States.

CHAPTER EIGHTEEN

THE LEGAL PROFESSION

1 INTRODUCTION

Law is a profession as distinguished from a business or occupation. Historically, the three learned professions are law, medicine, and theology. Each involves a dedication to mankind in which the character of the service performed is more important than any remuneration received for the service. In these professions, the individual practitioner assumes duties and responsibilities which exceed those of other callings. In the practice of law, these duties extend to the courts, to the public, and to the client.

A lawyer's first duty is to the administration of justice. As an officer of the court, it is his obligation to see that proceedings are conducted in a dignified and orderly manner and that issues are tried on their merits only. The practice of law is not a game or mere battle of wits, but rather a means to promote justice.

The lawyer's duties to his client are such as to require the highest degree of fidelity, loyalty, and integrity. These duties, which among other things prevent an attorney from testifying against his client, are more fully discussed in section 2.

To engage in the practices of law is not a natural or constitutional right, but a privilege conferred upon one as a result of his knowledge of the law and possession of good moral character. The latter involves a proper conception of the nature and duties of the office of attorney and also of the ethics of the profession. It has sometimes been described as absolute obedience to the unenforceable. Absolute honesty and integrity are minimum standards for the profession. In addition, loyalty to the United States and to the Constitution on the part of a lawyer has been an inalienable condition to the privilege of practicing law. It has been ruled that an inquiry into one's affiliation with the Communist Party is relevant to the determination of good citizenship and the ability to take the oath of a lawyer in good conscience. A recent case was contrary, however.

Beyond the requirement of good moral character, there are others such as residence requirements and satisfactory knowledge of the law as evidenced by an examination. But it is clear that the most important requirement is "good moral character" as determined by the appropriate court.

Courts are given a great deal of discretion in determining what constitutes good moral character. This is necessary so that they can attempt to further the public interest, the administration of justice, in the best possible manner.

The right to practice law may be suspended or revoked by the court. An attorney may be disbarred for crimes of moral turpitude or for violating his responsibilities to the court or to his clients. Professional misconduct may include conduct in and out of court. Grounds for disbarment are not limited to professional misconduct, but also include acts committed in an attorney's nonprofessional capacity which may reflect adversely on his profession and the system of law he represents. An attorney may engage in commercial pursuits of an honorable character, but his conduct in relation to a business must not be immoral, dishonest, or in violation of private interests or the public good. In the disbarment proceeding of an attorney who was a partner in a social club that conducted gambling games, the court said, "It would be a travesty if the courts were powerless to restrain rogues from parading as its officers, simply because they were clever enough to divorce their professional lives from their private lives." The court did not find that the respondent was a common gambler within the meaning of the criminal statutes, but held that he degraded his profession by maintaining his interest in the club. The court decided that his conduct was not in keeping with that of a member of the profession who is conscious of the dignity and standing of his calling.

The sections which follow will deal further with the duties and responsibilities of lawyers and judges. An acquaintance with these matters should provide an insight into the attitudes and practices of lawyers which will be valuable to both the readers who are potential clients and those who intend to enter the legal profession. In addition, section 4 deals with the questions raised when unlicensed lay persons give legal advice and perform other legal services. This is especially important to those who are or intend to be accountants, insurance brokers, real estate brokers, or bankers.

2   PROFESSIONAL ETHICS OF LAWYERS

Lawyers by the very nature of their profession are privy to their client's most important secrets and affairs. Lawyers are often actively involved in the personal lives of their clients ranging from their family affairs and divorce to their alleged violations of the criminal law. These relationships dictate that lawyers meet the highest standards of professional and ethical conduct. In order to assist members of the profession, the American Bar Association has promulgated the Canons of Professional Ethics, some of which follow. These canons, together with judicial decisions and similar ethical rules adopted by state bar associations, serve to regulate lawyers in the practice of their profession.

CANONS OF PROFESSIONAL ETHICS

PREAMBLE.

In America, where the stability of Courts and of all departments of government rests upon the approval of the people, it is peculiarly essential that the system for establishing and dispensing Justice be developed to a high point of efficiency and so maintained that the public shall have absolute confidence in the integrity and impartiality of its administration. The future of the Republic, to a great extent, depends upon our maintenance of Justice pure and unsullied. It cannot be so maintained unless the conduct and the motives of the members of our profession are such as to merit the approval of all just men.

No code or set of rules can be framed, which will particularize all the duties of the lawyer in the varying phases of litigation or in all the relations of professional life. The following canons of ethics are adopted by the American Bar Association as a general guide, yet the enumeration of particular duties should not be construed as a denial of the existence of others equally imperative, though not specifically mentioned.

1   THE DUTY OF THE LAWYER TO THE COURTS

It is the duty of the lawyer to maintain towards the Courts a respectful attitude, not for the sake of the temporary incumbent of the judicial office, but for the maintenance of its supreme importance. Judges, not being wholly free to defend themselves, are peculiarly entitled to receive the support of the Bar against unjust criticism and clamor. Whenever there is proper ground for serious complaint of a judicial officer, it is the right and duty of the lawyer to submit his grievances to the proper authorities. In such cases, but not otherwise, such charges should be encouraged and the person making them should be protected. . . .

5   THE DEFENSE OR PROSECUTION OF THOSE ACCUSED OF CRIME

It is the right of the lawyer to undertake the defense of a person accused of crime, regardless of his personal opinion as to the guilt of the accused; otherwise innocent persons, victims only of suspicious circumstances, might be denied proper defense. Having undertaken such defense, the lawyer is bound, by all fair and honorable means, to present every defense that the law of the land permits, to the end that no person may be deprived of life or liberty, but by due process of law.

The primary duty of a lawyer engaged in public prosecution is not to convict but to see that justice is done. The suppression of facts or the secreting of witnesses capable of establishing the innocence of the accused is highly reprehensible.

6   ADVERSE INFLUENCES AND CONFLICTING INTERESTS

It is the duty of a lawyer at the time of retainer to disclose to the client all the circumstances of his relations to the parties, and any interest in or connection with the controversy, which might influence the client in the selection of counsel.

It is unprofessional to represent conflicting interests, given after a full disclosure of the facts. Within the meaning of this canon, a lawyer represents conflicting interests when, in behalf of one client, it is his duty to contend for that which duty to another client requires him to oppose.

The obligation to represent the client with undivided fidelity and not to divulge his secrets or confidences forbids also the subsequent acceptance of retainers or employment from others in matters adversely affecting any interest of the client with respect to which confidence has been reposed. . . .

8   ADVISING UPON THE MERITS OF A CLIENT'S CASE

A lawyer should endeavor to obtain full knowledge of his client's cause before advising thereon, and he is bound to give a candid opinion of the merits and probable result of pending or contemplated litigation. The miscarriages to which justice is subject by reason of surprises and disappointments in evidence and witnesses, and through mistakes of juries and errors of Courts, even though only occasional, admonish lawyers to beware of bold and confident assurances to clients, especially where the employment may depend upon such assurance. Whenever the controversy will admit of fair judgment, the client should be advised to avoid or to end the litigation.

9   NEGOTIATIONS WITH OPPOSITE PARTY

A lawyer should not in any way communicate upon the subject of controversy with a party represented by counsel; much less should he undertake to negotiate or compromise the matter with him, but should deal only with his counsel. It is incumbent upon the lawyer most particularly to avoid everything that may tend to mislead a party not represented by counsel, and he should not undertake to advise him as to the law.

10   ACQUIRING INTEREST IN LITIGATION

The lawyer should not purchase any interest in the subject matter of the litigation which he is conducting. . . .

15   HOW FAR A LAWYER MAY GO IN SUPPORTING A CLIENT'S CAUSE

Nothing operates more certainly to create or to foster popular prejudice against lawyers as a class, and to deprive the profession of that full measure of public esteem and confidence which belongs to the proper discharge of its duties than does the false claim, often set up by the unscrupulous in defense of questionable transactions, that it is the duty of the lawyer to do whatever may enable him to succeed in winning his client's cause.

It is improper for a lawyer to assert in argument his personal belief in his client's innocence or in the justice of his cause.

The lawyer owes "entire devotion to the interest of the client, warm zeal in the maintenance and defense of his rights and the exertion of his utmost learning and ability," to the end that nothing be taken or be withheld from him, save by the rules of law, legally applied. No fear of judicial disfavor or public unpopularity should restrain him from the full discharge of his duty. In the judicial forum the client is entitled to the benefit of any and every remedy and defense that is authorized by the law of the land, and he may expect his lawyer to assert every such remedy or defense. But it is steadfastly to be borne in mind that the great trust of the lawyer is to be performed within and not without the bounds of the law. The office of attorney does not permit, much less does it demand of him for any client, violation of law or any manner of fraud or chicane. He must obey his own conscience and not that of his client. . . .

22   CANDOR AND FAIRNESS

The conduct of the lawyer before the Court and with other lawyers should be characterized by candor and fairness.

It is not candid or fair for the lawyer knowingly to misquote the contents of a paper, the testimony of a witness, the language or the argument of opposing counsel, or the language of a decision or a textbook; or with knowledge of its invalidity, to cite as authority a decision that has been overruled, or a statute that has been repealed; or in argument to assert as a fact that which has not been proved, or in those jurisdictions where a side has the opening and closing arguments to mislead his opponent by concealing or withholding positions in his opening argument upon which his side then intends to rely.

It is unprofessional and dishonorable to deal other than candidly with the facts in taking the statements of witnesses, in drawing affidavits and other documents, and in the presentation of causes.

A lawyer should not offer evidence which he knows the Court should reject, in order to get the same before the jury by argument for its admissibility, nor should he address to the judge arguments upon any point not properly calling for determination by him. Neither should he introduce into an argument, address to the court, remarks or statements intended to influence the jury or bystanders.

These and all kindred practices are unprofessional and unworthy of an officer of the law charged, as is the lawyer, with the duty of aiding in the administration of justice. . . .

30 JUSTIFIABLE AND UNJUSTIFIABLE LITIGATION

The lawyer must decline to conduct a civil cause, or to make a defense when convinced that it is intended merely to harass or to injure the opposite party or to work oppression or wrong. But otherwise it is his right, and, having accepted retainer, it becomes his duty to insist upon the judgment of the Court as to the legal merits of his client's claim. His appearance in Court should be deemed equivalent to an assertion on his honor that in his opinion his client's case is one proper for judicial determination.

31 RESPONSIBILITY FOR LITIGATION

No lawyer is obliged to act either as adviser or advocate for every person who may wish to become his client. He has the right to decline employment. Every lawyer upon his own responsibility must decide what employment he will accept as counsel, what causes he will bring into Court for plaintiffs, what cases he will contest in Court for defendants. The responsibility for advising as to questionable transactions, for bringing questionable suits, for urging questionable defenses, is the lawyer's responsibility. He cannot escape it by urging as an excuse that he is only following his client's instructions.

32 THE LAWYER'S DUTY IN ITS LAST ANALYSIS

No client, corporate or individual, however powerful, nor any cause, civil or political, however important, is entitled to receive nor should any lawyer render any service or advice involving disloyalty to the law whose ministers we are, or disrespect of the judicial office, which we are bound to uphold, or corruption of any person or persons exercising a public office or private trust, or deception or betrayal of the public. When rendering any such improper service or advice, the lawyer invites and merits stern and just condemnation. Correspondingly, he advances the honor of his profession and the best interests of his client when he renders service or gives advice tending to impress upon the client and his undertaking exact compliance with the strictest principles of moral law. He must also observe and advise his client to observe the statute law, though until a statute shall have been construed and interpreted by competent adjudication, he is free and is entitled to advise as to its validity and as to what he conscientiously believes to be its just meaning and extent. But above all a lawyer will find his highest honor in a deserved reputation for fidelity to private trust and to public duty, as an honest man and as a patriotic and loyal citizen. . . .

37 CONFIDENCES OF A CLIENT

It is the duty of a lawyer to preserve his client's confidences. This duty outlasts the lawyer's employment, and extends as well to his employees; and neither of them should accept employment which involves or may involve the disclosure or use of these confidences, either for the private advantage of the lawyer or his employees or to the disadvantage of the client, without his knowledge and consent, and even though there are other available sources of such information. A lawyer should not continue employment when he discovers that this obligation prevents the performance of his full duty to his former or to his new client.

If a lawyer is accused by his client, he is not precluded from disclosing the truth in respect to the accusation. The announced intention of a client to commit a crime is not included within the confidences which he is bound to respect. He may properly make such disclosures as may be necessary to prevent the act or protect those against whom it is threatened.

3 JUDICIAL ETHICS

In addition to the Canons of Professional Ethics for lawyers, the American Bar Association has adopted Canons of Judicial Ethics for judges. As we have seen, on many occasions the judiciary not only decides disputes between litigants but also plays a major role in bringing about social, economic, and political changes. In a real sense, the security of the republic and our way of life is entrusted to those people who wield judicial power. Some of the guidelines which lawyers believe that judges should follow in the conduct of their office and in their daily lives are set forth here.

CANONS OF JUDICIAL ETHICS

---

1 RELATIONS OF THE JUDICIARY

The assumption of the office of judge casts upon the incumbent duties in respect to his personal conduct which concern his relation to the state and its inhabitants, the litigants before him, the principles of law, the practitioners of law in his court, and the witnesses, jurors and attendants who aid him in the administration of its functions.

2 THE PUBLIC INTEREST

Courts exist to promote justice, and thus to serve the public interest. Their administration should be speedy and careful. Every judge should at all times be alert in his rulings and in the conduct of the business of the court, so far as he can, to make it useful to litigants and to the community. He should avoid unconsciously falling into the attitude of mind that the litigants are made for the courts instead of the courts for the litigants. . . .

4   AVOIDANCE OF IMPROPRIETY

A judge's official conduct should be free from impropriety and the appearance of impropriety; he should avoid infractions of law; and his personal behavior, not only upon the Bench and in the performance of judicial duties, but also in his everyday life, should be beyond reproach.

5   ESSENTIAL CONDUCT

A judge should be temperate, attentive, patient, impartial, and, since he is to administer the law and apply it to the facts, he should be studious of the principles of the law and diligent in endeavoring to ascertain the facts.

6   INDUSTRY

A judge should exhibit an industry and application commensurate with the duties imposed upon him.

7   PROMPTNESS

A judge should be prompt in the performance of his judicial duties, recognizing that the time of litigants, jurors and attorneys is of value and that habitual lack of punctuality on his part justifies dissatisfaction with the administration of the business of the court. . . .

14   INDEPENDENCE

A judge should not be swayed by partisan demands, public clamor or considerations of personal popularity or notoriety, nor be apprehensive of unjust criticism. . . .

19   JUDICIAL OPINIONS

In disposing of controverted cases, a judge should indicate the reasons for his action in an opinion showing that he has not disregarded or overlooked serious arguments of counsel. He thus shows his full understanding of the case, avoids the suspicion of arbitrary conclusion, promotes confidence in his intellectual integrity and may contribute useful precedent to the growth of the law.

It is desirable that Courts of Appeals in reversing cases and granting new trials should so indicate their views on questions of law argued before them and necessarily arising in the controversy that upon the new trial counsel may be aided to avoid the repetition of erroneous positions of law and shall not be left in doubt by the failure of the court to decide such questions.

But the volume of reported decisions is such and is so rapidly increasing that in writing opinions which are to be published judges may well take this fact into consideration, and curtail them accordingly, without substantially departing from the principles stated above.

It is of high importance that judges constituting a court of last resort should use effort and self-restraint to promote solidarity of conclusion and the consequent influence of judicial decision. A judge should not yield to pride of opinion or value more highly his individual reputation than that of the court to which he should be loyal. Except in case of conscientious difference of opinion on fundamental principle, dissenting opinions should be discouraged in courts of last resort.

20 INFLUENCE OF DECISIONS UPON THE DEVELOPMENT OF THE LAW

A judge should be mindful that his duty is the application of general law to particular instances, that ours is a government of law and not of men, and that he violates his duty as a minister of justice under such a system if he seeks to do what he may personally consider substantial justice in a particular case and disregards the general law as he knows it to be binding on him. Such action may become a precedent unsettling accepted principles and may have detrimental consequences beyond the immediate controversy. He should administer his office with a due regard to the integrity of the system of the law itself, remembering that he is not a depository of arbitrary power, but a judge under the sanction of law. . . .

28 PARTISAN POLITICS

While entitled to entertain his personal views of political questions, and while not required to surrender his rights or opinions as a citizen, it is inevitable that suspicion of being warped by political bias will attach to a judge who becomes the active promoter of the interests of one political party as against another. He should avoid making political speeches, making or soliciting payment of assessments or contributions to party funds, the public endorsement of candidates for political office and participation in party conventions.

He should neither accept nor retain a place on any party committee nor act as party leader, nor engage generally in partisan activities.

Where, however, it is necessary for judges to be nominated and elected as candidates of a political party, nothing herein contained shall prevent the judge from attending or speaking at political gatherings, or from making contributions to the campaign funds of the party that has nominated him and seeks his election or re-election. . . .

33 SOCIAL RELATIONS

It is not necessary to the proper performance of judicial duty that a judge should live in retirement or seclusion; it is desirable that, so far as reasonable attention to the completion of his work will permit, he continue to mingle in social intercourse, and that he should not discontinue his interest in or appearance at meetings of members of the Bar. He should, however, in pending or prospective litigation before him be particularly careful to avoid such action as may reasonably tend to awaken the suspicion that his social or business relations or friendships constitute an element in influencing his judicial conduct.

34   A SUMMARY OF JUDICIAL OBLIGATION

In every particular his conduct should be above reproach. He should be conscientious, studious, thorough, courteous, patient, punctual, just, impartial, fearless of public clamor, regardless of public praise, and indifferent to private political or partisan influences; he should administer justice according to law, and deal with his appointments as a public trust; he should not allow other affairs or his private interests to interfere with the prompt and proper performance of his judicial duties, nor should he administer the office for the purpose of advancing his personal ambitions or increasing his popularity.

35   IMPROPER PUBLICIZING OF COURT PROCEEDINGS

Proceedings in court should be conducted with fitting dignity and decorum. The taking of photographs in the court room, during sessions of the court or recesses between sessions, and the broadcasting or televising of court proceedings are calculated to detract from the essential dignity of the proceedings, distract the witness in giving his testimony, degrade the court, and create misconceptions with respect thereto in the mind of the public and should not be permitted.

Provided that this restriction shall not apply to the broadcasting or televising, under the supervision of the court, of such portions of naturalization proceedings (other than the interrogation of applicants) as are designed and carried out exclusively as a ceremony for the purpose of publicly demonstrating in an impressive manner the essential dignity and the serious nature of naturalization.

36   CONDUCT OF COURT PROCEEDINGS

Proceedings in court should be so conducted as to reflect the importance and seriousness of the inquiry to ascertain the truth.

The oath should be administered to witnesses in a manner calculated to impress them with the importance and solemnity of their promise to adhere to the truth. Each witness should be sworn separately and impressively at the bar or the court, and the clerk should be required to make a formal record of the administration of the oath, including the name of the witness.

Some of the canons are controversial and subject to much debate. For example, Judicial Canon No. 35 which prohibits televising court proceedings is under rather constant attack from the news and broadcasting media. The canons of ethics technically are not laws but are generally respected and followed by courts and attorneys.

4   UNAUTHORIZED PRACTICE OF LAW

A person may prepare his own contracts, will or other legal documents and may appear in court to handle his own case. However, only one who is duly licensed by the judicial branch of government can serve as an attorney at law for another. Persons who render legal services without the requisite license are guilty of a crime and also may be enjoined from such practices.

The fact that a corporation is an artificial person which can act only through its agents has created the issue of whether or not unlicensed corporate officers are guilty of unauthorized practice for appearing in behalf of their company. In the case which follows corporate officials argued that they should have the same privilege as the one individuals have in representing themselves.

SIMBRAU, INC. V. UNITED STATES
367 F.2d 373 (1966)

PER CURIAM: The sole question in this appeal as stated by the attorney at law representing appellant corporation is "Must a corporation, to litigate its rights in a court of law, employ an attorney at law to appear for it and represent it in the court or courts before whom its rights need to be adjudicated?" As appellant's brief states, "Plaintiff attempted to represent itself by its President, Walter T. Savoye, Sr." The unequivocal answer to the above question is Yes.

The basic statute is 28 U.S.C. § 1654 which reads:

Appearance personally or by counsel
In all courts of the United States the parties may plead and conduct their own cases personally or by counsel as, by the rules of such courts, respectively, are permitted to manage and conduct causes therein. As amended May 24, 1949, c. 139, § 91, 63 Stat. 103.

The qualification requirements for attorneys and counselors at law in order to be admitted to practice in the United States District Court for the Middle District of Pennsylvania are set out in Rules 1, 2 and 3, of that Court. Rule 8(1) of this Court's Rules covers the admission requirements for attorneys and counselors at law to practice in this Court.

Osborn v. United States Bank President, 22 U.S. 738 (1824), is relied on as supporting the theory that the corporate plaintiff can sue by an agent who need not be an attorney at law. Chief Justice Marshall in *Osborn,* p. 839, said "A corporation, it is true, can appear only by attorney, while a natural person may appear for himself." Because the Chief Justice did not use the full phrase "attorney at law," appellant insists that any person so authorized by a corporation can start and carry through a law suit. There is no basis whatsoever in the *Osborn* opinion for that conclusion. The particular problem involved was whether the lawyer for the Bank needed to file evidence of his authority to institute the litigation. Immediately prior to the above quoted sentence the Chief Justice in the same sequence made it plain that he was talking solely of attorneys at law. He said p. 828:

Natural persons may appear in court, either by themselves, or by their attorney. But no man has a right to appear as the attorney of another, without the authority of that other. In ordinary cases, the authority must be produced, because there is, in the nature of things, prima facie evidence that one man is in fact the attorney of another. The case, of an attorney-at-law, an attorney for the purpose of representing another in court, and prosecuting or defending a suit in his name, is somewhat different. The power must indeed exist, but its production has not been considered as indispensable. Certain gentlemen, first licensed by government, are admitted, by order of court, to stand at the bar, with a general capacity to represent all the suitors in the court. The appearance of any one of these gentlemen in a cause, has always been received as evidence of his authority; and no additional evidence, so far as we are informed, has ever been required. This practice, we believe, has existed from the first establishment of our courts, and no departure from it has been made in those of any state, or of the Union.

Osborn has been referred to in reported opinions many times on its various phases but never as upholding appellant's stated view. As recently as 1962 the Circuit Court of Appeals for the Tenth Circuit in *Flora Constr. Co. v. Fireman's Fund Ins. Co.*, 307 F.2d 413, 414, depended on *Osborn* primarily (mentioning eight later decisions to the same effect) for its statement "The rule is well established that a corporation can appear in a court of record only by an attorney at law."

In *Acme Poultry Corp. v. United States*, 146 F.2d 738, 740 (4 Cir. 1944), Judge Parker for the Court held: "The handling of the case in court for the corporation was a matter for its counsel, not for its officers." In the only other case we have found in this Circuit dealing with the precise problem, *MacNeil v. Hearst Corp.*, 160 F.Supp. 157 (D.C.D. Del. 1958), the first question to be answered by District Judge Rodney was "1. May a corporate plaintiff institute and prosecute a civil action in Court by its corporate officers alone?" The Court said regarding this:

The answer to the first question must be in the negative. The authorities in the Federal Courts which have determined the question are uniform in holding that a corporation can do no act except through its agents and that such agents representing the corporation in Court must be attorneys at law who have been admitted to practice, are officers of the Court and subject to its control.

Judge Nealon in his sound District Court opinion in this appeal rightly points out that "The confusion that has resulted in this case from pleadings awkwardly drafted and motions inarticulately presented likewise demonstrates the wisdom of such a policy."

The judgment of the District Court will be affirmed.

More difficult questions are presented in matters which do not involve court appearances. It is relatively easy to define the practice of medicine or dentistry but it is extremely difficult to define the practice of law because it involves the giving of advice. Advice can be given by anyone and is almost inherent in certain business functions. For example, an accountant preparing an income tax return applies certain legal principles in the course of his work. A trust officer of a bank uses legal knowledge when discussing the bank's services in connection with estates and trusts. Do these activities constitute unauthorized practice of law? Among those who have been held to be guilty of unauthorized practice of law in the performance of their services are: (1) a business consultant who prepared corporate charters and related documents, (2) real estate brokers in preparing contracts and deeds, (3) union representatives in handling workmen's compensation cases, (4) insurance brokers in preparing estate plans, (5) a "debt-pooler" who gave advice on bankruptcy, (6) a collection agency that sued in its own name to collect accounts for others, (7) an accountant who researched the law in order to give tax advice, or when faced with a difficult tax question, (8) a title company which prepared deeds and mortgages, and (9) a bank in preparing estate plans and documents to implement such plans. Lay specialists object to the narrowing of their activities by the courts, and attempts are being made to define more clearly the proper role of "business specialists" such as those listed above. National organizations such as the American Institute of Certified Public Accountants are working with the American Bar Association to set appropriate guidelines for the scope of activities of members of the bar as well as the lay specialists. The case below indicates the policy behind the rule permitting only licensed persons to perform legal services for others, and illustrates some of the difficulties which arise because those activities which constitute the practice of law have not been precisely defined.

CHICAGO BAR ASS'N V. QUINLAN & TYSON, INC.
214 N.E.2d 771 (Ill. 1966)

PER CURIAM: The Chicago Bar Association filed a complaint in the circuit court of Cook County to enjoin a real-estate brokerage firm, Quinlan and Tyson, Inc., from engaging in the unauthorized practice of law. After a lengthy hearing before a master in chancery it was found that the activities in question, performed in connection with negotiating purchases and sales of real estate for customers, constitute the practice of law. A decree was entered as prayed, except that the defendant was permitted to fill in the blanks of customary offer forms and contract forms as a necessary incident to its business. Upon review in the appellate court that part of the decree was reversed which allowed the filling in of forms, the court holding that none of the challenged services could be performed by persons not licensed to practice law. We have granted leave to appeal. The Illinois State Bar Association, the Chicago Real Estate Board and others have appeared and filed briefs as *amici curiae*.

The defendant is a corporation employing some fifty or sixty persons of which three are licensed real-estate brokers and twenty-three are licensed real-estate salesmen. In conducting its business defendant prepares offers to purchase real estate, draws contracts of purchase and sale, prepares deeds and other instruments necessary to clear or transfer title, and supervises the closing of the transaction. No separate fee is charged for these services, the defendant's compensation consisting solely of brokerage commissions.

The documents ordinarily used—consisting of the contract of sale, the deed, bill of sale for personalty, escrow agreement, application for a mortgage and affidavits waiving possible objections to title—come in standardized forms which defendant's brokers, real-estate salesmen and office personnel fill out for the parties involved. The forms are completed by inserting pertinent factual information and by deleting or striking out portions which do not apply. The forms themselves have been drawn or composed by lawyers.

Defendant contends such services do not amount to the practice of law because their performance by real-estate men has become an established custom and no harm is shown to have resulted. It is argued that they are a necessary incident of the real-estate business and that the filling in of these forms is a simple matter, for which ordinary business intelligence is sufficient. Relied upon also is the assertion that no compensation is charged for the service. Cited and discussed, State by State, are decisions from other jurisdictions tending to support the position taken by the defendant.

We have considered the authorities referred to but find it unnecessary to discuss them at length. The question is not one of first impression in this State. It was settled by our decision in *People v. Schafer,* 404 Ill. 45, 87 N.E.2d 773, where a licensed real-estate broker was held in contempt of court for preparing contracts, deeds, notes and mortgages in transactions for which he received a broker's commission. This court found unacceptable the contention that the drawing of such instruments was proper because done in connection with his real-estate business. Rejected also was the argument which considers those acts to be more or less mechanical and routine, requiring no legal knowledge or skill. We pointed out that "Those who prepare instruments which affect titles to real estate have many points to consider. A transaction which at first seems simple may upon investigation be found to be quite involved. One who merely fills in certain blanks when other pertinent information should be elicited and considered is rendering little service but is acting in a manner calculated to produce trouble."

Except for the matter of filling in blanks on the customary preliminary contract-of-sale form, which we shall hereinafter discuss, we agree with the appellate court that the *Schafer* case is not distinguishable from the case at bar. The fact that other kinds of unauthorized practice were also involved in that case does not affect the holding. Nor are we convinced from defendant's arguments that this authority should be overruled. It is not decisive that defendant is compensated only by its commission, making no special charge for the services in question; nor is it relevant that the services are customarily provided by real-estate men and that no identifiable harm is proved to have ensued. As the appellate court pointed out, it is the character of the acts themselves that determines the issue. If by their nature they require a lawyer's training for their proper performance it does not matter that there may have been a widespread disregard of the requirement or that considerations of business expediency would be better served by a different rule.

We think, however, that in one respect the prohibition in the appellate court's opinion is too broad. In the *Schafer* case this court did not in so many words discuss the preliminary or earnest money contract form, nor did we specifically condemn the mere filling in of the blanks on such forms. The decree of the trial court in the case at bar, permitting real-estate brokers to fill in the blanks of whatever form of such contract is customarily used in the community and to make appropriate deletions from such contract to conform to the facts, is approved. In the usual situation where the broker is employed to find a purchaser he performs this service when he produces a prospect ready, willing and able to buy upon the terms proposed by the seller. The execution of an offer or preliminary contract is an evidencing or recording of this service in bringing together the buyer and seller. It coincides with the job the broker was employed to perform and which he is licensed to perform, and in practice it marks the point at which he becomes entitled to his commission. It seems reasonable therefore that he be authorized to draft this offer or preliminary contract, where this involves merely the filling in of blank forms.

In *Gustafson v. V. C. Taylor & Sons,* 138 Ohio St. 392, 35 N.E.2d 435, a real-estate broker followed the practice of filling in the blanks of a printed "offer to purchase" form which, like those involved in the case at bar, had been prepared by a regularly admitted attorney-at-law. In a suit to enjoin this as unauthorized practice of law the court held that where the broker did nothing more than fill in simple factual material such as the date, price, name of the purchaser, location of the property, date of giving possession and duration of the offer he was not engaging in the practice of law. It was pointed out that such services require no more than ordinary business intelligence and do not require the skill peculiar to one trained and experienced in the law. The *Gustafson* case was cited and fully stated in the opinion of this court in the *Schafer* case, where we proceeded to say that if a particular service performed by the broker "requires legal skill or knowledge, or more than ordinary business intelligence, it constitutes the practice of law" but that "when filling in blanks as directed he may not by that simple act be practicing law. . . ." We think, therefore, that the broker may properly fill in the usual form of earnest money contract or offer to purchase where this involves merely the supplying of simple factual data.

But when the broker has secured the signatures on the usual form of preliminary contract or offer to purchase, completed by the insertion of necessary factual data, he has fully performed his obligation as broker. The drawing or filling in of blanks on deeds, mortgages and other legal instruments subsequently executed requires the peculiar skill of a lawyer and constitutes the practice of law. Such instruments are often muniments of title and become matters of permanent record. They are not ordinarily executed and delivered until after title has been examined and approved by the attorney for the purchaser. Their preparation is not incidental to the performance of brokerage services but falls outside the scope of the broker's function.

The defendant and the real-estate board *amici* argue that all the forms in question are so standardized that only ordinary business intelligence is required to complete them. If the question were merely one of skill in filling out forms the argument would be persuasive. But more is involved than this simple operation and the question cannot realistically be viewed in such isolation. The legal problems involved often depend upon the context in which the instrument is placed, and only a lawyer's training gives assurance that they will be identified or pointed out. The mere completion of a form can readily be done by a stenographer. But it requires a lawyer's advice to determine whether it will accomplish the desired result under all the circumstances. As this court emphasized in the *Schafer* case, 404 Ill. at p. 52, 87 N.E.2d at p. 777 quoting from a Missouri decision: " 'Any one who wants to pay the price may purchase a set of form books and read and copy them. He may use them in his own business if he so desires. But when he advises others for a consideration, that this or that is the law, or that this form or that is the proper form to be used in a certain transaction, then he is doing all that a lawyer does when a client seeks his advice.' "

Drafting and attending to the execution of instruments relating to real-estate titles are within the practice of law, and neither corporations nor any other persons unlicensed to practice the profession may engage therein.

Nor does the fact that standardized forms are usually employed make these services an incident of the real-estate broker business. Many aspects of law practice are conducted through the use of forms, and not all of the matters handled require extensive investigation of the law. But by his training the lawyer is equipped to recognize when this is and when it is not the case. Neither counsel nor *amici* have suggested any practicable way in which an exception to the general rule can be made where only the use of forms is involved, or where the transaction is a "simple" one. Mere simplicity cannot be the basis for drawing boundaries to the practice of a profession. A pharmacist, for example, might be competent to prescribe for many of the simpler ailments, but it takes a medical background to recognize when the ailment is simple. Protection of the public requires that only licensed physicians may prescribe or treat for any ailment, regardless of complexity or simplicity. And protection of the public requires a similar approach when the practice of law is involved. . . .

Appellate court affirmed in part and reversed in part; circuit court affirmed.

5   THE ATTORNEY–CLIENT PRIVILEGE

It is obvious that if an attorney is to give competent advice and adequate representation he must know to the extent possible all of the facts involved in any legal problem presented to him by his client. In attempting to ensure that an attorney may be fully advised of his client's problems, and all matters affecting them, the rules of evidence provide that certain confidential communications to an attorney are privileged. The law does not permit an attorney to reveal such facts and testify against his client, even if called to the stand to do so at a trial. This is called the attorney-client privilege, and may extend to communications made to employees of the attorney in certain cases. The decision which follows discusses the rationale behind the attorney-client privilege, as well as its historical development and application to corporate clients.

RADIANT BURNERS, INC. V. AMERICAN GAS ASS'N
320 F.2d 314 (1963)

The plaintiff, Radiant Burners, Inc., brought this antitrust action against the defendants, the American Gas Association, a trade association, its members and others, alleging that they were involved in a conspiracy and combination in restraint of trade in violation of Section 1 of the Sherman Act, which had the purpose of controlling the market and foreclosing the plaintiff from competition. For this violation, the plaintiff sought an injunction and treble damages. In the pretrial discovery proceedings, each of the parties made available to the others upon their request, the unprivileged documents it had on file relating to the case. However, a dispute arose concerning certain documents in the possession of the defendants. The defendants contended that these were not discoverable by the plaintiff, since they were within the scope of the attorney-client privilege. The trial court held that privilege was not available to corporations and ruled in favor of the plaintiff. The defendants appealed.

HASTINGS, CHIEF JUDGE: . . . The broad question for decision on this interlocutory appeal is whether the district court erred in holding that in a private antitrust action a corporation may not claim the attorney-client privilege to bar discovery of documents. . . .

The rationale of the district court's holding on the merits of the question was that the privilege is not available to corporations because it is historically personal in nature and may be claimed only by natural persons. Further, that since secrecy or confidentiality is essential to a claim of the privilege in any event, it is not possible to maintain this relationship because of the possibility of disclosure to persons who constitute or are necessarily related to the corporate entity. . . .

Dean Wigmore teaches that the history of the attorney-client privilege finds its origin in the reign of Elizabeth I, "where the privilege already appears as unquestioned." It arose from "a consideration for *oath and the honor* of the attorney rather than for the apprehensions of his client." The doctrine that the privilege was that of the attorney rather than the client began to give way to a new concept in the 1700's. The "new theory looked to the necessity of *providing subjectively for the client's freedom of apprehension* in consulting his legal adviser. It proposed to assure this by removing the risk of disclosure by the attorney even at the hands of the law." By the middle of the 1800's, the privilege became substantially recognized as that of the client "to include communications made, first, during any other litigation; next, in contemplation of litigation; next, during a controversy but not yet looking to litigation; and, lastly, in any consultation for legal advice, wholly irrespective of litigation or even of controversy." 8 Wigmore, Evidence § 2290 (McNaughton Rev. 1961).

The policy of the privilege has been grounded on subjective considerations since the latter part of the 1700's. "In order to promote freedom of consultation of legal advisers by clients, the apprehension of compelled disclosure by the legal advisers must be removed; hence the law must prohibit such disclosure except on the client's consent. Such is the modern theory." 8 Wigmore § 2291.

There seems to be general acceptance of the four fundamental conditions recognized as necessary by Wigmore "to the establishment of a privilege against the disclosure of communications:"

1   *The communications must originate in a* confidence that they will
    not be disclosed.
2   *This element of* confidentiality must be essential *to the full and sat-
    isfactory maintenance of the relation between the parties.*
3   *The* relation *must be one which in the opinion of the community
    ought to be sedulously* fostered.
4   *The* injury *that would inure to the relation by the disclosure of the
    communications must be* greater than the benefit *thereby gained for
    the correct disposal of litigation.*

Only if these four conditions are present should a privilege be recog-
nized.

*That they are present in most of the recognized privileges is plain
enough; and the absence of one or more of them serves to explain why certain
privileges have failed to obtain the recognition sometimes demanded for them.
In the privilege for communications between attorney and client, for example, all four are present, the only condition open to any dispute being the
fourth.* 8 Wigmore § 2285.

Finally, on the attorney-client privilege itself, Wigmore makes a sum-
mation "of the general principle so as to represent all its essentials" in
the following sequence:

(1) *Where legal advice of any kind is sought* (2) *from a professional
legal adviser in his capacity as such,* (3) *the communications relating to that
purpose,* (4) *made in confidence* (5) *by the client,* (6) *are at his instance
permanently protected* (7) *from disclosure by himself or by the legal adviser,*
(8) *except the protection be waived.* 8 Wigmore § 2292.

We turn now to the application of this deep rooted privilege—recognized for more than a century as existing between attorney and client for
the benefit of a natural person—to a corporate client. . . .

Plaintiff argues that the privilege developed before the utilization of
the corporation as a business entity and that it finds its origin in terms of
a personal immunity. We believe this is a misconception of the principles
underlying the privilege. Our conclusion is that the privilege is that of a
"client" without regard to the non-corporate or corporate character of the
client, designed to facilitate the workings of justice.

It is argued that because corporations have been denied the protection
of the constitutional privilege against self-incrimination, because of their
impersonal character, that by analogy they are to be denied the protection
of the attorney-client privilege. We shall not attempt to reconcile the
scholarly divergence of views on this proposition. In *White,* the Supreme
Court was moved to its conclusion because it found the constitutional privilege against self-incrimination to be essentially personal in character,
"applying only to natural individuals." It is our view, as we have previously

stated, that the attorney-client privilege derives from a regard for the rights of a client, personal or impersonal in character, fostering a social policy concerned with facilitating the workings of justice.

Plaintiff urges that the benefits to society through the application of the privilege are outweighed by the superior benefits of full disclosure. There is eminent authority in support of this view. . . . These are in essence forceful arguments urged against recognition of the attorney-client privilege in any form. Plaintiff argues; "It would seem a universally accepted proposition that the dubious value of the attorney-client privilege requires its contraction rather than expansion. Most of the commentators agree that the doctrine even as applied to individuals should be abolished and would be, but for the hue and cry that lawyers would raise about such denigration of their prime status symbol."

Plaintiff follows this thought to urge that the privilege be contracted rather than expanded to include corporations. We do not regard the resolution of the question before us as requiring an expansion of the privilege. We think it already is in existence and has been for more than a hundred years. We cannot agree that the proper remedy is annihilation. If, on the other hand, a change in social policy dictated by modern liberalization of discovery procedures is in order, the cure would seem to lie in the area of accommodation of the privilege to modern business practice.

It is our considered judgment that based on history, principle, precedent and public policy the attorney-client privilege in its broad sense is available to corporations, and we so hold.

Giving recognition to what we believe is already an established rule of law, requires the acknowledgment that it is an obstruction to full and free discovery. We have chosen to follow Wigmore, with whom several noted scholars have disagreed. We, therefore, quote his admonition:

> *Nevertheless, the privilege remains an exception to the general duty to disclose. Its benefits are all indirect and speculative; its obstruction is plain and concrete. Even the answers to Bentham's argument concede that the privilege is well founded in its application to a certain proportion of cases. It is worth preserving for the sake of a general policy, but it is nonetheless an obstacle to the investigation of the truth. It ought to be strictly confined within the narrowest possible limits consistent with the logic of its principle.* 8 Wigmore § 2291, at 554, citing *Foster v. Hall*, 12 Pick. 89, 29 Mass. 89, 97 (1831), ("*The rule of privilege, having a tendency to prevent the full disclosure of the truth, ought to be construed strictly*").

The district court has asked us to spell out the answers to questions relating to confidentiality in the corporate chain of command. We are asked "to apply the elements of simple common law personal privilege to complex corporate transactions." With due respect, we must decline the invitation to decide, in a vacuum, the limitations to be imposed in the application of the privilege by a corporation. If there be a place for a "guide-lines" opinion at our court's level, this is not it. . . .

Where a corporation is the client it must act through its officers and agents. The character of the corporate organization and management will vary from the small, family type, one-man variety to the giant with its thousands of employees. The problems concerning confidentiality will necessarily vary accordingly. . . .

There is no reason to believe that the required confidentiality cannot properly be maintained within the corporate family. It can just as readily be dissipated. These matters will all have to be resolved on a case-by-case basis. No one is wise enough to decide them in advance.

Certainly, the privilege would never be available to allow a corporation to funnel its papers and documents into the hands of its lawyers for custodial purposes and thereby avoid disclosure. Likewise, it seems well settled that the requisite professional relationship is not established when the client seeks business or personal advice, as opposed to legal assistance.

In balancing the competing goals of the free and unobstructed search for the truth with the right and absolute necessity for confidential disclosure of information by the client to its attorney to gain the legal advice sought thereby, the courts will realize that they are not dealing with a blanket privilege. . . .

A corporation is entitled to the same treatment as any other "client" —no more and no less. If it seeks legal advice from an attorney, and in that relationship confidentially communicates information relating to the advice sought, it may protect itself from disclosure, absent its waiver thereof. . . . [REVERSED]

6   THE ROLE OF THE SUPREME COURT

In recent years particularly, the Supreme Court has become a subject of controversy. There have even been suggestions that certain of its members be impeached. Many of the reasons for the controversy have been previously discussed in this book. As the Court has tended to move from a policy of judicial restraint to one of judicial activism, it is not surprising that criticism has followed. In the years to come, the Court will in all probability continue to play a significant role in the formulation of governmental policy and its actions will continue to be the subject of major debate. Following are portions of an article and a speech of two prominent authorities on the Supreme Court which focus on the role it has recently played in shaping our political and social institutions.

THE CHANGING ROLE OF THE SUPREME COURT OF THE U.S.A. [1]
Anthony Lewis [2]

INTRODUCTION

The subject of this article concerns that most curious institution in the American system of government—the Supreme Court of the United States. I say curious, first of all, because of some surface distinctions between the Court and other agencies of Government that are obvious to any newspaper man in Washington.

In a city thick with publicists, the Supreme Court is a last holdout from Madison Avenue. It is the only news beat in Washington where officials do not cultivate the press, and spoon-feed it. Reporters may be pals of Senators, and even of Presidents, but not of Supreme Court justices. . . .

Alone among Government agencies, the Supreme Court seems to have escaped Parkinson's law. The reader may remember Professor Parkinson's thesis—that the number of employees in any office continuously expands, and the amount of work automatically increases to keep the new hands busy. The work at the Supreme Court is still done by nine men, assisted by eighteen young law clerks. Nothing is delegated to committees of ghost writers or task forces.

The Court is at the same time the most aloof of Washington agencies and the most approachable. The great marble palace which houses it seems cold and inflated, and there is a formal, ceremonial air to the Court's public sessions. But during an oral argument in the courtroom, for all the austerity of the pillars and the pseudo-classical friezes, the atmosphere is remarkably intimate as court and counsel converse. It really is conversation—as direct, searching, focused discussion as can be found anywhere in Washington.

POWER OF THE SUPREME COURT

But beyond those surface distinctions there is the deeper curiosity about the Supreme Court. That is the grant of power—in a society that proudly calls itself a democracy—to nine men appointed for life. For the power given to Supreme Court justices is great indeed, undoubtedly greater than that given to any other judges anywhere.

De Tocqueville wrote a century ago, "Scarcely any political question arises in the United States that is not resolved, sooner or later, into a

[1] 51 *Ill. B.J.* 8 (1962). Used by permission from Mr. Anthony Lewis and the *Illinois Bar Journal.*
[2] Mr. Anthony Lewis is a New York newspaperman who has been assigned to cover the Supreme Court.

judicial question." And so issues that would be decided in most countries by parliament or prime ministers come to the Supreme Court of the United States.

One question before the Court this term was whether the public schools of New York State may constitutionally open each day with a prayer. As I heard counsel argue that case, ranging over all the policy reasons for and against strict secularism in our schools, it occurred to me that here was the kind of question committed to political decision in most countries—the kind it would be unthinkable to take to a court. (I may add that the unhappy history of political controversy in Europe over the religion in schools does not argue the wisdom of political resolution of such problems.) . . .

GRIST OF SUPREME COURT'S ROLE

Of course, the Supreme Court does not spend all its time deciding great constitutional questions. The grist of its docket is statutory construction— deciding what Congress meant in some statute. But even that routine-sounding job can pose large and delicate problems in a governmental system as complex as ours.

In construing a statute the Court may be resolving a contest of power between the Federal Government and the States, as it does, for example, when it says whether the Taft-Hartley law permits a state court to entertain a case arising from a labor dispute or whether, instead, it commits the problem to the National Labor Relations Board.

One of the most important pieces of statutory construction in recent years took one sentence in the Taft-Hartley Act—a sentence that on its face simply gave the Federal courts jurisdiction over suits for violation of collective bargaining agreements—and made that sentence a charter for the Federal courts to fashion a whole new structure of law for labor con-tracts. Sometimes, under the heading of statutory construction, the Court has to resolve a head-on clash between two agencies of the same Federal Government. It did that this term when it held that the Federal Power Com-mission had no right to approve a merger of two natural gas companies, while a Justice Department suit attacking the merger as an antitrust vio-lation was before the courts.

CONGRESS OFTEN VAGUE

The basic difficulty for the Supreme Court in saying what Congress meant is that so often Congress meant nothing at all. It simply never envisaged the problem before the Court. The Congress that wrote the Sherman Act back in 1890, prohibiting "every contract or combination in restraint of trade," simply gave the Court a blank check to fill in with contemporary legal and economic theory. It is hardly surprising that the Court has had some difficulty deciding what is an antitrust violation, or that the justices have disagreed.

The increasing demands on Congress have aggravated the problem. The fact is that Congress does not have time these days to legislate in detail. When it comes to a difficult problem, its tendency is to fuzz things over and let the Court resolve the difficulty under the guise of discovering what Congress "intended." I remember the offshore oil legislation, when Congress could have stated right in the statute how far out into the Gulf of Mexico state mineral rights should run. But it was too difficult politically to make that decision, and so Congress asked the Court to do it on the basis of some ambiguous history. At the argument Justice Frankfurter said something about Congress passing the buck. . . .

I turn to an area of judicial decision so new that one must read about it in the newspapers rather than the law reports—legislative apportionment.

In a 1946 decision, *Colegrove v. Green*—The Supreme Court seemed to close the doors of the Federal courts to complaints by urban and suburban voters that legislative districts were so unequal in population as to violate their constitutional rights. Justice Frankfurter's opinion said that trying to deal with unfair apportionments would lead the courts into a "political thicket," and he advised the city voters to work for reform through the political process. In a dozen cases after 1946 the Court followed the *Colegrove* doctrine of keeping hands off apportionment issues.

Then, last March 26, the Court suddenly told us that the doors were not closed after all. In *Baker v. Carr* it held that a suit challenging the apportionment of Tennessee's legislature stated a constitutional claim triable in the Federal courts. The opinion explained away all the earlier cases, starting with *Colegrove v. Green,* but for at least one reader the explanation did not explain. In fact, if not in theory, *Colegrove v. Green* and the other cases were overruled. Their spirit of abstention was rejected . . . and . . . Justice Frankfurter's advice to work for political change was useless; the political system provided no way of escape. The Supreme Court opened the way for political as well as legal forces to work for orderly change.

That was the moral seen by Attorney General Robert F. Kennedy in *Baker v. Carr.* "When people criticize the courts for invading spheres of action which supposedly belong to other parts of our constitutional system," he said of the Tennessee case, "they often overlook the fact that the courts must act precisely because the other organs of government have failed to fulfill their responsibilities."

Perhaps in 1946, when *Colegrove v. Green* was decided, it still seemed possible that the rural oligarchies in control of state legislatures would listen to reason. But by 1962 that hope had passed. It was plain that only the Supreme Court could begin to cure the disease of malapportionment eating away at the vitals of American democracy.

CONCLUSION

There, in impressionistic summary, . . . [is an area] of the law in which the Supreme Court's construction of the Constitution is contributing to profound changes in American government and society. Just as clearly, . . . [this case] represent[s] a shift to the Court's conception of its own role. . . .

The Court has begun to enforce new restraints on state action. And how different are the interests involved in these restraints from those that concerned the Supreme Court only a generation ago.

Just recall the dominant mood of the Court before 1937. The issues then were the right of the states to set maximum hours and minimum wages, the right of the Federal Government to use its tax and commerce powers against the great Depression. The Court's concern seemed to be with property, not with what we today would call human liberty.

Which brings us again to the question why. Why has there been this dramatic change in Supreme Court doctrine during the last quarter-century? Surely the area of decision at which we have looked suggests some answers.

First, it is clear that there has been an ethical element in the Court's motivation. In intervening in behalf of . . . the citizen disenfranchised by malapportionment, the Court has been responding to what it deemed a moral demand—a demand of the natural conscience.

Moreover, the national conscience had found no way to express itself except through the courts. The Supreme Court moved in only when the political system was stymied—when there was no other way out of the moral dilemma.

SUPREME COURT AS INSTRUMENT OF NATIONAL MORAL VALUES

The conclusion is that the Supreme Court has tended in recent years to act as the instrument of national moral values that have not been able to find other governmental expression. If the Court has changed, it is because we have changed.

The unhappy recent history of the world *has* changed the values of Americans, and so it should be no great surprise that the Supreme Court puts its emphasis on different interests. We are more concerned, now, about abuse of official authority, mistreatment of racial minorities and sabotage of democracy than we are about the sanctity of property or even about state powers in a Federal system.

And the Framers drew our Constitution in deliberately vague terms so that it could reflect the values of each generation. The courts have inevitably drawn on the moral consensus of their own time to give content to such phrases as "due process" and "equal protection."

Of course, not everyone agrees on moral goals, much less ones that are judicially attainable. The nine justices cannot be expected to march in happy unanimity toward a legal heaven whose definition all applaud.

Only in the field of race relations—where, ironically, public reaction has been the most divisive—have the justices regularly been in agreement. They have apparently found the moral imperative here more obvious. But even in race relations it seems doubtful to me that unanimity can long be preserved as the Court reaches the difficult questions of how to distinguish "private" from "public" discrimination.

COURT DEEPLY DIVIDED

Outside the racial area the Court has been deeply divided. Justice Frankfurter has been the principal spokesman for the view that the Court should be hesitant to impose its moral ideals upon a complex political structure. He dissented not only from *Baker v. Carr* but, for example, from last year's decision outlawing illegally seized evidence in state criminal trials.

This does not mean that Justice Frankfurter likes unfair apportionments or illegal evidence—far from it. He is simply a believer in the independent power of the states, wisely or unwisely used; sometimes I think he is the last person in the country who holds that view as a matter of deep intellectual belief. And he is enough of a skeptic about the perfection of judges so that he hesitates to bind government to rigid judicial formulas.

Justice Frankfurter's fears can hardly be dismissed out of hand. The role now being played by the Supreme Court puts the justices—and the lower court judges who must carry out their decisions—on the frontiers of social change. And that may not always be a natural locale for a judge. Not every man trained to construe a contract will feel at home weighing great social problems. Judges will be strained to their intellectual and moral limits. Care in the selection of judges becomes even more crucially important.

But for all the difficulties, I myself see no satisfactory alternative to the role being taken up by the Court. I think it is better to take the risks of judicial intervention than to be satisfied with doing nothing. . . .

In this great country, so often riven by local interests with which Congress has neither the time nor the desire to deal, some agency has to bring local action into harmony with overriding national ideals. Its very remoteness, its freedom from sectional and political pressures have rightly made us choose as that instrument the Supreme Court of the United States.

RECENT TRENDS IN UNITED STATES SUPREME COURT DECISIONS [3]
Philip B. Kurland [4]

Looking over the last decade of the Supreme Court's work—roughly the period between the school desegregation cases in 1954 and the reapportionment cases of 1964—one quickly discovers that the justices have wrought more fundamental changes in the political and legal structure of the United States than during any period in our history since Mr. Chief Justice Marshall first wrote meaning into the abstractions of the Constitution's language. And, to make my essential point at the outset, the problem is not primarily whether in your eyes or mine these changes are good or bad, but rather whether the Supreme Court, constituted as it is by nine lawyers with life tenure and politically irresponsible, is the proper organ of government to accomplish the goals it may decide to set for this country.

Three dominant movements are evident in the court's recent work. First, and foremost has been the emerging primacy of equality as a guide to constitutional decision. Perhaps an offshoot of the Negro revolution that the court helped to sponsor in *Brown v. Board of Education,* the equalitarian revolution in judicial doctrine has made dominant the principles to be read into the equal protection clause of the 14th amendment rather than the due process clause, heretofore the polestar of Supreme Court action. . . . The decisions in the school segregation cases, the sit-in cases, and the reapportionment cases are merely the most prominent of a very large number of decisions pushing this egalitarian theme. Quite clearly the movement is at its inception; certainly it is nowhere near its conclusion.

Two fundamental difficulties face the court in this effort, or would face the court were it more conscious of its obligation to justify and explain its judgments. The first is the question whether the equal protection clause empowers the court to eliminate not only the inequalities imposed by law but the inequalities that derive from nongovernmental action or inaction, the social and economic inequalities as well as the political inequalities. . . . The second major problem . . . is the task of adequately reconciling the competing claims of equality on the one hand with liberty and other fundamental guaranties on the other. . . .

The second prominent theme of current Supreme Court adjudication, however important, is hardly novel. I am referring to the effective subordination, if not destruction, of the federal system. This movement is not entirely disparate from the egalitarian push. For each is a drive to uniformity and away from diversity. Equality demands uniformity of rules. Uniformity cannot exist if there are multiple rulemakers. It follows that the objective of

[3] Address delivered Jan. 7, 1965, before the Governmental Affairs Council of the Chicago Association of Commerce and Industry. Used by permission from Professor Philip B. Kurland and the *Chicago Tribune.*
[4] Professor Kurland is a member of the faculty of the Law School of the University of Chicago.

equality cannot be achieved except by the elimination of authorities not subordinate to the central power. It, too, is an important part of our political and social and economic movement away from diversity toward conformity. . . . Perhaps the most amazing fact about the court's recent infringements on state authority is that, having taken so much power away from the states, it continues to find more to take away. . . .

The third of the major trends discernible from a study of the court's efforts over the last 10 years . . . [is] the enhancement of the judicial dominion at the expense of the power of other branches of government, national as well as state. . . . There was, at one time, a fairly substantial area of governmental action that the court had wisely declared off-limits for itself. The reapportionment cases seem to have dealt a fatal blow to the idea that there are certain functions of government beyond the competence of the court to perform. . . . It is only fair to note, however, that the court treats its own precedents with no less disdain than it accords congressional legislation. Indeed, a court that considers its pronouncements to be "the law of the land" might be expected to pay more respect to its own opinions. The fact of the matter is that the number of its own cases overruled by the court in the past decade, either openly or covertly, have accelerated at such a rate as almost to remove the hyperbole from Mr. Justice Roberts' charge that the court's judgments were coming to be like railroad excursion tickets, good for this day only. . . .

The solution of the problem of excessive judicial power . . . must be found in making the judicial branch of the government politically more responsible without impinging on its independence. It should be remembered . . . that the success of Anglo-American democracies has depended in no small part on the independence of the judiciary.

Such an answer, if it is to be found anywhere, is most likely to be found in the responsible utilization of the amending process, a prerequisite that will both justify the process and, in many instances, make it superfluous. That prerequisite is a real comprehension on the part of the electorate of the role and performance of the Supreme Court. And the obligation of this understanding falls particularly on the leaders of the community. For, I think I can say without fear of being proved wrong, that the press has failed in its obligation to educate the public about the decisions of the court. It is also unfortunately true that the bar has failed in this regard. . . .

Only an educated public can understand whether judicial decisions appropriately call for constitutional amendment. At the same time, an educated and aroused public may make the court politically more responsible than it has been.

INDEX

751